a Wolters Kluwer business

Revenue Recognition Guide

by Scott Taub

Highlights

Revenue Recognition Guide is a comprehensive reference manual covering key concepts and issues that arise in determining when and how to recognize revenue. It covers the litany of existing authoritative literature related to revenue recognition and clarifies those revenue recognition concepts that are vague. *Revenue Recognition Guide* also provides examples of key points, includes excerpts from the financial statements of public companies to illustrate key concepts and judgments, and discusses revenue recognition projects on the agendas of the various accounting standard-setters.

2010 Edition

This edition covers new revenue-related accounting standards, issued in response to specific revenue recognition problems or other prevalent accounting issues. It also includes cross-references to the FASB's new Accounting Standards Codification, which replaced the original pronouncements as the authoritative source of U.S. Generally Accepted Accounting Principles on July 1, 2009.

Accounting Research Manager

Accounting Research Manager is the most comprehensive, up-to-date, and objective online database of financial reporting literature. It includes all authoritative and proposed accounting, auditing, and SEC literature, plus independent, expert-written interpretive guidance.

Our Weekly Summary e-mail newsletter highlights the key developments of the week, giving you the assurance that you have the most current information. It provides links to new FASB, AICPA,

SEC, PCAOB, EITF, and IASB authoritative and proposal-stage literature, plus insightful guidance from financial reporting experts.

Our outstanding team of content experts takes pride in updating the system on a daily basis, so you stay as current as possible. You'll learn of newly released literature and deliberations of current financial reporting projects as soon as they occur! Plus, you benefit from their easy-to-understand technical translations.

With **Accounting Research Manager**, you maximize the efficiency of your research time, while enhancing your results. Learn more about our content, our experts and how you can request a FREE trial by visiting us at **http://www.accountingresearchmanager.com.**

CCH Learning Center

CCH's goal is to provide you with the clearest, most concise, and up-to-date accounting and auditing information to help further your professional development, as well as a convenient method to help you satisfy your continuing professional education requirements. The CCH Learning Center* offers a complete line of self-study courses covering complex and constantly evolving accounting and auditing issues. We are continually adding new courses to the library to help you stay current on all the latest developments. The CCH Learning Center courses are available 24 hours a day, seven days a week. You'll get immediate exam results and certification. To view our complete accounting and auditing course catalog, go to: **http://cch.learningcenter.com.**

---

* CCH is registered with the National Association of State Boards of Accountancy (NASBA) as a sponsor of continuing professional education on the National Registry of CPE Sponsors. State boards of accountancy have final authority on the acceptance of individual courses for CPE credit. Complaints regarding registered sponsors may be addressed to the National Registry of CPE Sponsors, 150 Fourth Avenue North, Nashville, TN 37219-2417. Telephone: 615-880-4200.

* CCH is registered with the National Association of State Boards of Accountancy as a Quality Assurance Service (QAS) sponsor of continuing professional education. Participating state boards of accountancy have final authority on the acceptance of individual courses for CPE credit. Complaints regarding QAS program sponsors may be addressed to NASBA, 150 Fourth Avenue North, Suite 700, Nashville, TN 37219-2417. Telephone: 615-880-4200.

12/09

2010

Revenue Recognition Guide

Scott Taub

This publication is designed to provide accurate and authoritative information in regard to the subject matter covered. It is sold with the understanding that the publisher is not engaged in rendering legal, accounting, or other professional services. If legal advice or other professional assistance is required, the services of a competent professional person should be sought.

—From a *Declaration of Principles* jointly adopted by a Committee of the American Bar Association and a Committee of Publishers and Associations

ISBN: 978-0-8080-2110-0

No claim is made to original government works; however, within this Product or Publication, the following are subject to CCH's copyright: (1) the gathering, compilation, and arrangement of such government materials; (2) the magnetic translation and digital conversion of data, if applicable; (3) the historical, statutory and other notes and references; and (4) the commentary and other materials.

Portions of this work were published in a previous edition.

Printed in the United States of America

Contents

Preface

Revenue recognition…The mere mention of the topic elicits thoughts of complex accounting and difficult judgments fraught with the potential for unfavorable high-profile financial statement restatements. Revenue is the top line in the income statement, and one of the most important indices of financial health to both preparers and users of financial statements. Reporting the correct amount of revenue on a timely basis is also one of the most difficult tasks in financial reporting.

Despite the importance of revenue recognition to the financial statements of virtually all companies, the accounting literature addressing revenue recognition is not as well-developed as the literature addressing many other areas of financial reporting. Although many accounting pronouncements directly or indirectly address revenue recognition, most of the guidance is extremely narrow in scope and addresses a particular issue or narrowly defined transaction. This lack of authoritative literature addressing certain issues and industries has resulted in the development of revenue recognition for some transactions on the basis of industry practice.

The lack of comprehensive guidance combined with the variety and complexity of revenue transactions has resulted in a large number of issues in revenue recognition, including many financial statement restatements and SEC enforcement cases. In fact, two reports issued by the SEC staff in 2003 illustrate that revenue recognition is an area prone to problems: (1) Report pursuant to Section 704 of the Sarbanes-Oxley Act of 2002 (the Section 704 Report) and (2) Summary by the Division of Corporate Finance of Significant Issues Addressed in the Review of the Periodic Reports of the Fortune 500 Companies (the Fortune 500 Report). The Section 704 Report showed that improper revenue recognition was the area where the SEC brought the greatest number of enforcement actions during the report period and the Fortune 500 Report found that accounting policy disclosures related to revenue recognition was an area frequently questioned by the SEC's Division of Corporate Finance. These reports confirmed the findings from several other studies conducted in recent years.

In response to the growing number of problems in the area of revenue recognition, the SEC Staff issued Staff Accounting Bulletin No. 101 (SAB 101), *Revenue Recognition in Financial Statements,* in late 1999. SAB 101 summarized the existing revenue recognition guidance and the SEC Staff's views on the application of that guidance. In addition to causing a number of companies to change their revenue recognition policies, SAB 101 also helped to focus the attention of nearly every public company, as well as analysts and other financial statement users, on revenue recognition.

As a result of these developments, many accounting standard-setters around the world have begun a number of new projects on revenue recognition. Although many of these projects are limited in scope and address very specific revenue recognition issues, the ultimate goal of one project (the FASB's Revenue Recognition project) is to address revenue recognition on a comprehensive basis. However, until that project is completed, available revenue recognition guidance will remain incomplete and scattered throughout the accounting literature.

The principal objective of *Revenue Recognition Guide* is to fill this void. This book addresses the key issues faced in revenue recognition, identifies the appropriate accounting literature, explains both the required accounting and the reasons for that guidance, and often illustrates the application through recourse to disclosures and excerpts from the financial statements of publicly traded companies. For issues not addressed in the accounting literature, this book suggests accounting treatments that are consistent with general revenue recognition concepts and principles. This book also highlights the problem areas noted in the Section 704 and the Fortune 500 Reports.

The 2010 edition of the *Revenue Recognition Guide* incorporates changes in accounting literature and interpretive developments through May 2009. It also includes, in Chapter 13, "Future Expectations and Projects," a discussion of revenue-related projects on the standard-setters' agendas. A comprehensive discussion is provided of the most significant of these projects, the FASB's Revenue Recognition project. In addition, Chapter 13 includes discussion related to the following current EITF issues, which could affect revenue recognition guidance in the near future:

- EITF Issue No. 08-1, *Revenue Arrangements with Multiple Deliverables*
- EITF Issue No. 08-9, *Milestone Method of Revenue Recognition*
- EITF Issue No. 09-3, *Applicability of SOP 97-2 to Certain Arrangements That Include Software Elements*

Within the 13 chapters of the book, a number of Observations, Practice Pointers, and Practice Alerts highlight key consequences of the accounting guidance and identify issues to watch for when dealing with certain revenue transactions. SEC Registrant Alerts highlight issues that the SEC is particularly focused on, as well as additional guidance provided by the SEC beyond the guidance typically followed by non-public companies.

The book also includes a topical index as well as a cross-reference to the authoritative literature that indicates the chapters where specific pieces of authoritative literature are discussed. In addition, the text includes references to the paragraphs of the authoritative literature that address key points.

Abbreviations

The following abbreviations are used throughout the text to represent the various sources of authoritative literature discussed in this book:

AAG	AICPA Audit and Accounting Guide
AcSEC	AICPA Accounting Standards Executive Committee
AICPA	American Institute of Certified Public Accountants
APB	Accounting Principles Board Opinion
ARB	Accounting Research Bulletin
ASC	FASB Accounting Standards Codification
CIRP	SEC Current Issues and Rulemaking Projects
CON	FASB Statement of Financial Accounting Concepts
EITF	Emerging Issues Task Force
FAS	FASB Statement of Financial Accounting Standards
FASB	Financial Accounting Standards Board
FSP	FASB Staff Position
FTB	FASB Technical Bulletin
IAS	IASB International Accounting Standard
IASB	International Accounting Standards Board
IFRIC	International Financial Reporting Interpretations Committee
REG S-X	SEC Regulation S-X
SAB	SEC Staff Accounting Bulletin
SEC	Securities and Exchange Commission
SOP	AICPA Statement of Position
TPA	AICPA Technical Practice Aid

Acknowledgments

Scott Taub thanks all of the members of the Professional Standards Group at Arthur Andersen for their guidance, counsel, and friendship. A better group of people will never be found. Most important,

Scott thanks his wife, Lynn, for her endless patience during the writing of this book and her support of Scott in every one of his career decisions.

About the Author

AUTHOR

Scott A. Taub is a Managing Director of Financial Reporting Advisors, LLC (FRA), which provides consulting services related to accounting and SEC reporting and litigation support services. FRA specializes in applying generally accepted accounting principles to complex business transactions and also provides litigation support and expert services. Mr. Taub is also a member of the IASB's International Financial Reporting Interpretations Committee.

Prior to writing the first edition of this book in 2002, Mr. Taub was a partner in Arthur Andersen's Professional Standards Group (PSG), where he consulted on complex financial reporting matters, helped to establish and disseminate Andersen's policies regarding financial reporting matters, and represented the firm before various standards setters, including the FASB, SEC, AICPA, and IASB. Mr. Taub also authored interpretive guidance for Andersen on a wide variety of accounting and reporting issues.

From September 2002 through January 2007, Mr. Taub was a Deputy Chief Accountant at the Securities and Exchange Commission (SEC) and twice served as Acting Chief Accountant for a total of 14 months. He played a key role in the SEC's implementation of the accounting reforms under the landmark Sarbanes-Oxley Act and was responsible for the day-to-day operations of the Office of the Chief Accountant. Mr. Taub represented the SEC in many venues, including the FASB and IASB's advisory committees, and served as the SEC Observer to the FASB's Emerging Issues Task Force (EITF) and as Chair of the Accounting and Disclosure committee of the International Organization of Securities Commissions (IOSCO).

Mr. Taub is a frequent speaker, having addressed numerous audiences sponsored by a variety of organizations, and writes a periodic column for *Compliance Week* on financial reporting developments. He is a licensed CPA in Michigan and Illinois and is a member of the American Institute of Certified Public Accountants.

CONTRIBUTING AUTHOR

Ashwinpaul (Tony) C. Sondhi is the Founder and president of A. C. Sondhi & Associates, LLC, a Financial Advisory Services firm located in New Jersey. He is currently a member of the Emerging Issues Task Force (EITF) of the Financial Accounting Standards Board (FASB), the EITF Agenda Committee and its 2008 Working Group on EITF 08-01. He is also a member of the Expert Advisory Panel on Fair

Value of the International Accounting Standards Board (IASB). From 2001–2003, he was a member of the Accounting Standards Executive Committee (AcSEC) of the American Institute of Certified Public Accountants (AICPA) and the Planning Subcommittee of the AcSEC. He has also been a member of the Global Financial Reporting Advocacy Committee and Chairman of the Financial Accounting Policy Committee of the CFA Institute.

Mr. Sondhi served on the FASB Task Force on Accounting for Impairments of Long-lived Assets and on the Steering Committee for the Statement of Cash Flows of the International Accounting Standards Committee. Mr. Sondhi was also an advisor to the FASB on its project comparing U.S. and International Financial Reporting Standards.

Mr. Sondhi received his Ph.D. in Accounting and Economics/ Management Science from New York University. He has taught at New York University, Columbia University, and Georgetown University. He has been a Visiting Professor at Stockholm University, Sweden, and Copenhagen Business School, Denmark. His research has been published in several accounting and finance journals.

In addition to co-authoring the 2006–2009 editions of CCH's *Revenue Recognition Guide*, Mr. Sondhi co-authored *The Analysis and Use of Financial Statements*, Third Edition, which is a recommended text for the Chartered Financial Analysts (CFA) program. Mr. Sondhi has also edited *Credit Analysis of Nontraditional Debt Securities*, co-authored *Impairments and Write-offs of Long-Lived Assets*, and co-edited *CFA Readings in Financial Statement Analysis*, and *Off-Balance Sheet Financing Techniques*.

Mr. Sondhi serves on the Board of Directors of an investment advisory services firm and one charitable foundation. He is also an advisor to several U.S. and foreign companies. His consulting activities include revenue recognition, valuation, and comparative analyses of financing and capital structure alternatives, creation and operation of finance, securitization, intellectual property, and investment subsidiaries, analyses of covenants, and the development of debt agreements. Mr. Sondhi has also served as an expert witness on many financial reporting issues.

CHAPTER 1
INTRODUCTION

CONTENTS

OVERVIEW

Revenue is one of the most important indicators of a successful business. It is a key statistic used in the assessment of a company's financial health. The source, amount, and timing of reported revenue is relevant to all parties interested in financial data: company management, regulators, auditors, and users of financial statements. However, the determination of when and how much revenue to recognize remains difficult for accountants and industry professionals. The principal objective of *Revenue Recognition Guide* is to help all parties become more efficient and effective users of the revenue recognition and reporting literature. The *Guide* will also help its users develop more comprehensive revenue recognition policies.

The *Guide* comprehensively addresses the most important revenue reporting issues. It describes the appropriate accounting for each issue and explains the reason for that accounting. The *Guide* also provides practical examples and financial statement disclosures from public companies that illustrate the application of key concepts and judgments.

WHY A BOOK ON REVENUE RECOGNITION

Revenue Recognition Is Important to Financial Statement Users

Revenue-generating transactions are varied and can be extremely complicated. Because revenue reporting directly affects a company's results of operations and financial position, a thorough knowledge of the underlying concepts and practices is essential to the preparation and understanding of a company's financial statements.

The importance of revenue to the assessment of company performance has long been clear to the financial world. During the late 1990s, revenue was often viewed as the main driver of value for many companies, particularly those that were Internet-based. Small changes in revenue could often lead to huge changes in the market value of these companies. When the technology bubble burst in 2000, the steep stock price declines of many publicly traded Internet companies were attributed, in part, to the fact that their revenue numbers were not sustainable and, in some cases, misleading.

The Authoritative Literature Does Not Address All of the Issues

Despite the importance of revenue recognition to the financial statements of virtually all companies, the accounting literature on revenue recognition is neither comprehensive nor easy to apply. The revenue recognition guidance was originally published in over 200 separate documents by multiple standard-setters, including the Accounting Principles Board (APB), the Financial Accounting Standards Board (FASB), the Emerging Issues Task Force (EITF), and others. The introduction of the FASB Accounting Standards Codification (ASC) has significantly reduced the chances of being unable to identify relevant literature for a transaction, but other difficulties remain.

Most of the revenue recognition guidance is narrow in scope and only addresses specific issues or types of transactions. As a result, there is detailed guidance on some issues and little or no guidance on others. In addition, the development of revenue recognition guidance has occurred on an industry-by-industry basis, with the result that the models used by different industries are often inconsistent with one another.

Revenue Recognition Is a Leading Cause of Financial Reporting Errors

The lack of comprehensive guidance, combined with the variety and complexity of these transactions, has resulted in a large number of financial reporting errors. The staff of the Securities and Exchange Commission (SEC) issued two reports in early 2003 that highlighted revenue recognition as an area prone to problems: (1) Report Pursuant to Section 704 of the Sarbanes-Oxley Act of 2002 (the Section 704 Report) and (2) Summary by the Division of Corporation Finance of Significant Issues Addressed in the Review of the Periodic Reports of the Fortune 500 Companies (the Fortune 500 Report).

In developing the Section 704 Report, the SEC staff studied enforcement actions filed during the period July 31, 1997, through July 30, 2002. Improper revenue recognition was the area where the SEC brought the greatest number of enforcement actions during this period. The types of improprieties ranged from the improper timing of revenue recognition (e.g., improper recognition of revenue related to bill-and-hold sales and consignment sales) to fictitious revenue (e.g., falsification of sales documents, failure to consider side letter agreements) to improper valuation of revenue (e.g., failure to appropriately consider rights of return). Other revenue-related areas where the SEC brought a significant number of actions were nondisclosure of related party transactions and the accounting for nonmonetary and round-trip transactions.

The Fortune 500 Report resulted from the SEC's Division of Corporation Finance's (Corp Fin) review of all annual reports filed by Fortune 500 companies. This report provides insight into areas commonly questioned by Corp Fin during their reviews of annual reports. Revenue recognition accounting policy disclosures was an area frequently questioned by Corp Fin. In many cases, Corp Fin requested that companies significantly expand these disclosures. Industries where these requests were common included computer software, computer services, computer hardware, communications equipment, capital goods, semiconductor, electronic instruments and controls, energy, pharmaceutical, and retail. The revenue-related topics precipitating these requests included accounting for software, multiple-element arrangements, rights of return, price protection features, requirements for installation of equipment, customer acceptance provisions, and various types of sales incentive programs.

In addition, several other studies have shown that revenue recognition issues, more than any other issues, are the cause of the most financial statement restatements. Several high-profile revenue restatements over the last few years have reinforced the focus of regulators and the investing public on revenue recognition policy and disclosure.

The Authoritative Literature Is Changing

Largely in response to these problems, the SEC issued Staff Accounting Bulletin No. 101 (SAB 101), *Revenue Recognition in Financial Statements*, in late 1999, which explained the SEC staff's views on the application of the existing revenue recognition guidance. As a result, some companies were required to change their revenue recognition policies. The most significant impact of SAB 101, whose updated guidance is included in Topic 13, *Revenue Recognition*, of the Codification of Staff Accounting Bulletins, however, is that it focused the attention of most public companies on their revenue recognition policies and procedures. Even companies whose revenue recognition policies did not change as a result of the guidance in SAB Topic 13 have paid more attention to their revenue recognition policies and procedures since it was issued.

The FASB has made considerable progress on its project to provide comprehensive guidance on revenue recognition. This project may result in substantive changes to revenue reporting. See Chapter 13, "Future Expectations and Projects," for a discussion of this FASB project.

Tying the Literature Together

Because the revenue accounting literature is incomplete and was originally issued in many different pronouncements, it is often difficult to understand how it all fits together. This product makes it easier to identify the appropriate literature to follow (or analogize to) by: (a) addressing the issues in a topical manner, (b) providing references to the authoritative literature where appropriate, (c) providing guidance in areas that have not yet been addressed by standard-setters, and (d) providing explanations beyond those in the authoritative literature.

Seeing the Big Picture

The discussion above provides several good reasons why a product on revenue recognition is timely. This product addresses revenue recognition on a comprehensive basis, instead of issue-by-issue or transaction-by-transaction, making it easier to understand the fundamental principles and see common threads in the literature.

Focusing on the fundamental principles can also reveal the underlying logic that sometimes generates seemingly inconsistent conclusions. For example, although the same principles may be used to account for two different revenue transactions, the facts and circumstances related to each transaction will determine how to apply these principles and ultimately account for the transactions.

HOW THIS PRODUCT IS ORGANIZED

Introduction and Framework of Revenue Recognition

After an introduction and brief survey of the authoritative accounting literature in Chapter 2, Chapter 3, "General Principles," provides a detailed explanation of the FASB's conceptual framework on revenue recognition and a discussion of the criteria for revenue recognition that commonly appear in the revenue recognition literature and how these conditions are consistent with the conceptual framework. In addition, guidance is provided on how to evaluate satisfaction of these conditions.

Applying the Literature to Specific Transactions

The framework discussed in Chapter 3, "General Principles," is enhanced in Chapters 4–8, which discuss application of the general principles and criteria to specific types of transactions and issues. Chapter 4, "Multiple-Element Arrangements," addresses multiple-element transactions and explains when and how to account for separate deliverables. Chapters 5–7 discuss product, service, and intellectual property deliverables and explain how the general principles and criteria should be applied to these types of transactions. Chapter 8, "Miscellaneous Issues," addresses assorted issues that can affect revenue recognition in certain types of transactions. The discussion in these chapters is presented in the context of the conceptual framework.

Detailed Models in the Accounting Literature

Chapter 9, "Contract Accounting," and Chapter 10, "Software—A Complete Model," discuss two revenue recognition models that are comprehensively addressed in the accounting literature. Each model applies to a narrow group of transactions—accounting for certain long-term contracts (Chapter 9) and software revenue recognition (Chapter 10). Unlike the discussion of other issues in this product that is based, to a large extent, on analogy to common principles and concepts in revenue accounting, the guidance on contract accounting and software revenue recognition is taken directly from the accounting literature that was created to address these transactions. The recognition guidance in Chapters 5–8 generally does not apply to these transactions.

Financial Reporting

Chapter 11, "Presentation," and Chapter 12, "Disclosures," deal with issues that directly affect the financial statements. Chapter 11 focuses on an issue that is perhaps just as important as revenue recognition—the determination of what amounts should be reported on the revenue line of the financial statements as opposed to some other line. Chapter 12 discusses revenue recognition disclosures that are either required or desirable in the financial statements.

A Look Toward the Future

The product closes with a discussion of projects that have not yet been completed by the various accounting standard-setters. Given the ever-changing nature of the accounting literature on revenue recognition and the broad implications that certain projects-in-progress will have on revenue recognition, readers should closely monitor these projects.

CHAPTER 2
A BRIEF SURVEY OF REVENUE-RELATED
LITERATURE

CONTENTS

BACKGROUND

Revenue recognition receives more attention than any other accounting topic. Despite this, standard-setters have never attempted to provide comprehensive, internally-consistent, and broadly applicable accounting standards for revenue. Instead, revenue recognition has been addressed on a fragmented basis, with various pieces of literature that deal with a wide range of topic- or industry-specific issues. Given the multitude of ways that companies earn revenue, it is not surprising that separate standards have been developed for specific types of transactions. For example, selling real estate is very different than selling software and leasing a product is different than originating loans. Accordingly, divergent approaches have been developed to address revenue recognition in these and other situations.

> **PRACTICE ALERT:** In response to the level of attention paid to revenue recognition and the state of the authoritative literature on the topic, the FASB has undertaken a project to comprehensively address this subject. The tentative conclusions reached to date by the FASB would result in a significant departure from current practice. Chapter 13, "Future Expectations and Projects," discusses the status of this project, including the FASB's key preliminary decisions and the differences between these decisions and current practice.

OVERVIEW

This chapter provides an overview of the revenue recognition guidance in existence today. The literature has been classified into three categories: (1) literature that provides general guidance applicable to all (or most) revenue transactions, (2) literature that addresses specific transactions or types of revenue, and (3) literature that addresses specific issues in revenue recognition that may arise in various types of transactions.

> **PRACTICE ALERT:** This chapter only identifies current authoritative literature. However, several current projects will likely have a significant effect on accounting for revenue. These projects are discussed in Chapter 13, "Future Expectations and Projects."

Topics identified in this survey of literature that are too narrow or complex for a book intended to broadly address revenue recognition are not discussed in this publication. Readers should consult the "Cross-Reference to GAAP" at the end of this book for a complete listing of accounting literature discussed and the chapter(s) in which the discussion can be found. Guidance not listed in the cross-reference list is not covered in any detail in this book.

GENERALLY ACCEPTED ACCOUNTING PRINCIPLES

The body of literature that companies in the Unites States follow is commonly referred to as U.S. generally accepted accounting principles (GAAP). U.S. GAAP is made up of guidance originally published in many individual pronouncements by a number of different standard-setting bodies over seven decades. Needless to say, the results are sometimes uncoordinated or even contradictory. It is not unusual for standard-setters to have used differing logic in resolving various issues over time.

The FASB, recognizing this problem, undertook a project beginning in the early 1980s to create a Conceptual Framework for accounting standards. The purpose of the Conceptual Framework, which is documented in the FASB's Statements of Financial Accounting Concepts, is to describe the objectives and principles that should underlie accounting standards. In this book, references are often made to the Conceptual Framework to help explain the theory behind accounting standards. However, while the Conceptual Framework is very useful in understanding accounting standards, it is not part of authoritative U.S. GAAP. As such, it is not included in the FASB Accounting Standards Codification (ASC), which is discussed in more detail below.

Original Pronouncements

As noted above, U.S. GAAP was developed over a long period of time by several different bodies, each of which has promulgated its guidance in multiple types of documents. The result of this, after many decades of work, was that U.S. GAAP was spread across over 2,000 pronouncements in at least a dozen different forms. The accounting standard-setters and the categories of documents they have produced include:

- AICPA Committee on Accounting Procedure:
  - Accounting Research Bulletins (ARB).
- Accounting Principles Board:
  - Accounting Principles Board Opinions (APB).
- AICPA Accounting Standards Executive Committee (AcSEC):
  - Accounting and Audit Guides (AAG);
  - AICPA Statements of Position (SOP);
  - AICPA Practice Bulletins (PB); and
  - Technical Practice Aids (TPA).
- Financial Accounting Standards Board:
  - Statements of Financial Accounting Standards (FAS);
  - FASB Interpretations (FIN);
  - FASB Technical Bulletins (FTB);
  - EITF Consensuses (EITF);
  - FASB Staff Positions (FSP); and
  - FASB Staff Implementation Guides.

The Accounting Standards Codification

Particularly when combined with the lack of consistency in the scope and style of the guidance, this array of guidance could be difficult to navigate. Historically, the U.S. GAAP hierarchy was in place to help those applying U.S. GAAP to determine which of the many different pronouncements should carry greater weight in assessing how to handle a particular accounting issue. The different types of pronouncements were categorized into Levels A through D to indicate their relative authority. In general, Level A documents were those that had gone through the most extensive public review and comment process, with each successive level indicating a reduced amount of public discussion and input. Although the GAAP hierarchy was often helpful in resolving inconsistencies among different pieces of literature, it did not help practitioners ensure that they were considering all of the relevant guidance.

In January 2008, the FASB launched the verification phase of its Accounting Standards Codification (ASC) project. The ASC uses a consistent structure to display its reorganization of the existing U.S. GAAP literature into approximately 90 topics. The ASC is now the single source of authoritative accounting literature in the United States for all reporting periods, interim and annual, ending after September 15, 2009. The ASC incorporates all of the accounting standards that were previously listed in Levels A through D of the U.S. GAAP hierarchy.

The ASC is organized by topic, rather than by standard. Whereas all of the previous documents were numbered sequentially when issued, future standard-setting projects will update various sections of the ASC. As such, the ASC will always include the current authoritative guidance in full, eliminating the need to consult multiple sources to identify relevant guidance.

The ASC uses a numerical classification scheme with a four-level hierarchy—Topic-Subtopic-Section-Paragraph (referenced as XXX-YY-ZZ-PP). The topics reside in four main areas as follows:

1. Presentation (Topics 205–299). These topics relate only to presentation matters and do not address recognition, measurement, and derecognition matters. Topics include Income Statement, Balance Sheet, Earnings per Share, and so forth.

2. Financial Statement Accounts (Topics 305–700). The ASC organizes topics in a financial statement order, including Assets, Liabilities, Equity, Revenue, and Expenses. Topics include Receivables, Revenue Recognition, Inventory, and so forth.

3. Broad Transactions (Topics 805–899). These topics relate to multiple financial statement accounts and are generally transaction-oriented. Topics include Business Combinations, Derivatives, Nonmonetary Transactions, and so forth.

4. Industries (Topics 905–999). These topics relate to accounting that is unique to an industry or type of activity. Topics include Airlines, Software, Real Estate, and so forth.

Subtopics represent subsets of a topic to which different guidance applies. For example, Products and Services are separate subtopics of the Revenue Recognition topic in the ASC. ASC sections represent the nature of the content in a subtopic, such as Recognition, Measurement, Disclosure, and so forth. The section numbers are the same for each subtopic as follows:

- XXX-YY-00 Status
- XXX-YY-05 Overview and Background
- XXX-YY-10 Objectives
- XXX-YY-15 Scope and Scope Exceptions
- XXX-YY-20 Topical Definitions—Glossary
- XXX-YY-25 Recognition
- XXX-YY-30 Initial Measurement
- XXX-YY-35 Subsequent Measurement
- XXX-YY-40 Derecognition
- XXX-YY-45 Other Presentation Matters
- XXX-YY-50 Disclosure
- XXX-YY-55 Implementation Guidance and Illustrations
- XXX-YY-60 Relationships
- XXX-YY-65 Transition and Open Effective Date Information
- XXX-YY-70 Links to Grandfathered Material

One of the benefits of the ASC is that all U.S. GAAP is now accessible in one place, reducing the chances that guidance relevant to an issue will be missed. In addition, access to the ASC is free at http://asc. fasb.org/home or through a link on the FASB's website (http:// www.fasb.org). Further information about the structure and features of the ASC is also available on the FASB website.

SEC Guidance

Pursuant to U.S. law, the SEC has the authority and responsibility to prescribe accounting standards to be used by public companies. Virtually since its inception, the SEC has looked to private-sector bodies to set standards. It is because the SEC looks to the FASB that FASB standards are required to be applied by public companies. Nonetheless, the SEC retains both the responsibility and the authority to prescribe the standards to be used by public companies. As such, rules, interpretations, and other guidance issued by the SEC must be applied by public companies in the financial statements they include in SEC filings. Much of the accounting-related guidance that the SEC has issued is included in Regulation S-X.

In addition to official releases by the SEC itself, the SEC staff periodically issues Staff Accounting Bulletins (SABs) that explain the staff's interpretations of existing accounting literature. Because SABs are not intended to contradict or supersede existing accounting literature, the guidance in a SAB should not contradict guidance in accounting standards issued by the FASB or other accounting standard-setters. Both releases of the SEC itself, as well as SABs, are included for convenience in the ASC. While it is expected that the ASC will be kept up-to-date with any changes in SEC guidance, the official version of this guidance will continue to be maintained by the SEC and its staff, and may be found at the SEC's website (http://www.sec.gov).

In December 1999, the SEC staff issued a significant SAB related to revenue recognition. This guidance, which has been updated several times since it was released, is codified in SAB Topic 8A, *Retail Companies—Sales of Leased or Licensed Departments*, and SAB Topic 13, *Revenue Recognition*.

The interaction of these SAB Topics with other authoritative literature is clearly described in SAB Topic 13A1. In summary, if other authoritative literature applies to the situation, it should be followed. If no other authoritative literature applies to the situation, the guidance in the SAB Topics should be followed in lieu of analogizing to other authoritative literature.

REVENUE RECOGNITION LITERATURE

As mentioned previously, revenue recognition guidance has been published in a great many standards. The balance of this section of this chapter lists those publications, grouped into topics or industries, and identifies where each publication's guidance now resides in the ASC. Documents are referenced using the defined abbreviation and their number, while ASC citations use the classification scheme and numbering system in the ASC.

Not all of the literature identified below is discussed further in this book. Refer to the U.S. GAAP cross-reference index at the end of the book to determine whether a particular piece of literature is discussed further.

In addition to the authoritative guidance in U.S. GAAP identified below, two of the FASB Concepts Statements provide overall context and guidance:

1.   FASB Statement of Financial Accounting Concepts No. 5, *Recognition and Measurement in Financial Statements of Business Enterprises* (CON-5), provides broad recognition guidance.

2. FASB Statement of Financial Accounting Concepts No. 6, *Elements of Financial Statements* (CON-6), provides broad presentation guidance.

GENERAL REVENUE RECOGNITION GUIDANCE

General Guidance

Publication	ASC	ASC Topic
SAB Topic 13, *Revenue Recognition*	605-10-S99	Revenue Recognition

Product Sales

Publication	ASC	ASC Topic
FAS-48, *Revenue Recognition When Right of Return Exists*	605-15-25-1	Revenue Recognition
FAS-49, *Accounting for Product Financing Arrangements*	470-40	Debt
EITF 95-1, *Revenue Recognition on Sales with a Guaranteed Minimum Resale Value*	840-10-55-12	Leases
EITF 95-4, *Revenue Recognition on Equipment Sold and Subsequently Repurchased Subject to an Operating Lease*	605-15-25-5	Revenue Recognition
EITF 01-8, *Determining Whether an Arrangement Contains a Lease*	845-10-15	Nonmonetary Transactions
EITF 03-12, *Impact of FASB Interpretation No. 45 on Issue No. 95-1*	460-10-55-17	Guarantees

Service Transactions

Publication	ASC	ASC Topic
SAB Topic 13, *Revenue Recognition*	605-10-S99	Revenue Recognition
EITF 01-8, *Determining Whether an Arrangement Contains a Lease*	845-10-15	Nonmonetary Transactions
EITF D-96, *Accounting for Management Fees Based on a Formula*	605-20-S99-1	Revenue Recognition

Publication	ASC	ASC Topic
ITC-Service, *FASB Invitation to Comment: Accounting for Certain Service Transactions*	N/A	N/A

Licenses of Intellectual Property Not Addressed Elsewhere

Publication	ASC	ASC Topic
SAB Topic 13, *Revenue Recognition*	605-10-S99	Revenue Recognition
EITF 07-1, *Accounting for Collaborative Arrangements*	808-10	Collaborative Arrangements

Multiple-Element Arrangements

Publication	ASC	ASC Topic
EITF 00-21, *Revenue Arrangements with Multiple Deliverables*	605-25	Revenue Recognition
SAB Topic 13, *Revenue Recognition*	605-10-S99	Revenue Recognition
EITF 01-8, *Determining Whether an Arrangement Contains a Lease*	840-10-15	Leases
EITF 03-5, *Applicability of AICPA Statement of Position 97-2 to Nonsoftware Deliverables in an Arrangement Containing More-Than-Incidental Software*	985-605-15-3	Software

Sales Incentives

Publication	ASC	ASC Topic
EITF 01-9, *Accounting for Consideration Given by a Vendor to a Customer (Including a Reseller of the Vendor's Products)*	605-50	Revenue Recognition
EITF 02-16, *Accounting by a Customer (Including a Reseller) for Certain Consideration Received from a Vendor*	605-50	Revenue Recognition
EITF 03-10, *Application of Issue No. 02-16 by Resellers to Sales Incentives Offered to Consumers by Manufacturers*	605-50-45	Revenue Recognition

Publication	ASC	ASC Topic
EITF 06-1, *Accounting for Consideration Given by a Service Provider to Manufacturers or Resellers of Equipment Necessary for an End-Customer to Receive Service from the Service Provider*	605-50	Revenue Recognition

Presentation

Publication	ASC	ASC Topic
REG S-X, *Rule 5-03, Income Statements*	225-10-S99-2	Income Statement
SAB Topic 8, *Retail Companies*	605-15-S99-2 and S99-3	Revenue Recognition
SAB Topic 13, *Revenue Recognition*	605-10-S99	Revenue Recognition
EITF 99-19, *Reporting Revenue Gross as a Principal versus Net as an Agent*	605-45	Revenue Recognition
EITF 00-10, *Accounting for Shipping and Handling Fees and Costs*	605-45-45-19	Revenue Recognition
EITF 01-9, *Accounting for Consideration Given by a Vendor to a Customer (Including a Reseller of the Vendor's Products)*	605-50	Revenue Recognition
EITF 01-14, *Income Statement Characterization of Reimbursements Received for "Out-of-Pocket" Expenses Incurred*	605-45-45-22	Revenue Recognition
EITF 02-3, *Issues Involved in Accounting for Derivative Contracts Held for Trading Purposes and Contracts Involved in Energy Trading and Risk Management Activities*	815-10-45-9	Derivatives and Hedging
EITF 02-16, *Accounting by a Customer (Including a Reseller) for Certain Consideration Received from a Vendor*	605-50	Revenue Recognition
EITF 03-10, *Application of Issue No. 02-16 by Resellers to Sales Incentives Offered to Consumers by Manufacturers*	605-50-45	Revenue Recognition

Publication	ASC	ASC Topic
EITF 03-11, *Reporting Realized Gains and Losses on Derivative Instruments That Are Subject to FASB Statement No. 133 and Not "Held for Trading Purposes" as Defined in Issue No. 02-3*	815-10-55-62	Derivatives and Hedging
EITF 06-1, *Accounting for Consideration Given by a Service Provider to Manufacturers or Resellers of Equipment Necessary for an End-Customer to Receive Service from the Service Provider*	605-50	Revenue Recognition
EITF 06-3, *How Taxes Collected from Customers and Remitted to Governmental Authorities Should Be Presented in the Income Statement (That Is Gross versus Net Presentation)*	605-45-15-2	Revenue Recognition

INDUSTRY-BASED GUIDANCE

Airlines

Publication	ASC	ASC Topic
AAG-AIR, *Industry Audit Guide for Audits of Airlines*	908-605	Airlines

Agriculture

Publication	ASC	ASC Topic
SOP 85-3, *Accounting by Agricultural Producers and Agricultural Cooperatives*	905-605	Agriculture
AAG-APC, *Audit and Accounting Guide for Audits of Agricultural Producers and Agricultural Cooperatives*	905-605	Agriculture

Broadcasting

Publication	ASC	ASC Topic
FAS-63, *Financial Reporting by Broadcasters*	920-605	Entertainment—Broadcasters

Cable Television

Publication	ASC	ASC Topic
FAS-51, *Financial Reporting by Cable Television Companies*	922-605	Entertainment— Cable Television

Casinos

Publication	ASC	ASC Topic
AAG-CAS, *Audit and Accounting Guide for Audits of Casinos*	924-605	Entertainment— Casinos

Construction Contracts

Publication	ASC	ASC Topic
ARB-45, *Long-Term Construction-Type Contracts*	605-35	Revenue Recognition
SOP 81-1, *Accounting for Performance of Construction-Type and Certain Production-Type Contracts*	605-35	Revenue Recognition
AAG-CON, *Audit and Accounting Guide for Construction Contractors*	910-605	Contractors— Construction

Contributions Received

Publication	ASC	ASC Topic
FAS-116, *Accounting for Contributions Received and Contributions Made*	958-605	Not-for-Profit Entities
AAG-NPO, *Audit and Accounting Guide for Not-for-Profit Organizations*	958-605	Not-for-Profit Entities

Employee Benefit Plans

Publication	ASC	ASC Topic
SOP 92-6, *Accounting and Reporting by Health and Welfare Benefit Plans*	962 and 965	Plan Accounting— Defined Contribution Pension Plans/Plan Accounting— Health and Welfare Benefit Plans

Publication	ASC	ASC Topic
AAG-EBP, *Audit and Accounting Guide for Audits of Employee Benefit Plans*	960 and 962	Plan Accounting— Defined Contribution Pension Plans/Plan Accounting— Health and Welfare Benefit Plans

Federal Government Contractors

Publication	ASC	ASC Topic
ARB-43, *Restatement and Revision of Accounting Research Bulletins,* Chapter 11, *Government Contracts*	912-605	Contractors— Federal Government
AAG-FGC, *Audit and Accounting Guide for Audits of Federal Government Contractors*	912-605	Contractors— Federal Government

Financial Services

Publication	ASC	ASC Topic
FAS-91, *Accounting for Nonrefundable Fees and Costs Associated with Originating or Acquiring Loans and Initial Direct Costs of Leases, an amendment of FASB Statements No. 13, 60, and 65 and a rescission of FASB Statement No. 17*	310-20	Receivables
FAS-140, *Accounting for Transfers and Servicing of Financial Assets and Extinguishments of Liabilities, a replacement of FASB Statement No. 125*	405-20	Liabilities
FAS-156, *Accounting for Servicing of Financial Assets, an amendment of FASB Statement No. 140*	860-50	Transfers and Servicing
SAB Topic 5DD, *Miscellaneous Accounting—Loan Commitments Accounted for as Derivative Instruments*	815-10-S99	Derivatives and Hedging
FIN-45, *Guarantor's Accounting and Disclosure Requirements for Guarantees, Including Indirect Guarantees of Indebtedness of*	460	Guarantees

Publication	ASC	ASC Topic
Others, an interpretation of FASB Statements No. 5, 57, and 107, and rescission of FASB Interpretation No. 34		
SOP 01-6, *Accounting by Certain Entities (Including Entities with Trade Receivables) That Lend to or Finance the Activities of Others*	860-50	Transfers and Servicing
SOP 03-3, *Accounting for Certain Loans or Debt Securities Acquired in a Transfer*	310-30	Receivables
AAG-DEP, *Audit and Accounting Guide for Depository and Lending Institutions: Banks and Savings Institutions, Credit Unions, Finance Companies and Mortgage Companies*	942-605	Financial Services— Depository and Lending
AAG-INV, *Audit and Accounting Guide for Audits of Investment Companies*	946	Financial Services— Investment Companies
AAG-BRD, *Audit and Accounting Guide for Brokers and Dealers in Securities*	940-605	Financial Services— Brokers and Dealers
EITF 84-20, *GNMA Dollar Rolls*	860-10	Transfers and Servicing
EITF 85-13, *Sale of Mortgage Service Rights on Mortgages Owned by Others*	860-50-40-10 and 40-11	Transfers and Servicing
EITF 85-20, *Recognition of Fees for Guaranteeing a Loan*	605-20-25-9	Revenue Recognition
EITF 85-24, *Distribution Fees by Distributors of Mutual Funds That Do Not Have a Front-End Sales Charge*	946-605-25-8	Financial Services— Investment Companies
EITF 86-8, *Sale of Bad-Debt Recovery Rights*	860-10-55-73	Transfers and Servicing
EITF 88-22, *Securitization of Credit Card and Other Receivable Portfolios*	860-20-55-16	Transfers and Servicing

Publication	ASC	ASC Topic
EITF 95-5, *Determination of What Risks and Rewards, If Any, Can Be Retained and Whether Any Unresolved Contingencies May Exist in a Sale of Mortgage Loan Servicing Rights*	860-50-40-3 through 40-5	Transfers and Servicing
EITF 97-3, *Accounting for Fees and Costs Associated with Loan Syndications and Loan Participations after the Issuance of FASB Statement No. 125*	310-20-25-19 and 25-20	Receivables
FSP FIN 45-2, *Whether FASB Interpretation No. 45, "Guarantor's Accounting and Disclosure Requirements for Guarantees, Including Indirect Guarantees of Indebtedness of Others," Provides Support for Subsequently Accounting for a Guarantor's Liability at Fair Value*	460-10-35-2	Guarantees
FSP FIN 45-3, *Application of FASB Interpretation No. 45 to Minimum Revenue Guarantees Granted to a Business or Its Owners*	460-10-55-10 and 55-11	Guarantees
FASB Staff Implementation Guide, *A Guide to Implementation of Statement 91 on Accounting for Nonrefundable Fees and Costs Associated with Originating or Acquiring Loans and Initial Direct Costs of Leases: Questions and Answers*	310-20	Receivables
FSP EITF 85-24-1, *Application of EITF Issue No. 85-24, "Distribution Fees by Distributors of Mutual Funds That Do Not Have a Front-End Sales Charge," When Cash for the Right to Future Distribution Fees for Shares Previously Sold Is Received from Third Parties*	946-605	Financial Services— Investment Companies

Franchises

Publication	ASC	ASC Topic
FAS-45, *Accounting for Franchise Fee Revenue*	952-605	Franchisors

Freight

Publication	ASC	ASC Topic
EITF 91-9, *Revenue and Expense Recognition for Freight Services in Process*	605-20-25-13	Revenue Recognition

Health Care

Publication	ASC	ASC Topic
AAG-HCO, *Audit and Accounting Guide for Health Care Organizations*	954-605	Health Care Entities

Insurance

Publication	ASC	ASC Topic
FAS-60, *Accounting and Reporting by Insurance Enterprises*	944-605	Financial Services— Insurance
FAS-97, *Accounting and Reporting by Insurance Enterprises for Certain Long-Duration Contracts and for Realized Gains and Losses from the Sale of Investments*	944-605	Financial Services— Insurance
FAS-113, *Accounting and Reporting for Reinsurance of Short-Duration and Long-Duration Contracts*	944-605	Financial Services— Insurance
SOP 03-1, *Accounting and Reporting by Insurance Enterprises for Certain Nontraditional Long-Duration Contracts and for Separate Accounts*	944-20 and 944-80	Financial Services— Insurance
FTB 90-1, *Accounting for Separately Priced Extended Warranty and Product Maintenance Contracts*	605-20-25-1 through 25-6	Revenue Recognition

Publication	ASC	ASC Topic
FSP FAS 97-1, *Situations in Which Paragraphs 17(b) and 20 of FASB Statement No. 97, "Accounting and Reporting by Insurance Enterprises for Certain Long-Duration Contracts and for Realized Gains and Losses from the Sale of Investments," Permit or Require Accrual of an Unearned Revenue Liability*	944-605-25-8 through 25-11	Financial Services— Insurance

Motion Pictures

Publication	ASC	ASC Topic
SOP 00-2, *Accounting by Producers or Distributors of Films*	926-605	Entertainment— Films

Music

Publication	ASC	ASC Topic
FAS-50, *Financial Reporting in the Record and Music Industry*	928-605	Entertainment— Music

Oil and Gas

Publication	ASC	ASC Topic
FAS-19, *Financial Accounting and Reporting by Oil and Gas Producing Companies*	932	Extractive Activities—Oil and Gas
SAB Topic 12, *Oil and Gas Producing Activities*	932-360-S99	Extractive Activities—Oil and Gas
FAS-69, *Disclosures about Oil and Gas Producing Activities, an amendment of FASB Statements 19, 25, 33, and 39*	932-235	Extractive Activities—Oil and Gas
AAG-OGP, *Audit and Accounting Guide for Audits of Entities with Oil and Gas Producing Activities*	932-605	Extractive Activities—Oil and Gas

Real Estate

Publication	ASC	ASC Topic
FAS-66, *Accounting for Sales of Real Estate*	360-20	Property, Plant, and Equipment

Publication	ASC	ASC Topic
FAS-67, *Accounting for Costs and Initial Rental Operations of Real Estate Projects*	970-605-25	Real Estate— General
FAS-98, *Accounting for Leases, an amendment of FASB Statements No. 13, 66, and 91 and a rescission of FASB Statement No. 26 and Technical Bulletin 79-11*	840-40	Leases
FIN-43, *Real Estate Sales, an interpretation of FASB Statement No. 66*	360-20	Property, Plant, and Equipment
SOP 92-1, *Accounting for Real Estate Syndication Income*	970-605	Real Estate— General
SOP 04-2, *Accounting for Real Estate Time-Sharing Transactions*	978-605	Real Estate— Time Sharing Activities
AAG-CIR, *Audit and Accounting Guide for Common Interest Realty Associations*	972-360	Real Estate— Common Interest Realty Associations
EITF 84-17, *Profit Recognition on Sales of Real Estate with Graduated Payment Mortgages or Insured Mortgages*	360-20-40-35	Property, Plant, and Equipment
EITF 85-27, *Recognition of Receipts from Made-Up Rental Shortfalls*	970-360	Real Estate— General
EITF 86-6, *Antispeculation Clauses in Real Estate Sales Contracts*	360-20-40-39	Property, Plant, and Equipment
EITF 86-7, *Recognition by Homebuilders of Profit from Sales of Land and Related Construction Contracts*	970-360-55-4	Real Estate— General
EITF 87-9, *Profit Recognition on Sales of Real Estate with Insured Mortgages or Surety Bonds*	360-20-40-11	Property, Plant, and Equipment
EITF 88-12, *Transfer of Ownership Interest as Part of Down Payment under FASB Statement No. 66*	360-20-55-66	Property, Plant, and Equipment
EITF 88-21, *Accounting for the Sale of Property Subject to the Seller's Preexisting Lease*	840-40-55-37	Leases

Publication	ASC	ASC Topic
EITF 88-24, *Effect of Various Forms of Financing under FASB Statement No. 66*	360-20-40-14	Property, Plant, and Equipment
EITF 07-6, *Accounting for the Sale of Real Estate Subject to the Requirements of FASB Statement No. 66 When the Agreement Includes a Buy-Sell Clause*	360-20-55-21	Property, Plant, and Equipment

Research and Development Arrangements

Publication	ASC	ASC Topic
FAS-68, *Research and Development Arrangements*	730-20	Research and Development
REG S-X, Rule 5-03, *Income Statements*	225-10-S99-2	Income Statement
SAB Topic 13, *Revenue Recognition*	605-10-S99	Revenue Recognition

Software

Publication	ASC	ASC Topic
SOP 97-2, *Software Revenue Recognition*	985-605	Software
EITF 00-3, *Application of AICPA Statement of Position 97-2 to Arrangements That Include the Right to Use Software Stored on Another Entity's Hardware*	985-605-55-120 through 55-125	Software
EITF 03-5, *Applicability of AICPA Statement of Position 97-2 to Nonsoftware Deliverables in an Arrangement Containing More-Than-Incidental Software*	985-605-15-3	Software
FSP FIN 45-1, *Accounting for Intellectual Property Infringement Indemnifications under FASB Interpretation No. 45, "Guarantor's Accounting and Disclosure Requirements for Guarantees, Including Indirect Guarantees of Indebtedness of Others"*	460-10-55-31 through 55-34	Guarantees
TPA 5100, Various AICPA Technical Practice Aids	985-605	Software

Utilities

Publication	ASC	ASC Topic
FAS-71, *Accounting for the Effects of Certain Types of Regulation*	980-605	Regulated Operations
EITF 91-6, *Revenue Recognition of Long-Term Power Sales Contracts*	980-605-25	Regulated Operations
EITF 92-7, *Accounting by Rate-Regulated Utilities for the Effects of Certain Alternative Revenue Programs*	980-605-25	Regulated Operations
EITF 96-17, *Revenue Recognition under Long-Term Power Sales Contracts That Contain both Fixed and Variable Pricing Terms*	980-605-25	Regulated Operations

MISCELLANEOUS ISSUES

Customer Acceptance Provisions

Publication	ASC	ASC Topic
SAB Topic 13, *Revenue Recognition*	605-10-S99	Revenue Recognition
FAS-5, *Accounting for Contingencies*	460-10-25	Guarantees

Equity Received as Compensation in Revenue Transaction

Publication	ASC	ASC Topic
EITF 00-8, *Accounting by a Grantee for an Equity Instrument to Be Received in Conjunction with Providing Goods or Services*	505-50	Equity

Guarantees and Indemnifications

Publication	ASC	ASC Topic
FAS-5, *Accounting for Contingencies*	460-10	Guarantees
FIN-45, *Guarantor's Accounting and Disclosure Requirements for Guarantees, Including Indirect Guarantees of Indebtedness of Others, an interpretation of FASB Statements No. 5, 57, and 107, and rescission of FASB Interpretation No. 34*	460-10	Guarantees

Publication	ASC	ASC Topic
EITF 03-12, *Impact of FASB Interpretation No. 45 on Issue No. 95-1*	460-10-55-17	Guarantees
FSP FIN 45-1, *Accounting for Intellectual Property Infringement Indemnifications under FASB Interpretation No. 45, "Guarantor's Accounting and Disclosure Requirements for Guarantees, Including Indirect Guarantees of Indebtedness of Others"*	460-10-55-31 through 55-34	Guarantees
FSP FIN 45-2, *Whether FASB Interpretation No. 45, "Guarantor's Accounting and Disclosure Requirements for Guarantees, Including Indirect Guarantees of Indebtedness of Others," Provides Support for Subsequently Accounting for a Guarantor's Liability at Fair Value*	460-10-35-2	Guarantees
FSP FIN 45-3, *Application of FASB Interpretation No. 45 to Minimum Revenue Guarantees Granted to a Business or Its Owners*	460-10-55	Guarantees

Installment Method of Accounting

Publication	ASC	ASC Topic
APB-10, *Omnibus Opinion—1966, Installment Method of Accounting*	605-10-25-3 through 25-5	Revenue Recognition

Leases

Publication	ASC	ASC Topic
FAS-13, *Accounting for Leases*	840	Leases
FAS-29, *Determining Contingent Rentals, an amendment of FASB Statement No. 13*	840-10-55-38	Leases
FAS-91, *Accounting for Nonrefundable Fees and Costs Associated with Originating or Acquiring Loans and Initial Direct Costs of Leases, an amendment of FASB Statements No. 13, 60,*	310-20	Receivables

Publication	ASC	ASC Topic
and 65 and a rescission of FASB Statement No. 17		
FAS-98, *Accounting for Leases, an amendment of FASB Statements No. 13, 66, and 91 and a rescission of FASB Statement No. 26 and Technical Bulletin No. 79-11*	840-40	Leases
SAB Topic 13, *Revenue Recognition*	605-10-S99	Revenue Recognition
FTB 85-3, *Accounting for Operating Leases with Scheduled Rent Increases*	840-20-25-2	Leases
FTB 88-1, *Issues Relating to Accounting for Leases*	840	Leases
EITF 84-37, *Sale-Leaseback Transaction with Repurchase Option*	840-40-S99	Leases
EITF 85-27, *Recognition of Receipts from Made-Up Rental Shortfalls*	970-360-55	Real Estate— General
EITF 86-17, *Deferred Profit on Sale-Leaseback Transaction with Lessee Guarantee of Residual Value*	840-40-55-26	Leases
EITF 95-1, *Revenue Recognition on Sales with a Guaranteed Minimum Resale Value*	840-10-55-12 through 55-25	Leases
EITF 95-4, *Revenue Recognition on Equipment Sold and Subsequently Repurchased Subject to an Operating Lease*	605-15-25-5	Revenue Recognition
EITF 98-9, *Accounting for Contingent Rent*	840-10-50-5	Leases
EITF 01-8, *Determining Whether an Arrangement Contains a Lease*	840-10-15	Leases
EITF 01-12, *The Impact of the Requirements of FASB Statement No. 133 on Residual Value Guarantees in Connection with a Lease*	840-10-15-20	Leases
EITF 03-12, *Impact of FASB Interpretation No. 45 on Issue No. 95-1*	460-10-55-17	Guarantees

Publication	ASC	ASC Topic
EITF Topic D-107, *Lessor Consideration of Third-Party Residual Value Guarantees*	840-30-S99	Leases
FASB Staff Implementation Guidance, *A Guide to Implementation of Statement 91 on Accounting for Nonrefundable Fees and Costs Associated with Originating or Acquiring Loans and Initial Direct Costs of Leases: Questions and Answers*	310-20	Receivables
FSP FAS-13-2, *Accounting for a Change or Projected Change in the Timing of Cash Flows Relating to Income Taxes Generated by a Leveraged Lease Transaction*	840-30-35-37 through 35-47	Leases

Nonmonetary Transactions

Publication	ASC	ASC Topic
APB-29, *Accounting for Nonmonetary Transactions*	845-10	Nonmonetary Transactions
EITF 87-10, *Revenue Recognition by Television "Barter" Syndicators*	920-845	Entertainment— Broadcasters
EITF 93-11, *Accounting for Barter Transactions Involving Barter Credits*	845-10-30-17 through 30-20	Nonmonetary Transactions
EITF 99-17, *Accounting for Advertising Barter Transactions*	605-20-25-14 through 25-18	Revenue Recognition
EITF 01-2, *Interpretations of APB Opinion No. 29*	845-10	Nonmonetary Transactions
EITF 04-13, *Accounting for Purchases and Sales of Inventory with the Same Counterparty*	845-10-25-4	Nonmonetary Transactions

Rights of Return or Cancellation

Publication	ASC	ASC Topic
FAS-48, *Revenue Recognition When Right of Return Exists*	605-15-25	Revenue Recognition
SAB Topic 13, *Revenue Recognition*	605-10-S99	Revenue Recognition

Sales of Future Revenues

Publication	ASC	ASC Topic
EITF 88-18, *Sales of Future Revenues*	470-10-25	Debt

Warranties

Publication	ASC	ASC Topic
FAS-5, *Accounting for Contingencies*	460-10-25-5 through 25-7	Guarantees
FTB 90-1, *Accounting for Separately Priced Extended Warranty and Product Maintenance Contracts*	605-20-25-1 through 25-6	Revenue Recognition
FIN-45, *Guarantor's Accounting and Disclosure Requirements for Guarantees, Including Indirect Guarantees of Indebtedness of Others, an interpretation of FASB Statements No. 5, 57, and 107, and rescission of FASB Interpretation No. 34*	460-10	Guarantees

REVENUE RECOGNITION UNDER INTERNATIONAL FINANCIAL REPORTING STANDARDS

Another source of revenue recognition literature is International Financial Reporting Standards (IFRS). IFRS is the most commonly used set of accounting standards outside the United States. IFRS has been promulgated by the International Accounting Standards Board (IASB) and its predecessor, the International Accounting Standards Committee (IASC), and their respective interpretive bodies, the International Financial Reporting Interpretations Committee (IFRIC) and the Standing Interpretations Committee (SIC).

A detailed discussion of IFRS revenue recognition literature is beyond the scope of this publication. However, it can be useful to refer to IFRS on certain matters (as the book does in several subsequent chapters) to understand how other standard-setters have resolved those issues. This can help in applying relevant U.S. GAAP guidance.

The following pages describe (at a very basic level) IFRS revenue recognition guidance and identify relevant IFRS pronouncements.

IFRS Framework

The IASB's framework defines income as "increases in economic benefits during the accounting period in the form of inflows or enhancements of assets and decreases of liabilities that result in increases in equity, other than those relating to contributions from equity participants." The framework goes on to distinguish between the two main components of income—revenue and gains. Revenue arises "in the course of the ordinary activities of an entity." In contrast, gains are "other items that meet the definition of income and *may or may not* arise in the course of the ordinary activities of an entity [emphasis added]." The framework goes on to explain that because gains are not different in nature from revenues, they are not regarded as a separate element.

Although similar to U.S. GAAP in most aspects, the lack of a distinction between revenue and gains is a difference. However, this rarely results in significantly different treatment of particular transactions.

Applicable Standards

The most striking difference between U.S. GAAP and IFRS concerning revenue recognition is the volume of guidance. Although U.S. GAAP, as laid out above, has many standards on revenue recognition, IFRS has very little guidance, and what guidance exists is often so high-level that many different ways of applying the literature have developed.

IAS 18, *Revenue*, is a general statement that addresses revenue recognition for three significant types of revenue: (1) product sales, (2) service transactions, and (3) rights to use assets. IAS 18 defines revenue as the "gross inflow of economic benefits during the period arising from the course of the ordinary activities of the entity when those inflows result in an increase in equity, other than increases resulting from contributions by equity participants." IAS 18 notes that such inflows must be on the entity's own account; revenue does not include amounts collected on behalf of a third party. Three additional IASB standards address, in detail, other significant types of revenue: (1) IAS 11, *Construction Contracts*, (2) IAS 17, *Leases*, and (3) IAS 41, *Agriculture*. Limited revenue recognition guidance for the insurance industry also is provided in IFRS 4, *Insurance Contracts*.

Several interpretations that address revenue recognition topics may also be useful to those using U.S. GAAP, as they address issues or questions that may arise but for which U.S. GAAP is incomplete. These include IFRIC 13, *Customer Loyalty Programmes*, covering the accounting for award credits issued in connection with a revenue transaction; IFRIC 12, *Service Concession Arrangements*, dealing with revenue recognition and many other issues that often arise in public-private infrastructure and service arrangements; and IFRIC 15, *Agreements for the Construction of Real Estate*, which provides guidance on selecting a revenue recognition model for contracts to build and sell real estate.

To the extent that a topic or issue is covered by both U.S. and international GAAP literature, a U.S. company must follow the guidance in U.S. literature. To the extent a topic or issue is not covered in U.S. literature but is covered in IASB literature, however, a U.S. company can refer to IASB literature for accounting guidance and policies that are likely to be acceptable in the U.S. GAAP framework. Referring to IASB literature provides the perspective of a standard-setter that has specifically focused on and addressed an accounting topic or issue. This perspective can be helpful to a U.S. company in determining how to account for a particular topic or issue that is not covered in U.S. GAAP.

Presentation and Other Issues

Presentation of revenue on the income statement is addressed in IAS 1, *Presentation of Financial Statements*. IAS 1 gives preparers of financial statements considerable flexibility on the introduction of additional revenue line items, sub-totaling, and ordering.

IAS 14, *Segment Reporting*, defines "segment result" as "segment revenues less segment expenses" and has definitions of both segment revenues and expenses with specific items to be included or excluded from those amounts. For example, segment revenue includes "an entity's share of profits and losses of associates, joint ventures, or other investments accounted for under the equity method if those items are included in consolidated or total entity revenue" and segment expenses specifically excludes these amounts. This is relevant regarding where such profit and losses should appear on the consolidated statement of income.

Listing of IFRS Revenue Recognition Literature

IAS 18	*Revenue*
IAS 11	*Construction Contracts*
IAS 17	*Leases*
IAS 41	*Agriculture*
IFRS 4	*Insurance Contracts*
SIC-13	*Jointly Controlled Entities—Nonmonetary Contributions by Venturers*
SIC 15	*Operating Leases—Incentives*

SIC-27   *Evaluating the Substance of Transactions Involving the Legal Form of a Lease*

SIC 29   *Service Concession Arrangements—Disclosure*

SIC-31   *Revenue—Barter Transactions Involving Advertising Services*

IFRIC 4   *Determining Whether an Arrangement Contains a Lease*

IFRIC 12   *Service Concession Arrangements*

IFRIC 13   *Customer Loyalty Programmes*

IFRIC 15   *Agreements for the Construction of Real Estate*

IFRIC 18   *Transfers of Assets from Customers*

CHAPTER 3
GENERAL PRINCIPLES

CONTENTS

BACKGROUND

Revenue, which appears on the top line of the income statement, is one of the most important measures of a company's health to preparers, auditors, and users of financial statements. The amount and timing of revenue recognition have a significant effect on the results of a company's operations. The changing nature of business operations (and revenue-generating transactions) suggests that accounting for revenue will continue to generate significant questions. Basic guidance on revenue recognition is addressed in the FASB Concepts Statements, which say that revenue should be recognized when it is both earned and either realized or realizable (CON-5, par. 83).

The following are examples of situations where revenue is earned and realized at, or almost at, the same time:

- A restaurant's revenue generally is earned and realizable after a meal has been eaten and paid for by the diner.

- A retail store's revenue generally is earned and realizable when the customer pays for the merchandise at the cash register.

- A manufacturer's revenue generally is earned and realizable for COD orders upon delivery.

- For plumbers and for providers of lawn care and similar services, revenue generally is earned and realizable as the services are performed and paid for by the customer.

In some cases, revenue is realized before it is earned. For example:

- Magazine subscriptions are often paid for in advance. The revenue is realized before the magazines are delivered and earned when the magazines are delivered.

- Airlines generally require payment when a ticket is purchased, at which time revenue is realized. Revenue is earned when the airline provides the transportation.

In other cases, revenue is earned before it becomes realizable. For example:

- A manufacturer that sells products on credit earns revenue from the sale upon delivery. The revenue may not be immediately realizable if the customer's ability to pay is in question.

- Some retailers provide products to customers on a trial basis, in which case the customer has no commitment to pay for the products unless he or she keeps them for a particular period of time. Although the earnings process may arguably be complete when the product is delivered, the revenue does not become realizable until the trial period lapses.

Because these fundamental concepts are easily applied to many transactions, the accounting standard-setters have not provided much other general guidance. Instead, additional guidance has been focused on the application of the basic concepts to more complex transactions and on how certain issues affect the application of the basic concepts. As discussed in Chapter 2, "A Brief Survey of Revenue-Related Literature," existing revenue recognition guidance is limited to a small portion of transactions. However, the number and complexity of transactions continues to expand and the basic concepts are not always readily applicable to the transactions that are common today.

SURVEY OF ACCOUNTING LITERATURE

The general principles on revenue reporting under U.S. generally accepted accounting principles (GAAP) are set forth in the FASB's Conceptual Framework. The Framework provides a conceptual basis upon which the FASB and other accounting standard-setters can develop detailed accounting standards. As a result, the

Concepts Statements are not intended to provide sufficient guidance for preparers to determine the proper accounting treatment in a particular transaction.

The basic principle of revenue reporting as set forth in CON-5, paragraph 83, is that "recognition involves consideration of two factors, (a) being realized or realizable and (b) being earned, with sometimes one and sometimes the other being the more important consideration." This conceptual guidance has been unchanged since it was first issued by the FASB in 1984.

For many revenue transactions, the conceptual guidance is augmented by Statements on Financial Accounting Standards that provide more detailed guidance on applying the basic concepts. Additional general guidance on revenue recognition comes from SAB Topic 13, *Revenue Recognition* (ASC 605-10-S99).

REVENUE RECOGNITION LITERATURE

Publication	ASC	ASC Topic	Subject
SAB Topic 13	605-10-S99	Revenue Recognition	Revenue Recognition
CON-5	N/A	N/A	Recognition and Measurement in Financial Statements of Business Enterprises
ARB-45	605-35	Revenue Recognition	Long-Term Construction-Type Contracts
APB-10	605-10-25-3	Revenue Recognition	Installment and Cost Recovery Methods of Revenue Recognition
FAS-48	605-15-25	Revenue Recognition	Revenue Recognition When Right of Return Exists
FAS-49	470-40-05	Debt	Product Financing Arrangements
FAS-50	928-605-25-2	Entertainment— Music	Music License Fees
FAS-66	360-20	Property, Plant, and Equipment	Accounting for Sales of Real Estate
SOP 81-1	605-35	Revenue Recognition	Accounting for Performance of Construction-Type and Certain Production-Type Contracts

SOP 97-2	985-605	Software	Software Revenue Recognition
SOP 00-2	926-605	Entertainment— Films	Accounting by Producers or Distributors of Films
EITF D-96	605-20-S99	Revenue Recognition	Management Fees Based on a Formula
EITF 01-9 and EITF 06-1	605-50	Revenue Recognition	Customer Payments and Incentives

SUPPORTING LITERATURE

Publication	ASC	ASC Topic	Subject
FAS-5	460-10-25	Guarantees	Warranty Obligations Incurred in Connection with the Sale of Goods or Services
FAS-5	450-20-25	Contingencies	Loss Contingencies
FAS-13	840	Leases	Leases
FAS-71	980-605-30	Regulated Operations	Regulated Operations—Revenue Collected Subject to Refund
FAS-133	815-10-15	Derivatives and Hedging	Definition of a Derivative
FAS-140	405-20	Liabilities	Extinguishment of Liabilities
EITF 01-8	840-10-15	Leases	Determining Whether an Arrangement Contains a Lease
SEC FRR 23	N/A	N/A	The Significance of Oral Guarantees to the Financial Reporting Process

OVERVIEW

The two concepts—earned and realized or realizable—are meant to ensure that a company does not recognize revenue (1) until it has performed under the terms of the arrangement, thereby earning the right to receive and retain payment as contractually documented, and (2) unless it will indeed receive and retain (realize) payment in a form that has value to the company.

Earned

As stated in CON-5, "revenues are considered to have been earned when the entity has substantially accomplished what it must do to be entitled to the benefits represented by the revenues." This may be delivering goods, performing services, providing information, or any other activity for which one entity would pay another entity. The acts the seller performs to fulfill the earned criterion constitute the "earnings process."

To meet the earned criterion, the earnings process must be completed, at least in part. Until the company has performed a service, it should not recognize revenue related to amounts it has been paid in advance or will be paid in return for that performance. In most cases, the point at which revenue is earned is fairly clear from the terms of the transaction. For example:

- An automobile part manufacturer's revenue is earned when it delivers parts to its customers.

- A car rental agency's revenue is earned via the passage of time as it allows a customer to use one of its cars.

- A grocery store's revenue is earned when the customer proceeds through the checkout line with groceries.

In many other transactions, however, it is unclear when revenue has been earned. For example, an executive recruiter performs many activities as part of a search, including contacting potential candidates, setting up interviews, and assisting in salary negotiations. However, it is not until someone has been hired that the customer benefits from all these activities. Similarly, a sales agent performs many activities to line up purchasers of its customer's products. However, it is not until the products are purchased that the customer benefits from these activities. In these situations, it is not immediately clear whether revenue is earned over time (e.g., the period over which the search for candidates or purchasers is performed), or only upon successful completion of all necessary activities (e.g., acceptance by a candidate or orders placed by a purchaser).

Completion of the earnings process also may have nothing to do with the timing of the payments under the contract. For example, the receipt of a deposit or upfront fee in an arrangement does not necessarily indicate that revenue has been earned, even if the deposit or fee is nonrefundable. On the other hand, the fact that payment in an arrangement is not due for some period of time does not necessarily indicate that the revenue has not yet been earned. In some cases, although performance on one component may be complete, revenue may not be recognized if payment for that performance is contingent upon completion of performance on other components of the contract. See Chapter 4, "Multiple-Element Arrangements" for a discussion of contingent revenue.

Realized or Realizable

Revenue is considered realized or realizable when the seller receives either cash from the customer or an asset, such as a note receivable, that is convertible into cash. In addition, the receipt of nonmonetary assets that are not readily convertible into cash may also meet the realizability criterion as long as the fair values of such assets are readily determinable (see further discussion in Chapter 8, "Miscellaneous Issues").

The requirement that revenue must be realized or realizable before it is recognized should be common sense. If the company has not received a benefit from the arrangement, it would be illogical to recognize the related revenue. Determining whether the realizable criterion has been met can often be fairly easy. In general, this occurs when either a cash payment is received or the customer becomes legally obligated to make such a payment because the seller has fulfilled its responsibilities under the contract.

However, many provisions can exist in arrangements that raise questions about the realizability of revenue. For example, when payment is received but the customer has a right of return, the right of return may make realizability uncertain. In other arrangements, the fee may vary based on one or more events whose outcome will not be known until after initial payment or delivery. In transactions with vendor financing and/or extended payment terms, the fee may not be realizable because of the extent of the seller's involvement with the financing of payments made (or to be made) by the customer.

Four Conditions for Recognition

The accounting literature that has been developed since the conceptual framework guidance was introduced has attempted to provide additional conditions for determining when revenue has been earned and is realizable. As previously mentioned, some of this literature is transaction-specific (e.g., SOP 00-2 (ASC 926-605) on the licensing of motion pictures), while some is issue-specific (e.g., FAS-49 (ASC 470-40-05), on product financing arrangements). In contrast, SAB Topic 13 (ASC 605-10-S99) is more general in nature.

Although different pieces of literature use different terms, each generally requires that the following four conditions are met in order for revenue to be both earned and realizable (e.g., SAB Topic 13A1; SOP 97-2, par. 8; SOP 00-2, par. 7; FAS-50, par. 7) (e.g., ASC 605-10-S99; 985-605-25-3; 926-605-25-1; 928-605-25-2):

1. Persuasive evidence of an arrangement exists.

2. The arrangement fee is fixed or determinable.

3. Delivery or performance has occurred.

4. Collectibility is reasonably assured.

> **OBSERVATION:** Each of the above four conditions must be met by the end of an accounting period in order to recognize revenue from a particular transaction. If any condition fails to be satisfied, revenue recognition must be deferred until the period in which the final condition is met.[1]

Each of the four criteria will be discussed in this chapter. Generally speaking, the analyses of the collectibility and persuasive evidence criteria do not change significantly based on the type of transaction involved. Therefore, the discussion of these conditions in this chapter applies to all transactions, and there is no material discussion of these conditions in Chapters 4–7 and 9–10, which address specific issues and transaction types.

By contrast, the analyses of the fixed or determinable fee and delivery or performance criteria can differ significantly based on the type of transaction involved. Therefore, the basic discussion of these criteria included in this chapter is supplemented by significant additional discussion by transaction type in Chapters 4–7 and 9–10.

PERSUASIVE EVIDENCE OF AN ARRANGEMENT

To determine whether the "earned" criterion has been met—that is, to assess whether the seller has substantially completed what it has

---

[1] Meeting the revenue recognition conditions after the end of the period is a "Non-recognized Subsequent Event," as discussed in Paragraph 10 of FAS-165, *Subsequent Events* (ASC 855). Nonrecognized subsequent events "provide evidence with respect to conditions that did *not* exist at the date of the balance sheet but arose after the balance sheet date."

agreed to do—it is necessary to identify what obligations the seller has undertaken. For this reason, revenue cannot be recognized until there is persuasive evidence of an arrangement. The existence of persuasive evidence of an arrangement permits identification of the seller's obligations and facilitates an analysis of whether the seller has fulfilled these obligations and earned the related revenue.

Persuasive evidence of an arrangement also helps ensure that the realizability criterion is met because it provides the legal basis on which the seller can demand payment from the customer. If no arrangement exists under which the buyer has agreed to pay the seller for performing under the contract, any revenue the seller believes he or she is owed may not be realizable and the seller may not have a right to payment under the law.

What Constitutes "Persuasive Evidence"

The accounting literature does not specify the types of evidence that qualify as persuasive evidence of an arrangement. Rather, the evidence used to document a sales transaction provides the evidence necessary for revenue recognition.

Many companies routinely document sales arrangements by written contracts. For these companies, persuasive evidence of an arrangement generally would exist upon execution of the final contract by both parties. Thus, despite the fact that the seller may have delivered the products or services specified and billed the customer, no revenue should be recognized if the final contract is pending.

ILLUSTRATION: PERSUASIVE EVIDENCE OF AN ARRANGEMENT

(Adapted from SAB Topic 13A2, ques. 1 (ASC 605-10-S99, A2, ques. 1))

Facts: Company A has product available to ship to customers prior to the end of its current fiscal quarter. Customer Beta places an order for the product, and Company A delivers the product prior to the end of its current fiscal quarter. Company A's normal and customary business practice for this class of customer is to enter into a written sales agreement that requires the signatures of the authorized representatives of the Company and its customer to be binding. Company A prepares a written sales agreement, and its authorized representative signs the agreement before the end of the quarter. However, Customer Beta does not sign the agreement because Customer Beta is awaiting the requisite approval by its legal department. Customer Beta's purchasing department has orally agreed to the sale and stated that the contract will be formally approved the first week of Company A's next fiscal quarter. Company A expects that payment will be made on normal credit terms.

Discussion: In view of Company A's business practice of requiring a written sales agreement for this class of customer, persuasive evidence of an arrangement would require a final agreement that has been executed by the properly authorized personnel of the customer. Customer Beta's execution of the sales agreement after the end of the quarter causes the transaction to be considered a transaction of the subsequent period.

EXAMPLE: PERSUASIVE EVIDENCE OF AN ARRANGEMENT

Citrix Systems Form 10-K—Fiscal Year Ended December 31, 2007

Persuasive evidence of the arrangement exists. The Company recognizes revenue on packaged products and appliances upon shipment to distributors and resellers. For packaged product and appliance sales, it is the Company's customary practice to require a purchase order from distributors and resellers who have previously negotiated a master packaged product distribution or resale agreement. For electronic and paper license arrangements, the Company typically requires a purchase order from the distributor, reseller, or end-user (depending on the arrangement) and an executed product license agreement from the end-user. For technical support, product training, and consulting services, the Company requires a purchase order and an executed agreement. For online services, the Company requires the customer or the reseller to electronically accept the terms of an online services agreement or execute a contract.

If a company does not have a standard or customary business practice of using written contracts to document a sales arrangement, there would usually be other forms of written or electronic evidence to document the transaction. Such evidence might be as simple as a restaurant check, a cash register receipt, or a click on the "submit order" button on an internet site (SAB Topic 13A2, ques. 1) (ASC 605-10-S99, A2, ques. 1).

The methods used to document sales transactions may vary from location to location within a company, or may vary based on the type of customer (e.g., corporate vs. individual) or transaction (e.g., product vs. service). Therefore, each transaction should be evaluated based upon the documentation that would be expected to exist for the type of transaction.

EXAMPLE: PERSUASIVE EVIDENCE OF AN ARRANGEMENT

8X8, Inc. Form 10-K—Fiscal Year Ended March 31, 2007

For all sales, except those completed via the Internet, we use either a binding purchase order or other signed agreement as evidence of an arrangement.

For sales over the Internet, we use a credit card authorization as evidence of an arrangement, and recognize revenue upon settlement of the transaction, if there are no customer acceptance conditions. We do not settle credit card transactions until equipment related to the transaction, if any, is shipped to a customer.

In some instances, a company may enter into a transaction in which the documentation is not consistent with the company's standard practice. In these cases, judgment must be applied in assessing whether persuasive evidence of an arrangement exists. For example, if a company that normally uses written contracts to document its arrangements delivers its product and receives payment and acceptance of the product from its customer, persuasive evidence of an arrangement may very well exist, even if the formal contract was never signed due to the customer's desire for quick delivery.

DELIVERY

To ensure that the earned criterion is met, delivery or performance must occur before revenue is recognized. This requirement helps assess whether the obligations undertaken by the vendor have been completed. Each obligation is generically referred to as an element or deliverable. This assessment must be done individually for each deliverable in an arrangement. However, when multiple deliverables exist, certain issues must be considered when allocating the arrangement fee to the individual deliverables. These issues are discussed in Chapter 4, "Multiple-Element Arrangements."

Basic Models

Delivery of an element occurs when the seller has fulfilled its obligations related to that element and the customer has realized value from the element. Delivery of some elements may occur all at once, while delivery of others may occur over a period of time. Although an infinite variety of deliverables can be included in a revenue arrangement, the delivery or performance condition is evaluated for accounting purposes using one of two models. The decision of which model to use is based on whether the vendor's obligations are completed and whether the value transferred to the customer all at once or over a period of time. The first model, referred to in this product as the Completed Performance model, is used when a single point in time can be identified as the point when the vendor completes its obligation and the customer realizes value all at once. The second model, referred to as the Proportional Performance model, is used when (1) the seller completes the performance obligation, and (2) the customer receives value over a period of time.

> ☞ **PRACTICE POINTER:** No matter which model is used, the delivery condition is not met until the vendor's obligation to the customer is fulfilled. Therefore, if the vendor hires a third party to fulfill the obligation, revenue cannot be recognized until the third party actually fulfills the obligation. Merely hiring an outside party to provide a deliverable to the customer does not constitute delivery, because hiring a third party does not provide value to the customer. Value is not provided unless and until the customer actually receives the deliverable.

Choosing a Model

The choice of which model to use is a key step toward recognizing revenue. In some cases, the identification of an appropriate model is easy, because the performance pattern is clear. Other situations require significant judgment. Although some generalizations can be made about what kind of deliverables should be evaluated under each model, it is important to review the substance of each deliverable to determine when delivery occurs for that deliverable.

The discussion below focuses on different types of deliverables, since it is necessary to separately assess delivery for each deliverable in an arrangement. When an arrangement includes multiple deliverables, the delivery condition is not met for a particular deliverable if it does not have value to the customer on a standalone basis. This is discussed further in Chapter 4, "Multiple-Element Arrangements."

Products

The delivery of products generally is evaluated using the Completed Performance model, because the customer realizes all of the value at once—that is, when the product is physically delivered to the customer. At that time, the vendor completes its entire obligation with respect to the deliverable. The Completed Performance model is sometimes referred to as the product model.

Although a manufacturer may take a number of actions related to an arrangement before delivering the product, these actions generally do not provide value to the customer until delivery occurs. Therefore, it is usually not appropriate to recognize revenue using the Proportional Performance Model as the product is being manufactured. However, delivery of a product must be evaluated using the Proportional Performance model when the arrangement qualifies for percentage of completion accounting. This method of accounting is discussed in Chapter 9, "Contract Accounting."

Products may also be evaluated under the Proportional Performance model when the arrangement involves a subscription. See Chapter 5, "Product Deliverables," for further discussion on delivery of products.

Services

The delivery of a service generally is evaluated using the Proportional Performance model, because the vendor fulfills a portion of its obligations and the customer receives value as each part of the service is performed. As a result, revenue is earned as each part of the service is performed. For example, a home health service that agrees to visit a patient once a week for a year should recognize a portion of the revenue with each visit (provided the other conditions for revenue recognition have been met). In situations where service is provided over a period of time, delivery may occur ratably throughout that time period. For example, the fee in an arrangement to provide high-speed internet access for one year would be recognized ratably over the year (provided the other conditions for revenue recognition have been met).

The correct model to use for some service transactions, however, is less clear. For example, in certain service transactions, although the service is performed over a period of time, the customer realizes value only if and when the final act of the service is performed. This may be true in the case of installation services, where the customer may not realize any value from the installation until it is completed. Similarly, a sales agent generally would not be considered to have delivered services until the customer makes a purchase from the supplier. These types of services may be most appropriately evaluated under the Completed Performance model.

See Chapter 6, "Service Deliverables," for additional discussion on the delivery of services.

> **PRACTICE ALERT:** Situations may arise where arrangements that purport to cover only the sale of products or the delivery of services actually contain a lease. See EITF 01-8 (ASC 840-10-15), which provides guidance on how to determine whether an arrangement contains a lease. When an arrangement has a lease, the lease component must be accounted for as such using lease accounting guidelines even though the arrangement is characterized as a product sale or a service transaction. Because of the differences in the accounting treatment of product sales, service transactions, and leases, the determination that a lease exists will likely have a significant effect on the amount and timing of revenue recognition. The provisions of EITF 01-8 (ASC 840-10-15) are discussed under "Leases" later in this chapter.

Intellectual Property

Intellectual property licensing presents challenges in determining when delivery occurs. For example, in a transaction involving the right to use copyrighted material for a two-year period, does delivery occur when the license term begins, or does delivery occur ratably over the two-year period? For certain types of intellectual property transactions, industry- or transaction-specific accounting literature provides guidance on which model to use for assessing delivery. However, there is little authoritative guidance for the majority of intellectual property licenses. A detailed discussion of this topic can be found in Chapter 7, "Intellectual Property Deliverables." In addition, delivery of software is discussed in Chapter 10, "Software—A Complete Model."

Leases

For certain transactions, the model to use for evaluating delivery is specified in the accounting literature. One major category of transactions for which significant guidance exists is leasing. Lease transactions are primarily addressed in FAS-13 (ASC 840), which specifies that the lessor should treat certain leases as operating leases and others as sales-type leases.[2] In substance, an operating lease is evaluated under the Proportional Performance model, with revenue generally being recognized ratably over the lease term. Conversely, revenue recognition in a sales-type lease is based on the Completed Performance model, with performance deemed complete upon physical delivery of the item being leased.

When an arrangement that purports to be only a sale of products or services in effect contains a lease, the accounting treatment of the lease component will likely have a significant effect on the amount and timing of revenue recognition. As a result, and to add clarity to the definition and determination of whether an arrangement contains a lease, supplemental guidance exists in EITF 01-8 (ASC 840-10-15). This guidance builds upon the fundamental definition of a lease in FAS-13 (ASC 840) and requires consideration of the following characteristics in order to determine whether an arrangement contains a lease:

- Only property, plant, or equipment (which includes only land and/or depreciable assets) can be the subject of a lease, and a lease only exists if fulfillment of the arrangement

---

[2] Lease accounting is not addressed in this product. CCH has other sources of guidance that should be consulted for sales-type vs. operating lease classification.

is dependent on the use of specific property, plant, or equipment (the property, plant, or equipment can be either explicitly or implicitly identified) (EITF 01-8, pars. 9–11) (ASC 840-10-15-5 and 15-6).

* A right to use property, plant, or equipment has been conveyed and, therefore a lease exists, if the purchaser/lessee has the right to control use of the underlying property, plant, or equipment. The right to control the use of the property, plant, or equipment exists if either of the following conditions exist:

— The purchaser/lessee (a) has the right to operate the subject assets (either itself or through directing others) in a manner it determines, or (b) has the ability or right to control physical access to the subject assets, while obtaining or controlling more than a minor amount of the output or other utility of the subject assets; or

— It is remote that another party or other parties will take more than a minor amount of the output or other utility of the property, plant, or equipment during the arrangement, and the price the purchaser will pay for the output is neither contractually fixed per unit nor equal to the current market price per unit as of the time of delivery of the output (EITF 01-8, par. 12) (ASC 840-10-15-6).

EITF 01-8 (ASC 840-10-15-17) also notes that executory costs fall within the scope of FAS-13 (ASC 840).

When an arrangement has a lease, the lease deliverable must be accounted for using FAS-13 (ASC 840) even though the overall arrangement is characterized as a product sale or the delivery of services. Separation of the lease element (or elements) from the other elements in the arrangement is discussed in Chapter 4, "Multiple-Element Arrangements."

Construction and Other Long-Term Contracts

Another type of transaction for which U.S. GAAP provides specific guidance on revenue recognition is construction and other long-term contracts. This guidance, in ARB-45 and SOP 81-1 (ASC 605-35), provides factors to consider for determining whether to use the Completed Performance or Proportional Performance model. For long-term contracts, the two models are referred to as the Completed Contract and Percentage-of-Completion methods, respectively. Discussion of the scope and application of long-term contract accounting is included in Chapter 9, "Contract Accounting."

ILLUSTRATION: CHOOSING THE APPROPRIATE MODEL FOR ASSESSING DELIVERY OF PRODUCTS AND SERVICES

The following examples illustrate the typical factors that must be taken into account when choosing which model to use.

EXAMPLE 1

Facts: Company A manufactures and sells furniture. It has a standard product line and customers may choose various colors, fabrics, and finishes from Company A's product catalog. Company A manufactures the furniture only after a customer places an order.

Discussion: Company A performs several activities in fulfilling a customer order, including manufacturing the furniture and physically delivering it to the customer. However, the customer only receives value upon the actual delivery of the furniture. Therefore, delivery or performance does not occur while the furniture is manufactured. Company A should evaluate delivery under the Completed Performance model.

EXAMPLE 2

Facts: Company B charges users a fee for nonexclusive access to its web site containing proprietary databases. The fee allows access to the web site for a one-year period. After the customer is provided a user ID, there are no other specific actions Company B must perform related to an individual customer. Rather, Company B must only continue to allow the customer access to the databases.

Discussion: The only specific action Company B performs with respect to a customer is providing the customer a user ID. However, the customer receives value over the course of the year that access to the databases is provided. Therefore, Company B should evaluate delivery under the Proportional Performance model.

EXAMPLE 3

Facts: Company C, a telecommunications service provider, enters into an arrangement to sell its business customer a number of generic telephones and to provide basic telephone service for one year.

Discussion: The customer receives some value from the arrangement when the telephones are delivered and additional value over the year that service will be provided. Company C should therefore evaluate delivery of the telephones under the Completed Performance model and should evaluate delivery of the telephone service under the Proportional Performance model. Chapter 4, "Multiple-Element Arrangements," should be consulted for purposes of determining whether the telephones and basic telephone service should be treated as separate elements for accounting purposes.

EXAMPLE 4

Facts: Company D provides training to corporate boards of directors on carrying out their responsibilities. When Company D gets a new client, it spends time learning about the company, its management personnel, and the industries in which it operates. Company D uses this information to customize the training course for that company's board of directors. Company D then delivers the training to the board during a day-long session.

Discussion: Company D performs several activities in the course of fulfilling its responsibilities, some of which involve the design of customer-specific content. However, the customer receives value only when the final act, the delivery of the training, occurs. Therefore, Company D should use the Completed Performance model to evaluate delivery for its transactions.

EXAMPLE 5

Facts: Company E publishes guidance on accounting for various transactions. Company E updates its materials once per year and prints a hard-copy book after each update. Customers either purchase the most recent hard-copy version of the materials or purchase online access to the information for one year.

Discussion: Customers who buy the hard-copy book receive value from the transaction when the book is delivered, and Company E has no further obligations once the book is delivered. However, online subscribers receive value throughout the year that access is provided, and Company E fulfills a portion of its obligation each day of the year. Therefore, the Completed Performance model is appropriate for sales of books, and the Proportional Performance model is appropriate for sales of online subscriptions.

Applying the Completed Performance Model

As noted above, the Completed Performance model is used when a single point in time can be identified at which the vendor completes its obligation. This should coincide with the point in time that the customer has realized value by obtaining an asset, the results of a service, or other benefits. Under this model, the delivery criterion is met, in total, at that particular point in time. Therefore, the Completed Performance model is used when performance takes place all at once or when it takes place over a period of time, but value is not transferred to the customer until the final act is completed. Because all revenue is recognized at that time, large differences in revenue for a financial reporting period can occur depending on whether delivery occurs just before or just after period-end.

In a product sale, performance generally is completed when the product is delivered to the customer. Determining exactly when that occurs, however, is not always straightforward. For example, when a product is shipped through the mail or by a third-party carrier, delivery may occur when the product leaves the seller's premises or when it arrives at the buyer's location, depending on the shipping terms. In other situations, a seller may retain certain risks and rewards so that performance is not actually complete, despite physical delivery. The resolution of these types of issues and uncertainties is required to apply the Completed Performance model to a product sale appropriately.

When the Completed Performance model is applied to a service transaction, it is generally because the final act of the service is the act that allows the customer to realize the benefits of the service. Therefore, if the Completed Performance model is appropriate for a service, the point at which delivery is deemed to occur (i.e., completion of the final act) must be identified.

In other transactions where the completed performance model is applied, the issues that are likely to be important for determining when to recognize revenue are similar to those in a product sale. The application of the Completed Performance model to various transactions is more fully discussed in Chapters 5–10.

Applying the Proportional Performance Model

In the Proportional Performance model, revenue is recognized as performance occurs, based on the relative value of the performance that has occurred to that point in time. This model is useful when the vendor fulfills its obligation over a period of time, and the customer receives value throughout the performance period.

In applying the Proportional Performance model to a service transaction, the key issue is generally the pattern of performance. For example, if a service transaction involves a specified number of similar acts, such as mowing a lawn once a week for an entire summer, an equal amount of revenue should be recognized upon completion of each act. However, when the acts are not similar, revenue should be allocated based on their relative values. In other situations, value may be transferred to a customer ratably over a period of time, such as when the service is insurance coverage or access to a health club. The application of the Proportional Performance model to various transactions is discussed more fully in Chapters 5–10.

EXAMPLE: APPLYING THE PROPORTIONAL PERFORMANCE MODEL

Costco Wholesale Corporation Form 10-K—Fiscal Year Ended September 2, 2007

Membership fee revenue represents annual membership fees paid by substantially all of the Company's members. The Company accounts for membership fee revenue on a deferred basis, whereby, revenue is recognized ratably over the one-year membership period. In 2007, the Company performed a detailed analysis of the timing of recognition of membership fees based on each member's specific renewal date, as this methodology represented an improvement over the historical method, which was based on the period in which the fee was collected. This review resulted in a $56,183 reduction in membership fee revenue in 2007 and a corresponding increase to deferred membership fees on the Company's consolidated balance sheet.

FIXED OR DETERMINABLE FEE

Ensuring that a fee is fixed or determinable prior to revenue recognition is at the crux of the realizability criterion. For example, if the fee is dependent upon future events, it is unclear whether it will indeed be paid. As a result, it is uncertain whether the fee is realizable. However, a fee that is not fixed or determinable may also suggest that revenue has not yet been earned, if the seller is still required to perform in some manner.

Meaning of Fixed or Determinable

Although several pieces of accounting literature, including SOP 97-2 (ASC 985-605), SOP 00-2 (ASC 926-605), and SAB Topic 13 (ASC 605-10-S99), refer to the fixed or determinable fee criterion, there is no clear definition of fixed or determinable fees. Instead, the literature provides examples that illustrate certain concepts relevant to determining whether a fee is fixed or determinable.

Many arrangement terms raise questions about whether the fee is fixed or determinable. For example, customer rights of return or cancellation introduce uncertainty into the arrangement. Similarly, fees subject to change based upon the future success or failure of the work performed may indicate that a fee is not fixed or determinable. In addition, arrangements may have penalty or bonus clauses that introduce potential variability into the arrangements.

Whether a fee is fixed or determinable is not always an "all or nothing" answer. In many arrangements, a portion of the fee is not subject to change for any reason, while another portion may vary based on one or more factors. In these instances, the portion of the fee that is not subject to change should be considered fixed or determinable.

> **OBSERVATION:**   The requirement of a fixed or determinable fee refers to whether the fee can vary based upon future events. In certain situations, a fee that cannot change based upon future events may not be quantifiable until certain information related to past events is collated and evaluated. For example, consider an arrangement in which a company provides trans-action processing services that are priced based on the number of transactions processed each month for its customers. At month-end, although the fee cannot change based on future events, the amount owed by every customer will only be deter-mined after it has been calculated using monthly activity reports from the company's various locations.
>
> In other cases, a vendor may base revenue estimates on historical transactions or use information provided by licensees or resellers of its intellectual property in order to estimate roy-alty or fee revenue. However, changing market and technolog-ical conditions as well as a lack of adequate information from new users may not allow the vendor to develop reasonable estimates. Under these conditions, revenue cannot be recog-nized until the vendor receives actual use or resale information from licensees or resellers.
>
> In these situations, the fact that information about past events must be gathered and analyzed does not preclude a conclusion that the fee is fixed or determinable. Instead, the company should record its best estimate of the revenue at period-end and adjust that estimate when information is completely analyzed to calculate the precise fee amount. If this analysis is completed before the financial statements are released, it should be incorporated into those financial statements.[3]

Evaluating Terms That Allow for Variable Fees

Any term in an arrangement that could change the arrangement fee should be analyzed to determine whether that fee (in whole or in

---

[3] The analysis of information about events that occurred before the end of the account-ing period is a "Recognized" subsequent event, as discussed in Paragraph 8 of FAS-165, *Subsequent Events* (ASC 855). Recognized subsequent events are "subsequent events that provide additional evidence about conditions that existed at the date of the balance sheet, including the estimates inherent in the process of preparing financial statements."

part) is not fixed or determinable. Although the accounting literature provides no direct guidance on how to make such a determination, existing guidance and concepts applied in the accounting for related issues can be used to identify the following four categories of factors that might cause a fee to be variable:

1. *Factors within the customer's control.* For example, general return rights and incentive fees based on the customer's usage of a product.

2. *Factors within the seller's control.* For example, certain forms of price protection and bonuses relating to cumulative performance over the term of a contract.

3. *Factors within control of a specified third party.* For example, an agent's fee might be partially refundable based on whether the end customer exercises a right of return; or, a lease agreement may require additional payments if the lessee exceeds certain sales levels (in this situation the additional lease payments are in control of the lessee's customers).

4. *Factors based on an index or other underlying.* For example, fees based on investment return as compared to an index, fees that vary with changes in the CPI or the inflation rate, and contingencies based on the weather.

Factors within the Customer's Control

General Rule

If an arrangement fee can be increased by future customer actions, the increase is not fixed or determinable until the customer takes the action. This is the case for a vendor that receives a bonus based on the usage of a delivered product or a licensor of intellectual property that is due a fee for each sale of a product incorporating the licensed technology. Thus, even if most customers do use the product or incorporate the licensed technology in the manner specified, revenue cannot be recognized until that usage or incorporation occurs.

> **OBSERVATION:** Arrangements involving factors within the customer's control may be specified in different ways to achieve the same result. For example, an arrangement could entitle the seller to a $20,000 bonus if the customer uses the product more than 20 times in the first year. Alternatively, an economically similar arrangement could be created if the arrangement started with a $20,000 higher fee and specified that a penalty of $20,000 would occur if the customer did not use the product more than 20 times in the first year. Both of

these arrangements should be accounted for as if the $20,000 at risk is not fixed or determinable until the customer uses the product 20 times.

There are other situations in which customer actions or rights could reduce the amount of revenue that will ultimately be realized by the seller. Volume or other rebates and rights of return are examples. When a customer has such a right, the portion of the fee at risk generally should not be considered fixed or determinable until the customer's right has expired.

Exception—Ability to Estimate Breakage

Generally, fees subject to change based on customer actions are not fixed or determinable. However, there are many situations where customers' actions can be predicted. For example, many customers do not take advantage of the rights they have in an arrangement. This is called "breakage." FAS-48 (ASC 605-15-25-1 through 25-4), which addresses rights to return products, in certain circumstances permits revenue recognition based on estimated breakage as long as the estimate is reasonable and reliable. This guidance has been used by analogy, extending the application of breakage estimates to other rights as well. The breakage exception, however, only applies when the customer's future action would reduce the fee. In other words, absent the customer's action, the fee would be higher.

> **SEC REGISTRANT ALERT:** A related issue is when the vendor can derecognize a deferred revenue obligation in the absence of performance. Generally, the SEC staff has stated that the derecognition guidance of FAS-140 (ASC 405-20) governs the accounting treatment for this consideration. However, in a December 5, 2005, speech at the 2005 AICPA National Conference on Current SEC and PCAOB Developments, the SEC staff indicated that derecognition may also be acceptable when the vendor can demonstrate that it is remote that the customer will require performance. The staff discussed the application of this concept to sales of gift cards, some percentage of which would not be redeemed. Although recognition of breakage at the time of sale would not be appropriate (no performance has occurred), breakage could be recognized as the vendor was legally released from the obligation (by redemption or expiration). Alternatively, the staff indicated that breakage for unused gift cards could be recognized on the basis of actual redemption experience (reasonable and objective determination of the amount and the time period of actual redemption would be a prerequisite).

EXAMPLE: ESTIMATE OF BREAKAGE

Limited Brands Form 10-K—Fiscal Year Ended February 2, 2008

The Company's brands sell gift cards with no expiration dates to customers. The Company does not charge administrative fees on unused gift cards. The Company recognizes income from gift cards when they are redeemed by the customer. In addition, the Company recognizes income on unredeemed gift cards when it can determine that the likelihood of the gift card being redeemed is remote and that there is no legal obligation to remit the unredeemed gift cards to relevant jurisdictions (gift card breakage). The Company determines the gift card breakage rate based on historical redemption patterns. The Company accumulated enough historical data to determine the gift card breakage rate at Bath & Body Works and Express during the fourth quarter of 2005 and Victoria's Secret during the fourth quarter of 2007. Gift card breakage is included in Net Sales in the Consolidated Statements of Income.

During the fourth quarter of 2005, the Company recognized $30 million in pre-tax income related to the initial recognition of gift card breakage at Express and Bath & Body Works. During the fourth quarter of 2007, the Company recognized $48 million in pre-tax income related to the initial recognition of gift card breakage at Victoria's Secret.

Limited Brands Form 10-K—Fiscal Year Ended February 3, 2007

All of the Company's brands sell gift cards with no expiration dates. The Company recognizes income from gift cards when they are redeemed by the customer. In addition, the Company recognizes income on unredeemed gift cards when it can determine that the likelihood of the gift card being redeemed is remote and that there is no legal obligation to remit the unredeemed gift cards to relevant jurisdictions (gift card breakage). The Company determines the gift card breakage rate based on historical redemption patterns. During the fourth quarter of 2005, the Company accumulated enough historical data to determine the gift card breakage rate at both Express and Bath & Body Works. Once the breakage rate is determined, it is recognized over a 36-month period based on historical redemption patterns of each brand's gift cards. Gift Card breakage is included in net sales in the Consolidated Statements of Income.

During the fourth quarter of 2005, the Company recognized $30 million in pre-tax income related to the initial recognition of gift card breakage at Express and Bath & Body Works. The Company will recognize gift card breakage at Victoria's Secret and Limited Stores when adequate historical data exist.

Rights of return When a customer has the right to receive a full refund by returning a product, the fee may not be fixed or determinable. Indeed, some might also suggest that there is no persuasive evidence of an arrangement under these circumstances. Nevertheless, despite the existence of such rights, revenue can often be recognized before the right of return expires. These rights have been specifically addressed in FAS-48, which concludes that revenue may be recognized upon delivery as long as a reliable estimate of returns can be made and certain other conditions are met. If a company enters into a large number of homogeneous transactions, a reliable estimate may be developed based on its historical experience. In this situation, the company must defer only revenue in the amount expected to be refunded. Further information about accounting for rights of return, including a discussion of factors that may indicate a reliable estimate of returns cannot be made, is provided in Chapter 5, "Product Deliverables."

Rights to cancel service transactions   In some service transactions, customers have a right (similar to a product return right)—to cancel the remainder of the service and receive a full refund (i.e., not just a refund based on the remaining service to be performed). This is common in the sale of certain memberships (such as warehouse club memberships) and may exist for a limited time in the sales of insurance policies, warranties, and similar items. FAS-48 does not provide guidance for cancellation rights in service transactions; its scope is limited to product returns. However, the application of concepts similar to those in FAS-48 may allow a company to make reliable estimates of refunds or cancellations. When this is the case, recognition of revenue excluding the amount the company expects to refund is acceptable, although not required.

> **SEC REGISTRANT ALERT:**   In question 1 of SAB Topic 13A4a (ASC 605-10-S99, A4a), the SEC staff expressed its view that, while recognition of revenue based on a reliable estimate of breakage may be acceptable, deferral of all revenue until the refund period ends is preferable in these situations.

Other service transactions may include a right to cancel the remainder of the service for a pro-rata refund (i.e., a refund of only a portion of the fee) based on the proportion of the service remaining to be provided. In these situations, the fee becomes fixed or determinable ratably throughout the service period, as the amount of the refund the customer could receive decreases. Because the service is delivered on a proportional basis throughout the period, these types of cancellation rights generally do not cause further delays in revenue recognition.

Additional information about the accounting for service cancellation rights, including a discussion of factors that may indicate a reliable estimate of refunds cannot be made, is provided in Chapter 6, "Service Deliverables."

Coupons and rebates   Certain revenue arrangements give the customer the ability to send in a form or other documentation of their purchase to obtain a full or partial rebate of the purchase price (e.g., a $20 mail-in rebate found in the box of a computer printer). In other arrangements, a vendor may sell products to a retailer and also issue coupons to the retailers' customers (e.g., a newspaper coupon for 50 cents off a box of cereal). In both of these instances, the fee from the sale can change after the seller has performed under the arrangement. In general, the existence of a coupon or rebate indicates that the purchase price is not fixed or determinable.

Redemption rates on coupons and rebates are much lower than 100%. Therefore EITF 01-9 (ASC 605-50) concludes that revenue potentially subject to rebate or refund may be recognized as long as a reliable estimate of breakage can be made. The following factors may impair a company's ability to make a reasonable estimate of coupon or rebate redemptions (EITF 01-9, par. 23) (ASC 605-15-25-3):

- Significant possibility of external factors, such as obsolescence or regulatory changes, affecting the product;

- A long offer period;

- A lack of relevant historical experience; and

- An absence of a large volume of relatively homogeneous transactions.

Other sales incentives involve an offer to rebate or refund a specified amount of cash only if the customer makes a specified cumulative level of purchases or remains a customer for a minimum time period. Like rebates that are exercisable based on a single purchase, revenue subject to volume rebates may be recognized based on estimated breakage as long as the estimate is reasonable and reliable.

If a reliable estimate of the rebate liability cannot be made for either single or volume purchases, the related revenue is not considered fixed or determinable. As a result, this revenue cannot be recognized until the rebate rights lapse.

Further information about the accounting for rebate rights, including a more detailed discussion of factors that may indicate a reliable estimate of rebates cannot be made, is included in Chapter 8, "Miscellaneous Issues."

EXAMPLE: ESTIMATE OF REBATE LIABILITY

Abaxis Form 10-K—Fiscal Year Ended March 31, 2009

Distributor and Customer Rebates

We offer distributor pricing rebates and customer incentives from time to time. The distributor pricing rebates are offered to distributors upon meeting the sales volume requirements during a qualifying period. The distributor pricing rebates are recorded as a reduction to gross revenues during a qualifying period. Cash rebates are offered to distributors or customers who purchase certain products or instruments during a promotional period. Cash rebates are recorded as a reduction to gross revenues.

The distributor pricing rebate program is offered to distributors in the North America veterinary market, upon meeting the sales volume requirements of veterinary products during the qualifying period. Factors used in the rebate calculations include the identification of products sold subject to a rebate during the qualifying period and which rebate percentage applies. Based on these factors and using historical trends, adjusted for current changes, we estimate the amount of the rebate that will be paid and record the liability as a reduction to gross revenues when we record the sale of the product. Settlement of the rebate accruals from the date of sale ranges from one to three months after sale. At March 31, 2009, 2008 and 2007, the accrual balances related to distributor pricing rebates were $74,000, $140,000 and $229,000, respectively. The changes in the rebate accrual at each fiscal year end are based upon distributors meeting the purchase requirements during the quarter.

Other rebate programs offered to distributors or customers vary from period to period in the medical and veterinary markets. Generally, the rebate program relates to the sale of certain products during a specified promotional period. As part of the rebate program, a distributor or customer receives a cash rebate upon purchasing the products in the North America market during a promotional period. Factors used in the rebate calculations include the identification of products sold subject to a rebate during the qualifying period and the estimated lag time between the sale and payment of a rebate. We estimate the amount of the rebate that will be paid, and record the liability as a reduction of gross revenues when we record the sale of the product. Settlement of the rebate accruals from the date of sale ranges from one to six months after sale. At March 31, 2009, 2008 and 2007, the accrual balances related to rebates were $22,000, $0 and $168,000, respectively. The changes in the rebate accrual were due to the type of marketing promotions offered during the fiscal year and timing of the rebate obligations paid to customers.

The following table is an analysis of the rollforward activities for the distributor and customer rebate accruals (in thousands):

	Balance at Beginning of Year	Provisions	Payments	Balance at End of Year
Year Ended March 31, 2009:				
Distributor rebates	$140	$ 264	$(330)	$ 74
Customer rebates	–	30	(8)	22
Total distributor and customer rebates	$140	$ 294	$(338)	$ 96
Year Ended March 31, 2008:				
Distributor rebates	$229	$ 498	$(587)	$140
Customer rebates	168	–	(168)	–
Total distributor and customer rebates	$397	$ 498	$(755)	$140

Year Ended March 31, 2007:

Distributor rebates	$ 90	$ 781	$(642)	$229
Customer rebates	36	328	(196)	168
Total distributor and customer rebates	$126	$1,109	$(838)	$397

Other situations   The concept of reliably estimating breakage has only been addressed in the specific situations discussed above. Analogizing to FAS-48 (ASC 605-15-25-1 through 25-4), question 1 of SAB Topic 13A4a (ASC 605-10-S99, A4a), or EITF 01-9 (ASC 605-50) may be appropriate in a limited number of other situations.

However, no amount of evidence is sufficient to allow the recognition of revenue that will be received if a customer takes a specific action in the future. For example, if a fee in a license arrangement is $100 for a three-month license, and the customer has an option to extend the license to one year for an additional $50, the $50 extension fee cannot be considered fixed or determinable until the option is exercised, no matter how likely it is that the extension will be exercised.

Factors within the Seller's Control

In some cases, the fee in an arrangement may vary based upon the seller's performance. For example, in an arrangement to deliver a large amount of equipment, there may be fixed fees for the equipment, plus a bonus payment if the seller completes all deliveries (or a penalty if the seller does not complete all deliveries) within a specified period. In other situations, a seller may offer price protection to the buyer by agreeing to return a portion of the arrangement fee if the seller subsequently sells the same product or service to another customer at a lower price.

General Rule

The fee may not be fixed or determinable if it depends on the seller's future actions. For example, if a seller can earn a bonus by completing a service ahead of schedule, that bonus should not be recognized until the service is completed ahead of schedule and the bonus is earned.

> **OBSERVATION:** Arrangements like this may be specified in different ways to achieve the same result. For example, an arrangement could entitle the seller to a $20,000 bonus if the service is completed by a particular date. Alternatively, an economically similar arrangement could be created if it started with a $20,000 higher fee and specified that the seller

would be penalized $20,000 if it did not finish by the same date. Both of these arrangements should be accounted for as if the $20,000 at risk is not fixed or determinable until the project is completed by the specified date.

Exception—Ability to Predict or Control Actions

FAS-48 (ASC 605-15-25-1 through 25-4) and related literature provide exceptions that permit revenue recognition when future customer actions can change the arrangement fee. Because a seller's actions are easier to predict than a customer's, a lower threshold of evidence is required. However, if a reliable estimate cannot be made—for example, because the arrangement is unique or contains atypical performance criteria—the vendor's future actions should be interpreted such that they result in the least amount of revenue recognized by the vendor. The accounting literature provides specific guidance on this topic in certain situations.

Conditional rights of return Revenue attributable to delivered items in an arrangement may be refundable if the seller fails to deliver some or all of the other items in the arrangement. The accounting for conditional rights of return in multiple-element arrangements is discussed in Chapter 4, "Multiple-Element Arrangements."

Price protection based solely on sellers' prices Sellers may agree to refund a portion of the purchase price to customers if the sellers' standard prices decrease. Because the seller will determine whether to lower its prices, it may be possible to estimate the effect of this price protection. When this is the case, a vendor may conclude that the fee is fixed in whole or in part. However, if the vendor has shown an inability to predict price decreases or an inability to keep its prices at preferred levels (perhaps due to aggressive competition), then the fee should not be considered fixed or determinable (SOP 97-2, par. 30) (ASC 985-605-25-36).

Exception—Recognition Based on Current Measurements

In some cases, a service provider may agree to a time-based fee arrangement. For example, a hotel manager may agree to compensation based partially on the hotel's operating income for a calendar year or a sales agent may be entitled to a bonus if he or she increases sales by a certain percentage relative to the prior year. In these situations, the question is whether any portion of the incentive fee is fixed or determinable before the end of the measurement period. The SEC staff commented on this situation in EITF D-96 (ASC 605-20-S99) and indicated that such fees may be considered fixed and determinable at any point in time (using the formula and contract terms at that date) even if the vendor cannot predict the results of its future actions. Nonetheless, the SEC staff noted a preference for the conclusion that the incentive fee is not fixed or determinable until the end of the measurement period.

> **OBSERVATION:** In an arrangement where a bonus or additional fee is earned upon meeting a particular threshold, no part of the bonus or additional fee is fixed or determinable until the threshold is met, even if the progress to date indicates that this will occur. Recognition at interim dates would be acceptable only if there are termination provisions that call for a final measurement based on progress to date (SAB Topic 13A4c) (ASC 605-10-S99, A4c).

> **DISCLOSURE ALERT:** See Chapter 12, "Disclosures," for information about required disclosures.

ILLUSTRATION: ACCOUNTING FOR FEES BASED ON A FORMULA

Facts: Investment Advisor A manages Fund B and is paid a flat fee per month, plus 20% of Fund B's returns in excess of 12% annually. The contract may be terminated by either party with reasonable notice at the end of each quarter. In the event of a termination, the amount due for the incentive fee will be calculated as of the termination date based on the fund returns to date by comparing them with a 12% annual return prorated for the portion of the year that has passed.

Assume that Fund B's returns exceed the annual target by $120,000 in the first quarter, $60,000 in the second quarter, $50,000 in the fourth quarter, and are $80,000 less than the target in the third quarter. Thus, the total return of Fund B for the year exceeds the 12% target return by $150,000. Advisor A's 20% share of the $150,000 is $30,000.

Discussion: Advisor A may choose from two accounting policies. The first is not to recognize incentive fee revenue until the end of the one-year measurement period under the theory that none of it is fixed or determinable until then because future poor performance in a subsequent interim period could decrease the incentive fee revenue earned in a prior interim period. This method, which is preferred by the SEC staff, would result in the recognition of $30,000 in incentive fee income on the last day of the year.

The second method is to record incentive fee revenue as the amount that would be due under the formula at the point in time when the contract could be terminated—in this example, at the end of the quarter. Accordingly, Advisor A would record $24,000 of incentive fee revenue in the first quarter and $12,000 in the second quarter. In the third quarter, however, $16,000 of the previously recognized revenue would be reversed. Finally, $10,000 of incentive fee revenue would be recognized in the fourth quarter.

Factors within Control of a Third Party

Certain contracts have fees that vary based on the actions of a party other than the buyer or seller (e.g., agency contracts). In these arrangements, a sales agent may agree to refund its commission if the end customer returns the product. Alternatively, the agent may receive a bonus if a customer the agent introduces to the supplier makes additional purchases from the supplier or renews his or her subscription. Other arrangements, particularly if they are long-term in nature, may contain pricing terms that vary with changes in tax law or industry regulations.

General Rule

Third-party actions are likely to be even more difficult to predict than customer actions. As a result, it is not appropriate to assume that third parties will take actions resulting in additional payments from the customer to the vendor in an arrangement. However, if a third party can take an action that reduces a company's revenue, it is generally appropriate to assume the third party will take such an action.

For example, in an operating lease that provides for additional rent when sales exceed a certain level, the lessor should not recognize this additional amount until the specified level of sales is reached, even if sales trends suggest that this will occur. Similarly, an agent whose fee is at risk if the end customer cancels its arrangement with the seller should generally not recognize the fee as revenue until the end customer's cancellation right lapses.

Exception—Ability to Estimate Breakage

Third-party cancellation and return rights Revenue recognition is acceptable in arrangements that include certain third-party return or cancellation rights as long as the amount of refunds can be reliably estimated. The criteria to determine the reliability of these estimates are similar to those required for estimating breakage in other service transactions (e.g., using the existence of a large pool of homogeneous transactions to derive the estimate). Further discussion on estimating breakage in these situations is included in Chapter 6, "Service Deliverables."

Price-matching Certain retailers, such as electronic stores, routinely offer a form of price protection based on their competitors' prices. These retailers offer to refund the difference between the price paid by a customer and a lower price on the same product offered by a competitor within the next 30 days. Unlike price protection based on the particular vendor's future prices, estimating the effects of a price-matching offer is likely to be very difficult.

However, if a sufficient history exists and the competitive environment is stable, it may be possible to estimate the effects of a price-matching policy. If reliable estimates can be made, revenue may be recognized net of the expected price-matching payments. If a reliable estimate cannot be made, as is likely to be the case, no revenue should be recognized until the price-matching period ends.

ILLUSTRATION: THIRD-PARTY ACTIONS AND FIXED OR DETERMINABLE FEES

(Adapted from SAB Topic 13A4a, ques. 2 (ASC 605-10-S99, A4a, ques. 2))

EXAMPLE 1: A leasing broker's commission from the lessor upon a commercial tenant's signing of a lease agreement is refundable under lessor cancellation privileges if the tenant fails to move into the leased premises by a specified date.

EXAMPLE 2: A talent agent's fee receivable from its principal (a celebrity) for arranging an endorsement for a five-year term is cancelable by the celebrity if the customer breaches the endorsement contract with the celebrity.

EXAMPLE 3: An insurance agent's commission received from the insurer upon selling an insurance policy is entirely refundable for the 30-day period required by state law, and it is subsequently refundable on a declining pro rata basis until the consumer has made six monthly payments.

Discussion: In all of these cases, the arrangement fee can vary based upon the actions of a third party named in the contract. Thus, absent a large volume of homogeneous transactions sufficient to allow a reliable estimate of the effects of these rights, the fee in question should only be recognized as the third party takes actions or as the right to take these actions lapses.

Because of the unique nature of the transactions in Examples 1 and 2, it is unlikely that such a large volume of homogeneous transactions would exist to allow for a reliable estimate of cancellations.

However, in Example 3, a sufficient history may exist. Therefore, the company should evaluate whether it has sufficient evidence to make a reliable estimate of cancellations and thereby recognize revenue. If a sufficient history does not exist, no revenue should be recognized until the 30-day full refund period has lapsed. The revenue would then become fixed or determinable on a ratable basis until the customer has made six payments.

Exception—Regulators' Approval of Rate Increases

In some cases, a regulated company, such as a utility, is permitted to bill requested rate increases before the regulator has ruled on the request. The fact that the regulator has the power to deny the request raises a question about whether the possible increased rates are fixed or determinable. The FASB addressed this question in the context of regulated businesses within the scope of FAS-71 (ASC 980). The FASB concluded that contingent refundability should be treated as a collectibility issue rather than a fixed or determinable issue. Thus, the criteria in paragraph 8 of FAS-5 (ASC 450-20-25) would determine whether a provision for estimated refunds should be recognized (see "Collectibility" in this chapter).

Exception—Fees at Risk Due to Changes in Law or Regulation

When the third-party action that could change the arrangement fee is a legal or regulatory change, it is generally appropriate to assume that no such change will occur. Thus, revenue should be recognized on the basis of existing laws and regulations. For example, in providing guidance on the effects of potential changes in tax law on income tax calculations, FAS-109, *Accounting for Income Taxes* (ASC 740, *Income Taxes*; 740-10-25-47), specifically prohibits the assumption of any changes until they are enacted. However, if changes that would result in a reduced fee are considered probable, a reserve for refunds may be required under FAS-5 (ASC 450-20-25-2).

Other Exceptions

If unique circumstances make it unlikely that the portion of the fee at risk will actually be lost, it may be possible to conclude that the fee is fixed or determinable, despite the existence of the contingency. Each set of facts and circumstances should be carefully analyzed to determine whether this is the case.

ILLUSTRATION: FEE MAY VARY BASED ON THIRD-PARTY ACTIONS

Facts: Company X acts as a sales representative for Company Y. Company X's commission is earned on a sliding scale such that its commission on the first 10,000 units of Company Y's products sold in a year is $5 per unit and the commission for each unit beyond that is $7 per unit. Company X has been selling Company Y's products for several years and has always sold at least 20,000 units. At the end of the first quarter, Company X has sold 5,000 units of Company Y's product and collected $25,000 from Company Y. Company X believes that it will sell approximately 5,000 units per quarter for the rest of the year.

Discussion: Company X believes that it will eventually realize $120,000 in commissions during the year (10,000 units at $5, plus another 10,000 units at $7), an average of $6 per unit, and has historical experience that supports this estimate. Therefore, Company X may believe that it should record a receivable of $5,000 at the end of the first quarter, in addition to the revenue it has already collected. However, whether Company X meets its estimated sales is at least partially in control of third parties, that is, the customers who purchase Company Y's product. The additional revenue is not fixed or determinable and Company X should only recognize the $25,000 it has collected as revenue in the first quarter. Revenue attributable to additional sales should be recorded only when those sales occur.

Factors Based on an Index

Many leases have rent escalation clauses tied to the inflation rate or consumer price index. Other arrangements, such as those to deliver commodities, may include fees that are based on the market price of the commodity on a particular date. These are examples of factors unrelated to a specific party's actions that may nonetheless cause an arrangement fee to be variable.

> **PRACTICE ALERT:** Some sales arrangements include embedded rights and obligations that may meet the definition of a derivative in FAS-133 (ASC 815-10-15). Depending on their nature and economic relationship to the remainder of the arrangement, these embedded features may have to be accounted for separately, similar to a freestanding derivative. Such an embedded derivative is subject to the same accounting requirements as a freestanding derivative, and the remaining host arrangement is accounted for using applicable revenue recognition principles.

Like the other types of variable fees discussed previously, fees that vary based upon future changes in an index or other underlying may not be fixed or determinable, because it is generally not appropriate to recognize revenue using predictions of future events. However, as noted above, there are situations where it is permissible to recognize revenue based on predictions of future customer, seller, or third-party actions, particularly when a sufficient body of evidence exists such that reliable estimates can be made. This evidence, however, does not usually exist to predict future changes in an index or other underlying. Therefore, revenue should be recognized in these situations based on the then-current measurement, which assumes no future increases or decreases. The effects of changes in the index or underlying should be recognized as soon as such changes occur (FAS-13, par. 5n) (ASC 840-10-55-11).

EXHIBIT 3-1
FIXED OR DETERMINABLE FEES

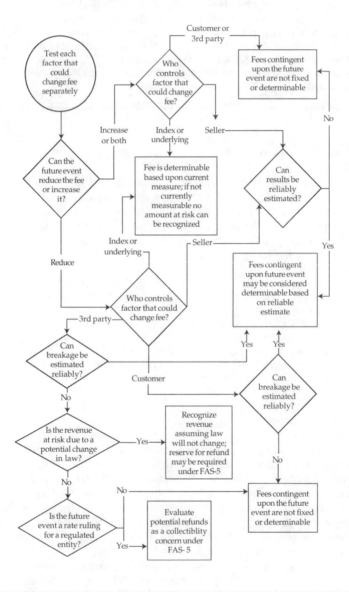

Fees Affected by Multiple Factors

Many arrangements have fees that can vary based on multiple factors, each of which may be under the control of a different party or tied to a different index. In general, each factor should be evaluated separately, with revenue being recognized only if none of the factors preclude the fee from being considered fixed or determinable.

COLLECTIBILITY

The final condition that must be met before revenue can be recognized is that collection of the fee must be reasonably assured. This condition is at the crux of whether the arrangement fee is indeed realizable. Clearly, when a fee is uncollectible, no revenue should be recognized, as the company will not receive an economic benefit from the arrangement.

The accounting literature, however, does not provide specific criteria that should be used to evaluate whether collection is reasonably assured. The same factors used to develop a bad debt reserve for accounts receivable also should be helpful in determining whether collection of an arrangement fee is reasonably assured. This evaluation should be performed when the other three conditions for revenue recognition are met.

Accounting if Collectibility Is Not Reasonably Assured

If collectibility is not reasonably assured at the time the other three revenue recognition conditions are met, revenue should not be recognized until collection becomes reasonably assured or occurs. In general, the direct costs of the transaction should be expensed as if revenue had been recognized. When collection has been deemed less than reasonably assured, such costs generally will not meet the definition of an asset and should not be capitalized or recorded on the balance sheet.[4]

---

[4] In rare circumstances, recognition of revenue and costs under the installment or cost recovery methods may be appropriate (APB-10, par. 12) (ASC 605-10-25-3 and 25-4). However, the use of these methods is usually limited to sales of real estate (FAS-66, par. 22) (ASC 360-20-40-27 through 40-34).

EXAMPLE: COLLECTIBILITY NOT REASONABLY ASSURED

Covad Communications Form 10-K—Fiscal Year Ended December 31, 2007

Revenue Recognition

The Company recognizes revenues from recurring services when (i) persuasive evidence of an arrangement between the Company and the customer exists, (ii) service has been provided to the customer, (iii) the price to the customer is fixed or determinable, and (iv) collectibility of the sales price is reasonably assured. If a customer is experiencing financial difficulties and, (a) is not current in making payments for the Company's services or, (b) is essentially current in making payments but, subsequent to the end of the reporting period, the financial condition of such customer deteriorates significantly or such customer files for bankruptcy protection, then, based on this information, the Company may determine that the collectibility of revenues from this customer is not reasonably assured or its ability to retain some or all of the payments received from a customer that has filed for bankruptcy protection is not reasonably assured. Accordingly, the Company classifies this group of customers as "financially distressed" for revenue recognition purposes. The Company recognizes revenues from financially distressed customers when it collects cash for the services, assuming all other criteria for revenue recognition have been met, but only after the collection of all previous outstanding accounts receivable balances. Payments received from financially distressed customers during a defined period prior to their filing of petitions for bankruptcy protection are recorded in the consolidated balance sheets caption "Unearned revenues" if the Company's ability to retain these payments is not reasonably assured.

The Company has billing disputes with some of its customers. These disputes arise in the ordinary course of business in the telecommunications industry and their impact on the Company's accounts receivable and revenues can be reasonably estimated based on historical experience. In addition, certain revenues are subject to refund if the end-user terminates service within 30 days of service activation. Accordingly, the Company maintains allowances, through charges to revenues, based on the Company's estimates of (i) the ultimate resolution of the disputes and (ii) future service cancellations. The allowances for service credits and bad debt are calculated generally as a percentage, based on historical trends, of balances that meet certain criteria plus specific reserves for known disputes. As stated above, revenues from financially distressed customers are recognized when cash for the services to those customers is collected but only after the collection of all previous outstanding accounts receivable balances.

Upon determining that a customer is financially distressed, the Company establishes an allowance, through a charge to bad debt expense (included in selling, general and administrative expenses in the consolidated statements of operations), based on such customer's outstanding balance.

Accounts receivable consisted of the following:

	December 31,	
	2007	**2006**
Gross accounts receivable	$33,190	$34,123
Allowance for service credits	(2,787)	(2,729)
Allowance for bad debts	(217)	(243)
Accounts receivable, net	$30,186	$31,151

The Company's accounts receivable valuation accounts were as follows:

	December 31,		
	2007	**2006**	**2005**
Allowance for service credits:			
Balance at beginning of period	$2,729	$2,838	$1,405
Provision	4,537	4,536	9,333
Write-offs	(4,479)	(4,645)	(7,330)
Recoveries	—	—	(570)
Balance at end of period	$2,787	$2,729	$2,838
Allowance for bad debts:			
Balance at beginning of period	$243	$486	$161
Provision	453	173	800
Write-offs	(461)	(416)	(329)
Recoveries	(18)	—	(146)
Balance at end of period	$217	$243	$486

Wholesaler Financial Difficulties   In 2007, 2006 and 2005, the Company issued billings to its financially distressed customers aggregating $2,353, $2,161 and $2,897, respectively, which were not recognized as revenues or accounts receivable in the accompanying consolidated financial statements at the time of such billings. However, in accordance with the revenue recognition policy described above, the Company recognized revenues from certain of these customers when cash was collected aggregating $2,154, $2,218 and $2,757 in 2007, 2006 and 2005, respectively. For 2007, 2006 and 2005, revenues from customers that filed for bankruptcy accounted for approximately 0.1%, 0.1% and 0.3%, respectively, of the Company's total net revenues. As of December 31, 2007 and 2006, the Company had contractual receivables from its financially distressed customers totaling $521 and $470, respectively, which are not reflected in the accompanying consolidated balance sheet as of such date.

The Company has identified certain of its customers who were essentially current in their payments for the Company's services prior to December 31, 2007, or have subsequently paid all or significant portions of the respective amounts that the Company recorded as accounts receivable as of December 31, 2007, that the Company believes may be at risk of becoming financially distressed. For 2007, 2006 and 2005, revenues from these customers collectively accounted for approximately 1.8%, 1.3% and 11.0%, respectively, of the Company's total net revenues. As of December 31, 2007 and 2006, receivables from these customers collectively accounted for 3.0% and 1.4%, respectively, of the Company's gross accounts receivable balance. If these customers are unable to demonstrate their ability to pay for the Company's services in a timely manner in periods ending subsequent to 2007, revenue from such customers will only be recognized when cash is collected, as described above.

Uncollectible Amounts and Bad Debts

It is important to evaluate collectibility before revenue is initially recognized so that collectibility problems existing before revenue recognition can be separated from similar problems that arise later. If collection is not reasonably assured at the inception of the arrangement, no revenue would be recognized. If collection is reasonably assured initially and revenue is recognized but subsequent events require a change in the accounts receivable reserve or write-off, the related bad debt expense should be adjusted accordingly. See Chapter 11, "Presentation," for a discussion of income statement classification of bad debt expense.

EVALUATING THE REVENUE RECOGNITION CONDITIONS

Arrangement-by-Arrangement Analysis

When evaluating the four conditions discussed in this chapter, it is important to consider all aspects of the arrangement. To accomplish this, the contracts underlying the arrangement should be reviewed in detail to ensure that all contractual terms are properly interpreted. For most companies, this review should begin with the company's standard sales contract. However, any modifications to the standard contract must be evaluated for their effects on revenue recognition. Modifications to standard contracts could require a company to recognize revenue differently for each contract. For example, if a company sells products with different FOB terms, revenue on those shipped FOB Shipping Point may generally be recognized upon shipment, while revenue on those shipped FOB Destination may not be recognized until the customer receives the products. Similarly, different customer acceptance provisions or cancellation rights in various contracts may cause otherwise similar contracts to be accounted for differently.

> ☞ **PRACTICE POINTER:** Many provisions can affect the timing of revenue recognition. Therefore, companies should have controls in place to limit the types of provisions that sales personnel can add to the standard contract. In addition, controls should be in place to ensure that all sales contracts are reviewed by accounting personnel who can appropriately evaluate whether any nonstandard terms will affect revenue recognition.

All Contractual Terms Must Be Considered

Some companies use contracts that contain terms that customers generally ignore in practice. For example, a contract may provide a customer with the right to have an equipment vendor's engineering staff on-site for a limited period of time after installation of the equipment. However, as long as installation goes smoothly, customers may not take advantage of this right. In other situations, an arrangement may provide the customer with the right to a certain amount of service. History, however, may show that customers on average do not use the maximum amount of service to which they are entitled. This often occurs, for example, in wireless telephone plans that provide a basket of monthly minutes.

In most situations, delivery should be evaluated under the assumption that the vendor will have to fulfill all of its obligations under the arrangement, including those that are only to be performed if requested by the customer. However, if the company has significant historical experience with a large volume of homogeneous contracts that include similar terms and that experience allows the company to reliably estimate breakage, it is acceptable to recognize revenue, assuming that such breakage will occur. There must be significant objective evidence available to support a conclusion that obligations will not have to be fulfilled.

> **SEC REGISTRANT ALERT:** In a December 2002 speech, the SEC staff discussed the issue of breakage in situations where customers make a nonrefundable prepayment for services or goods that they ultimately do not demand. The SEC staff observed that under FAS-140 (ASC 405-20), only performance or legal release will extinguish the vendor's liability. This approach would result in no recognition of income for products or services paid for, but not demanded by the customer, until the end (or expiration) of the performance period. Alternatively, the SEC staff indicated that it will not object to revenue

recognition prior to the expiration of the performance period provided both the following conditions exist:

- Management can demonstrate that the demand for future performance is remote based on a large population of homogeneous transactions; and

- There is objective reliable historical evidence supporting the estimate of breakage.

The SEC staff also indicated that (a) it would be skeptical of an accounting model that results in immediate income for breakage and (b) whether breakage represents revenue or a gain (i.e., other income) depends on the facts and circumstances.

Even if sufficient evidence exists to estimate breakage, it should be an extremely rare occurrence where consideration of breakage results in immediate income recognition. Instead, the arrangement fee should be recognized as the products or services are delivered to the customer over the performance period. For example, consider a situation in which a customer prepays $10,000 for 100 hours of professional services to be provided over the course of one year, but the professional services provider has sufficient history and experience to demonstrate that the customer will ultimately demand only 80 hours of services. In this situation, the professional services provider may adopt an accounting policy that would result in recognizing the $10,000 of revenue over the 80 hours of services as they are rendered—$125 per hour of service rendered. Alternatively, the professional services provider may adopt an accounting policy that would result in recognizing $8,000 of revenue over the 80 hours of services as they are rendered and $2,000 of breakage income upon expiration of the arrangement. However, the professional services provider may not adopt an accounting policy that would result in recognizing $2,000 of breakage income upon initiation of the arrangement and $8,000 of revenue over the 80 hours of services as they are rendered. To do so would be to recognize revenue before performance has occurred.

EXAMPLE: RELIABLE ESTIMATE OF BREAKAGE

Learning Tree Form 10-K—Fiscal Year Ended October 3, 2008

Revenue Recognition

We offer our customers a multiple-course sales discount referred to as a Learning Tree Training Passport. A Learning Tree Training Passport allows an individual Passport holder to attend up to a specified number of courses over a one- to two-year period for a fixed price. For a Training Passport, the amount of revenue recognized for each attendance in a course is based upon the selling price of the Training Passport, the list price of the course taken, the weighted average list price of all courses taken and the estimated average number of courses Passport holders will actually attend. Upon expiration of each individual Training Passport, we record the difference, if any, between the revenues previously recognized and that specific Training Passport's selling price. The estimated attendance rate is based upon the historical experience of the average number of course events that Training Passport holders have been attending. The actual Training Passport attendance rate is reviewed at least semi-annually, and if the Training Passport attendance rates change, the revenue recognition rate for active Training Passports and for Training Passports sold thereafter is adjusted prospectively.

We believe it is appropriate to recognize revenues on this basis in order to most closely match revenue and related costs, as the substantial majority of our Passport holders do not attend the maximum number of course events permitted under their Training Passports. We believe that the use of recent historical data is reasonable and appropriate because of the relative stability of the average actual number of course events attended by Passport holders. The average actual attendance rate for all expired Training Passports has closely approximated the estimated rate we utilize. Although we have seen no material changes in the historical rates as the number of course titles has changed, we monitor such potential effects. In general, determining the estimated average number of course events that will be attended by a Training Passport holder is based on historical trends that may not continue in the future. These estimates could differ in the near term from amounts used in arriving at the reported revenue. If the estimates are wrong, we would record the difference between the revenues previously recognized for that Training Passport and the Training Passport selling price upon expiration of that Training Passport. Thus, the timing of revenue recognition may be affected by an inaccurate estimation, but the inaccuracy would have no effect on the aggregate revenue recognized over the one- to two-year life of each Training Passport.

For newer Passport products for which historical utilization data is not available, we assume that the estimated average number of courses to be attended is equal to the number of courses available on the Passport. This assumed utilization rate may be revised in future periods after sufficient time has passed to amass historical trends.

Multiple Contracts and Side Letters

Most of the time, the boundaries of an arrangement are clearly defined by the contract between the parties. However, to ensure that all appropriate terms are considered prior to revenue recognition, it may be necessary to evaluate multiple contracts as part of a single arrangement. For example, a contract for the sale of products may not specifically provide any rights of return. However, the existence of a master supply agreement with the same customer may grant that customer significant return rights on all purchases.

In other situations, a company may enter into a side letter with the customer that effectively amends the contract between the parties and grants the customer additional rights, requires the seller to provide additional products or services, or alters the payment terms. Any revenue accounting process must consider such a side letter in order to facilitate a thorough analysis.

> **SEC REGISTRANT ALERT:** In early 2003, the SEC staff issued the Report Pursuant to Section 704 of the Sarbanes-Oxley Act of 2002 (the Section 704 Report). In compiling the information in the Section 704 Report, the SEC staff studied enforcement actions filed during the period July 31, 1997, through July 30, 2002. The greatest number of enforcement actions related to improper revenue recognition. A common theme in these enforcement actions related to side letters that were not considered, or inappropriately considered, in recognizing revenue. This is a strong indication that more attention should be given to uncovering the existence and understanding the terms of side agreements and the effects they have on revenue recognition. (Also see SEC FRR 23, *The Significance of Oral Guarantees to the Financial Reporting Process.*)

Further guidance on combining contracts for revenue recognition purposes, including factors that should be considered in deciding whether to combine contracts, is included in Chapter 4, "Multiple-Element Arrangements."

Noncontractual Terms

Although the rights and obligations of both parties to a revenue arrangement are often contractually documented, there are some situations where rights and obligations are established by common business practice, local law, or custom. For example, rights of return are often unspecified in a sales arrangement, but nonetheless offered for a limited time if the customer is not satisfied. Similarly, products that are not covered by a written warranty will often be replaced or repaired by the seller if they do not function properly. All such rights and obligations should be considered in the revenue recognition process.

CHAPTER 4
MULTIPLE-ELEMENT ARRANGEMENTS

CONTENTS

BACKGROUND

Sellers increasingly enter into arrangements that have a combination of obligations such as delivering a product, providing a service, granting a license or other right, or taking (or refraining from taking) certain actions. Arrangements with multiple-seller obligations (deliverables) are generally referred to as "Multiple-Element Arrangements." These arrangements can be as simple as the sale of a shirt and pants (two product deliverables) or as complex as a hospital construction contract that includes the installation of sophisticated diagnostic tools, the sale of related software and a contract to operate the hospital upon completion.

Multiple-element arrangements present unique accounting issues that do not exist in single-element contracts, such as how to allocate the arrangement consideration among the various deliverables.

SURVEY OF ACCOUNTING LITERATURE

Some industry and transaction-specific guidance includes assistance on how to account for arrangements with multiple elements that fall within the scope of that literature. In addition, EITF 00-21 (ASC 605-25) provides guidance on accounting for multiple-element arrangements. All of this literature relies on the same underlying principles to determine whether the deliverables can be treated separately for accounting purposes. The interaction of EITF 00-21 (ASC 605-25) and other guidance is discussed later in this chapter.

REVENUE RECOGNITION LITERATURE

Publication	ASC	ASC Topic	Subject
SAB Topic 13	605-10-S99	Revenue Recognition	Revenue Recognition
CON-5	N/A	N/A	Recognition and Measurement in Financial Statements of Business Enterprises
CON-6	N/A	N/A	Elements of Financial Statements
FAS-45	952-605	Franchisors	Accounting for Franchise Fee Revenue
FAS-48	605-15-25	Revenue Recognition	Revenue Recognition When Right of Return Exists
FAS-66	360-20	Property, Plant, and Equipment	Accounting for Sales of Real Estate
FIN-45	460	Guarantees	Guarantees
SOP 81-1	605-35	Revenue Recognition	Accounting for Performance of Construction-Type and Certain Production-Type Contracts
SOP 97-2 and EITF 03-5	985-605	Software	Software Revenue Recognition
SOP 00-2	926-605	Entertainment— Films	Accounting by Producers or Distributors of Films
EITF 85-20	605-20-25	Revenue Recognition	Recognition of Fees for Guaranteeing a Loan
EITF 00-21	605-25	Revenue Recognition	Revenue Arrangements with Multiple Deliverables
TPA 5100.39	985-605-55-4	Software	Combining Separate Software Customer Contracts

---

SUPPORTING LITERATURE

Publication	ASC	ASC Topic	Subject
FAS-5	450-20	Contingencies	Loss Contingencies
FAS-13	840	Leases	Leases
FAS-133	815	Derivatives and Hedging	Derivatives and Hedging
FAS-133 Guide	815-10-15-8 and 15-9	Derivatives and Hedging	Combining Separate Financial Contracts
EITF 01-8	840-10-15	Leases	Determining Whether an Arrangement Contains a Lease

---

OVERVIEW

CON-5 sets forth the guidance that revenue should be recognized when it is both realized (or realizable) and earned. In discussing the "earned" criterion, CON-5 goes on to say, "revenues are considered to have been earned when the entity has substantially accomplished what it must do to be entitled to the benefits represented by the revenues" (CON-5, par. 83b). This concept is not easily applied to multiple-element arrangements. A narrow interpretation would not permit revenue recognition until a seller has completed substantially all of its obligations. The accounting literature, however, recognizes that a delivered element *may* represent a separate earnings process that provides value to the customer, even if other items in the arrangement remain to be delivered. The specific conditions that must be met to account for a delivered element separately are discussed at length later in the chapter.

This chapter focuses on determining whether a multiple-element arrangement should be separated for accounting purposes and, if so, how the arrangement consideration should be allocated to the delivered elements.

SCOPE

EITF 00-21 (ASC 605-25) applies to all types of deliverables (products, services, rights to use assets including intellectual property) in all industries, unless the deliverables in a multiple-element arrangement are subject to the requirements of other guidance that contains separation and/or allocation guidance. This is discussed in a subsequent section of this chapter titled, "Interaction between EITF 00-21 (ASC 605-25) and Other Guidance."

EITF 00-21 (ASC 605-25) also does not apply to the following types of vendor offers:

- Those involving free or discounted products or services to be delivered at a future date, or a rebate or refund of a determinable cash amount, if the customer reaches a predefined threshold of cumulative revenue transactions with the vendor or continues to be a customer of the vendor for a predefined period of time; and

- Those related to point and loyalty programs (regardless of whether the vendor is the program operator) (EITF 00-21, 4(b)) (ASC 605-25-15-3).

However, as discussed in Chapter 8, "Miscellaneous Issues," a company is not precluded from adopting the provisions of EITF 00-21 (ASC 605-25) as its accounting policy for these types of offers.

DEFINING THE ARRANGEMENT

Generally, the unit of accounting in multiple-element arrangements is a single contract between the parties. However, it may be necessary to combine two or more contracts when the *substance of the arrangement* would be distorted by accounting for the contracts separately. The principle underlying this guidance is that the substance of an arrangement is more important than its form. As a result, a combination of multiple contracts should not change the accounting for the overall arrangement.

When various elements of a single arrangement are documented in multiple contracts, these contracts must be combined and evaluated as one multiple-element arrangement. EITF 00-21 (ASC 605-25) presumes that separate contracts with the same entity or related parties entered into at or near the same time have been negotiated as a package and should therefore be evaluated as a single arrangement (EITF 00-21, par. 2) (ASC 605-25-25-3).

U.S. generally accepted accounting principles (GAAP) provides guidance on when it is appropriate to combine certain types of contracts. For example, TPA 5100.39 (ASC 985-605-55-4) addresses the combination of contracts in software revenue recognition (see Chapter 10, "Software—A Complete Model"). In addition, Question K-1 of the FAS-133 Guide, *Guide to Implementation of Statement 133 on Accounting for Derivative Instruments and Hedging Activities* (ASC 815-10-15-8 and 15-9), deals with the combination of separate contracts for the purposes of applying the derivatives and hedging literature.

The following guidance is a non-exhaustive list of factors that should be used to determine whether separate contracts should be combined and evaluated as a single multiple-element arrangement:

Timing of the Execution of the Contracts:

1. The contracts or agreements were negotiated or executed within a short time frame of each other or in contemplation of each other (TPA 5100.39) (ASC 985-605-55-4); and FAS-133 Guide, Question K-1 (ASC 815-10-15-8 and 15-9).

Definition of "Customer":

2. The contracts are with the same customer (or affiliates of each other) (FAS-133 Guide, Question K-1) (ASC 815-10-15-8 and 15-9).

Substance and the Composition of the Contract:

3. The contracts relate to the same elements, or what is, in essence, the same project (TPA 5100.39) (ASC 985-605-55-4) and FAS-133 Guide, Question K-1 (ASC 815-10-15-8 and 15-9).

4. The different elements are closely interrelated or interdependent in terms of design, technology, or function (TPA 5100.39) (ASC 985-605-55-4).

5. One or more elements in one contract or agreement are essential to the functionality of an element in another contract (TPA 5100.39) (ASC 985-605-55-4).

Arrangement Consideration and the Payment Terms:

6. The fee for one or more contracts or agreements is subject to refund or forfeiture or other concession if another contract is not satisfactorily completed (TPA 5100.39) (ASC 985-605-55-4).

7. Payment terms under one contract or agreement coincide with performance criteria of another contract or agreement (TPA 5100.39) (ASC 985-605-55-4).

> **PRACTICE ALERT:** Although TPA 5100.39 (ASC 985-605-55-4) was issued by the AICPA for the software industry, its principles (and those in the FAS-133 Guide, Question K-1) should be considered in other situations as well. The evaluation of whether multiple contracts should be combined for purposes of evaluating revenue recognition is particularly challenging in, and relevant to, contracts in the biotech, intellectual property, and services industries.

ILLUSTRATION: EVALUATING MULTIPLE CONTRACTS

EXAMPLE 1

Facts: Company G manufactures and sells computer printers. These printers use a proprietary ink cartridge design, such that the cartridges cannot be provided by any other manufacturer. The printers are sold by retailers for $100 each and the ink cartridges sell for $40 each. When a printer is sold, it includes one cartridge. Company G's printers and ink cartridges are readily available from retail distributors of Company G's products. Company G enters into a contract to supply a customer with 100 printers for $80 each. Six months later, Company G signs a contract with the same customer to provide ink cartridges for the printers on an as-needed basis for $30 each for two years.

Discussion: A review of the indicators described above shows that the contracts are with the same customer (indicator 2) and that the "Substance of the Deliverables" indicators (3, 4, and 5) are present, suggesting that the contracts should be combined. However, the "Fee and Payment Terms" indicators (6 and 7) do not exist, and it is not clear that indicator 1 exists. Additional factors that Company G should consider include the fact that ink cartridges can be purchased by the customer from parties other than Company G, and the fact that Company G routinely sells printers and ink cartridges separate from each other. In this situation, Company G would likely conclude that the arrangement for the sale of printers and the arrangement for the sale of ink cartridges should not be combined. However, a slight change in the facts (e.g., if the arrangements were signed less than 1 month apart) might change this conclusion.

EXAMPLE 2

Facts: Company R owns the rights to a proprietary chemical compound used to make various products. It licenses the right to use the compound in a particular product line to a customer for three years, which is the remaining life of the patent on the compound. However, Company R does not provide the customer with a license to manufacture the proprietary compound or have it manufactured—Company R maintains those rights exclusively until the patent expires. The customer will be responsible for developing the product and marketing it. An initial payment under the license is due at signing, with further payments due ratably over the term of the license. In a separate contract, contemplated at the time of the license, but negotiated and signed three months later, Company R agrees to supply the chemical compound to this customer at market prices for three years.

Discussion: A review of the indicators described above shows that indicators 1 through 5 are present and suggests that the contracts should be combined. However, the "Fee and Payment Terms" indicator 6 does not exist. In this case, Company R would likely conclude that the two contracts should be combined and evaluated as one arrangement for revenue recognition purposes.

DELIVERABLES

Once the scope of the arrangement has been determined, the vendor must identify all of the deliverables in the arrangement. This step is necessary because each deliverable must be evaluated to determine whether it should be treated separately or combined with other deliverables for purposes of revenue recognition. After this determination has been made, a deliverable will qualify for separate revenue recognition only if specific criteria indicate that the deliverable represents a separable earnings process.

What makes this analysis difficult is that the accounting literature does not define a "deliverable." The term, however, has generally been interpreted to mean any performance obligation on the part of the seller. Therefore, obligations to, for example, perform services, grant licenses, and deliver products, are all considered deliverables.

The absence of a definition means that considerable judgment is required to identify a deliverable and, in effect, separate it from other deliverables in the arrangement. For example, in an arrangement involving the sale of a specialized product, the vendor may promise not to sell a similar product to any of the customer's competitors. It is not clear whether the exclusivity provision is a separate deliverable apart from the product deliverable. Similarly, a company licensing its technology may explicitly agree to assist the customer in patent infringement allegations from third parties. In this case, it is not clear that the obligation to assist a customer in legal defense should be considered a deliverable independent of the licensing deliverable.

In addition to the problem of distinguishing between deliverables, the lack of a definition also suggests that two vendors may differ in their identification of deliverables. The conditions that must be met to treat deliverables separately, however, should minimize the likelihood of potentially different conclusions about the number of deliverables in an arrangement. A vendor also must determine whether the existence of undelivered items in the arrangement precludes recognition of revenue allocated to a specific deliverable. As a result, each deliverable must be evaluated to determine whether it should be treated separately or bundled together with other deliverables in the arrangement both at the inception of the arrangement and as each item in the arrangement is delivered (EITF 00-21, par. 8) (ASC 605-25-25-4). The absence of a definition of a "deliverable" and the requirement to identify all of the deliverables in an arrangement is further complicated by the fact that no deliverable may be treated as inconsequential or perfunctory for separation and allocation purposes.

Once the identified deliverables have been separated and the total arrangement consideration has been allocated to those deliverables, the appropriate revenue recognition principles (as discussed in other chapters of this product) should be used to determine when the revenue allocated to each deliverable must be recognized as if it were the only deliverable in the arrangement.

In some cases, the separation criteria may not be met at the level of individual deliverables and two or more deliverables must be combined. The increasing number of multiple-element arrangements (consider, for example, the proliferation of "solutions" offered today in lieu of a single product or service) yields combined deliverables with greater frequency.

SEPARATING MULTIPLE-ELEMENT ARRANGEMENTS

Determining the Model to Apply

EITF 00-21 (ASC 605-25) provides the general principles as well as a model for the separation of multiple element arrangements into individual units of accounting and the allocation of the arrangement consideration to the elements in the arrangement. Other authoritative literature also describes models for separating multiple element arrangements and/or the allocation of the arrangement consideration. Identifying the correct model is straightforward for arrangements that only have elements within the scope of other parts of U.S. GAAP: SOP 97-2 (ASC 985-605), SOP 81-1 (ASC 605-35), and FAS-13 (ASC 840) are examples of literature that provide separation and allocation guidance for deliverables in multiple element arrangements within their scope. As a result, arrangements that *only* have elements within the scope of such literature must be separated pursuant to that guidance.

The appropriate separation model is more difficult to identify, however, when some elements are in the scope of specific guidance that covers separation and other elements are not. In general, the correct model to use depends on:

- The nature of the elements involved, and

- Whether the specific literature provides separation guidance for arrangements that have elements within and outside its scope.

Interaction Between EITF 00-21 (ASC 605-25) and Other Guidance

The decision on which guidance to apply to a multiple-element arrangement is a function of whether guidance other than EITF 00-21 (ASC 605-25) includes separation and/or allocation guidance. In some cases, there is guidance on both when to separate and how to allocate consideration among the elements in the arrangement. In these situations, that guidance should be applied to determine whether the elements within and outside its scope should be separated and, if so, how the arrangement consideration should be allocated (see EITF 00-21, par. 4(a)(i)) (ASC 605-25-15-3).

FIN-45 (ASC 460) is an example of guidance that covers both separation of and allocation to deliverables within and outside its scope. If an arrangement includes a guarantee or indemnification required to be recognized and measured pursuant to FIN-45 (ASC 460), the guarantee or indemnification must be treated as a separate element and measured initially at its fair value (for additional discussion related to FIN-45 (ASC 460), see "Guarantees and Indemnifications in Multiple-Element Arrangements" later in this chapter). In this situation, FIN-45 requires: (1) a separation of the guarantee or indemnification from the other elements in the arrangement; and (2) the allocation of a defined amount (i.e., fair value) to the guarantee or indemnification.

Most of the accounting literature provides guidance that is limited to deliverables or elements within a clearly stated scope. For example, SOP 97-2 (and EITF 03-05) (ASC 985-605) provides separation and allocation guidance for multiple-element arrangements that fall within its scope (i.e., arrangements that include software and software-related elements).

However, when other guidance is silent on whether and how arrangement consideration should be split between elements within its scope and those outside its scope, the guidance in EITF 00-21 (ASC 605-25) should be used to separate the elements within the scope of the other guidance from those outside the scope of the other guidance (EITF 00-21 par. 4 (a)(iii)) (ASC 605-25-15-3).

SOP 97-2 (ASC 985-605) does not provide guidance on how to separate multiple-element arrangements with elements outside its scope (e.g., hardware deliverables where software is not essential to the functionality of the hardware). In this situation, the guidance in EITF 00-21 (ASC 605-25) should be used to initially separate the software elements from the non-software elements. Further separation should be based on SOP 97-2 (ASC 985-605) for the software elements and other guidance for the non-software elements.

If, based on the guidance in EITF 00-21 (ASC 605-25), elements that fall within the scope of specific guidance cannot be separated from other elements, the appropriate recognition of revenue should be determined for these combined deliverables as a single unit of accounting (EITF 00-21, pars. 4 and 10) (ASC 605-25-15-3 and 605-25-25-6).

SEC REGISTRANT ALERT: In a December 2003 speech, the SEC Staff discussed (a) the scope interaction of SOP 97-2 (ASC 985-605) and EITF 00-21 (ASC 605-25), and (b) the scope interaction of SOP 97-2 (ASC 985-605) and FAS-13 (ASC 840).

The SEC Staff noted that prior to the issuance of EITF 00-21 (ASC 605-25), bundled information technology consulting arrangements including software license, customization, installation, and continuing information technology management services (a service element) were usually accounted for a single deliverable under SOP 81-1 (ASC 605-35). The EITF 00-21 (ASC 605-25) guidance should be applied to bundled arrangements that include significant customization of software to determine whether the SOP 97-2 (ASC 985-605) elements should be separated from other elements.

The SEC Staff also noted that the hardware and executory cost elements of a leased customized software arrangement should be unbundled and accounted for separately using FAS-13 (ASC 840).

PRACTICE ALERT: The model that should be applied to a multiple-element arrangement including software and software-related elements depends on whether some or all of the other elements in the arrangements are software-related. Depending on the nature of the elements in the arrangement, it may be appropriate initially to apply the EITF 00-21 (ASC 605-25) (in case one or more elements are not software-related) or the SOP 97-2 (ASC 985-605) multiple-element arrangement model (when all the elements are software-related). Note that an arrangement involving software that requires significant production, modification, or customization (a software element) and other software or software-related elements is subject to SOP 97-2 (ASC 985-605) and the guidance in EITF 00-21 (ASC 605.25) does not apply. See Chapter 10, "Software—A Complete Model," for a comprehensive discussion of this subject.

Often, there is specific guidance on when to separate elements but not on how to allocate arrangement consideration. In these situations, the specific guidance should be applied to determine whether the elements within and outside its scope should be separated. If the elements should be separated, the relative fair value method must be used to allocate arrangement consideration. Fair values for the elements in these situations must be determined based on the best estimate of fair value available. (These cases correspond to interaction issues discussed in EITF 00-21, par. 4(a)(ii) (ASC 605-25-15-3)). In other words, the residual method should only be used when there is an insufficiency of fair value evidence (as is the case in certain circumstances under EITF 00-21 (ASC 605-25), as discussed later in this chapter).

FAS-13 (ASC 840) is an example of specific literature that provides separation but not allocation guidance. In an arrangement including FAS-13 (ASC 840) elements (e.g., the lease and maintenance of leased equipment) and other elements, the FAS-13 (ASC 840) elements must be separated from the other elements using the guidance in EITF 00-21 (ASC 605-25). However, FAS-13 (ASC 840) does not specify how the arrangement consideration should be allocated among these elements. In this situation, the arrangement consideration should be allocated using the relative fair value method.

EXAMPLE: FAS-13 AND NON-FAS-13 DELIVERABLES

Excerpts from the Xerox Corporation Annual Report—Fiscal Year Ended December 31, 2007

Revenue Recognition under Bundled Arrangements

We sell the majority of our products and services under bundled lease arrangements, which typically include equipment, service, supplies, and financing components for which the customer pays a single negotiated fixed minimum monthly payment for all elements over the contractual lease term.

Revenues under these arrangements are allocated considering the relative fair values of the lease and nonlease deliverables included in the bundled arrangement, based upon the estimated relative fair values of each element. Lease deliverables include maintenance and executory costs, equipment and financing, while nonlease deliverables generally consist of the supplies and nonmaintenance services.

Once the elements within the scope of the specific guidance have been separated from the elements outside the scope of that guidance:

- Further separation of the elements within the scope of the specific guidance is governed by the multiple-element arrangement model within that guidance; and

- Further separation of the elements not within the scope of the specific guidance is governed by EITF 00-21 (ASC 605-25).

Paragraph 4(a)(iii) (ASC 605-25-15-3) deals with the case where other literature covers the accounting for certain deliverables but does not provide guidance on the separation or allocation of arrangement consideration to deliverables within and outside its scope. In these cases, the separation and allocation guidance of EITF 00-21 (ASC 605-25) must be applied.

Basic Model

The existence of multiple deliverables in an arrangement raises three issues. The first is that the customer might not receive value from the delivery of a particular item because the delivered item works together with one of the undelivered items in the arrangement. The second stems from the fact that the arrangement fee generally is negotiated for the entire package of deliverables in the contract rather than deliverable-by-deliverable, and therefore it may not be clear how much revenue is specifically allocable to each deliverable. The third issue arises when a portion of the arrangement fee related to the delivered element may be refundable, withheld by the customer, or the vendor may have to grant a concession upon non-performance of one or more undelivered elements in the arrangement.

> **OBSERVATION:** Contingent revenue is a function of the vendor's performance with respect to *undelivered elements* and should not be confused with refunds or concessions stemming from customer acceptance (performance, other mutually agreed-upon or subjective criteria) and warranties (conformity with published specifications) that relate to *delivered elements*. Contingent revenue is discussed in greater detail later in this chapter.

These concerns, however, are rendered moot once all deliverables in the arrangement have been delivered. Therefore, the allocation of revenue to the various deliverables in an arrangement is only important if some of the items will be delivered before others.

Because these issues concern the relationship between delivered and undelivered items, the accounting analysis is designed to determine whether this interrelationship prevents either (1) the customer from having full use of the delivered item prior to the delivery of one or more undelivered elements in an arrangement or (2) the vendor from properly allocating the arrangement fee to the delivered items. When contingent revenue is present, the amount and timing (but not allocation) of revenue recognition is at issue.

In order to address these concerns, a delivered item should be treated as a separate deliverable for accounting purposes only if all of the following conditions are met (EITF 00-21, par. 9) (ASC 605-25-25-5):

1. The *delivered item(s)* has value to the customer on a standalone basis. Standalone value exists if the deliverable is sold separately by the vendor or if the customer could resell the delivered item on a standalone basis. Satisfaction of this condition does not depend on the existence of an observable market for the deliverable.

2. There is objective and reliable evidence of the fair value of the *undelivered item(s)*.

3. If the arrangement includes a general right of return related to the delivered item, delivery or performance of the *undelivered*

item(s) is considered probable and substantially in the control of the vendor.

The first condition applies only to delivered items whereas the second and third conditions apply only to undelivered items. Consider an arrangement in which both the delivered and undelivered elements have standalone value and delivery of the undelivered element is in the control of the vendor (i.e., the third condition is met). Furthermore, assume that there is objective and reliable evidence of fair value (OREFV) for all the elements in the arrangement. In such an arrangement, the elements must be separated for accounting purposes.

Alternatively, assume that the vendor does not have OREFV for the delivered item. This does not hinder its separation from the undelivered element(s) (using the residual method) for which there is OREFV. If the order of delivery were reversed in this arrangement, however, the elements could not be separated because there would be no OREFV of the undelivered element. Note that the vendor does not have the option of bundling deliverables for accounting purposes if those deliverables meet all of the separation conditions of paragraph 9 of EITF 00-21 (ASC 605-25-25-5).

> **PRACTICE ALERT:** The prohibition on separating deliverables in a multiple-element arrangement simply because of a lack of sufficient evidence of the fair value of the undelivered items has often been cited as a provision of US GAAP that can distort reported results. In large part because of these concerns, the EITF in Issue 08-1, *Revenue Recognition Arrangements with Multiple Deliverables*, is rethinking this requirement. See Chapter 13, "Future Expectations and Projects," for a discussion of this project, which is likely to remove the prohibition on separation due to a lack of sufficient evidence of fair value of the undelivered item(s).

EXAMPLE: BASIC MODEL

Affymetrix Inc. Form 10-K—Fiscal Year Ended December 31, 2007

The Company derives the majority of its revenue from product sales of GeneChip® probe arrays, reagents, and related instrumentation that may be sold individually or combined with any of the product or product related revenue items listed below. When a sale combines multiple elements, the Company accounts for multiple element arrangements under Emerging Issues Task Force Issue No. 00-21 (EITF 00-21), *Revenue Arrangements with Multiple Deliverables*.

EITF 00-21 provides guidance on accounting for arrangements that involve the delivery or performance of multiple products, services and/or rights to use assets. In accordance with EITF 00-21, the Company allocates revenue for transactions or collaborations that include multiple elements to each unit of accounting based on its relative fair value, and recognizes revenue for each unit of accounting when the revenue recognition criteria have been met. The price charged when the element is sold separately generally determines fair value. In the absence of fair value of a delivered element, the Company allocates revenue first to the fair value of the undelivered elements and the residual revenue to the delivered elements. The Company recognizes revenue for delivered elements when the delivered elements have standalone value and the Company has objective and reliable evidence of fair value for each undelivered element. If the fair value of any undelivered element included in a multiple element arrangement cannot be objectively determined, revenue is deferred until all elements are delivered and services have been performed, or until fair value can objectively be determined for any remaining undelivered elements.

Product Related Revenue

Product related revenue includes subscription fees earned under GeneChip® array access programs; license fees; milestones and royalties earned from collaborative product development and supply agreements; equipment service revenue; product related scientific services revenue; and revenue from custom probe array design fees.

The identification of deliverables in an arrangement should be initially performed at the inception of the agreement. This analysis will help assess whether each condition of the basic model will be met when certain items are delivered. However, the final determination of whether a deliverable may be treated separately for accounting purposes should be made at the time revenue on that item would otherwise be recognizable, aside from the concerns raised by the existence of undelivered items. Thus, as each item is delivered, the vendor in a multiple-element arrangement should review the conditions based on the status of the arrangement at that time (EITF 00-21, par. 8) (ASC 605-25-25-4).

> **DISCLOSURE ALERT:** See Chapter 12, "Disclosures," for information about required disclosures.

> **SEC REGISTRANT ALERT:** In early 2003, the SEC staff issued the Report Pursuant to Section 704 of the Sarbanes-Oxley Act of 2002 (the Section 704 Report). In compiling the information in the Section 704 Report, the SEC staff studied enforcement actions filed during the period July 31, 1997, through July 30, 2002. The greatest number of enforcement actions brought by

the SEC related to improper revenue recognition. One of the common revenue recognition issues highlighted in the Section 704 Report related to improper recognition of revenue from multiple-element arrangements or bundled contracts. One of the two actions discussed in the Section 704 Report in this regard involved improper allocation of arrangement consideration, and the other involved improper separation of interdependent elements. This finding is a strong indication that more attention should be given to accounting for multiple-element arrangements.

In addition, in early 2003, the SEC staff issued the Summary by the Division of Corporation Finance of Significant Issues Addressed in the Review of the Periodic Reports of the Fortune 500 Companies (the Fortune 500 Report). This report resulted from the SEC's Division of Corporation Finance's (Corp Fin) review of all annual reports filed by Fortune 500 companies. The report provides insight into areas commonly questioned by Corp Fin during its reviews of annual reports. One area specifically mentioned in the Fortune 500 Report relates to accounting for multiple-element arrangements. Corp Fin specifically indicated that companies in the computer software, computer services, computer hardware, and communications equipment industries could improve their disclosures by expanding the discussion related to multiple-element arrangements.

Standalone Value to the Customer

Significant judgment is required to evaluate whether elements have value to the customer on a standalone basis. This involves determining whether the item being sold by a company is sold separately by any vendor or whether that item could be resold by the customer on a standalone basis. To conclude that an element has standalone value to the customer because the element is sold separately by another vendor, that other element should provide the same quality and value to the customer as the element sold by the company. Factors to consider by way of comparison include (but are not limited to) pricing, functionality, features, quality grades/assessments, ease of installation and delivery, warranty and acceptance provisions, and availability of post-sale support. To conclude that the customer could resell the deliverable on a standalone basis, the company must consider the nature of the market in which the deliverable can be resold, the value to be received on resale, and whether reselling the deliverable would affect its quality or utility. The examples below and those included in an appendix to EITF 00-21 (ASC 605-25) illustrate the application of the concept of "standalone value to the customer" in various situations.

ILLUSTRATION: STANDALONE VALUE TO THE CUSTOMER

The following represent arrangements where the delivered item does not have value to the customer on a standalone basis:

Example 1: The arrangement involves the sale of a satellite television receiver and one year of service. The receiver operates on a proprietary network and therefore can only be used with the service provided by the vendor in the arrangement. In addition, there is no secondary market for separate sales of the satellite television receiver since each receiver is uniquely identified to a particular customer and that customer's service contract. As such, the receiver does not have value to the customer on a standalone basis (i.e., absent the ongoing satellite television service).

Example 2: The arrangement involves the sale and installation of equipment. The equipment is highly specialized and will not operate until certain adjustments are made during installation. Because of the unique nature and specialization of the equipment, only one vendor manufactures or installs the equipment. This effectively prohibits the customer from reselling the equipment on a standalone basis. As such, the equipment does not have value to the customer on a standalone basis (i.e., absent the installation service).

The following represent arrangements where the delivered item does have value to the customer on a standalone basis:

Example 3: The arrangement involves the sale of office equipment by Vendor D and a contract to provide maintenance on that office equipment. Vendor D, as well as other vendors, sells the office equipment without the maintenance contract. As such, the office equipment has value to the customer on a standalone basis (i.e., absent the maintenance contract).

Example 4: The arrangement involves the sale of two pieces of manufacturing equipment by Vendor E. Both pieces of equipment are needed to manufacture the intended product. Vendor E only sells the two pieces of equipment together. However, other vendors sell separately equipment that is comparable to, and compatible with each piece of Vendor E's equipment. This also effectively results in the customer being able to resell Vendor E's equipment on a standalone basis if it chose to do so. As such, each piece of equipment has value to the customer on a standalone basis (i.e., absent the delivery of the other piece of equipment).

EXAMPLE: LACK OF STANDALONE VALUE TO THE CUSTOMER

K12 Inc. Form 10-K—Fiscal Year Ended June 30, 2008

Revenue Recognition

In accordance with SEC Staff Accounting Bulletin No. 104 (SAB No. 104), we recognize revenues when the following conditions are met: (1) persuasive evidence of an arrangement exists; (2) delivery of physical goods or rendering of services is complete; (3) the seller's price to the buyer is fixed or determinable; and (4) collection is reasonably assured. Once these conditions are satisfied, the amount of revenues we record is determined in accordance with Emerging Issues Task Force (EITF 99-19), *Reporting Revenue Gross as a Principal versus Net as an Agent.*

We generate almost all of our revenues through long-term contracts with virtual public schools. These schools are generally funded by state or local governments on a per student basis. Under these contracts, we are responsible for providing each enrolled student with access to our OLS, our online lessons, offline learning kits and student support services required for their complete education. In most cases, we are also responsible for providing complete management and technology services required for the operation of the school. The revenues derived from these long-term agreements are primarily dependent upon the number of students enrolled, the extent of the management services contracted for by the school, and the level of funding provided to the school for each student.

We have determined that the elements of our contracts are valuable to schools in combination, but do not have standalone value. In addition, we have determined that we do not have objective and reliable evidence of fair value for each element of our contracts. As a result, the elements within our multiple-element contracts do not qualify for treatment as separate units of accounting. Accordingly, we account for revenues received under multiple element arrangements as a single unit of accounting and recognize the entire arrangement based upon the approximate rate at which we incur the costs associated with each element.

Fair Value Evidence

In general where the accounting literature discusses multiple-element arrangements, the objective is to allocate the arrangement consideration to the individual elements based on their relative fair values.[1] This approach is described in EITF 00-21 (ASC 605-25-30-2). As a result, allocation of arrangement consideration may not be based on the cost of those deliverables, the prices stated in the arrangement, or the time or effort expended to provide the deliverables. Using these, or any other non-fair value measure, to allocate arrangement consideration is inappropriate because they may not represent the amount at which an individual element would be sold on a standalone basis (i.e., the fair value of the individual element).

---

[1] For example, fair value allocation is discussed in FAS-13 (ASC 840), FAS-45 (ASC 952-605), FAS-66 (ASC 360-20), FIN-45 (ASC 460), SOP 81-1 (ASC 605-35), SOP 97-2 (ASC 985-605), and SOP 00-2 (ASC 926-605).

To ensure that the revenue allocation process is as objective as possible, allocated amounts must be based on "objective and reliable" evidence (EITF 00-21, par. 9b) (ASC 605-25-25-5). Such evidence often consists of vendor-specific objective evidence (VSOE) of fair value, as discussed in the literature on software revenue recognition (see Chapter 10, "Software—A Complete Model"). VSOE of fair value is limited to (SOP 97-2, par. 10) (ASC 605-25-30-8):

1. The price charged when the same element is sold separately.

2. For an element not yet sold separately, the price established by management, if it is probable that the price, once established, will not change before the separate introduction of the element into the marketplace.

Although VSOE is required to allocate revenue in a software arrangement, it is not required in non-software arrangements. However, VSOE is always considered the best evidence of fair value and sufficiently objective and reliable to meet the second condition of the multiple-element model (EITF 00-21, par. 16) (ASC 605-25-30-9). For example, if a company separately sells an element for $100, it should use $100 as the element's fair value in the allocation of arrangement consideration even if its competitors sell that item for $120 or $80.

If VSOE of fair value is not available, a company should consider all other available evidence including third-party sales of the same item and its own sales of similar items (EITF 00-21, par. 16) (ASC 605-25-30-9). For many deliverables, such evidence may not be available. For example, objective and reliable evidence of fair value is generally not available if (1) the vendor does not sell the product or service separately, (2) the product or service is unique to the vendor, thereby eliminating the availability of third party evidence, and (3) the vendor does not sell a similar product or service on a standalone basis.

When evaluating whether sufficient evidence of fair value exists, a company should not refer to measures that are not objective or reliable. For example, third-party sales prices may not be reliable measures if the items are not exactly the same and differences in quality, brand, or other factors could suggest different fair values. Also, a measurement based on cost plus a "normal" gross margin is not an acceptable estimate of fair value as (1) different deliverables would be expected to have different gross margins and (2) costs incurred are rarely a good measure of the fair value of an item. Similarly, separate prices stated in a contract do not usually constitute sufficient evidence of fair value since a contract is negotiated as a whole and the parties most likely did not separately bargain for each item. However, in the rare circumstance where the elements of the contract were each separately bid and the customer could have accepted or rejected the companies bid for each element without affecting the other elements, such prices may be objective evidence of fair value (SOP 81-1, par. 40) (ASC 605-35-25-10 through 25-13).

EXAMPLE: FAIR VALUE EVIDENCE

Xerox Corporation Annual Report—Fiscal Year Ended December 31, 2008

Revenue Recognition under Bundled Arrangements

We sell the majority of our products and services under bundled lease arrangements, which typically include equipment, service, supplies and financing components for which the customer pays a single negotiated monthly fixed price for all elements over the contractual lease term. Typically, these arrangements include an incremental, variable component for page volumes in excess of contractual page volume minimums, which are often expressed in terms of price per page. Revenues under these arrangements are allocated, considering the relative fair values of the lease and nonlease deliverables included in the bundled arrangement, based upon the estimated relative fair values of each element. Lease deliverables include maintenance and executory costs, equipment and financing, while nonlease deliverables generally consist of supplies and nonmaintenance services. Our revenue allocation for lease deliverables begins by allocating revenues to the maintenance and executory costs plus profit thereon. The remaining amounts are allocated to the equipment and financing elements.

We perform extensive analyses of available verifiable objective evidence of equipment fair value based on cash selling prices during the applicable period. The cash selling prices are compared to the range of values included in our lease accounting systems. The range of cash selling prices must be reasonably consistent with the lease selling prices, taking into account residual values, in order for us to determine that such lease prices are indicative of fair value.

Our pricing interest rates, which are used in determining customer payments, are developed based upon a variety of factors including local prevailing rates in the marketplace and the customer's credit history, industry and credit class. We reassess our pricing interest rates quarterly based on changes in the local prevailing rates in the marketplace. These interest rates have been historically adjusted if the rates vary by 25 basis points or more, cumulatively, from the last rate in effect. The pricing interest rates generally equal the implicit rates within the leases, as corroborated by our comparisons of cash to lease selling prices. In light of worldwide economic conditions prevailing at the end of 2008, we expect to continually review this methodology in 2009 to ensure that our pricing interest rates are reflective of changes in the local prevailing rates in the marketplace.

Measurement and Allocation of Arrangement Consideration

The amount of total arrangement consideration is based on the terms and conditions of the contract. A vendor should assume that customer actions (specific refund rights and customer cancellation provisions) and performance bonuses that may be earned will not result in any incremental consideration (EITF 00-21, par. 11) (ASC 605-25-30-6). However, see Chapter 9, "Contract Accounting," for a discussion of SOP 81-1 (ASC 605-35), which permits the inclusion of expected performance bonuses (that are reasonably and reliably determinable) in the measurement of estimated contract revenue.

Two methods exist for the purpose of allocating arrangement consideration to deliverables that should be treated separately for accounting purposes—the relative fair value method and the residual method. Use of one method versus the other is dictated by the facts and circumstances. However, if generally accepted accounting principles require one of the elements to be initially recognized at its fair value and subsequently marked-to-market for accounting purposes, the amount allocated to that element should be its fair value. The remaining unallocated arrangement consideration is then allocated to the remaining elements in the arrangement using either the relative fair value or the residual method, as appropriate (EITF 00-21, par. 13) (ASC 605-25-30-4).

Relative Fair Value Method

If sufficient evidence of fair value exists for all elements (deliverables), the arrangement consideration should be allocated to the individual elements based on their relative fair values (EITF 00-21, par. 12) (ASC 605-25-30-2). The result of this process is that when a multiple-element arrangement has a total fee that is less than the fee that would be determined by adding up the fair values of the individual elements, the discount is allocated pro rata across each of the elements.

ILLUSTRATION: ALLOCATION OF ARRANGEMENT CONSIDERATION—RELATIVE FAIR VALUE METHOD

General Facts: Company W manufactures equipment that is used to make widgets. The widget-making process involves two pieces of equipment, both of which Company W manufactures. In an arrangement with a new customer, Company W sells both pieces of equipment, along with 10 days of training for the customer's employees, for a total fee of $900,000. Title to each machine transfers upon shipment. Company W does not grant general or specific refund rights to its customers.

VARIATION 1

Additional Facts: Company W also sells each piece of equipment separately. In addition, competitors manufacture machines that perform the same functions as Machine 1 and 2, and machines from different manufacturers are interchangeable. Company W sells Machine 1 separately for $400,000, and Machine 2 separately for $550,000. No amount of the arrangement consideration is contingent upon performance of undelivered components.

Company W sells training services separately to customers who already have equipment installed and want additional training for new employees. Company W charges $5,000 per day for training. However, not all customers purchase training, as Company W includes operating manuals with its equipment.

Company W delivers Machine 1 first, then Machine 2, then the training, using the installed machines to demonstrate the machines' functionality. Payment terms are $400,000 upon delivery of Machine 1, $475,000 upon delivery of Machine 2, and $25,000 upon providing the training.

Discussion: Since Company W and other vendors sell each of the machines separately and since the customer can learn how to operate the machines without buying training from Company W, Machine 1 has value to the customer on a standalone basis (i.e., absent Machine 2 and the training), and Machine 2 has value to the customer on a standalone basis (i.e., absent the training).

Evidence of fair value exists for all three deliverables in the arrangement, because Company W sells each one separately. As such, the relative fair value method should be used to allocate the arrangement consideration. The allocation of the consideration to the three elements is as follows:

Fair Value of Machine 1	$ 400,000	(40% of total FV)
Fair Value of Machine 2	550,000	(55% of total FV)
Fair Value of Training	50,000	(5% of total FV)
Total Fair Value	$1,000,000	(100% of total FV)
Less: Arrangement Fee	900,000	
Discount in the Arrangement	$ 100,000	
Discount as a Percentage of Fair Value	−10%	
Allocation to Machine 1 = $400,000 − 10% (40% of arrangement fee)	$ 360,000	
Allocation to Machine 2 = $550,000 − 10% (55% of arrangement fee)	495,000	
Allocation to Training = $50,000 − 10% (5% of arrangement fee)	45,000	
Total Arrangement Fee	$ 900,000	

In addition, the allocation of arrangement consideration is not affected by payment terms or specific refund rights since the amount otherwise allocable to delivered items is not contingent upon the delivery of subsequent items.

Company W should recognize the arrangement consideration allocated to each item when the recognition criteria discussed in other chapters of this product (i.e., Chapter 5, "Product Deliverables," for Machines 1 and 2; and Chapter 6, "Service Deliverables," for the training) have been satisfied.

VARIATION 2

Additional Facts: The customer needs the machines to operate in a unique environment. As such, Machines 1 and 2 are manufactured to unique customer specifications. Company W does not sell Machine 1 and Machine 2 separately. Company W's competitors do not manufacture similar machines. Due to the unique customer specifications, there is not a secondary market in which the customer could resell the machines individually. Company W sells Machine 1 and Machine 2 together for $950,000.

Company W sells training services separately to customers who already have equipment installed and want additional training for new employees. Company W charges $5,000 per day for training. However, not all customers purchase training, as Company W includes operating manuals with its equipment. The unique customer specifications related to Machines 1 and 2 do not alter the manner in which training would take place.

Company W delivers Machine 1 first, then Machine 2, then the training, using the installed machines to demonstrate the machines' functionality. Payment terms are $400,000 upon delivery of Machine 1, $475,000 upon delivery of Machine 2, and $25,000 upon providing the training.

Discussion: Machine 1 does not have value absent Machine 2 since (a) machines from different suppliers do not work with each other, (b) Company W does not sell the machines separately, and (c) the customer cannot resell Machine 1 on a standalone basis. Because the customer can learn to operate the machines without buying training from Company W, the combination of Machines 1 and 2 has value to the customer absent delivery of the training. For accounting purposes, this arrangement has two elements: (1) Machines 1 and 2 (the machines), and (2) training. The machines are considered one bundled element instead of two separate elements because Machine 1 does not have value to the customer on a standalone basis (i.e., absent Machine 2).

Evidence of fair value exists for both deliverables in the arrangement. The allocation of the consideration to the elements would be as follows:

Fair Value of Machines 1 and 2	$ 950,000	(95% of total FV)
Fair Value of Training	50,000	(5% of total FV)
Total Fair Value	$1,000,000	(100% of total FV)
Less: Arrangement Fee	900,000	

Discount in the Arrangement	$ 100,000
Discount as a Percentage of Fair Value	− 10%
Allocation to Machines 1 and 2 = $950,000 − 10% (95% of arrangement fee)	855,000
Allocation to Training = $50,000 − 10% (5% of arrangement fee)	45,000
Total Arrangement Fee	$ 900,000

In addition, the allocation of arrangement consideration is not affected by payment terms or specific refund rights since the amount otherwise allocable to delivered items is not contingent upon the delivery of subsequent items.

Company W should not recognize the arrangement consideration allocated to the machines until the recognition criteria discussed in Chapter 5, "Product Deliverables," have been satisfied for *both* machines. Arrangement consideration allocated to the training should be recognized when the recognition criteria discussed in Chapter 6, "Service Deliverables," have been satisfied.

Residual Method

If sufficient evidence of fair value exists for all undelivered items, but does not exist for one or more delivered items, the arrangement consideration should be allocated to the various elements of the arrangement using the residual method (EITF 00-21, par. 12) (ASC 605-25-30-2 and 30-3). Under this method, the amount of arrangement consideration allocated to the delivered elements should be the total arrangement consideration less the aggregate fair values of the undelivered elements. Thus, any potential discount on the arrangement taken as a whole is allocated entirely to the delivered elements. In addition, if the sum of the fair values of the undelivered elements is greater than the total arrangement consideration, no arrangement consideration is allocated to the delivered items. This process ensures that the amount of revenue recognized is not overstated at any point in time.

> **OBSERVATION:** The residual method works in only one direction, when evidence of fair value exists for all undelivered elements. If evidence of fair value exists for delivered elements, but does not exist for one or more undelivered elements, the residual method cannot be used because it is not possible to ensure that all of the potential discount in the arrangement will be allocated to the delivered elements. The use of the "reverse" residual method is limited to bundled arrangements involving the delivery of one or more financial instruments that must be initially recognized at fair value and subsequently marked-to-market under U.S. GAAP (ASC 605-25-30-4).

ILLUSTRATION: ALLOCATION OF ARRANGEMENT CONSIDERATION—RESIDUAL METHOD

General Facts: Company X sells three deliverables to Customer Y— Product P, Product Q, and Product R. Company X does not grant general or specific refund rights to Customer Y. Total arrangement consideration is $500,000. Based on its facts and circumstances, Company X concludes that each of the products has value to the customer on a standalone basis.

VARIATION 1

Additional Facts: Sufficient objective and reliable evidence is available to support the fair values of Products Q and R. However, sufficient objective and reliable evidence is not available to support the fair value of Product P. Due to its production schedule, Company X delivers Product P first, then Product Q, then Product R.

The evidence available to support the fair values of Products Q and R indicates the fair values of those products are $100,000 and $250,000, respectively. Payment terms are $200,000 upon delivery of Product P, $150,000 upon delivery of Product Q, and $150,000 upon delivery of Product R.

Discussion: Company X should treat each of the products as separate elements for accounting purposes since (a) each of the products has value to the customer on a standalone basis, (b) fair value evidence exists for the undelivered products, and (c) there is no general right of return to consider.

In addition, the allocation of arrangement consideration is not affected by payment terms or specific refund rights because the amount otherwise allocable to delivered items is not contingent upon the delivery of subsequent items.

Evidence of fair value exists only for the undelivered products in the arrangement. As such, the residual method would be used to allocate the arrangement consideration as follows:

Total Arrangement Consideration	$500,000
Fair Value of Product Q = Amount Allocated to Product Q	100,000
Fair Value of Product R = Amount Allocated to Product R	250,000
Residual = Amount Allocated to Product P	$150,000

Company X should recognize the arrangement consideration allocated to each product when the recognition criteria discussed in Chapter 5, "Product Deliverables," have been satisfied for each individual product.

VARIATION 2

Additional Facts: Sufficient objective and reliable evidence is available to support the fair values of Products Q and R. However, sufficient objective and reliable evidence is not available to support the fair value of Product P. Due to its production schedule, Company X delivers Product P first, then Product Q, then Product R.

The evidence available to support the fair values of Products Q and R indicates the fair values of those products are $300,000 and $250,000, respectively. Payment terms are $50,000 upon delivery of Product P, $250,000 upon delivery of Product Q, and $200,000 upon delivery of Product R.

Discussion: Company X should treat each of the products as separate elements for accounting purposes since (a) each of the products has value to the customer on a standalone basis, (b) fair value evidence exists for the undelivered products, and (c) there is no general right of return to consider.

Evidence of fair value exists only for the undelivered products in the arrangement. As such, the residual method would be used to allocate the arrangement consideration. However, the sum of the fair values of Products Q and R ($550,000) is greater than the arrangement consideration. As such, no arrangement consideration is allocated to Product P. The amount allocated to Product Q (the second product delivered) is determined using the residual method as follows:

Total Arrangement Consideration	$500,000
Fair Value of Product R = Amount Allocated to Product R	250,000
Residual = Amount Allocated to Product Q	$250,000

In addition, the allocation of arrangement consideration is not affected by payment terms or specific refund rights since the amount otherwise allocable to delivered items is not contingent upon the delivery of subsequent items.

Company X should recognize the arrangement consideration allocated to each product ($0 for Product P, $250,000 for Product Q, and $250,000 for Product R) when the recognition criteria discussed in Chapter 5, "Product Deliverables," have been satisfied for each individual product.

VARIATION 3

Additional Facts: Sufficient objective and reliable evidence is available to support the fair values of Products P and Q. However, sufficient objective and reliable evidence is not available to support the fair value of Product R. Due to its production schedule, Company X delivers Product P first, then Product Q, then Product R.

The evidence available to support the fair values of Products P and Q indicates the fair values of those products are $100,000 and $250,000, respectively. Payment terms are $150,000 upon delivery of Product P, $250,000 upon delivery of Product Q, and $100,000 upon delivery of Product R.

Discussion: None of the products can be treated as a separate element for accounting purposes since fair value evidence is not available for Product R, an undelivered item, at the time both Products P and Q are delivered. Instead, all three products should be bundled together and accounted for as a single element. As such, no revenue should be recognized until the recognition criteria discussed in Chapter 5, "Product Deliverables," have been satisfied related to all three products. In other words, no amounts may be recognized related to Products P and Q prior to delivery of Product R since appropriate fair value evidence does not exist for Product R.

Contingent Consideration

Contingent consideration includes specific refund rights and performance bonuses. Specific refund rights are contractual provisions that provide a customer with the right to return a delivered product for a refund (or to avoid payment for previously delivered items) or that would require any other concession if the vendor failed to deliver or provide any remaining undelivered items in the arrangement (EITF 00-21, par. 14) (ASC 605-25-30-5). For example, the customer may be entitled to return all elements for a refund, even if only one of several elements is not delivered. In other situations, the customer may have the right to a refund or liquidated damages in the event a particular item is not delivered. Performance bonuses, by contrast, are payments due from customers only if specified performance conditions are met. For example, the customer may be required to pay additional consideration if the vendor completes performance by a specified date or below specified costs. Performance bonuses should not be considered in the measurement and allocation of arrangement consideration until the performance criteria have been met.

> **OBSERVATION:**   Rights triggered by nonperformance may result from existing laws or be explicitly stated in the contract. However, rights may also exist as a matter of business practice or by implicit agreement between the parties. All rights should be considered, not merely those that are legally documented. This is consistent with the general notion of accounting for the substance of an arrangement, rather than its form.

The amount *allocated* to a delivered item is limited to the lesser of (a) the amount otherwise allocable to that item (based on using the relative fair value or residual method, as appropriate) or (b) the amount that is not contingent upon the delivery of additional items or meeting other specified performance conditions (EITF 00-21, par. 14)

(ASC 605-25-30-5). This limitation has no effect on the allocation of arrangement consideration if the amount that may be withheld or refunded is equal to or less than the amount of arrangement consideration allocated to the specified undelivered item since the arrangement consideration allocated to the delivered item is not at risk. If, however, the payment that may be withheld or refunded is greater than the amount of arrangement consideration allocated to the specified undelivered item, then some amount of the arrangement consideration allocated to the delivered item is at risk. Effectively, the amount that is at risk should not be allocated to the delivered item. The section later in this chapter entitled "Distinction Between General and Specific Refund Rights" provides additional information related to why general and specific refund rights are approached differently in the context of separating multiple-element arrangements.

ILLUSTRATION: ALLOCATION OF ARRANGEMENT CONSIDERATION—EFFECTS OF SPECIFIC REFUND RIGHTS

(Adapted from Exhibit A in the SEC staff's frequently asked question and answer document on SAB 101, *Revenue Recognition in Financial Statements*. Although most of this FAQ document was ultimately codified in SAB Topic 13 by way of SAB 104, *Revenue Recognition*, Exhibit A was not included in the codification. The examples included in Exhibit A continue to be used in this product, as adapted, because of their continued relevance in the context of EITF 00-21 (ASC 605-25).)

General Facts: Company A develops, manufactures, and sells complex manufacturing equipment. Company A enters into a sales contract with Customer B to sell and install a specific piece of equipment for $20 million. Company A does not provide Customer B with a general right of return. Company A concludes that the equipment has value to the customer on a standalone basis. Company A has developed its own internal specifications for the model of equipment Customer B ordered and has previously demonstrated that the equipment meets those specifications. There are no special operational specifications in the contract with Customer B and the equipment does not need to be integrated with other equipment. Title to the equipment passes to the customer upon delivery. Company A sells the equipment separately for $19,500,000. In those cases, a general contractor installs the equipment, charging $500,000.

VARIATION 1

Additional Facts: The contract with Customer B includes a customer acceptance provision that obligates Company A to demonstrate that the installed equipment meets its standard criteria before customer acceptance. If customer acceptance is not achieved within 120 days of delivery of the equipment, Customer B can require Company A to remove the equipment and refund all payments. Payment terms are 80% due upon delivery and 20% due after installation and customer acceptance.

Discussion: Company A should treat the equipment and installation as separate elements for accounting purposes since (a) the equipment has value to the customer on a standalone basis, (b) fair value evidence exists for both the equipment and installation, and (c) there is no general right of return to consider. However, Company A has a specific refund right related to the equipment that becomes exercisable if installation is not successfully completed within 120 days. As such, the amount allocated to the equipment is limited to the lesser of (a) the amount otherwise allocable to the equipment using the relative fair value method or (b) the amount that is not contingent upon performance of the installation. While $19,500,000 is otherwise allocable to the equipment (i.e., absent the specific refund right), 100% of that amount is contingent upon performance of the installation due to the specific refund right. As such, Company A ultimately should not allocate any arrangement consideration to the equipment. All of the arrangement consideration is effectively allocated to the installation service.

The arrangement consideration allocated to installation should not be recognized until the recognition criteria discussed in other chapters of this product (i.e., Chapter 5, "Product Deliverables," for the equipment, and Chapter 6, "Service Deliverables," for the installation) have been satisfied.

VARIATION 2

Additional Facts: Company A is an experienced provider of installation services related to its equipment. It has never failed to install the equipment as required in a contract within 120 days of delivery. The $20,000,000 arrangement fee is due upon delivery of the equipment. However, if installation is not successfully performed within 120 days of delivery of the equipment, Customer B may cancel the installation portion of the contract with Company A and receive a $750,000 refund from Company A. Customer B does not have the right to return the equipment based on Company A's failure to perform installation. In addition, Customer B has no general refund rights.

Discussion: Company A should treat the equipment and installation as separate elements for accounting purposes since (a) the equipment has value to the customer on a standalone basis, (b) fair value evidence exists for both the equipment and installation, and (c) there is no general right of return to consider. However, Company A has a specific refund right related to the equipment that becomes exercisable if installation is not successfully completed within 120 days. As such, the amount allocated to the equipment is limited to the lesser of (a) the amount otherwise allocable to the equipment using the relative fair value method or (b) the amount that is not contingent upon performance of the installation. While $19,500,000 is otherwise allocable to the equipment (i.e., absent the specific refund right), $250,000 of that amount is contingent upon performance of the installation due to the specific refund right. As such, Company A ultimately should only allocate $19,250,000 of the arrangement consideration to the equipment. This results in $750,000 of the arrangement consideration ultimately being allocated to the installation.

The arrangement consideration allocated to the equipment should not be recognized until the recognition criteria discussed in Chapter 5, "Product Deliverables," have been satisfied. The arrangement consideration allocated to the installation should not be recognized until the recognition criteria discussed in Chapter 6, "Service Deliverables," have been satisfied.

Customer Cancellation Provisions

In some cases, an arrangement includes a provision allows the customer to cancel or terminate the arrangement upon payment of a fee. When such a provision exists in a multiple-element arrangement, a company should assume that the customer will not cancel the arrangement for purposes of allocating arrangement consideration among the deliverables. However, to the extent an amount is recorded as an asset for the excess of revenue recognized over the amount of cash received from the customer since the inception of the arrangement, that asset should not exceed the cancellation fee to which the vendor is entitled under the arrangement. In these situations, the vendor's right to the cancellation fee must be legally enforceable, and the vendor should have the intent to enforce its contractual right to collect the cancellation fee for purposes of supporting recognition of the asset (EITF 00-21, par. 15) (ASC 605-25-30-6).

General Refund Rights

In many arrangements, a customer can exercise certain general rights even after a product is delivered. For example, general rights of return and standard warranty provisions represent uncertainties and potential future obligations that exist at the time of delivery. Typically, such rights are evaluated for each deliverable in an arrangement, pursuant to the appropriate guidance (e.g., FAS-48 (ASC 605-15-25-1 through 25-4) for returns and FAS-5 (ASC 460) for warranties). This guidance is discussed in other chapters of this product.

If an arrangement includes a general refund right, delivery or performance of the undelivered item(s) must be considered probable and substantially within the vendor's control to treat a delivered item separately for accounting purposes (EITF 00-21, par. 9c) (ASC 605-25-25-5). If general refund rights exist and delivery or performance of the undelivered item(s) are considered probable and substantially in the vendor's control, then those rights should be accounted for as discussed in Chapter 5, "Product Deliverables," and Chapter 6, "Service Deliverables," as appropriate. The existence of these rights does not, in and of itself, preclude treating a delivered item separately for accounting purposes. If general refund rights exist and delivery or performance of the undelivered item(s) are not considered probable and substantially in the vendor's control, then the delivered item should not be treated separately for accounting purposes.

An assessment of whether performance of the undelivered element(s) is probable and substantially in the vendor's control is required after *each* element in the arrangement is delivered. The vendor's ability to meet this criterion is a function of the nature of the undelivered elements and the specific characteristics of the vendor. Factors that determine performance of undelivered elements include the amount of time to complete, degree of customization, reliance on subcontractors, and the availability of components. The vendor's history of performance and financial condition must also be considered in the assessment.

Distinction Between General and Specific Refund Rights

An important distinction is made between general and specific refund rights in EITF 00-21 (ASC 605-25). The existence of a general refund right creates a connection between the deliverables that must be considered from the perspective of the *vendor*. As a result, the vendor must assess whether performance related to undelivered items is probable and substantially within its control.

By contrast, the existence of a specific refund right creates a connection between the deliverables that the vendor should consider from the *customer's* perspective. A specific refund right expressly connects the deliverables in a multiple-element arrangement, because it specifically ties the vendor's right to consideration (or the right to retain consideration) to whether the vendor provides the undelivered items. This express link indicates that there is a stronger connection between deliverables in a multiple-element arrangement containing a specific refund right than in a multiple-element arrangement containing only a general refund right. To address the accounting implications of this stronger connection, the amount allocated to a delivered item is limited to the lesser of (a) the amount otherwise allocable to that item (based on using the relative fair value or residual method, as appropriate) or (b) the amount that is not contingent upon the delivery of additional items or meeting other specified performance conditions (EITF 00-21, par. 14) (ASC 605-25-30-5).

Deferred Costs

As noted previously, there are instances when revenue in a multiple-element arrangement may not be recognized even though some of the elements have already been delivered. This can occur for many reasons, including a delivered item not having standalone value to a customer, a lack of evidence of fair value, or the existence of a specific refund right. When revenue cannot be recognized upon delivery of the element, an issue arises regarding how to treat the costs incurred related to that element.

When costs are minimal, this issue is not significant. However, for many deliverables, the related direct and incremental costs are significant. The accounting literature does not provide detailed guidance on the deferral of costs multiple-element arrangements, although the costs must meet the definition of an asset as defined in CON-6 in order to qualify for deferral. Authoritative literature that provides guidance on cost deferral in other revenue transactions must be consulted for additional guidance. This discussion is provided in Chapter 8, "Miscellaneous Issues."

Guarantees and Indemnifications in Multiple-Element Arrangements

FIN-45 (ASC 460) provides initial accounting and disclosure requirements related to guarantees and indemnifications. FIN-45 (ASC 460) requires accounting for the both the contingent and non-contingent aspects of the guarantee or indemnification and mandates extensive disclosures.

Some entities, such as financial institutions or insurance companies, are in the "business" of providing guarantees or indemnifications. Other entities provide guarantees or indemnifications in connection with their other, primary business activities. This section of the chapter focuses on the accounting considerations for the latter set of entities. Specifically, it focuses on the accounting by entities that enter into multiple-element arrangements where one of the elements is a guarantee and the other elements relate to their primary activities.

FIN-45's (ASC 460's) broad scope makes it applicable to many common arrangements. For example, equipment manufacturers often guarantee the loans their customers obtain from third-party lenders to purchase the manufacturers' equipment. The accounting for such guarantees is covered by FIN-45 (ASC 460). Another, more common example is a warranty provided by a retailer or product manufacturer to a customer. Such warranties are a guarantee as defined in FIN-45 (ASC 460) and are subject to certain disclosure requirements. Chapter 12, "Disclosures," discusses the disclosure requirements related to guarantees.

Scope

As mentioned above, FIN-45 (ASC 460) provides a broad definition of what constitutes a guarantee. However, certain guarantees are specifically excluded from the requirements, despite meeting this definition, while certain other guarantees are excluded from the initial recognition and measurement (IR&M) provisions of FIN-45 (ASC 460) but not the disclosure provisions. Given this complexity, the first step in accounting for a guarantee or indemnification is to determine whether it falls within the scope of the IR&M provisions of FIN-45 (ASC 460). A set of basic characteristics and defined exceptions provide the foundation for making this determination.

Basic characteristics If a guarantee or indemnification possesses any of the following basic characteristics, it initially falls within the scope of FIN-45 (ASC 460) (FIN-45, par. 3) (ASC 460-10-15-4):

- Contracts that contingently require the guarantor to make payments (either in cash, financial instruments, other assets, shares of its stock, or provision of services) to the guaranteed party based on changes in an underlying that is related to an asset, liability, or equity security of the guaranteed party.

- Contracts that contingently require the guarantor to make payments (either in cash, financial instruments, other assets, shares of its stock, or provision of services) to the guaranteed party based on another entity's failure to perform under an obligating agreement (performance guarantees).

- Indemnification agreements (contracts) that contingently require the indemnifying party (the guarantor) to make payments to the indemnified party (guaranteed party) based on changes in an underlying that is related to an asset, liability, or equity security of the indemnified party.

- Indirect guarantees of the indebtedness of others even though the payment to the guaranteed party may not be based on changes in an underlying that is related to an asset, liability, or equity security of the guaranteed party.

Certain guarantees and indemnifications that possess one of the basic characteristics listed above, however, are specifically excluded from all of the provisions of FIN-45 or just the IR&M provisions of FIN-45, as discussed below.

Exclusions from all provisions The following types of guarantees that may be found in revenue arrangements are excluded from all of the provisions of FIN-45 (ASC 460) (i.e., neither the IR&M nor disclosure provisions apply to these guarantees), even if they possess one of the basic characteristics discussed above (FIN-45, par. 6) (ASC 460-10-15-7):

- Guarantees of the residual value of leased property at the end of a lease term by the lessee if the lessee accounts for the lease as a capital lease.

- Guarantees involved in leases that are accounted for as contingent rent.

- Guarantees (or indemnifications) that are issued by either an insurance company or a reinsurance company and accounted for under the related industry-specific authoritative literature, including guarantees embedded in either insurance contracts or investment contracts.

- Vendor rebates where the contract contingently requires the vendor to make payments to the customer based on the customer's sales revenues, number of units sold, or similar events.

- Guarantees (or indemnifications) whose existence prevents the guarantor from being able to either account for a transaction as the sale of an asset or recognize the profit from that sale transaction.

Exclusions from IR&M provisions FIN-45 (ASC 460) provides additional exclusions from its IR&M provisions. The following types of guarantees or indemnifications that may be found in revenue arrangements are subject to the disclosure provisions of FIN-45 (ASC 460), but are not subject to the IR&M provisions (see Chapter 12, "Disclosures" for a discussion of the disclosure requirements) (FIN-45, par. 7) (ASC 460-10-15-9 and ASC 460-10-25-1):

- Guarantees that meet the definition of a derivative and are accounted for at fair value.

- Product warranties related to the product's ability to function but not its value.

- Guarantees by an original lessee when the lease is modified (as discussed in the authoritative literature addressing lease accounting) such that the original lessee becomes secondarily liable instead of being primarily liable (i.e., primary obligor role shifts from original lessee to new party).

Guarantees and indemnifications that possess one of the basic characteristics but are included on the preceding list are only subject to the disclosure provisions of FIN-45 (ASC 460).

Scope provisions and revenue-related guarantees and indemnifications Some of the more common guarantees and indemnifications found in sales arrangements are as follows:

- *A manufacturer's guarantee of a loan obtained by its customer from a third-party lender to buy the manufacturer's product.* Such a guarantee contains one of the basic characteristics of a guarantee because it requires the manufacturer to make payments to the lender if the customer fails to perform under an obligating agreement (i.e., the customer's loan agreement with the third-party lender). This guarantee does not contain any of the characteristics that would exclude it from any of the provisions of FIN-45 (ASC 460).

- *A fixed-price trade-in right offered by a vendor to its customer.* Such a right contains one of the basic characteristics of a guarantee because it may require the seller to make a payment to the purchaser based on changes in the price of the asset purchased. This guarantee does not contain any of the characteristics that would exclude it from any of the provisions of FIN-45 (ASC 460) unless the existence of such a guarantee prevents revenue recognition.

- *A product warranty.* As noted above, a product warranty is excluded from FIN-45's (ASC 460's) IR&M provisions, but the disclosure provisions apply. See Chapter 12, "Disclosures," for a discussion of these disclosure requirements.

- *An indemnification in a software licensing agreement that indemnifies the licensee against liability and damages arising from any claims of patent, copyright, trademark, or trade secret infringement by the software vendor's software.* As discussed in FSP FIN-45-1 (ASC 460-10-55-30 through 55-34), such an indemnification is akin to a product warranty. FIN-45's (ASC 460's) disclosure provisions apply to this indemnification, while its IR&M provisions do not. See Chapter 12, "Disclosures," for a discussion of the disclosure requirements of FIN-45.

- *Vendor rebates based on the volume of purchases made by a customer over a period of time.* Such a provision does not contain any of the basic characteristics of a guarantee because the contingent payment provision relates to an asset of the vendor, not the purchaser. Payment provisions related to a company's own assets are not guarantees covered by FIN-45 (ASC 460).

- *Arrangements that provide for contingent payments to the purchaser such that the contingency prevents revenue recognition.* This is a specific scope exclusion from all of FIN-45 (ASC 460). Examples include provisions in product sales arrangements that require the transaction to be accounted for as a consignment or a financing (see Chapter 5, "Product Deliverables"), and software arrangements where the software vendor participates in the customer's financing through either (a) indemnifying the financing party against claims beyond the software vendor's standard indemnifications or (b) guaranteeing the customer's loan with the financing party, thus preventing the recognition of revenue when the presumption that the fee is not fixed or determinable cannot be overcome (see Chapter 10, "Software—A Complete Model").

There are many other types of guarantees or indemnifications in revenue arrangements. Companies should be very diligent in evaluating the provisions of their contracts against the criteria in FIN-45 (ASC 460). Consultation with auditors or other experts in this regard may be necessary due to the broad and complex nature of the scope provisions.

Initial Recognition and Measurement

FIN-45 (ASC 460) provides guidance for guarantees and indemnifications that fall within the scope of its IR&M provisions. However, FIN-45 (ASC 460) does not provide guidance related to the subsequent accounting for any guarantee liability recognized as a result of applying these provisions. In initially accounting for any guarantee or indemnification, FIN-45 (ASC 460) notes that there are two distinct liabilities (FIN-45, par. 8) (ASC 460-10-25-2):

1. *Noncontingent liability*—The guarantor's obligation to stand ready to perform under the terms of the guarantee.

2. *Contingent liability*—The guarantor's potential obligation to make payments in the future related to the guarantee.

Noncontingent liability If a guarantee or indemnification falls within the scope of the IR&M provisions of FIN-45 (ASC 460), the related noncontingent liability must be initially recognized at its fair value. If the guarantee or indemnification is the only element in the transaction with an unrelated party, the liability recognized is the fee received by the guarantor for providing that guarantee or indemnification. If the guarantee or indemnification is part of a multiple-element arrangement, the liability recognized should be an estimate of the guarantee or indemnification's fair value (e.g., if the guarantee or indemnification was the only element in the transaction, the fee received by the guarantor) (FIN-45, par. 9) (ASC 460-10-30-2).

A multiple-element arrangement containing a guarantee or indemnification that falls within the scope of the IR&M provisions of FIN-45 (ASC 460) must be separated from the other elements in the arrangement and recorded at its fair value. In these instances, the guarantee or indemnification's fair value should first be allocated to the guarantee and then the relative fair value method should be used to allocate the remaining consideration among the other elements in the arrangement.

Contingent liability Accounting for the contingent liability continues to be governed by FAS-5 (ASC 450-20). Therefore, a contingent liability should only be recognized when occurrence of the liability becomes probable and the amount is reasonably estimable. It would be unusual for a contingent liability to be recognized initially (i.e., at the same time as the noncontingent liability). However, if this occurs, the total liability recognized for the guarantee or indemnification should be the greater of (a) the noncontingent liability (i.e., the fair value of the guarantee or indemnification) or (b) the probable and reasonably estimable contingent liability (FIN-45, par. 10) (ASC 460-10-30-3).

Subsequent Measurement

Although FIN-45 (ASC 460) does not provide any requirements related to the subsequent measurement of the recorded noncontingent liability, it does provide insight regarding the "typical" subsequent accounting. FIN-45 (ASC 460) indicates that the noncontingent liability would typically be taken into income as the guarantor's risk is reduced, which would be (a) when the related guarantee or indemnification expires or is settled (the Settlement Approach), (b) over the term of the guarantee or indemnification based on a systematic and rational amortization method (the Earnings Process Approach), or (c) over the term of the guarantee as the fair value of the guarantee changes, but only if this approach is supported by other authoritative literature, such as guarantees that meet the definition of a derivative (the Fair Value Approach) (FIN-45, par. 12) (ASC 460-10-35-2). The application of the Fair Value Approach to guarantees where other authoritative literature supports subsequently marking a guarantee to fair value is supported by FSP FIN-45-2 (ASC 460-10-35-2). Each of these approaches is discussed below. By contrast, subsequent measurement of the contingent liability is governed by FAS-5 (ASC 450) and is beyond the scope of this publication.

Settlement Approach   This approach would result in the elimination of the noncontingent liability when the guarantor's obligation under the guarantee is settled or when it expires based on the terms of the guarantee.

Earnings Process Approach   This approach results in the reduction of a noncontingent liability over the period the guarantor stands ready to honor the guarantee. In a sense, this method treats the noncontingent liability as a deferred fee for providing a service. EITF 85-20 (ASC 605-20-25-9) indicates that the pattern over which such a fee should be recognized depends on the nature of the guarantee.

Fair Value Approach   This approach results in an increase or decrease in the guarantee's carrying amount during the period of the guarantee based on periodic remeasurements. As discussed above, a guarantee "qualifies" for this approach only if there is other supporting authoritative literature. For example, a guarantee that meets the definition of a derivative must be accounted for under FAS-133 (ASC 815), which requires it to be subsequently re-measured based on its fair value. While guarantees that meet the definition of a derivative in FAS-133 (ASC 815) are excluded from the IR&M provisions of FIN-45 (ASC 460), they are subject to the disclosure requirements.

The approach that should be used to subsequently measure the noncontingent liability component of a guarantee is a matter of judgment that depends on both the type of guarantee and the facts and circumstances. The approach selected should be disclosed and consistently applied in similar situations.

> **DISCLOSURE ALERT:**   See Chapter 12, "Disclosures," regarding accounting policy disclosure requirements.

ILLUSTRATION: MULTIPLE-ELEMENT ARRANGEMENT CONTAINING A GUARANTEE

Facts: On January 1, 20X1, Manufacturer A sells product to Company B for $100,000. Company B arranges financing with Lender C. Lender C requests and receives a guarantee from Manufacturer A. The guarantee calls for Manufacturer A to make Lender C whole if Company B defaults on its loan with Lender C. Manufacturer A determines that the fair value of the guarantee is $10,000 on January 1, 20X1. The term of Company B's loan with Lender C is two years. Manufacturer A is released from the guarantee obligation gradually as Company B makes its payments. Manufacturer A determines that the conditions for revenue recognition are met on January 1, 20X1 (including the collectibility condition). Company B makes the scheduled payments to Lender C for the first year of the loan, totaling $50,000. At the end of 20X1, Manufacturer A determines that the fair value of the guarantee is $3,000. Manufacturer A also concludes that recognition of a contingent liability related to the guarantee is not required at December 31, 20X1. Company B defaults on the first payment due in 20X2, at which point Manufacturer A concludes it will have to make Lender C whole for the remaining balance of Company B's loan. For ease of illustration, the effects of interest are not considered.

Accounting: Manufacturer A recognizes receipt of payment, revenue, and guarantee liability on January 1, 20X1:

Cash	$100,000	
Product Revenue		$90,000
Guarantee (Noncontingent) Liability		$10,000

The entries recorded during 20X1 and 20X2 depend on the approach used by Manufacturer A to subsequently measure the noncontingent guarantee liability. As such, the entries under the Settlement and Earnings Process Approaches are presented below, with a comparison of both approaches that follow. Manufacturer A may not use the Fair Value Approach since that approach is not supported by other authoritative literature in relation to Manufacturer A's transaction (e.g., the guarantee does not meet the definition of a derivative under FAS-133 (ASC 815)).

Settlement Approach

During 20X1, Manufacturer A would not reduce the noncontingent guarantee liability, even though it has been released from half of the guarantee obligation, since the guarantee obligation has not expired or been settled.

Upon Company B's default in 20X2, Manufacturer A would record the contingent loss:

Guarantee Loss	$50,000	
Guarantee (Contingent) Liability		$50,000

Upon Manufacturer A's settlement of the guarantee in 20X2, Manufacturer A would record the cash payment to Lender C to pay off Company B's outstanding loan balance and record the noncontingent guarantee liability as guarantee income since it has been settled:

Guarantee (Contingent) Liability	$50,000	
Cash		$50,000
Guarantee (Noncontingent) Liability	$10,000	
Guarantee Income		$10,000

Earnings Process Approach

During 20X1, Manufacturer A would reduce the noncontingent guarantee liability and recognize guarantee income based on the guidance in EITF 85-20 (assume straight-line amortization for ease of illustration):

Guarantee (Noncontingent) Liability	$5,000	
Guarantee Income		$5,000

Upon Company B's default in 20X2, Manufacturer A would record the contingent loss:

Guarantee Loss	$50,000	
Guarantee (Contingent) Liability		$50,000

During 20X2, Manufacturer A would continue to reduce the noncontingent guarantee liability and recognize guarantee income:

Guarantee (Noncontingent) Liability	$5,000	
Guarantee Income		$5,000

Upon Manufacturer A's settlement of the guarantee in 20X2, Manufacturer A would record the cash payment to Lender C to pay off Company B's outstanding loan balance:

Guarantee (Contingent) Liability	$50,000	
Cash		$50,000

Comparison	**Approach**	
	Settlement	**Earnings Process**
Guarantee Liability at 12/31/20X1	$10,000	$5,000
Guarantee Liability upon Company B's Default	$60,000	$55,000
Guarantee Income During 20X1	$0	$5,000
Guarantee Income During 20X2	$10,000	$5,000
Guarantee Loss During 20X2	$50,000	$50,000

The primary difference between the approaches is the timing of the reduction (or changes) in the noncontingent guarantee liability. Under the Settlement Approach, Manufacturer A does not reduce the noncontingent guarantee liability until it settles the guarantee obligation. However, under the Earnings Process Approach, the noncontingent guarantee liability will change prior to the guarantee's actual settlement since Manufacturer A amortizes the noncontingent guarantee liability over the period it remains obligated to perform—the guarantee period. Under these two approaches, the guarantee income (noncontingent liability) and guarantee loss (contingent liability) are effectively viewed as two separate amounts related to two separate occurrences. Whether the guarantee income and loss are recognized gross or net on the income statement in these two approaches is a matter of judgment that depends on the facts and circumstances.

RECOGNITION WHEN ELEMENTS CANNOT BE SEPARATED

In several situations discussed earlier, revenue from a delivered element cannot be recognized due to its interaction with undelivered elements. When this occurs, the arrangement consideration allocable to a delivered item(s) that cannot be treated separately for accounting purposes should be combined with the arrangement consideration allocable to the other applicable undelivered item(s) within the arrangement. The appropriate pattern of revenue recognition should then be determined for that bundled group of deliverables (EITF 00-21, par. 10) (ASC 605-25-25-6). This pattern of recognition may differ depending upon (a) whether any of the performance obligations in the multiple-element arrangement may be considered inconsequential or perfunctory and (b) the reason the elements in the multiple-element arrangement were not separated for accounting purposes.

Inconsequential or Perfunctory Performance Obligations

When an element in a multiple element arrangement cannot be treated separately for accounting purposes, a question may arise regarding whether that element is so inconsequential or perfunctory that it should not affect the recognition of revenue related to other elements in the arrangement.

Consider a situation where equipment is sold subject to installation and the vendor cannot separate these deliverables due to a lack of fair value evidence for the installation. In this case, the vendor believes that installation is an inconsequential or perfunctory obligation. As a result, the vendor believes that it has substantially completed or fulfilled the terms specified in the arrangement and, therefore, despite the absence of fair value for the installation, recognition of equipment related revenue should not be deferred.

Whether a remaining performance obligation may be viewed as inconsequential or perfunctory and, thereby, not affect the recognition of revenue related to the other elements in the arrangement, is not addressed in EITF 00-21 (ASC 605-25) or any other authoritative literature applicable to private companies. However, the SEC staff has addressed this question in SAB Topic 13A3c (ASC 605-10-S99). This guidance is not mandatory for private companies, although they should still consider its application given the absence of other guidance.

In SAB Topic 13A3c (ASC 605-10-S99), the SEC staff indicates that if the only remaining performance obligation on the part of the vendor is inconsequential or perfunctory, the vendor can still conclude that it has met the delivery or performance criterion necessary to recognize revenue for the delivered elements (SAB Topic 13A3c, ques. 1) (ASC 605-10-S99).

Inconsequential or Perfunctory Criteria

A remaining performance obligation may not be considered inconsequential or perfunctory if (a) it is essential to the functionality of a delivered item, (b) the vendor's failure to fulfill the remaining performance obligation would result in the customer receiving a full or partial refund or rejecting (or a right to a refund or to reject) delivered items, or (c) the vendor does not have a demonstrated history of fulfilling the remaining performance obligation in a timely manner and reliably estimating the remaining costs (SAB Topic 13A3c, ques. 1 and 2) (ASC 605-10-S99). Further information on these criteria is provided below with information on other factors that must also be considered.

Essential to the functionality In determining whether a remaining performance obligation is essential to the functionality of a delivered item, the vendor should consider both the "standalone value to the customer" guidance in EITF 00-21 (ASC 605.25) (as discussed earlier in this chapter) and the "essential to the functionality" guidance in SOP 97-2 (ASC 985-605) (see Chapter 10, "Software—A Complete Model"). It is instructive to consult both of these sources given their conceptual similarity and common objective. In addition, it would be a rare situation where consistent conclusions would not be reached when analyzing each piece of guidance individually (e.g., concluding that a delivered element has value to the customer on a standalone basis when an undelivered element is essential to its functionality).

For example, if the arrangement includes equipment and installation that should not be treated separately for accounting purposes, factors that would indicate that either (1) the equipment does not have standalone value to the customer absent the installation, or (2) that the installation is essential to the functionality of the equipment, include (a) the installation involves significant changes to the features or capabilities of the equipment or building complex interfaces or connections, and (b) the installation services are unavailable from other vendors. Conversely, factors that would indicate that either (1) the equipment does have standalone value to the customer absent the installation, or (2) the installation is not essential to the functionality of the equipment, include (a) the equipment is a standard product, (b) installation does not significantly alter the equipment's capabilities, and (c) other companies are available to perform the installation (SAB Topic 13A3c, ques. 3) (ASC 605-10-S99).

> **OBSERVATION:** If the reason that equipment and installation must be combined for accounting purposes is the fact that the equipment does not have standalone value to the customer, it will generally follow that installation is essential to the equipment's functionality. As a result, the installation could not be viewed as inconsequential or perfunctory and revenue would

be deferred until the installation is performed, provided the other criteria for revenue recognition have been met.

Refund right   Whether a refund right exists if the remaining performance obligation is not fulfilled is often documented in the sales contract. However, such rights may also exist due to industry practice, company policy, or laws and regulations. In addition, the relationship between the buyer and the seller should be evaluated in full to determine whether unstated refund rights might exist. Therefore, all rights that exist, whether explicit or implicit, must be considered.

Other criteria   Other factors should also be considered in determining whether a remaining performance obligation is inconsequential or perfunctory, including (SAB Topic 13A3c, ques. 2) (ASC 605-10-S99):

- Has the cost or time to fulfill the remaining performance obligation in similar contracts historically varied significantly from one instance to another?

- Are the skills required to fulfill the remaining performance obligation specialized or not readily available in the marketplace?

- Is the cost of fulfilling the remaining performance obligation, or the fair value of that remaining performance obligation, more than insignificant in relation to such items as the contract fee, gross profit, and operating income allocable to the other items in the arrangement?

- Is the period before the remaining performance obligation is fulfilled lengthy?

- Is the timing of payment of a portion of the sales price coincident with fulfilling the remaining performance obligation?

A "yes" answer to any of these questions is an indication that the remaining performance obligation is more than inconsequential or perfunctory.

This evaluation is highly subjective and, as a result, different vendors might reach different conclusions. Because the timing of revenue recognition is affected by the conclusion reached, a conservative approach should be used. A company should also consider consulting with experts before reaching a final conclusion.

DISCLOSURE ALERT: See Chapter 12, "Disclosures," regarding accounting policy disclosure requirements.

ILLUSTRATION: EFFECTS OF CONCLUDING THAT REMAINING PERFORMANCE OBLIGATION IS INCONSEQUENTIAL OR PERFUNCTORY

General Facts: Vendor A sells a piece of equipment and installation services related to that equipment to Customer B. Total arrangement consideration is $100,000 and is paid in full by Customer B upon delivery of the equipment. The equipment's carrying value in inventory is $75,000. The installation services are not complex and do not significantly alter the equipment's capabilities. Customer B has purchased this equipment from Vendor A in the past and could install the equipment itself using an installation and operation manual provided by Vendor A. As a matter of convenience, however, Customer B purchases the installation services from Vendor A. Vendor A has a history of providing the installation services in a timely manner and reliably estimating the costs of providing the installation. The costs of providing the installation services to other customers for the same piece of equipment have not varied significantly. Vendor A anticipates providing the installation services within one week of the equipment being delivered. There are no general or specific return/refund rights included in this arrangement. Vendor A delivers the equipment on December 31, 20X1 and provides the installation services on January 6, 20X2. When the installation services should not be treated separately for accounting purposes, Vendor A has an accounting policy that requires it to evaluate whether those services should be treated as an inconsequential or perfunctory remaining performance obligation. Aside from the effects of the installation services, Vendor A concludes that the general conditions for recognizing revenue related to the equipment are met upon delivery of the equipment on December 31, 20X1. Similarly, Vendor A concludes that the general conditions for recognizing revenue related to the installation services are met upon performance of those services on January 6, 20X2.

VARIATION 1

Additional Facts: Vendor A has never sold the equipment without the installation and has never provided standalone installation services. Since another vendor has never installed Vendor A's equipment and since Vendor A has never provided standalone installation services, Vendor A does not have evidence to support the fair value of the installation services. Vendor A incurs $1,000 of costs when providing the installation services.

Discussion: Vendor A should not treat the equipment and installation services as separate elements for accounting purposes due to the lack of fair value evidence for the installation services (the undelivered element). Factors supporting a potential conclusion that the installation services are an inconsequential or perfunctory remaining performance obligation include:

- The installation services are not essential to the functionality of the equipment since (a) the installation is not complex and does not significantly alter the equipment's capabilities, and (b) Customer B could install the equipment on its own. While no other vendors have provided the installation service, Customer B could perform this service for itself or, in theory, provide this service for other customers of Vendor A.

- There are no general or specific refund rights and therefore Vendor A's failure to perform the installation services would not result in Customer B receiving a full or partial refund or rejecting (or a right to a refund or to reject) the equipment.

- Vendor A has a demonstrated history of providing the installation services in a timely manner and reliably estimating the remaining costs.

- Vendor A's costs of providing the installation services to other customers for the same piece of equipment have not varied significantly.

- The skills required to provide the installation services are not specialized. This is supported by the fact that Customer B could install the equipment itself using the installation and operation manual provided by Vendor A.

- Vendor A's costs of providing the installation services ($1,000) are insignificant in relation to the contract's overall fee (1% of $100,000), gross profit (4.2% of $24,000), and operating income.

- At the time the equipment is delivered to Customer B, Vendor A anticipates that the installation services will be provided within one week. This is a typical timeframe for Vendor A to provide these installation services to its customers.

- The $100,000 arrangement fee is paid in full upon delivery of the equipment. In other words, no portion of this payment is contingent upon Vendor A providing the installation services.

One factor that cannot be evaluated in this analysis is whether the fair value of providing the installation services is insignificant in relation to the contract fee, gross profit, and operating income allocable to the equipment. This is due to Vendor A's conclusion that it does not have appropriate fair value evidence for the installation services, which precludes the vendor from allocating the arrangement consideration for purposes of analyzing this factor. However, Vendor A believes the other factors present in the arrangement compensate for its inability to evaluate this factor and provide sufficient evidence to conclude that the installation services are an inconsequential or perfunctory remaining performance obligation.

Accounting: On December 31, 20X1, Vendor A records the entire arrangement consideration as revenue, recognizes the equipment's inventory costs as costs of sales, and accrues the costs of performing the installation:

Cash	$100,000	
Equipment Revenue		$100,000
Cost of Sales	$76,000	
Inventory		$75,000
Accrued Costs of Installation Services		$1,000

On January 6, 20X2, Vendor A relieves the accrual related to providing the installation services:

Accrued Costs of Installation Services	$1,000	
Cash or Liability (depending on nature of costs)		$1,000

VARIATION 2

Additional Facts: Vendor A has never sold the equipment without the installation and has never provided standalone installation services. Since another vendor has never installed Vendor A's equipment and since Vendor A has never provided standalone installation services, Vendor A does not have fair value evidence for the installation services. Vendor A incurs $15,000 of costs when providing the installation services.

Discussion: Vendor A should not treat the equipment and installation services as separate elements for accounting purposes due to the lack of fair value evidence for the installation services (the undelivered element). The analysis of whether the installation services are an inconsequential or perfunctory performance obligation is similar to that in Variation 1, with one significant exception. In Variation 2, Vendor A is not able to conclude that its costs of providing the installation services ($15,000) are insignificant in relation to the contract's overall contract fee (15% of $100,000), gross profit (150% of $10,000), and operating income. As a result, Vendor A concludes that the installation services are more than inconsequential or perfunctory.

Accounting: On December 31, 20X1, Vendor A records receipt of the cash from Customer B, recognizes deferred revenue for that amount, and reclassifies the equipment to an account that signifies it is being held by others:

Cash	$100,000	
Deferred Revenue		$100,000
Inventory Held by Others	$75,000	
Inventory		$75,000

On January 6, 20X2, Vendor A recognizes the arrangement consideration as revenue and records the related equipment inventory costs and costs of performing the services as cost of sales:

Deferred Revenue	$100,000	
Equipment and Installation Services Revenue		$100,000
Cost of Sales—Equipment	$75,000	
Cost of Sales—Installation Services	$15,000	
Inventory Held by Others		$75,000
Cash or Liability (depending on nature of costs)		$15,000

VARIATION 3

Additional Facts: Historically, Vendor A has sold the equipment without the installation. In those situations, the customer has either performed the installation itself using the installation and operation manual provided by Vendor A or hired a professional installer to perform the installation for $2,000. Vendor A charges $98,000 for the equipment when it sells it on a standalone basis. When providing the installation services Vendor A incurs $1,000 of costs.

Discussion: Vendor A should treat the equipment and installation services as separate elements for accounting purposes since (a) the equipment has value to Customer B on a standalone basis (i.e., Customer B could perform the installation services itself or could hire a professional installer to perform the installation services), (b) appropriate fair value evidence exists to allocate the arrangement consideration (i.e., the relative fair value method should be used since objective and reliable evidence of fair value exists for both the equipment and installation), and (c) no general right of return or refund exists. The amount allocated to the equipment is $98,000 and the amount allocated to the installation services is $2,000.

Accounting: On December 31, 20X1, Vendor A records the arrangement consideration allocated to the equipment as revenue, defers the arrangement consideration allocated to the installation, and recognizes the equipment's inventory costs as costs of sales:

Cash	$100,000	
Deferred Revenue		$ 2,000
Equipment Revenue		$98,000
Cost of Sales—Equipment	$ 75,000	
Inventory		$75,000

On January 6, 20X2, Vendor A records the arrangement consideration allocated to the installation services as revenue and the costs of providing those services as cost of sales:

Deferred Revenue	$2,000	
Installation Services Revenue		$2,000
Cost of Sales—Installation Services	$1,000	
Cash or Liability (depending on nature of costs)		$1,000

COMPARISON OF VARIATIONS

These variations illustrate how the timing of revenue recognition can differ depending on the conclusions reached about whether the multiple-element arrangement should be separated and, if not, whether the remaining performance obligation may be considered inconsequential or perfunctory:

	Timing of Revenue Recognition
Variation 1—Should not treat equipment and installation services as separate elements, and installation services are inconsequential or perfunctory.	All arrangement consideration is recognized as revenue when equipment is delivered.
Variation 2—Should not treat equipment and installation services as separate elements, and installation services are more than inconsequential or perfunctory.	All arrangement consideration is recognized as revenue when installation services are performed.
Variation 3—Should treat equipment and installation services as separate elements.	A portion of the arrangement consideration is recognized as revenue when equipment is delivered, and the remainder as installation services are performed.

Analysis of Multiple Remaining Performance Obligations

Generally, if there is more than one remaining performance obligation, the evaluation of whether these obligations are inconsequential or perfunctory should be performed for the entire group, because, in the aggregate, these obligations may represent a significant portion of the value of the arrangement. However, if, for example, four items as a group, are not inconsequential or perfunctory, the company may then evaluate three of the four as a group to determine whether the group of three is inconsequential or perfunctory as a whole, and so on. In addition, a remaining performance obligation should generally not be considered inconsequential or perfunctory if it is one of a number of similar items that are not inconsequential or perfunctory as a group.

Accounting for Remaining Performance Obligations Considered Inconsequential or Perfunctory

A vendor should develop a policy that is consistent across similar arrangements and similar performance obligations to determine whether the remaining obligations are inconsequential or perfunctory. The cost of any remaining performance obligations considered inconsequential or perfunctory should be recognized (with the expense recorded as part of cost of sales) when revenue from the arrangement is first recognized (SAB Topic 13A3c, ques. 1) (ASC 605-10-S99).

Delivered Item Does Not Have Standalone Value to the Customer

When a delivered item does not have value to the customer on a standalone basis, arrangement consideration otherwise allocable to the delivered item should not be recognized. This component of the arrangement consideration should be recognized, assuming all other revenue recognition criteria have been met, when another item(s) has been provided such that the two (or more) items have value to the customer on a standalone basis. At this point, the timing or pattern of recognition will depend on the nature of the items involved.

> **OBSERVATION:** In the situation where a delivered element does not have value to the customer on a standalone basis (i.e., absent the delivery of one or more undelivered elements), it is generally the case that there is at least one undelivered element that is essential to the functionality of the delivered element. This is due to the similarity between the two concepts and their common objective. It would be a rare situation where inconsistent conclusions would be reached when analyzing the concepts individually (e.g., concluding that a delivered element has value to the customer on a standalone basis when an undelivered element is essential to its functionality). As a result, when the delivered element does not have value to the customer on a standalone basis absent the undelivered element, the undelivered element should not be considered an inconsequential or perfunctory remaining performance obligation since it is likely to be essential to the functionality of the delivered element.

Sufficient Evidence of Fair Value Does Not Exist

When sufficient evidence of fair value does not exist to allocate arrangement consideration among the elements in a multiple-element arrangement (where these elements are not treated as inconsequential or perfunctory remaining performance obligations for accounting purposes), some portion of revenue generally is recognized upon delivery of the final element for which evidence of fair value does not exist, assuming that all other revenue recognition criteria have been met. Therefore, once the last element for which sufficient evidence of fair value does not exist has been delivered, either the seller's performance under the arrangement will be complete or all of the remaining items will be those for which sufficient evidence of fair value exists, in which case the residual method may be applied.

For example, if an arrangement consists of only a product and related post-delivery maintenance services (where the services are

not treated as inconsequential or perfunctory remaining performance obligations for accounting purposes) and there is insufficient
evidence of fair value to allocate arrangement consideration
between the two elements, the revenue from the entire arrangement
should be recognized as the maintenance is delivered. In most cases,
revenue would be recognized ratably over the maintenance period
using the Proportional Performance Model (see Chapter 6, "Service
Deliverables"). If the final element to be delivered in a similar situation is a product for which evidence of fair value does not exist, all
revenue from the arrangement would often be deferred until the
revenue recognition criteria for product sales (see Chapter 5, "Product Deliverables") have been satisfied for that final element.

General Refund Right Exists and Performance of Undelivered Item(s) Not Probable or Substantially within Vendor's Control

When a general refund right exists and the delivery or performance
of the undelivered items is not considered probable or substantially
within the control of the vendor, arrangement consideration
otherwise allocable to the delivered item should not be recognized.
That arrangement consideration should be recognized, assuming all
other revenue recognition criteria have been met, at the earlier of (a)
the expiration of the general refund right (i.e., the general refund
right is no longer a factor in determining whether the delivered item
should be treated separately for accounting purposes) or (b) the
performance of the undelivered items becoming probable *and* substantially within the control of the vendor (i.e., the company will
have satisfied the separation condition). At this point, the timing or
pattern of recognition will depend on the nature of the items
involved.

This approach is consistent with the conclusion that would be
reached in applying FAS-48 (ASC 605-15-25-1 through 25-4). As discussed in Chapter 5, "Product Deliverables," the criterion that must
be met to recognize revenue when a right of return exists, is the
ability to reasonably estimate the amount of future returns. If performance of an undelivered item is not probable or substantially in
the vendor's control, making reasonable estimates of the amount of
future returns would not be possible. Failure to meet this criterion
(or any of the other necessary criteria under FAS-48 (ASC 605-15-25-
1 through 25-4)) results in the deferral of revenue until the earlier of
(a) expiration of the return right or (b) subsequently concluding that
the criterion is met. Although not explicitly noted, it is this guidance
that resulted in the inclusion of the general refund right condition in
EITF 00-21 (ASC 605-25).

OBSERVATION: In the situation where a multiple-element arrangement is not separated because a general refund right exists and performance of the undelivered item(s) is not probable or substantially in the vendor's control, it is highly unlikely that the undelivered item(s) could be considered inconsequential or perfunctory, because evaluation of many of the "inconsequential or perfunctory" indicators described earlier in this section would not be possible. As a result, the inability to evaluate these indicators would suggest that the undelivered item(s) is more than inconsequential or perfunctory.

RECOGNITION WHEN SPECIFIC REFUND RIGHT EXISTS

When a specific refund right results in some or all of the amount otherwise allocable to a delivered element (the at-risk amount) not being allocated to that element, the at-risk amount should only be recognized, provided the other criteria for recognition have been met, upon the earlier of (a) the expiration of the specific refund right (i.e., the specific refund right is no longer a factor in determining the amount of revenue that should be allocated to the delivered element) or (b) delivery of the undelivered element on which the specific refund right is based (i.e., the basis for the specific refund right no longer exists). The timing or pattern of recognition at this point will depend on the nature of the items involved.

Given the cost deferral issues that may arise when a specific refund right exists, a question may arise regarding recognition of the amount allocated to a delivered element that is not at-risk (i.e., there is not a specific refund right that could result in the refund of the amount ultimately allocated to the delivered element). For example, assume the following: (1) there are two elements in the arrangement—Element 1 and Element 2, (2) total arrangement consideration is $100, (3) the amounts otherwise allocable to Element 1 and Element 2 based on their relative fair values are $70 and $30, respectively, (4) Element 1 is delivered before Element 2, (5) $100 is due upon receipt of Element 1, (6) if Element 2 is not delivered, the vendor must refund $60, and (7) Element 1 and Element 2 otherwise meet the separation criteria in EITF 00-21 (ASC 605-25). In this situation, the amount ultimately allocated to Element 1 is $40. The $70 that would otherwise have been allocable to Element 1 is reduced to $40 (a reduction of $30) because the amount otherwise allocated to the undelivered element ($30) is less than the amount that would be refunded if the undelivered element is not delivered ($60, for a difference of $30). Depending on the cost of Element 1 and how that cost is recognized, the recognition of $40 of revenue related to Element 1 could result in a negative profit margin. As a result, a question has arisen regarding whether the $40 of revenue ultimately allocated to Element 1 (and the related cost) could be deferred until the revenue ultimately allocated to Element 2 (and the related cost) is recognized. In this situation, it would be inappropriate to defer the $40 of revenue ultimately allocated to Element 1 if it otherwise meets the applicable revenue recognition criteria. To allow deferral of the revenue in this situation would effectively make the conclusion reached based on applying the guidance in EITF 00-21 (ASC 605-25) (i.e., that elements should be treated separately) optional, which was specifically rejected in the deliberations that led to this guidance. Whether some or all of the cost of Element 1 can be deferred in this situation is discussed in Chapter 8, "Miscellaneous Issues."

> **OBSERVATION:** The existence of a specific refund right related to an as-yet-undelivered element precludes treatment of that element as inconsequential or perfunctory since the vendor's failure to fulfill the remaining performance obligation would result in the customer receiving a full or partial refund or rejecting (or a right to a refund or to reject) delivered items.

CHAPTER 5
PRODUCT DELIVERABLES

CONTENTS

BACKGROUND

The most basic (and probably the most common) sales transaction is the sale of a product for cash. Although the transaction may be simple, the accounting for it is not necessarily straightforward. For example, a retail sale in which the customer pays cash for a product at the checkout counter would seem to require clear-cut accounting. When the customer leaves the store, the goods have been delivered and paid for, so it would appear that the revenue has been both earned and realized, thereby allowing recognition at that time. However, even this simple transaction typically includes terms that can present revenue recognition issues. For example, most retailers grant customers a right of return for a limited period of time. In addition, there may be both explicit and implicit warranties on the products purchased. These and other common sales terms raise questions about the amount and timing of revenue recognition. More complicated product sale arrangements, such as those between a manufacturer and a reseller or between a parts supplier and its major customers, can introduce a myriad of other obligations and terms that further complicate the amount and timing of revenue recognition.

> **PRACTICE ALERT:** Situations may arise where arrangements that purport to cover only the sale of products actually contain a lease. EITF 01-8 (ASC 840, *Leases*; 840-10-15), discussed in Chapter 3, "General Principles," provides guidance to help determine whether an arrangement contains a lease. Regardless of the formal characterization of an arrangement, the portion of the arrangement that represents a lease must be accounted for using lease accounting principles. Separation of the lease element from the other elements in the arrangement is discussed in Chapter 4, "Multiple-Element Arrangements."

This chapter explores significant accounting issues that are common in but unique to product transactions. Where a product transaction includes multiple deliverables, these accounting issues must be evaluated separately for each deliverable in the arrangement. As discussed in Chapter 4, "Multiple-Element Arrangements," the interrelationship between deliverables in a multiple-element arrangement may give rise to issues beyond those that exist in a single-element transaction.

SURVEY OF ACCOUNTING LITERATURE

U.S. generally accepted accounting principles (GAAP) does not comprehensively address general product sale issues. General guidance is found in the FASB Concepts Statements and SAB Topic 13, *Revenue Recognition* (ASC 605-10-S99). Despite the lack of general guidance, many pronouncements address specific product transaction issues. For example, FAS-48 (ASC 605-15-25) addresses sales with a right of return and EITF 95-4 (ASC 605-15-25-5) addresses equipment sold and subsequently repurchased subject to an operating lease. Other guidance on product sale transactions has been developed based on industry practice. In addition, international standards, most notably IAS 18, provide guidance on certain issues not covered in U.S. GAAP. Although companies reporting under U.S. GAAP are not required to follow international standards, they are good sources for policies that may be acceptable within the U.S. GAAP framework.

REVENUE RECOGNITION LITERATURE

Publication	ASC	ASC Topic	Subject
SAB Topic 13	605-10-S-99	Revenue Recognition	Revenue Recognition
FAS-48	605-15-25	Revenue Recognition	Revenue Recognition When Right of Return Exists
FAS-49	470-40	Debt	Product Financing Arrangements
FTB 90-1	605-20-25	Revenue Recognition	Separately Priced Extended Warranty and Product Maintenance Contracts
EITF 95-1	815-10-55-12	Derivatives and Hedging	Revenue Recognition on Sales with a Guaranteed Minimum Resale Value
EITF 95-4	605-15-25	Revenue Recognition	Revenue Recognition on Equipment Sold and Subsequently Repurchased Subject to an Operating Lease

SUPPORTING LITERATURE

Publication	ASC	ASC Topic	Subject
APB-21	835-30	Interest	Interest on Receivables and Payables
FAS-5	460	Guarantees	Product Warranties
FIN-45	460	Guarantees	Guarantees
EITF 01-8	840-10-15	Leases	Determining Whether an Arrangement Contains a Lease

GENERAL CONDITIONS FOR RECOGNITION

As with all revenues, product sales revenue should be recognized when it has been earned and is realized or realizable. Revenue from product sales is generally earned when the products are delivered to the customer. Such revenue is usually considered realizable once the customer has committed to pay for the products and the customer's ability to pay is not in doubt. However, various types of uncertainties may exist that affect *when* (timing) and *how much* (amount) revenue is recognized (CON-5, pars. 83–84).

As discussed in Chapter 3, "General Principles," revenue is considered earned and realizable when all of the following conditions are met:

1. Persuasive evidence of an arrangement exists.
2. The arrangement fee is fixed or determinable.
3. Delivery or performance has occurred.
4. Collectibility is reasonably assured.

In addition, the delivery condition in a product sale should generally be evaluated under the Completed Performance model. This means that delivery occurs at a single point in time, rather than over an extended period. Although this point in time usually is when physical delivery of the product occurs, there are many arrangements where this is not the case.

The guidance in this chapter addresses most product deliverables. However, certain contracts to deliver products should be accounted for using contract accounting principles. These contracts are typically for building a customized product that will take an extended period of time to complete. Contract accounting is discussed in Chapter 9, "Contract Accounting."

Risks and Rewards of Ownership

In a product sale, all of the general conditions for revenue recognition are usually present at the time the product is delivered (i.e., when the buyer takes physical possession of the product from the seller). In general, the delivery requirement for purposes of recognizing revenue is satisfied when substantial risks and rewards of ownership of the goods have passed from the seller to the buyer.

The term "risks and rewards of ownership" refers to all of the things that would normally accrue to an owner of products. For example, risks of ownership include a loss of market value, obsolescence, theft, physical damage, and excess inventory. Rewards of ownership include gains due to increases in value, the right to use and restrict the use of the product, the right to sell or otherwise determine the disposition of the product, the right to enhance the existing product, and the ability to grant security interests in the product.

The physical transfer of a product does not always indicate that revenue has been earned. For example, in some transactions, the seller may retain specified risks or benefits after the product has been transferred to the customer; in other transactions, all risks and benefits may be transferred to the buyer before the product is delivered to the buyer. The issues discussed in this chapter generally relate to whether the retention by the seller of a specific risk or reward precludes revenue recognition.

EXHIBIT 5-1
OVERVIEW OF PRODUCT REVENUE RECOGNITION

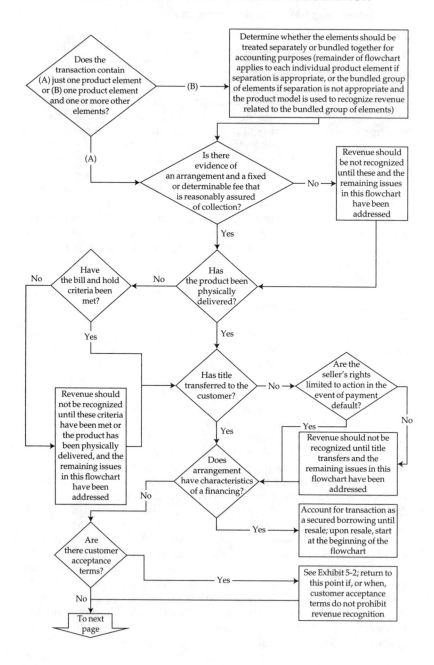

EXHIBIT 5-1 continued

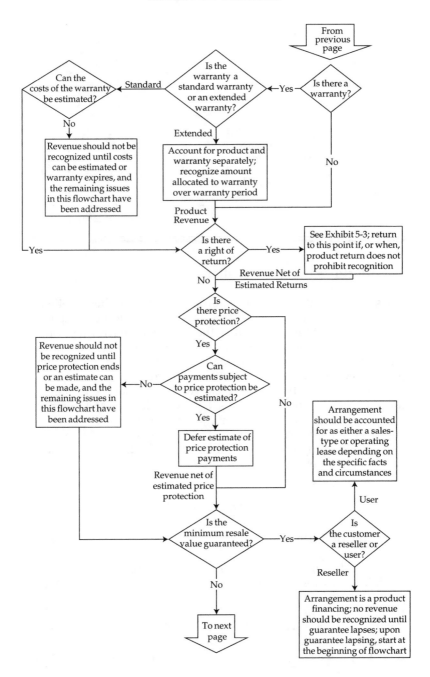

EXHIBIT 5-1 continued

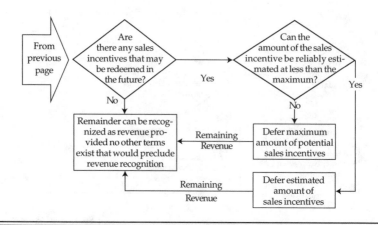

Manufacturers versus Resellers

The same general revenue recognition guidance applies whether the products being sold have been manufactured by the company or were purchased for resale. Thus, the act of manufacturing or building a product is not an earnings event, except in the case of long-term contracts accounted for under the Percentage-of-Completion model (see Chapter 9, "Contract Accounting").

The identity of the customer, however, may have some effect on the revenue recognition analysis. For example, although the principles of revenue recognition are the same whether the customer is an end-user or a reseller, the results of applying those principles (e.g., to rights of return) can vary significantly depending on whether the customer is an end-user or a reseller.

DELIVERY

Transfer of Title

As noted above, physical delivery is often the time when revenue is considered earned, because the risks and rewards of ownership generally rest with the holder of the products and, therefore, pass to the buyer at delivery. However, with rare exceptions (see "Title Retained after Delivery," below), physical delivery must be accompanied by the passage of "title" from the seller to the buyer before revenue can be recognized. "Title" is a term that generally pertains to the ownership of goods in a legal sense. The party that has title to goods is assumed to control their use and be at risk of loss, absent contractual arrangements stating otherwise. Therefore, for accounting purposes, products generally are considered delivered when title passes from the seller to the buyer. In many transactions, such as retail purchases, passage of title is not documented in any formal manner, but the timing of title transfer is clear from the transaction (e.g., title passes at the register when the customer pays for the merchandise).

However, the timing of title transfer is not as clear in many other transactions. For example, without analyzing the specific contract, it is not clear when title transfers for goods delivered by mail; in some cases, title transfers when the goods are put in the mail and in others, title transfers only upon receipt by the buyer. A similar situation exists for manufacturers who ship to their customers by modes of transportation such as truck or train using a third-party shipping agent. Because the transfer of title is basically a legal concept, it may be necessary to consult with legal experts to determine when title transfers. In most situations, however, a basic understanding of local laws and the terms agreed upon by the buyer and seller are enough to determine when title has transferred.

> **OBSERVATION:** Transfer of title is important in revenue recognition for product sales, because it generally determines when the risk of loss and control of the products passes from the seller to the buyer. However, contractual arrangements can separate the transfer of certain risks or rights from the transfer of title. As discussed above, when risks and rewards of ownership remain with the seller, revenue recognition often is not appropriate. This is true even if title has been transferred. For further discussion, see "Consignment Sales" below.

Free-on-Board Terms

Free-on-Board (FOB) terms generally designate which party pays for shipping the products. "FOB shipping point" means that the shipping is paid for by the buyer. "FOB destination" means that the shipping is paid for by the seller. In most cases, the party that pays for shipping owns (i.e., has title to) the products during shipment. Therefore, FOB destination indicates that title to the product passes upon delivery to the customer. FOB shipping point signifies that title passes when the products leave the seller's premises. The FOB terms are usually specified in a contract between the parties, the purchase order, the bill of lading, or some other documentation of the sales transaction.

> **OBSERVATION:**   Although rare, some contracts specify that title transfers at a different point during transit—for example, when a particular border is crossed. Other contracts may specify that title transfers either before the goods leave the seller's premises or some time after they are received by the buyer.

If the risks and rewards of ownership transfer at the same time that the title transfers, FOB terms specify the point at which revenue can be considered earned. For accounting purposes, products shipped FOB shipping point can generally be considered delivered when the goods leave the seller's premises. Products shipped FOB destination are considered delivered when the goods reach the customer. As such, FOB terms indicate whether outbound shipments in transit should be recognized as a sale at period-end. FOB shipping point terms result in recognition of revenue and cost of sales at the end of a reporting period for shipments in transit at that date (provided the other criteria for recognition have been met); FOB destination terms result in shipments in transit not being recorded until the subsequent reporting period (SAB Topic 13A3a) (ASC 605-10-S99, A3a).

> **OBSERVATION:**   Even when FOB destination terms are used such that title does not transfer until the buyer receives the products, the risk of physical loss on the products may be held by a third-party shipping agent and not the seller. However, this does not allow the seller to recognize revenue before the shipping agent completes delivery to the buyer because the shipper is the seller's agent and the seller will not have fulfilled its obligations to the buyer until the products are delivered.

> ☛ **PRACTICE POINTER:**   A majority of companies routinely record all sales transactions when they leave the company's premises. This is done even if the goods are shipped FOB destination, because it is far easier to determine the point at which goods are shipped than it is to determine when the customer receives them. When this procedure is used on FOB destination shipments, the company should evaluate the amount of outbound shipments in transit at a period-end and reverse the recognition of sales and cost of sales for those transactions if the effects are material.

Local Laws

Because title is essentially a legal concept, laws sometimes specify the point at which title transfers. In certain jurisdictions, these laws can be overridden by contractual language; in others, the laws override any documentation of title transfer. As a result, local laws must be taken into account to determine when title has transferred. This is especially important in transactions where the seller and buyer are in different jurisdictions.

EXAMPLES: DELIVERY

Apple, Inc. Form 10-K—Fiscal Year Ended September 27, 2008

Product is considered delivered to the customer once it has been shipped and title and risk of loss have been transferred. For most of the Company's product sales, these criteria are met at the time the product is shipped. For online sales to individuals, for some sales to education customers in the U.S., and for certain other sales, the Company defers revenue until the customer receives the product because the Company retains a portion of the risk of loss on these sales during transit.

Electronics for Imaging, Inc. Form 10-K—Fiscal Year Ended December 31, 2005

Delivery for hardware generally occurs when product is delivered to the customer's common carrier. In some instances, products are also sold under terms included in sales arrangements that result in different timing for revenue recognition, assuming all other recognition criteria are met: a) if title and risk of loss is transferred at the customer's destination (CIP Destination), revenue is recognized when the product(s) arrives at the customer site; and b) if title is retained after product delivery until payment is received, revenue is recognized at the time when passage of title occurs upon payment receipt.

Subscriptions

When products are sold under a subscription arrangement, the delivery condition should be evaluated under the Proportional Performance model and revenue should be allocated to each product in proportion to its value. In many cases, each item is allocated the same amount of revenue because their individual values do not vary significantly (e.g., a magazine or newspaper subscription). As each item is delivered, revenue allocated to that item should be recognized, unless other terms of the transaction prohibit recognition. Subscription revenue may not be recognized when the subscription is received or billed with an accrual of the estimated costs to fulfill the subscription, even when the subscription price is completely nonrefundable. In this case, revenue is realized at the inception of the subscription, but only earned as the products are delivered.

Delivery to an Alternate Site or Third Party

A seller's performance may generally be considered complete upon delivery to a third party designated by the buyer, unless the seller retains an explicit or implicit obligation to deliver the product to the customer. For example, a company that purchases inventory in excess of its currently available storage space may direct the seller to deliver the products to a third-party warehouse for storage. As long as full payment is due on normal terms upon delivery to the third party, and the customer is responsible for storage costs and transporting the product to its own facilities when needed, the delivery criterion would be met.

However, if a significant portion of the purchase price is not payable until the product reaches the customer, delivery to the third party should not result in revenue recognition, even when the buyer has chosen the third party. The delay in payment until final delivery indicates that the seller retains risk until the customer receives the product at the final delivery point. If this is the case, a partial payment received upon delivery to the third party should be reflected as a liability, rather than as revenue (SAB Topic 13A3a) (ASC 605-10-S99, A3a).

When a product is delivered to a third party selected by the seller, revenue recognition must usually be delayed until the product is delivered to the customer. For example, a mail order catalog company may deliver goods to an outside fulfillment house, which will then package and ship the goods to the customer. In this type of arrangement, revenue should only be recognized upon final delivery to the customer, because the fulfillment house is merely an agent of the seller. However, if the buyer specifically acknowledges that, upon delivery to the third party, the seller has no further obligation with respect to the transaction and that the buyer must look solely to the third party to obtain final delivery of the products, the delivery criterion will generally be satisfied.

Title Retained after Delivery

In some situations, sellers retain title after goods are delivered. The most common example is in consignment arrangements. Generally, delivery does not occur on a consignment until title passes to the buyer. However, there are instances where the delivery condition is met even though title is retained. In these limited circumstances, all significant risks and rewards of ownership must still transfer to the buyer, even though title does not pass.

One example is when the seller retains title to provide security for the collection of the purchase price and the seller's rights are limited to taking action only in the event of nonpayment. This may occur in countries where local laws and customs do not provide the seller with a security interest in products that have been sold but not yet paid for. If the seller retains title, but its rights are limited to recovering the goods only in the event of nonpayment—that is, the seller cannot, for example, rescind the transaction or prohibit the customer from doing what it wishes with the goods, despite holding title—revenue can be recognized upon delivery provided that the other conditions for revenue recognition have also been met. In the U.S., however, the Uniform Commercial Code provides the seller with a security interest in goods that have not yet been paid for even after passage of title, so title generally need not be retained for this purpose (SAB Topic 13A2, ques. 3) (ASC 605-10-S99, A2, ques. 3).

Other transactions in which the seller retains title after delivery should be analyzed as leasing transactions. If the transaction can be classified as a sales-type lease under the leasing literature, revenue recognition upon delivery may be appropriate.

> ☞ **PRACTICE POINTER:** Some companies sell their products pursuant to standard contracts with clauses that enhance the seller's rights to payment for the products sold. Although the clause is included for a sound business purpose, the retention of title generally exposes the seller to certain risks and entitles it to certain rights (in addition to a security interest in the event of nonpayment) that could affect the timing of revenue recognition. Therefore, companies that retain title to products after shipment but before payment should determine the legal effect of such an arrangement. If title retention is solely meant to ensure timely payment by the customer, revenue recognition may still be appropriate. However, if title retention exposes the seller to any additional risks or rights, regardless of whether the seller intends to exercise its rights, the product should not be considered delivered until payment is received and title passes.

EXAMPLE: TITLE RETENTION TO RECOVER PRODUCTS IN EVENT OF CUSTOMER DEFAULT

Unisys Corporation Form 10-K—Fiscal Year Ended December 31, 2007

Revenue from hardware sales with standard payment terms is recognized upon shipment and the passage of title. Outside the United States, the company recognizes revenue even if it retains a form of title to products delivered to customers, provided the sole purpose is to enable the company to recover the products in the event of customer payment default and the arrangement does not prohibit the customer's use of the product in the ordinary course of business.

DELIVERY WITHOUT A TRANSFER OF RISK

Consignment Sales

A consignment "sale" is not a sale at all. A shipment of goods "on consignment" generally means that payment (and title passage) is expected only when the purchaser resells the inventory to a customer or uses it in production. As a result, the seller retains ownership of the inventory and unsold items may be returned by the purchaser. Because the seller retains title and all risks and rewards of ownership, except perhaps custodial risks (e.g., the risk of physical loss), the shipment of goods on consignment does not constitute delivery for accounting purposes and does not trigger the recognition of revenue (SAB Topic 13A2, ques. 2) (ASC 605-10-S99, A2, ques. 2).

Consignment sales usually are specified in a contract. However, a contract need not be labeled as a consignment to be treated as one for accounting purposes. For example, with rare exception (see "Title Retained After Delivery" above), a purported sale in which title remains with the seller until the buyer resells, pays for, or uses the goods should be treated as a consignment, because the lack of title transfer will usually mean that significant risks and rewards remain with the seller.

Even when title transfers to the buyer upon delivery, the arrangement terms may nonetheless indicate that the transaction is a consignment and should be treated as one. This frequently occurs in the sale of high-priced items, which often involves the buyer acting as an agent for the seller. For example, an arrangement in which title passes to the customer upon shipment and the customer has unlimited rights of return and need not pay for the goods until resale occurs is, in substance, a consignment. In these cases, revenue should not be recognized until the goods are resold. However, determining when a transaction is substantively similar to a consignment is a matter of significant judgment. Some factors that may be indicative of an in-substance consignment are as follows:

> **OBSERVATION:** Although these factors may be explicitly detailed in the sales agreement, they can also exist by custom or historical practice between the parties. For example, a small manufacturer whose product is mainly distributed by a large retailer may have little or no leverage to enforce specific terms in the sales agreement and, therefore, agree to accept returns or give sales discounts that are not explicitly documented. In this situation, an evaluation of whether these implicit rights create an in-substance consignment should be conducted.

1. *Payment is not due until the goods have been resold.* The buyer has no risk of loss.

2. *The buyer lacks substance, or uses financing or guarantees from the seller to purchase the products.* In this situation, the seller retains the risk of loss through its financing-related commitments.

> **OBSERVATION:** If the seller guarantees debt incurred by the buyer to purchase the seller's products and the arrangement is not a product financing, the seller has entered into a multiple-element arrangement with the buyer. The elements in this arrangement consist of the product and the guarantee. The application of FIN-45 (ASC 460) to this situation is discussed in Chapter 4, "Multiple-Element Arrangements."

3. *The buyer has, in substance, an unlimited right of return.* This removes the buyer's risk of loss because the product can be returned if the item is not resold.

4. *The buyer pays more than other customers or makes purchases above and beyond its normal needs.* This indicates that some type of side arrangement may exist between the seller and buyer.

5. *The seller imposes constraints on the buyer's sales, pricing, credit, and advertising policies.* This indicates that the seller has retained some control over the use and disposition of the product and, therefore, not enough risks and rewards of ownership have passed to the buyer to permit revenue recognition.

6. *The seller agrees to take returns from the buyer if the buyer gets returns from its customers.* This removes some of the buyer's risk for the product and may indicate that the buyer is essentially acting as the seller's agent.

7. *The seller agrees to assume the credit risk that exists in the buyer/ reseller's sales to end customers.* The reseller may, in substance, be acting as the seller's agent.

8. *The payment due the seller varies based on its customer's success in reselling the product.* The reseller may, in substance, be acting as the seller's agent.

> **OBSERVATION:** None of the factors discussed above definitively indicate that an arrangement should be accounted for as a consignment sale. However, all transactions with any of the above characteristics should be carefully evaluated to determine their substance. It is also important to analyze a company's history of ultimately resolving these transactions. For example, if the buyer/reseller has a long right of return but payment for the products is made promptly and returns are small and predictable, this right of return may not be indicative of an arrangement that is, in substance, a consignment. Conversely, if payment is not due until the end of a long return period or if significant returns frequently occur just before the

return period lapses, the arrangement would appear to be an in-substance consignment.

> **SEC REGISTRANT ALERT:**   In early 2003, the SEC staff issued the Report Pursuant to Section 704 of the Sarbanes-Oxley Act of 2002 (the Section 704 Report). In compiling the information in this Report, the SEC staff studied enforcement actions filed during the period July 31, 1997, through July 30, 2002. The greatest number of enforcement actions related to improper revenue recognition, and one of the issues highlighted in the Report was the accounting for consignment sales. The SEC staff noted that the accounting for consignment sales (and other contingency sales) "generally failed to meet the criteria under U.S. GAAP for recognizing revenue because the seller had not actually assumed the risks and rewards of ownership, the terms of the sale were modified, or the revenue was otherwise not realized (or realizable) and earned." This finding is a strong indication that more attention should be given to the identification of and accounting for consignment sales.

EXAMPLES: IN-SUBSTANCE CONSIGNMENTS

Advanced Micro Devices, Inc. Form 10-K—Fiscal Year Ended December 29, 2007

The Company sells to distributors under terms allowing the distributors certain rights of return and price protection on unsold merchandise held by them. The distributor agreements, which may be cancelled by either party upon specified notice, generally contain a provision for the return of those of the Company's products that the Company has removed from its price book or that are not more than twelve months older than the manufacturing code date. In addition, some agreements with distributors may contain standard stock rotation provisions permitting limited levels of product returns. Accordingly, the Company defers the gross margin resulting from the deferral of both revenue and related product costs from sales to distributors with agreements that have the aforementioned terms until the merchandise is resold by the distributors.

The Company also sells its products to distributors with substantial independent operations under sales arrangements whose terms do not allow for rights of return or price protection on unsold products held by them. In these instances, the Company recognizes revenue when it ships the product directly to the distributors.

Stryker Corporation Form 10-K—Fiscal Year Ended December 31, 2007

Revenue Recognition

A significant portion of the Company's Orthopaedic Implants revenue is generated from consigned inventory maintained at hospitals or with field representatives. For these products, revenue is recognized at the time the Company receives appropriate notification that the product has been used or implanted. The Company records revenue from MedSurg Equipment product sales when title and risk of ownership have been transferred to the customer, which is typically upon shipment to the customer.

Silicon Image, Inc. Form 10-K—Fiscal Year Ended December 31, 2007

Revenue from products sold directly to end-users, or to distributors that do not receive price concessions and rights of return, is generally recognized when title and risk of loss has passed to the buyer which typically occurs upon shipment. Reserves for sales returns are estimated based primarily on historical experience and are provided at the time of shipment.

For products sold to distributors with agreements allowing for price concessions and product returns, we recognize revenue based on our best estimate of when the distributor sold the product to its end customer. Our estimate of such distributor sell-through is based on point of sales reports received from our distributors. Revenue is not recognized upon shipment since, due to various forms of price concessions, the sales price is not substantially fixed or determinable at that time. Price concessions are recorded when incurred, which is generally at the time the distributor sells the product to an end-user. Additionally, these distributors have contractual rights to return products, up to a specified amount for a given period of time. Revenue is earned when the distributor sells the product to an end-user, at which time our sales price to the distributor becomes fixed. Pursuant to our distributor agreements, older or end-of-life products are sold with no right of return and are not eligible for price concessions. For these products, revenue is recognized upon shipment and title transfer assuming all other revenue recognition criteria are met.

At the time of shipment to distributors, we record a trade receivable for the selling price since there is a legally enforceable right to payment, relieve inventory for the carrying value of goods shipped since legal title has passed to the distributor and record the gross margin in "deferred margin on sale to distributors", a component of current liabilities in our consolidated balance sheet. Deferred margin on the sale to distributor effectively represents the gross margin on the sale to the distributor. However, the amount of gross margin we recognize in future periods will be less than the originally recorded deferred margin on sale to distributor as a result of negotiated price concessions. We sell each item in our product price book to all of our distributors worldwide at a relatively uniform list price. However, distributors resell our products to end customers at a very broad range of individually negotiated price points based on customer, product, quantity, geography, competitive pricing and other factors. The majority of our distributors' resale are priced at a discount from list price. Often, under these circumstances, we remit back to the distributor a portion of their original purchase price after the resale transaction is completed. Thus, a portion of the "deferred margin on the sale to distributor" balance represents a portion of distributors' original purchase price that will be remitted back to the distributor in the future. The wide range and variability of negotiated price concessions granted to distributors does not allow us to accurately estimate the portion of the balance in the

Deferred margin on the sale to distributor that will be remitted back to the distributors. We reduce deferred margin by anticipated or determinable future price concessions.

Product Financing Arrangements

In the consignment arrangements discussed above, payment to the vendor is delayed until the products are used or resold. When payment is due upon delivery or shortly thereafter, a transaction would generally not be considered a consignment. However, certain terms included in the sales agreement may indicate that, substantively, the sale is actually a financing arrangement—that is, a secured borrowing with the inventory serving as collateral. Sales of inventory should be analyzed as financing arrangements when payment is due under normal terms but the risks and rewards of ownership have not been transferred to the purchaser.

FAS-49 (ASC 470-40) addresses product financing arrangements and specifies that a financing, rather than a sale, exists if the following two conditions are met (FAS-49, par. 5) (ASC 470-40-15-2):

1. *The arrangement requires the seller to repurchase the product (or a substantially identical product), or processed goods that the product is a component of, at specified prices, and the prices are not subject to change except for fluctuations due to financing and holding costs.* This condition indicates that the seller has retained risks related to the market value of the product, because it will be forced to repurchase the product, regardless of market demand.

2. *The amount the seller will pay to repurchase the products covers (or will be adjusted to cover) the buyer's purchasing and holding costs (including interest).* This indicates that the buyer's return from the transaction is essentially a financing return, rather than one a company would expect from purchasing and reselling inventory.

The above terms need not be explicitly stated for the arrangement to be treated as a product financing. FAS-49 (ASC 470-40-15-2) notes that a repurchase obligation substantively exists in any of the following situations:

- The seller agrees to make up any difference between certain specified resale prices and the actual resale price for products when they are sold by the buyer.

- The seller has an option, but not an obligation, to repurchase the product, but there is a significant incentive for the seller to exercise the repurchase option. An example is an arrangement that provides for a significant penalty if the seller does not exercise its option.

- The buyer has a put option whereby it can require the seller to repurchase the product.

> **OBSERVATION:** Many product financing arrangements can be difficult to identify. However, these transactions all share a common characteristic—they are largely motivated by the seller's immediate need for cash, even when responsibility for the products being sold is retained by the seller. As a result, product financing arrangements can often be identified by determining whether the seller retains the responsibility (either in real or financial terms) for the products, even after they are paid for by the buyer. Similarly, a buyer's motivation in a product financing arrangement is to earn a return from the seller (that is similar to what a lender would receive) on the money it spends to purchase and hold the product. For example, a sales transaction in which the buyer has a right of return that enables it to recover more than the purchase price (plus any processing costs) of the inventory items may be indicative of a financing arrangement

When an arrangement is accounted for as a product financing, payments received from the customer should be recorded as a liability and generally classified as debt (see Chapter 11, "Presentation") and the inventory delivered to the buyer should remain on the seller's books. As the buyer incurs holding costs (such as insurance) and processing costs, the seller should record a payable to the buyer as if the buyer had incurred the costs on the seller's behalf. The seller should then account for the costs consistent with their nature and the seller's normal policies. Repurchase payments in excess of the original debt recorded and the accrued holding and processing costs should be treated as interest expense.

ILLUSTRATION: PRODUCT FINANCING ARRANGEMENT

Facts: The Grenache Co. sells 100 cases of its 2005 vintage Grenache to AMS Cellars for $500 per case, receiving $50,000 cash upon delivery. The Grenache Co. agrees to repurchase any unsold cases of the 2005 Grenache from AMS in six months at $525 per unit. The Grenache Co. estimates, based on its history of selling Grenache to AMS, that AMS will resell 94 of the 100 cases within six months and, therefore, The Grenache Co. believes it will repurchase six cases in six months at $525 per case. Market interest rates are approximately 10% for secured borrowings. AMS sells 50 of the 100 cases of the 2005 Grenache to a third party three months later and sells another 44 cases just before the six months are up. The remaining six units are sold back to The Grenache Co. at the stipulated $525 per case price. Holding costs for the 2005 Grenache are negligible.

Accounting: Because The Grenache Co. has granted AMS the right to put unsold inventory back to it at a price that equals the original sales price increased by an amount that represents a financing rate of return, the transaction should be treated as a product financing arrangement. Therefore, no revenue can be recognized upon delivery, despite The Grenache Co.'s ability to estimate its ultimate obligation under the arrangement. Because no revenue is recognized, the inventory remains on The Grenache Co.'s books. The accounting is as follows:

- At the inception of the arrangement, The Grenache Co. records the cash received:

Cash	$50,000	
Debt		$50,000

- For three months, The Grenache Co. records interest on the entire debt ($50,000 × 10% effective rate × ¼ of a year = $1,250)

Interest Expense	$1,250	
Interest Payable		$1,250

- When AMS sells the first 50 units, The Grenache Co. recognizes revenue and eliminates that portion of the debt:

Debt	$25,000	
Interest Payable	$625	
Revenue		$25,625

- For the remaining three months, The Grenache Co. records interest on the remaining debt ($25,000 × 10% effective rate × ¼ of a year = $625):

Interest Expense	$625	
Interest Payable		$625

- When AMS sells the next 44 units, The Grenache Co. recognizes revenue and eliminates that portion of the debt:

Debt	$22,000	
Interest Payable	$1,100	
Revenue		$23,100

- The Grenache Co. records the repurchase of the remaining six units:

Debt	$3,000	
Interest Payable	$150	
Cash		$3,150

The accounting is the same as if The Grenache Co. borrowed $50,000 for three months and another $50,000 for six months at a 10% interest rate, and then sold 50 cases of the 2005 Grenache at $512.50 per unit in three months and another 44 cases of the 2005 Grenache at $525 per cases in the next three months. This is consistent with the conclusion that the original transaction is essentially a financing transaction, rather than a true product sale.

REVENUE RECOGNITION BEFORE DELIVERY

"Bill and Hold" Sales

In certain situations, revenue may be recognized before shipment if delivery is delayed at the buyer's request and the buyer takes title and agrees to pay for the goods in advance. This type of transaction is called a "bill and hold" sale. Both the SEC and the IASB have addressed these sales transactions; they have not been addressed by a U.S. accounting standard-setter. As a result, private companies preparing financial statements under U.S. GAAP are not subject to any specific requirements. Nonetheless, private companies should adopt a consistent accounting policy and the SEC and IFRS models provide the best policy frameworks available. The IFRS model is found in IAS 1, par. 14 and appendix par. 1, while the SEC model is found in SAB Topic 13A3a (ASC 605-10-S99, A3a).

Both models attempt to ensure that revenue is only recognized if the substance of the transaction (apart from the physical location of the goods) is exactly the same as if the products had been shipped to the buyer. The criteria are, therefore, restrictive and generally result in recognition only upon delivery to the buyer. This is particularly the case with the SEC model. Public companies in the U.S., however, must use the SEC's model when preparing financial statements for SEC filings. Details of both models are as follows:

1. *(IFRS and SEC) Risks of ownership must have passed to the buyer.* This is a standard criterion that must be met before recognizing revenue in any product sale transaction.

2. *(IFRS) The amount of revenue can be measured reliably.* This is a standard criterion that must be met before recognizing revenue in any transaction.

   (SEC) Although the SEC's position on bill and hold sales does not specifically include a similar requirement, the requirement that the fee be fixed or determinable (see Chapter 3, "General Principles") covers this point.

3. *(IFRS) The seller does not continue to exercise managerial responsibility or control over the products.* If the seller retains control or

involvement, this indicates that the risks and rewards did not transfer as they would if the products had been delivered.

(SEC) The seller cannot retain any specific performance obligations such that the earnings process is not complete. Although the SEC focuses on the risks of continuing involvement rather than the control that such involvement provides, the intent is similar. If the seller has any performance obligations remaining, the revenue has not been earned.

4. *(IFRS) It is probable that the seller will realize revenue on the sale.* This is a standard criterion that must be met before recognizing revenue in any sale.

   (SEC) The customer must have made a fixed commitment to purchase the goods, preferably in writing. The SEC states the same provision more definitively because the staff is concerned that any conditions or contingencies may indicate that the transaction has not yet been consummated. Thus, revenue recognition on a bill and hold transaction would be precluded if, for example, the customer has a right of return.

5. *(IFRS) Any costs to be incurred related to the sale can be measured reliably.* If the seller expects to incur costs of an uncertain amount, it is difficult to conclude that all of the seller's significant obligations have been fulfilled.

   (SEC) The goods must be complete and ready for shipment. This effectively prohibits the incurrence of any future costs, other than those related to delivery.

6. *(IFRS) It is probable that delivery will be made.* If delivery is not probable, the existence of the transaction is called into question, especially if payment has not yet been received.

   (SEC) There must be a fixed delivery schedule that is consistent with the buyer's business purpose. The SEC believes that the delivery date (s) must be set before revenue can be recognized, a more restrictive requirement than the comparable IFRS requirement.

7. *(IFRS) The goods are on hand, identified, and ready for delivery.* If the goods are not currently available for delivery, revenue recognition is not appropriate because delivery cannot yet be fulfilled.

   (SEC) The goods must be segregated from remaining inventory so that they cannot be used to fill orders for others. This criterion, which requires that the goods be treated as if they have been delivered to the customer, is somewhat more explicit than the comparable IFRS criterion.

8. *(IFRS) The buyer specifically acknowledges the deferred delivery instructions.* Without this acknowledgement, it is difficult to substantiate that a contractual arrangement for the sale exists.

(SEC) The buyer, not the seller, must request (typically in writing) that the transaction be on a bill and hold basis and the buyer must have a substantial business purpose for ordering on a bill and hold basis. The SEC's model is more restrictive because the SEC believes that bill and hold provisions must be acknowledged and requested by the buyer and that the reason for the request should be disclosed.

9. *(IFRS) The usual payment terms apply.* Deferred payment terms may indicate that payment is tied to delivery and that the substance of the transaction is a purchase upon shipment.

(SEC) The date by which the seller expects payment and whether the seller has modified its normal billing and credit terms for this buyer. If the seller has modified its normal billing and credit terms, the transaction should be evaluated to determine whether payment terms have been extended and the seller should determine whether payment is unlikely or specifically tied to delivery. The latter would indicate that it is a bill and hold transaction for which revenue recognition is inappropriate.

If the seller determines that revenue recognition is appropriate, the SEC model requires assessment of whether the related receivable should be discounted in accordance with APB-21 (ASC 835-30).

> **SEC REGISTRANT ALERT:** In early 2003, the SEC staff issued the Report Pursuant to Section 704 of the Sarbanes-Oxley Act of 2002 (the Section 704 Report). In compiling the information in the Section 704 Report, the SEC staff studied enforcement actions filed during the period July 31, 1997, through July 30, 2002. The greatest number of enforcement actions related to improper revenue recognition and one of the issues highlighted in the report was the accounting for bill and hold transactions. The SEC staff noted that, "Improper accounting for bill-and-hold transactions usually involves the recording of revenue from a sale, even though the customer has not taken title of the product and assumed the risks and rewards of ownership of the products specified in the customer's purchase order or sales agreement. . . . These transactions may be recognized legitimately under U.S. GAAP when special criteria are met, including being done pursuant to the buyer's request." This finding underscores the requirement that the above conditions be met prior to recognizing revenue on a bill and hold transaction. It also indicates common shortcomings in bill and hold transactions from a revenue recognition perspective, including items 1 and 8 as discussed above.

The criteria discussed above have been specifically identified by the IASB and the SEC and must be met to recognize revenue on a bill and hold basis. However, other factors might also be useful in assessing whether the substance of the bill and hold agreement is that of a consummated transaction for which revenue recognition is appropriate, or that of a (potential) future transaction for which revenue should not yet be recognized. For example, SAB Topic 13A3a (ASC 605-10-S99, A3a) identifies a number of examples of additional factors that might be relevant:

- *Past experiences with bill and hold transactions.* If payments in past transactions were received late or not at all, the substance of the transactions may have been agreements to make purchases at a later date or upon delivery.

- *Whether the buyer bears the risk of loss in the event of a decline in the market value of the goods.* If the buyer does not bear this risk, all the risks of ownership have not been transferred. This may occur if the transaction has a price-protection clause.

- *Whether the seller's custodial risks are insurable and insured.* If the risk of holding the product is so high that insurance is unavailable or prohibitively expensive, the custodial risk may be too high to conclude that all substantive risks of ownership have passed to the buyer.

- *Whether the buyer's business reasons for the bill and hold have introduced a contingency to the buyer's commitment.* For example, if the buyer requests a bill and hold transaction, because it does not yet have a license to own or take custody of the products, this might indicate that the transaction will never be completed.

☛ **PRACTICE POINTER:** Any company that enters into bill and hold transactions should ensure that it has very strong controls over the process of negotiating and signing contracts with customers, because small changes to a contract can cause the arrangement to fail the bill and hold criteria. For example, if a salesperson negotiates extended payment terms or a right of return, the timing of revenue recognition on a bill and hold transaction would likely be affected, even though such clauses might not affect revenue recognition on a standard sales transaction. A company's internal controls should also ensure that revenue from a bill and hold transaction is limited to transactions where the arrangement was specifically requested by the customer, rather than suggested by the salesperson.

SEC REGISTRANT ALERT: In December 2005, an SEC release on vaccine bill and hold transactions allowed vaccine stockpile participants to recognize revenue despite not meeting bill and hold requirements. This guidance may not be analogized to for any other type of bill and hold transaction.

DISCLOSURE ALERT: See Chapter 12, "Disclosures," for information about disclosures that may be required.

EXAMPLE: SEC ENFORCEMENT ACTION RELATED TO BILL AND HOLD SALES

Excerpts Taken from Accounting and Auditing Enforcement Release No. 1911—November 13, 2003

Improper Bill-and-Hold Sale

Gateway also solicited an arrangement with one of its larger customers, a rent-to-own consumer leasing company, in mid-September 2000.

On September 21, 2000, Gateway's sales representative sent an e-mail to the consumer leasing company confirming that the consumer leasing company would issue a purchase order for $16.5 million of PCs, for which it would receive a 5% discount, that the consumer leasing company would be billed by September 30, 2000, and would take the PCs by October 31, 2000. The e-mail did not reference warehousing arrangements. The parties agreed the consumer leasing company would not take the product until the fourth quarter, after it issued subsequent purchase orders from individual stores, as had been its practice. They also agreed that the consumer leasing company would be invoiced and pay on subsequent store purchase orders, not the $16.5 million purchase order.

On September 21, 2000, the consumer leasing company issued a purchase order for $16.5 million in PCs and peripherals. The purchase order provided that the equipment would be shipped to "local warehousing for subsequent distribution," and stated that the order was FOB destination. Gateway then "shipped" the products by segregating them in the third-party warehouses located adjacent to Gateway's manufacturing facilities. . . . The consumer leasing company did not make any arrangements with the warehouses, or have any contact with the warehouses.

Gateway improperly recognized revenue of $16.5 million on the third quarter purported sale (and also failed to apply the 5% discount on the sale until the fourth quarter). Thus, Gateway increased its third quarter reported revenue by $16.5 million.

The transaction failed to satisfy three critical GAAP criteria for revenue recognition on a bill-and-hold transaction.[4] First, revenue recognition was inappropriate because the consumer leasing company lacked any substantial business purpose for ordering the goods on bill-and-hold basis. Second, Gateway had specific performance obligations concerning the purchase order that it did not discharge during the third quarter, including (1) upon receipt of a second purchase order from the consumer leasing company, an obligation to remove the product from the warehouse inventory, send it back to Gateway's manufacturing facility for re-entry into Gateway's computer system, and then ship the product to the individual store specified on the order; and (2) an obligation to reverse the September 21, 2000, sale of the PC out of its system and issue a second invoice to the consumer leasing company. These specific performance obligations precluded revenue recognition. Third, revenue recognition was inappropriate because the consumer leasing company did not request that the transaction be on a bill-and-hold basis and did not pay the cost for warehousing the inventory.

[4] *Footnote Omitted.*

Layaway Sales

Layaway sales are a type of bill and hold transaction. In a layaway transaction, a buyer makes a partial payment (typically nonrefundable) on an item to be delivered in the future upon payment of the remaining purchase price, and the seller sets the buyer's item aside for a period of time. However, if the buyer does not make the remaining payment within the required period, the initial deposit will be forfeited and the seller may sell the item to another customer.

Layaways are bill and hold transactions because the seller collects a portion of the purchase price without delivering the item. It is clear that under the SEC's bill and hold model, a layaway transaction could not qualify for revenue recognition before the last payment is received and the product is delivered. This is because the buyer has not made a final commitment to purchase the goods, as he or she may elect to cease making payments and thereby not purchase the goods (SAB Topic 13A3e) (ASC 605-10-S99, A3e).

Because this specific condition is only included in the SEC's bill and hold model, nonpublic companies may be able to justify revenue recognition on a layaway sale if they can show that the basic revenue recognition criteria have been met. IAS 18 specifically allows recognition of revenue on layaway transactions if the first five requirements of the IAS bill and hold accounting model are met (see prior discussion) and both of the following conditions exist:

1. *A significant deposit is received* (IAS 18, App. par. 3). The buyer in a layaway transaction has the right to stop making payments under the arrangement. Therefore, the buyer's risk of loss due to a decline in market value is limited to the dollar amount of payments to date. As a result, some of the risk of a market price decline remains with the seller and might only be partially covered by the forfeited payments. Therefore, the size of the initial deposit must be carefully considered to ensure that it effectively transfers enough of the risk of loss to the buyer.

2. *Experience indicates that most layaway transactions are eventually consummated* (IAS 18, App. par. 3). Without historical evidence that most customers complete required payments and take delivery, it is difficult to conclude that a sale has occurred.

Payments received before revenue can be recognized should be recorded as deposit liabilities, and the related inventory should remain on the books. In the event that initial payments are forfeited because the buyer does not complete the required payments, the deposit liability should be eliminated and income credited by the same amount. This credit generally should not be classified as revenue because no earnings event occurred. Instead, it should be reflected as a gain classified below gross margin.

POST-DELIVERY PRODUCT-RELATED OBLIGATIONS

Customer Acceptance Provisions

Customer acceptance provisions allow the customer to cancel an arrangement when the product delivered does not meet the customer's needs or desires. The existence of such provisions raises questions as to whether the earnings process is complete at the time of shipment or only after customer acceptance has been obtained. When products are sold subject to these provisions, the nature of the provisions should be analyzed to determine which accounting model applies to the transaction. Generally, customer acceptance provisions and the related accounting take one of the four forms discussed below.

Product Shipped for Trial or Evaluation Purposes

In these arrangements, the seller delivers a product (before finalizing a sales agreement) and allows the customer to evaluate it prior to acceptance. When products are shipped on this basis, a purchase is consummated only upon customer acceptance. In some cases, acceptance occurs as long as the customer does not reject the product within a specified period of time. For example, a book club may ship its members a book every month for a 14-day trial period. If the member does not return the book within the trial period, the member is deemed to have accepted the book and is obligated to pay for it. In other cases, an affirmative acceptance from the customer is necessary to trigger a purchase obligation. This is more common if the product is equipment that is intended for a specific use.

EXHIBIT 5-2
CUSTOMER ACCEPTANCE PROVISIONS

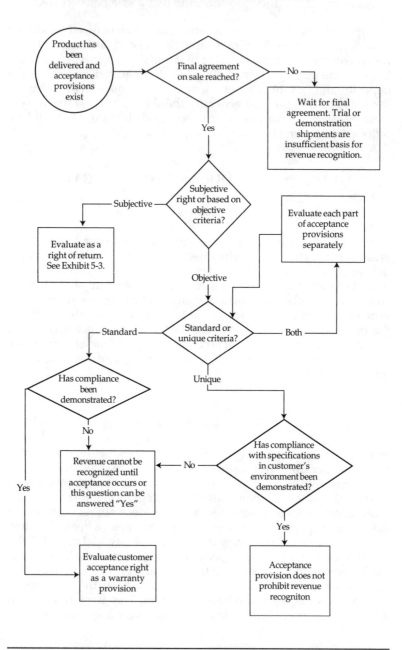

Regardless of whether title passes upon shipment, these arrangements do not constitute a sale until acceptance occurs. This is because until acceptance, there is no persuasive evidence of an arrangement. Accordingly, in arrangements where products are delivered for trial or evaluation purposes, revenue should not be recognized until acceptance occurs, either by notification from the customer or by passage of time without rejection, provided the other conditions for revenue recognition have been met (SAB Topic 13A3b, ques. 1) (ASC 605-10-S99, A3b, ques. 1).

> ☞ **PRACTICE POINTER:** The reason shipment on a trial basis or for evaluation purposes does not trigger revenue recognition is because the arrangement does not even purport to be a sale until acceptance occurs. Therefore, historical experience at estimating how many of these shipments will ultimately result in sales, no matter how accurate, cannot be used to justify revenue recognition prior to acceptance. By contrast, subjective customer acceptance clauses and rights of return (discussed later in this chapter) do not absolutely preclude revenue recognition during the return period because a sale agreement is in place before the products are delivered. Since rights of return provide many of the same protections as an arrangement with a trial or evaluation period, companies may wish to change their sales contracts accordingly. This may allow a company to recognize revenue at an earlier point in time.

Subjective Right of Return

Certain customer acceptance provisions give the buyer a right to reject the product if he or she is dissatisfied for any reason. An example of such a provision is one that allows the customer to return a product with "no questions asked." Acceptance provisions based on wholly subjective terms are, in substance, general rights of return. Thus, this class of acceptance provisions should be accounted for in accordance with FAS-48 (ASC 605-15-25), and related interpretations. (See SAB Topic 13A3b, ques. 1 (ASC 605-10-S99, A3b, ques. 1), and "Rights of Return" in this chapter).

Customer Acceptance Based on Meeting Standard Seller-Specified Performance Criteria

These provisions give the customer a right of return or replacement if the delivered product is defective, fails to meet advertising claims, or does not meet the *vendor's* published specifications for the product. In some cases, the seller may have the right to refund the purchaser's money or repair the product rather than provide a replacement. This type of acceptance provision is generally used in a situation where identical rights are granted to every customer of a particular class and involves seller-specified performance criteria that the seller is reasonably certain the product will meet. If the seller has previously demonstrated that the product meets these criteria, the customer acceptance provision is no different from a product warranty. Under these circumstances, the customer acceptance provision should be accounted for as a warranty (see "Product Warranties" in this chapter).

However, if the seller has not previously demonstrated that the delivered product meets the stated specifications, warranty accounting is not appropriate, because it is uncertain whether the company has delivered the product specified in the arrangement. Therefore, revenue should be deferred until the specifications have been achieved or the customer has accepted the product (SAB Topic 13A3b, ques. 1 and 2) (ASC 605-10-S99, A3b, ques. 1 and 2).

Customer Acceptance Based on Customer-Specified or Negotiated Criteria

This type of customer acceptance provision is the most difficult to analyze. Provisions like these are common in sales of equipment to be used in manufacturing, and in sales of industrial goods designed for a specific location, such as an air conditioning system designed for a particular building. Prior to installation and product testing at the customer's location, it is often unclear whether the product meets the specified criteria. This is because, no matter how much testing is done before shipment, it may not be possible to replicate the conditions of the customer's environment. These types of arrangements usually allow the seller a period of time after installation and testing to resolve any problems that might exist in meeting the criteria. As a result, the seller may need to perform additional work after installation in order to meet the specifications. If a substantive amount of additional work is likely to be required, revenue recognition upon shipment is inappropriate because the seller has not met its obligations.

Therefore, when an arrangement has customer-specified acceptance provisions, the seller must be able to reliably demonstrate that the delivered product meets these specified criteria before revenue can be recognized. If the criteria are sufficiently objective and the seller can replicate conditions under which the customer will operate the product, it may be possible to objectively demonstrate compliance with the acceptance provisions prior to shipment. In this case, revenue may be recognized upon delivery, provided that all other revenue recognition conditions have been met.

However, if unique aspects of the customer's environment could affect the assessment of whether the product meets the criteria or if other circumstances exist that prohibit the seller from verifying compliance with the acceptance provisions until delivery or installation, revenue should not be recognized until compliance can be verified. Verification often consists of a formal customer sign-off to indicate that the acceptance provisions have been met. However, if the seller can verify that the product meets the acceptance criteria and, thereby, believes it would be able to enforce a claim for payment even though formal customer sign-off has not occurred, revenue may be recognized because the seller has fulfilled all terms of the contract. As with other accounting that is based on a legal interpretation, consultation with legal experts may be necessary to determine the appropriate treatment (SAB Topic 13A3b, ques. 1) (ASC 605-10-S99, A3b, ques. 1).

EXAMPLE: CUSTOMER ACCEPTANCE PROVISIONS

KLA-Tencor Corporation Form 10-K—Fiscal Year Ended June 30, 2008

We recognize revenue when persuasive evidence of an arrangement exists, delivery has occurred or services have been rendered, the seller's price is fixed or determinable, and collectibility is reasonably assured. We derive revenue from three sources—system sales, spare part sales and service contracts. We typically recognize revenue for system sales upon acceptance by the customer that the system has been installed and is operating according to predetermined specifications. We also recognize revenue prior to written acceptance from the customer, as follows:

- When system sales to independent distributors have no installation requirement, contain no acceptance agreement, and 100% payment is due upon shipment, revenue is recognized upon shipment;

- When the installation of the system is deemed perfunctory, revenue is recognized upon shipment. The portion of revenue associated with installation is deferred based on estimated fair value, and that revenue is recognized upon completion of the installation;

- When the customer fab has already accepted the same tool, with the same specifications, and it can be objectively demonstrated that the tool meets all of the required acceptance criteria upon shipment, revenue is recognized upon shipment. The portion of revenue associated with installation is deferred based on estimated fair value, and that revenue is recognized upon completion of the installation;

- When the customer withholds signature on our acceptance document due to issues unrelated to product performance, revenue is recognized when the system is performing as intended and meets all published and contractually-agreed specifications;

- When the system is damaged during transit and title has passed to the customer, revenue is recognized upon receipt of cash payment from the customer.

Total revenue recognized without a written acceptance from the customer was approximately 16%, 14% and 4% of total revenues for the fiscal years ended June 30, 2008, 2007 and 2006, respectively. The increase in revenue recognized without a written acceptance is primarily driven by increased shipments of tools that have already met the required acceptance criteria at those customer fabs as well as an increase in sales of systems with perfunctory installation, primarily with respect to sales of products of companies that we have acquired during the past two fiscal years. Shipping charges billed to customers are included in system revenue, and the related shipping costs are included in costs of revenues.

EXAMPLE: CUSTOMER ACCEPTANCE—ABILITY TO ESTIMATE RETURN RATE

8x8, Inc. Form 10-K—Fiscal Year Ended March 31, 2007

Historically, the Company recognized new subscriber revenue from its Packet8 service offerings upon the expiration of the applicable acceptance period. Under the terms of the Company's typical subscription agreement, new customers can terminate their service within 30 days of order placement and receive a full refund of fees previously paid. During the first few years of the Company's Packet8 service, it lacked sufficient history to apply a return rate and reserve against new order revenue. Accordingly, the Company deferred new subscriber revenue 30 days to ensure that the 30-day acceptance period has expired. In the first quarter of 2007, the Company evaluated two years of historical data related to the termination of service during the 30-day acceptance period. By June 2006, the Company determined that it had sufficient history of subscriber conduct to make reasonable estimates of cancellations within the 30-day trial period. Therefore, in the first quarter of fiscal 2007, the Company began recognizing new subscriber revenue in the month in which the new order was shipped, net of an allowance for expected cancellations. As a result of this change in revenue recognition, the Company recognized an additional $68,000 of new order service revenue, $280,000 of new order product revenue and $466,000 of new order cost of product during the first quarter of fiscal 2007.

OBSERVATION: Acceptance provisions based on specific criteria must be evaluated on a contract-by-contract basis. As a result, the timing of revenue recognition may differ for otherwise similar contracts. For example, in an arrangement to deliver multiple machines, each of which operate to identical specifications, it may not be possible to determine whether the first machine meets the specifications until it is tested in the customer's plant. Therefore, revenue recognition would need to be deferred on the first machine until after installation and testing. However, if the other machines in the order are identical to the first and any modifications that were necessary on the first machine are made to the others before shipment, revenue recognition on these machines may be appropriate upon shipment. If the contract specified unique acceptance provisions for each machine delivered, the analysis of the timing of revenue recognition would be different for each machine.

DISCLOSURE ALERT: See Chapter 12, "Disclosures," for information about disclosures that may be required.

SEC REGISTRANT ALERT: In early 2003 the SEC staff issued the Summary by the Division of Corporation Finance of Significant Issues Addressed in the Review of the Periodic Reports of the Fortune 500 Companies (the Fortune 500 Report). This report resulted from the SEC's Division of Corporation Finance's (Corp Fin) review of all annual reports filed by Fortune 500 companies. The report provides insight into areas commonly questioned by Corp Fin during its reviews of annual reports. One area specifically mentioned in this report relates to customer acceptance clauses. Corp Fin noted that the quality of disclosures on these provisions requires improvement, particularly in the capital goods, semiconductor, and electronic instruments and controls industries.

ILLUSTRATION: EFFECTS OF CUSTOMER ACCEPTANCE PROVISIONS ON REVENUE RECOGNITION

(Adapted from SAB Topic 13A3b, ques. 3 through 5 (ASC 605-10-S99, A3b, ques. 3 through 5))

Facts: Company E is an equipment manufacturer whose main product is generally sold in a standard model. The contracts for sale of that model provide for customer acceptance to occur after the equipment is received and tested by the customer. The acceptance provisions state that if the equipment does not perform to Company E's published specifications, the customer may return the equipment for a full refund or a replacement unit, or may require Company E to repair the equipment so that it performs up to published specifications. Customer acceptance is indicated by either a formal sign-off by the customer or by the passage of 90 days without a claim under the acceptance provisions. Title to the equipment passes upon delivery to the customer. Company E does not perform any installation or other services on the equipment it sells and tests each piece of equipment against its specifications before shipment. Payment is due under Company E's normal payment terms for that product—30 days after customer acceptance.

EXAMPLE 1

Additional Facts: Company E receives an order from a new customer for a standard model of its main product. Based on the customer's intended use of the product, location, and other factors, there is no reason that the equipment would operate differently in the customer's environment than it does in Company E's facility.

Discussion: Although the arrangement includes a customer acceptance provision, acceptance is based on meeting Company E's published specifications for a standard model. Because Company E demonstrates that the equipment shipped meets the specifications before shipment, and the equipment is expected to operate the same in the customer's environment as it does in Company E's, Company E should evaluate the customer acceptance provision as a warranty under FAS-5 (ASC 460). If Company E can reasonably and reliably estimate the amount of warranty obligations, Company E should recognize revenue upon delivery of the equipment (provided the other criteria for recognition are met) with an appropriate liability for probable warranty obligations.

EXAMPLE 2

Additional Facts: Company E enters into an arrangement with a new customer to deliver a version of its standard product modified as necessary to fit into a space of specific dimensions while still meeting all of the published vendor specifications with regard to performance. In addition to the customer acceptance provisions relating to the standard performance specifications, the customer may reject the equipment if it does not conform to the specified dimensions. Company E creates a testing chamber of the exact same dimensions as specified by the customer and makes simple design changes to the product so that it fits into the testing chamber. The equipment still meets all of the standard performance specifications.

Discussion: The contract effectively includes two customer acceptance clauses—one based on a customer-specific criterion and one based on standard performance specifications. For the customer acceptance clause based on the customer-specific criterion, Company E demonstrates that the equipment shipped meets that objective criterion before shipment. As such, there are no uncertainties related to that customer acceptance clause that affect revenue recognition. For the customer acceptance clause based on the standard performance specifications, Company E demonstrates that the equipment shipped meets those specifications before shipment as well. This customer acceptance clause should be evaluated under FAS-5 (ASC 460) as a warranty obligation. If Company E can reasonably and reliably estimate the amount of warranty obligations, it should recognize revenue upon delivery of the equipment with an appropriate liability for probable warranty obligations (provided the other criteria for recognition are met).

EXAMPLE 3

Additional Facts: Company E enters into an arrangement with a new customer to deliver a version of its standard product modified as necessary to be integrated into the customer's new assembly line while still meeting all of the standard published vendor specifications with regard to performance. The customer may reject the equipment if it fails to meet the standard published performance specifications or cannot be satisfactorily integrated into the new line. Company E has never modified its equipment to work on an integrated basis in the type of assembly line the customer has proposed. In response to the request, Company E designs a version of its standard equipment that is modified as believed necessary to operate in the new assembly line. The modified equipment still meets all of the standard published performance specifications, and Company E believes the equipment will meet the requested specifications when integrated into the new assembly line. However, Company E is unable to replicate the new assembly line conditions in its pre-shipment testing.

Discussion: This contract includes a customer acceptance clause based, in part, on a customer-specific criterion and Company E cannot demonstrate that the equipment shipped meets that criterion before shipment. Accordingly, Company E may not recognize revenue before the product is successfully integrated at its customer's location and meets the customer-specific criterion.

Product Warranties

Many product sale arrangements include a warranty provision that provides the purchaser with some protection in the event the product does not perform as expected or requires post-sale servicing. Under a normal warranty, the seller assumes an obligation to repair or replace the product if it fails to perform as advertised or according to published specifications. However, not all warranty provisions involve the same type of obligation and it is important to understand the substance of these obligations to facilitate the proper accounting. For example, if the seller commits to ensure that the product will meet certain specifications that have not yet been demonstrated, revenue should not be recognized until compliance with these specifications is achieved. Furthermore, if the warranty is based on meeting criteria specific to a particular customer or product sale, the warranty obligation should be evaluated as a customer acceptance provision based on customer-specified criteria (see "Customer Acceptance Provisions" above).

In addition, certain warranties may include obligations other than ensuring that the product continues to operate according to specifications. For example, a warranty provision in a software arrangement may include the right to upgrades or updates to the product or a warranty on an automobile may include oil changes and other preventative maintenance during the warranty term. Neither of these specific provisions should be accounted for as part of the warranty. Rather, the sale of a product, along with a promise to provide upgrades or services after the sale, should be treated as a multiple-element arrangement (see Chapter 4, "Multiple-Element Arrangements"). Therefore, a portion of the sales prices in these situations generally should be allocated to the additional elements and deferred until the seller fulfills its obligations to provide the other products or services.

Most warranty provisions, however, merely require that the seller repair or replace the item if it fails to perform in the way it was designed and manufactured to perform. These provisions are usually explicitly identified in the documentation that comes with the product, but warranties may also be implied or required by laws or regulations (e.g., the "lemon laws" that cover automobiles in many states are a type of warranty). Because of a warranty commitment, the seller's involvement with the product may not end after delivery. At a minimum, the seller must be prepared to honor the warranty for whatever period of time it is in force.

One method of accounting for a product sale with a warranty would be to treat it as a multiple-element arrangement; the product would be one element and the warranty another. Revenue would be allocated between the product and the warranty, with the amount allocated to the warranty recognized as revenue over the warranty period, consistent with other service transactions. Another possible method of accounting for a warranty would be to treat it as a part of the product and not account for it separately. If analyzed this way, a question arises as to whether the warranty obligation is significant enough to prevent revenue recognition on the product. If the obligation is significant, revenue would not be recognized until the warranty expires. Conversely, if the warranty obligation were deemed insignificant, all revenue would be attributed to the product and recognized upon delivery (or when all revenue recognition criteria are met). U.S. GAAP recognizes the merit of both accounting approaches, depending on the facts and circumstances.

> **OBSERVATION:** Although warranties are conceptually within the scope of FIN-45 (ASC 460), they are exempted from its accounting requirements through an exception.

Standard Warranties

In many cases, a sale of goods in the normal course of business includes a standard warranty for all buyers of the product. This warranty is not treated as a separate service; rather, it is considered an integral part of the product sale. Revenue may be recognized upon product delivery when a standard warranty is included in the transaction, provided that the costs of honoring the warranty can be reliably estimated and that the other conditions for revenue recognition have been met. The estimated costs of honoring the warranty must be accrued to cost of sales when revenue is recognized, and these costs should be updated as estimates change.

However, if the costs of honoring the warranty cannot be reliably estimated and the potential range of loss is wide, revenue should be deferred until either a reliable estimate of the costs can be made or the warranty period expires (FAS-5, par. 25) (ASC 460-10-25-6). Indicators that costs may not be reliably estimable include (a) the introduction of new products or significant modifications that have been made to old products, (b) the extension of the scope of a warranty beyond what has normally been given in the ordinary course of business, and (c) undertaking new obligations.

> **DISCLOSURE ALERT:** See Chapter 12, "Disclosures" for information about required disclosures.

Separately Priced Extended Warranty and Product Maintenance Contracts

The preceding discussion applies only to standard warranties offered to all purchasers of a product without an extra charge. Revenue from separately priced extended warranty and product maintenance contracts should be deferred and recognized in income over the contract period. A warranty is priced separately any time a customer may purchase the product with or without the warranty. For example, assume that all purchasers of a particular model of television receive a one-year warranty and can purchase a three-year warranty for an added charge. The arrangement should be accounted for as having a one-year standard warranty and a two-year separately priced extension. As such, the fee paid for the two-year extension should be deferred and recognized as revenue after the television is delivered in years two and three. The purchase price of the television with the standard one-year warranty should be recognized as revenue upon delivery as long as all other revenue recognition conditions are met and the costs of honoring the one-year warranty can be reliably estimated.

The recognition pattern for revenue attributable to a separately priced extended warranty contract should be on a straight-line basis, unless historical evidence indicates that the costs of performing services under the contract are incurred on other than a straight-line basis. If costs are incurred on other than a straight-line basis, revenue should be recognized over the contract period in proportion to the costs expected to be incurred in performing services under the contract (FTB 90-1, par. 3) (ASC 605-20-25-1 through 25-6).

EXAMPLES: WARRANTIES

Dell, Inc. Form 10-K—Fiscal Year Ended January 30, 2009

Warranty Liability and Related Deferred Service Revenue

Revenue from extended warranty and service contracts, for which Dell is obligated to perform, is recorded as deferred revenue and subsequently recognized over the term of the contract or when the service is completed. Dell records warranty liabilities at the time of sale for the estimated costs that may be incurred under its standard warranty. Changes in Dell's deferred revenue for extended warranties, and warranty liability for standard warranties which are included in other current and non-current liabilities on Dell's Consolidated Statements of Financial Position, are presented in the following tables:

	Fiscal Year Ended		
	January 30, 2009	February 1, 2008	February 2, 2007
	(in millions)		
Deferred service revenue:			
Deferred service revenue at beginning of year	$5,260	$4,221	$3,707
Revenue deferred for new extended warranty and service contracts sold[b]	3,545	3,806	3,188
Revenue recognized[c]	(3,156)	(2,767)	(2,674)
Deferred service revenue at end of year	$5,649	$5,260	$4,221
Current portion	$2,649	$2,486	$2,032
Non-current portion	3,000	2,774	2,189
Deferred service revenue at end of year	$5,649	$5,260	$4,221

	Fiscal Year Ended		
	January 30, 2009	February 1, 2008	February 2, 2007
Warranty liability:			
Warranty liability at beginning of year	$ 929	$ 958	$ 951
Costs accrued for new warranty contracts and changes in estimates for pre-existing warranties[a][b]	1,180	1,176	1,255
Service obligations honored[c]	(1,074)	(1,205)	(1,248)
Warranty liability at end of year	$1,035	$ 929	$ 958
Current portion	$ 721	$ 690	$ 768
Non-current portion	314	239	190
Warranty liability at end of year	$1,035	$ 929	$ 958

(a) Changes in cost estimates related to pre-existing warranties are aggregated with accruals for new standard warranty contracts. Dell's warranty liability process does not differentiate between estimates made for pre-existing warranties and new warranty obligations.

(b) Includes the impact of foreign currency exchange rate fluctuations.

(c) Fiscal 2008 and Fiscal 2007 amounts have been revised to include foreign currency exchange rate fluctuations in revenue deferred for new extended warranty and service contracts sold and costs accrued for new warranty contracts and changes in estimates for pre-existing warranties to conform to the current period presentation.

General Electric Co. Form 10-K—Fiscal Year Ended December 31, 2008

We sell product services under long-term agreements in our Technology Infrastructure and Energy Infrastructure segments, principally in Aviation, Energy and Transportation, where costs of performing services are incurred on other than a straight-line basis. We also sell product services in Healthcare, where such costs generally are expected to be on a straight-line basis. These agreements are accounted for under Financial Accounting Standards Board (FASB) Technical Bulletin (FTB) 90-1, *Accounting for Separately Priced Extended Warranty and Product Maintenance Contracts.* For the Aviation, Energy and Transportation FTB 90-1 agreements, we recognize related sales based on the extent of our progress towards completion measured by actual costs incurred in relation to total expected costs. We routinely update our estimates of future costs for agreements in process and report any cumulative effects of such adjustments in current operations. For the Healthcare FTB 90-1 agreements, we recognize revenues on a straight-line basis and expense-related costs as incurred. We provide for any loss that we expect to incur on any of these agreements when that loss is probable.

OBSERVATION: In many cases, a company that sells an extended warranty will purchase insurance to cover its potential losses. Although purchasing insurance transfers the risk of loss under the contract to the insurance company, the seller remains liable for the warranty obligation in the event that the insurance company cannot or does not honor the policy. Because the seller has neither fulfilled its obligation nor been released by the buyer from that obligation (i.e., the buyer was not a party to the insurance contract), purchasing insurance to cover the risk of loss under a warranty contract should not trigger revenue recognition. The accounting treatment for the warranty contract and the insurance coverage should be considered separately.

DISCLOSURE ALERT: See Chapter 12, "Disclosures," for information about required disclosures.

Products Shipped Subject to Other Conditions

Product sales can include various other conditions. For example, products may be sold subject to installation or performance of other services. When a product is sold together with post-delivery services, the arrangement should be accounted for as a multiple-element arrangement. If the product and service deliverables meet the requirements for separate accounting treatment, the revenue allocated to the product element should be recognized at the appropriate time, without regard to the service element. However, if the deliverables do not meet the requirements for separate accounting treatment, no revenue should be recognized until the product is delivered *and* the service has been performed. See Chapter 4, "Multiple-Element Arrangements," for further discussion.

RIGHTS OF RETURN

Return rights are very common in product transactions. For example, almost any retail purchase can be returned for a limited period of time. Resellers and distributors are often granted rights of return to reduce their risk of loss if the product is difficult to resell. Similarly, sales of commercial products may have rights of return related to quality, performance testing, or other factors.

> ☞ **PRACTICE POINTER:** Return rights are often documented in the sales contract. However, such rights may also exist due to industry practice, company policy, or laws and regulations. In addition, the relationship between the buyer and seller should be evaluated in full to determine whether unstated rights of return might exist. For example, a large customer of a company may have enough leverage to return goods beyond the limited period stated in the contract. Although the seller may be within its rights to deny such returns, it is common for a seller to accept such a return from an important customer. Therefore, all rights of return, whether or not explicitly stated in a contract, must be considered.

General Rights of Return

FAS-48 (ASC 605-15) provides accounting guidance for a subjective right of return, such as a "100% satisfaction guarantee," that may be exercised at will by the purchaser. This guidance prohibits recognition of revenue if there is significant uncertainty as to whether, or to what extent, the return right will be exercised. However, this guidance does not apply to exchanges by ultimate customers (i.e., end users) of one item for another of the same kind, quality, and price. These types of exchange rights are not treated as returns for accounting purposes and generally should have no effect on revenue recognition (FAS-48, fn. 3) (ASC 605-15-15-2).

Although the return right creates a question as to whether the transaction has been completed, the seller records revenue upon delivery when specific criteria are met. However, this is only acceptable when the terms of the arrangement make it clear that a sale has occurred, there are no other contingencies, and the likelihood of the customer exercising the right of return can be estimated. If any of these three conditions is not met, the existence of the return right renders the transaction as incomplete until the return right lapses. Specifically, revenue should be recognized at the time of sale, net of estimated returns, only if all of the following conditions (and the remaining general conditions for revenue recognition) are met (FAS-48, par. 6) (ASC 605-15-25-1):

1. *The sales price to the buyer is fixed or determinable.* This shows that the return period is not just part of the transaction's pricing negotiations. If the arrangement does not meet this criterion, no revenue should be recognized because a fixed or determinable fee is one of the prerequisites to recognizing revenue.

2. *Payment is not contractually or otherwise excused until the product is resold.* If payment is not required until the product is resold, the transaction takes on characteristics of a consignment, for which no revenue should be recognized.

   > **OBSERVATION:** Although payment may contractually be due within a specified period of time, a company may have a business practice of not pursuing payment until the customer actually resells the products. If this is the case, the business practice must be considered in the evaluation, and revenue may not be recognized until the right of return expires or payment is received.

3. *The buyer holds the risks of destruction, damage, or theft of the property.* If the buyer does not hold these risks, then all of the risks and rewards of ownership have not passed, and revenue recognition is prohibited.

4. *The buyer has economic substance apart from the seller.* A sale with a right of return to a company with little substance raises significant questions about the buyer's ability to pay. In this case, the buyer would appear to be acting as a sales agent for the seller, rather than as a substantive purchaser. As a result, the seller should not record any sale to the nonsubstantive purchaser.

5. *The seller does not have significant obligations for future performance relating to the resale of the product by the buyer.* If the seller is required to assist the buyer in the product's resale, the seller has not completed its obligations under the arrangement until resale has occurred and should not recognize revenue until then, provided the other conditions for recognition have been met.

6. *The amount of future returns and costs expected in connection with any returns can be reasonably predicted.* This criterion requires the most judgment and is the one that most often cannot be met. See below for further discussion.

Estimating Returns

Determining whether a reasonable estimate of returns can be made is sometimes quite easy. For example, a product that has been sold to the same group of customers and has generated a consistent rate of return for many years can probably be expected to have the same level of returns in the future, as long as there are no external changes that might affect customers' return habits. On the other hand, a start-up company selling a newly invented product that is not similar to any other product on the market may quickly conclude that it cannot estimate the level of returns that will occur (SAB Topic 13A4a, ques. 4 (ASC 605-10-S99, A4a, ques. 4)).

> **OBSERVATION:** There is no specific level of returns that would prohibit recognition of revenue on sales with a right of return. The accounting literature focuses entirely on the ability of a company to estimate returns in determining whether revenue may be recognized upon delivery. When the percentage of customers exercising return rights is high, it may be more difficult to estimate the rate of returns, but this is just one of many factors a company would take into account in determining whether it can make a reliable estimate of returns (SAB Topic 13A4a, ques. 5) (ASC 605-10-S99, A4a, ques. 5).

When evaluating whether a reasonable estimate of returns can be made, all available information should be considered. The following factors, the existence of any of which may cause the seller to conclude that returns cannot be reasonably predicted, should be considered by a seller when estimating the amount of returns:

1. *The product is susceptible to significant external factors, such as technological obsolescence or changes in demand* (FAS-48, par. 8) (ASC 605-15-25-3). When the return period is lengthy, it may be difficult to predict the economic and technological life of (i.e., demand for) the product. It may also be harder to forecast competitors' actions and customers' responses to market factors.

2. *The return period is long* (FAS-48, par. 8) (ASC 605-15-25-3). The longer the return period, the more difficult it becomes to predict the level of returns. Whether a return period is long should be

determined based on the nature of the product, industry practice, and the type of customer.

3. *The absence of relevant historical experience* (FAS-48, par. 8) (ASC 605-15-25-3). Without historical experience to reference, predicting customer actions is virtually impossible. However, in the absence of company-specific experience, industry experience may be relevant.

4. *The absence of a large volume of relatively homogeneous transactions* (FAS-48, par. 8) (ASC 605-15-25-3). It is generally difficult to predict the actions of a particular customer. However, it is much easier to predict, on average, the actions of a large number of similar customers.

5. *Increases in or excess levels of inventory at distributors, or a lack of information about the levels of inventory at distributors* (SAB Topic 13A4b, ques. 1) (ASC 605-10-S99, A4b, ques. 1). Either of these situations indicates that historical experience is less likely to have sufficient predictive ability to guide future actions given the problems with inventory management.

6. *Importance of sales by and to a particular distributor to the reporting entity (overall or to a specific reportable segment)* (SAB Topic 13A4b, ques. 1) (ASC 605-10-S99, A4b, ques. 1). Trends in sales by and to an important distributor or significant changes in inventory levels at a new distributor may have implications for the vendor's ability to estimate returns.

7. *Expected introductions of new products* (SAB Topic 13A4b, ques. 1) (ASC 605-10-S99, A4b, ques. 1). If the product subject to the return right is near the end of its life due to the planned introduction of a new or upgraded version, it is possible that more returns will occur as customers opt for the new or upgraded version.

8. *The product is new* (SAB Topic 13A4b, ques. 1) (ASC 605-10-S99, A4b, ques. 1). The newer the product, the less likely it is that relevant return experience exists. Depending upon the circumstances, return experience with other, similar, products may be useful.

> **OBSERVATION:** The ability to estimate returns could vary from product to product, location to location, customer to customer, and arrangement to arrangement. In addition, it may be possible for a company to estimate returns for certain transactions but not others. Thus, a company that sells various products or serves different market segments whose return rates are expected to vary should develop different return estimates for each type of product or market segment.

EXHIBIT 5-3
RIGHTS OF RETURN

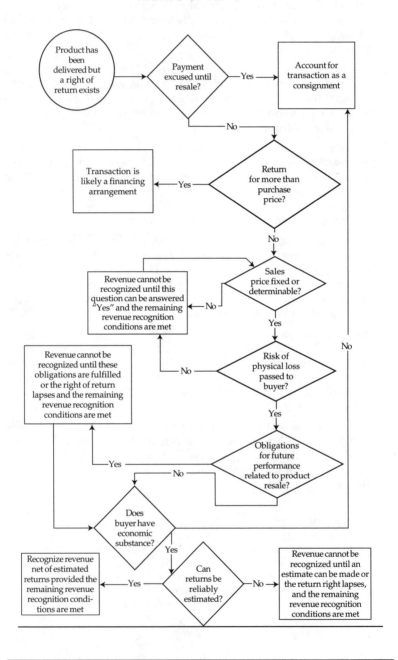

☞ **PRACTICE POINTER:** U.S. GAAP requires a reliable estimate of returns before any revenue can be recognized. Some have suggested that, even in the absence of a good estimate, revenue recognition should be allowed if a company assumes an unusually conservative (i.e., high) level of returns that is unlikely to be exceeded. However, this treatment is not consistent with the accounting literature. Therefore, it is critical that the company develop and sustain the ability to reliably estimate returns to recognize any revenue at delivery (SAB Topic 13A4b, ques. 5) (ASC 605-10-S99, A4b, ques. 5).

In some arrangements, however, a company may sell a large number of products to a single customer with a capped right of return. For example, if the customer is only permitted to return up to 20% of the products shipped, revenue may be recognized upon delivery for the 80% to which the return rights do not apply, assuming all other revenue recognition criteria are met. The 20% of products to which the rights of return do apply should be evaluated to determine whether revenue may be recognized upon delivery.

EXAMPLE: INABILITY TO ESTIMATE RETURNS

Dell, Inc. Form 10-K—Fiscal Year Ended January 30, 2009

During Fiscal 2008, we began selling our products through retailers. Sales to our retail customers are generally made under agreements allowing for limited rights of return, price protection, rebates, and marketing development funds. We have generally limited the return rights through contractual caps. Our policy for sales to retailers is to defer the full amount of revenue relative to sales for which the rights of return apply as we do not currently have sufficient historical data to establish reasonable and reliable estimates of returns, although we are in the process of accumulating the data necessary to develop reliable estimates in the future. All other sales for which the rights of return do not apply are recognized upon shipment when all applicable revenue recognition criteria have been met. To the extent price protection and return rights are not limited, all of the revenue and related cost are deferred until the product has been sold by the retailer, the rights expire, or a reliable estimate of such amounts can be made.

Accounting for Rights of Return

When revenue is not recognized at the time of sale because an estimate of returns cannot be made, the seller should delay recognition until the earlier of when the return privilege has expired or information allowing the company to make a reasonable estimate of returns becomes available, provided the other conditions for revenue recognition have been met (FAS-48, par. 6) (ASC 605-15-25-1). In this situation, the inventory "sold" should remain on the company's books, and any cash collected should be reflected as a liability, rather than as revenue. The inventory should be evaluated for impairment under the assumption that the customer will return the products to the company and consider any anticipated repackaging or other costs to put the merchandise in saleable condition.

> **OBSERVATION:** U.S. GAAP is clear that when an estimate of returns cannot be made, no revenue can be recognized. To be consistent with this approach, no cost of sales should be recognized. It is not appropriate in such a situation to merely defer the margin on the sale by recognizing revenue equal to cost of sales. While deferring only the gross margin ensures that net income is not overstated, it results in the recognition of revenue for a transaction that is, essentially, incomplete (SAB Topic 13A4b, ques. 1) (ASC 605-10-S99, A4b, ques. 1). It also misrepresents various balance sheet components.

When a transaction meets all of the criteria for revenue recognition upon delivery despite the existence of a return right, revenue and cost of sales should be recognized net of the expected returns. Any inventory expected as a return should be evaluated for impairment and this evaluation should consider any anticipated repackaging or other costs to put the merchandise in saleable condition. As estimates of returns change, the anticipated refund liability should be adjusted to reflect this new information.

> **DISCLOSURE ALERT:** See Chapter 12, "Disclosures," for information about disclosures that may be required.

> **SEC REGISTRANT ALERT:** In early 2003 the SEC staff issued the Summary by the Division of Corporation Finance of Significant Issues Addressed in the Review of the Periodic Reports of the Fortune 500 Companies (the Fortune 500 Report). This report resulted from the SEC's Division of Corporation Finance's (Corp Fin) review of all annual reports filed by Fortune 500 companies. The report provides insight into areas commonly questioned by Corp Fin during its reviews of annual reports. One area specifically mentioned in this report relates to rights of return. Corp Fin noted that the quality of disclosures on rights of return requires improvement, particularly in the capital goods, semiconductor, electronic instruments and controls, and pharmaceutical industries.

ILLUSTRATION: PRODUCT SOLD WITH RIGHT OF RETURN

Facts: Example Company sells 100 units of Product A at $100 per unit. Product A has an inventory cost of $87 per unit, and repackaging any returned units for resale will cost $15 per unit. Customers get a 30-day right of return on Product A and, ultimately, 5 of the 100 units are returned. The right of return is the only issue that can affect when revenue should be recognized.

EXAMPLE 1

Additional Facts: Example Company determines at the time of sale that it cannot estimate the amount of returns it will receive.

Accounting:

Upon delivery:

- No revenue is recognized and the inventory remains on the company's books.

- The inventory is evaluated for impairment, under the assumption it will be returned. As the inventory cost plus anticipated repackaging costs ($87 + $15 = $102/unit) exceeds the anticipated sales price of the products ($100/unit), an impairment of $2 per unit, or $200 total, is recorded.

Cost of Sales (Impairment)	$200	
Inventory		$200

- Payment is received.

Cash	$10,000	
Deposit Liability		$10,000

At the end of the return period:
- Revenue for products not returned is recognized.

Deposit Liability	$9,500	
Revenue		$9,500

- Inventory is reduced and cost of sales recorded for products not returned.

Cost of Sales	$8,075	
Inventory ($85 × 95 units)		$8,075

- Cash is refunded on the returned products.

Deposit Liability	$500	
Cash		$500

- Repackaging costs are incurred on the returned products.

Inventory	$75	
Cash		$75

EXAMPLE 2

Additional Facts: Example Company determines that it can estimate the amount of returns and this estimate is initially determined to be 6% of sales.

Accounting:

Upon delivery:

- Revenue is recognized for products not expected to be returned and a refund liability is recorded for products expected to be returned.

Cash	$10,000	
Revenue		$9,400
Deposit Liability		$600

- Cost of sales is recognized for products not expected to be returned.

Cost of Sales	$8,178	
($87 × 94 units)		
Inventory		$8,178

- Units expected to be returned are evaluated for impairment and take repackaging costs into account. An impairment of $2 per unit is calculated.

Cost of Sales	$12	
Inventory		$12

At the end of the return period:

- Additional revenue and cost of sales are recognized because returns were less than expected.

Deposit Liability	$100	
Revenue		$100
Cost of Sales	$85	
Inventory		$85

- Cash refunds are made for returned products.

Deposit Liability	$500	
Cash		$500

- Repackaging costs on returned products are incurred.

Inventory	$75	
Cash		$75

SALES WITH MARKET VALUE PROTECTION

Certain clauses in a product sales arrangement mitigate some of the buyer's risk of a decline in market value of the goods. However, when these clauses cause the seller to retain a substantial amount of the risks and rewards of ownership, sale accounting will be precluded.

Price Protection

A price protection clause provides the buyer a credit (either in cash or as a discount on future purchases) if there is a price decrease during a specified period of time or until the buyer resells the goods. Some price protection clauses (sometimes called "Most Favored Nation" clauses) require a payment only if the seller lowers its prices during the price protection period. Other terms result in a direct payment to the customer if a competitor offers the same or a similar product at a lower price. Retailers in competitive market segments, such as appliances and electronics, commonly offer the latter form of price protection.

The accounting for price protection depends on whether the seller can estimate the amount of refunds to be granted under the price protection terms. If the seller can develop a reasonable and reliable estimate, revenue should be recognized upon delivery (assuming all other revenue recognition criteria are met) net of a provision for estimated price protection refunds. If the seller cannot develop a reasonable and reliable estimate, revenue should not be recognized until either such an estimate can be made or the price protection period ends. When the price protection clause allows for refunds based on the actions of a competitor, it may be difficult to make a reasonable and reliable estimate because the payments can be triggered by a third party rather than the seller. At a minimum, the factors discussed under "Rights of Return" should be considered in these situations.

DISCLOSURE ALERT: See Chapter 12, "Disclosures," for information about disclosures that may be required.

SEC REGISTRANT ALERT: In a December 2001 speech, the SEC staff indicated that it would focus on the accounting for price protection clauses. Specifically, the staff suggested that it will be highly skeptical in a situation where a company has developed an estimate of payments to be granted without relevant historical experience. In addition, in early 2003, the SEC staff issued the Summary by the Division of Corporation Finance of Significant Issues Addressed in the Review of the Periodic Reports of the Fortune 500 Companies (the Fortune 500 Report). This report resulted from the SEC's Division of Corporation Finance's (Corp Fin) review of all annual reports filed by Fortune 500 companies. The report provides insight into areas commonly questioned by Corp Fin during its reviews of annual reports. One area specifically mentioned in this report relates to price protection clauses. Corp Fin noted that the quality of disclosures on price protection clauses requires improvement, particularly in the capital goods, semiconductor, and electronic instruments and controls industries.

EXAMPLES: PRODUCT RETURNS AND PRICE PROTECTION

Intel Corporation Form 10-K—Fiscal Year Ended December 29, 2007

Because of frequent sales price reductions and rapid technology obsolescence in the industry, we defer sales made to distributors under agreements allowing price protection and/or right of return until the distributors sell the merchandise.

Activision, Inc. Form 10-K—Fiscal Year Ended March 31, 2007

Revenue Recognition

We recognize revenue from the sale of our products upon the transfer of title and risk of loss to our customers. Certain products are sold to customers with a street date (i.e., a date on which products are made widely available by retailers). For these products we recognize revenue no earlier than the street date. Revenue from product sales is recognized after deducting the estimated allowance for returns and price protection.

We may permit product returns from, or grant price protection to, our customers under certain conditions. In general, price protection refers to the circumstances when we elect to decrease the wholesale price of a product by a certain amount and, when granted and applicable, allows customers a credit against amounts owed by such customers to us with respect to open and/or future invoices. The conditions our customers must meet to be granted the right to return products or price protection are, among other things, compliance with applicable payment terms, and consistent delivery to us of inventory and sell-through reports. We may also consider other factors, including the facilitation of slow-moving inventory and other market factors. Management must make estimates of potential future product returns and price protection related to current period product revenue. We estimate the amount of future returns and price protection for current period product revenue utilizing historical experience and information regarding inventory levels and the demand and acceptance of our products by the end consumer. The following factors are used to estimate the amount of future returns and price protection for a particular title: historical performance of titles in similar genres; historical performance of the hardware platform; historical performance of the brand; console hardware life cycle; Activision sales force and retail customer feedback; industry pricing; weeks of on-hand retail channel inventory; absolute quantity of on-hand retail channel inventory; our warehouse on-hand inventory levels; the title's recent sell-through history (if available); marketing trade programs; and competing titles. The relative importance of these factors varies among titles depending upon, among other items, genre, platform, seasonality, and sales strategy. Significant management judgments and estimates must be made and used in connection with establishing the allowance for returns and price protection in any accounting period. Based upon historical experience we believe our estimates are reasonable. However, actual returns and price protection could vary materially from our allowance estimates due to a number of reasons including, among others, a lack of consumer acceptance of a title, the release in the same period of a similarly themed title by a competitor, or technological obsolescence due to the emergence of new hardware platforms. Material differences may result in the amount and timing of our revenue for any period if factors or market conditions change or if management makes different judgments or utilizes different estimates in determining the allowances for returns and price protection. For example, a 1% change in our March 31, 2007 allowance for returns and price protection would impact net revenues by $0.9 million.

Guaranteed Resale or Residual Value

To induce a purchaser to buy its product, a company may offer what amounts to a blanket guarantee on the value of the product for some period of time after delivery. Such guarantees can take several forms. For example, the company may agree to repurchase the product from its customer for a set price after several years of use. Alternatively, a company could agree to make up the difference between the actual selling price when its customer resells the product and the guaranteed price. These kinds of price guarantees must be evaluated as part of the original sale transaction, rather than as a separate purchase transaction or loss contingency.

The accounting for a resale price or residual value guarantee generally depends on whether the purchaser (i.e., the beneficiary of the guarantee) intends to use the products or resell them. If the purchaser is a reseller, the seller should account for the transaction as a product financing arrangement (see the discussion earlier in this chapter).

When the purchaser intends to use the products, the seller should account for the transaction as a lease. This is because the purchaser has essentially agreed to pay the difference between the initial purchase price and the guaranteed residual value for use of the product during the guarantee period.

Unless the residual value guarantee is less than 10% of the original sales price or the term of the guarantee is at least 75% of the useful life of the product, the lease accounting literature will classify this type of arrangement as an operating lease, rather than a sales-type lease. As a result, the asset will remain on the seller's books and be depreciated, the cash received will be recorded as a liability, and the difference between the initial sales price and the guaranteed residual value will be recognized as revenue over the guarantee period. If the guarantee can be exercised at various dates, with amounts declining over time, each decrease in guaranteed value should be considered rental income for the applicable period. If the residual value guarantee expires, any remaining liability should be recognized as revenue at that time, and the remaining asset value should be treated as cost of sales (EITF 95-1) (ASC 840-10-55-12 through 55-25).

> **OBSERVATION:** The residual value guarantee in a sales arrangement does not fall within the scope of FIN-45 (ASC 460) because FIN-45 (ASC 460) does not apply to a guarantee for which the underlying is related to an asset of the guarantor. For example, if a sales arrangement with a residual value guarantee is deemed an operating lease based on applying the guidance in EITF 95-1 (ASC 840-10-55-12 through 55-25), the equipment (i.e., the underlying) will remain on the lessor's books, which exempts the guarantee from the scope of FIN-45 (ASC 460). If a sales arrangement with a residual value guarantee is deemed a sales-type lease, the lessor continues to recognize the guaranteed equipment's (the underlying's) residual value as an asset through its net investment in the lease (EITF 03-12) (ASC 460-10-55-17), which also exempts the guarantee from the scope of FIN-45 (ASC 460).

ILLUSTRATION: RESIDUAL VALUE GUARANTEE ON USED EQUIPMENT

Facts: Equipment Co. sells Product X for $100,000. It also offers its customer a residual value guarantee on Product X that is exercisable three years after the original sale. The guaranteed value is $55,000 after three years.

Product X has a cost basis of $60,000, and an estimated useful life of ten years. Equipment Co. generally uses straight-line depreciation. Since the residual value guarantee is more than 10% of the original sales price and the term of the guarantee is less than 75% of the useful life of the product, Equipment Co. concludes that the agreement should be treated as an operating lease.

EXAMPLE 1

Additional Facts: The customer uses the equipment for three years, and then sells it to a third party for $50,000. Equipment Co. therefore makes a $5,000 payment related to the residual value guarantee.

Accounting:

Original Sale:

- Equipment Co. recognizes the receipt of payment, but no revenue.

Cash	$100,000	
Deposit Liability		$100,000

Each of the three years following the original sale:
- Equipment Co. recognizes the difference between the original sales price and the first residual value guarantee amount as lease income as follows:

Original sales price		$100,000
Residual value guarantee in three years		55,000
Income to recognize over three years		$ 45,000
Income to recognize each year		$ 15,000
Deposit Liability	$15,000	
Lease Revenue		$ 15,000

- Equipment Co. records depreciation expense on Product X based on Product X's carrying value of $60,000 and a ten-year life.

Depreciation Expense	$6,000	
Accum. Depreciation—Product X		$6,000

At the end of year three:
- Equipment Co. records its payment under the guarantee.

Deposit Liability	$5,000	
Cash		$5,000

- Equipment Co. records the remaining liability as revenue, along with cost of sales for the remaining carrying value of Product X.

Deposit Liability	$50,000	
Product Sale Revenue		$50,000
Cost of Sales	$42,000	
Accum. Depreciation—Product X	$18,000	
Historical Cost—Product X		$60,000

EXAMPLE 2

Additional Facts: The customer keeps the equipment longer than three years. Equipment Co. therefore makes no payment on its residual value guarantee.

Accounting:

Original sale and each of the three years following the original sale:

- See Example 1.

At the end of year three:

- Equipment Co. records the remaining liability as revenue, along with cost of sales for the remaining carrying value of Product X.

Deposit Liability	$55,000	
Product Sale Revenue		$55,000
Cost of Sales	$42,000	
Accum. Depreciation—Product X	$18,000	
Historical Cost—Product X		$60,000

Sales with Fixed-Price Trade-In Rights

One variant on a guaranteed residual value is a fixed-price trade-in right, which allows the customer to exchange the purchased product for a specified credit toward another of the manufacturer's products after some period of time. This type of right is a guarantee under FIN-45 (ASC 460). As a result, the fixed-price trade-in right should be initially recognized and measured at fair value provided that it does not prohibit revenue recognition on the arrangement in general. In effect, a sales contract that includes a fixed-price trade-in right is a multiple-element arrangement; one element is the sale of the product and the other is the trade-in right or guarantee. Multiple-element arrangements and FIN-45 (ASC 460) are discussed in more detail in Chapter 4, "Multiple-Element Arrangements."

SELLER-PROVIDED FINANCING AND GUARANTEES

Sales with Extended Payment Terms

Some sellers elect to finance their customers' purchases by agreeing to receive fixed payments over an extended period of time, rather than receiving the purchase price per normal payment terms shortly after delivery. Except in the sale of software products (see Chapter 10, "Software—A Complete Model"), U.S. GAAP does not provide specific guidance about when extended payment terms should prevent revenue recognition. However, extended payment terms can affect two of the four basic conditions for revenue recognition—a fixed or determinable fee and that collectibility is reasonably assured.

Extended Payment Terms and Fixed or Determinable Fees

Extended payment terms raise the risk that the seller will agree to provide additional products or services or reduce the arrangement fee to ensure payment according to the stated terms, even for a creditworthy customer. Consider the example of a customer who is dissatisfied with the product but does not have a warranty or return right. The customer may instead elect to withhold payments and require the seller to negotiate to receive additional amounts that are due. Therefore, extended payment terms should be carefully considered along with warranty, return, customer acceptance, and other terms in the arrangement to determine whether they result in a conclusion that the arrangement fee is not fixed or determinable.

> **OBSERVATION:** The above discussion applies only to payment terms that are fixed at the time of delivery. Terms that are extended until the products are used or resold generally indicate the existence of a consignment arrangement, as previously discussed in this chapter.

Extended Payment Terms and Collectibility

The longer the payment terms, the more difficult it is to conclude that revenue collection is reasonably assured. Significant judgment must be applied in these situations. If a seller concludes that collection is not reasonably assured, no revenue or receivable should be recorded. It is not acceptable in these instances to record revenue and a selling expense for the anticipated bad debt because the threshold criteria for revenue recognition were never met.

Discounting Long-Term Receivables

When products are sold on extended payment terms and it is acceptable to recognize revenue upon delivery, APB-21 (ASC 835-30-25-7) requires the long-term receivable and, therefore, the revenue, to be recorded at the present value of the payments, rather than at the nominal value. Interest income should then be accrued on the receivable until all payments are made. Therefore, when extended payment terms are stated at their nominal values, a portion of the payments will be attributed to interest income, as opposed to revenue (APB-21, par. 12) (ASC 835-30-25-10).

Guaranteeing a Loan in Connection with a Sale of Products

Some companies agree to guarantee the loan a buyer uses to purchase the seller's products. Although the company has collected the purchase price in cash, the probability of ultimately realizing the purchase price is the same as if it had sold the product on extended payment terms per the loan terms. Therefore, before recognizing any revenue, the company should evaluate whether collectibility is reasonably assured as if it were the lender under the loan.

If the company still concludes that collection is reasonably assured and that all other revenue recognition criteria have been met, FIN-45 (ASC 460) requires the transaction to be treated as a multiple-element arrangement; one element is the product sale and the other is the loan guarantee. This type of multiple-element arrangement is discussed in more detail in Chapter 4, "Multiple-Element Arrangements."

> **DISCLOSURE ALERT:** See Chapter 12, "Disclosures," for information about required disclosures.

Sale/Repurchase/Lease Transactions

In certain situations, especially those involving a manufacturer that sells its products through a dealer network, the manufacturer will provide financing to the end users of the product. The manufacturer (or its finance affiliate) may accomplish this by (re)purchasing the product from the dealer and leasing it to the end user. If the manufacturer recognizes revenue on the original sale to the dealer and then also recognizes revenue from the lease to the end user, it will recognize revenue twice on the same physical product. In EITF 95-4 (ASC 605-15-25-5), the EITF concluded that this is acceptable and that the manufacturer may recognize a sale at the time the product is transferred to the dealer, despite the possibility it will repurchase the product to lease it to an end user, if all of the following conditions exist:

1. The dealer is a substantive and independent enterprise that transacts business separately with the manufacturer and end users.

2. The manufacturer has delivered the product to the dealer and the risks and rewards of ownership, including responsibility for the ultimate sale of the product, insurability, theft, or damage, have passed to the dealer.

3. An end user's failure to enter into a lease with the finance affiliate (or manufacturer) would not allow the dealer to return the product to the manufacturer.

4. The finance affiliate (or manufacturer) has no legal obligation to provide a lease arrangement to a potential end user.

5. The end user may choose to obtain financing from parties unaffiliated with the manufacturer, and it is feasible for the end user to do so.

CHAPTER 6
SERVICE DELIVERABLES

CONTENTS

BACKGROUND

Although the U.S. economy has been historically product-based, service-based deliverables have become an integral part of the economy over the past several decades. The number of businesses that offer services to the public continues to increase and the range of these services has consistently expanded. Personal services include those provided by health clubs, lawn care companies, retirement homes, and painters. Business services include architectural and engineering services, outsourcing of functions such as payroll and information technology, advertising, sales and marketing, and storage. Businesses charge for these services using various methods, such as calculating fees based on time, activity and success.

This chapter explores accounting issues that are common in but unique to service transactions. When a service transaction includes multiple deliverables, these accounting issues must be evaluated separately for each deliverable in the arrangement. As discussed in Chapter 4, "Multiple-Element Arrangements," the interrelationship between deliverables in a multiple-element arrangement may give rise to issues beyond those that exist in a single-element transaction.

> **PRACTICE ALERT:** Some arrangements that purport to cover only the sale of services may contain lease deliverables. See Chapter 3, "General Principles" for a discussion of EITF 01-8 (ASC 840, *Leases*; 840-10-15) which provides guidance on how to determine whether an arrangement contains a lease. When an arrangement contains lease deliverables, the lease components must be accounted for as such. This is the case even though the arrangement is not formally characterized as a lease. Separation of the lease element from the other elements in an arrangement is discussed in Chapter 4, "Multiple-Element Arrangements."

SURVEY OF ACCOUNTING LITERATURE

U.S. GAAP addresses certain specific transactions. Additional general guidance has been derived from the FASB Concepts Statements and SAB Topic 13, *Revenue Recognition* (ASC 605-10-S99). This chapter provides a discussion of both the specific and the applicable general guidance.

In the late 1970s, the AICPA and the FASB attempted to develop standards on common accounting issues in service transactions. The AICPA developed an exposure draft of a proposed SOP, which was subsequently issued as an FASB Invitation to Comment (1978). Although this document is sometimes referenced for suggested accounting guidance, it never went beyond the Invitation to Comment stage and, therefore, is not authoritative literature.

REVENUE RECOGNITION LITERATURE

Publication	ASC	ASC Topic	Subject
SAB Topic 13	605-10-S99	Revenue Recognition	Revenue Recognition
CON-5	N/A	N/A	Recognition and Measurement in Financial Statements of Business Enterprises
FAS-48	605-15-25	Revenue Recognition	Revenue Recognition When Right of Return Exists
FAS-68	730-20	Research and Development	Research and Development Arrangements
FTB 90-1	605-20-25	Revenue Recognition	Separately Priced Extended Warranty and Product Maintenance Contracts
SOP 81-1	605-35	Revenue Recognition	Construction-Type and Certain Production-Type Contracts
EITF 91-6	980-605-25	Regulated Operations	Long-Term Power Sales Contracts
EITF 91-9	605-20-25-13	Revenue Recognition	Revenue and Expense Recognition for Freight Services
EITF 00-21	605-25	Revenue Recognition	Revenue Arrangements with Multiple Deliverables

SUPPORTING LITERATURE

Publication	ASC	ASC Topic	Subject
APB-21	835-30	Interest	Interest on Receivables and Payables
FAS-5	460	Guarantees	Warranties
FAS-140	405-20	Liabilities	Extinguishments of Liabilities

Publication	ASC	ASC Topic	Subject
FIN-45	460	Guarantees	Guarantees
EITF 88-18	470-10-25	Debt	Sales of Future Revenues
EITF 01-8	840-10-15	Leases	Determining Whether an Arrangement Contains a Lease

GENERAL CONDITIONS FOR REVENUE RECOGNITION

Revenue from service transactions should be recognized when it has been earned and is realized or realizable. Revenue from services is generally earned either as the services are performed or when they are complete and is usually considered realizable once the customer has committed to pay for the services and the customer's ability to pay is not in doubt. However, many uncertainties may exist in service transactions that affect the amount and timing of revenue recognition (CON-5, pars. 83–84).

As discussed in Chapter 3, "General Principles," revenue is considered earned and realizable when all of the following conditions are met:

1. Persuasive evidence of an arrangement exists.

2. The arrangement fee is fixed or determinable.

3. Delivery or performance has occurred.

4. Collectibility is reasonably assured.

The analysis of the first and fourth conditions does not change significantly based on the type of transaction involved. See Chapter 3, "General Principles," for discussion of the persuasive evidence and collectibility conditions. The balance of this chapter focuses on the analysis of the performance and fixed or determinable fee conditions in service transactions.

PERFORMANCE

The evaluation of a service transaction requires an understanding of the pattern of delivery or performance. Performance determines the extent to which the earnings process is complete and whether the customer has received value from the service. The key question in service transactions is whether performance involves single or multiple acts. As discussed in Chapter 3, the Proportional Performance model often is applied to service transactions because delivery or performance occurs over time. However, the pattern of delivery or performance is not always clear or determinative. In certain service transactions, the customer does not receive any value from the service until it is completed. In these cases, revenue recognition should occur pursuant to the Completed Performance model.

Performance Is a Single Act

In some service transactions, performance consists of a single act. For example, a customer may pay a stylist for a haircut. Determining when performance has occurred for this type of transaction is not difficult and using either the Completed Performance or Proportional Performance model will result in the recognition of the same amount of revenue at essentially the same time.

Performance Involves Multiple Acts

When performance involves multiple acts, it is necessary to determine whether the Completed Performance model or Proportional Performance model should be used to evaluate when the delivery criterion has been met and revenue earned. When the performance of multiple acts spans more than one accounting period, this determination will affect the amount and timing of revenue recognized in each period.

The Proportional Performance model is often appropriate for service transactions because the customer typically receives value as the services are performed. For example, when a company purchases transaction-processing services for one year, it receives value each time a transaction is processed. Similarly, a company that purchases data warehousing services receives a benefit each time data are stored on the service provider's hardware.

However, the Completed Performance model should be used if services are performed in more than a single act, but the final act is so significant in relation to the overall transaction that substantive performance only takes place when the final act is completed. For example, a real estate agent hired to sell a house performs many acts—running advertisements in newspapers, scheduling showings, assisting in contract negotiations, and coordinating open houses. However, the final act—actually closing on the sale—is so significant that revenue should generally only be recognized at that time, even if a nonrefundable fee was collected when the house was first listed (see the discussion of "Advance Fees" in this chapter).

Determining whether to use the Completed Performance model or the Proportional Performance model requires significant judgment. However, the following factors, if present in a service arrangement, may indicate that the Completed Performance model should be used:

1. *If the seller fails to perform the final act, the customer (or the customer's new service provider) would need to "start over," rather than just pick up where the original vendor left off.* If revenue is truly earned as services are provided, neither the customer nor the customer's new service provider should have to perform activities or services already completed by the original vendor.

2. *Payment terms indicate that no payment is due until the final act is performed.* This may indicate that the parties have agreed that the final act is particularly significant.

3. *The final act is significantly different in nature from the other acts to be performed.* This may indicate that the other acts are simply performed to allow the final and important act to be performed.

4. *The contracts underlying the transaction specify only the final act (i.e., completion of service) and other acts are performed at the seller's discretion.* If the interim acts are not discussed in the contracts, they are unlikely to be important to the customer.

5. *There is significant uncertainty as to whether the vendor can complete all of the acts in the arrangement.* If the vendor is uncertain of its ability to complete the final act or acts, this may indicate that these acts are more difficult and potentially more significant to the arrangement.

ILLUSTRATION: CHOOSING THE DELIVERY MODEL IN A SERVICE TRANSACTION

(Adapted from SAB Topic 13A4d (ASC 605-10-S99, A4d))

Facts: Company M performs claims processing and medical billing services for healthcare providers. In this role, Company M is responsible for preparing and submitting claims to third-party payers, tracking outstanding billings, and collecting amounts billed. Company M's fee is a fixed percentage (e.g., 5%) of the amount collected. If no collections are made, no fee is due to Company M. Company M has historical evidence indicating that the third-party payers pay 85% of the billings submitted with no further effort by Company M.

Discussion: Company M must wait until collections occur before recognizing revenue. Despite the fact that Company M estimates it will not need to put forth any further efforts in 85% of the billings, the fact remains that the final act—collecting on the receivables—is of such significance that revenue should not be recognized until it is completed. The importance of collection, as compared to sending the bills and the other acts Company M performs, is evidenced by the fact that payment is not due until collection occurs.

Applying the Completed Performance Model

Revenue Recognition

When the Completed Performance model is used to assess the delivery criterion, a specific act provides evidence that performance is complete. Revenue is earned at the time this act is completed, provided all other revenue recognition criteria are met.

Recognition of Direct and Incremental Costs

When revenue is not recognized until performance is completed, a question arises about how to account for the direct and incremental costs related to performance. These costs are similar to the costs incurred by a manufacturer to produce inventory for sale. Inventory costs are capitalized on incurrence and expensed as cost of sales as revenues on the product sales are earned and recognized.

When the Completed Performance model is used, costs similar to inventory costs can generally be capitalized (provided they are realizable) and recognized as an expense when the related revenue is recognized. Costs that can generally be capitalized include those that are (a) directly related to the performance of services under the arrangement and (b) incremental to costs that the vendor would have incurred if it did not need to fulfill the contract in question. For additional discussion of cost recognition in these and other situations, see Chapter 8, "Miscellaneous Issues."

Applying the Proportional Performance Model

When delivery in a service transaction is evaluated using the Proportional Performance model, the pattern of performance must be determined. This determination should focus on the pattern of service provided to the customer, rather than on when resources or effort are expended by the service provider.

> **PRACTICE ALERT:** The application of the Proportional Performance model (as discussed in this chapter) should not be confused with the percentage-of-completion method of accounting. As discussed later in this section under "Recognition of Direct Costs," the percentage-of-completion method results in a constant gross margin percentage. This is not necessarily the case when the Proportional Performance model is used. The percentage-of-completion method should only be applied to service contracts that fall within the scope of SOP 81-1 (ASC 605-35). Such contracts are limited to architectural or engineering design services and construction consulting services.

ILLUSTRATION: RECOGNITION BASED ON PATTERN OF SERVICE, NOT PATTERN OF COSTS

(Adapted from SAB Topic 13A3f, ques. 1 (ASC 605-10-S99, A3f, ques. 1))

Example 1:   A company charges users a fee for nonexclusive access to its web site, which contains proprietary databases. The fee allows access to the web site for a one-year period. After the customer is provided with an identification number and trained in the use of the database, there are no incremental costs that will be incurred in serving this customer.

Example 2:   An Internet company charges a fee to users for advertising a product for sale or auction on certain pages of its web site. The company agrees to maintain the listing for a period of time. The cost of maintaining the advertisement on the web site for the stated period is minimal.

Example 3:   A company charges a fee to host another company's web site for one year. The arrangement does not involve exclusive use of any of the hosting company's servers or other equipment. Almost all of the projected costs will be incurred upon the initial loading of information on the host company's Internet server and setting up appropriate links and network connections.

Discussion: In these instances, some argue that revenue should be recognized when the initial setup is completed because the ongoing obligation involves minimal cost or effort and is therefore perfunctory or inconsequential. However, the substance of each of these transactions indicates that the purchaser pays for a service that is delivered over time. As a result, revenue recognition should also occur over time, reflecting the pattern of provision of service rather than in proportion to the costs incurred or efforts expended.

Identifying the Acts That Trigger Revenue Recognition

Acts that actually provide value to the customer are the only ones that should trigger revenue recognition in a service transaction. Setup or administrative activities generally should not trigger revenue recognition. The following factors may indicate that a particular task is insufficient to trigger revenue recognition:

1. *The task is not identified in the service contract.* In general, an unspecified task is less likely to represent an item that provides value to the customer and more likely to be an internal process of the vendor.

2. *The task relates to building the vendor's infrastructure or training its employees to be able to perform services for the customer.* These are tasks that are performed to allow the provision of service during

the contract term. They generally do not independently provide value to the customer.

3. *The task is purely administrative in nature.* Administrative tasks, such as setting up a customer account, billing the customer, and responding to routine information requests are only *indirectly* related to providing the contracted-for service.

4. *The customer would not be aware that the task was performed.* Tasks that provide value to the customer and thus appropriately trigger revenue recognition should generally be visible to the customer.

There is not necessarily a link between the level of costs incurred related to a particular act and whether that act should trigger revenue recognition. For example, if an act results in the incurrence of substantive costs, that fact alone should not result in the conclusion that the act triggers revenue recognition (SAB Topic 13A3f, ques. 1) (ASC 605-10-S99, A3f, ques. 1). That determination should generally be based on whether value is provided to the customer, not on the level of costs associated with the act.

> **OBSERVATION:**   Selecting which acts in a service arrange-
> ment should trigger revenue recognition is very similar to iden-
> tifying the various deliverables in a multiple-element arrangement
> (see Chapter 4, "Multiple-Element Arrangements"). In fact, service
> transactions with multiple activities are, in substance, multiple-
> element arrangements. Whether the contract is analyzed as a
> multiple-element arrangement or not, the result should be the
> same—actions that do not contribute toward providing value to
> the customer should not trigger revenue recognition.

Pattern of Revenue Recognition

Once the acts triggering revenue recognition have been identified, it is necessary to determine the pattern of revenue recognition as these acts are performed.

> **DISCLOSURE ALERT:**   See Chapter 12, "Disclosures," for
> information about disclosures that may be required.

Specified number of similar acts   If the transaction involves a specified number of identical or similar acts (e.g., the processing of bi-weekly payroll checks by a payroll processor), an equal amount of revenue should be recognized for each act. Even if the cost to provide each act varies—for example, because of a learning curve faced by the service provider—the same amount of revenue should be recognized each time the act is performed.

In some arrangements, the customer does not take advantage of all of the service to which it is entitled. This is referred to as "breakage." For example, if the arrangement is to process mortgage payments for the life of a mortgage, the service provider may be able to estimate, based on typical early payoff experience, that the mortgage will last for much less than its stated 30-year term. A service provider that believes it will actually perform fewer acts than the maximum number specified in the arrangement may also believe that revenue should be recognized based on this lower estimate, thereby allocating more revenue to each act. In certain circumstances, this is permissible. See the discussion in the "Evaluating the Revenue Recognition Conditions" Section of Chapter 3, "General Principles," for more information.

Specified number of non-similar acts Some service transactions involve multiple dissimilar acts. For example, consider a lawn care company offering complete landscaping services on an annual basis. The service includes mowing, watering, fertilizing, trimming, and replanting. When a service transaction involves a specified number of defined acts that are not identical or similar, revenue should be allocated on the basis of the relative value of each act. In substance, this type of transaction is a multiple-element arrangement (see Chapter 4, "Multiple-Element Arrangements"). If there is insufficient evidence to determine the fair values of each of the separable acts, revenue should be recognized on a systematic and rational basis over the estimated period (generally the service or contract term) during which the acts will be performed. One such basis may be the residual method discussed in Chapter 4. Where no systematic and rational basis well represents the pattern in which performance takes place, revenue should be recognized on a straight-line basis.

> **OBSERVATION:** As noted above, if a single service requires multiple acts that *are not* similar in nature and there is insufficient fair value evidence to allocate the arrangement consideration to each act, it may be appropriate to recognize revenue on a straight-line basis over the performance period. If, however, an arrangement includes two separate *services* for which there is insufficient evidence of fair value to facilitate the allocation of revenue using either the relative fair value or residual method, revenue recognition is unlikely to be appropriate until the performance period for *both* services has begun. This situation must be analyzed as a multiple-element arrangement, as discussed in Chapter 4.

Determining whether a situation involves a single service with multiple acts or multiple services requires judgment. For example, a vendor that replaces transmissions performs two or more acts in doing so (e.g., removes old transmission, installs new transmission). However, the replacement of the transmission is generally viewed as one service. Conversely, a vendor that agrees to replace a customer's transmission and provide an oil change is clearly providing two services.

> **OBSERVATION:** When a service provider constructs assets that it will own and operate to provide contractual services, these assets should not be considered separate deliverables. As discussed earlier, the construction of these assets represents a setup activity that the service provider must perform in order to provide the contractual services. Therefore, these acts should not trigger revenue recognition.

> **SEC REGISTRANT ALERT:** In a December 2002 speech, the SEC staff discussed service contract revenue recognition. The SEC staff stressed that registrants should consider whether service contracts contain multiple elements that should be evaluated for separation in accordance with EITF 00-21 (ASC 605-25). As a result, registrants should not default to treating a service contract as one bundled arrangement for revenue recognition purposes.

Unspecified number of similar acts for a specified period If a service transaction involves an unspecified number of identical or similar acts with a fixed period of performance (e.g., a maintenance contract on office equipment), revenue should be recognized ratably over the specified period during which the acts will be performed, unless evidence suggests that some other method is more representative of the pattern in which performance takes place. The seasonality of service or prior experience regarding the pattern of performance may constitute such evidence. For example, an annual contract to provide road maintenance in a cold-weather location would likely involve a higher percentage of services provided during winter months compared with the summer.

Unspecified number of similar acts for an unspecified period Some service contracts provide for a service to continue indefinitely or for the lifetime of the service provider or the customer. For example, a muffler shop may offer a lifetime guarantee on its service for an extra fee. This unlimited extended warranty could require the muffler shop to perform an unspecified amount of additional work over a long period of time. Similarly, a health club may offer a lifetime membership in exchange for a large one-time fee (either with or without ongoing periodic fees).

In these situations, the contractual service period is indefinite. When this is the case, it is generally appropriate to recognize revenue over an estimated service period. To the extent that sufficient data exists to estimate the expected service period or the amount of service that will be provided, revenue should be allocated to each act or time period based on these estimates.

However, if there is no basis upon which to estimate either the service period or the amount of service that will be provided, revenue should only be recognized when performance is complete, or when breakage actually occurs (e.g., the health club member terminates his or her membership).

Recognition of Direct and Incremental Costs

Long-term service contracts are fairly common and are frequently used in outsourcing arrangements. For example, a business may hire a service provider to manage its information technology or transportation functions. Long-term service contracts are also used in the management of certain projects, such as testing programs for new drugs and health care products.

As discussed in Chapter 9, "Contract Accounting," long-term contracts to deliver products or equipment are accounted for under the percentage-of-completion method, a particular application of the Proportional Performance model, if the scope criteria in SOP 81-1 (ASC 605-35-15) are met. Except in the case of engineering or architectural design and construction consulting services, which produce an end-product in the form of intellectual property, percentage-of-completion accounting should not be applied to service contracts. Therefore, although the application of the Proportional Performance model to service transactions frequently results in revenue recognition based on the percentage of completion of the service, it is not appropriate to recognize costs in the same manner. Direct and incremental costs of services accounted for under the Proportional Performance model should, in most cases, be recognized as incurred, even if they are not incurred ratably as services are provided.

> **SEC REGISTRANT ALERT:** In a December 2002 speech, the SEC staff discussed the issue of applying percentage-of-completion accounting to service contracts that are outside the scope of SOP 81-1 (ASC 605-35). The SEC staff stressed that SOP 81-1 (ASC 605-35) and, therefore percentage-of-completion accounting, should not be applied to service contracts that do not fall within its scope. The only service contracts that fall within the scope of SOP 81-1 (ASC 605-35) are those for architectural or engineering design services and construction consulting services.

In many of these contracts, the service provider expects the contract to be profitable over the contract term. This is because productivity increases over the course of the contract, which lowers the direct cost of providing the service and makes the final years of the contract more profitable than the early years. If the percentage-of-completion method were applied, gross margin would be recognized based on the estimated revenues and costs over the term of the contract. However, for a service contract, this method of accounting is not acceptable. Direct and incremental costs of providing the service should be expensed as incurred, rather than spread over the contract term. Therefore, margins are likely to vary over the course of a long-term service contract; however, the varying margins appropriately reflect performance in the different periods.

> ☛ **PRACTICE POINTER:**   Because the costs in a long-term service contract are likely to be higher in the initial years, some service providers structure their contracts to have higher payments in the early years (or require a significant upfront payment or incorporate liquidated damages clauses) in order to balance the contract's cash inflows and cash outflows. However, changes in the timing of customer payments do not result in a similar change to when revenue should be recognized. In general, revenue should still be recognized ratably over the service period unless the service to the customer is also greater in the beginning of the contract.

Recognition of Initial and Setup Costs

As discussed earlier, vendors sometimes perform acts that do not trigger revenue recognition but result in costs. For example, a company that agrees to manage a database may incur costs to convert the data into a format that works with its systems. Other companies may incur costs related to contract procurement, such as a sales commission. Under certain conditions, these costs may be capitalized as an asset and expensed as revenue is recognized over the term of the service arrangement. For a detailed discussion on this topic, see Chapter 8, "Miscellaneous Issues."

EXAMPLE: COSTS OF SETUP ACTIVITIES

Electronic Data Systems Corporation Form 10-K—Fiscal Year Ended December 31, 2007

The Company also defers and subsequently amortizes certain setup costs related to activities that enable the provision of contracted services to the client. Such activities include the relocation of transitioned employees, the migration of client systems or processes, and the exit of client facilities acquired upon entering into the client contract. Deferred contract costs, including setup costs, are amortized on a straight-line basis over the remaining original contract term unless billing patterns indicate a more accelerated method is appropriate. The recoverability of deferred contract costs associated with a particular contract is analyzed on a periodic basis using the undiscounted estimated cash flows of the whole contract over its remaining contract term. If such undiscounted cash flows are insufficient to recover the long-lived assets and deferred contract costs, including contract concessions paid to the client, the deferred contract costs and contract concessions are written down by the amount of the cash flow deficiency. If a cash flow deficiency remains after reducing the balance of the deferred contract costs and contract concessions to zero, any remaining long-lived assets are evaluated for impairment. Any such impairment recognized would equal the amount by which the carrying value of the long-lived assets exceeds the fair value of those assets.

EXAMPLE: SETUP ACTIVITIES

Acxiom Corporation Form 10-K—Fiscal Year Ended March 31, 2009

The Company provides database management and IT management services under long-term arrangements. These arrangements may require the Company to perform setup activities such as the design and build of a database for the customer under the database management contracts and migration of the customer's IT environment under IT management contracts. In the case of database management contracts, the customer does not acquire any ownership rights to the Company's intellectual property used in the database and the database itself provides no benefit to the customer outside of the utilization of the system during the term of the database management arrangement. In some cases, the arrangements also contain provisions requiring customer acceptance of the setup activities prior to commencement of the ongoing services arrangement.

Upfront fees billed during the setup phase for these arrangements are deferred and setup costs that are direct and incremental to the contract are capitalized and amortized on a straight-line basis over the service term of the contract. Revenue recognition does not begin until after customer acceptance in cases where contracts contain acceptance provisions. Once the setup phase is complete and customer acceptance occurs, the Company recognizes revenue over the remaining service term of the contract. In situations where the arrangement does not require customer acceptance before the Company begins providing services, revenue is recognized over the contract period and no costs are deferred.

ADVANCE FEES

Service Fee Paid in Advance

Service providers may require payment in advance. The advance payment may be either refundable (i.e., the customer may cancel the arrangement and receive a refund) or nonrefundable (i.e., the customer is not entitled to cancel the arrangement and receive a refund). In the case of a refundable advance fee, revenue should not be recognized upon collection of the fee because the fee is neither earned nor realizable.

When a nonrefundable advance fee is paid, the realizability condition for revenue recognition is satisfied. However, the fact that an advance payment is nonrefundable does not overcome the fact that performance has not yet occurred. Therefore, revenue should not be recognized until performance occurs and the revenue is earned.

> ☞ **PRACTICE POINTER:** Some contracts that include a fee to be paid upon signing specify that the fee is intended to compensate the service provider for services rendered prior to contract execution. In general, it is not appropriate to allocate a fee in a service arrangement to activities that occurred before the arrangement was signed.

Initiation and Installation Fees

A service transaction may require a nonrefundable initiation fee with subsequent periodic payments for future services (e.g., an activation fee for a cellular telephone with monthly payments based on usage) or a nonrefundable fee for installation of equipment essential to providing the future services with subsequent periodic payments for the services (e.g., a fee charged to install and connect a security alarm with monthly payments for the ongoing security monitoring).

Initiation and installation services may be services in and of themselves. This is the case when installation or initiation services meet the conditions necessary for separation from the other services in the contract, pursuant to the model discussed in Chapter 4, "Multiple-Element Arrangements." If these conditions are met, revenue allocated to the initiation or installation services may be recognized when these services are provided as long as the other conditions for revenue recognition have been met. If the initial fee is greater than the amount allocated to initiation or installation services, the difference should be treated as an advance fee for the other services in the arrangement and recognized as these services are provided.

In other instances, no separate services are provided at the outset of the arrangement in return for the initiation or installation fee, or, if services are performed, they do not meet the separation conditions discussed in Chapter 4, "Multiple-Element Arrangements" (e.g., the services do not provide standalone value to the customer). When this is the case, the fee charged for the installation or initiation service should be deferred and recognized as the other services in the arrangement are performed. In substance, the initial fee is an advance charge for future services, rather than a charge for a separate service.

The period over which the deferred upfront fee should be recognized should extend beyond the initial contractual period if the relationship with the customer is expected to extend beyond the initial term and the customer continues to benefit from the payment of the upfront fee (e.g., if subsequent renewals do not include a similar fee) (SAB Topic 13A3f, ques. 1) (ASC 605-10-S99, A3f, ques. 1). In addition, customers may pay a higher upfront fee for additional services, custom features, or functionality. Upon renewal, the customers would continue to benefit from these incremental services, features, or functionality. Therefore, it would be appropriate to recognize the upfront fees over the *expected* customer relationship term rather than the initial term.

EXAMPLES: SERVICE AND ACTIVATION FEES PAID IN ADVANCE

Covad Communications Group, Inc. Form 10-K—Fiscal Year Ended December 31, 2007

The Company recognizes upfront fees associated with service activation over the expected term of the customer relationship, which is presently estimated to be twenty-four to forty-eight months using the straight-line method. The Company includes revenue from sales of CPE and other activation fees for installation and setup as upfront fees because neither is considered a separate unit of accounting. Similarly, the Company treats the incremental direct costs of service activation, which consist principally of CPE, service activation fees paid to other telecommunications companies and sales commissions, as deferred charges in amounts no greater than the aggregate upfront fees that are deferred, and such incremental direct costs are amortized to expense using the straight-line method over a range of twenty-four to forty-eight months.

United States Cellular Corporation Form 10-K—Fiscal Year Ended December 31, 2008

Activation fees charged with the sale of service only, where U.S. Cellular does not also sell a handset to the end user, are deferred and recognized over the average service period. U.S. Cellular defers recognition of a portion of commission expenses related to activations in the amount of deferred activation fee revenues. This method of accounting provides for matching of revenues from activations to direct incremental costs associated with such activations within each reporting period.

License or Processing Fees

Fees may be received in exchange for a license or other intangible right or for the performance of certain administrative tasks related to a future service (e.g., processing a health club membership application). In many cases, the license provided or the services performed do not constitute deliverables that a customer would pay for, absent an ongoing service arrangement. In these situations, the upfront deliverables do not result in revenue recognition upon delivery, because they do not have value to the customer on a standalone basis (see Chapter 4, "Multiple-Element Arrangements," for further discussion). Like initiation or installation fees that cannot be separately accounted for, these fees should also be deferred and recognized over the performance period of the remaining services in the arrangement. As noted above, this period may extend beyond the initial contractual performance period if renewals are expected and the customer continues to benefit from payment of the up front fee.

ILLUSTRATION: UPFRONT FEES

(Adapted from SAB Topic 13A3f, questions 1 and 2 (ASC 605-10-S99, A3f, ques. 1 and 2), and questions 11 and 12 in the SEC staff's frequently asked question and answer document on SAB 101, *Revenue Recognition in Financial Statements*. Although not codified in SAB Topic 13 presently, the examples continue to be relevant in understanding the accounting for upfront fees.)

Facts: An arrangement provides a lifetime membership to a health club. An initiation payment compensates the health club for processing the application, providing a membership kit to the member and assigning the member a locker. The member then pays a monthly fee for continued access to the facility. Assume that this arrangement is a single unit of accounting under EITF 00-21 (ASC 605-25) (see Chapter 4, "Multiple-Element Arrangements").

Discussion: This transaction should be accounted for under the Proportional Performance model, because service is provided throughout the term of the arrangement. The customer receives no separate value from the application processing and the membership kit and would not pay for them absent the contract to use the club. Therefore, these acts do not trigger revenue recognition. Instead, the fee charged should be deferred and recognized as the rest of the services (health club access) are provided.

Because the arrangement is a lifetime membership, the upfront fee that is deferred should be recognized over the estimated customer relationship period, assuming that this period can be estimated. If it cannot be estimated, the initiation fee should be deferred until the relationship period can be estimated or the customer's membership terminates because he or she stops making monthly payments.

Facts: An arrangement involves the installation of an additional telephone jack at a residence and the activation and provision of local phone service to the new owners. The installation of the additional jack may be performed at the same time as activation of phone service or at a different time. The customer pays an activation fee, a fee to install the additional jack, and a monthly fee for the local telephone service.

Discussion: The provision of telephone service should be accounted for under the Proportional Performance model. The activation services do not provide the customer with any value absent the ongoing telephone service and therefore no revenue should be recognized upon activation. The activation services and ongoing telephone service represent a single unit of accounting under EITF 00-21 (ASC 605-25) (see Chapter 4, "Multiple-Element Arrangements"). The additional telephone jack, however, provides added value to the homeowner (by increasing the value of his or her home), regardless of the provision of service. Therefore, revenue may be recognized upon the installation of the additional jack. The amount allocated to the installation of the additional telephone jack should be determined using the guidance in Chapter 4, "Multiple-Element Arrangements." Any amount received upfront in excess of the amount allocated to the installation of the additional telephone jack (perhaps some or all of the amount labeled an activation fee) should be deferred and recognized over the period that telephone service will be provided. Because this period is unspecified, the deferred fee should be recognized over the estimated service period, assuming this period can be estimated.

Facts: Company A provides its customers with activity tracking or similar services (e.g., tracking of property tax payment activity, sending delinquency letters on overdue accounts) for a ten-year period. Company A requires customers to prepay for all of the services for the term specified in the arrangement. The ongoing services to be provided are generally automated after the initial customer setup. At the outset of the arrangement, Company A performs setup procedures to facilitate delivery of its ongoing services to customers. These procedures consist primarily of establishing the necessary records and files in Company A's pre-existing computer systems. Once the initial customer setup activities are complete, Company A provides its services in accordance with the arrangement. Company A is not required to refund any portion of the fee if the customer terminates the services or does not utilize all of the services to which it is entitled. Assume that this arrangement is a single unit of accounting under EITF 00-21 (AC 605-25) (see Chapter 4, "Multiple-Element Arrangements").

Discussion: The customer cannot, and would not, separately purchase the setup services without the ongoing services. The customer contracted for the ongoing activity tracking service, not for the setup activities. Provided all other revenue recognition criteria are met, service revenue should be recognized on a straight-line basis, unless evidence suggests that the revenue is earned or obligations are fulfilled in a different pattern over the contractual term of the arrangement or the expected period during which those specified services will be performed, whichever is longer.

POST-PERFORMANCE OBLIGATIONS

Customer Acceptance Provisions

Customer acceptance provisions generally allow the customer to cancel the arrangement if the service does not meet expectations. The existence of such provisions raises questions as to whether the earnings process is complete when the service is performed, or only after customer acceptance has been obtained. When services are subject to customer acceptance, the terms of these provisions determine what accounting model to apply. Generally, customer acceptance provisions and the related accounting take one of the four forms discussed below (for a flow chart on evaluating customer acceptance provisions, see Exhibit 5-2 in Chapter 5, "Product Deliverables").

Service Performed for Trial or Evaluation Purposes

Sellers often provide their services on a trial basis to potential customers to facilitate an evaluation. For example, a health club may offer a trial period during which the customer has access to all the benefits of membership before being obligated to pay for membership.

Demonstration or trial arrangements do not constitute sales and no revenue can be recognized prior to acceptance by the customer. The passage of a specified interval without rejection or affirmative acceptance by the customer is required to trigger a purchase obligation and provide persuasive evidence of an arrangement. Revenue may be recognized after acceptance provided the other conditions for revenue recognition have been met (SAB Topic 13A3b, ques. 1) (ASC 605-10-S99, A3b, ques. 1).

☛ **PRACTICE POINTER:** No amount of evidence of the ability to develop reasonable and reliable estimates of the percentage of demonstration or trial arrangements that result in sales will permit revenue recognition prior to acceptance because a trial or demonstration arrangement is not a sale. By contrast, subjective customer acceptance clauses and refund rights do not absolutely preclude revenue recognition because a sales agreement is in place before the services are performed.

Because these rights provide customers with protections similar to those in a trial or evaluation period, companies may want to change their trial contracts accordingly. This may allow a company to recognize revenue at an earlier point in time.

Subjective Right of Return

Certain customer acceptance provisions permit the buyer to request a refund or refuse payment in the event he or she is dissatisfied with the service for any reason. An example of such a provision is a "100% satisfaction guarantee." Acceptance provisions based on wholly subjective terms are, in substance, general rights of return. Thus, this class of acceptance provisions should be accounted for in accordance with FAS-48 (ASC 605-15-25) and related interpretations. (See SAB Topic 13A3b, question 1 (ASC 605-10-S99, ques. 1), and "Cancellation or Refund Rights" in this chapter).

Customer Acceptance Based on Meeting Standard Seller-Specified Performance Criteria

These provisions give customers the right to a refund or to withhold payment for a service that is ineffective, fails to meet advertising claims, or does not meet the vendor's published specifications. For example, an Internet service provider may guarantee that certain up-time targets will be met, which would give a customer the right to cancel the arrangement and receive a refund if they are not. In other cases (e.g., a car repair with a guarantee), the seller may have the right to perform the service a second time, rather than refund the purchaser's money.

This type of acceptance provision is usually offered (a) when the seller is reasonably certain the service will meet the applicable specifications, and (b) to every customer of a particular class. If the seller has previously demonstrated its ability to meet the specified criteria, the customer acceptance provision should be accounted for as a warranty (see "Service Warranties" in this chapter).

However, revenue recognition (and warranty accounting) is not appropriate when the seller has not previously demonstrated that it can perform the service to the stated specifications because it is not yet clear that the specified service has been delivered. Revenue should be deferred until the specifications have been achieved or the customer accepts the service (SAB Topic 13A3b, ques. 1) (ASC 605-10-S99, A3b, ques. 1).

Customer Acceptance Based on Customer-Specified or Negotiated Criteria

This type of acceptance provision, which is the most complex, is generally included in arrangements with customized services. These provisions usually give the seller a period of time after initially performing the service to resolve any problems that might exist in meeting the criteria. Because the service provider must continue to work until the performance conditions are satisfied, it may not be possible to conclude that obligations under the arrangement have been substantially performed until these specifications are met.

Therefore, when customer-specified acceptance provisions exist, the seller must be able to reliably demonstrate that the service meets (or will meet upon completion, if revenue on the service is to be recognized using the Proportional Performance model) the acceptance criteria prior to revenue recognition. This may be possible if the criteria are objective or if the company has provided similar services to the customer in the past.

However, if unique aspects of the customer's environment could affect whether the service meets the specified criteria, or if other circumstances exist that prohibit the seller from verifying compliance with the acceptance provisions until the service has been completed, revenue should not be recognized until compliance can be verified. Verification often consists of formal customer sign-off that the acceptance provisions have been met. However, if the seller can verify that the service meets the acceptance criteria and therefore believes it would be able to enforce a claim for payment even though formal customer sign-off has not occurred, revenue may be recognized because the seller has fulfilled all terms of the contract. As with any accounting treatment that is based on a legal interpretation, consultation with legal experts may be necessary to determine the appropriate treatment (SAB Topic 13A3b, ques. 1) (ASC 605-10-S99, A3b, ques. 1).

> **OBSERVATION:** Acceptance provisions based on criteria specific to a particular contract or customer must be evaluated on a contract by contract basis. Therefore, the timing of revenue recognition may not be the same for different contracts.

> **DISCLOSURE ALERT:** See Chapter 12, "Disclosures," for information about disclosures that may be required.

> **SEC REGISTRANT ALERT:** In early 2003, the SEC staff issued the Summary by the Division of Corporation Finance of Significant Issues Addressed in the Review of the Periodic Reports of the Fortune 500 Companies (the Fortune 500 Report). This report resulted from the SEC's Division of Corporation

Finance's (Corp Fin) review of all annual reports filed by Fortune 500 companies and provides insight into areas commonly questioned by the SEC staff during its reviews of annual reports. One area specifically mentioned in this report relates to customer acceptance clauses. The SEC staff noted that the quality of disclosures related to customer acceptance clauses requires improvement.

Service Warranties

Many service arrangements include a warranty provision that gives the purchaser some protection in the event the service does not provide the expected benefits. Automobile mechanics, carpenters, and electricians are among the service providers that often provide these warranties. Usually, a service warranty requires the vendor to perform the service a second time if the work does not produce results in accordance with published specifications for some period. Because warranty provisions may involve different types of obligations, it is important to understand the substance of these obligations in order to properly account for the warranty. For example, if the seller commits to ensure that the service will meet certain specifications beyond those that it usually meets, the seller will likely be unable to determine how much performance will be required to meet the specifications. In these cases, revenue should only be recognized when the specifications are achieved.

In addition, certain warranties may include obligations other than ensuring that the service continues to meet specifications. These additional deliverables should not be accounted for as part of the warranty. Rather, an arrangement that includes the right to future additional products or services should be accounted for as a multiple-element arrangement (see Chapter 4, "Multiple-Element Arrangements"). Therefore, a portion of the arrangement fee in these situations should be allocated to the additional deliverables and deferred until the seller fulfills its obligations related to the additional products or services.

As noted above, most service warranty provisions merely require that the seller perform the service a second time if it does not provide the intended results (and fix any damage caused, if applicable). Warranty obligations are usually explicit in the service contract, but may also be implied or required by laws or regulations (e.g., many states require certain licensed service providers to provide a limited warranty with their services). Because of an explicit or implicit warranty commitment, the seller's performance obligation may not end when the initial service is completed. At the very least, the seller must stand ready to honor the warranty for whatever period of time it is in force.

One possible method of accounting for a sale with a warranty would be to treat it as a multiple-element arrangement with the initial service and the warranty as separate deliverables. The amount of revenue allocated to the warranty would then be recognized over the warranty period. Another method would be to consider the warranty part of the original service, rather than as a separate service. If analyzed this way, a question arises as to whether the warranty obligation is significant enough to prevent revenue recognition on the original service. If it is significant, then revenue could not be recognized until the warranty expires. Conversely, if the warranty obligation were deemed insignificant, all revenue would be attributed to the original service and recognized when that service is performed, assuming all other revenue recognition criteria are met.

U.S. generally accepted accounting principles (GAAP) recognizes the merit in both of these approaches. When a standard warranty is given to all customers, it is considered inseparable from the service. However, when the warranty is separately priced so that some customers may opt to pay for it while others do not, the warranty is considered a separate service (i.e., a separate deliverable) consistent with the way it is sold.

Standard Warranties

When a service provider offers a standard warranty to all of its customers, the warranty is not treated as a separate service. Instead, it is considered an integral part of providing the service under the arrangement. Revenue may be recognized as the service is performed (assuming other revenue recognition conditions are also met) when a standard warranty is included in the transaction, provided that the costs of honoring the warranty can be reliably estimated. In these cases, the estimated costs of honoring the warranty must be accrued as a cost of sales when revenue is recognized. Accrued costs should be updated as estimates change.

However, if the costs of honoring the warranty cannot be reliably estimated and the potential range of loss is wide, revenue should be deferred until either a reliable estimate of the costs can be made or the warranty period expires (FAS-5, par. 25) (ASC 460-10-25-4). Indicators that costs may not be reliably estimable include (a) the service is new or is being provided by new personnel, (b) the scope of a warranty has been extended beyond what has normally been given in the ordinary course of business, and (c) new obligations have been undertaken.

> **DISCLOSURE ALERT:** See Chapter 12, "Disclosures," for information about required disclosures.

Separately Priced Extended Warranty and Product Maintenance Contracts

Revenue from separately priced extended warranties and product maintenance contracts should be deferred and recognized over the contract period. A warranty is priced separately any time a customer has the option to buy the service with or without the warranty. For example, assume that everyone who has their brakes replaced at a national chain gets a one-year warranty on the work, but that three-year protection is available for an additional charge. The arrangement should be accounted for as having a one-year standard warranty and a two-year separately priced extension. As a result, the fee paid for the two-year extension should be deferred and recognized as revenue in years two and three after the brake job has been performed. The charge for the brake job with the standard one-year warranty should be recognized as revenue when the job is completed, as long as the other revenue recognition conditions are met *and* the costs of honoring the one-year warranty can be reliably estimated.

Revenue attributable to a separately priced extended warranty contract should be recognized on a straight-line basis unless historical evidence indicates that the costs of performing services under the contract are incurred on other than a straight-line basis. If costs are incurred on other than a straight-line basis, revenue should be recognized over the contract period in proportion to the costs expected to be incurred in performing services under the contract (FTB 90-1, par. 3) (ASC 605-25-25-3).

> **OBSERVATION:** A company that sells an extended warranty may purchase insurance to cover its potential losses. Although purchasing insurance may transfer the risk of loss under the contract to the insurance company, the seller remains liable for the warranty obligation in the event that the insurance company cannot or will not honor the insurance coverage. Because the seller has neither fulfilled its obligation nor been released by the buyer from that obligation (i.e., the buyer was not a party to the insurance contract), purchasing insurance to cover the risk of loss under a warranty contract should not trigger revenue recognition. The accounting for the warranty contract and the accounting for the insurance should be considered separately.

> **DISCLOSURE ALERT:** See Chapter 12, "Disclosures," for information about required disclosures.

Other Post-Performance Obligations

Service providers may assume obligations that continue after the main service has been completed. For example, a transaction processor may agree to provide information about the transactions it processes over a specified period. Whenever a service provider agrees to perform multiple services, or takes on continuing performance obligations, the arrangement should be accounted for as multiple-element arrangement. See Chapter 4, "Multiple-Element Arrangements," for further discussion.

CANCELLATION OR REFUND RIGHTS

In product sales, customers often have the right to return a product and receive a full refund if they are not satisfied. Although not as common, service transactions may have similar provisions. For example, membership warehouse clubs typically charge an annual fee that is wholly refundable for some period of time after the beginning of the term. Other service providers may offer "100% satisfaction guarantee or your money back." The accounting for product return rights is addressed in FAS-48 (ASC 605-15-25), which allows revenue recognition when a return right exists, provided that certain conditions are met (see Chapter 5, "Product Deliverables"). However, this guidance does not apply to service transactions (FAS-48, par. 4) (ASC 605-15-15-3).

> **OBSERVATION:** The guidance in this section applies to service transactions with full refund rights. However, some service transactions may have cancellation provisions that reduce the refundable amount as time passes or as service is provided. These refund rights only need to be considered if some revenue that would be recognizable absent the refund right is potentially subject to refund. Because refund rights in these situations generally expire ratably and the service is usually delivered ratably, such rights do not usually limit revenue recognition.

> ☛ **PRACTICE POINTER:** Cancellation or refund rights are often documented in the sales contract. However, these rights may also exist due to industry practice, company policy, or federal, state, and local laws and regulations. In the evaluation of cancellation or refund rights, all rights, whether or not explicitly stated, must be considered.

Potential Accounting Treatments

Although FAS-48 (ASC 605-15-15) specifically excludes service transactions from its scope, many companies have applied similar accounting to refundable service transactions. As a result, revenue is recognized upon performance of the service and an estimate of refunds is accrued. Some, however, believe this treatment is not acceptable for service transactions.

There are strong arguments on both sides of this issue. Supporters of the analogy to FAS-48 (ASC 605-15-15) note that the standard allows revenue recognition on a product sale even though a right of return exists in situations where the vendor has fulfilled its obligations and the amount of revenue is reasonably estimable. They believe the same conditions often exist in a service transaction with refund rights.

Those who believe the analogy is inappropriate argue that the differences between product and service transactions warrant different treatment of refund rights. They also believe that a refund obligation is within the scope of FAS-140 (ASC 405-20), which only allows financial liabilities to be derecognized if (1) the debtor pays the creditor and is relieved of its obligation for the liability (*paying the creditor* includes delivery of cash, other financial assets, goods or services, or reacquisition by the debtor of its outstanding debt securities) or (2) the debtor is legally released from being the primary obligor under the liability (FAS-140, par. 16) (ASC 405-20-40). Since a refund obligation is only relieved when it is paid or expires, such an analysis would result in no amount potentially subject to refund being recognized as revenue. A second argument is that unlike a product refund wherein the product is returned to the seller, a service transaction cannot be undone once it has been performed. Thus, the customer ultimately keeps the results of the service without paying for it.

In the end, the decision regarding which model to apply to refundable service transactions is an accounting policy decision that a company must make (SAB Topic 13A4a, ques. 3) (ASC 605-10-S99, A4a, ques. 3).

> **DISCLOSURE ALERT:** Companies should disclose their choice of accounting policy for service transactions with a right of refund. See Chapter 12, "Disclosures," for additional discussion of accounting policy disclosures.

Applying FAS-48 (ASC 605-15-25) by Analogy

If a company elects to apply a policy similar to the accounting specified in FAS-48 (ASC 605-15-25), it must determine whether the applicable requirements have been met. The criteria of FAS-48, par. 6 (ASC 605-15-25-1), are as follows, as they would be applied to a service transaction:

1. *The sales price to the buyer is fixed or determinable.* This shows that the refund period is not part of the transaction's pricing negotiations. If the arrangement does not meet this criterion, no revenue should be recognized because a fixed or determinable price is a prerequisite to revenue recognition.

2. *The buyer has economic substance apart from the seller.* A sale to a company with little substance (or primarily that provided by the seller) raises significant questions about the buyer's ability to pay. In such a case, the seller should not record the sale.

3. *The seller does not have significant obligations for future performance relating to the refundable service.* If the seller is required to continue performing additional work for the customer until the refund right lapses, the performance criterion may not have been met.

4. *The amount of future cancellations and refunds can be reasonably predicted.* This is the most subjective criterion and is often not met. See below for further discussion.

Estimating Refunds

It is often straightforward to determine whether a reasonable estimate of refunds can be made. For example, if a service has been provided to the same group of customers and has generated a consistent rate of refund requests for many years, this rate can be expected to continue in the future, provided there are no external factors that might change this experience. By contrast, a start-up company or one that sells a new service may not be able to estimate the level of refunds. The following factors should be considered in the evaluation of whether an estimate of refunds can be reasonably made (FAS-48, par. 8) (ASC 605-15-25-3):

1. *The service is susceptible to significant external factors, such as the introduction of competitors' services with superior technology or greater expected market acceptance, that affect market demand for the seller's service offerings.* When the cancellation period is lengthy, it may be difficult to predict the economic and technological life of (i.e., demand for) the service. It may also be harder to forecast competitors' actions and customers' responses to market factors.

2. *The cancellation period is long.* The longer the cancellation or refund period, the more difficult it becomes to predict the level of refund requests. The determination of length should be based on the nature of the service, industry practice, and the type of customer.

3. *The absence of relevant historical experience.* Without historical experience to reference, customer actions may be impossible to predict. In the absence of company-specific experience, industry experience may be relevant. However, because the identity of the service provider may greatly affect customer satisfaction, industry experience may be less relevant in service transactions than in product transactions.

4. *The absence of a large volume of relatively homogeneous transactions.* It is generally difficult to predict the actions of a particular customer. However, it is easier to predict the actions of a large number of customers.

5. *The service is new.* The newer the service offering, the less specific refund experience that exists. Depending upon the circumstances, refund experience for similar services may be relevant.

> **OBSERVATION:** The ability to estimate refunds may vary from location to location, customer to customer, and arrangement to arrangement. Thus, it is possible that a company may be able to estimate refunds for certain transactions but not others. In addition, when a company sells various types of services or serves market segments whose cancellation rates are expected to vary, the company should develop different estimates for each type of service or market segment.

> **SEC REGISTRANT ALERT:** The SEC staff believes that it is preferable to apply FAS-140 (ASC 405-20) to refundable service transaction fees and thereby defer revenue recognition until the refund period expires (SAB Topic 13A4a, ques. 4) (ASC 605-10-S99, A4a, ques. 4). However, the SEC staff will accept an analogy to FAS-48 (ASC 605-15-25) if the criteria discussed above under are satisfied. With respect to estimating the refunds to be provided, the staff believes all of the following must be true for an acceptable estimate to be made (SAB Topic 13A4a, ques. 1) (ASC 605-10-S99, A4a, ques. 1):

> • The estimates of terminations or cancellations and refunded revenues are being made for a large pool of homogeneous items (e.g., membership or other service transactions with the same characteristics such as terms, periods, class of customers, nature of service).

> • There is a sufficient company-specific historical basis upon which to estimate the refunds and the company believes that such historical experience is predictive of future events. The SEC staff generally believes that a company introducing new services or servicing a new class of customer should wait until it has at least two years of experience before concluding that sufficient company-specific historical evidence exists.

> • Reliable estimates of the expected refunds can be made on a timely basis. The SEC staff considers any of the following to be indicative of an inability to make reliable estimates:

> —There are recurring, significant differences between actual experience and estimated cancellation or termination rates (e.g., an actual cancellation rate of 40% versus an estimated rate of 25%) even if the effect of the difference on

the amount of estimated refunds is not material to the consolidated financial statements.

—There are recurring variances between the actual and estimated amount of refunds that are material to either revenue or net income in quarterly or annual financial statements.

—There is more than a remote chance that material adjustments (both individually and in the aggregate) to previously recognized revenue would be required.

—The customer's termination or cancellation and refund privileges exceed one year.

DISCLOSURE ALERT: See Chapter 12, "Disclosures," for information about required disclosures.

Accounting for Refund Rights

If revenue is not recognized when the service is performed because of the inability to estimate refunds, the seller should defer revenue recognition until either the cancellation period has expired or information allowing the company to make a reasonable estimate becomes available (FAS-48, par. 6) (ASC 605-15-25-1). In this situation, any cash collected should be reflected as a liability, rather than as revenue. Costs related to providing the service should still be recognized as incurred, because unlike refund rights in product transaction, the seller cannot reclaim anything of value from the customer in the event the customer requests a refund.

When a company chooses the FAS-48 (ASC 605-15-25) method of accounting, it must meet the conditions discussed earlier to recognize revenue net of estimated refunds. Although revenue is reduced for the amount of estimated refunds, a similar reduction is generally not reflected in cost of sales. If revenue is recognized in earnings over the service period, adjustments for changes in estimated refunds should be recorded by adjusting the revenue, deferred revenue, and refund obligations at each financial statement date to the amounts that are appropriate based on the latest refund estimate (SAB Topic 13A4a, ques. 1) (ASC 605-10-S99, A4a, ques. 1).

ILLUSTRATION: SERVICE SOLD WITH RIGHT OF REFUND

Facts: Marketing Company sells 100 memberships to its travel club at $120 per membership. Customers may cancel their membership at any time during the one-year term of the membership. Any customer who does so receives a full refund of the membership fee. Ten customers request a refund after three months and 30 others request a refund just before the end of the membership period.

EXAMPLE 1

Additional Facts: Marketing Company has a policy of waiting until the refund period expires before recognizing revenue, thereby treating the refund provision as a monetary liability pursuant to FAS-140 (ASC 405-20).

Accounting:

Upon sale:

- Payment is received, but no revenue is recognized.

Cash	$12,000	
Deposit Liability		$12,000

After three months:

- Cash is refunded to the 10 customers that request refunds.

Deposit Liability	$1,200	
Cash		$1,200

At the end of the year:

- Cash is refunded to the 30 customers that requested refunds.

Deposit Liability	$3,600	
Cash		$3,600

- Revenue on the remaining memberships is recognized in full because the refund period has expired and performance has occurred.

Deposit Liability	$7,200	
Revenue		$7,200

EXAMPLE 2

Additional Facts: Marketing Company follows a policy of recognizing revenue on sales of memberships with a refund right as long as refunds can be estimated. This is similar to the accounting treatment under FAS-48 (ASC 605-15-25) for product sales with a right of return. Because this travel club is a new offering, Marketing Company concludes that it cannot reliably estimate the amount of refunds.

Accounting:

Same as in Example 1.

EXAMPLE 3

Additional Facts: Marketing Company follows a policy of recognizing revenue on sales of memberships with a refund right as long as refunds can be estimated. In this case, Marketing Company originally estimates a 30% refund rate, but changes the estimate to 40% when 10 customers request a refund after three months. Marketing Company has sufficient evidence to support its refund estimates.

Accounting:

Upon sale:

- Payment is received, but no revenue is recognized because performance has not occurred. Based on its estimates of expected refunds, Marketing Company records both deferred revenue and a monetary liability.

Cash	$12,000	
Deferred Revenue		$8,400
Deposit Liability		$3,600

During the first three months of the membership:

- Revenue is recognized ratably on those memberships for which refunds are not expected.

Deferred Revenue	$2,100	
Revenue		$2,100

After three months:

- Cash is refunded to the 10 customers that request refunds.

Deferred Liability	$1,200	
Cash		$1,200

- Based on its new estimate of refunds, Marketing Company adjusts the remaining deferred revenue and deposit liability balances, as well as the revenue recognized in the three months that have elapsed.

Deferred Revenue	$900	
Revenue		$300
Deposit Liability		$1,200

During the remaining nine months of the membership:

- Revenue is recognized ratably on those memberships for which refunds are not expected.

Deferred Revenue	$5,400	
Revenue		$5,400

• Cash is refunded to the 30 customers that request refunds.

Deposit Liability	$3,600	
Cash		$3,600

SELLER-PROVIDED FINANCING AND GUARANTEES

Sales with Extended Payment Terms

Some sellers may provide financing for their customers' purchases by agreeing to receive fixed payments over a long period of time, rather than in advance (see "Advance Fees") or in accordance with normal payment terms. Except in sales of software products, (see Chapter 10, "Software—A Complete Model"), U.S. GAAP does not provide specific guidance on when extended payment terms should prevent revenue recognition. However, extended payment terms can affect two of the four conditions for revenue recognition: (1) a fixed or determinable fee and (2) collectibility is reasonably assured.

Extended Payment Terms and Fixed or Determinable Fees

Extended payment terms raise the risk that the service provider will offer additional products or services or reduce the arrangement fee to ensure payment according to the stated terms, even for a credit-worthy customer. For example, a dissatisfied customer, who does not have a warranty, may withhold payment and require the seller to renegotiate the terms of the arrangement. Therefore, extended payment terms should be evaluated, along with warranty, refund, customer acceptance, and similar provisions, to determine whether the arrangement fee is fixed or determinable. If both the payment terms and performance of the service are extended such that the payment terms mirror the performance, revenue recognition may not be delayed. However, if the payment terms extend beyond completion of the service or are disproportionately delayed until the end of a long service period, the timing of revenue recognition may be affected.

Extended Payment Terms and Collectibility

The longer the payment terms, the more difficult it is to conclude that collection is reasonably assured. If collection is not reasonably assured, no revenue or receivable should be recorded. It is

unacceptable to record revenue and a selling expense for the anticipated bad debt because the threshold criteria for revenue recognition
have not been met.

Discounting Long-Term Receivables

When services are sold on terms that extend significantly beyond the
point in time that revenue is recognized, the long-term receivable,
and therefore the revenue, should be recorded at the present value
of the payments, rather than the nominal value. Interest income
would be accrued on the receivable until all payments are made.
Therefore, when extended payment terms are stated at their
nominal values, a portion of the payments will be attributed to
interest income, as opposed to revenue (APB-21, par. 12) (ASC
835-30-25). However, if the payment terms are extended but merely
reflect the proportional performance of the contract, no discounting
is required.

Guaranteeing a Loan in Connection with a Sale of Services

A company may agree to guarantee amounts borrowed (from third-
party lenders) by a customer to buy the company's services.
Although the company has collected cash, it has effectively sold
the services on extended payment terms pursuant to the loan
terms. Therefore, prior to recognizing any revenue, the company
should evaluate whether collectibility is reasonably assured as if it
were the lender in the transaction.

If the company concludes that collection is reasonably assured
and all other revenue recognition criteria have been met, FIN-45
(ASC 460) requires the transaction to be treated as a multiple-
element arrangement—the elements are the sale of services and
the loan guarantee. This type of multiple-element arrangement is
discussed in Chapter 4, "Multiple-Element Arrangements."

> **DISCLOSURE ALERT:** See Chapter 12, "Disclosures," for
> information about required disclosures.

REVENUE RECOGNITION FOR SPECIFIC TRANSACTIONS

Accounting standard-setters have addressed the application of the
general revenue recognition guidance (specifically, whether and
when revenue has been earned) to certain service transactions.
This guidance also provides insight, by analogy, into how the general

guidance might be applied to other types of service transactions. The discussion below focuses on two types of service transactions that are addressed in the literature. For a comprehensive listing of the literature that addresses specific transactions, see Chapter 2, "A Brief Survey of Revenue-Related Literature."

Transportation Revenues

One type of transaction for which the application of the Completed Performance or Proportional Performance model is not clear is the provision of freight or shipping services. One argument in favor of assessing the delivery condition using the Proportional Performance model is the fact that the goods get closer to their destination as they progress in the shipping process. However, an argument in favor of assessing the delivery condition using the Completed Performance model is the fact that the customer will not receive value until the goods are delivered to their destination.

Revenue recognition for freight providers in discussed in EITF 91-9 (ASC 605-20-25-13). The EITF concluded that the following four methods of accounting for freight services are acceptable:

1. *Revenue is recognized when freight is received from the shipper or when freight leaves the carrier's terminal with accrual of the estimated direct costs to complete delivery.* This method is considered least preferable by the SEC staff because revenue is recognized before performance. This outcome is also inconsistent with the general revenue recognition principles. Although freight carriers may use this method, other companies should not analogize to this guidance to support revenue recognition before performance.

2. *Revenue and direct costs are recognized when the shipment reaches its destination.* This method applies the Completed Performance model and treats costs as an asset when they are incurred. As a result, costs are recognized at the same time as revenue.

3. *Revenue is recognized when shipment is completed with expenses recognized as incurred.* This method also applies the Completed Performance model, but does not treat costs incurred as an asset. Although acceptable, this method does not match revenue and expenses and may therefore distort results.

4. *Revenue is recognized based on relative transit time in each reporting period with expenses recognized as incurred.* This method applies the Proportional Performance model to the transaction.

> **DISCLOSURE ALERT:** Because freight companies may adopt any of the above four revenue recognition policies, the choice of policy should be disclosed. See Chapter 12, "Disclosures," for additional discussion of accounting policy disclosures.

EXAMPLES: FREIGHT REVENUES

Union Pacific Corporation Form 10-K—Fiscal Year Ended December 31, 2007

Revenue Recognition

We recognize commodity revenue on a percentage-of-completion basis as freight moves from origin to destination. The allocation of revenue between reporting periods is based on the relative transit time in each reporting period with expenses recognized as incurred.

United Parcel Service, Inc. Form 10-K—Fiscal Year Ended December 31, 2007

Revenue Recognition

U.S. Domestic and International Package Operations—Revenue is recognized upon delivery of a letter or package, in accordance with EITF 91-9, *Revenue and Expense Recognition for Freight Services in Process.*

Forwarding and Logistics—Freight forwarding revenue and the expense related to the transportation of freight is recognized at the time the services are performed, and presented in accordance with EITF 99-19, *Reporting Revenue Gross as a Principal Versus Net as an Agent.* Material management and distribution revenue is recognized upon performance of the service provided. Customs brokerage revenue is recognized upon completing documents necessary for customs entry purposes.

Freight—Revenue is recognized upon delivery of a less-than-truckload ("LTL") or truckload ("TL") shipment, in accordance with EITF 91-9.

Swift Transportation Co., Inc. Form 10-K—Fiscal Year Ended December 31, 2006

Cumulative Effect Adjustments

The Company previously recognized operating revenues and related direct costs as of the date freight is picked up for shipment. This revenue recognition policy was consistent with method two under EITF 91-9. Historically, the Company evaluated the materiality of revenue recognition in accordance with method two of EITF 91-9 as compared to a more preferable method (i.e. method three or five) on both a quarterly and annual basis utilizing the rollover method. The Company believes the prior years quarterly and annual consolidated financial statements derived from the application of method two do not differ materially from the results that would have been derived under method three discussed within EITF 91-9 due to the Company's relatively short length of haul, under the rollover method. Pursuant to SAB 108, the Company assessed the materiality using both the rollover and iron-curtain methods. Under the iron-curtain method, the difference between method two under EITF 91-9 and the more preferable method three under EITF 91-9 was considered material to our consolidated financial statements as of and for the year ended December 31, 2006. Accordingly, the Company recorded an adjustment to reduce the opening 2006 retained earnings by $10.2 million to reflect the implementation of SAB 108.

Research and Development Arrangements

Companies often provide research and development (R&D) services in various types of arrangements. In some cases, a customer owns all rights to the results of the R&D. In other cases, the customer funds all or a portion of the R&D and receives some rights to the results of the activities. Certain arrangements also give the company that performs the R&D a right or the obligation to purchase the results of the R&D from the customer.

Because these arrangements are complex, it may be difficult to determine whether revenue should be recognized as R&D is performed or only upon its successful completion. Indeed, because of the existence of a purchase option as described above, it may be unclear whether the payments from the funding party are merely loans, rather than payments for services. Even if it is determined that the payments are for services, the pattern of revenue recognition may still be unclear, particularly if some payments are contingent upon reaching future milestones. Many of the issues on R&D arrangements were addressed in FAS-68 (ASC 730-20). Other issues were addressed in SAB Topic 13 (ASC 605-10-S99) and through the development of industry practice.

> **DISCLOSURE ALERT:** See Chapter 12, "Disclosures," for information about disclosures that are required for companies that perform research and development for others.

Determining the Nature of the Obligation

Payments received from the funding party may be recognized as revenue (using the Proportional Performance model) as R&D services are performed, if the company determines that it has undertaken an obligation to provide services, rather than to repay a loan or to provide a developed product (i.e., an obligation not only to provide services, but to succeed in doing whatever the R&D hopes to do). To reach this conclusion, it must be clear that the funding party bears the risk of the R&D not producing the expected results.

If the company performing the R&D is obligated to repay any of the funds provided by the other parties regardless of the outcome of the research and development, all or part of the risk has not been transferred. The following are examples in which an entity has committed to repay (FAS-68, par. 6) (ASC 730-20-25-4):

- The company guarantees, or has a contractual commitment that assures, repayment of the funds provided by the other parties, regardless of the outcome of the research and development.

- The other parties can require the entity to purchase their interests in the research and development, regardless of the outcome.

- The other parties automatically will receive debt or equity securities of the entity on termination or completion of the research and development, regardless of the outcome.

In each of these cases, it is clear that the "customer" is only lending the company money to fund the R&D, rather than paying the company to perform it, because the "customer" has the ability to get its money back if the R&D fails.

Even if written agreements under the arrangement do not require the entity to repay any funding, other conditions may indicate that the entity is likely to bear the risk of failure. If these conditions suggest that it is probable[1] the company will be required to repay the funding if the R&D fails, there is a presumption that the entity has such an obligation. As discussed under "Cancellation or Refund Rights" in this chapter, refundable service fees should not be recognized as revenue unless the potential refunds can be reliably estimated. Given the customer-specific nature of R&D arrangements, it is unlikely that reliable estimates can be made. The following conditions create the presumption that the entity will repay the other parties if the R&D fails (FAS-68, par. 8) (ASC 730-20-25-6):

- *The entity has indicated the intent to repay all or a portion of the funds provided.*

- *The entity would suffer a severe economic penalty if it failed to repay any of the funds provided to it, regardless of the outcome of the research and development.* An economic penalty is considered "severe" if, in the normal course of business, an entity would probably choose to pay the other parties rather than incur the penalty. For example, if the entity would lose valuable rights to existing products in the event it did not purchase the funding party's interest in the R&D, the funds received should be considered a loan rather than payment for services.

---

[1] Probable is used here consistent with its use under FAS-5 (ASC 450), to mean repayment is likely.

- *A significant related-party relationship between the entity and the parties funding the research and development exists at the time the entity enters into the arrangement.* This indicator is particularly strong if the entity also has the right to purchase the results of the R&D on anything other than a fair value basis. See Chapter 8, "Miscellaneous Issues," for further discussion of related-party revenue transactions.

- *The entity has essentially completed the project before entering into the arrangement.* In this case, it would appear that the funding party is purchasing the results of the R&D, rather than contracting with the company to perform R&D. The payment received is effectively a prepayment for future R&D results if that R&D is successful.

- *The entity is required to make royalty payments to the funding party based on the revenues from products other than (or in addition to) those stemming from the products developed with the funds provided by that party.* In this situation, it would appear that the funding party is purchasing a future payment stream, rather than merely purchasing R&D services. Payments for a future payment stream are generally accounted for as debt (EITF 88-18) (ASC 470-10-25).

Accounting If There Is Deemed to Be an Obligation to Repay the Funding

If the company has an obligation to repay the funding, revenue should not be recognized using the Proportional Performance model. Instead, a liability to repay the funding should be recognized. Revenue might, in these cases, be appropriately recognized under the Completed Performance model if the liability is repaid by delivery of the successful results of the R&D, instead of by paying cash to the funding party.

Accounting If the Obligation Is to Perform R&D Services

If the repayment of any funds provided by the funding parties depends solely on success of the R&D (e.g., royalty payments), the entity should assess performance under the Proportional Performance model and recognize revenue as services are performed, assuming that all other revenue recognition criteria have been met. However, determining the pattern of performance is not always straightforward. In addition, payments may not mirror the pattern of performance, because they are often triggered only when (and if) specific milestones are reached. Such payments are not fixed or determinable until these milestones are achieved and, as a result, the amount of revenue that may be recognized is limited.

Three methods are generally accepted for purposes of determining the pattern of revenue recognition in R&D arrangements.

> **OBSERVATION:** Whether an arrangement to perform R&D services consists of a single unit or multiple units of accounting should be based on the guidance in EITF 00–21 (ASC 605-25) (see Chapter 4, "Multiple-Element Arrangements"). After the units of accounting have been identified, one of the three methods discussed below should be used to determine the pattern of revenue recognition.

Performance-Based Methods

Two of the methods rely on the model in EITF 91-6 (ASC 980-605-25). An analogy is appropriate because the transactions addressed therein also involve situations in which payments under the contract do not mirror performance. The model in EITF 91-6 (ASC 980-605-25) mandates the recognition of revenue based on the lesser of the amount calculated using the proportional performance to date and the amount due under the terms of the contract for work that has already been performed. Thus, if 60% of the service has been provided, but only 55% of the total fee is due, revenue is limited to 55% of the total fee. Conversely, if 60% of the service has been provided, but 65% of the total fee is due, only 60% of the total fee may be recognized.

As noted above, EITF 91-6 (ASC 980-605-25) is the basis for two methods of accounting for R&D service contracts. One of the methods—the Expected Revenue method—uses total expected revenue in applying the model. This calculation bases the estimate of the amount of revenue earned at any point in time on the total revenue the company expects to earn from the contract, including payments that have not yet become due because the milestones to which they relate have not yet been reached. The other method—the Payments Received method—only uses upfront payments and payments related to milestones already reached. Both methods limit the amount of revenue recognized at any point in time to amounts that have become due (and are nonrefundable) under the terms of the contract.

The following steps illustrate the application of these two performance-based methods to R&D contracts:

1. Estimate the percentage of total services that have already been provided.

OBSERVATION: Over time, the estimate of total effort to be expended may change. If this happens, the change in estimate should be accounted for using either the cumulative catch-up method or the prospective method. The cumulative catch-up method effectively provides for a true-up to the new estimate in the current period by calculating revenue as if the new estimate were used all along. The prospective method effectively provides for revenue to be recognized in the current and future periods using the remaining fees to be recognized and the remaining effort to be expended.

☞ **PRACTICE POINTER:** As discussed earlier in this chapter, there may be situations in which the total amount of service to be provided is not estimable, either from a time-based or efforts-based perspective. In these cases, it is not possible to recognize any revenue under the EITF 91-6-(ASC 980-605-25) based methods until performance is complete or the amount of performance that will be required can be reliably estimated. However, the milestone method, discussed below, may be appropriate in these situations.

2. Multiply that percentage by either the total expected payments (Expected Revenue method), or the nonrefundable payments to-date (including those that are contractually due, but have not yet been made, as long as collectibility is reasonably assured) (Payments Received method), depending on which method is to be used.

3. Compare the result of step 2 with the nonrefundable payments received to date (including payments that are contractually due but not yet paid, as long as collectibility is reasonably assured). The lesser of the two is the amount of revenue that should be recognized, cumulatively, on the contract.

An illustration of these methods follows the discussion of the milestone-based method.

EXAMPLES: INITIAL FEE IN A RESEARCH ARRANGEMENT

Immunogen, Inc. Form 10-K—Fiscal Year Ended December 31, 2007

Generally, upfront payments on single-target licenses are deferred over the period of our substantial involvement during development. Our employees are available to assist the Company's collaborators during the development of their products. We estimate this development phase to begin at the inception of the collaboration agreement and conclude at the end of non-pivotal Phase II testing. We believe this period of involvement is, depending on the nature of the license, on average six and one-half years. Quarterly, we reassess our periods of substantial involvement over which we amortize our upfront license fees. In the fiscal year ended June 30, 2007, this reassessment increased the recognition of license and milestone fees by approximately $56,000 from the prior year's estimate. In the event that a single-target license were to be terminated, we would recognize as revenue any portion of the upfront fee that had not previously been recorded as revenue, but was classified as deferred revenue at the date of such termination.

We defer upfront payments received from our broad licenses over the period during which the collaborator may elect to receive a license. These periods are specific to each collaboration agreement, but are between seven and twelve years. If a collaborator selects an option to acquire a license under these agreements, any option fee is deferred and recorded over the life of the option, generally 12 to 18 months. If a collaborator exercises an option and we grant a single target license to the collaborator, we defer the license fee and accounts for the fee as it would for an upfront payment on a single-target license, as discussed above.

In the event a broad-license agreement were to be terminated, we would recognize as revenue any portion of the upfront fee that had not previously been recorded as revenue, but was classified as deferred revenue at the date of such termination. In the event a collaborator elects to discontinue development of a specific product candidate under a single-target license, but retains its right to use our technology to develop an alternative product candidate to the same target or a target substitute, we would cease amortization of any remaining portion of the upfront fee until there is substantial preclinical activity on another product candidate and our remaining period of substantial involvement can be estimated.

Milestone-Based Method

The milestone-based method separates, rather than combines, the upfront and milestone payments. Because the upfront fee does not relate to a discrete earnings process, it should be recognized over the performance period on a systematic and rational basis. If information on efforts expended and total efforts to be expended is available, a percentage-of-efforts based method should most likely be used. If this information is not available, the most likely systematic and rational basis would be a time-based method where the upfront fee is recognized ratably over the performance period. The milestone payments, however, are deemed to relate to the portion of the performance period that is dedicated to achieving the specific milestone. As a result, each milestone is, in substance, treated as if it were a separate contract to be evaluated using a Completed Performance model.

The milestone-based method assumes that each milestone is substantive. If any milestones are not, this method cannot be used. This is because customers would not separately pay for achieving a nonsubstantive milestone. The following questions should be considered in the assessment of whether a milestone is substantive:

- Is substantive effort required to reach the milestone?
- What labor and other costs must be incurred to achieve the milestone?
- What type of skill is required to achieve the milestone?
- How certain is achievement of the milestone?
- Does the amount of the milestone payment seem reasonable in light of the effort required to achieve that milestone?
- How does the elapsed time between the payments compare to the effort required to reach the milestone?

☞ **PRACTICE POINTER:** The milestone-based method, while commonly used, is difficult to justify in most instances. The various milestones would be unlikely to meet the criteria under EITF 00-21 (ASC 605-25) to be separate units of accounting. (See Chapter 4, "Multiple-Element Arrangements.") However, the EITF is currently working on a project that would formally add the milestone method to U.S. GAAP. See Chapter 13, "Future Expectations and Projects," for a discussion of EITF 08-9, *Milestone Method of Revenue Recognition.*

Comparison of Methods

ILLUSTRATION: COMPARISON OF PERFORMANCE-BASED AND MILESTONE-BASED MODELS

Facts: Biotech Company (Biotech) enters into an agreement with Pharmaceutical Company (Pharma) to license Compound A to Pharma for a period of three years. In addition, Biotech agrees to perform research and development for Pharma with the goal of using Compound A to develop a medicinal treatment for acne. Biotech receives $100,000 up front and $200,000 as it meets each of two milestones. For purposes of this example, assume that the milestones are substantive and meaningful. None of these payments ($500,000 in total) are refundable under any circumstances once received. No other continuing performance obligations exist. Biotech estimates that it will spend $50,000, $40,000, and $60,000 of labor costs in Years 1, 2, and 3, respectively, in performing R&D for Pharma. During Year 2, the first milestone is reached. Biotech incurred $50,000 and $40,000 of labor costs in Years 1 and 2, respectively.

Accounting: The license of Compound A and the R&D services are two elements in a multiple-element arrangement. Biotech concludes that these elements cannot be separated given the lack of fair value evidence and the interrelated nature of the license and the research and development activities. Biotech calculates revenue for Year 1 and Year 2 using the two performance-based methods and the milestone-based method as follows:

	Year 1	Year 2
Labor Dollars Expended to Date	$ 50,000	$ 90,000
Total Expected Labor Dollars	150,000	150,000
Percent Complete at End of Year	33%	60%
Upfront Payment Received	100,000	100,000
Milestone Payments Received (Cumulative)	—	200,000
Total Payments Received to Date	100,000	300,000
"Earned" Amount Using the Payments Received Method (Cumulative)	33,333	180,000
Amount to be Recognized Using Payments Received Method (lesser of "earned" amount and payments received) (Cumulative)	**33,333**	**180,000**
Total Expected Payments	500,000	500,000
"Earned" Amount Using the Expected Revenue Method (Cumulative)	166,667	300,000
Amount to be Recognized Using the Expected Revenue Method (lesser of "earned" amount and payments received) (Cumulative)	**100,000**	**300,000**
Amount to be Recognized using Milestone-Based Method (All milestone payments received plus a portion of upfront payment based on percent complete at the end of year) (Cumulative)	**33,333**	**260,000**

Therefore, Biotech calculates revenue for Year 1 and Year 2 using each of the three methods as follows.

	Expected Revenue	Payments Received	Milestone
Year 1	$100,000	$ 33,333	$ 33,333
Year 2	200,000	146,667	226,667
Cumulative through Year 2	$300,000	$180,000	$260,000

Each of the three methods results in a different pattern of revenue recognition over the two-year period. The different patterns result from each method being more or less reliant on certain facts. The performance-based—expected revenue—method's variations are tied primarily to level of effort. However, if the milestone payments do not keep pace with the level of effort expended, the method's variance may also be dependent on the timing of milestone payments. The performance-based—payments received—method's variations are tied primarily to level of effort and timing of milestone payments. The timing of milestone payments affects this method because revenue is calculated based on receipts. This also results in a greater amount of backended revenue (i.e., recognized towards the end of the service period). The milestone-based method's variations depend in part on the approach used to recognize the upfront fee. If an efforts-based approach is used to recognize the upfront fee (as is the case in the illustration above), the milestone-based method's variations will be caused by both level of effort and timing of milestone payments. If a time-based approach is used to recognize the upfront fee, then the milestone-based method's variations will be due solely to the timing of milestone payments.

Which of these methods is preferable depends to a certain extent on the facts and circumstances. However, the performance-based—expected revenue—method is generally preferable in most situations because it results in the ratable recognition of revenue as service is performed, except to the extent that such revenue is not fixed or determinable because its realization depends on achieving a future milestone. Critics of this approach have suggested that the method inappropriately considers revenue from future milestones and therefore violates the fixed or determinable condition. However, because revenue recognition at any point in time is limited to the cumulative nonrefundable payments that have been received (or have become due), only the portions of the fee that are in fact fixed or determinable are recognized.

☞ **PRACTICE POINTER:** The method selected to account for R&D contracts is considered an accounting policy choice. As a result, any change from this method to another must be treated as a change in accounting principle. Such change would have to be considered preferable in order to be effected.

EXAMPLE: COLLABORATION AGREEMENT—LICENSE FEE AND MILESTONE PAYMENTS

Viropharma, Inc. Form 10-K—Fiscal Year Ended December 31, 2007

Wyeth Agreement

In December 1999, the Company entered into a licensing agreement with Wyeth for the discovery, development and commercialization of hepatitis C drugs. In connection with the signing of the agreement, the Company received $5.0 million from Wyeth. This amount is nonrefundable and a portion of it was recorded as deferred revenue at December 31, 1999. This revenue is being recognized as certain activities are performed by the Company over the estimated performance period. The original performance period was 5 years. In 2002, the Company and Wyeth extended the compound screening portion of the agreement by two years, and as a result the Company extended the performance period from 5 years to 7 years. The unamortized balance of the deferred revenue will be amortized over the balance of the extended performance period. Of this deferred revenue, the Company recognized $0.6 million as revenue in each 2006, 2005 and 2004. The revenue was fully amortized as of December 31, 2006, resulting in no deferred revenue on the consolidated balance sheet. In September 2006, the Company agreed to renew some limited preclinical screening activity with Wyeth. The amortization period was not extended to reflect this renewal as the economic benefit of the initial $5.0 million payment is no longer being earned and the Company's involvement with the activity is de minimus.

If drug candidates are successfully commercialized, the Company has the right to co-promote the products and share equally in the net profits in the U.S. and Canada. The Company is entitled to milestone payments upon the achievement of certain development milestones and royalties for product sales, if any, outside of the U.S. and Canada.

In 2000, the Company sold an aggregate of 200,993 shares of common stock to Wyeth for aggregate proceeds of $6.0 million. The sales of common stock were as a result of progress made under the companies' hepatitis C virus collaboration. In August 2006, Wyeth and the Company announced that data indicated that HCV-796 has achieved a "proof of concept" milestone under the companies' agreements. In connection with meeting the proof of concept milestone, Wyeth purchased 981,836 shares of ViroPharma's common stock for a purchase price of $10.0 million which represents the final stock purchase milestone outlined in the companies' agreements.

In June 2003, the Company amended its collaboration agreement with Wyeth to, among other things, focus the parties' screening activity on one target, to allocate more of the collaboration's pre-development efforts to the Company (subject to the Company's cost sharing arrangement with Wyeth for this work), and to clarify certain of the reconciliation and reimbursement provisions of the collaboration agreement. In addition, under the amended agreement both companies are permitted to work outside the collaboration on screening against targets other than the target being addressed by each company under the collaboration. While, in connection with the Company's restructuring in January 2004, it agreed with Wyeth that both parties would cease screening compounds against HCV under the collaboration, in September 2006, the Company agreed to renew some limited preclinical screening activity with Wyeth. During the term of the agreement, the two parties will work exclusively with each other on any promising compounds and in one particular HCV target.

CHAPTER 7
INTELLECTUAL PROPERTY
DELIVERABLES

CONTENTS

BACKGROUND

Many companies earn revenue by permitting others to use their assets. These assets can be tangible or intangible. Some examples include:

- A car rental agency that allows customers to rent vehicles.
- A computer software developer that allows customers to license software products.

- A movie production company that allows customers to license film rights.

- A franchisor that allows customers to use its name and processes.

- A developer of a drug that allows a marketer to sell the drug.

The accounting for transactions in which one company sells the right to use its assets has been debated for many years. However, this debate has not produced a universally applicable model. This is the result of key differences across transaction types, including:

- The term of the arrangement (i.e., limited or in perpetuity);

- The nature of the asset (i.e., tangible versus intangible);

- Whether the right to use is exclusive or nonexclusive;

- Variable or fixed fees; and

- Cancellation and modification provisions.

Certain licenses of intangible assets are addressed in the accounting literature (see "Revenue Recognition for Specific Intellectual Property Transactions" later in this chapter), but many others are not. When a company licenses intellectual property that is not the subject of a specific authoritative pronouncement, the company must consider the license's specific facts and circumstances, the general revenue recognition guidance contained in the FASB Concepts Statements, and the individual pieces of topic-specific guidance that address accounting for the sale of rights to use specific types of assets. SEC registrants must also consider the guidance provided in SAB Topic 13, *Revenue Recognition* (ASC 605-10-S99), as might private companies developing accounting policies.

This chapter explores significant accounting issues that are common in but unique to the sale or licensing of intellectual property assets. Where an intellectual property asset transaction includes multiple deliverables, these accounting issues must be evaluated separately for each deliverable in the arrangement. As discussed in Chapter 4, "Multiple-Element Arrangements," the interrelationship between deliverables in a multiple-element arrangement may give rise to issues beyond those that exist in a single-element transaction.

SURVEY OF ACCOUNTING LITERATURE

The accounting literature that addresses the sale or licensing of intellectual property assets is almost entirely transaction- or industry-based. For example, there is a significant amount of guidance on leasing tangible assets and licensing motion picture rights.

Conversely, with the exception of SAB Topic 13 (ASC 605-10-S99), which addresses several narrow issues on intellectual property licenses in general, there is little or no implementation guidance for transactions that fall outside the scope of the industry- or transaction-based literature.

REVENUE RECOGNITION LITERATURE

Publication	ASC	ASC Topic	Subject
SAB Topic 13	605-10-S99	Revenue Recognition	Revenue Recognition
FAS-45	952-605	Franchisors	Franchise Fee Revenue
FAS-48	605-15-25	Revenue Recognition	Revenue Recognition When Right of Return Exists
SOP 97-2	985-605	Software	Software Revenue Recognition
SOP 00-2	926-605	Entertainment—Films	Accounting by Producers or Distributors of Films
EITF 00-3	985-605-55-119	Software	Arrangements That Include the Right to Use Software Stored on Another Entity's Hardware
EITF 00-21	605-25	Revenue Recognition	Revenue Arrangements with Multiple Deliverables
EITF 03-5	985-605-15-3	Software	Non-Software Deliverables in an Arrangement Containing More-Than-Incidental Software
EITF 07-1	808	Collaborative Arrangements	Accounting for Collaborative Arrangements

SUPPORTING LITERATURE

Publication	ASC	ASC Topic	Subject
APB-21	835-30	Interest	Interest on Receivables and Payables
FAS-13	840	Leases	Leases
FIN-45	460	Guarantees	Guarantees
FSP FIN 45-1	460-10-55-30	Guarantees	Intellectual Property Infringement Indemnifications

GENERAL CONDITIONS FOR RECOGNITION

Revenue from intellectual property transactions should be recognized when it has been earned and is realized or realizable. Revenue is generally earned at either the beginning or throughout the license term, depending upon the nature of the license and the other obligations taken on by the licensor. Such revenue is usually considered realizable once the customer has committed to pay for the license, provided the customer's ability to pay is not in doubt. In licenses of intellectual property, it is common to only have a commitment to make partial payments at the inception of the license, with the customer becoming obligated to make additional payments based on performance milestones, use of the property, or the passage of time. These and other uncertainties may determine the amount and timing of revenue recognition.

As discussed in Chapter 3, "General Principles," revenue is considered earned and realizable when all of the following conditions are met:

1. Persuasive evidence of an arrangement exists.

2. The arrangement fee is fixed or determinable.

3. Delivery or performance has occurred.

4. Collectibility is reasonably assured.

The analysis of the first and fourth conditions above does not change significantly based on the type of transaction involved. Therefore, this chapter primarily focuses on the analysis of the fixed or determinable and delivery conditions in intellectual property transactions.

DELIVERY

The key revenue recognition issue in intellectual property arrangements is whether delivery occurs when the lease or license term begins (Completed Performance model) or throughout the term of the lease or license (Proportional Performance model). To make this determination, it is necessary to assess whether the arrangement is, in substance, the sale of an asset. If the transaction is deemed a sale, the Completed Performance model should be applied. If the seller/licensor does not transfer substantially all of the risks and rewards at the inception of the arrangement, a Proportional Performance model should be applied.

Each arrangement and asset type can have unique characteristics that make this assessment difficult. For a sale of the right to use tangible assets (i.e., leases), detailed guidance is provided in the accounting literature on how to determine whether the Completed Performance or Proportional Performance model applies. This guidance may also be useful, by analogy, in accounting for sales of the right to use intangible assets (i.e., intellectual property licenses).

> **OBSERVATION:** Software and other types of intellectual property are often delivered via a tangible medium. This, however, does not change the fact that the value to the customer is the intellectual property. For example, computer software delivered on a compact disc is actually the sale or license of the software program. The compact disc is merely the tangible medium used to provide the customer access to the intangible computer software program.

Possible Analogies in the Accounting Literature

The accounting literature addresses several types of transactions involving rights to use assets. These transactions include leases, licenses to software, and motion pictures and franchise arrangements. The existing literature discusses when to apply the Completed Performance or Proportional Performance model to assess delivery.

Leases

FAS-13 (ASC 840), the cornerstone literature for accounting by a lessor, has been amended and supplemented by various pieces of other literature. A detailed listing of the relevant authoritative literature addressing a lessor's accounting for lease revenue is included in Chapter 2, "A Brief Survey of Revenue-Related Literature."

FAS-13 provides insight into the question of how to account for a license of intellectual property because the basic model focuses on which party (lessor or lessee) holds the risks and rewards of ownership. The basic model in FAS-13 (ASC 840) requires a lessor to determine whether the substance of the lease is the sale of the asset by focusing on which party (the lessee or lessor) holds the risks and rewards of ownership. If a lease transaction is essentially the sale of an asset, the analysis of delivery should be analogous to that in a product sale (Completed Performance model). If the lease effectively conveys the lessee the right to use the asset for a limited time, delivery should be evaluated as it is in many service transactions (Proportional Performance model).

A lessor uses the following decision tree to determine the appropriate delivery model for a lease:

EXHIBIT 7-1
LEASE FLOW CHART

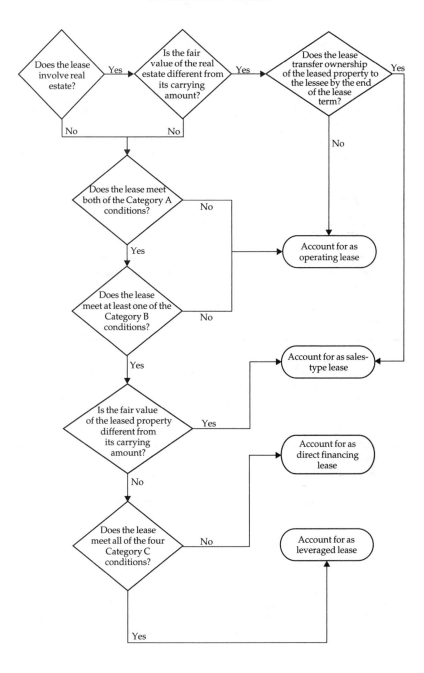

Category A Conditions (FAS-98, par. 22(f), FAS-13, par. 8) (ASC 840-10-25-42)

1. Collections of rentals must be reasonably predictable
2. Significant risks or commitments beyond those related to usual sales warranties cannot be retained or undertaken

Category B Conditions (FAS-13, par. 7) (ASC 840-10-25-1)

1. Title to the leased asset transfers to lessee at the end of the lease term
2. Lessee has option to purchase leased asset at a bargain price
3. Lease term is 75% or more of the estimated useful life of the property subject to the lease
4. Present value of minimum lease payments is 90% or more of the fair value of the leased property less any investment tax credit retained by the lessor

Category C Conditions (FAS-13, par. 42) (ASC 840-10-25-43)

1. Lease involves at least three parties: lessee, long-term creditor, and lessor
2. Long-term creditor financing is substantial and nonrecourse to lessor
3. Lessor's net investment declines during the early years and increases during the later years of the lease term
4. Lessor accounts for any retained investment tax credit as cash flow component of lease

---

The criteria (Category A, B, and C Conditions) focus on whether the lessor has transferred the significant risks and rewards of ownership to the lessee. If the lessor retains the significant risks and rewards, the lease must be treated as an operating lease—that is, the lessor must apply the Proportional Performance model whereby the operating lease payments are recognized as revenue over the lease term. If the lessor transfers the significant risks and rewards of ownership to the lessee, the Completed Performance model should be used. The lease is treated as a sales-type, direct financing, or leveraged lease, as appropriate. Each of these methods results in the application of a variation of the Completed Performance model.

Franchises, Software, and Motion Pictures

Franchise fee revenue recognition is discussed in FAS-45 (ASC 952-605); software revenue recognition is discussed in SOP 97-2, EITF 00-3, and EITF 03-05 (ASC 985-605); and recognition of revenue from the licensing of films is discussed in SOP 00-2 (ASC 926-605). In general, the Completed Performance model is used to evaluate the delivery condition unless certain factors exist. Further discussion of arrangements involving franchises and motion pictures is included later in this chapter. Software revenue recognition is discussed fully in Chapter 10, "Software—A Complete Model."

Choosing the Right Model

The software and motion picture models are comparable because the nature of the licensed property is similar. The franchise model, however, is different, because these arrangements invariably involve a continuing relationship between the parties. Certain characteristics of the FAS-13 (ASC 840) lease model set it apart from each of the above models.

The determination as to which of these models is the best analogy for intellectual property licenses depends on the type of intellectual property involved. For example, content is central to both a manuscript for a novel and a film. Although the content is presented differently (written word versus picture), the nature of the intellectual property involved is the same. As a result, the company trying to sell or license the manuscript should consider applying the guidance in SOP 00-2 (ASC 926-605) to determine when the fees received from sale or licensing should be recognized.

Finding the appropriate analogy for other types of intellectual property is not quite as easy. For example, the value in the formula for a candy bar is realized through the product that the formula produces. SOP 00-2 (ASC 926-605) does not apply because there are no significant similarities between a candy bar formula and a film. The nature of the candy bar formula, however, is somewhat similar to a software program since a computer code works much like a formula. However, the value provided by the software program is completely different from the value provided by a candy bar formula. As a result, SOP 97-2 (ASC 985-605) may not be directly applicable. A franchise agreement may include the rights to food or other formulas. However, there is much more involved in a franchise than merely the transfer of rights to intellectual property such as a candy bar formula. In this instance, FAS-45 (ASC 952-605) is not a clean analogy. A candy bar formula is clearly intellectual property and not a tangible asset. It is, therefore, difficult to apply the FAS-13 (ASC 840) model.

While analogizing to a particular part of the literature can help answer questions that arise, all facts and circumstances related to the intellectual property license must be analyzed in the context of the general revenue recognition concepts and conditions discussed above (see "General Conditions for Recognition") to determine when delivery occurs under the license.

Key Factors in Evaluating Delivery of Intellectual Property

Delivery generally occurs when value is transferred to the customer. In intellectual property transactions, it may be unclear whether value transfers all at once or over time as the right to use the asset is provided. The factors discussed below should be used to determine which model applies and when to begin recognizing revenue.

Commencement of License Term

The earliest point at which delivery can occur is the first day of the license term. For example, if a license arrangement is consummated on March 15, but the license term begins on April 1, the licensor may not recognize any revenue prior to April 1. This approach is consistent with one of the general conditions that must be met to recognize revenue from the sale or license of software and films. This point applies to intellectual property transactions under either the Completed Performance model or the Proportional Performance model. In both cases, no revenue should be recognized until the beginning of the license term (SAB Topic 13A3d and TPA 5100.70) (ASC 605-10-S99, A3d and ASC 985-605-55-103).

Risks and Rewards of Ownership

As discussed above, intellectual property is sometimes delivered on a physical medium. When this is the case, many of the considerations typically involved in product sales are relevant to recognition of revenue from the intellectual property license. For example, intellectual property delivered on a physical medium (e.g., a CD, a book, or printed data) is generally not complete until title transfers, along with the related risks and rewards of ownership of the physical medium containing the intellectual property. See Chapter 5, "Product Deliverables," for discussion of these issues. Chapter 10, "Software—A Complete Model," also discusses how these issues are addressed in the software revenue recognition literature.

Exclusivity

The rights to use tangible assets fundamentally differ from rights to use intangible assets. A specific tangible asset may be used by only one user at a time, whereas a specific intangible asset can be used concurrently by many users. To illustrate this concept, consider an automobile and computer software. The automobile (the tangible asset) may only be rented to and used by one driver at a time, whereas the computer software (the intangible asset) may be licensed to and operated by many users at the same time. This basic distinction has resulted in the development of different accounting models for the sale of rights to use tangible and intangible assets.

However, an arrangement that provides exclusive rights to intellectual property is similar to a product sale because it can only be licensed (or sold) once. An arrangement that provides non-exclusive rights to intellectual property, however, is similar to software and film sales because it can be sold to more than one concurrent user. Therefore, the leasing literature can be used to determine when delivery occurs in an arrangement with exclusivity and the software literature can be used to determine when delivery occurs in a non-exclusive arrangement.

Duration of the Arrangement

Comparing the term of the arrangement with the life of the intellectual property enables the licensor to evaluate whether the arrangement is more similar to the outright sale of a product or a short-term operating lease.

Arrangement term Because licenses of intellectual property (other than those discussed above) are not addressed in the authoritative literature, there is no guidance on how to determine the life of an arrangement that has options or potential extensions. For example, the stated term of the arrangement may be five years. However, provisions in the arrangement may automatically (or on achievement of certain milestones or targets, for example, if neither party has defaulted) extend the term in perpetuity. In this situation, the seller or licensor should carefully consider whether the term of the arrangement is effectively the life of the intellectual property.

Intellectual property life The life of the intellectual property is the time period over which it provides benefits to its owner or users. To establish the life of the intellectual property, the seller or licensor should consider the nature of (1) the legal rights it possesses to the intellectual property and (2) the intellectual property itself. For example, if the intellectual property rights are subject to a patent, the seller or licensor should consider when the patent will expire and whether it will or can be renewed. In addition, the seller or licensor should consider whether the intellectual property rights relate to a technology susceptible to obsolescence, which could result in the economic life being shorter than the legal life.

An arrangement whose duration is for the life of the intellectual property has an attribute similar to a product sale—neither the customer's right to use the intellectual property nor its ownership of the product revert back to the owner after a limited period of time. Duration of the arrangement is also relevant in lease accounting. One of the conditions that qualify an arrangement for sales-type lease treatment is whether the lease term is 75% or more of the estimated useful life of the property subject to the lease.

An arrangement whose duration is shorter than the life of the intellectual property has attributes similar to an operating lease because the rights to use the property will lapse before the end of the property's useful life. (Software sales are often for durations shorter than the life of the software and the software revenue recognition literature relies predominantly on a Completed Performance model.) The primary benefit of considering the duration of the arrangement arises when it is evaluated in conjunction with exclusivity.

Exclusivity/Duration Matrix

Different combinations of exclusivity and duration affect the analysis of which model—Competed Performance or Proportional Performance—is most appropriate. The following matrix outlines which model(s) can be justified in accounting for the sale or license of intellectual property based on the confluence or divergence of exclusivity and duration:

	Term equal to life of intellectual property	Term less than life of intellectual property
Exclusive	**Quadrant I** **Completed Performance**	**Quadrant II** **Proportional Performance**
Non-exclusive	**Quadrant III** **Completed or Proportional Performance**	**Quadrant IV** **Completed or Proportional Performance**

Quadrant I

When intellectual property is licensed to a customer for the duration of its life and on an exclusive basis, it is very similar to an outright product sale. Therefore, a Completed Performance model is generally most appropriate. In an outright product sale, except for normal rights of return that are accounted for separately in accordance with FAS-48 (ASC 605-15-25), the product will not revert to the seller.

Similarly, the right to use the intellectual property will not revert to the seller or licensor during the intellectual property's life if the license is exclusive and its term is equal to the intellectual property's remaining useful life. Furthermore, as in an outright product sale where the specific product is sold only to one customer, intellectual property sold on an exclusive basis is only licensed to one customer.

> **OBSERVATION:** Intellectual property may be licensed on an exclusive basis for use in either specific geographic areas or specific applications. For example, a specific medical compound may be licensed exclusively to one researcher for use in developing a treatment for one medical condition and also exclusively licensed to a second researcher for use in developing a treatment for a different medical condition. Similarly, a candy bar formula may be licensed exclusively to one company for the North American region and licensed exclusively to a second company for the European region.

Quadrant II

When intellectual property is licensed to a customer for less than the duration of its life and on an exclusive basis, a Proportional Performance model is generally most appropriate, because the license is similar to an operating lease. In an operating lease, the right to use the asset will revert to the lessor at the end of the lease term. Similarly, the right to use the intellectual property will revert to the seller or licensor at the end of the license arrangement term if the term is less than the life of the intellectual property. The presumption, in both cases, is that the leased asset or licensed intellectual property will have value to the lessor or licensor at that point in time. Furthermore, in an operating lease the asset is only leased to one customer. Likewise, the intellectual property is only licensed to one customer when the terms are exclusive.

> **OBSERVATION:** Although transactions with these characteristics appear similar to operating leases, both SOP 97-2 (ASC 985-605) and SOP 00-2 (ASC 926-605) generally require the use of a Completed Performance model in these situations. Therefore, the operating lease analogy should not be applied to all intellectual property licenses that are exclusive and limited in duration. Each license should be analyzed carefully to reach an appropriate conclusion.

Quadrants III and IV

When a sale or license of intellectual property is non-exclusive, it is not clear whether a Completed Performance model or a Proportional Performance model should be applied. For instance, non-exclusivity is prevalent in software and motion picture arrangements and a Completed Performance model is generally used in both cases. However, the leasing literature requires certain conditions to be met (which are unlikely in the typical intellectual property licensing arrangement) in order to treat the right to use a tangible asset as a sale. This is because ownership of the intellectual property does not usually transfer to the licensee at the end of the arrangement term, the licensee does not usually have the option to purchase the intellectual property at a bargain price, and it is usually not possible to determine whether the present value of the payments under the arrangement are 90% or more of the fair value of the intellectual property due to the complexity of deriving a fair value for these assets. If the term of the arrangement represents 75% or more of the estimated life of the intellectual property, one of the criteria may be satisfied. If this is the case, a Completed Performance model may be the most appropriate.

In many of the Quadrant III and IV situations, a legitimate case might be made for using either the Completed Performance model or the Proportional Performance model. As a result, a seller should determine which model *best* fits the specific facts and circumstances and select it as the accounting policy for the arrangement (and other similar arrangements). If neither model is clearly the best analogy, a seller or licensor of intellectual property will have to choose one of the models to use as its accounting policy in these (and other similar) situations.

> ☞ **PRACTICE POINTER:** Companies in this situation should determine their accounting policy choice after careful consideration. Any change to this policy (i.e., going from a Proportional Performance model to a Completed Performance model or vice versa) is treated as a change in accounting principle. See FAS-154 (ASC 250, *Accounting Changes and Error Corrections*) for the appropriate accounting treatment.

> **DISCLOSURE ALERT:** See Chapter 12, "Disclosures," for information about disclosures that may be required.

> **SEC REGISTRANT ALERT:** In a December 2002 speech, the SEC staff discussed the quality of accounting policy disclosures on revenue recognition. In general, the SEC staff indicated that these disclosures needed to be more complete and precise, particularly with regard to circumstances that could affect the timing and amount of revenue recognized.

FIXED OR DETERMINABLE FEES

Variable Fees

It is common for the fee in a license of intellectual property to depend upon how the property is used by the customer. For example, the fee related to a drug under development may increase if the customer receives FDA approval to begin the next stage of testing. Similarly, fees that result from licensing a customer list may be tied to a specific amount of sales that the licensee generates. These fees, like other fees that depend upon the occurrence of a future event (e.g., receipt of FDA approval), are not fixed or determinable. Chapter 3, "General Principles," includes a general discussion on this topic.

Refund, Return, and Cancellation Rights

General Model

Intellectual property licenses often include rights of return, cancellation, or refund. These rights are generally included in arrangements where intellectual property is licensed to many end customers. For example, the purchase of a movie on DVD usually includes a limited time right of return and the purchase of an annual license to view internet content may include a right that allows a full refund if the purchaser cancels within the first 30 days. Other intellectual property transactions may have specially designed refund or return rights. For example, a license of the rights to a technology being developed may be cancelable by the customer for a full or partial refund if certain milestones in the development of the technology are not reached.

> ☛ **PRACTICE POINTER:** Return rights are often documented in the sales contract. However, such rights may also exist due to industry practice, company policy, or federal, state, and local laws and regulations. In addition, the relationship between the buyer and seller should be evaluated to determine whether unstated rights of return might exist and whether the company has a practice of accepting returns that it is not required to by the contract. All rights of return, whether or not explicitly stated, must be considered. See the return rights Examples in Chapter 5.

Both SOP 97-2 (ASC 985-605) and SOP 00-2 (ASC 926-605) specifically require the use of the guidance in FAS-48 (ASC 605-15-25) when accounting for returns on sales of software and movies. By analogy, FAS-48 (ASC 605-15-25) may be applied to sales of other intellectual property when a right of return exists.

Although a right of return or refund creates a question as to whether the transaction has been completed, the seller records revenue upon delivery when specific criteria are met. However, this is only acceptable when the terms of the arrangement make it clear that a sale has occurred, there are no other contingencies and the likelihood of the customer exercising the right of return can be reliably estimated. If any of these three conditions are not met, the return right makes the transaction incomplete until the return right lapses. Specifically, revenue should be recognized at the time of sale, net of estimated returns, only if all of the following conditions are met (FAS-48, par. 6) (ASC 605-15-25-1):

1. The sales price to the buyer is fixed or determinable.

2. Payment is not contractually or otherwise excused until the product is resold.

3. The buyer holds the risks of destruction, damage, or theft of the property. If not, all of the risks and rewards of ownership have not passed to the buyer and revenue recognition is prohibited.

4. The buyer has economic substance apart from the seller.

5. The seller does not have significant obligations for future performance relating to the resale of the product by the buyer.

6. The amount of future returns and costs expected in connection with any returns can be reasonably predicted.

A detailed discussion of these criteria is provided in Chapter 5, "Product Deliverables." Except for the sixth criterion, the analysis is effectively the same in an intellectual property transaction as it would be in a product sale. The third criterion is relevant in intellectual property transactions when the intellectual property is provided on a physical medium, such as a compact disc. The right-of-return analysis in these situations is essentially the same as in a product sale, including the need to consider whether the buyer holds the "physical risks" related to the tangible medium on which the intellectual property is provided. However, analysis of the sixth criterion in an intellectual property license presents unique challenges, which are discussed below.

Estimating Returns

As discussed in Chapter 5, "Product Deliverables," a large volume of homogeneous transactions is required to estimate the extent to which customers will exercise return or refund rights. In certain types of intellectual property transactions, such as the sales of computer software or videotapes to end-users, there may be a large volume of homogeneous transactions on which an estimate of returns can be based.

However, other licenses of intellectual property, such as licenses to use technology to develop products, or rights to access data such as membership or customer lists, are unlikely to have the requisite large volume of homogeneous transactions. Instead, these transactions are more likely to be "one-off" transactions that include mostly customized terms. To the extent that fees paid by the licensee in these types of arrangements are refundable, they are not recognizable, because a reasonable and reliable estimate of returns cannot be made.

Even when a large volume of homogeneous transactions does exist, other factors might affect the ability to make a reliable estimate of the number of customers that will exercise their rights. These factors are discussed in detail in Chapter 5.

CONTINUING PERFORMANCE OBLIGATIONS

Regardless of the delivery model used to account for the sale or licensing of intellectual property, the seller or licensor must understand the nature of any continuing performance obligations whether related to the license of intellectual property or in separate agreements, such as research and development or contract manufacturing arrangements. Unless the continuing performance obligation meets the requirements to be treated as a separate element in a multiple-element arrangement, the existence of such an obligation affects the timing of revenue recognition. Chapter 4, "Multiple-Element Arrangements," provides an in-depth discussion of the conditions that must be met to conclude that multiple elements can be separated for accounting purposes. Two continuing performance obligations that are common in intellectual property licenses are discussed below.

When-and-If-Available Deliverables

A when-and-if-available clause requires the seller or licensor to make enhancements or other information related to the licensed intellectual property available to the buyer or licensee if it becomes available. For example, if the owner of the rights to a drug licenses them to a third party for use in Japan, a when-and-if-available clause may require the company to provide the customer with the results of any work it performs to improve the drug or get it approved in the U.S. to treat additional conditions.

If delivery of any additional rights or information is required under a when-and-if-available clause, a continuing performance obligation exists in the arrangement. However, in some cases, a when-and-if-available clause is included in an arrangement, but the seller/licensor has no intent to improve upon the product or to develop additional information. Despite this fact, when-and-if-available clauses represent a continuing performance obligation that will be fulfilled over the time period that the clause is in force.

Because a when-and-if-available clause is considered an incremental deliverable, the license agreement must be evaluated under the multiple-element arrangement guidance discussed in Chapter 4, "Multiple-Element Arrangements," to determine whether the intellectual property initially provided under the license agreement should be treated separately from the when-and-if-available deliverable for accounting purposes. As discussed in Chapter 4, a delivered item(s) should be considered a separate deliverable for accounting purposes if all of the following conditions are met (EITF 00-21, par. 9) (ASC 605-25-25-5):

1. The delivered item(s) has value to the customer on a standalone basis. That item(s) has value on a standalone basis if it is sold separately by any vendor or the customer could resell the deliverable on a standalone basis.

2. There is objective and reliable evidence of the fair value of the undelivered item(s).

3. If the arrangement includes a general right of return relative to the delivered item, delivery or performance of the undelivered item(s) is considered probable and substantially within the control of the vendor.

As discussed in Chapter 4, EITF 00-21 (ASC 605-25) applies to all revenue-generating multiple-element arrangements, except for those covered by other authoritative literature, such as SOP 97-2 (ASC 985-605) (see Chapter 10, "Software—A Complete Model"), SOP 00-2 (ASC 926-605) (see "Motion Pictures" later in this chapter), FAS-45 (ASC 952-605) (see "Franchises" later in this chapter), and FAS-13 (ASC 840) (see "Leases" earlier in this chapter). The interaction of this literature and EITF 00-21 (ASC 605-25) is discussed in detail in Chapter 4.

When-and-if available deliverables do not usually impact the assessment of standalone value for the initially licensed intellectual property. However, the second criterion is far more difficult to meet when the undelivered element is a when-and-if-available deliverable. This is because objective evidence of fair value for a when-and-if-available clause often does not exist in industries where these clauses are used infrequently. An exception is the software industry (see Chapter 10, "Software—A Complete Model").

It is possible, however, for the licensor to conclude that a when-and-if-available clause is an inconsequential obligation. If the only remaining obligation is inconsequential, the licensor may determine that it has met the delivery or performance criterion necessary to recognize revenue (SAB Topic 13A3c, ques. 1) (ASC 605-10-S99, A3c, ques. 1). The factors that must be considered are discussed in Chapter 4, "Multiple-Element Arrangements."

A when-and-if-available clause should not be considered inconsequential simply because it does not result in any incremental costs to the licensor. Instead, the analysis should be based on whether any delivery requirements or other obligations (e.g., refunds or concessions) are expected to result from it. If the likelihood that any substantive items will be delivered is remote, then the when-and-if-available clause should be considered inconsequential. In addition, the seller or licensor should be able to explain why the when-and-if-available clause deemed inconsequential was negotiated into the arrangement.

> **OBSERVATION:** SOP 97-2 (ASC 985-605) provides guidance on how to determine when post-contract customer support, including unspecified upgrades and enhancements, may be considered inconsequential. Paragraph 60 of SOP 97-2 (ASC 985-605-25-73) states that:
>
> A determination that unspecified upgrades/enhancements offered during the PCS arrangement are expected to be minimal and infrequent should be evidenced by the patterns of minimal and infrequent unspecified upgrades/enhancements offered in previous PCS arrangements. A conclusion that unspecified upgrades/enhancements are expected to be minimal and infrequent, should not be reached simply because unspecified upgrades/enhancements have been, or are expected to be, offered less frequently than on an annual basis. Regardless of the vendor's history of offering unspecified upgrades/enhancements to initial licensees, PCS should be accounted for separately from the initial licensing fee if the vendor expects to offer upgrades/enhancements that are greater than minimal or more than infrequent to the users or resellers of the licensed software during the PCS arrangement.

Based on the inherent difficulties in assessing the value of a when-and-if-available clause, the seller or licensor must often (a) combine the intellectual property license and the unspecified when-and-if-available deliverables for revenue recognition purposes and (b) conclude that the when-and-if-available clause represents a more than inconsequential performance obligation. This results in the recognition of all revenue over (at a minimum) the term of the when-and-if-available provisions using a Proportional Performance model.

> **DISCLOSURE ALERT:** See Chapter 12, "Disclosures," for information about disclosures that may be required.

Combined License and Research and Development Arrangements

Arrangements that involve licensing intellectual property and providing related research and development services are increasingly common. The licensor typically receives nonrefundable upfront fees, milestone payments, royalties, or a combination of all three. These transactions are multiple-element arrangements with two deliverables: (a) the intellectual property license and (b) the R&D services. Whether these deliverables may be accounted for separately should be determined using the general model discussed earlier under "When-and-If Available Deliverables."

In most cases, the elements in a combined license and R&D arrangement will not meet the necessary conditions for separate accounting treatment. The main reason is that the intellectual property license will rarely have value to the customer on a standalone basis. This is because the owner of the license is usually the only one who has the expertise to perform the R&D. Furthermore, objective evidence of the fair value of the R&D services does not usually exist and, therefore, fair value cannot be determined. When the two elements in this type of arrangement cannot be separated, any initial payment received (often termed a license payment) should be treated as an advance payment for the services and recognized over the performance period (determined based on all of the elements in the arrangement), which may be equal to or greater than the period over which the R&D services are provided. Revenue recognition for R&D services is discussed in detail in Chapter 6, "Service Deliverables."

> **SEC REGISTRANT ALERT:** In a December 2007 speech, the SEC Staff discussed whether a vendor's participation on a joint steering committee (to monitor progress on the R&D) established through a collaborative arrangement constitutes a deliverable under EITF 00-21 (ASC 605-25). The SEC Staff noted that if a contract requires the vendor to participate on such a committee or if the failure to do so would question the vendor's performance under the arrangement, then a presumption exists that participation is obligatory, and, therefore, it should be evaluated as a potential deliverable. This can be important to the revenue recognition period, because such steering committees generally are intended to continue in operation long after the product has been approved, sometimes for the product's entire life.

> **SEC REGISTRANT ALERT:** The SEC Staff has concluded that a nonrefundable upfront payment in an arrangement involving the license of intellectual property and performance of R&D

activities, may not be recognized up front (SAB Topic 13A3f, ques. 1) (ASC 605-10-S99, A3f, ques. 1).

DISCLOSURE ALERT: See Chapter 12, "Disclosures," for information about disclosures that may be required.

EXAMPLES: COMBINED LICENSE AND RESEARCH AND DEVELOPMENT ARRANGEMENTS

Affymetrix Form 10-K—Fiscal Year Ended December 31, 2007

F. Hoffmann-La Roche Ltd.

In February 1998, the Company entered into a non-exclusive collaborative development agreement with F. Hoffmann-La Roche Ltd. ("Roche") to initially develop human probe array-based diagnostic products. Under the terms of the agreement the parties are collaborating to develop mutually agreed upon arrays, as well as associated instrumentation, software, and reagents. In January 2003, the Company expanded its collaboration with Roche by granting Roche access to our GeneChip® technologies to develop and commercialize GeneChip® diagnostic laboratory tests for DNA analysis, genotyping and resequencing applications, as well as for RNA expression analysis, in a broad range of human disease areas. Using our GeneChip® technologies, Roche intends to develop and market diagnostic tests for diseases such as cancer and osteoporosis and cardiovascular, metabolic, infectious and inflammatory diseases. Affymetrix and Roche believe that developing targeted microarray expression profiles for cancer, plus genotyping and resequencing profiles for other diseases will enable the creation and commercialization of novel standardized diagnostic solutions. These solutions ultimately will allow physicians to better diagnose and treat human disease. Under the terms of the collaborative agreement, Roche paid the Company an access fee of $70 million and the agreement also includes a broad range of other compensation payable by Roche to Affymetrix throughout the life of the agreement based on royalties on sales of diagnostic kits and milestone payments for technical and commercial achievements. As part of the agreement, Affymetrix will manufacture and supply Roche with microarrays and related instrumentation based on Affymetrix' GeneChip® platform. In 2003, Roche launched the AmpliChip® CYP450 array product initially for research use only, but in late 2004 obtained CE marking and FDA regulatory approvals of the product for in-vitro diagnostic use.

The parties amended the collaborative development agreement in December 2006. Under the terms of the amendment, Roche is relieved of certain future license installment payments that would have been payable by Roche to Affymetrix under the agreement beginning in 2008, Affymetrix is relieved of certain "most favorable terms and conditions" obligations to Roche, and Roche has agreed to pay to Affymetrix additional milestone payments related to future commercial achievements. The license agreement is subject to Roche's option to terminate on December 31, 2010 or any time on or after December 31, 2015, with one year's prior notice. As part of the arrangement between the parties, Affymetrix will continue to manufacture and supply Roche with microarrays and related instrumentation based on Affymetrix' GeneChip® platform.

The Company has assessed the revenue recognition of the December 2006 collaborative agreement amendment in accordance with EITF 00-21 to account for the multiple deliverables in the arrangement and to evaluate the revenue allocated to each of the units of accounting (the research and development period and the manufacturing and supply period). The Company has established objective and reliable evidence of fair market value for the manufacturing and supply period undelivered unit of accounting based on analysis of the pricing for similar manufacturing and supply agreements sold to other Powered by Affymetrix™ partners on a standalone basis that do not contain a research and development period. The Company has determined that the product transfer pricing, royalties on sales of diagnostic kits and milestone payments for technical and commercial achievements for the manufacturing and supply period unit of accounting in the amended Roche collaborative agreement reflects the established fair market value for these deliverables. In addition, the Company re-assessed the estimated remaining research and development period and determined that Roche's one-time, upfront payment of $70 million under the license agreement, which was paid to Affymetrix in the first quarter of 2003, should continue to be recognized as a component of product related revenue over the remaining estimated research and development period which was estimated to be through fiscal 2007. Research revenue under this contract was approximately $14.2 million for each of the three years ended December 31, 2007, 2006 and 2005, respectively. The amortization of this license agreement was completed in December 2007. The associated research costs are not significant for each of the years presented.

Medarex, Inc. Form 10-K—Fiscal Year Ended December 31, 2007

Pfizer

In September 2004, the Company entered into a series of agreements with Pfizer, Inc. ("Pfizer"). The first agreement amended the Company's existing collaborative research and license and royalty agreements with Pfizer to provide for the discovery and development of up to 50 antibody products over ten years. The second and third agreements were a sublicense from the Company to Pfizer and a cross-license of certain patents and patent applications solely relating to the companies' respective anti-CTLA-4 antibody programs. The fourth agreement was a stock purchase agreement also related to the anti-CTLA-4 programs. Pursuant to certain of these agreements, Pfizer made a cash payment to the Company of $80.0 million and purchased 4,827,808 shares of the Company's common stock at a purchase price equal to $6.21 per share for an aggregate purchase price of $30.0

million. The purchase price represented a small premium to market price at the time the Company entered into the collaboration.

The Company accounts for revenue arrangements that include multiple deliverables in accordance with EITF 00-21. The Company has concluded that because the Pfizer collaboration contains multiple deliverables (licenses to technology and research services) EITF 00-21 applies. The Company considers the arrangement with Pfizer to be a single unit of accounting under EITF 00-21 for purposes of recognizing the initial $80.0 million payment. For the years ended December 31, 2007, 2006 and 2005, the Company recognized $10.7 million, $10.5 million and $9.3 million of revenue under the agreements with Pfizer.

Patent Defense and Maintenance

Intellectual property licenses often require the licensor to defend the validity and legality of underlying intellectual property (patent, trademark, etc.) against future claims. This ongoing obligation might be thought to impact revenue recognition for two reasons. First, it could be considered a separate deliverable in the arrangement. The SEC staff, however, accepts that, although the promise to defend against legal challenges is an obligation, it does not represent a separate deliverable because the licensee receives no additional value from these actions beyond that which was delivered initially. As a result, the presence of such a provision does not, in and of itself, require the licensor to use a Proportional Performance model to account for the arrangement (SAB Topic 13A3g) (ASC 605-10-S99, A3g).

Alternatively, the promise to defend against legal challenges could affect revenue recognition because it appears to be a guarantee within the scope of FIN-45 (ASC 460). However, because the guarantee relates to the performance of an asset of the customer, it scoped out of FIN-45 (ASC 460) for recognition and measurement purposes (FSP FIN 45-1) (ASC 460-10-55-33). The disclosure requirements of FIN-45 (ASC 460) apply, however.

> **OBSERVATION:** If, at the time the license is entered into, the licensor believes that its patent may not be valid or aware that its ownership of the intellectual property may not be legal, it should consider whether revenue should be deferred.

> **DISCLOSURE ALERT:** See Chapter 12, "Disclosures," regarding the disclosure requirements of FIN-45 (ASC 952-605).

Warranties and Customer Acceptance Clauses

Some intellectual property licenses may include warranties and customer acceptance clauses. For example, a customer acceptance clause may allow the customer to cancel the license for a full refund if the technology does not perform to specifications in the license arrangement.

When these clauses are included, their effect on revenue recognition should be evaluated in the same manner as similar clauses in a product sale arrangement. Chapter 5, "Product Deliverables," provides detailed guidance on the accounting for these clauses.

> **DISCLOSURE ALERT:** See Chapter 12, "Disclosures," for information about disclosures that may be required.

SELLER-PROVIDED FINANCING AND GUARANTEES

Licenses with Extended Payment Terms

Some licensors provide financing for their customers' purchases by agreeing to receive fixed payments over a long period of time, rather than full payment at the inception of the license. Except in the sale of software products (see Chapter 10, "Software—A Complete Model"), U.S. generally accepted accounting principles (GAAP) does not provide specific guidance about when extended payment terms should preclude revenue recognition. However, extended payment terms can affect the evaluation of two conditions for revenue recognition: (1) a fixed or determinable fee and (2) collectibility.

Extended Payment Terms and Fixed or Determinable Fees

Extended payment terms raise the risk that, in order to ensure payment according to the stated terms, the licensor will agree to extend the license or otherwise provide the licensee with additional rights related to the intellectual property. For example, a customer that earns less revenue than expected from the licensed technology because of increased competition might withhold a license payment in the hope of terminating the license early, or receiving additional value from the licensor.

If the combination of extended payment terms and risks inherent in the license create a significant likelihood of concessions, payments should only be considered fixed or determinable as they are made. Therefore, revenue related to future payments under extended payment terms would not be recognized, even if delivery has already occurred.

OBSERVATION: SOP 97-2 (ASC 985-605) specifically addresses extended payment terms in the context of software arrangements. The presumption is that the fee is not fixed or determinable if payment terms extend beyond the earlier of the expiration of the license term or one year after delivery. Although no similar presumption exists outside of software arrangements, the guidance in SOP 97-2 (ASC 985-605-25-33 through 25-35) may be a useful analogy for other intellectual property licenses. See Chapter 10, "Software—A Complete Model," for a complete discussion.

Extended Payment Terms and Collectibility

The longer the payment terms, the more difficult it is to conclude that collection is reasonably assured. If collection is not reasonably assured, no revenue or receivable should be recorded. It is unacceptable in these instances to record revenue and a selling expense for the anticipated bad debt because the threshold criteria for revenue recognition have not been met.

Discounting Long-Term Receivables

When intellectual property is licensed on terms that extend significantly beyond the point in time that revenue is recognized, the long-term receivable and the related revenue should be recorded at the present value of the payments, rather than the nominal value. Interest income should be accrued on the receivable until all payments are received. Therefore, when extended payment terms are stated at their nominal values, a portion of the payments will be attributed to interest income, as opposed to revenue (APB-21, par. 12) (ASC 835-30-25-7). In effect, product or service revenue is earned on delivery and as other criteria are satisfied. The recognition of interest income acknowledges the financing provided to the customer. If the payment terms are extended but merely reflect the proportional performance of the contract, no discounting is required. In this case, the extended payments are earned as services are delivered over time; no financing has been provided to the customer.

Guaranteeing a Loan in Connection with a License

A company may agree to guarantee amounts borrowed by a customer to license the company's intellectual property. Although the company has collected cash in this situation, it has effectively licensed the property on extended payment terms pursuant to the loan terms. Therefore, prior to recognizing any revenue, the company should evaluate whether collectibility is reasonably assured as if it were the lender in the loan transaction.

If the company concludes that collection is reasonably assured and all other revenue recognition criteria have been met, FIN-45 (ASC 460) requires the transaction to be treated as a multiple-element arrangement. The two elements are the intellectual property license and the loan guarantee. This type of multiple-element arrangement is discussed in Chapter 4, "Multiple-Element Arrangements."

> **DISCLOSURE ALERT:** See Chapter 12, "Disclosures," for information about required disclosures.

REVENUE RECOGNITION FOR SPECIFIC INTELLECTUAL PROPERTY TRANSACTIONS

As noted in the introductory sections of this chapter, revenue recognition for certain intellectual property transactions is addressed in the accounting literature. These models are generally consistent because revenue is recognized when the four basic conditions for recognition are met. However, because each model was developed to address a narrow set of transactions, the analysis of when the conditions are met is somewhat different in each instance.

Collaborative Arrangements

Significant operating and financial risks of developing and successfully marketing products and services based on intellectual property (as well as other assets) have resulted in the proliferation of the use of collaborative arrangements to share these risks in the biotechnology, pharmaceutical, motion picture, software, and computer hardware industries. The collaborative arrangements involve a wide range of activities from research and development to marketing and distribution and are often conducted through a "virtual joint venture" that does not always include the formation of a legal structure. Within this "virtual joint venture," however, specific activities or operations in certain geographic locations may be conducted through legal structures. Contractual terms governing the sharing of operating responsibilities and the allocation of revenues, expenses, and profits or losses between participants in the arrangement vary widely across arrangements.

Financial reporting of these arrangements is diverse. The diversity often leads to a lack of comparability of arrangements across companies within the same industry. Revenues, reimbursements, and expenses are variously classified and reported either gross or net in the income statements of participants. Some arrangements have been reported under the equity method using APB-18 (ASC 323, *Investments—Equity Method and Joint Ventures*).

In EITF 07-1 (ASC 808), a collaborative arrangement is defined as a contractual arrangement between two or more parties involving a joint operating activity conducted wholly or partly through a legal entity wherein the parties have the following two significant characteristics:

1. They are active participants in the arrangement, with each party doing significantly more than just providing financial resources.

2. They are exposed to significant risks and rewards that are based on the success of the endeavor.

A collaborative arrangement may be subject to EITF 07-1 (ASC 808) even when it is partially conducted through a separate legal entity. The requirements of ARB-51 and FAS-94 (ASC 810, *Consolidation*), APB-18 (ASC 323), FIN-46(R) (ASC 810), or other related accounting standards may apply to the part of the arrangement conducted through a legal entity.

> **DISCLOSURE ALERT:** The disclosure requirements of EITF 07-1 (ASC 808) apply to the *entire* collaborative arrangement even if a part of the arrangement is conducted through a legal entity.

The financial reporting requirements of EITF 07-1 (ASC 808) do not apply to arrangements within the scope of other authoritative accounting literature. This Issue also does not provide any guidance related to recognition and measurement issues (for example, determination of the appropriate units of accounting, the appropriate recognition requirements, or when recognition criteria are satisfied) related to collaborative arrangements.

Participants should evaluate the substance of contractual arrangements at inception to determine whether they are collaborative arrangements. A reconsideration of this assessment would be required whenever changes in the facts and circumstances change either the role of the participants or their exposure to risks and rewards of the arrangement. However, a collaboration agreement can begin at any point in the life cycle of an operating activity.

The determination of whether an entity is (1) an active participant in, and (2) exposed to significant risks and rewards of a collaborative arrangement, and therefore subject to the requirements of EITF 07-1 (ASC 808), calls for significant judgment and is a function of the facts and circumstances specific to the arrangement, including, but not limited to, the terms and conditions of the arrangement.

The Task Force provides the following indicators (not intended to be an exhaustive list) of active participation:

- Directing and conducting the activities of the joint operating activity,
- Sharing responsibilities of a steering committee or other governance mechanism, and
- Ownership or control of a contractual or other legal right to the underlying intellectual property.

The following terms and conditions may indicate that the participants are not subject to significant risks and rewards of the arrangement:

- Compensation for services provided is commensurate with market rates,
- The arrangement permits recovery of all (or substantially all) of the cumulative economic contribution to date in the event a participant quits the arrangement without cause,
- A single participant receives all of the initial profits, and
- A participant is subject to limit risks and/or rewards.

The stage in the life cycle of the endeavor and the expected duration or extent of the participants' financial participation in the arrangement relative to the endeavor's aggregate expected life or total expected value are other factors that should be evaluated in determining whether a participant is exposed to significant risks and benefits of a collaborative arrangement.

The guidance in EITF 99-19 (ASC 605-45) should be used to determine whether revenues generated and costs incurred in transactions with third parties should be reported gross or net on the income statement. All revenues and costs that are subject to other authoritative accounting literature should be accounted for in accordance with that literature.

The income statement characterization of payments between participants in a collaborative arrangement should be based on:

- The nature and contractual terms of the arrangement,
- The nature of each participant's business operations, and
- Whether the payments are subject to other authoritative literature on income statement characterization.

Payments subject to other authoritative literature should be reported pursuant to that literature. The income statement characterization of payments not subject to other authoritative literature should be based on analogy to authoritative literature or a reasonable and rational accounting policy election that must be consistently applied.

Participants in a collaborative arrangement should disclose the following in the initial period and annually thereafter:

- Information about the nature and the purpose of its collaborative arrangements,

- Its rights and obligations in the collaborative arrangements,

- The accounting policy for collaborative arrangements per APB-22 (ASC 235, *Notes to Financial Statements*; 235-10), and

- The income statement classification and amounts attributable to transactions between the participants in the arrangement for each period an income statement is presented.

Separate disclosure is required of information related to individually significant collaborative arrangements.

Software

SOP 97-2 (ASC 985-605) provides two models—Completed Performance and Proportional Performance—to account for software revenue. The correct model to use is dictated by whether the software sold or licensed involves significant production, modification, or customization (collectively referred to as significant changes). If no significant changes are required, a Completed Performance model is used. If significant changes to the software are required, SOP 97-2 (ASC 985-605) requires the use of contract accounting, which generally results in the application of a Proportional Performance model. Software revenue recognition is discussed in Chapter 10, "Software—A Complete Model."

Franchises

FAS-45 (ASC 952-605) provides guidance on the recognition of franchise fee revenue. A franchisor earns franchise fee revenue from the franchisee pursuant to the terms of the franchise agreement. The franchise agreement generally conveys rights to the franchisee such as the right to operate a business using the franchisor's name, the right to use the franchisor's processes, and the right (or requirement) to purchase products or services from the franchisor.

Scope

The arrangement must possess certain characteristics to meet the definition of a franchise agreement in U.S. GAAP.[1] Any arrangement that has these characteristics is a franchise agreement, regardless of whether it is labeled as such and regardless of whether the company in question considers itself to be in the franchising business (FAS-45, par. 26) (ASC 952-605-20):

- The agreement must be written and establish the rights and responsibilities of the franchisor and franchisee for a defined period of time.

- The agreement must have as its purpose the distribution of a product or service, or an entire business concept, within a particular market area.

- The agreement must provide for the franchisor and franchisee to contribute resources for establishing and maintaining the franchise.

- The agreement must outline and describe the specific marketing practices to be followed, specify the contribution of each party to the operation of the business, and set forth certain operating procedures with which both parties agree to comply.

- The agreement must establish the franchised outlet as a business entity requiring and supporting the full-time business activity of the franchisee (i.e., if the outlet is merely an authorized distributor or representative to sell a particular good or service, it is not a franchise).

- The agreement must establish a common identity for the franchisor and franchisee.

> ☞ **PRACTICE POINTER:** It is common for a purported franchise agreement to be missing one or more of the characteristics described above. For example, a trademark license agreement may not require the licensor to do anything other than transfer the trademark to the licensee. As a result, the trademark licensing arrangement would not be considered a franchise agreement for accounting purposes. Other agreements may have the purported franchisee enter into an agency relationship with the franchisor to sell the franchisor's products, or to identify potential franchisees. To the extent that a license agreement does not possess *all* of the characteristics listed above, it is not

---

[1] The need for such an agreement to be in place fulfills the persuasive evidence of an arrangement condition that is a part of all revenue recognition analyses.

considered a franchise agreement under FAS-45 (ASC 952-605). In such cases, revenue should be recognized using the general guidance for intellectual property or service transactions, depending upon the nature of the arrangement.

Franchise Fees

Franchise fees are generally characterized as either initial or continuing. The initial fees are usually paid up front in conjunction with the transfer of intellectual property rights, the performance of initial services, and the sale of proprietary equipment. The continuing fees are usually paid over the life of the franchise agreement. These fees may be paid as the franchisor sells products or services to the franchisee or can be based on a percentage of the franchisee's revenues or another quantitative operating measure. In most cases, the franchise agreement specifies a combination of some or all of these types of fees.

> **DISCLOSURE ALERT:** See Chapter 12, "Disclosures," for information about disclosures that may be required.

EXAMPLE: TYPES OF FRANCHISE FEES

Buffalo Wild Wings, Inc. Form 10-K—Fiscal Year Ended December 30, 2007

(m) Revenue Recognition

Franchise agreements have terms ranging from ten to twenty years. These agreements also convey multiple extension terms of five or ten years, depending on contract terms and if certain conditions are met. We provide the use of the Buffalo Wild Wings trademarks, system, training, preopening assistance, and restaurant operating assistance in exchange for area development fees, franchise fees, and royalties of 5% of a restaurant's sales.

Franchise fee revenue from individual franchise sales is recognized upon the opening of the franchised restaurant when all material obligations and initial services to be provided by us have been performed. Area development fees are dependent based on the number of restaurants in the territory, as are our obligations under the area development agreement. Consequently, as obligations are met, area development fees are recognized proportionally with expenses incurred with the opening of each new restaurant and any royalty-free periods. Royalties are accrued as earned and are calculated each period based on restaurant sales.

Allocation of Initial Franchise Fees

Initial franchise fees compensate the franchisor for providing a bundle of deliverables. These deliverables may include the transfer of rights to certain intellectual property (e.g., restaurant name, logos, formulas) and services necessary to assist the franchisee in opening a franchised outlet (e.g., training, site identification). Specific equipment, products, or supplies may also be included. The initial franchise fee does not necessarily only relate to these initial deliverables. A portion of the fee may also relate to products or services that will be provided to the franchisee in the future. The key to correctly recognizing (with respect to the amount and timing) an initial franchise fee is to allocate it to the various products and services provided.

The initial franchise fee should be allocated based on the following sources of value for each deliverable:

Deliverable	Source of Value
Equipment, supplies and products to be furnished initially	Fair value of the assets
Products to be sold in the future	Either the selling price of the same product to other customers or the cost of the product plus a reasonable profit on the sale
Services to be provided in the future	Cost of providing the service plus a reasonable profit margin
Services and intellectual property rights provided initially	Residual

The method used to allocate the initial franchise fee in a franchise agreement is a residual method. This type of method starts with the total amount to be allocated (the initial franchise fee) and subtracts the values of some, but not all, of the deliverables (equipment, supplies, and products to be provided initially, products to be sold in the future, and services to be provided in the future), leaving the residual to represent the value of the remaining elements (services and intellectual property rights to be provided initially).

> ☛ **PRACTICE POINTER:**   Although using cost plus a reasonable profit margin for purposes of estimating the fair value of products or services provided under a franchise agreement is appropriate, it is generally an inappropriate measure of fair value when allocating consideration among deliverables in other multiple-element arrangements (see Chapter 4, "Multiple-Element Arrangements").

ILLUSTRATION: INITIAL FRANCHISE FEE ALLOCATION

Facts: Franchisor Inc. (Franchisor) enters into a franchise agreement with Franchisee Co. (Franchisee). This agreement meets the conditions of FAS-45 (ASC 952-605-20) and is considered a franchise agreement for accounting purposes. The franchise agreement conveys the right to open a franchised outlet that bears Franchisor's trademark name and that produces and sells Franchisor's secret recipe breads. The term of the agreement is five years. The franchise agreement requires Franchisee to make the following payments to Franchisor: (1) an initial fee of $1,000,000, (2) royalty payments equal to 2% of Franchisee's sales, (3) $50,000 per year for 50,000 pounds of unique organic flours, and (4) $60,000 per year for four seasonal marketing campaigns. The franchise agreement requires Franchisor to provide the following to Franchisee: (1) rights to use its trademark and secret recipes, (2) initial services, including site-selection and site-design assistance and employee training on baking methods, (3) equipment necessary for Franchisee to produce the secret recipe breads, including a specifically designed oven and oven implements, (4) 50,000 pounds annually of unique organic flours, and (5) four seasonal marketing campaigns. The fair value of the specifically designed oven and oven implements is $140,000. The selling price of 50,000 pounds of the unique organic flours to other customers is $60,000. The cost of providing the four seasonal marketing campaigns plus a reasonable profit margin is $75,000.

Allocation: The $1,000,000 initial fee is allocated as follows:

Franchise Element		Amount of Initial Fee Allocated to Element
Oven and oven implements (equipment)		$140,000
Products (organic flours) to be sold in the future		
Selling price to other customers over the term of the franchise agreement ($60,000 per year for 5 years)	$300,000	
Selling price to Franchisee ($50,000 per year for 5 years)	250,000	50,000
Future services (marketing campaigns)		
Cost plus a reasonable profit margin ($75,000 per year for 5 years)	375,000	
Selling price to Franchisee ($60,000 per year for 5 years)	300,000	75,000
Initial services and rights to use trademark and secret recipes (residual)		$735,000

Recognition of Fees Related to Initial Services and Intellectual Property Rights

The portion of the initial franchise fee allocated to the initial services and intellectual property rights should be recognized when the franchisor has substantially performed or satisfied its obligations under the franchise agreement. The franchisor must consider the following questions when assessing whether it has substantially performed:

1. Does the franchisor have any obligation or intent to refund cash received or forgive notes or receivables due from the franchisee?

2. Has the franchisor performed less than substantially all of the initial services required under the franchise agreement?

3. Are there any remaining material conditions or obligations that would preclude the franchisor from concluding that it has substantially performed?

4. Does the franchise agreement include an option for the franchisor to purchase the franchisee's business that the franchisor expects to exercise?

If the answer to any of these questions is "yes," the franchisor has not substantially performed. For example, answering "yes" to the first question indicates that a portion of the initial franchise fee is refundable. When any portion of the fee is refundable, it should not be recognized. Answering "yes" to the last question means that the initial fee is effectively a reduction of the future purchase price of the business. In this case, the initial fee should not be recognized as revenue at all.

It is presumed that the earliest point a franchisor can achieve substantial performance is upon commencement of operations by the franchisee. This presumption can only be overcome if the franchisor can demonstrate that all obligations, both explicit and implicit, have been fulfilled before the franchisee starts its operations (FAS-45, par. 5) (ASC 952-605-25-3).

> **OBSERVATION:** In answering the questions above, a franchisor must determine whether there are any services that the franchisor is expected to perform, either as a matter of practice or due to regulatory considerations, even if these services are not explicit in the franchise agreement. If these obligations exist, the franchisor does not achieve substantial performance until these services are either performed or no longer required.

EXAMPLE: RECOGNITION OF INITIAL FEES

Yum Brands, Inc. Form 10-K—Fiscal Year Ended December 29, 2007

We recognize initial fees received from a franchisee or licensee as revenue when we have performed substantially all initial services required by the franchise or license agreement, which is generally upon the opening of a store.

There are many different types of services and intellectual property rights provided by a franchisor as part of the initial services. However, franchisors are precluded from allocating the residual amount of the initial franchise fee to any individual initial services or intellectual property rights provided (even if separate prices are stated in the franchise agreement) unless there have been separate sales of the individual services. This restriction exists because initial services and intellectual property rights are often so interrelated and interdependent that assigning individual values would be difficult and essentially meaningless (FAS-45, par. 13) (ASC 952-605-25-11). Therefore, a Completed Performance model is used for the initial services and intellectual property rights and delivery of both must occur before revenue attributable to either may be recognized.

> **OBSERVATION:** The conclusion in FAS-45 (ASC 952-605) is that neither initial services nor rights to be delivered have value to the franchisee on a standalone basis (e.g., absent the other initial services and rights). This is consistent with the general guidance for multiple-element transactions discussed in Chapter 4, "Multiple-Element Arrangements."

Recognition of Fees Related to Equipment, Supplies, and Products

Revenue from the sale of equipment, supplies, and products delivered either initially or in the future should be recognized when these products meet the requirements for revenue recognition as discussed in Chapter 5, "Product Deliverables."

Recognition of Fees Related to Future Services to Be Provided

Continuing franchise fees should be recognized when earned and realized or realizable (FAS-45, par. 14) (ASC 952-605-25-12). For royalty-based fees, this will generally occur when the royalties accrue and become receivable to the franchisor. For services that are not part of the initial services, consult Chapter 6, "Service Deliverables," for guidance on how to determine when such fees are earned and realized or realizable. Any initial franchise fee allocated to future services (i.e., services that are not part of the initial services) should be deferred and recognized over the life of the franchise (FAS-45, par. 7) (ASC 952-605-25-4).

> ☞ **PRACTICE POINTER:** When franchisors sell inventory, equipment, or continuing services to franchisees, the role of the franchisor must be understood to determine whether such sales should be recognized gross or net in the income statement. To the extent the franchisor acts as an agent in these sales, no revenues and expenses should be recognized. For example, a franchisor may place orders for equipment on behalf of its franchisees. In this situation the franchisor should *not* recognize equipment sales and cost of equipment sales. Instead, this transaction should be accounted for on the balance sheet using receivables and payables. Additional guidance on recognizing revenue and expenses gross or net in the income statement can be found in Chapter 11, "Presentation."

ILLUSTRATION: FRANCHISE FEE RECOGNITION

Facts: Assume the same facts as those in the earlier Initial Franchise Fee Allocation illustration. In addition, Franchisee's revenues for Year 1 under the franchise agreement were $5,000,000.

Accounting: The accounting for the initial and continuing franchise fees in Year 1 is as follows:

- At the inception of the franchise agreement, Franchisor records the initial franchise fee received:

Cash or Receivable	$1,000,000	
Deferred Revenue		$1,000,000

- Upon achieving substantial completion related to the initial services and intellectual property rights, Franchisor recognizes the portion of the initial franchise fee allocated to those initial deliverables:

Deferred Revenue	$735,000	
Initial Franchise Fee Revenue		$735,000

- Upon delivery of the specifically designed oven and oven implements and transfer of title to Franchisee, Franchisor recognizes the portion of the initial franchise fee allocated to that equipment:

Deferred Revenue	$140,000	
Equipment Sales		$140,000

- During Year 1, upon delivery of the unique organic flours and transfer of title to Franchisee, Franchisor recognizes one-fifth of the initial franchise fee allocated to that deliverable and the incremental amount paid by or due from Franchisee for those deliveries:

Deferred Revenue	$10,000	
Cash or Receivable	$50,000	
Product Sales		$60,000

- During Year 1, upon earning the revenue related to the four seasonal marketing programs, Franchisor recognizes one-fifth of the initial franchise fee allocated to that deliverable and the incremental amount paid by or due from Franchisee for those services:

Deferred Revenue	$15,000	
Cash or Receivable	$60,000	
Service Fees		$75,000

- During Year 1, upon earning the royalties and the royalties becoming receivable from Franchisee, Franchisor recognizes royalty revenues:

Cash or Receivable	$100,000	
Royalty Revenues		$100,000

Area Franchise Fees

Area franchise agreements grant rights that allow a franchisee to open multiple franchised outlets within a defined geographic area. The key questions to answer before recognizing the initial franchise fee are:

- Do the franchisor's substantial obligations under the area franchise agreement relate to the area franchise as a whole?
- Are the effort and cost of the initial services to be provided under the area franchise agreement significantly independent of the number of individual franchises to be established?

If the answer to both of these questions is "yes," then the initial franchise fee under the area franchise agreement should be treated similarly to the initial franchise fee under an individual franchise agreement. However, if the answer to either or both questions is "no," the franchisor must allocate the initial franchise fee to each franchised outlet based on the expected total number. This method effectively breaks down an area franchise agreement into individual franchise agreements.

ILLUSTRATION: AREA FRANCHISE FEE

Facts: Franchisor M enters into an area franchise agreement with Franchisee D. This agreement meets the definition in FAS-45 (ASC 952-605-20) and is considered a franchise agreement for accounting purposes. The area franchise agreement conveys Franchisee D the right to open up to ten franchised outlets in the metropolitan Detroit area, as defined in the franchise agreement. Each of these franchised outlets will bear Franchisor M's trademark name and sell Franchisor M's specialized baby products. The term of the agreement is five years. The franchise agreement requires Franchisee D to make an initial franchise fee payment of $5,000,000. The initial services and intellectual property rights to be provided by Franchisor M include transferring trademarks and providing site-selection and site-design assistance. Franchisee D expects to open all ten franchise outlets.

Assessment: The effort and cost relating to the site-selection and site-design assistance are significantly dependent on the number of individual franchises to be established. Each incremental franchised outlet to be opened by Franchisee D results in Franchisor M having to put forth the effort and expend the cost necessary to select and design a site. As a result, Franchisor M concludes that it must allocate the initial franchise fee among the ten franchised outlets Franchisee D expects to open. This results in the allocation of the $500,000 initial franchise fee ($5,000,000 total initial franchise fee divided by ten expected franchised outlets) to each franchised outlet. Each franchised outlet will be treated as an individual franchise agreement for purposes of recognizing the $500,000.

As previously noted, allocating an initial franchise fee under an area franchise agreement often involves estimating the number of franchised outlets to be opened by the franchisee. If this estimate is subsequently revised due to a change in circumstances, the remaining fees should be recognized as revenue in proportion to the remaining services to be performed.

Refund rights attached to an initial franchise fee in an area franchise agreement are treated the same as refund rights in an individual franchise agreement. As a result, the franchisor may not recognize revenue from any portion of an initial franchise fee that may be refunded to the franchisee. Under an area franchise agreement, refund rights may not mirror the method used to allocate the initial franchise fee (e.g., more revenue is refundable at any given point in time than the amount that otherwise can be considered earned). This underscores the need to ensure that refund rights have been appropriately considered in an area franchise agreement.

EXAMPLE: AREA FRANCHISE FEE

Panera Bread Company Form 10-K—Fiscal Year Ended December 25, 2007

Franchise Operations

Panera began a broad-based franchising program in 1996. Panera continues to extend its franchise relationships beyond its current franchisees and annually files a Franchise Disclosure Document to facilitate sales of additional franchise and area development agreements, which we refer to as ADAs. The Panera franchise agreement typically requires the payment of a franchise fee of $35,000 per bakery-cafe (generally broken down into $5,000 at the signing of the ADA and $30,000 at or before the bakery-cafe opens) and continuing royalties of 4 to 5 percent of sales from each bakery-cafe. Panera franchise-operated bakery-cafes follow the same standards for in-store operating standards, product quality, menu, site selection, and bakery-cafe construction as do Panera Company-owned bakery-cafes. The franchisees are required to purchase all of their dough products from sources approved by Panera. Panera's fresh dough facility system supplies fresh dough products to substantially all Panera franchise-operated bakery-cafes. Panera does not finance franchisee construction or ADA payments. In addition, Panera does not hold an equity interest in any of the Panera franchise-operated bakery-cafes.

We have entered into franchise ADAs with 39 Panera franchisee groups, or area developers, as of December 25, 2007. Also, as of December 25, 2007, there were 666 Panera franchise-operated bakery-cafes open and commitments to open 293 additional Panera franchise-operated bakery-cafes. Panera expects these bakery-cafes to open according to the timetables established in the various ADAs with franchisee groups, with the majority opening in the next four to five years. Panera expects its area developers to open approximately 55 new Panera franchise-operated bakery-cafes in 2008. The ADAs require an area developer to develop a specified number of bakery-cafes on or before specific dates. If a franchisee fails to develop bakery-cafes on schedule, Panera has the right to terminate the ADA and develop Company-owned locations or develop locations through new area developers in that market. Panera may exercise one or more alternative remedies to address defaults by area developers, including not only development defaults, but also defaults in complying with Panera's operating and brand standards and other covenants under the ADAs and franchise agreements. At the present time, Panera does not have any international franchise development agreements.

Motion Pictures

Arrangements to license or sell films are varied. They may include the rights to a single film or many films. They may allow exploitation on an exclusive or non-exclusive basis in defined or undefined geographic regions. They may provide the customer with only limited control over the actual distribution of a film. Fees under these agreements may be paid up front or over time and may be fixed, variable, or a combination of fixed and variable. Understanding the terms of an arrangement to license or sell films is an integral part of determining when fees should be recognized as revenue. SOP 00-2 (ASC 926) provides such guidance.

The provisions of SOP 00-2 (ASC 926-605) apply to sales or licenses of film rights by producers and distributors of films who own or control these rights. The definition of films includes feature or animated films, television specials, television series, or similar products. Films may be housed on a variety of media including film, video tape, and that used to provide digitized content (e.g., DVDs).

A producer or distributor of films should recognize revenue related to the sale or license of films only when all of the following conditions have been met (SOP 00-2, par. 7) (ASC 926-605-25-1):

1. There is persuasive evidence of a sale or licensing arrangement with a customer;

2. The film is complete and, in accordance with the terms of the arrangement, has been delivered or is available for immediate and unconditional delivery;

3. The license period of the arrangement has begun and the customer can begin its exploitation, exhibition, or sale;

4. The arrangement fee is fixed or determinable; and

5. Collection of the arrangement fee is reasonably assured.

These conditions are similar to those required in most transactions, although they are modified slightly to address the unique characteristics of film licenses and sales.

Persuasive Evidence of an Arrangement

The evaluation of the persuasive evidence condition is generally no different for films than it is for any other revenue arrangement. However, regardless of the form of the documentation for an arrangement, such documentation must be in place and legally enforceable before any revenue is recognized (SOP 00-2, par. 9) (ASC 926-605-25-4). For additional discussion, see Chapter 3, "General Principles."

Completion

SOP 00-2 (ASC 926-605) requires the use of a Completed Performance model for evaluating when revenue is earned. This evaluation is fairly straightforward. However, any modification to the film that must be made before it is ready for the customer should be evaluated to determine whether it is significant. If the modifications are significant, the film is not considered complete and revenue cannot be recognized (SOP 00-2, par. 13) (ASC 926-605-25-8).

Significant modifications are those changes that add new or additional content to a film. Thus, modifying a film by reshooting a scene or adding special effects would be considered significant because content is added or changed. On the other hand, modifying a film by inserting subtitles, formatting it to fit a television screen, or adjusting it to allow the insertion of a commercial would not be considered significant, as none of these actions add content to the film itself (SOP 00-2, par. 18) (ASC 926-605-20).

Delivered or Available for Delivery

Revenue should not be recognized prior to physical delivery when a licensing arrangement calls for or is silent about delivery (SOP 00-2, par. 11; also see Chapter 5, "Product Deliverables," for a discussion of physical delivery) (ASC 926-605-25-6). Some licensing arrangements may directly or indirectly (through a film laboratory access letter) grant the customer immediate and unconditional access to a film print. In this type of arrangement, the delivery criterion is satisfied when the film is complete and immediately available (SOP 00-2, pars. 7 and 12) (ASC 926-605-25-7).

> **OBSERVATION:** While the exception discussed above allows for revenue recognition before delivery in some circumstances, U.S. GAAP rarely permits this. As such, this provision should generally not be analogized to. See Chapter 5, "Product Deliverables" for another exception to the delivery requirement with regards to bill-and-hold transactions that meet very restrictive criteria.

License Period Has Begun

This condition prohibits revenue recognition until the license period of the arrangement has started and the customer is free to begin exploitation, exhibition, or sale of the film. A common restriction in a film license or sales arrangement is the inclusion of a street date. A street date generally restricts a customer from exploiting, exhibiting, or selling a film prior to the date the producer or distributor plans to market the film on a broader basis. For example, a distributor may ship copies of a hit movie on DVD to a reseller in September, but restrict their sale until October 1, to synchronize availability throughout the country and tie that availability to a marketing program. Revenue related to the DVDs shipped in September may not be recognized before the street date of October 1 (SOP 00-2, par. 14) (ASC 926-605-25-10).

Many producers enter into arrangements where they license the rights to market film-related products. These arrangements are often entered into well before the release date of the related film. However, producers should not recognize revenue from these types of arrangements prior to the release of the related film (SOP 00-2, par. 26) (ASC 926-605-25-30). Until this occurs, the license period on the film-related products has not substantively begun.

EXAMPLE: SATISFACTION OF AVAILABILITY CONDITION

Viacom, Inc. Form 10-K—Fiscal Year Ended December 31, 2007

Revenue in connection with the exhibition of feature films by the Filmed Entertainment segment is accounted for in accordance with Statement of Position ("SOP") No. 00-2, *Accounting by Producers or Distributors of Films* ("SOP 00-2"). Revenue is recognized from theatrical distribution of motion pictures upon exhibition. For home entertainment product sold by the Filmed Entertainment and Media Networks segments, revenue is recognized on the later of the shipment or the date that those products are made widely available for sale by retailers. Revenue from the licensing of feature films and original programming for exhibition in television markets is recognized upon availability for telecasting by the licensee. Revenue for video-on-demand and similar pay-per-view arrangements are recognized as the feature films are exhibited based on end-customer purchases as reported by the distributor.

Allocation of Fees in Multiple-Film Arrangements

A producer or distributor often licenses or sells multiple films to customers in one arrangement. These films may or may not be produced or completed upon commencement of the arrangement. In these situations, any fee received must be allocated among the individual films. The allocation of a fee among the individual films in a multiple-film arrangement is based on refundable amounts for incomplete or unproduced films and estimated relative fair values for complete films (SOP 00-2, par. 16) (ASC 926-605-25-12).

OBSERVATION: Each film in a multiple-film arrangement is, in substance, a separate deliverable. The process of allocating a flat fee between films in a multiple-film arrangement is similar to the allocation methodology used in other multiple-element arrangements. See Chapter 4, "Multiple-Element Arrangements." However, one significant difference exists. This relates to using the amount that is refundable if an unproduced film is ultimately not produced for purposes of allocating a portion of the flat fee to the unproduced film. This methodology is used to address specific factors often present in film arrangements and should not be used in other multiple-element transactions.

ILLUSTRATION: ALLOCATION OF FLAT FEE TO MULTIPLE FILMS

Facts: Producer B enters into a license agreement with Customer K. The license agreement grants exploitation and exhibition rights to Customer K for three separate films. Two of the films, *Action-Packed* and *Romance,* are complete. The remaining film, *Political Thriller,* is not yet complete. The license agreement requires Customer K to pay a flat fee of $10,000,000. If Producer B does not complete *Political Thriller,* it must refund $2,500,000. The fair values of the exploitation and exhibition rights related to *Action-Packed* and *Romance* are $6,000,000 and $4,000,000, respectively.

Allocation: The $10,000,000 flat fee is first allocated to *Political Thriller* based on the refundable amount of $2,500,000. The remaining $7,500,000 is allocated based on the relative fair values of *Action-Packed* and *Romance,* resulting in 60% of that amount, or $4,500,000, being allocated to *Action-Packed*, and 40%, or $3,000,000, being allocated to *Romance.*

When available, a producer or distributor should use the quoted market price of each completed film as its fair value for allocation purposes. If a quoted market price is not available, the producer or distributor should use the best available information to determine fair value. One valuation technique often used in this situation is a discounted cash flow methodology (SOP 00-2, par. 17) (ASC 926-605-25-16).[2]

OBSERVATION: SOP 00-2 (ASC 926-605) specifically permits the use of valuation techniques, such as a discounted cash flow methodology, to determine the fair value of a film in a multiple-film arrangement. However, these valuation methodologies may not be appropriate to determine the fair

---

[2] SOP 00-2 (ASC 926-605) includes guidance on the application of a discounted cash flow methodology to estimate fair value. Additional guidance may be found in FAS-157 (ASC 820, *Fair Value Measurements and Disclosures*).

values of elements in other (i.e., non-film) multiple-element arrangements. See the "Fair Value Evidence" section of Chapter 4, "Multiple-Element Arrangements," and the "Vendor-Specific Objective Evidence (VSOE) of Fair Value" section of Chapter 10, "Software—A Complete Model," for additional discussions.

If a producer or distributor concludes that it cannot determine the fair value for an individual completed film, it is prohibited from recognizing any of the flat fee until it can determine fair value and complete the allocation.

Fixed or Determinable Fees

Flat fees   Flat fees are payable regardless of the success or failure of the film and are neither contingent upon future performance by the producer or distributor nor subject to change based on rights held by the customer. Flat fees are considered fixed and determinable because the amount of the fee is not dependent upon any future events (SOP 00-2, par. 15) (ASC 926-605-25-11).

Variable fees   Variable fees are those based on some measure of the film's performance, such as a percentage of a customer's revenue from exploiting or exhibiting a film. These fees are considered fixed or determinable as the customer exhibits or exploits the film (SOP 00-2, par. 18) (ASC 926-605-25-18). Until then, the fees are not fixed or determinable because they are dependent upon future events.

Nonrefundable minimum guarantees   The fee in some arrangements can be essentially variable, except to the extent that the customer guarantees it will pay some minimum amount. Generally, the nonrefundable minimum guarantees are treated as flat fees and any amounts over and above this minimum are treated as variable fees. However, in some arrangements, the nonrefundable minimum guarantee is cross-collateralized (i.e., it can be applied to a number of films, territories, and/or markets and the exploitation results (revenues) for all applicable films, territories, and/or markets are aggregated for purposes of determining the variable fees payable to the producer or distributor under the arrangement). To the extent that a nonrefundable guaranteed minimum exists in an arrangement that has been cross-collateralized, the nonrefundable minimum guarantee is effectively the same as a variable fee and is only considered fixed and determinable as the customer exhibits or exploits the films, or at the end of the license (SOP 00-2, par. 134) (ASC 926-605-25-20).

Returns and price concessions   A producer or distributor should account for returns and price concessions based on the provisions of

FAS-48 (ASC 605-15-25). To recognize revenue net of estimated product returns and price concessions, the following conditions must be met (FAS-48, par. 6) (ASC 605-15-25-1):

1. The seller's price to the buyer is substantially fixed or determinable at the date of sale.

2. The buyer has paid the seller, or the buyer is obligated to pay the seller and the obligation is not contingent on resale of the product.

3. The buyer's obligation to the seller would not be changed in the event of theft or physical destruction or damage of the product.

4. The buyer acquiring the product for resale has economic substance apart from that provided by the seller.

5. The seller does not have significant obligations for future performance to directly bring about resale of the product by the buyer.

6. The amount of future returns and price concessions can be reasonably estimated.

The producer or distributor must consider both the contract terms and its customary business practices when identifying return rights or price concession obligations. If the producer or distributor does not meet all of the foregoing conditions, the fees under the arrangement are not fixed or determinable. For additional discussion of these conditions, see Chapter 5, "Product Deliverables."

Arrangement Modifications

It is not uncommon for film arrangements to be modified for various reasons. For example, the term of the arrangement may be extended, the territory expanded, the number of allowable showings increased, or the basis on which the fee is calculated changed. The type of modification determines the appropriate accounting.

If an arrangement modification solely involves extending the term of an existing arrangement, fees related to the modification should be recognized after the modification has been finalized, based on the type of fee involved (e.g., flat, variable) as discussed above (SOP 00-2, par. 22) (ASC 926-605-25-23 through 25-25).

All other modifications make the revised arrangement a new arrangement. To the extent any refunds or concessions are granted by the producer or distributor through the arrangement modifications, previously reported revenue in the amount of the refunds or concessions should be reversed (SOP 00-2, par. 23) (ASC 926-605-25-26).

OBSERVATION: The accounting for refunds or concessions in a modified arrangement effectively results in the producer or distributor recognizing revenue as if the new financial terms had been in place at the beginning of the original arrangement. As a result, a cumulative catch-up adjustment is recorded in the year of the modification for the difference between cumulative revenue recognized under the old financial terms and cumulative revenue that would have been recognized under the new financial terms.

ILLUSTRATION: ARRANGEMENT MODIFICATION INVOLVING CONCESSION

Facts: Producer T had a license agreement with Customer D. Only one film was involved in the license agreement. The original license agreement had a term of three years and provided a flat fee of $50,000 and variable fees of 10% based on Customer D's gross receipts. Customer D's gross receipts in Year 1 were $1,000,000. In Year 1, Producer T recognized the $50,000 flat fee and $100,000 of variable fees as revenue. At the beginning of Year 2, Producer T and Customer D modified the terms of the original license agreement. The modified license agreement changed the flat fee to $20,000 and the variable fee rate to 12%.

Accounting: At the beginning of Year 2, Producer T should reverse $10,000 of revenue. This is based on the following calculation:

Revenue recognized in Year 1	
Flat fee	$ 50,000
Variable fee	100,000
Total	150,000
Revenue that would have been recognized in Year 1 under the modified terms	
Flat fee	20,000
Variable fee	120,000
Total	140,000
Concession	$ 10,000

CHAPTER 8
MISCELLANEOUS ISSUES

CONTENTS

OVERVIEW

Chapters 4–7 have provided a detailed discussion of specific types of revenue transactions. This chapter addresses four important issues related to various types of revenue transactions:

1. Deferral of costs of revenue transactions;
2. Sales incentives;
3. Related-party sales; and
4. Nonmonetary transactions.

LISTING OF APPLICABLE LITERATURE

Publication	ASC	ASC Topic	Subject
SAB Topic 13	605-10-S99	Revenue Recognition	Revenue Recognition
CON-6	N/A	N/A	Elements of Financial Statements
ARB-43, Ch. 4	330-10	Inventory	Inventory Pricing
FAS-60	944	Financial Services— Insurance	Accounting and Reporting by Insurance Enterprises
FAS-91	310-20	Receivables	Nonrefundable Fees and Costs Associated with Originating or Acquiring Loans and Initial Direct Costs of Leases
FTB 90-1	605-20-25	Revenue Recognition	Accounting for Separately Priced Extended Warranty and Product Maintenance Contracts

| EITF 99-5 | 340-10 | Deferred Costs and Other Assets | Accounting for Pre-Production Costs Related to Long-Term Supply Arrangements |
| EITF 00-21 | 605-25 | Revenue Recognition | Revenue Arrangements with Multiple Deliverables |

DEFERRING THE COSTS OF REVENUE TRANSACTIONS

The accounting for many costs associated with revenue transactions is well established. U.S. generally accepted accounting principles (GAAP) addresses the following types of costs:

Cost	Primary Literature
Advertising costs	SOP 93-7, *Reporting on Advertising Costs* (ASC 720, *Other Expenses*; 720-35); and PB-13, *Direct-Response Advertising and Probable Future Benefits* (ASC 340-20)
Start-up costs	SOP 98-5, *Reporting on the Costs of Start-Up Activities* (ASC 720-15)
Inventory costs	ARB-43, *Chapter 4* and FAS-151, *Inventory Costs, an Amendment of ARB-43, Chapter 4* (ASC 330)
Intangible assets	FAS-142, *Goodwill and Other Intangible Assets* (ASC 350, *Intangibles—Goodwill and Other*)
Internal-use software costs	SOP 98-1, *Accounting for the Costs of Computer Software Developed or Obtained for Internal Use* (ASC 350-40)
Web site development costs	EITF 00-2, *Accounting for Web Site Development Costs* (ASC 350-50)
External-use software costs	FAS-86, *Accounting for the Costs of Computer Software to Be Sold, Leased, or Otherwise Marketed* (ASC 985, *Software*; 985-20)
Film-related costs	SOP 00-2 (ASC 926, *Entertainment—Films*; 926-20)
Real estate project costs	FAS-67 (ASC 970, *Real Estate—General*)
Insurance enterprise costs	FAS-60 (ASC 944)
Lease inducements	FTB 88-1, *Issues Relating to Accounting for Leases* (ASC 840, *Leases*)

Pre-production costs related to long-term supply arrangements	EITF 99-5, *Accounting for Pre-Production Costs Related to Long-Term Supply Arrangements* (ASC 340-10)
Credit-card-related costs	EITF 88-20 (ASC 310-10)

Despite the guidance noted above that covers specific kinds of costs, there is no guidance on how to account for many costs in revenue transactions. Certain costs (for example, the cost of soliciting a customer, negotiating the terms of a contract, and paying a sales commission) may be incurred before the related revenue is recognized. Other costs are incurred before performance begins, during the setup phase of a service transaction, or during delivery of a component in a multiple-element arrangement that cannot be treated separately for accounting purposes. In general, the following cost categories are often considered candidates for deferral or capitalization:

- *Solicitation costs*—Costs incurred by a vendor to solicit or acquire a *specific* customer or revenue stream (excluding advertising). An example of a solicitation cost is a sales commission.

- *Direct origination costs*—Direct costs incurred to consummate a specific revenue transaction. Examples of origination activities include the evaluation of a customer's credit rating, negotiation of the sales contract, and preparation and processing documentation of the transaction.

- *Multiple-element costs*—Costs related to a delivered element in a multiple-element arrangement, where the delivered element either (1) cannot be treated separately for accounting purposes, or (2) should be treated separately but the amount of revenue allocated to it is restricted because all or a portion of the revenue for that element is contingent upon performance on an undelivered element. For example, if a vendor sells equipment subject to installation but concludes that the equipment does not have value to the customer absent the installation (that is, on a standalone basis), no revenue can be recognized upon delivery of the equipment. The cost of the equipment is an example of a multiple-element cost.

- *Setup and other direct and incremental costs of installation*—Costs related to activities that enable a vendor to perform under the terms of the arrangement. These activities (a) are performed (and the related costs incurred) at the inception of an arrangement, (b) do not represent a separate earnings process, and (c) are arrangement specific. An example of setup and installation costs are those incurred by a vendor in a human resource outsourcing contract for conversion of the customer's historical data to the vendor's software platform.

The key issue with regard to these costs is whether the costs may be capitalized or deferred until revenue is recognized. The accounting literature answers this question for some transactions and certain types of costs. For example, FAS-60 (ASC 944-30) provides guidance for insurance companies, FAS-91 (ASC 310-20) provides guidance on the deferral of loan origination costs, and FTB 90-1 (ASC 605-20) provides guidance on deferral of costs related to the sale of extended warranties. However, this guidance is narrow in scope and does not address the majority of situations in which costs are incurred before revenue is recognized.

The question of cost deferral has arisen more frequently since the issuance of SAB Topic 13, *Revenue Recognition* (ASC 605-10-S99), which underscored the SEC staff's view that the incurrence of costs should not necessarily result in revenue recognition, thereby leading to more situations in which costs are incurred before revenue can be recognized. SAB Topic 13 (ASC 605-10-S99) directly addresses cost deferral by suggesting that in certain arrangements, the models in FAS-91 (ASC 310-20) and FTB 90-1 (ASC 605-20) may be appropriate.

EXAMPLES: SETUP COSTS

Acxiom Corporation Form 10-K—Fiscal Year Ended March 31, 2009

The Company provides database management and IT management services under long-term arrangements. These arrangements may require the Company to perform setup activities such as the design and build of a database for the customer under the database management contracts and migration of the customer's IT environment under IT management contracts. In the case of database management contracts, the customer does not acquire any ownership rights to the Company's intellectual property used in the database and the database itself provides no benefit to the customer outside of the utilization of the system during the term of the database management arrangement. In some cases, the arrangements also contain provisions requiring customer acceptance of the setup activities prior to commencement of the ongoing services arrangement.

Upfront fees billed during the setup phase for these arrangements are deferred and setup costs that are direct and incremental to the contract are capitalized and amortized on a straight-line basis over the service term of the contract. Revenue recognition does not begin until after customer acceptance in cases where contracts contain acceptance provisions. Once the setup phase is complete and customer acceptance occurs, the Company recognizes revenue over the remaining service term of the contract. In situations where the arrangement does not require customer acceptance before the Company begins providing services, revenue is recognized over the contract period and no costs are deferred.

Computer Sciences Corp. Form 10-K—Fiscal Year Ended March 28, 2008

Capitalization of outsourcing contract costs

Certain costs incurred upon initiation of an outsourcing contract are deferred and amortized over the contract life. These costs consist of contract acquisition and transition/setup costs, and include the cost of due diligence activities after competitive selection, costs associated with installation of systems and processes, and amounts paid to clients in excess of the fair market value of acquired assets (premiums). Finance staff, working with program management, review costs to determine appropriateness for deferral in accordance with relevant accounting guidance.

Key estimates and assumptions that we must make include assessing the fair value of acquired assets in order to calculate the premium and projecting future cash flows in order to assess the recoverability of deferred costs. We utilize the experience and knowledge of our professional staff in program management, operations, procurement and finance areas, as well as third parties on occasion, to determine fair values of assets acquired. To assess recoverability, undiscounted estimated cash flows of the contract are projected over its remaining life and compared to the unamortized deferred cost balance. Such estimates require judgment and assumptions, which are based upon the professional knowledge and experience of our personnel. Key factors that are considered in estimating the undiscounted cash flows include projected labor costs and productivity efficiencies. A significant change in an estimate or assumption on one or more contracts could have a material effect on our results of operations. Amortization of such premiums is recorded as a reduction to revenues.

Depreciation and Amortization

The Company's depreciation and amortization policies are as follows:

Outsourcing contract costs–Contract life, excluding option years

Outsourcing Contract Costs

Costs on outsourcing contracts, including costs incurred for bid and proposal activities, are generally expensed as incurred. However, certain costs incurred upon initiation of an outsourcing contract are deferred and expensed over the contract life. These costs represent incremental external costs or certain specific internal costs that are directly related to the contract acquisition or transition activities. Such capitalized costs can be separated into two principal categories: contract acquisition costs and transition/setup costs. The primary types of costs that may be capitalized include labor and related fringe benefits, subcontractor costs, travel costs, and asset premiums.

The first principal category, contract acquisition costs, consists mainly of due diligence activities after competitive selection as well as premiums paid. Premiums are amounts paid to clients in excess of the fair market value of acquired assets. Fixed assets acquired in connection with outsourcing transactions are capitalized at fair value and depreciated consistent with fixed asset policies described above. Premiums are capitalized as outsourcing contract costs and amortized over the contract life. The amortization of outsourcing contract cost premiums is accounted for as a reduction in revenue.

The second principal category of capitalized outsourcing costs is transition/ setup costs. Such costs are primarily associated with installation of systems and processes.

In the event indications exist that an outsourcing contract cost balance related to a particular contract may be impaired, undiscounted estimated cash flows of the contract are projected over its remaining term, and compared to the unamortized outsourcing contract cost balance. If the projected cash flows are not adequate to recover the unamortized cost balance, the balance would be adjusted to equal the contract's fair value in the period such a determination is made. The primary indicator used to determine when impairment testing should be performed is when a contract is materially underperforming, or is expected to materially underperform in the future, as compared to the original bid model or subsequent annual budgets.

Terminations of outsourcing contracts, including transfers either back to the client or to another I/T provider, prior to the end of their committed contract terms are infrequent due to the complex transition of personnel, assets, methodologies, and processes involved with outsourcing transactions. In the event of an early termination, the Company and the client, pursuant to certain contractual provisions, engage in discussions to determine the recovery of unamortized contract costs, lost profits, transfer of personnel, rights to implemented systems and processes, as well as other matters

---

Definition of an Asset

The conceptual framework makes clear that costs should not be deferred if they do not create or add value to an asset. Assets are defined as "...probable future economic benefits obtained or controlled by a particular entity as a result of past transactions or events" (CON-6, par. 25). The costs addressed in this section do not independently result in the creation of any tangible assets. However, when the costs are part of a revenue-generating arrangement, the arrangement itself could be considered an asset because the revenue provides a future economic benefit and the arrangement is controlled by the company and is legally binding.

Costs Eligible for Deferral

The only costs eligible for deferral are those that directly relate to a specific revenue arrangement (SAB Topic 13A3f, ques. 3) (ASC 605-10-S99, A3f, ques. 3).

FAS-91 (ASC 310-20) addresses the accounting for loan solicitation and direct origination costs, and allows such costs to be capitalized. Costs eligible for deferral are those that relate directly to a specific loan and are either: (1) incremental direct costs incurred with third parties, or (2) certain internal direct costs related to origination activities. Internal direct costs are limited to a portion of the salaries and benefits of employees involved in the origination process (FAS-91, par. 6) (ASC 310-20-20). This amount is calculated by multiplying the percentage of the employees' time spent on origination activities and the employee's total compensation (salary plus commissions plus benefits). Commissions paid to internal salespeople may be capitalized to the extent that the salesperson performs origination (as opposed to just solicitation) activities.

FTB 90-1 (ASC 605-20) addresses the accounting for costs to acquire separately priced extended warranty and product maintenance contracts. It specifies that only incremental direct costs incurred for a specific contract should be deferred (FTB 90-1, par. 4) (ASC 605-20-25-4). This would appear to be slightly inconsistent with the costs allowed to be deferred under the FAS-91 (ASC 310-20) model, as discussed above, as it seems to effectively preclude the deferral of any portion of employee salaries and benefits.

However, FTB 90-1, paragraph 12 (background information not in ASC), may be read to suggest that, despite the use of different terms and wording, the cost deferral models in FAS-91 (ASC 310-20) and FTB 90-1 (ASC 605-20-25-4) are intended to be the same. This latter view appears to be the view held by the staff of the FASB and is reflected in the Accounting Standards Codification (ASC).

Choosing an Accounting Policy

The capitalization of customer acquisition costs, and other costs incurred before performance begins, is generally not required, with the exception of those transactions directly covered by accounting literature identified previously. Expensing as incurred is always acceptable for the other costs that are not covered explicitly in the accounting literature (SAB Topic 13A3f, ques. 3) (ASC 605-10-S99, A3f, ques. 3). However, it is also generally acceptable to analyze these costs using a model similar to that described in FAS-91 (ASC 310-20). The objective would be to defer costs that are directly related to the transaction until the revenue is recognized. In some cases, a company may believe that a model other than the FAS-91 (ASC 310-20) model best meets this objective. This may be appropriate depending on the nature of costs incurred. The policy should be selected based on an analysis of the arrangements and the costs incurred, rather than on a goal of capitalizing (or expensing) a certain amount of costs.

> **OBSERVATION:** Direct costs of a delivered product that cannot be treated separately from the undelivered elements in the

arrangement (see Chapter 4, "Multiple-Element Arrangements," for additional information) should be capitalized, subject to the realizability test discussed in a subsequent section. Expensing these costs, which are actually costs of performance rather than acquisition or setup, would be inconsistent with the guidance in paragraph 4 of ARB-43, Ch. 4, which states: "the inventory at any given date is the balance of costs applicable to goods on hand remaining after the matching of absorbed costs with concurrent revenues. This balance is appropriately carried to future periods provided it does not exceed an amount properly chargeable against the revenues expected to be obtained from ultimate disposition of the goods carried forward [ASC 330-10-05-3]." The multiple-element costs associated with this exception should not be confused with those that arise when a delivered element should be treated separately, but the amount of revenue allocated to it is restricted because all or a portion of the payment for that delivered element is contingent upon delivery of an undelivered element. See the section entitled, "Special Considerations for Certain Multiple-Element Costs," for a discussion of this type of multiple-element cost.

ILLUSTRATION: COST DEFERRAL

Facts: Satellite TV Company (Satellite) sells receivers and satellite dishes and provides satellite television programming to customers. Satellite enters into a transaction with Customer M (M) where M purchases a satellite dish and receiver and signs a contract to receive one year of satellite programming. M installs the satellite dish and receiver itself. Amounts to be paid by M include a $50 upfront, nonrefundable fee and $30 per month for the duration of the contract. If the customer cancels the contract early, a $200 cancellation fee is due to Satellite. The costs incurred by Satellite include:

- $150 related to its purchase of the receiver and satellite dish from a third party

- $15 of origination costs (allocated employee costs for one-quarter hour spent by an employee to perform a credit check and process paperwork)

- $25 of setup costs (allocated employee costs for one-half hour spent activating the receiver and satellite dish to receive Satellite's signals)

- $100 commission paid to an internal employee dedicated solely to selling activities

Satellite has concluded that it should not separate the sale of the receiver and satellite dish from the satellite programming services. Furthermore, Satellite has concluded that the upfront fee should be deferred over a period of three years (expected customer relationship period) using the straight-line method.

Discussion: Each of the costs listed above should be evaluated as follows:

- Receiver and satellite dish—The costs of the receiver and satellite dish are incremental direct costs paid to a third party. They are eligible for deferral.

- Performing credit check and processing paperwork—The amounts related to an internal employee performing a credit check and processing paperwork are direct internal origination costs. These costs are generally eligible for deferral.

- Activating receiver and satellite dish—The amount related to an internal employee activating the receiver and satellite dish to receive Satellite's signals represents direct payroll-related costs incurred in connection with setup activities. These costs are generally eligible for deferral.

- Commission—The commission paid to an internal employee dedicated solely to selling activities is likely eligible for deferral as long as the commission is paid only for successful efforts—that is, only when a contract is generated.

Based on this evaluation, the total amount of capitalizable costs is $290. As discussed above, the receiver and dish costs would be required to be capitalized. Satellite could elect to capitalize the other costs or expense them as incurred. In addition, Satellite might conclude that capitalizing only some of the setup, commission and/or origination costs would provide the most transparent presentation to investors and could likely justify a policy reflecting that judgment. For example, Satellite might decide to capitalize only the incremental costs of a new contract, which would cause Satellite to expense the setup and origination costs, but capitalize the sales commissions.

DISCLOSURE ALERT: Companies should disclose their choice of accounting policy related to the capitalization or expensing of customer acquisition and other costs addressed in this section. See Chapter 12, "Disclosures," for additional discussion of accounting policy disclosures.

EXAMPLE: COSTS ELIGIBLE FOR DEFERRAL

salesforce.com, inc. Form 10-K—Fiscal Year Ended January 31, 2009

If a consulting arrangement does not qualify for separate accounting, we recognize the consulting revenue ratably over the remaining term of the subscription contract. Additionally, in these situations we defer the direct costs of the consulting arrangement and amortize those costs over the same time period as the consulting revenue is recognized. The deferred cost on our consolidated balance sheet totaled $17.3 million at January 31, 2009 and $13.9 million at January 31, 2008. Such amounts are included in prepaid expenses and other current assets and other assets.

Accounting for Deferred Commissions. We defer commission payments to our direct sales force. The commissions are deferred and amortized to sales expense over the non-cancelable terms of the related subscription contracts with our customers, which are typically 12 to 24 months. The commission payments, which are paid in full the month after the customer's service commences, are a direct and incremental cost of the revenue arrangements. The deferred commission amounts are recoverable through the future revenue streams under the non-cancelable customer contracts. We believe this is the preferable method of accounting as the commission charges are so closely related to the revenue from the non-cancelable customer contracts that they should be recorded as an asset and charged to expense over the same period that the subscription revenue is recognized.

During fiscal 2009, we deferred $63.7 million of commission expenditures and we amortized $58.7 million to sales expense. During the same period a year ago, we deferred $62.7 million of commission expenditures and we amortized $42.2 million to sales expense. Deferred commissions on our consolidated balance sheet totaled $57.1 million at January 31, 2009 and $52.1 million at January 31, 2008.

Realizability Test

Like all assets, deferred costs must be evaluated for realizability. Both FAS-91 (ASC 310-20) and FTB 90-1 (ASC 605-20-25) require the deferral of costs due to the existence of a contractual revenue stream against which these costs must be matched. As a result, the nature of the terms of arrangements that fall within the scope of these statements supports the realizability of the deferred costs. For other transactions, the following questions should be considered to determine whether deferrable costs are realizable:

- Has any nonrefundable revenue related to the specific transaction been deferred?

- Is there a clause in the contractual arrangement that management intends to enforce (e.g., a liquidated damages clause) that would facilitate recovery of the deferred costs?

Deferrable costs up to the amount of nonrefundable deferred revenue are considered realizable because the recognition of the deferred revenue will offset the recognition of deferred costs. If deferrable costs are in excess of nonrefundable deferred revenue (or if there is no deferred revenue), these excess costs should only be considered realizable under the following circumstances:

1. The contractual arrangement contains a specific clause related to the deferrable costs;

2. The clause is legally enforceable;

3. Management intends to enforce the clause; and

4. Probable and objectively supportable net margins exist during the base term of the contractual arrangement to support the amount of deferrable costs (where net margins represent revenues net of related direct costs).

One question that arises in applying this test is whether any revenue in addition to contractual minimums should be included. For example, in the satellite television arrangement discussed above, the customer may be able to purchase additional services, such as premium movie channels or special event programming. It may be appropriate to include these additional revenues (and related costs) in the realizability test if the additional amounts are probable and objectively supportable. However, companies should be judicious when adopting a policy that considers revenues in excess of minimum contractual revenues to estimate net margins for purposes of the realizability test.

> **OBSERVATION:** Some companies have essentially eliminated the need for a realizability test by adopting a policy of deferring costs only to the extent of deferred revenues. This policy is less preferable than one that adopts a full cost deferral model or expenses all costs as incurred. However, a policy of deferring direct costs to the extent of deferred revenues is acceptable, if applied consistently.

EXAMPLE: LIMITING DEFERRED COSTS TO DEFERRED REVENUES

Qwest Communications International Form 10-K—Fiscal Year Ended December 31, 2007

We recognize revenue for services when the related services are provided. Recognition of certain payments received in advance of services being provided is deferred until the service is provided. These advance payments include wireline activation fees and installation charges, which we recognize as revenue over the expected customer relationship period ranging from one to five years. We also defer related costs for customer acquisitions. The deferral of customer acquisition costs is limited to the amount of deferral of revenue on advance payments. Costs in excess of advance payments are recorded as expense in the period such costs are incurred. Expected customer relationship periods are estimated using historical experience. Termination fees or other fees on existing contracts that are negotiated in conjunction with new contracts are deferred and recognized over the new contract term.

ILLUSTRATION: APPLICATION OF THE REALIZABILITY TEST

Facts: Assume the same facts and conclusions as those presented earlier in the examples involving Satellite TV Company (Satellite). In addition, assume the following:

- The monthly costs incurred by Satellite to provide programming services to M are $12.

- Satellite has received a letter from its external legal counsel indicating that its programming services contracts are legally enforceable.

- Satellite has a history of enforcing its contracts and intends to enforce its contract with M.

Also, Satellite does not have a policy of including revenues expected in excess of contractual minimums (e.g., specialty programming fees) when determining whether deferred costs are realizable.

Application: Based on its accounting policies, Satellite has determined that $290 of costs are deferrable in the arrangement it has with M. An amount equal to the upfront nonrefundable fee of $50 is considered realizable. Satellite also expects net margins of $216 during the contract period ($360 of contractual revenue [$30 per month for 12 months] less $144 of related direct costs ([$12 per month for 12 months]). Satellite can support its expectations of $216 in net margins under this contract with a large volume of company-specific history for similar contracts. An additional $216 of deferrable costs are also considered realizable since (a) this amount represents probable and objectively supportable net margins, (b) Satellite's contract with M is legally enforceable, (c) Satellite intends to enforce its contract with M, and (d) Satellite's intentions are reasonable in light of its demonstrable history of enforcing its contracts.

Based on this analysis, the amount of deferrable costs that are realizable is $266 ($50 supported by the upfront nonrefundable fee and $216 supported by probable and objectively supportable net margins). The remainder of the deferrable costs, $24 ($290 total deferrable costs less $266 realizable deferrable costs), should be expensed as incurred.

Special Considerations for Certain Multiple-Element Costs

When specific refund rights exist in a multiple-element arrangement, the amount of revenue allocable to a delivered element is limited to the lesser of: (a) the amount otherwise allocable to that element (on the basis of the relative fair value or the residual method, as appropriate), or (b) the amount that is not contingent upon the delivery of additional items or meeting other specified performance conditions (EITF 00-21, par. 14) (ASC 605-25-30-5) (see Chapter 4, "Multiple-Element Arrangements"). These situations raise the following question: What is the proper accounting treatment for the costs associated with the delivered element (referred to in this section as the delivered element costs)?

This discussion can be illustrated with the following numerical examples:

> **Common Facts:** There are two elements in the arrangement—Element 1 and Element 2. Total arrangement consideration is $100. The amounts otherwise allocable to Element 1 and Element 2 based on their relative fair values are $70 and $30, respectively. Vendor delivers Element 1 before Element 2. The cost of Element 1 is $50. The cost of Element 2 is $10. Element 1 and Element 2 otherwise meet the separation criteria in EITF 00-21. All of the revenue recognition conditions have been met for Element 1 upon its delivery.
>
> > **Example 1 Additional Facts:** $100 is due upon delivery of Element 1. Vendor must refund the entire amount if Element 2 is not delivered.
> >
> > **Example 2 Additional Facts:** $100 is due upon delivery of Element 1. If Element 2 is not delivered, Vendor must refund $60.

Example 1

In this example, no revenue should be allocated to Element 1 because the entire amount of arrangement consideration is refundable if Element 2 is not delivered. The question is whether the cost of Element 1 ($50) should be deferred or expensed upon delivery of Element 1. Deferring the $50 until delivery of Element 2 (assuming this occurs) would result in revenue of $100, costs of $60, and a profit margin of $40 for the entire transaction, all recognized at the same point in time. Expensing the $50 upon delivery of Element 1 results in a negative profit margin of—$50 for the Vendor upon delivery of Element 1 and a higher positive profit margin of $90 upon delivery of Element 2. However, the total profit margin of $40 for the entire transaction is the same upon delivery of Element 2 regardless of whether the $50 is deferred or expensed upon delivery of Element 1.

In this example, application of the realizability test indicates that the delivered element costs are not realizable. First, there is no non-refundable deferred revenue in this arrangement, because the $100 the Vendor receives upon delivery of Element 1 must be refunded in the event of non-performance of Element 2. Second, although there is a contractual arrangement supporting the transaction, the arrangement has a contingency related to the realization of revenue for the delivered element. The existence of this contingency may make it difficult to conclude that probable and objectively support-able net margins exist to justify the realizability of Element 1's costs. This does not, however, mean that the cost of Element 1 must be expensed upon delivery. See the discussion below on "Accounting for Delivered Element Costs."

Example 2

In this example, $40 of revenue is allocated to Element 1. The $70 that would otherwise have been allocated to Element 1 is reduced to $40 (a reduction of $30) because the amount otherwise allocated to the undelivered element ($30) is less than the amount that would be refunded if the undelivered element is not delivered ($60, for a difference of $30). The question is how the cost of Element 1 should be treated and whether this treatment is affected by the fact that some amount of revenue is allocated to Element 1.

In Example 2, the cost of Element 1 ($50) exceeds the revenue allo-cated to it ($40) by $10. In this situation, deferring the entire cost of Element 1 would not be appropriate. It would also be inappropriate to defer the $40 of revenue allocated to Element 1 because the conditions for revenue recognition have been met (see Chapter 4, "Multiple-Element Arrangements"). However, because expensing the entire $50 upon delivery of Element 1 would result in negative profit margin of—$10 for Vendor on Element 1, should some portion of Element 1's cost be deferred? If so, how should this be determined?

Application of the realizability test to Example 2 is awkward. First, there is no nonrefundable deferred revenue. All of the nonre-fundable revenue is allocated to Element 1 and will be recognized upon delivery. Second, although there may be a contractual arrange-ment supporting the transaction, the arrangement contains a con-tingency related to the realization of revenue for the delivered element. The existence of this contingency may make it difficult to conclude that probable and objectively supportable net margins exist to justify the realizability of Element 1's costs. This does not, however, mean that the cost of Element 1 must be expensed upon its delivery. See the discussion below on "Accounting for Delivered Element Costs."

Accounting for Delivered Element Costs

The fact patterns in Examples 1 and 2 are relatively straightforward. However, the treatment of Element 1's cost in these Examples is not easily resolved. Consider the additional complexities that would be introduced if the cost of Element 1 were $40 or $30, or if a third element delivered after Element 2 had additional specific refund rights. Unfortunately, there is no accounting literature that specifically addresses these issues. Before any cost (including Element 1's cost) can be recognized, however, it must meet the definition of an asset in CON-6. In addition, how should one determine whether an asset exists and in what amount? There is no one right answer to this question. The critical objective is always the same—to develop a "reasoned" approach in a particular set of facts and circumstances.

Different approaches have been discussed on how to determine whether any delivered element costs in a particular set of facts and circumstances should be capitalized for accounting purposes. One approach comprises the following two steps:

> Step 1: Does the company have an asset?

> Step 2: If so, what is the company's impairment test for that asset?

In Step 1, the company must determine whether it has obtained or controlled future economic benefits as a result of the revenue transaction. In making this determination, the company should consider the contract it has with the customer to deliver a second element at a potentially higher profit margin than it otherwise would have. Does this contract result in the company obtaining or controlling future economic benefits? The answer depends on the facts and circumstances and requires the exercise of reasoned judgment.

In Step 2, the company must determine an appropriate impairment test. This requires the consideration of factors such as the margin that will be earned on the final element and the margin that will be earned on the final element in comparison to the margin that would typically be earned on this element if it were sold on a standalone basis. Another factor to consider is whether the delivered element is typically sold at a loss when sold on a standalone basis or in arrangements that do not include a specific refund right. Many factors, in addition to those discussed here, should be considered and analyzed to make this determination. The analysis should ultimately result in a reasoned approach to assessing whether the carrying amount of the company's asset is realizable.

Another approach to determining whether any of the delivered element costs in a particular set of facts and circumstances should be capitalized involves analyzing different accounting treatments and identifying the most appropriate. The potential accounting treatments that are typically considered include:

- *Expense the delivered element costs upon delivery*—In the case of Example 2, this would result in the recognition of $40 of revenue and $50 of cost of goods sold upon the delivery of Element 1.

- *Capitalize the delivered element costs upon delivery*—In the case of Example 2, this would result in the recognition of $40 of revenue and $50 of deferred costs upon the delivery of Element 1.

- *Expense delivered element costs up to the amount of revenue allocated to the delivered element and capitalize the delivered element costs in excess of the amount of revenue allocated to the delivered element (i.e., capitalize the delivered element costs to the extent of any loss) upon delivery*—In the case of Example 2, this would result in the recognition of $40 of revenue, $40 of cost of goods sold, and $10 of deferred costs upon delivery of Element 1.

- *Expense/Capitalize the costs of Element 1 on a pro rata basis upon delivery (i.e., costs would be expensed based on the proportion of revenue allocated to the delivered element and revenue that otherwise would have been allocated to the delivered element)*—In the case of Example 2, this would result in the recognition of $40 of revenue, $29 ($40 ÷ $70 × $50) of cost of goods sold, and $21 of deferred costs upon delivery of Element 1.

These potential accounting treatments should not be viewed as acceptable alternatives in every set of facts and circumstances. For example, it is not appropriate in Example 2 to conclude that the Vendor should capitalize the entire amount of Element 1's costs upon delivery because only $40 of revenue (57% of the amount of revenue otherwise allocable to Element 1) can be recognized upon delivery. However, when the analysis demonstrates that some or all of the delivered element costs should be capitalized, this amount must meet the definition of an asset and be realizable.

These are not the only approaches to accounting for delivered element costs, nor are they mutually exclusive. Each approach could be used to substantiate the results of the others. This relationship exists because (a) any capitalized costs must meet the definition of an asset and be realizable and (b) these approaches should result in identifying the accounting treatment that is most appropriate for a particular set of facts and circumstances. Consultation with experts to determine the most appropriate accounting treatment may be necessary in certain circumstances.

> **SEC REGISTRANT ALERT:** In a December 2003 speech, the SEC staff provided the following examples of situations where it may be appropriate to conclude that delivered element costs represent an asset: (1) the arrangement is effectively a consignment (in which case the delivered element costs would represent consignment inventory), (2) the loss incurred is considered an investment in the remainder of the contract, supported by the fact that the revenue allocated to the remaining elements is greater than the fair value of these elements, or (3) the costs incurred are contractually guaranteed reimbursable costs (similar to those costs discussed in EITF 99-5 (ASC 340-10)). In these examples, the application of Step 1 in the approach discussed above results in the conclusion that an asset exists. In addition, under the second approach discussed above, an analysis of the potential accounting treatments would likely result in the

conclusion that some or all of the delivered element costs should be capitalized.

When a decision is made to recognize delivered element costs as an asset, a key issue for the SEC staff involves the method selected to evaluate the asset for impairment. Other issues include (1) the nature of the costs that should be considered in calculating the loss on a delivered item and (2) how and over what periods the asset should be amortized.

In this speech, the SEC staff acknowledged that there is no one-size-fits-all solution to the treatment of delivered element costs. Given the analytical complexities and level of judgment required to determine whether these costs should be deferred, the SEC staff encouraged registrants to discuss the approaches they have taken with the SEC staff.

EXAMPLE: DEFERRED COSTS

Lasercard, Inc. Form 10-K—Fiscal Year Ended March 31, 2007

In the fourth quarter of fiscal year 2006, the Company entered into a subcontract covering an anticipated $11 million worth of product and services with a prime contractor for a Middle Eastern country to provide them with card personalization workstation integration for use in that country's personalized national ID program which includes optical memory cards, hardware, and software. The contract calls for multiple deliverables, installation, and certain client acceptance criteria, as defined in the agreement. In applying the guidance within EITF 00-21, the Company determined the deliverables are not to be accounted for as separate units, but rather as a bundled arrangement as the fair value of the undelivered items cannot be readily determined. Therefore, revenue recognition on this contract and the associated contract costs were deferred until the predominant undelivered element, the card personalization, is delivered and accepted, commencing with the installation and acceptance of the card personalization system. The Company determined that once the card personalization system is accepted, contract revenue would be recognized ratably based on actual cards personalized and accepted. The Company began recognizing revenue under this contract during the quarter ended March 31, 2007 as the card personalization system was accepted during that period. Revenue was recognized based upon the total number of cards accepted up to that time. We recognized revenue totaling $4 million in fiscal year 2007 based upon the total number of cards accepted through March 31, 2007. As of March 31, 2007 there remained $1 million of deferred revenue and $0.9 million of deferred contract costs relating to this contract. The components of the deferred contract costs as of March 31 are (in thousands):

	2007	2006
Optical memory cards and freight	$ —	$ 592
Hardware and other costs	954	449
Total deferred contract costs	$954	$1,041

Amortization

Deferred costs should generally be amortized as revenue related to the applicable contract is recognized. Thus, if the deferred costs are equal to or less than deferred revenue related to the same contract, the costs should be amortized over the same period and in the same manner as the related deferred revenue (SAB Topic 13A3f, ques. 5) (ASC 605-10-S99, A3f, ques. 5). If there are no deferred revenues, or if the amount of deferred costs exceeds the related deferred revenues, the cost, or excess costs, should be amortized in proportion to the revenue realized during the base contract term, excluding extensions. In these situations, the pattern of recognition for deferred costs should generally mirror the revenue to be recognized under the contract and if no pattern of revenue recognition can be predicted, the costs should be amortized on a straight-line basis over the contract period.

ILLUSTRATION: AMORTIZATION OF DEFERRED COSTS

Facts: Assume the same facts and conclusions as those presented earlier in the examples involving Satellite TV Company (Satellite).

Amortization: Satellite should amortize $50 of deferred costs over the same period and in the same manner that the $50 upfront nonrefundable fee will be recognized as revenue. This results in the recognition of $50 of deferred costs on a straight-line basis over a three-year period. The remaining $216 of deferred costs should be amortized on a straight-line basis over the one-year contract period.

Summary: Revenues and costs recognized over the expected period of the customer relationship (assuming that the revenue recognition criteria have been met) is as follows:

	Year 1	Year 2	Year 3	Total
Revenue:				
Amortization of upfront nonrefundable fee	$ 17	$ 17	$ 16	$ 50
Monthly programming fees	360	360	360	1,080
Total	377	377	376	1,130
Costs:				
Amortization of deferred costs				
$50 over three years	17	17	16	50
$216 over one year	216			216

Excess of deferrable costs over realizable costs	24	—		24
Monthly programming costs	144	144	144	432
Total	401	161	160	722
Net margin	$(24)	$216	$216	$408

EXAMPLE: AMORTIZATION OF DEFERRED COSTS

[*Readers should see the Computer Sciences Corp. example under "Costs of Revenue Transactions" for an example of the amortization of deferred costs.*]

SALES INCENTIVES

Many companies offer incentives to induce sales. Some common incentives include:

- Coupons and rebates in a single purchase transaction.
- Rights to discounts on future purchases.
- Volume discounts resulting in a cash rebate when a cumulative level of purchases is reached.
- "Free" products or services with the purchase of one or more products or services.
- "Points" (or "Miles") that can be accumulated and exchanged for free products or services, sometimes including products or services provided by parties other than the vendor.

This section discusses recognition of the costs of these incentives.[1]

---

[1] Proper classification of the costs of these incentives is also important. Classification is discussed in Chapter 11, "Presentation."

LISTING OF APPLICABLE LITERATURE

Publication	ASC	ASC Topic	Subject
SAB Topic 13	605-10-S99	Revenue Recognition	Revenue Recognition
FAS-140	405-20	Liabilities	Extinguishments of Liabilities
EITF 00-21	605-25	Revenue Recognition	Revenue Arrangements with Multiple Deliverables
EITF 01-9 and EITF 02-16	605-50	Revenue Recognition	Customer Payment and Incentives
TPA 5100.50	985-605-55-82	Software	Definition of More-Than-Insignificant Discount
TPA 5100.51	985-605-55-83	Software	Accounting for Significant Incremental Discounts

Coupons and Rebates

Coupons (e.g., a newspaper coupon for 50 cents off a box of cereal) and rebates (e.g., a $20 mail-in rebate found in the box of a computer printer) are examples of sales incentives that can be used by the beneficiary of the offer after a single purchase transaction. In many cases, the coupon or rebate user may not be the direct customer of the entity that offers the incentive. For example, newspaper coupons and mail-in rebates are generally offered by product manufacturers, but are redeemed by consumers who buy the product from a retail store. The retail store (or a distributor that acted as an intermediary) is the product manufacturer's direct customer; the end-user (consumer) is an indirect customer of the product manufacturer. The estimated cost of a single-purchase sales incentive must be recognized at the later of the date at which the related sale is recorded by the vendor or the date at which the sales incentive is offered (EITF 01-9, par. 22) (ASC 605-50-25-3). The rationale underlying this requirement stems from the possibility that the manufacturer may have sold the product to the vendor (or distributor) prior to offering the sales incentive.

Redemption rates on coupons and rebates are much lower than 100%. In fact, newspaper coupon redemption rates rarely exceed single-digit percentages. Therefore, if a company can reasonably estimate the expected redemption amount, it can record this estimate as a reduction in revenue. As estimates change, the accrual for the potential refund should also be adjusted. If reasonable estimates cannot be made, a liability should be recognized for the maximum potential amount of sales incentives that could be exercised or awarded. The following factors might impair a company's ability to make a reasonable estimate of coupon or rebate redemptions (EITF 01-9, par. 23) (ASC 605-50-25-4):

1. *The offer period is long.* The longer the offer period, the more difficult it becomes to predict the response rate. Whether an offer period is long should be determined based on the nature of the product, industry practice, and the type of customer.

2. *The absence of relevant historical experience.* Without historical experience to reference, predicting customer actions is virtually impossible. However, in the absence of company-specific experience, industry experience may be relevant.

3. *The absence of a large volume of relatively homogeneous transactions.* It is generally difficult to predict the actions of a particular customer. However, it is easier to predict the actions of a large number of customers.

> **OBSERVATION:** These factors are similar to those required for estimating product returns (see Chapter 5, "Product Deliverables") or service cancellations (see Chapter 6, "Service Deliverables") because, in both cases, the company is attempting to predict the actions of its customers.

Volume Rebates

Other sales incentives involve an offer to rebate or refund a specified amount of cash if the customer reaches a specified cumulative level of purchases or remains a customer for a certain time period. The cost of these incentives should be recognized as each of the required revenue transactions that results in progress by the customer toward earning the rebate occurs. The accrued cost should be limited to the estimated rebates potentially due, as long as an estimate can be made. If an estimate cannot be made, the maximum rebate potentially due customers should be accrued (EITF 01-9, par. 30) (ASC 605-50-25-8). Changes in the estimated amount of rebates or refunds and retroactive changes by a vendor to a previous offer should be recognized using a cumulative catch-up adjustment (EITF 01-9, par. 32) (ASC 605-50-25-9).

> **OBSERVATION:** Although estimating the amount of incentives to be used by a large group of consumers may be possible

because of historical experience, estimating volume rebates to be earned by a specific customer may be more difficult. This is particularly the case when the incentive plan is tailored for a specific customer. Therefore, companies that offer incentives to a small number of large customers are more likely to have difficulty estimating the amounts to be earned than companies that offer incentives to a large number of small customers.

Similar accounting should be followed by the customer receiving the volume rebate. The customer should recognize a reduction in cost of sales as each of the required revenue transactions that results in progress toward earning the rebate occurs, provided the rebate is (a) payable pursuant to a binding arrangement and (b) probable and reasonably estimable. If the rebate or refund is not probable and reasonably estimable, it should be recognized as the milestones are achieved (EITF 02-16, pars. 7 and 8) (ASC 605-50-25-10). Changes in the estimated amount of rebates or refunds and retroactive changes by a vendor to a previous offer should be recognized using a cumulative catch-up adjustment (EITF 02-16, par. 9) (ASC 605-50-25-12). See the SEC Registrant Alert in the Chapter 7 section entitled, "Combined License and Research and Development Arrangements."

EXAMPLE: VOLUME REBATES

BJ's Wholesale Club, Inc. Form 10-K—Fiscal Year Ended February 2, 2008

Vendor Rebates and Allowances

We receive various types of cash consideration from vendors, principally in the form of rebates based on purchasing or selling certain volumes of product; time-based rebates or allowances, which may include product placement allowances or exclusivity arrangements covering a predetermined period of time; price protection rebates and allowances for retail reductions on certain merchandise; and salvage allowances for product that is damaged, defective or becomes out-of-date. We recognize such vendor rebates and allowances based on a systematic and rational allocation of the cash consideration offered to the underlying transaction that results in progress by BJ's toward earning the rebates and allowances, provided the amounts to be earned are probable and reasonably estimable. Otherwise, rebates and allowances are recognized only when predetermined milestones are met. We recognize product placement allowances as a reduction of cost of sales in the period in which we complete the arranged placement of the product. Time-based rebates or allowances are recognized as a reduction of cost of sales over the performance period on a straight-line basis. All other vendor rebates and allowances are realized as a reduction of cost of sales when the merchandise is sold or otherwise disposed.

We also receive cash consideration from vendors for demonstrating their products in the clubs and for advertising their products, particularly in the

BJ's Journal, a publication sent to BJ's members periodically throughout the year. In both cases, such cash consideration is recognized as a reduction of selling, general and administrative ("SG&A") expenses to the extent it represents a reimbursement of specific, incremental and identifiable SG&A costs incurred by BJ's to sell the vendors' products. If the cash consideration exceeds the costs being reimbursed, the excess is characterized as a reduction of cost of sales. Cash consideration for product demonstrations is recognized in the period during which the demonstrations are performed. Cash consideration for advertising vendors' products is recognized in the period in which the advertising takes place.

Discounts on Future Purchases

A vendor may offer a discount on future purchases in conjunction with a current sales transaction. Some of these discounts may only be applied to future purchases of a particular product. Others may be applied to any future purchases during a defined time period.

The Software Model

The accounting for discounts offered on future purchases is addressed in the software revenue recognition literature (see Chapter 10, "Software—A Complete Model"). The software model requires a determination of whether the discount is incremental and *more-than-insignificant*. Revenue accounting for a transaction is affected only when the discount is deemed incremental and more-than-insignificant. In that case, a proportionate amount of the discount must be allocated to all the elements in the arrangement based on the relative fair value of each element. Although the software model does not apply to non-software transactions, it presents one view of the appropriate accounting for discounts that should be considered by companies outside the software industry.

> **DISCLOSURE ALERT:** Companies should disclose their choice of accounting policy for discounts offered to a customer in a current transaction that can be used for future purchases. See Chapter 12, "Disclosures," for additional discussion of accounting policy disclosures.

More-than-insignificant Incremental discounts   A future discount on purchases is considered a more-than-insignificant incremental discount if it meets all of the following criteria (ASC 985-605-15-3):

- *The future discount is incremental to the range of discounts reflected in the pricing of the other elements of the arrangement. If the* customer was able to negotiate a 30% discount on the elements in the current arrangement, offering a 30% discount on additional elements does not grant the customer anything that would not otherwise have been available.

- *The future discount is incremental to the range of discounts typically given in comparable transactions.* Discounts typically given in comparable transactions do not confer any value to the customer not currently available to the customer.
- *The future discount is significant.*

A future discount that does not meet all of these criteria should not receive any accounting recognition.

Accounting for more-than-insignificant incremental discounts
The basic principle for more-than-insignificant incremental discounts calls for a proportionate amount of the discount to be allocated to all the elements in the arrangement based on the relative fair value of each element. The application of this principle is straightforward when: (1) the products or services to which the discount applies are specified, and (2) there is sufficient evidence of the fair values of those products or services.

However, when either the products or services to which the discount applies are not specified or there is insufficient evidence of the fair values of those products or services, the accounting treatment is more complex and depends on whether the maximum amount of the discount can be quantified. When that maximum amount can be quantified, it should be allocated to the current and future purchases on the assumption that the customer will purchase the minimum amount necessary to be eligible for the maximum discount. The portion of the current transaction fee deferred is recognized proportionately as future purchases are delivered or provided (assuming that all other revenue recognition criteria are satisfied) ensuring that a consistent discount rate is applied. Any remaining deferred revenue is recognized when the discount expires.

When the maximum amount of the discount cannot be quantified (for example, when the quantity of future products or services to which the discount may apply is not specified), revenue allocated to current and future purchases should be net of the discount (note that revenue related to the initial purchase is deferred and, on future purchases, cash received determines the amount recognized as revenue). The portion of the fee deferred in conjunction with the current sales transaction should be recognized as revenue ratably over the discount period.

ILLUSTRATION: MORE-THAN-INSIGNIFICANT INCREMENTAL DISCOUNTS

EXAMPLE 1

Facts: Manufacturer X sells Product Y for $100 (its fair value) along with a right to a discount of $50 on Product Z, whose price and fair value is $150. The $50 discount is considered a significant incremental discount.

Accounting: Manufacturer X should allocate the $50 discount across Products Y and Z based on an overall discount rate of 20%. The overall discount rate is calculated as the ratio of the discount ($50) to the total of the fair values of Product Y and Z ($100 + $150 = $250). The amount of revenue that should be recognized for Product Y is $80 ($100 less the 20% discount) and $120 for Product Z ($150 minus the 20% discount). When the revenue recognition criteria have been met for the sale of each product, Manufacturer X will record the following journal entries:

- Upon sale of Product Y:

Cash or Receivable	$100	
Product Revenue		$80
Deferred Revenue		$20

- Upon sale of Product Z:

Cash or Receivable (sales price of $150 less $50 discount)	$100	
Deferred Revenue	$ 20	
Product Revenue		$120

EXAMPLE 2

Facts: Manufacturer L sells Product M for $250 (its fair value) along with a right to a discount of $100 that can be used on any of Manufacturer L's other Products—Products N through Z. The list prices of Products N through Z range from $150 to $350. The $100 discount is considered a significant incremental discount. Three months after the purchase of Product M, the customer uses the discount to purchase Product V, whose list price and fair value is $300.

Accounting: Manufacturer L should allocate the $100 discount across Product M and the future product purchase using the fair value of Product M and the lowest possible fair value of the future purchase on which the discount may be used ($150). The overall discount rate is 25%, calculated as the ratio of the discount ($100) to the total fair values of Product M and the lowest fair value ($250 + $150 = $400). The amount of revenue that should be recognized for Product M is $187.50 ($250 reduced by 25%) and for

Product V is $262.50 ($300 sales price less the $100 discount plus the $62.50 deferred in connection with the Product M sale). When the revenue recognition criteria have been met for the sale of each product, Manufacturer X will record the following journal entries:

- Upon sale of Product M:

Cash or Receivable	$250.00	
Product Revenue		$187.50
Deferred Revenue		$ 62.50

- Upon sale of Product V:

Cash or Receivable (sales price of $300 less $100 discount)	$200.00	
Deferred Revenue	$62.50	
Product Revenue		$262.50

EXAMPLE 3

Facts: Service Provider F sells Service G for $100 (its fair value) along with a right to a discount of 50% off all future purchases of Services H through W, with a maximum discount of $200. The 50% discount is considered a significant incremental discount by Service Provider F. Three months after the purchase of Service G, the customer uses the discount to purchase Service T, whose list price and fair value is $300.

Accounting: Service Provider F should assume that the customer will purchase the level of services necessary to take advantage of the maximum discount. This level of future purchases is $400 ($200 maximum discount divided by 50% discount rate). The overall discount rate is 40%, calculated as the ratio of the maximum discount ($200) to the total of the fair value of Service G and the level of future purchases necessary to earn the maximum discount ($100 + $400 = $500). The amount of revenue that should be recognized related to Service G is $60 ($100 reduced by 40%) and Service T is $180 ($300 sales price reduced by 40%, or $300 sales price less $150 cash discount plus 75% ($300 ÷ $400) of the $40 deferred in connection with the Service G sale). When the revenue recognition criteria have been met related to the sale of each service, Service Provider F records the following journal entries:

- Upon sale of Service G:

Cash or Receivable	$100	
Service Revenue		$60
Deferred Revenue		$40

- Upon sale of Service T:

Cash or Receivable (sales price of $300 less $150 discount)	$150	
Deferred Revenue	$30	
Service Revenue		$180

The remaining deferred revenue of $10 would be recognized upon future purchases totaling at least $100 or expiration of the discount.

Additional Examples: Additional examples of accounting for discounts on future purchases can be found in Chapter 10, "Software—A Complete Model."

Breakage

As described above and in Chapter 10, the software literature does not allow breakage (the portion of customers that will not use an offered discount) to be considered in the accounting for discounts on future purchases. This is due to the difficulty in making reasonable and reliable estimates of the breakage factor, as software transactions tend to be unique.

There are other areas of revenue accounting, however, in which the use of breakage is allowed, as long as reasonable and reliable estimates can be made. Several of these areas are discussed in Chapter 3, "General Principles." Companies that enter into a high volume of homogeneous transactions that include offers of discounts on future purchases may be able to make reliable estimates of breakage related to those offers. In these cases, it would likely be acceptable to use these estimates in the accounting for the offer.

> **SEC REGISTRANT ALERT:** In a December 2002 speech, the SEC staff discussed breakage in situations where customers make a nonrefundable prepayment for services or goods that they ultimately do not demand. The SEC staff observed that FAS-140 (ASC 405-20) requires either performance or legal release to extinguish a liability. Because a prepayment for future delivery of services or goods creates a liability, the application of FAS-140 (ASC 405-20) would result in no income recognition until the end (or expiration) of the performance period for products or services paid for, but not demanded, by the customer. Alternatively, the SEC staff indicated that it will not object to revenue recognition prior to the expiration of the performance period provided both the following conditions exist:
>
> 1. Management can demonstrate that the demand for future performance is remote based on a large population of homogeneous transactions; and
>
> 2. There is objective reliable historical evidence supporting the estimate of breakage.
>
> The SEC staff also indicated that (a) it would be skeptical of an accounting model that results in immediate income for breakage and (b) whether breakage represents revenue or a gain (i.e., other income) depends on the facts and circumstances.

In a December 2002 speech, the SEC staff discussed breakage in situations where customers make a nonrefundable prepayment for services or goods that they ultimately do not demand. The SEC staff observed that FAS-140 (ASC 405-20) requires either performance or legal release to extinguish a liability. Because a prepayment for future delivery of services or goods creates a liability, the application of FAS-140 (ASC 405-20) would result in no income recognition until the end (or expiration) of the performance period for products or services paid for, but not demanded, by the customer. Alternatively, the SEC staff indicated that it will not object to revenue recognition prior to the expiration of the performance period provided both the following conditions exist:

1. Management can demonstrate that the likelihood of a demand for future performance is remote; and

2. There is objective reliable historical evidence supporting the estimate of breakage.

The SEC staff also indicated that: (a) it would be skeptical of an accounting model that results in immediate income for breakage, and (b) whether breakage represents revenue or a gain (i.e., other income) will depend on the facts and circumstances.

The SEC staff used gift card redemption as an example, noting that recognition of breakage (the percentage of gift cards that will not be redeemed) on sale of the gift card is unacceptable (the delivery criterion is not satisfied at the inception of the arrangement). Gift card breakage can be recognized as the vendor is released from its obligation (e.g., at redemption or expiration) or when redemption is deemed remote. Another method recognizes breakage in proportion to actual redemption. In order to use this method, the vendor needs objective and reliable estimates of (1) breakage and (2) the period of gift card redemption. Registrants were encouraged to discuss specific facts and circumstances with the SEC staff.

EXAMPLES: GIFT CARD BREAKAGE

Limited Brands, Inc. Form 10-K—Fiscal Year Ended February 2, 2008

All of our brands sell gift cards with no expiration dates to customers in retail stores, through our direct channels and through third parties. We do not charge administrative fees on unused gift cards. We recognize income from gift cards when they are redeemed by the customer. In addition, we recognize income on unredeemed gift cards when we can determine that the likelihood of the gift card being redeemed is remote and there is no legal obligation to remit the unredeemed gift cards to relevant jurisdictions (gift card breakage). We determine the gift card breakage rate based on historical redemption patterns. We accumulated sufficient historical data to determine the gift card breakage rate at Bath & Body Works and Express during the fourth quarter of 2005 and Victoria's Secret during the fourth quarter of 2007. Gift card breakage is included in Net Sales in our Consolidated Statements of Income.

During the fourth quarter of 2005, we recognized $30 million in pre-tax income related to the initial recognition of gift card breakage at Express and Bath & Body Works. During the fourth quarter of 2007, we recognized $48 million in pre-tax income related to the initial recognition of gift card breakage at Victoria's Secret.

Williams-Sonoma, Inc. Form 10-K—Fiscal Year Ended February 3, 2008

Customer Deposits

Customer deposits are primarily comprised of unredeemed gift certificates, gift cards and merchandise credits and deferred revenue related to undelivered merchandise. We maintain a liability for unredeemed gift certificates, gift cards and merchandise credits until the earlier of redemption, escheatment or four years. During the second quarter of fiscal 2006, we completed an analysis of our historical gift certificate and gift card redemption patterns based on our historical redemption data. As a result of this analysis, we concluded that the likelihood of our gift certificates and gift cards being redeemed beyond four years from the date of issuance is remote. As a result, we changed our estimate of the elapsed time for recording income associated with unredeemed gift certificates and gift cards to four years from our prior estimate of seven years. This change in estimate resulted in the recording of income in selling, general and administrative expenses in the second quarter of fiscal 2006 of approximately $12,400,000. As of February 3, 2008 and January 28, 2007, customer deposits were $201,743,000 and $187,625,000, respectively.

Point and Loyalty Programs

Point and loyalty programs come in all shapes and sizes. Some programs involve a company granting points to their customers for every purchase with those points being redeemable in the future for goods or services provided by the company. The best known examples are airline frequent flyer programs.

There are also entities that specialize in operating point and loyalty programs. These entities (referred to as program operators) administer point and loyalty programs as a main revenue producing activity. Program operators sell points in their programs to third parties, and the third parties grant those points to their customers, employees, or others. These points are usually redeemable for a variety of goods or services. The program operator's obligations to its customers under these arrangements may solely involve redeeming the points. However, more often the program operator also provides a variety of administrative services to its customers such as tracking the point accumulation and redemption by the customer's participants in the program.

Some programs combine these basic elements. For example, in addition to granting "miles" to their customers based on purchases, many airlines also sell miles. The purchasers may be consumers who will redeem the points themselves or they may be other service providers, such as hotels or car rental agencies that will issue the miles to their customers.

The accounting considerations for these types of arrangements vary depending on the nature of the specific point and loyalty program. The more common considerations relate to (1) points granted to customers in connection with a current sales transaction, (2) points sold to third parties, (3) program operators, and (4) breakage.

> **DISCLOSURE ALERT:** Companies should disclose their accounting policy for the point and loyalty programs they offer and/or administer. See Chapter 12, "Disclosures," for additional discussion of accounting policy disclosures.

Points Granted as Part of Current Sales Transaction

The simplest point programs are those in which a customer earns points from purchases that are redeemable for additional products or services. In this transaction, the vendor has effectively sold two items to the customer: (1) the product or service delivered to the customer as part of that sales transaction, and (2) a portion of a product or service that will be provided in the future upon the redemption of the points issued. The fact that multiple items have been sold suggests that the arrangement should be accounted for as a multiple-element arrangement.

As discussed in Chapter 4, "Multiple-Element Arrangements," EITF 00-21 (ASC 605-25) provides criteria that must be met prior to treating elements in a multiple-element arrangement separately for accounting purposes. Although point and loyalty programs integrated with current sales transactions are multiple-element arrangements, they have specifically been excluded from the scope of EITF 00-21 (ASC 605-25) due to their unique nature. However, companies may elect to apply EITF 00-21 (ASC 605-25) to these types of arrangements. If points are treated as a separate element under EITF 00-21 (ASC 605-25), revenue allocated to the points must be deferred and recognized when the points are redeemed. If the points do not constitute a separate element and must be bundled with one or more other elements in the arrangement, the company may be able to conclude that the performance obligation related to the points is inconsequential.[2]

---

[2] An inconsequential performance obligation would not have to be considered when evaluating whether the delivery or performance criterion has been satisfied for the other elements in the arrangement (SAB Topic 13A3c, ques. 1) (ASC 605-10-S99, A3c, ques. 1). See Chapter 4, "Multiple-Element Arrangements," for a discussion of the criteria for determining whether a performance obligation is inconsequential.

If a company concludes that its performance obligation is inconsequential, it would accrue the costs related to the points at the time it recognizes revenue from the other elements in the arrangement. If a company concludes that the performance obligation related to the points is more than inconsequential, the earnings process must be taken into consideration when recognizing revenue for the bundled group of elements. As a result, revenue under the arrangement may not be recognizable until the points are redeemed.

> **OBSERVATION:** Many companies that issue points to their customers in programs such as the ones discussed, do not follow the guidance in EITF 00-21 (ASC 605-25). In practice, they use an accounting policy that results in: (1) no revenue allocation to the points, and (2) an accrual of associated costs at the point when revenue is recognized for the other elements in the arrangement. The measurement of the accrued liability varies across industries and companies within the same industry. It also changes over time for the same company.

EXAMPLES: INSIGNIFICANT DELIVERABLE

AMR Corp. Form 10-K—Fiscal Year Ended December 31, 2007

Frequent Flyer Program

American uses the incremental cost method to account for the portion of its frequent flyer liability incurred when AAdvantage members earn mileage credits by flying on American or its regional affiliates. In 2007, the Company changed its policy regarding the life of AAdvantage mileage credits. Effective December 15, 2007, AAdvantage members now must have mileage earning or redemption activity at least once every eighteen (18) months in order to remain active and retain their miles. Prior to this change, mileage credits automatically expired after thirty-six (36) months of inactivity in the AAdvantage member's account. The Company recorded a one-time benefit of $39 million as a component of passenger revenue in 2007 to reflect the impact of the additional miles expiring upon the change of expiration period for AAdvantage mileage.

American includes fuel, food, passenger insurance and reservations/ticketing costs in the calculation of incremental cost. These estimates are generally updated based upon the Company's 12-month historical average of such costs. American also accrues a frequent flyer liability for the mileage credits expected to be used for travel on participating airlines based on historical usage patterns and contractual rates.

Continental Airlines Form 10-K—Fiscal Year Ended December 31, 2007

Frequent Flyer Accounting

For those OnePass accounts that have sufficient mileage credits to claim the lowest level of free travel, we record a liability for either the estimated incremental cost of providing travel awards that are expected to be redeemed with us or the contractual rate of expected redemption on alliance carriers. Incremental cost includes the cost of fuel, meals, insurance and miscellaneous supplies, but does not include any costs for aircraft ownership, maintenance, labor or overhead allocation. A change to these cost estimates, the actual redemption activity, the amount of redemptions on alliance carriers or the minimum award level could have a significant impact on our liability in the period of change as well as future years. The liability is adjusted periodically based on awards earned, awards redeemed, changes in the incremental costs and changes in the OnePass program, and is included in the accompanying consolidated balance sheets as air traffic and frequent flyer liability. Changes in the liability are recognized as passenger revenue in the period of change.

American Express Company Form 10-K—Fiscal Year Ended December 31, 2007

Membership Rewards

The Membership Rewards program allows enrolled cardmembers to earn points that can be redeemed for a broad range of rewards, including travel, entertainment, retail certificates, and merchandise. The Company establishes balance sheet reserves which represent the estimated cost of points earned to date that are ultimately expected to be redeemed. Also, these reserves reflect management's judgment regarding overall adequacy. A weighted average cost per point redeemed during the previous 12 months is used to approximate future redemption costs and is affected by the mix of rewards redeemed. Management uses models to estimate ultimate redemption rates based on historical redemption statistics, card product type, year of program enrollment, enrollment tenure and card spend levels. During 2007, management enhanced the ultimate redemption rate models by incorporating more sophisticated statistical and actuarial techniques to better estimate ultimate redemption rates of points earned to date by current cardmembers given redemption trends and projected future redemption behavior. The provision for the cost of Membership Rewards points is included in marketing, promotion, rewards and cardmember services and the balance sheet reserves are included in other liabilities. The Company continually evaluates its reserve methodology and assumptions based on developments in redemption patterns, cost per point redeemed, and other factors.

Points Sold

As discussed above, a company may sell points to customers on a standalone basis. In other transactions, the points are included with a product or service, but are treated as a separate element for accounting purposes. In both situations, the sale and redemption of points do not represent separate earnings processes, as the customer would not pay for points without the ability to redeem them for valuable items.[3] Therefore, the earnings process related to the sale of points must be evaluated using a Completed Performance model, with performance only considered complete when the points are redeemed.

EXAMPLES: SALE OF POINTS

AMR Corp. Form 10-K—Fiscal Year Ended December 31, 2007

Revenue earned from selling AAdvantage miles to other companies is recognized in two components. The first component represents the revenue for air transportation sold and is valued at fair value. This revenue is deferred and recognized over the period the mileage is expected to be used, which is currently estimated to be 28 months. The second revenue component, representing the marketing services sold, is recognized as related services are provided.

The Company's total liability for future AAdvantage award redemptions for free, discounted or upgraded travel on American, American Eagle or participating airlines as well as unrecognized revenue from selling AAdvantage miles to other companies was approximately $1.6 billion at both December 21, 2007 and 2006 (and is recorded as a component of Air traffic liability in the consolidated balance sheets), representing 19.2 percent and 18.3 percent of AMR's total current liabilities, at December 31, 2007 and 2006, respectively.

The number of free travel awards used for travel on American and American Eagle was 2.6 million in 2007 and 2.6 million in 2006 representing approximately 7.5 percent of passengers boarded in each year. The Company believes displacement of revenue passengers is minimal given the Company's load factors, its ability to manage frequent flyer seat inventory, and the relatively low ratio of free award usage to total passengers boarded.

Changes to the percentage of the amount of revenue deferred, deferred recognition period, percentage of awards expected to be redeemed for travel on participating airlines, breakage or cost per mile estimates could have a significant impact on the Company's revenues or incremental cost accrual in the year of the change as well as in future years.

Continental Airlines Form 10-K—Fiscal Year Ended December 31, 2007

We also sell mileage credits in our frequent flyer program to participating entities, such as credit/debit card companies, alliance carriers, hotels, car rental agencies, utilities and various shopping and gift merchants. Revenue

---

[3] In certain programs, the issuer of points may be able to discontinue the program or change its terms without any liability to the point-holder. Even in these situations, the company has the obligation to redeem points presented for redemption before the terms are changed or the program is abandoned. Therefore, the accounting should reflect the redemption obligation.

from the sale of mileage credits is deferred and recognized as passenger revenue over the period when transportation is expected to be provided, based on estimates of its fair value. Amounts received in excess of the expected transportation's fair value are recognized in income currently and classified as other revenue. A change to the time period over which the mileage credits are used (currently six to 28 months), the actual redemption activity or our estimate of the amount or fair value of expected transportation could have a significant impact on our revenue in the year of change as well as future years.

During the year ended December 31, 2007, OnePass participants claimed approximately 1.5 million awards. Frequent flyer awards accounted for an estimated 7.2% of our total RPMs. We believe displacement of revenue passengers is minimal given our ability to manage frequent flyer inventory and the low ratio of OnePass award usage to revenue passenger miles.

At December 31, 2007, we estimated that approximately 2.4 million free travel awards outstanding were expected to be redeemed for free travel on Continental, Continental Express, Continental Connection, CMI or alliance airlines. Our total liability for future OnePass award redemptions for free travel and unrecognized revenue from sales of OnePass miles to other companies was approximately $318 million at December 31, 2007. This liability is recognized as a component of air traffic and frequent flyer liability in our consolidated balance sheets.

ILLUSTRATION: SALE OF PRODUCT AND POINTS

Facts: Company A sells a variety of household products. For each dollar of purchases, Company A's premier customers earn one point. The points may be accumulated and redeemed for a variety of Company A's household products. Point values are assigned to each of the household products for redemption purposes. Company A sells $50,000 of household products to Premier Customer D. As a result, Premier Customer D earns 50,000 points. The sales price of the household products to non-premier customers is $50,000. Company A regularly sells points on a standalone basis for $.25 per point. For purposes of this example, assume that Company A concludes that it should treat the sale of the household products separate from the sale of the points. Customer D eventually redeems the points for household products having a carrying amount of $6,000.

Accounting: Company A allocates revenue to the points based on the following calculation:

Fair value of household products	$50,000
Fair value of points (50,000 points @ $.25 per point)	12,500
Total fair value	62,500

Arrangement consideration	50,000
Portion allocable to household products based on relative fair values	80%
Consideration allocated to household products	40,000
Portion allocable to points based on relative fair values	20%
Consideration allocated to points	$10,000

Company A records the following journal entries:

* Upon meeting the revenue recognition criteria related to the sale of the household products to Customer A:

Cash or Receivable	$50,000	
Product Revenue		$40,000
Unredeemed Points Liability		$10,000

* Upon redemption of the points by Customer A:

Unredeemed Points Liability	$10,000	
Product Revenue		$10,000
Cost of Goods Sold	$ 6,000	
Product Inventory		$ 6,000

Program Operators

Program operators may agree to provide several deliverables to their customers, including the issuance and redemption of points as well as the provision of administrative services. Although these arrangements are specifically excluded from the scope of EITF 00-21 (ASC 605-25), they may still be evaluated as multiple-element arrangements, with the sale and redemption of the points considered one element and the administrative services as one or more elements. See Chapter 4, "Multiple-Element Arrangements," for guidance regarding separation of multiple-element arrangements under the EITF 00-21 (ASC 605-25) model.

If the administrative services are treated separately, the earnings process for the services will most likely be evaluated using a Proportional Performance model, with revenue recognized throughout the performance period. The revenue allocated to the points, however, would be recognized when the points are redeemed using a Completed Performance model. If the services and points are combined and treated as a single element, the revenue recognition accounting policy should take into consideration all of the program operators' obligations.

Breakage

As previously discussed, breakage is a term commonly used to describe the portion of customers that will not use all of the rights they obtain in a transaction. For point and loyalty programs, breakage refers to the points that will never be redeemed. This occurs because point holders may not accumulate a sufficient amount of points for redemption purposes, they may lose track of their points, or they may decide it is not worth their time or effort to redeem the points. Breakage presents a unique accounting issue—when should revenue be recognized for points that are not expected to be redeemed?

As discussed earlier, EITF 01-9 (ASC 605-50) addresses breakage related to the redemption of rebate offers. Under that guidance, a company may take breakage into consideration when accruing the liability related to redemption of rebate offers if reasonable and reliable estimates of the expected level of rebate redemptions can be made. Similar analyses allow breakage to be considered when accounting for rights of return or cancellation (see Chapter 5, "Product Deliverables," and Chapter 6, "Service Deliverables"). If a similar analysis yields a reliable estimate of breakage in a point program, that estimate may generally be taken into account in allocating revenue to points issued.

Even if sufficient evidence exists to estimate breakage, this should not result in immediate income recognition from points that are expected to go unredeemed. Instead, the sales price related to the points should be recognized based on the number of points expected to be redeemed by the customer over the redemption period.

ILLUSTRATION: FACTORING IN BREAKAGE

Facts: Airline J sells 1,000,000 miles to Customer D for $500,000. Airline J can make reasonable and reliable estimates of breakage and consequently determines that only 800,000 of these miles will ultimately be redeemed. During Airline J's first quarter, 250,000 of these miles are redeemed and used by Customer D.

Accounting: Airline J calculates the following amount of revenue that should be recognized for each mile as it is redeemed:

Arrangement consideration	$ 500,000
Reasonable and reliable estimate of miles to be redeemed	800,000
Revenue per mile	$ 0.625

Airline J records the following journal entries:

• Upon receiving cash from Customer D:

Cash or Receivable	$500,000	
Unredeemed Miles Liability		$500,000

• Upon redemption and use of miles by Customer D in first quarter (250,000 miles redeemed at $.625 of revenue per mile):

Unredeemed Miles Liability	$156,250	
Service Revenue		$156,250

☞ **PRACTICE POINTER:** In the above illustration, breakage was not factored into the revenue accounting by recognizing $100,000 ($500,000 arrangement consideration × [200,000 miles not expected to be redeemed/1,000,000 miles sold]) of revenue upon the sale of the miles. This approach is inappropriate because Airline J has not yet provided any services to earn that revenue.

If a company cannot make reasonable and reliable estimates of point redemption levels, it must assume that all of the points will eventually be redeemed for accounting purposes. This maximum point redemption liability is reduced over time as points are redeemed or as points expire unused. If points do not have an expiration date or if a company has a policy of honoring expired points, revenue might be deferred for a longer period of time, until the company is able to reliably estimate what percentage of points will ultimately be redeemed.

EXAMPLE: BREAKAGE

AMR Corp. Form 10-K—Fiscal Year Ended December 31, 2007

The Company considers breakage in its incremental cost calculation and recognizes breakage on AAdvantage miles sold over the estimated period of usage for sold miles that are ultimately redeemed. The Company calculates its breakage estimate using separate breakage rates for miles earned by flying on American and miles earned through other companies who have purchased AAdvantage miles for distribution to their customers, due to differing behavior patterns.

Management considers historical patterns of account breakage to be a useful indicator when estimating future breakage. Future program redemption opportunities can significantly alter customer behavior from historical patterns with respect to inactive accounts. Such changes may result in material changes to the deferred revenue balance, as well as recognized revenues from the program.

RELATED-PARTY SALES

Transactions reflected in financial statements are presumed to have been consummated on an arm's-length basis. This presumption is not justified when transactions are with related parties—even if the transactions are consummated on the same terms as those with unrelated parties—because the transactions may be the result of the relationship and may not have taken place without it. Accordingly, transactions with related parties require disclosure and, in certain cases, special accounting treatment.

General

In general, sales to related parties should be evaluated under the same general principles as other transactions. However, the fact that the customer is a related party can affect the judgment applied to many uncertainties that may otherwise exist in the transaction.

For example, sales to related parties with rights of return might not reasonably be expected to have the same return experience as other sales with rights of return. Therefore, reliable estimates of returns on these sales may not be available. Consignment arrangements with related parties, price protection clauses, warranties, acceptance provisions, and other uncertainties in related party transactions also warrant special consideration.

Noncontractual Terms

Every related party contract and transaction should be reviewed to determine whether, in substance, the rights and obligations (of both the customer and the vendor) are different from the rights and obligations in sales to unrelated parties.

Transactions That Lack Substance

The financial reporting system recognizes transactions when they have a substantive business purpose. Special accounting treatments are prescribed for transactions lacking a substantive business purpose.

Related party transactions should be carefully evaluated to establish the underlying business or economic rationale. For example, a sale with a limited right of return to a related party may, in substance, be an arrangement in which the "buyer" is acting as a sales agent for the "seller" or the right of return may be substantively unlimited, because the seller would accept returns from the related party beyond the contractual limitations. The accounting treatment for transactions lacking substance or a business purpose should reflect that fact, either by not recognizing the transaction at all (e.g., treat the arrangement as a shipment on consignment) or by altering the way it is treated (e.g., as one with an unlimited right of return, rather than a limited right of return).

Disclosures

The accounting literature requires specific disclosures about related party transactions. All parties in a related party transaction should ensure that the disclosures enable financial statement users to understand the magnitude of the transactions, the risks associated with them, and the reasons for them. Specific required disclosures for related party transactions are discussed in Chapter 12, "Disclosures."

> **SEC REGISTRANT ALERT:** In early 2003, the SEC staff issued the Report Pursuant to Section 704 of the Sarbanes-Oxley Act of 2002 (the Section 704 Report). In compiling the information in the Section 704 Report, the SEC staff studied enforcement actions filed during the period July 31, 1997, through July 30, 2002. One of the areas of improper accounting where a significant number of enforcement actions were brought by the SEC related to the disclosure of related party transactions. The SEC staff noted in the Section 704 Report that "Failure to disclose related party transactions hides material information from shareholders and may be an indicator of weaknesses in internal control and corporate governance procedures." This finding is a strong indication that more attention should be given to identifying and disclosing related party transactions. See Chapter 12 for a detailed discussion of required disclosures.

NONMONETARY TRANSACTIONS

A nonmonetary transaction involves an exchange of goods or services with little or no cash (or a financial instrument) changing hands. In general, any transaction in which less than 25% of the fair value is paid for with monetary consideration (i.e., cash or a financial instrument) should be considered a nonmonetary transaction. Although there are many types of nonmonetary transactions, this discussion focuses on nonmonetary transactions that may affect a company's revenues. In these cases, a company transfers products, services, or other revenue-generating items that constitute its ongoing major or central operations[4] in exchange for a nonmonetary asset. In most monetary transactions, measuring the total value of the transaction is not difficult because one of the parties in the transaction pays cash or another financial instrument. Because nonmonetary transactions involve little or no cash consideration, they raise measurement issues with respect to the value that should be assigned to the transaction.

> **OBSERVATION:** Nonmonetary revenue transactions do not affect the timing of revenue recognition, only the amount of revenue recognized.

> **PRACTICE POINTER:** In certain situations, purchase and sales agreements are entered into concurrently with the same party. In some cases these agreements require the transfer of cash between the parties. The substance of such agreements must be scrutinized to determine whether these agreements effectively represent a nonmonetary exchange transaction. For example, Company A agrees to sell $1,000,000 of inventory to Company B. Company B must make a payment to Company A in the amount of $1,000,000. At the same time, Company A agrees to purchase $1,000,000 of inventory from Company B. Company A must make a payment to Company B in the amount of $1,000,000. The sales and purchase agreements in this example effectively represent a nonmonetary transaction. The fact that cash was exchanged between the parties is meaningless in this transaction.

> **SEC REGISTRANT ALERT:** Round-trip transactions have received a significant amount of attention from the SEC staff. Round-trip transactions were an area of focus in the SEC staff's Report Pursuant to Section 704 of the Sarbanes-Oxley Act of 2002 (the Section 704 Report), issued in early 2003. The SEC staff studied enforcement actions filed during the period July 31, 1997, through July 30, 2002. In addition, round-trip transactions have also been a focus in recent SEC staff speeches. The SEC staff characterizes round-trip transactions

---

[4] Other nonmonetary transactions may result in the recognition of a gain or loss, but not revenue. See Chapter 11, "Presentation," for a discussion of the difference between revenues and gains.

in the Section 704 Report as transactions that "involve simultaneous pre-arranged sales transactions often of the same product in order to create a false impression of business activity and revenue." The SEC staff cited a number of enforcement actions in the Section 704 Report where registrants inappropriately used round-trip transactions to boost revenue. Essentially, the types of round-trip transactions identified by the SEC staff in the Section 704 Report should be treated as nonmonetary transactions. Nonmonetary transactions that lack substance should not result in the recognition of revenue. Registrants should carefully consider the accounting for such transactions and provide appropriate disclosure.

LISTING OF APPLICABLE LITERATURE

Publication	ASC	ASC Topic	Subject
CON-5	N/A	N/A	Recognition and Measurement in Financial Statements of Business Enterprises
APB-29	845-10	Nonmonetary Transactions	Nonmonetary Transactions
EITF 93-11	845-10	Nonmonetary Transactions	Barter Transactions Involving Barter Credits
EITF 99-17	605-20-25	Revenue Recognition	Accounting for Advertising Barter Transactions
EITF 00-8	505-50	Equity	Accounting by a Grantee for an Equity Instrument to Be Received in Conjunction with Providing Goods or Services
EITF 01-2	845-10	Nonmonetary Transactions	Interpretations of APB Opinion No. 29
FAS-153	845-10	Nonmonetary Transactions	Exchanges of Nonmonetary Assets
EITF 04-13	845-10	Nonmonetary Transactions	Accounting for Purchases and Sales of Inventory with the Same Counterparty

Basic Accounting Model

The first question that arises in a nonmonetary sale is whether any revenue should be recognized, as it is not clear that the "realized or realizable" criterion (see Chapter 3, "General Principles") can be met. CON-5 states:

> If product, services, or other assets are exchanged for nonmonetary assets that are not readily convertible into cash, revenues...may be recognized on the basis that they have been earned and the transaction is completed. Recognition...depends on the provision that the fair values involved can be determined within reasonable limits (CON-5, par. 84f).

An exchange (or exchange transaction) is a reciprocal transfer between entities where one entity obtains assets or services or incurs a liability by transferring assets or services or incurring other obligations to the other entity (APB-29, par. 3(c)) (ASC 845-10-20).

Revenue is generally recognized in a nonmonetary transaction if the fair values of the goods and services exchanged in the transaction can be determined. U.S. GAAP requires recognition of nonmonetary transactions at the fair value of the assets or services given up or those received, whichever is more readily determinable (APB-29, par. 18) (ASC 845-10-30-1). There are, however, exceptions to this treatment that may be relevant in a nonmonetary revenue transaction.

Exceptions

The recorded amount (carrying amount adjusted for impairment) of the nonmonetary asset(s) surrendered, rather than the fair values of the assets exchanged, must be used to measure a nonmonetary exchange under any of the following conditions (APB-29, par. 20) (ASC 845-10-30-3):

- Neither the fair value of the asset or service received nor the fair value of the asset or service given up is readily determinable.

- The exchange is of product or property held for sale in the ordinary course of business for product or property that will be sold in the same line of business to customers other than the parties to the exchange.

- The transaction has no commercial substance.

An exchange with commercial substance is a transaction that is expected to significantly change the entity's future cash flows. A transaction has a substantive effect on the entity's expected future cash if either of the following conditions are satisfied (APB-29, par. 21) (ASC 845-10-30-4):

1. The amount, timing, and risk of the future cash flows of the assets surrendered and those of the asset(s) received are significantly different.

2. The entity-specific values of the assets surrendered and those of the asset(s) received are significantly different and that difference is significant relative to the fair values of the assets exchanged. (CON-7 defines entity-specific values with reference to the economics and business activities of a specific entity (CON-7, par. 24(b).)

> **OBSERVATION:** If these exceptions did not exist, companies could artificially inflate earnings with transfers of inventory. Consider the situation where Company A transfers inventory to Company B in exchange for Company B's inventory. Both companies plan on selling the inventory they receive in the exchange to third-party customers in the normal course of their businesses. In the absence of these exceptions, both companies would be grossing up revenues, cost of sales, and profit by exchanging inventory for inventory. Grossing up these amounts is not appropriate if the exchange does not result in sales to third-party customers or change expected future cash flows.

> ☞ **PRACTICE POINTER:** Even in a nonmonetary exchange that is to be recognized based on the historical cost of the asset given up, a loss should be recognized if the transaction indicates that the fair value of the asset is less than its recorded amount. The loss in these instances is required to be recorded because the market price of the inventory has been shown to be less than its cost (ARB-43, Chapter 4, Statement 7) (ASC 330-10-35).

> **DISCLOSURE ALERT:** See Chapter 12, "Disclosures," for information about disclosures required for nonmonetary transactions.

Purchase and sale transactions with the same counterparty are required to be combined for the purpose of applying APB-29 (ASC 845-10) in certain circumstances.

1. Two or more inventory purchase and sales transactions with the same counterparty that were entered into in contemplation of each other, and

2. One transaction is *legally* contingent upon the performance of another inventory transaction with the same counterparty (EITF 04-13) (ASC 845-10-15-6).

The effect of combining these transactions is that they are likely to be looked at as an inventory-for-inventory exchange that must be recorded at the carrying amount of the inventory transferred. The EITF noted that the issuance of invoices and the exchange of offsetting cash consideration does not affect this consensus. Where a transaction is not legally contingent upon the performance of another inventory transaction, certain factors (the list is not exhaustive and no single factor is likely to be determinative) may indicate that the two transactions were entered into in contemplation of each other (EITF 04-13) (ASC 845-10-25-4):

- The transactions between the counterparties are subject to a specific (as opposed to a master netting arrangement) legal right of offset of obligations;
- These transactions are entered into the inventory purchase and sales transactions simultaneously;
- Inventory purchase and sales transactions were entered into at off-market terms; and
- There is relative certainty that the reciprocal inventory transactions will occur.

A transaction in which one entity transfers finished goods in a nonmonetary exchange for raw materials or work-in-process inventory within the same line of business does not qualify as an exchange transaction that facilitates sales to customers for the transferor of finished goods (see paragraph 20(b) of APB Opinion 29) (ASC 845-10-30-15). As a result, this type of transaction should be measured at fair value if:

- Fair value is determinable within reasonable limits; and
- The transaction has commercial substance (as discussed above).

The counterparties are required to disclose the revenues and costs (or gains and losses) related to this class of inventory transactions. All other nonmonetary exchanges of inventory in the same line of business must be reported at the carrying amount of the inventory transferred.

EXAMPLE: PURCHASES AND SALES OF INVENTORY WITH THE SAME COUNTERPARTY

Exxon Mobil Form 10-K—Fiscal Year Ended December 31, 2007

Effective January 1, 2006, the Corporation adopted the Emerging Issues Task Force (EITF) consensus on Issue No. 04-13, *Accounting for Purchases and Sales of Inventory with the Same Counterparty.* The EITF concluded that purchases and sales of inventory with the same counterparty that are entered into in contemplation of one another should be combined and recorded as exchanges measured at the book value of the item sold. In prior periods, the Corporation recorded certain crude oil, natural gas, petroleum product and chemical sales and purchases contemporaneously negotiated with the same counterparty as revenues and purchases. As a result of the EITF consensus, the Corporation's accounts "Sales and other operating revenue," "Crude oil and product purchases" and "Other taxes and duties" on the Consolidated Statement of Income were reduced prospectively from 2006 by associated amounts with no impact on net income. All operating segments were affected by this change, with the largest impact in the Downstream.

ILLUSTRATION: EXCHANGE OF INVENTORY FOR FIXED ASSET

Facts: Manufacturer A and Manufacturer B enter into a transaction where Manufacturer A provides inventory to Manufacturer B in exchange for a fixed asset that it intends to use in its production process. No cash or other monetary consideration is exchanged in this transaction. The readily determinable fair value of the inventory is $25,000 and it is recorded on Manufacturer A's books at $20,000.

Accounting: As the transaction is not an inventory-for-inventory exchange and the fair value can be readily determined, Manufacturer A should account for this transaction based on the fair value of the inventory surrendered. This results in the following journal entries being recorded by Manufacturer A upon consummation of the transaction:

Journal Entry	Debit	Credit
Fixed assets	$25,000	
Revenue		$25,000
Cost of goods sold	$20,000	
Inventory		$20,000

EXAMPLE: OTHER NONMONETARY EXCHANGES

Qwest Communications International Form 10-K—Fiscal Year Ended December 31, 2007

We have periodically transferred optical capacity assets on our network to other telecommunications service carriers. These transactions are structured as indefeasible rights of use, commonly referred to as IRUs, which are the exclusive right to use a specified amount of capacity or fiber for a specified term, typically 20 years. We account for the consideration received on transfers of optical capacity assets for cash and on all of the other elements deliverable under an IRU as revenue ratably over the term of the agreement. We have not recognized revenue on any contemporaneous exchanges of our optical capacity assets for other optical capacity assets.

Fair Value Considerations

To account for a revenue-generating nonmonetary transaction based on fair value, the fair value must be readily determinable within reasonable limits (APB-29, par. 20) (ASC 845-10-30-1). All evidence should be considered to determine the fair value of the transaction. In most cases, a nonmonetary transaction involving inventory or services that a company sells in its major ongoing central line of business can be valued based on the normal selling prices of such items. Other evidence might include quoted market prices or appraisals of the assets received in the transaction. If major uncertainties exist related to recoverability of the fair value assigned to an asset received in a nonmonetary transaction, such fair value should not be considered readily determinable within reasonable limits (APB-29, par. 26) (ASC 845-10-30-8).

Additional guidance on determining whether sufficient fair value evidence exists has been provided for exchanges of advertising space and for exchanges involving barter credits.

Advertising Exchange

One common type of nonmonetary transaction involves an exchange of advertising space. This is more common among Internet-based companies, but is observed in other industries as well. Companies engaging in advertising barter transactions should recognize revenue (and expense) at the fair value of the advertising space given up in the exchange transaction, provided that the fair value of that advertising space is determinable. If the fair value is not determinable, the transaction is recorded at the book value of the advertising space given up, which will generally be zero. The EITF has provided guidance on the development of fair value evidence. Fair value of advertising space surrendered must be based on recent historical cash transactions for the sale of similar advertising space to unrelated third parties (EITF 99-17) (ASC 605-20-25-14 through 25-18).

Historical cash transactions Only cash, marketable securities, or other consideration readily convertible to cash transactions occurring within the last six months may be considered for purposes of determining the fair value of the advertising surrendered. In addition, a company should consider whether there are any internal or external factors that would suggest that six months is too long of a period to look back to for purposes of finding representative cash transactions. Once a historical cash transaction has been used to substantiate the fair value of one advertising barter transaction, it may not be used to substantiate the fair value of another advertising barter transaction.

Similar advertising Advertising space surrendered in a nonmonetary transaction is deemed similar to advertising space sold in a cash transaction, only if both advertising spaces (EITF 99-17) (ASC 605-20-25-17):

1. Use the same media (e.g., a nonmonetary transaction where space is surrendered);
2. Use the same vehicle (e.g., a nonmonetary transaction where advertising space in Newspaper A is surrendered is not considered similar to a monetary transaction where advertising space in Newspaper B is surrendered); and
3. Are similar with respect to:
   a. Circulation, exposure, or saturation within an intended market;
   b. Timing (time of day, day of week, daily, weekly, 24 hours a day/7 days a week, and season of the year);
   c. Prominence (page on web site, section of periodical, location on page, and size of advertisement);
   d. Demographics of readers, viewers, or customers; and
   e. Duration (length of time advertising will be displayed).

DISCLOSURE ALERT: See Chapter 12, "Disclosures," for information about required disclosures.

EXAMPLE: BARTER TRANSACTION POLICY

Sinclair Broadcast Group, Inc. Form 10-K—Fiscal Year Ended December 31, 2008

Barter Arrangements

Certain program contracts provide for the exchange of advertising airtime in lieu of cash payments for the rights to such programming. The revenues realized from station barter arrangements are recorded as the programs are aired at the estimated fair value of the advertising airtime given in exchange for the program rights. Network programming is excluded from these calculations. Revenues are recorded as revenues realized from station barter arrangements and the corresponding expenses are recorded as expenses recognized from station barter arrangements.

We broadcast certain customers' advertising in exchange for equipment, merchandise and services. The estimated fair value of the equipment, merchandise or services received is recorded as deferred barter costs and the corresponding obligation to broadcast advertising is recorded as deferred barter revenues. The deferred barter costs are expensed or capitalized as they are used, consumed or received and are included in station production expenses and station selling, general and administrative expenses, as applicable. Deferred barter revenues are recognized as the related advertising is aired and are recorded in revenues realized from station barter arrangements.

Barter Credits

Nonmonetary transactions may involve barter credits that entitle the holder to receive goods or services in the future. The entity that redeems the barter credits may be the counterparty to the nonmonetary transaction or it may be a party whose business is operating barter credit programs. The basic nonmonetary transaction accounting model should be applied to nonmonetary transactions involving barter credits. Special considerations when applying this model to nonmonetary transactions involving barter credits include (EITF 93-11) (ASC 845-10-30-17 through 30-19):

* A presumption exists that the fair value of the nonmonetary asset exchanged is not greater than its carrying amount. This presumption can only be overcome if there is persuasive evidence to the contrary.

* The fair value of the nonmonetary asset in the transaction is generally considered to be more determinable than the fair value of the barter credits. The exception to this is if the barter

credit can be exchanged for cash or for items with independent quoted market prices (e.g., oil, gold).

- To record the transaction at fair value, there must be the expectation that the barter credits will be redeemed in a reasonable period of time and that the party that will provide goods or services upon the redemption of the barter credits will be in existence to honor its commitment.

ILLUSTRATION: EXCHANGE OF INVENTORY FOR BARTER CREDITS

Facts: Manufacturer C receives barter credits from Company Z in exchange for inventory. The carrying value of the inventory is $5,000. The fair value of the inventory is $4,500. Manufacturer C has received barter credits in previous nonmonetary transactions and has always redeemed these barter credits after a short period of time. The barter credits may not be redeemed for cash. Assume for purposes of this example that the barter credits will not be redeemed for inventory to be sold in the same line of business.

Accounting: Manufacturer C should account for this transaction based on the fair value of the inventory exchanged for the barter credits. This results in the following journal entries being recorded by Manufacturer A upon consummation of the transaction:

Journal Entry	Debit	Credit
Impairment loss on inventory	$ 500	
Inventory		$ 500
Cost of goods sold	$4,500	
Inventory		$4,500
Barter credits	$4,500	
Revenue		$4,500

Once barter credits have been recorded as part of a nonmonetary transaction, an impairment loss on the remaining amount of barter credits should be recognized if either (1) the fair value of the barter credits drops below their carrying amount or (2) the holder of the barter credits does not believe it is probable that it will redeem the barter credits (EITF 93-11) (ASC 845-10-30-19).

Receipt of Some Monetary Consideration

When both monetary and nonmonetary consideration is received in a transaction whose accounting should be based on fair values, the monetary consideration paid or received becomes part of the fair value determination.

When both monetary and nonmonetary consideration is received in a transaction whose accounting would otherwise not be based on fair values, the effect of the monetary consideration on the accounting for the transaction depends on the magnitude of the monetary consideration. As noted earlier, if the monetary consideration received in such a transaction is 25% or more of the fair value of the transaction, then the transaction should be accounted for as a monetary transaction. Monetary transactions are recorded at fair value.

If the monetary consideration is less than 25%, its effects depend on whether the company receives or pays the monetary consideration. If the company receives monetary consideration, the transaction should, in substance, be treated as a monetary transaction (at fair value) to the extent of the monetary consideration, and a nonmonetary transaction (at historical cost) for the balance. If the company is paying monetary consideration, it should not recognize any income. The recorded amount of the asset received in the nonmonetary transaction is based on the monetary consideration paid in the transaction plus the carrying amount of the asset surrendered in the transaction (APB-29, par. 22 and EITF 01-2) (ASC 845-10-30-6).

ILLUSTRATION: MONETARY CONSIDERATION LESS THAN 25% OF TRANSACTION'S FAIR VALUE

Facts: Manufacturer A and Manufacturer B enter into a transaction involving the exchange of inventory. Manufacturer A and Manufacturer B operate in the same line of business and plan on selling the inventory received in the exchange to end-users. Additional facts related to the transaction are as follows:

	Manufacturer A	B
Fair value of inventory provided	$15,000	$12,000
Fair value of inventory received	$12,000	$15,000
Recorded amount of inventory provided	$8,000	$7,000
Cash consideration received	$3,000	None
Cash consideration paid	None	$3,000

Accounting: Since this is an inventory-for-inventory exchange in the same line of business and the monetary consideration is less than 25% of the fair value of the transaction, it should not be accounted for as a monetary transaction.

Since Manufacturer A is receiving monetary consideration, it should account for the transaction as follows:

Monetary consideration received	$ 3,000	$ 3,000
Fair value of transaction	15,000	
Percentage of the transaction that is monetary	20%	
Recorded cost of inventory transferred	8,000	
Cost of sales for the portion of the inventory "sold" for monetary consideration		1,600
Profit to be recognized		$ 1,400

Journal Entry	Debit	Credit
Cost of Sales	$1,600	
Inventory		$1,600
Cash	$3,000	
Revenue		$3,000

These entries result in the inventory received by Manufacturer A having an initial carrying amount of $6,400. Manufacturer A only records revenue to the extent of cash consideration since this is an inventory-for-inventory exchange.

Since Manufacturer B is paying monetary consideration, it should account for the transaction as follows:

Journal Entry	Debit	Credit
Inventory	$3,000	
Cash		$3,000

No revenue or cost of sales results from this transaction for Manufacturer B since it is an inventory-for-inventory exchange where Manufacturer B is paying cash consideration.

EXAMPLE: NONMONETARY TRANSACTION ACCOUNTING POLICY

Seitel, Inc. Form 10-K—Fiscal Year Ended December 31, 2007

Revenue from Nonmonetary Exchanges
In certain cases, the Company will take ownership of a customer's seismic data or revenue interest (collectively referred to as "data") in exchange for a

non-exclusive license to selected seismic data from the Company's library. In connection with specific data acquisition contracts, the Company may choose to receive both cash and ownership of seismic data from the customer as consideration for the underwriting of new data acquisition. In addition, the Company may receive advanced data processing services on selected existing data in exchange for a non-exclusive license to selected data from the Company's library. These exchanges are referred to as nonmonetary exchanges. A nonmonetary exchange for data always complies with the following criteria:

- the data license delivered is always distinct from the data received;
- the customer forfeits ownership of its data; and
- the Company re3tains ownership in its data.

In nonmonetary exchange transactions, the Company records a data library asset for the seismic data received or processed at the time the contract is entered into or the data is completed, as applicable, and recognizes revenue on the transaction in equal value in accordance with its policy on revenue from data licenses, which is, when the data is selected by the customer, or revenue from data acquisition, as applicable. The data license to the customer is in the form of one of the four basic forms of contracts discussed above. These transactions are valued at the fair value of the data received or delivered, whichever is more readily determinable.

Fair value of the data exchanged is determined using a multi-step process as follows:

- First, the Company considers the value of the data or services received from the customer. In determining the value of the data received, the Company considers the age, quality, current demand and future marketability of the data and, in the case of 3D seismic data, the cost that would be required to create the data. In addition, the Company applies a limitation on the value it assigns per square mile on the data received. In determining the value of the services received, the Company considers the cost of such similar services that it could obtain from a third party provider.

- Second, the Company determines the value of the license granted to the customer. The range of cash transactions by the Company for licenses of similar data during the prior six months are evaluated. In evaluating the range of cash transactions, the Company does not consider transactions that are disproportionately high or low.

- Third, the Company obtains concurrence from an independent third party on the portfolio of all nonmonetary exchanges for data of $500,000 or more in order to support the Company's valuation of the data received. The Company obtains this concurrence on an annual basis, usually in connection with the preparation of its annual financial statements.

Payment in the Form of Equity Securities

One type of nonmonetary transaction that is somewhat common is the sale of products, services, or intellectual property for equity of the customer. In many cases, this transaction raises no questions other than those that exist in most nonmonetary transactions. However, an additional question that arises in certain sales for equity securities is what date to use in measuring the fair value of the equity instruments received. The question often arises because the instrument only vests as performance occurs or upon its completion. Thus, until that point, there is some question as to whether the vendor will ever receive the benefits embodied in the equity instrument.

In this situation, the vendor should measure the fair value of the equity instruments as of the earlier of the following dates (EITF 00-8, par. 4) (ASC 505-50-30-18):

1. The date the parties come to a mutual understanding of the terms of the equity-based compensation arrangement and a performance commitment is reached. A performance commitment is a commitment under which performance by the seller to earn the equity instruments is probable because of sufficiently large disincentives for nonperformance. Neither the forfeiture of the equity instruments, nor the ability to sue for nonperformance, in and of themselves, represents a sufficiently large disincentive.

2. The date the vendor completes the performance necessary to earn the equity instruments (i.e., the vesting date).

If, after the measurement date described above, the quantity or any of the terms of the equity instruments are dependent on the achievement of performance conditions, the initial measurement should be the one with the lowest value possible, as any amount above that would not be considered fixed or determinable. Changes in the fair value of the equity instrument that result from an adjustment to the instrument upon the achievement of a performance condition should be measured as additional revenue from the transaction by calculating the increase in the fair value of the instrument due to the changes (EITF 00-8, par. 6) (ASC 505-50-35-14).

> **OBSERVATION:** The instruments in these transactions may also experience changes in fair value after the measurement date for various other reasons. Changes in fair value of the equity instruments after the measurement date unrelated to the achievement of performance conditions should be accounted for in accordance with the relevant literature on the accounting and reporting for investments in equity instruments, and should not affect the amount of revenue recognized.

DISCLOSURE ALERT: See Chapter 12, "Disclosures," for information about required disclosures.

SEC REGISTRANT ALERT: As discussed earlier, round-trip transactions are receiving a significant amount of attention by the SEC staff. One round-trip transaction discussed by the SEC staff in a speech in December 2002 involved a vendor delivering cash and products or services and concurrently receiving cash and an equity interest in the customer. The substance of this transaction may be that the vendor is delivering products or services in exchange for an equity interest. If this is the substance of the transaction, the vendor should (a) record the investment in the counter-party at the fair value of either the shares received or the goods or services sold, whichever is more readily determinable, (b) record the net cash outlay or receipt, and (c) recognize as revenue the difference between the value of the investment received and the net cash outlay. The SEC staff has been clear that the substance of round-trip transactions should govern form. To the extent a registrant enters into round-trip transactions, the accounting for such transactions should be carefully considered and the details of such transactions should be appropriately disclosed.

CHAPTER 9
CONTRACT ACCOUNTING

CONTENTS

SURVEY OF APPLICABLE LITERATURE

Accounting for construction contracts is one of the few areas in which a comprehensive model for revenue recognition exists. The basic model was first provided in 1955. However, there was not much guidance on the application of the basic model or its scope. Standard-setters eventually determined that ARB-45 had not kept pace with the changing times and additional guidance was needed. As a result, SOP 81-1 was issued in 1981 and applies to both construction-type and certain production-type contracts.

The audit and accounting guides for construction contractors (AAG-CON) and federal government contractors (AAG-FGC) provide supplemental application guidance.[1]

---

[1] This chapter does not address the unique issues in accounting for government contracts.

LISTING OF APPLICABLE LITERATURE

Publication	ASC	ASC Topic	Subject
ARB-43, Ch. 11	912	Contractors—Federal Government	Government Contracts
ARB-45	605-35	Revenue Recognition	Long-Term Construction-Type Contracts
FAS-5	450-20	Contingencies	Loss Contingencies
SOP 81-1	605-35	Revenue Recognition	Performance of Construction-Type and Certain Production-Type Contracts
SOP 97-2	985-605	Software	Software Revenue Recognition
EITF 00-21	605-25	Revenue Recognition	Revenue Arrangements with Multiple Deliverables
AAG-CON	910	Contractors—Construction	Audit and Accounting Guide for Construction Contractors
AAG-FGC	912	Contractors—Federal Government	Audit and Accounting Guide for Audits of Federal Government Contractors
REG S-X, Rule 5-02	210-10-S99	Balance Sheet	Financial Statement Requirements, Commercial and Industrial Companies, Balance Sheets

OVERVIEW

Throughout this product, one of the most important questions affecting the timing of revenue recognition has been whether to use the Completed Performance or Proportional Performance model to determine when revenue has been earned. As noted in Chapter 3, "General Principles," product sales are generally analyzed under the Completed Performance model, such that revenue is not considered earned until the product is complete and delivered to the customer.

However, certain product transactions have characteristics that may make the use of the Proportional Performance model appropriate. This category of transactions calls for the delivery of a product that is built or constructed to the customer's specifications, rather than through the vendor's normal manufacturing and operating processes. Products built or constructed to customer specifications are generally not useful to the vendor apart from fulfilling the applicable contract, and the customer often has rights related to the products being constructed even before they are completed. Revenue in these transactions is considered earned during production, rather than only upon delivery of the completed product, as long as certain conditions are met.

The contract accounting literature generally specifies that costs should be recognized in proportion to revenue on a proportional (or ratable) basis throughout the term of the contract. This is very much unlike other applications of the Proportional Performance model where costs are recognized as incurred.

Although SOP 81-1 (ASC 605-35) does not specifically include discussion of the four general conditions for revenue recognition, all four criteria must be satisfied before revenue can be recognized.

SCOPE

Because of the significant differences in the way revenue and costs are recognized under contract accounting, it is important to carefully evaluate contracts to determine which guidance applies. Revenue from a product sale that does not fall within the scope of SOP 81-1 (ASC 605-35) may not be recognized under a Proportional Performance model. Further, while revenue on a service transaction is typically recognized under a Proportional Performance model, costs on a contract that does not fall within the scope of the contract accounting literature should be recognized as incurred, rather than smoothed over the contract's term.

The guidance in this chapter applies to construction-type and certain production-type contracts where facilities are built, goods are manufactured, or certain defined, related services are performed by a contractor[2] to customer specifications. However, contracts where a company uses its standardized manufacturing processes or regular marketing channels generally do not fall within the scope of SOP 81-1 (ASC 605-35) even if the subject of the contract is manufactured or performed by the company to customer specifications. This includes sales of goods from inventory or from homogeneous continuing production processes. Service contracts, other than those related to the construction industry, do not fall within the scope of SOP 81-1 (ASC 605-35).

> **SEC REGISTRANT ALERT:** As discussed above, it is generally not appropriate to analogize to SOP 81-1 (ASC 605-35)

---

[2] "Contractor" will be used throughout this chapter to describe the selling party in a contract that falls within the scope of this chapter's guidance.

with respect to linking revenue and cost recognition. In a December 2002 speech, the SEC staff stressed that percentage-of-completion accounting should not be applied to service contracts that are outside the scope of SOP 81-1 (ASC 605-35). Service contracts that fall within the scope of SOP 81-1 (ASC 605-35) are limited to contracts for architectural or engineering design services and construction consulting services (SOP 81-1, par. 13) (ASC 605-35-15-3).

Arrangements that fall within the scope of SOP 81-1 (ASC 605-35) must be supported with legally enforceable, binding agreements between the customer and contractor.[3] The duration of a contract (i.e., the period of time to construct, produce, or provide) is not a defining factor for purposes of determining whether a contract falls within the scope of SOP 81-1 (ASC 605-35). However, it may be a factor in determining whether the percentage-of-completion or completed-contract method should be used to account for the contract.

Examples of contracts that fall within the scope of this chapter include (SOP 81-1, par. 13) (ASC 605-35-15-3):

- Construction contracts, such as those of general building, heavy earth moving, dredging, demolition, design-build contractors, and specialty contractors (e.g., mechanical, electrical, or paving) and related service contracts, such as contracts for construction consulting services (e.g., agency contracts or construction management agreements), and contracts performed by architects, engineers, or architectural or engineering design firms.

- Contracts to design and build ships and transport vessels.

- Contracts to design, develop, manufacture, or modify complex aerospace or electronic equipment to a customer's specifications or to provide services related to the performance of such contracts.

Software and software-related arrangements that involve significant production, modification, or customization of software (SOP 97-2, par. 7) (ASC 985-605-15-3) are also accounted for under the guidance of SOP 81-1 (ASC 605-35). See Chapter 10, "Software—A Complete Model" for a comprehensive discussion of this class of arrangements.

As noted previously, contracts outside the scope of SOP 81-1 (ASC 605-35-15-6) include those involving the sale of products produced using the contractor's standardized manufacturing

---

[3] This is equivalent to the "persuasive evidence of an arrangement" condition that is generally required in order to recognize revenue on other transactions.

process (even if produced to the customer's specifications) and marketed using the contractor's regular marketing channels.

> **OBSERVATION:** Understanding the nature of the contract and determining whether the contract falls within or outside the scope of SOP 81-1 (ASC 605-35) is an important exercise because it could have a significant effect on the recognition of the related revenues and costs. A contract to build a piece of equipment that falls within the scope of SOP 81-1 (ASC 605-35) may be accounted for using a Proportional Performance model (percentage-of-completion method) resulting in the recognition of revenues as work is performed, and recognition of costs in proportion to revenues. However, if this contract is outside the scope of SOP 81-1 (ASC 605-35), the related revenue and costs may be recognized only at a single point in time under a Completed Performance model. Whether an arrangement is within the scope of SOP 81-1 (ASC 605-35) also has other important consequences for the amount and timing of revenue (e.g., different treatment of incentives) and cost (or, more precisely, expense) recognition.

ACCOUNTING METHODS

SOP 81-1 (ASC 605-35) describes two accounting methods—the percentage-of-completion method and the completed-contract method. Other methods, such as those where revenue is recognized based on progress billings or receipts and costs are recognized when incurred, are not acceptable. Under the percentage-of-completion method, contract revenues and contract costs should be recognized using a Proportional Performance model (i.e., as the contractor performs under the contract). By contrast, the completed-contract method specifies that contract revenues and contract costs should be recognized under a Completed Performance model (i.e., when the contract is complete or substantially complete). These two methods are not interchangeable for the same set of facts and circumstances. The decision about which method to apply must be based on an analysis of the arrangement using the specific criteria in SOP 81-1 (ASC 605-35); the determination is not a policy choice to be made by the contractor.

Circumstances of Use—Percentage-of-Completion

Percentage-of-completion is considered the model that best reflects the economics of most construction contracts. This is because, while not required in order to use percentage-of-completion accounting, these contracts (as well as certain other contracts) generally transfer ownership to the customer over time, as the asset is being built or manufactured. Furthermore, the contractor is usually compensated as the work is performed (through progress payments). The percentage-of-completion method synchronizes revenue recognition and transfer of ownership.

The percentage-of-completion method applies to contracts with the following characteristics (SOP 81-1, par. 23) (ASC 605-35-25-56 and 25-57):

- The contractor can consistently make reasonably dependable estimates of contract revenues, contract costs, and progress towards completion.

- The contract entered into by the contractor and the customer spells out the terms of the contract, including the specific rights and obligations of the customer and contractor, the contractor's compensation, and settlement terms.[4]

- The customer and contractor are both expected to satisfy their contractual obligations.

Ability to Make Estimates

The presumption is that the contractor can make reasonably dependable estimates in order to enter into profitable contracts and sustain its business model. This presumption can only be overcome if persuasive evidence exists to support the conclusion that it cannot make such estimates (SOP 81-1, par. 24) (ASC 605-35-25-58).

> **OBSERVATION:** When the ability to make estimates can affect revenue recognition, the accounting literature generally presumes that estimates cannot be made, unless persuasive evidence indicates they are reliable. As noted above, the contract accounting literature begins from a different perspective. The principle is the same—estimates should only be used if they are judged to be reasonable and reliable. However, the threshold of reliability for estimates used in percentage-of-completion is lower, resulting in estimates being used more often than they are in other situations.

Estimates, by their very nature, may deviate from actual results. However, when the deviation is consistently significant, the contractor should evaluate whether the estimates are reasonably dependable. This evaluation should attempt to (1) establish why the

---

[4] This point is generally consistent with the "fixed or determinable fee" condition generally required to recognize revenue on other transactions.

estimates are consistently and significantly different from actual results and (2) correct the estimation process, before discontinuing use of the percentage-of-completion method.

A contractor that can otherwise make reasonably dependable estimates may not be able to do so in isolated instances due to the existence of particular circumstances that inhibit the ability to make reasonable estimates on individual contracts. These "inherent hazards" may cast doubt on the ability of a customer or contractor to satisfy obligations under the contract and are different from normal recurring business risks. Examples of inherent hazards include contracts where completion is questionable due to external factors (e.g., pending legislation or litigation) and contracts where the item being manufactured or built is physically at risk due to external developments (e.g., condemnation or expropriation). Given the unique nature of inherent hazards, there must be specific, persuasive evidence that the existence of such a hazard prevents the development of reasonably dependable estimates (SOP 81-1, pars. 28–29) (ASC 605-35-25-65).

Circumstances of Use—Completed Contract

The completed-contract method may be used where the results would not differ materially from using the percentage-of-completion method, and it must be used where reasonably dependable estimates of contract revenues, contract costs, or progress towards completion cannot be made (SOP 81-1, pars. 31–32) (ASC 605-35-25-90 through 25-93).

A short-term contract is a situation where the application of the completed-contract method would not result in a materially different outcome from using the percentage-of-completion method. Therefore, if the contractor enters into predominantly short-term contracts, adopting the completed-contract method as its accounting policy would be appropriate. However, the contractor should carefully evaluate the affect of this reporting policy decision on interim financial statements.

EXAMPLE: COMPLETED CONTRACT
METHOD—BASIC MODEL

Crown Castle International Corp. Form 10-K—Fiscal Year Ended December 31, 2007

We provide network services, such as antenna installations and subsequent augmentation, network design and site selection, site acquisition services, site development and other services, on a limited basis. Network services revenues are generally recognized under a method which approximates the completed contract method. Under the completed contract method, revenues and costs for a particular project are recognized in total at the completion date. When using the completed contract method of accounting for network services revenues, we must accurately determine the completion date for the project in order to record the revenues and costs in the proper period. For antenna installations, we consider the project complete when the customer can begin transmitting its signal through the antenna. We must also be able to estimate losses on uncompleted contracts as such losses must be recognized as soon as they are known. The completed contract method is used for projects that require relatively short periods of time to complete (generally less than one year), such as our network services agreements and contracts. We do not believe that our use of the completed contract method for network services projects produces financial position and operating results that differ substantially from the percentage-of-completion method.

When the completed-contract method is used because the contractor cannot make reasonably dependable estimates of contract revenues, contract costs, or progress toward completion, this method must be applied for the duration of the contract. As a result, the contractor may not change to the percentage-of-completion method if reasonably dependable estimates of contract revenues, contract costs, and progress toward completion can subsequently be made.

Basic Accounting Policy

A company will generally determine its basic accounting model for contracts within the scope of SOP 81-1 (ASC 605-35) based on its standard agreements. However, a company may subsequently enter into a contract that is unique or atypical. In these situations, the company should consider whether a departure from its basic accounting model is necessary to account for the unique or atypical facts and circumstances. If a departure from its basic accounting model is necessary for such a contract, the contractor should disclose that departure (SOP 81-1, par. 31) (ASC 605-35-25-61; 605-35-25-95; 605-35-50-3; 605-35-50-5).

> **OBSERVATION:** A departure from the usual accounting model to account for a unique or atypical contract does not constitute a change in accounting policy. The contractor is merely using a different accounting policy for a different type of contract.

Other factors that may cause a contractor to depart from its basic accounting model include (1) the determination that reasonably dependable estimates cannot be made for a specific contract or (2) the existence of an inherent hazard related to a specific contract. These departures from the basic accounting model should also be disclosed.

COMBINING OR SEGMENTING CONTRACTS

Prior to applying either the percentage-of-completion or completed-contract method, the contractor must determine the proper unit of accounting. Normally, the unit of accounting is an individual contract. However, in certain situations, it may be appropriate to combine a group of contracts and account for them as if they were a single agreement. Conversely, a situation may arise where it is appropriate to segment a contract or group of contracts into two or more units of accounting and separately account for each unit of accounting as if it were an individual contract. Specific criteria have been developed to determine when contracts should be combined or segmented.

Combining Contracts

It is generally appropriate to combine contracts when accounting for them separately would misrepresent the economic substance of the arrangements as well as the amount and timing of the earned revenues, costs of earned revenues, and gross profit. Because of this interrelationship, the combined gross profit from the contracts should be recognized as the work is performed.

The following questions (based on the criteria in SOP 81-1, par. 37) (ASC 605-35-25-5 through 25-8) must be considered by a contractor to determine whether contracts should be combined for accounting purposes:

1. *Were the contracts negotiated as a single package in the same economic environment with an overall profit objective?* The time period between the negotiation of individual contracts should be reasonably short to lead to the conclusion that they were negotiated in tandem. If not, the likelihood that the contracts were negotiated in the same economic environment is diminished.

2. *Do the contracts, in essence, represent an agreement to perform a single project?* The elements, phases, or units of output of a group of contracts must be interrelated and interdependent to be considered a single project. The interrelationship and interdependence should extend to the design, technology, function, or ultimate purpose or use of the output from each contract.

3. *Do the contracts require closely related construction activities with substantial common costs that cannot be separately identified with,*

or reasonably allocated to, the individual contracts? Where two or more contracts have substantial costs in common, they may, in substance, be part of the same arrangement.

4. *Are the contracts performed concurrently or in a continuous sequence under the same project management at the same location or at different locations in the same general vicinity?*

5. *Do the contracts, in substance, constitute an agreement with a single customer?* An assessment of the other conditions that must be met to combine contracts should be considered in this context. The following questions are relevant:

   a. Did the different parties negotiate the contracts together?

   b. Do the different parties operate in the same economic environment?

   c. Is it reasonable to conclude that the contracts represent a single project that will benefit both parties?

In determining whether the contracts were effectively negotiated with a single customer, it is important to consider the mutual relationship and intentions of each party. For example, the more distant the relationship between the parties, the less likely it is that the contracts were negotiated with a single customer.

If the answer to each of the foregoing questions is "yes," a group of construction- or production-type contracts may be combined for accounting purposes. If the answer to any of the foregoing questions is "no" for a group of *construction-type* contracts, the contracts may not be combined for accounting purposes. If the answer to any of the questions is "no" when dealing with a group of *production-type* contracts, the contracts may still be combined into groupings such as production lots or releases for the purposes of accumulating and allocating production costs to units produced or delivered on the basis of average unit costs, if the following two conditions are met (SOP 81-1, par. 38) (ASC 605-35-25-9):

1. The contracts are with one or more customers for the production of substantially identical units of a basic item produced concurrently or sequentially, and

2. Revenue on the contracts is recognized under the percentage-of-completion method using the units-of-delivery approach discussed later in this chapter.

Segmenting a Contract or Group of Contracts

A contract or group of contracts may contain various elements or phases that have different profit margins. In addition, the contractor may agree to perform the various elements or phases independent of one another. In this situation, treating such a contract or group of contracts as a single unit for accounting purposes may distort the true economics of each element or phase. To address this situation, three sets of specific criteria have been established to determine whether a contract or group of contracts may be segmented for accounting purposes.

The first set of criteria allows a contract or group of contracts to be segmented if the following three actions (a) were taken during the negotiations, (b) were documented, and (c) are verifiable (SOP 81-1, par. 40) (ASC 605-35-25-12):

1. The contractor submitted bona fide proposals on the separate components of the project and on the entire project;

2. The customer had the right to accept the proposals on either basis; and

3. The aggregate amount of the proposals on the separate components approximated the amount of the proposal on the entire project.

If documentation is lacking, or if these steps were not taken, the contract or group of contracts may still be segmented if all of the following (second) set of criteria is met (SOP 81-1, par. 41) (ASC 605-35-25-13):

1. The terms and scope of the contract or project clearly call for separable phases or elements;

2. The separable phases or elements of the project are often bid or negotiated separately;

3. The market assigns different gross profit rates to the segments because of factors such as different levels of risk or differences in the relationship of the supply and demand for the services provided in the different segments;

4. The contractor has a significant history of providing similar services to other customers under separate contracts for each significant segment to which a profit margin higher than the overall profit margin on the project is ascribed;

5. The significant history with customers who have contracted for services separately is relatively stable in terms of pricing policy rather than unduly weighted by erratic pricing decisions;

6. The excess of the sum of the prices of the separate elements over the price of the total project is clearly attributable to cost savings incident to combined performance of the contract obligations; and

7. The similarity of services and prices in the contract segments and the prices of such services to other customers contracted separately should be documented and verifiable.

If neither the first nor second set of criteria has been satisfied for a *construction-type* contract or group of contracts, no segmentation is allowed. However, a *production-type* contract or group of contracts that do not meet either the first or second set of criteria may still be segmented into groupings such as production lots or releases for the purposes of accumulating and allocating production costs to units produced or delivered on the basis of average unit costs, when the following two conditions are met (SOP 81-1, pars. 38 and 42) (ASC 605-35-25-14):

1. The contracts are with one or more customers for the production of substantially identical units of a basic item produced concurrently or sequentially; and

2. Revenue on the contracts is recognized under the percentage-of-completion method using the units-of-delivery approach (discussed later in this chapter).

A production-type contract that does not satisfy any of the three sets of conditions provided herein may not be segmented.

> **OBSERVATION:** The segmentation criteria above are a specific methodology for separating elements in a multiple-element arrangement. The criteria are more restrictive and significantly different from the criteria applicable to other situations. Only the criteria discussed herein may be applied to segment contracts within the scope of the contract accounting literature.

> **PRACTICE ALERT:** As discussed in more detail in Chapter 4, "Multiple-Element Arrangements," EITF 00-21 (ASC 605-25) does not apply to arrangements that fall within the scope of SOP 81-1 (ASC 605-35). However, if an arrangement includes elements that fall within the scope of SOP 81-1 (ASC 605-35) *and* elements that fall outside the scope of SOP 81-1 (ASC 605-35), EITF 00-21 (ASC 605-25) should be applied to separate the SOP 81-1 (ASC 605-35) elements from the other elements. For further discussion, see Chapter 4, "Multiple-Element Arrangements," and Chapter 10, "Software—A Complete Model."

Discussion of Accounting Methods

Throughout the remainder of this chapter, it is assumed that the unit of accounting is an individual contract. This does not change the fact that when contracts are combined or segmented, the combined group of contracts or individual contract segment is the appropriate unit of accounting. It is to these units of accounting (in their combined or segmented form) that either the percentage-of-completion or completed-contract method should be applied.

PERCENTAGE-OF-COMPLETION METHOD

The use of the percentage-of-completion method results in the recognition of revenues and costs as the contractor performs under the contract. This method requires the contractor to estimate progress toward completion and calculate the amount of revenues, costs, or gross profit to be recognized in each accounting period. This characteristic of the percentage-of-completion method raises the following questions:

- What happens if the contractor cannot make reasonably dependable estimates?
- How may the contractor measure its progress toward completion?
- How should the contractor determine or calculate revenues, costs, or gross profit to be recognized in each accounting period?

Estimates of Contract Amounts

Contract revenues, contract costs, and progress toward completion must be estimated by the contractor to determine the amount of revenues, costs, or gross profits to recognize in a particular period. Normally, the contractor is able to determine and use its best estimates of these amounts. However, in some cases, the contractor may only be able to (1) determine a range of estimated amounts or (2) determine that it will not incur a loss. In extreme situations, the contractor may be unable to make any reasonably dependable estimates or even determine that it will not incur a loss. When this occurs, the completed-contract method must be used.

Range of Amounts

When a contractor can only estimate a range of revenues and costs, the contractor must determine which estimates within these ranges are most likely to occur. If the contractor can determine these amounts, they should be used. If the contractor cannot make such a determination, the amounts within the ranges that would result in the lowest probable profit margin (the lowest contract revenue estimate and the highest contract cost estimate) should be used (SOP 81-1, par. 25) (ASC 605-35-25-60).

ILLUSTRATION: LOWEST PROBABLE PROFIT MARGIN

Facts: Contractor A enters into a contract with Customer X to construct a unique building. This is the largest building by far that Contractor A has ever agreed to construct for a customer. Consequently, Contractor A is only able to estimate the range of revenues and costs expected under the contract. Contractor A estimates that its total contract revenues will range from $5.2 million to $5.5 million and that its total contract costs will range from $4.5 million to $4.8 million. Because of the lack of similarity between this contract and other contracts into which Contractor A has entered, Contractor A is not able to determine which point within these ranges is most likely to occur. At the end of the first reporting period, Contractor A has incurred $1.2 million of contract costs and estimates that the project is 25% complete.

Accounting: Because Contractor A cannot determine which amounts within the contract revenue and cost ranges are most likely to occur, it should use the combination of amounts that results in the lowest profit margin. Consider the following possibilities:

	(in thousands)			
Contract Revenues	Highest		Lowest	
Contract Costs	Highest	Lowest	Highest	Lowest
Percentage complete	25%	25%	25%	25%
Contract revenues	$ 5,500	$ 5,500	$ 5,200	$ 5,200
Calculated revenues	1,375	1,375	1,300	1,300
Contract costs	4,800	4,500	4,800	4,500
Calculated costs	1,200	1,125	1,200	1,125
Calculated profit margin	$ 175	$ 250	$ 100	$ 175

The combination of the lowest contract revenues and highest contract costs results in the lowest overall profit margin. As a result, these are the amounts Contractor A should use to calculate revenues earned under the percentage-of-completion method.

No Loss Incurrence

In some situations, it may be impractical for the contractor to estimate either specific amounts or ranges of contract revenues and costs. However, if the contractor can at least determine that it will not incur a loss, a zero profit model should be used. The zero profit model results in the recognition of an equal amount of revenues and costs. This method should only be used if more precise estimates cannot be made and its use must be discontinued when such estimates are obtainable. Once a contractor has more precise estimates, the change should be treated as a change in an accounting estimate (SOP 81-1, pars. 25 and 33) (ASC 605-35-25-60; 605-35-25-67 through 25-69).

> **OBSERVATION:**   If in the previous example, Contractor A was not able to determine a range of contract revenues and costs, but could at least ascertain that it would not incur a loss on the contract, Contractor A would recognize $1.2 million of revenue in the first reporting period affected by the contract.

> ☛ **PRACTICE POINTER:**   Before switching from the percentage-of-completion method to the completed-contract method (due to the inability to estimate), the contractor should review the contractual terms to determine whether there is protection from incurring a loss. If there is such a provision (e.g., contract terms provide for the contractor to be compensated on a cost-plus basis), the contractor should continue to use the percentage-of-completion method but with a zero profit model. To illustrate the significance of this decision, consider the previous example. Use of the percentage-of-completion method with a zero profit model results in the recognition of $1.2 million of revenue and expense in the first reporting period affected by the contract. By contrast, no revenue or expense would be recognized if Contractor A used the completed-contract method.

EXAMPLE: ZERO PROFIT MODEL

Electronic Data Systems Corp. Form 10-K—Fiscal Year Ended December 31, 2007

If a contract involves the provision of a single element, revenue is generally recognized when the product or service is provided and the amount earned is not contingent upon any future event. If the service is provided evenly during the contract term but service billings are irregular, revenue is recognized on a straight-line basis over the contract term. However, if the single service is a Construct Service, revenue is recognized under the percentage-of-completion method usually using a zero-profit methodology. Under this method, costs are deferred until contractual milestones are met, at which time the milestone billing is recognized as revenue and an amount of deferred costs is recognized as expense so that cumulative profit equals zero. If the milestone billing exceeds deferred costs, then the excess is recorded as deferred revenue. When the Construct Service is completed and the final milestone met, all unrecognized costs, milestone billings, and profit are recognized in full.

If the contract does not contain contractual milestones, costs are expensed as incurred and revenue is recognized in an amount equal to costs incurred until completion of the Construct Service, at which time any profit would be recognized in full. If total costs are estimated to exceed revenue for the Construct Service, then a provision for the estimated loss is made in the period in which the loss first becomes apparent.

Measuring Progress Toward Completion

A variety of acceptable methods have evolved to measure progress toward completion. These methods can be categorized as either input or output measures. Input measures are generally based on costs incurred or effort put forth. Output measures are generally based on units delivered or units of work performed (SOP 81-1, par. 46) (ASC 605-35-25-70). A contractor must exercise significant judgment in choosing the method it uses to measure progress toward completion for each type of contract. Once the method is selected, it should be consistently applied to contracts with similar characteristics. However, a contractor should use different methods to measure progress toward completion if doing so will provide the best estimates. Progress toward completion should be substantiated periodically through physical observation. However, physical observation should only be used in a corroborative way.

Input Measures

Cost-based measures are the most commonly used input measures. Costs incurred divided by total costs expected to be incurred provides the percentage-complete measure. This measure assumes that there is a relationship between project progress and the incurrence of costs (i.e., an additional dollar of contract cost incurred leads to increased productivity). This may not actually be the case, depending on the facts and circumstances. For example, if a contract has high initial costs related to the use of specialized labor but lower labor costs for the balance of the project, it may not be appropriate to measure progress based on the labor costs incurred.

An important component of a cost-to-cost calculation is determining what costs to include. The general rule requires all contract costs (including those related to subcontractors) to be included in the calculation (components of contract costs are discussed in more detail later in this chapter). When determining the amount of contract costs incurred that should be included, payments for work not yet performed and significant amounts of uninstalled materials not specifically produced or manufactured for the project should not be included (SOP 81-1, par. 50) (ASC 605-35-25-75 through 25-77).

ILLUSTRATION: COST-TO-COST MEASURE

Facts: Contractor B enters into a contract with Customer Y to construct a unique building. Contractor B determines that this contract falls within the scope of SOP 81-1 (ASC 605-35). Contractor B also concludes that it can use the percentage-of-completion method because reasonably dependable estimates of contract revenues, costs, and progress towards completion are determinable. Based on the information available, Contractor B decides to use a cost-to-cost method to estimate progress towards completion. Payments for contract costs through the end of the accounting period totaled $1.7 million. These payments included the following:

- $0.2 million to Subcontractor 1 for work already performed;

- $0.1 million of advance payments to Subcontractor 2 for work not yet performed;

- $1.0 million of standard materials purchased from third parties, $0.6 million of which has been used in the construction process and $0.4 million of which has not been used in the construction process; and

- $0.4 million of other contract costs relating primarily to labor and equipment.

Contractor B estimates that total contract costs expected to be incurred are $6.0 million.

Accounting: Progress toward completion using a cost-to-cost measure should be based on $1.2 million of the $1.7 million contract cost payments made through the end of the period. The advance payments to Subcontractor 2 for work not yet performed ($0.1 million) and the payments for standard materials purchased from third parties that have not yet been used in the construction process ($0.4 million) should be excluded from the calculation of progress toward completion. The percentage-complete at the end of the period is calculated as follows:

$1.2 million of contract costs / $6.0 million of total expected
contract costs
= 20% of contract is complete

Another commonly used input measure is based on efforts expended. The unit of measure in an efforts-based model may be labor dollars, labor hours, machine hours, material quantities, or any other unit of measure that reflects the usage of effort. The percentage complete is calculated based on total efforts expended (e.g., labor hours spent) divided by total efforts expected to be expended (e.g., total labor hours expected to be spent). Generally, an efforts-based model can be more closely linked to productivity than a cost-to-cost model. However, inefficiencies and other factors may weaken the link between efforts expended and productivity. When using an efforts-based measure, the contractor should include the efforts of subcontractors. If the efforts of subcontractors cannot be reasonably determined in the unit of measure necessary (e.g., labor hours), an efforts-based model should not be used (SOP 81-1, pars. 48-49) (ASC 605-35-25-72 and 73).

Output Measures

Output measures base progress toward completion on results achieved. The most common output measures are units produced or units delivered. Other output measures focus on value added to the project and achievement of contract milestones. Generally, output measures are regarded as better measures of progress toward completion than input measures. However, reliable measures of output are often unavailable (SOP 81-1, pars. 46–47) (ASC 605-35-25-71). For example, in a contract to produce a single piece of equipment or construct a single house, there is not likely to be any output measure on which progress toward completion can be measured.

The most common output measure is a units delivered approach, which results in the recognition of revenue as each unit of output is delivered. Costs are allocated to the delivered units based on an average unit cost, which may be based on costs incurred to date or costs expected to be incurred over the contract period. This method should be used in situations where products are manufactured or produced to the customer's specifications on a continuous or sequential basis (SOP 81-1, par. 4) (ASC 605-35-25-55). Use in other situations would generally be inappropriate.

One example of an output measure based on units delivered is a contract where the contractor has agreed to pave a ten-mile stretch of road for the customer. The output measure that could be used in this situation is miles of road paved in the current period divided by total miles to be paved under the contract. If the contractor agrees to pave ten miles of road and paves 2.5 miles in the first accounting period affected by the contract, the progress towards completion at the end of that period is 25% (2.5 miles of road paved in current accounting period divided by 10 miles of road to be paved in total under the contract).

EXAMPLE: USE OF UNITS-OF-DELIVERY AND COST-TO-COST

Lockheed Martin Corp. Form 10-K—Fiscal Year Ended December 31, 2007

Contract Accounting/Revenue Recognition

Approximately 84% of our sales are derived from long-term contracts for design, development and production activities, with the remainder attributable to contracts to provide other services that are not associated with design, development or production activities. We consider the nature of these contracts and the types of products and services provided when we determine the proper accounting method for a particular contract.

Accounting for Design, Development, and Production Contracts

Generally, we record long-term, fixed-price design, development and production contracts on a percentage of completion basis using units-of-delivery as the basis to measure progress toward completing the contract and recognizing sales. For example, we use this method of revenue recognition on our C-130J tactical transport aircraft program, and Multiple Launch Rocket System program. For certain other long-term, fixed-price design, development and production contracts that, along with other factors, require us to deliver minimal quantities over a longer period of time or to perform a substantial level of development effort in comparison to the total value of the contract, sales are recorded when we achieve performance milestones or using the cost-to-cost method to measure progress toward completion. Under the cost-to-cost method of accounting, we recognize sales based on the ratio of costs incurred to our estimate of total costs at completion. As examples, we use this methodology for our F-22 Raptor program and the AEGIS Weapon System program. In some instances, long-term production programs may require a significant level of development and/or a low rate of initial production units in their early phases, but will ultimately require delivery of increased quantities in later, full rate production stages. In those cases, the revenue recognition methodology may change from the cost-to-cost method to the units-of-delivery method as new contracts for different phases of a program are received after considering, among other factors, program and production stability. As we incur costs under cost-reimbursement-type contracts, we record sales and an estimated profit. Cost-reimbursement-type contracts include time and materials and other level-of-effort-type contracts. Examples of this type of revenue recognition include the F-35 Lightning II Joint Strike Fighter System Development and Demonstration (SDD) program and the THAAD missile defense program. Most of our long-term contracts are denominated in U.S. dollars, including contracts for sales of military products and services to foreign governments conducted through the U.S. Government (i.e., foreign military sales).

As a general rule, we recognize sales and profits earlier in a production cycle when we use the cost-to-cost and milestone methods of percentage of completion accounting than when we use the units-of-delivery method. In addition, our profits and margins may vary materially depending on the types of long-term contracts undertaken, the costs incurred in their performance, the achievement of other performance objectives, and the stage of performance at which the right to receive fees, particularly under incentive and award fee contracts, is finally determined.

Output measures should not be based on comparisons of progress billings to total expected billings or cash receipts to total expected cash receipts. Payment terms are established by contract and bear no direct relationship to the actual progress toward completion. Milestones, as stated in a contract, may not reflect output completed. Milestones often better reflect negotiated payment schedules and the budgetary or financial needs of a customer and/or the contractor. When using milestones as the basis of the output measure, it is important to ensure (by documentation and by noting verifiable evidence) that milestones are substantively correlated with output.

Determining Revenues and Costs to Be Recognized

One of two alternatives may be used to calculate earned revenue and costs of earned revenue under the percentage-of-completion method. A contractor should select one of the alternatives and apply it consistently to all contracts. Guidance on what constitutes contract revenues and contract costs for purposes of applying these alternatives is provided later in this chapter.

Alternative A

Under this alternative, both revenues and costs of sales are recognized based on the measure of progress toward completion. More specifically, revenue for any period equals total expected contract revenue multiplied by the percentage complete at the end of the period in question, less the amount of revenue recognized in prior periods. Similarly, cost of sales for any period equals total expected contract costs multiplied by the percentage complete at the end of the period in question, less the amount of contract costs recognized in prior periods (SOP 81-1, par. 80) (ASC 605-35-25-83).

Alternative B

Under this alternative, gross profit is the only measure based on progress toward completion. Cost of sales is based on actual costs incurred to date; revenues are then recorded in an amount equal to costs incurred plus the gross profit calculated based on the percentage complete. More specifically, cost of sales for any period equals the contract costs incurred in that period. Gross profit for any period equals total expected revenues less total expected costs, multiplied by the percentage complete at the end of the period in question, less gross profit recognized in prior periods. Revenue is merely the sum of the cost of sales for the period plus the gross profit for the period (SOP 81-1, par. 81) (ASC 605-35-25-84).

Comparison of Alternatives

The same amount of gross profit should result in any given period, regardless of the alternative selected. However, revenues and costs may vary given the different calculation methods under each alternative. As a result, the gross profit percentage may also vary.

Neither of the two methods applies the Proportional Performance model as it is applied in service and other transactions that are outside the scope of SOP 81-1 (ASC 605-35). For these transactions, the Proportional Performance model generally results in the recognition of revenues on a ratable basis and the recognition of costs as incurred. By contrast, Alternative A results in the ratable recognition of both revenues and costs, while Alternative B results in ratable recognition of gross profit, but not costs or revenues.

> ☞ **PRACTICE POINTER:** Because the application of Alternatives A and B can produce significantly different results from the Proportional Performance model in certain service transactions (see Chapter 6, "Service Deliverables"), it is very important to understand which transactions are within the scope of the contract accounting literature.

The similarities and differences between Alternatives A and B can best be illustrated through a numerical example.

ILLUSTRATION: COMPARISON OF ALTERNATIVES A AND B

Facts: Contractor C enters into a contract with Customer K to construct an office building. Assume for purposes of this example that contract accounting applies and that Contractor C meets the conditions to apply the percentage-of-completion method. The construction period is expected to span two years. The total amount due from Customer K under the contract is $10 million. The initial estimate of costs to construct the office building is $9 million. Other information necessary to determine earned revenues and costs of earned revenues for Year 1 and Year 2 of the contract is provided below.

	Year 1	Year 2
Total Expected Revenues	$10,000,000	$10,000,000
Total Expected Contract Costs	9,000,000	9,000,000
Total Expected Gross Profit	1,000,000	1,000,000
Current Period Actual Costs	4,000,000	5,000,000
Percent Complete	40%	100%
Progress Billings	$ 3,500,000	$6,500,000

Comparison of Alternatives: The amount of Current Period Revenues and Current Period Cost of Sales under Alternatives A and B for Years 1 and 2 are shown below.

Alternative A	Year 1	Year 2
Cumulative Revenues:		
Total Expected Revenues	$10,000,000	$10,000,000
Percent Complete	40%	100%
Cumulative Revenues	4,000,000	10,000,000
Current Period Revenues:		
Cumulative Revenues	4,000,000	10,000,000
Revenue Recognized in Prior Periods	—	4,000,000
Current Period Revenues	4,000,000	6,000,000

Cumulative Cost of Sales:

Total Expected Contract Costs	9,000,000	9,000,000
Percent Complete	40%	100%
Cumulative Cost of Sales	3,600,000	9,000,000
Current Period Cost of Sales:		
Cumulative Cost of Sales	3,600,000	9,000,000
Cost of Sales Recognized in Prior Periods	—	3,600,000
Current Period Cost of Sales	3,600,000	5,400,000
Current Period Gross Profit	$ 400,000	$ 600,000
Current Period Gross Profit Percentage	10%	10%

Under Alternative A, at the end of Year 1, the following amounts would be reflected as assets on Contractor C's balance sheet: (a) $500,000 of Unbilled Revenues ($4,000,000 Current Period Revenues, less $3,500,000 of Progress Billings), and (b) $400,000 of Costs of Uncompleted Contracts ($4,000,000 of Current Period Actual Costs incurred, less $3,600,000 Current Period Cost of Sales).

Alternative B	**Year 1**	**Year 2**
Cumulative Gross Profit:		
Total Expected Gross Profit	$1,000,000	$1,000,000
Percent Complete	40%	100%
Cumulative Gross Profit	400,000	1,000,000
Current Period Gross Profit:		
Cumulative Gross Profit	400,000	1,000,000
Gross Profit Recognized in Prior Periods	—	400,000
Current Period Gross Profit	400,000	600,000
Current Period Revenues:		
Current Period Cost of Sales	4,000,000	5,000,000
Current Period Gross Profit	400,000	600,000
Current Period Revenues	$4,400,000	$5,600,000
Current Period Gross Profit Percentage	9%	11%

Under Alternative B, at the end of Year 1, $900,000 of Unbilled Revenues ($4,400,000 Current Period Revenues less $3,500,000 of Progress Billings) would be reflected as an asset on Contractor C's balance sheet.

OBSERVATIONS:

1. Current Period Gross Profit is the same under each alternative in both Years 1 and 2. This should always be the case.

2. Current Period Gross Profit Percentages are not consistent between the alternatives in either Year 1 or Year 2. This will generally be the case given that revenues are calculated differently under each alternative.

3. Current Period Gross Profit Percentage is the same in both years under Alternative A. This is the case if there are no changes in estimates between periods. If there are changes in estimates between periods, the Current Period Gross Profit Percentage will be different year-over-year under Alternative A.

4. Current Period Gross Profit Percentage is different in both years under Alternative B. This is the case if a method other than cost-to-cost is used to measure progress towards completion.

5. The total debit reflected on Contractor C's balance sheet at the end of Year 1 is the same under both alternatives. This should always be the case.

COMPLETED-CONTRACT METHOD

Contract revenues and expenses are recognized under the completed-contract method when the contract is considered complete or substantially complete just as they are in any other application of a Completed Performance model (see Chapter 3, "General Principles"). In the interim, costs incurred and progress billings are reported on the balance sheet (SOP 81-1, par. 30) (ASC 605-35-25-88).

A contract is complete if there are no remaining costs or potential risks. A contract is substantially complete if any remaining costs or potential risks are considered insignificant. A contractor should use objective criteria to assess the completeness of a contract. These criteria should provide consistency in the contractor's determination of when a contract is complete. Factors that may be considered by the contractor include delivery of the product, acceptance by the customer, departure from the site, and compliance with performance specifications (SOP 81-1, par. 52) (ASC 605-35-25-96; 605-35-25-97). These criteria are similar to those that would be used in other applications of a Completed Performance model.

EXAMPLE: SUBSTANTIALLY COMPLETE

Computer Programs and Systems, Inc. Form 10-K—Fiscal Year Ended December 31, 2007

We do not record revenue upon the execution of a sales contract. Upon the execution of a contract to purchase a system from us, each customer pays a nonrefundable 10% deposit that is recorded as deferred revenue.

The customer pays 40% of the purchase price for the software and the related installation, training and conversion when we install the system and commence on-site training at the customer's facility, which is likewise recorded as deferred revenue. When the system begins operating in a live environment, the remaining 50% of the system purchase price for each module that has been installed is payable. Revenue from the sale of the software perpetual license and the system installation and training is recognized on a module-by-module basis after the installation and training have been completed and the system is functioning as designed for each individual module.

For the sale of equipment, we incur costs to acquire these products from the respective distributors or manufacturers. The costs related to the acquisition of equipment are capitalized into inventory and expensed upon the sale of equipment utilizing the average cost method.

To the extent that a contractor recognizes revenues and costs upon substantial completion, the contractor should provide an accrual for the estimated remaining costs to be incurred and for the estimated settlement of any outstanding claims or disputes that could result in payments. These accruals should be evaluated as contingencies using the guidance in FAS-5 (ASC 450-20).

REVENUE AND COST ELEMENTS

Contracts within the scope of this chapter can have many different revenue and cost elements. For example, contract revenues are often derived from the following pricing or billing mechanisms:

- Basic contract price
- Customer-furnished materials
- Contract options and additions
- Change orders
- Claims

Cost elements can include both direct and indirect costs of performance, as well as costs incurred before performance begins. A discussion of how these elements affect the recognition of revenues and costs under both the percentage-of-completion and the completed-contract method is provided below.

Basic Contract Price

In many instances, determining the basic contract price is relatively simple. For example, contracts are often structured such that the price will remain fixed even if the contractor's cost experience or performance is not as originally expected. In this type of a contract, the contractor bears all risks related to cost overruns or performance difficulties. As a result, a contractor may attempt to negotiate one or more of the following pricing elements in its basic fixed-price contracts to mitigate these risks (SOP 81-1, pars. 55–56 and App. B) (ASC 605-35-25-15 through 25-33):

- Economic price adjustments
- Prospective periodic redetermination of price
- Retroactive redetermination of price
- Firm target cost incentives
- Successive target cost incentives
- Performance incentives
- Level of effort adjustments

Other contracts include variable pricing components such as those based on time and materials. Total revenue under a time-and-materials priced contract varies based on time incurred, materials used, and any mark-up rates applied to these amounts. When revenues are determined based on costs, the contract may call for reimbursement of costs plus an incremental amount. That incremental amount may be fixed or variable based on the performance or ability to meet cost or performance targets.

Estimating the basic contract price requires an analysis of both the fixed and variable pricing elements. Given the amount of judgment involved, estimates of the basic contract price should be evaluated periodically to determine if any adjustments are necessary.

Subcontractor Involvement

When a subcontractor performs activities under a cost-type contract, a question arises as to whether the costs of the subcontractor should be included in the general contractor's income statement on a gross (as contract revenues and contract costs) or net (no net effect on contract revenues or contract costs if the general contractor does not mark up the subcontractor's costs) basis. The factors to consider in making this determination are (1) whether the general contractor acts as a principal or an agent vis-à-vis the subcontractor's costs and (2) the extent to which the general contractor bears the risks related to these costs. Generally, if the general contractor acts as a principal, it likely bears a substantive portion of the risks associated with these costs. In such a situation, the subcontractor costs should be reflected on a gross basis in the general contractor's income statement. Amounts paid to subcontractors should be recorded as contract costs and reimbursements of such amounts received from customers should be included in contract revenues. When the general contractor acts as an agent vis-à-vis the subcontractor's costs, it does not bear a substantive portion of the risks associated with these costs. As a result, the subcontractor costs should be reflected on a net basis in the general contractor's income statement. In other words, subcontractor costs should not be considered contract costs and reimbursements of such costs should not be considered contract revenues (SOP 81-1, pars. 58–59) (ASC 605-35-25-20; 605-35-25-21).

> **OBSERVATION:** Gross versus net reporting is addressed in EITF Issue No. 99-19 (ASC 605-50), which provides a framework for assessing whether revenue should be recognized gross or net. The two key issues within this framework are the role of the entity (principal or agent) and the risks assumed by that entity. This framework is discussed further in Chapter 11, "Presentation."

Customer-Furnished Materials

In certain instances, a customer may purchase materials for the contractor to use for a specific project. Whether the contractor should include the value of the materials in contract revenues and costs depends on the risks borne by the contractor relative to these materials. If the contractor is responsible for the nature, type, characteristics, or specifications of such materials, or if the contractor is ultimately responsible for the acceptability of the performance of such materials in the context of the overall project, the value of those materials should be included in contract revenues and contract costs (SOP 81-1, par. 60) (ASC 605-35-25-22 through 25-24).

EXAMPLE: CUSTOMER-FURNISHED MATERIALS AND SUBCONTRACTOR COSTS

Fluor Corporation Form 10-K—Fiscal Year Ended December 31, 2007

The company recognizes engineering and construction contract revenue using the percentage-of-completion method, based primarily on contract cost incurred to date compared with total estimated contract cost. Customer-furnished materials, labor and equipment, and in certain cases subcontractor materials, labor and equipment, are included in revenue and cost of revenue when management believes that the company is responsible for the ultimate acceptability of the project.

Contract Options and Additions

In some cases, a contract is changed after performance has begun. Such changes can provide for additional deliverables or changes to the originally contemplated deliverables. Whether contract options and additions should be treated as: (1) a separate contract, (2) part of the original contract, or (3) a change order depends on the facts and circumstances.

A contract option or addition is treated as a separate contract if any of the following circumstances exist (SOP 81-1, par. 64) (ASC 605-35-25-29):

1. The product or service to be provided differs significantly from the product or service provided under the original contract;

2. The price of the new product or service is negotiated without regard to the original contract and involves different economic judgments; or

3. The products or services to be provided under the exercised option or amendment are similar to those under the original contract, but the contract price and anticipated contract cost relationship are significantly different.

When these criteria are not met, a contract option or addition must be treated as a change order. In addition, a contract option or addition should only be combined with the original contract if it meets the criteria for combining contracts discussed earlier in this chapter.

Change Orders

Change orders are modifications of an original contract that effectively change the provisions of the contract without adding new provisions (SOP 81-1, par. 61) (ASC 605-35-25-25). Some change orders are approved by the contractor and customer on a timely basis, while others are not approved until after completion of the project. The timing of approval is often determined by the amount of uncertainty in a change order. The accounting treatment of change orders depends on whether the scope and pricing of the order have been approved by both the customer and the contractor. When the scope but not the pricing of the change order has been defined, the appropriate accounting treatment will depend on whether the contractor is using the completed-contract or percentage-of-completion method to account for the contract.

Approved Change Orders

If a change order has been approved with respect to both its scope and its pricing, the price of the change order should be included in contract revenues and the costs of the change order should be included in contract costs (SOP 81-1, par. 61) (ASC 605-35-25-27). Therefore, a change in estimate of both contract costs and contract revenues would occur at the time a change order is approved. This would generally result in a remeasurement of both the percentage complete and the recognized costs and expenses (see "Changes in Estimates" in this chapter).

Partially-Approved Change Orders

As noted above, the scope of a change order may be defined even though the pricing is not. The treatment of these unpriced change orders varies depending on whether the contractor is using the completed-contract or percentage-of-completion method to account for the contract.

Completed-contract method (SOP 81-1, par. 62) (ASC 605-35-25-98) The costs related to an unpriced change order should be deferred as contract costs if it is probable that total contract costs, including costs attributable to change orders, will be recovered from contract revenues. In making the judgment as to whether recovery is probable, the contractor should consider its historical ability to recover costs under change orders and the specific facts and circumstances surrounding the change order under review.

Percentage-of-completion method (SOP 81-1, par. 62) (ASC 605-35-25-87) The inclusion of costs and revenues related to change orders in the computation of earned revenues and costs depends, in part, on the contractor's assessment of whether change order costs will be recovered. If the contractor determines that it is *not* probable that the change order costs will be recovered through a change in the basic contract price, then the change order costs should be included in the percentage-of-completion computation related to the overall contract. Effectively, this assumes that the change order costs will be absorbed, or recovered, by the basic contract price. Therefore, a change in the estimate of contract costs would occur when the scope of a change order is defined.

If the contractor determines that it *is* probable that change order costs will be recovered through a change in the basic contract price, the contractor has the following options:

1. Defer the change order costs (and recognition of any revenue) until agreement on price has been reached; or
2. Treat the change order costs as contract costs in the period they are incurred for purposes of computing costs of earned revenues for that period and recognize contract revenues to the extent of these change order costs.

A contractor should select and consistently follow one of these options to account for unpriced change orders.

To the extent it is probable that the change order will be priced at an amount that exceeds the change order costs, the additional probable contract revenue in excess of the change order costs should only be included in contract revenues for purposes of computing earned revenues under the percentage-of-completion method if realization of that incremental amount is assured beyond a reasonable doubt (SOP 81-1, par. 62) (ASC 605-35-25-87).

Unapproved Change Orders

A change order in dispute or whose scope and price have not been approved should be evaluated as a claim for purposes of determining whether it should be included in contract revenues and contract costs (see discussion below) (SOP 81-1, par. 63) (ASC 605-35-25-28).

Claims

The basic contract price is negotiated using a set of project assumptions. When a contractor's experience differs from these assumptions (e.g., due to errors in customer specifications, delays caused by the customer), the contractor will often seek additional compensation from the customer. This additional compensation is sought either through a formal change order or through a claims process. As noted above, unapproved or contested change orders are accounted for as claims because they are substantively equivalent.

A contractor may adopt a policy where claims revenue is only recognized when a claim has been received or awarded. Alternatively, the contractor may adopt an accounting policy that includes claim amounts in contract revenues if, (a) it is probable that the claim will result in additional contract revenue and (b) this amount can be reliably estimated. Both of these requirements can only be met if all of the following conditions exist (SOP 81-1, par. 65) (ASC 605-35-25-30; 605-35-25-31):

1. The contract or other evidence provides a legal basis for the claim; or a legal opinion has been obtained, stating that under the circumstances there is a reasonable basis to support the claim;

2. Additional costs are caused by circumstances that were unforeseen at the contract date and are not the result of deficiencies in the contractor's performance;

3. Costs associated with the claim are identifiable or otherwise determinable and are reasonable in view of the work performed; and

4. The evidence supporting the claim is objective and verifiable, not based on management's "feel" for the situation or unsupported representations.

When these conditions are met, revenue from a claim may be recognized up to the extent of costs incurred related to the claim. However, if the estimate of the claim amount is greater than the costs incurred related to the claim, the excess amount should not be recognized as revenue until the claim is settled. This amount, as well as claims that do not meet the above conditions, represents contingent assets, which may not be recognized until they are realized (FAS-5, par. 17) (ASC 605-35-25-31).

Costs incurred related to a claim should be treated as costs of contract performance.

EXAMPLE: ACCOUNTING FOR CLAIMS

Jacobs Engineering Form 10-K—Fiscal Year Ended September 30, 2007

The nature of our business sometimes results in clients, subcontractors or vendors presenting claims to us for recovery of costs they incurred in excess of what they expected to incur, or for which they believe they are not contractually responsible. In those situations where a claim against us may result in additional costs to the contract, we would include in the total estimated costs of the contract (and therefore, the estimated amount of margin to be earned under the contract) an estimate, based on all relevant facts and circumstances available, of the additional costs to be incurred. Similarly, and in the normal course of business, we may present claims to our clients for costs we have incurred for which we believe we are not contractually responsible. In those situations where we have presented such claims to our clients, we include in revenues the amount of costs incurred, without profit, to the extent it is probable that the claims will result in additional contract revenue, and the amount of such additional revenue can be reliably estimated. Costs associated with unapproved change orders are included in revenues using substantially the same criteria used for claims.

Contract Costs

The identification of contract costs is important given the way costs are accounted for under the percentage-of-completion method (i.e., costs are recognized as the contractor performs) and completed-contract method (i.e., costs are deferred until the contractor is substantially complete). The general rule is that contract costs should only include direct costs related to the contract and indirect costs specifically identifiable or allocable to the contract. The following table lists different types of costs and whether these costs would be considered contract costs (SOP 81-1, par. 72) (ASC 605-35-25-34 through 25-38).

Cost	Contract Cost?	
	% of Compl.	**Compl. Contract**
Direct materials	Yes (Note 7)	Yes (Note 7)
Direct labor	Yes	Yes
Direct subcontracting costs	Yes (Note 8)	Yes (Note 8)
Indirect labor	Yes (Note 1)	Yes (Note 1)
Contract supervision	Yes (Note 1)	Yes (Note 1)
Tools and equipment	Yes (Notes 1, 6)	Yes (Notes 1, 6)
Supplies	Yes (Notes 1, 7)	Yes (Notes 1, 7)
Quality control	Yes (Note 1)	Yes (Note 1)
Inspection	Yes (Note 1)	Yes (Note 1)
Insurance	Yes (Note 1)	Yes (Note 1)
Repairs and maintenance	Yes (Note 1)	Yes (Note 1)
Depreciation	Yes (Note 1)	Yes (Note 1)
Amortization	Yes (Note 1)	Yes (Note 1)
Support costs	Yes (Note 1)	Yes (Note 1)
General and administrative	No (Note 2)	Accounting Policy (Note 3)
Selling costs	No (Note 4)	No (Note 4)
Interest	No (Note 5)	No (Note 5)

Note 1: These costs are indirect costs and are only considered contract costs if they are specifically identifiable with or allocable to the contract. The allocation methods used must be systematic and rational.

Note 2: General and administrative costs should be expensed as incurred under the percentage-of-completion method.

Note 3: General and administrative costs may be allocated to a contract and treated as contract costs when using the completed-contract method. The contractor should elect an accounting policy to either expense these costs as incurred or treat them as contract costs. This policy must be consistently followed for all contracts under the completed-contract method.

Note 4: Selling costs should be expensed as incurred, unless they qualify as precontract costs (see "Precontract Costs" in the next section).

Note 5:   Interest is not considered a contract cost. Interest capitalization is addressed in FAS-34 (ASC 835, *Interest*; 835-20)

Note 6:   The cost of equipment purchased for use on a contract should be allocated over the period of its expected use unless title to the equipment is transferred to the customer by terms of the contract (SOP 81-1, par. 50) (ASC 605-35-25-77).

Note 7:   Inventoriable costs (such as direct materials and supplies not yet used in the construction process) should not be carried at amounts, that when added to the estimated cost to complete, are greater than the estimated realizable value of the related contracts (SOP 81-1, par. 72) (ASC 605-35-25-37).

Note 8:   Whether subcontracting costs should be reflected in the general contractor's income statement gross or net is discussed earlier in this chapter under "Subcontractor Involvement."

The guidelines above apply to all contracts that fall within the scope of SOP 81-1 (ASC 605-35), including those that compensate the contractor based on costs. Whether a contractor is compensated for a specific type of cost in a cost-type contract does not affect whether it is considered a contract cost.

Precontract Costs

Precontract costs are costs incurred in anticipation of a contract. The nature of the cost and the probability of its recovery are important factors to consider when determining the appropriate accounting treatment. A list of various precontract costs and the appropriate accounting treatment for each is provided below (SOP 81-1, par. 75) (ASC 605-35-25-41).

Cost	Treatment
Costs (excluding start-up costs) incurred for a specific anticipated contract that will result in a benefit only if the contract is consummated	• Not initially included in contract costs or inventory • May be deferred if recoverability from specific contract is probable — If deferred, and contract is consummated, include in contract costs

Cost	Treatment
	— If deferred, and contract is not consummated or recovery is no longer probable, expense
	— If not deferred, and contract is subsequently consummated, do not reverse previously expensed costs
Costs incurred for assets (e.g., for the purchase of materials, production equipment, or supplies) in anticipation of a specific contract	• Capitalize cost of the asset subject to the recovery of the cost being probable
Costs incurred to acquire or produce goods in excess of the amounts required for an existing contract in anticipation of future orders for the same item	• Treat as inventory subject to the recovery of the cost being probable
Start-up costs (including training or learning costs) incurred in conjunction with an existing or anticipated contract	• Expense as incurred

Estimate of Costs to Complete

Estimates of costs to complete are important in accounting for a contract under both the percentage-of-completion and completed-contract methods. Such estimates are important under the percentage-of-completion method because total costs to complete (actual-to-date plus estimates to complete) are an integral factor in (1) the cost-to-cost method of measuring progress toward completion, (2) determining the costs of earned revenue recognized in any given period, and (3) determining whether a loss contract exists (also important under the completed-contract method).

Estimates of costs to complete should (SOP 81-1, par. 78) (ASC 605-35-25-44):

- *Be performed consistently across all contracts.* This requires having standard procedures in place.

- *Be reviewed periodically and compared to actual costs to complete.* This will enable the contractor to determine whether its estimation procedures require revision.

- *Contain the same complement of costs included in actual accumulated contract costs.* For example, if indirect labor is included in actual contract costs, it should be factored into the estimate of costs to complete.

• *Take into consideration expected cost increases.* If labor rates are expected to increase as a result of a new union contract, the higher rates should be used in the estimation process.

☛ **PRACTICE POINTER:** At any given point in time, contract costs are both costs that have been incurred and those that have yet to be incurred. Because both types of costs are important when accounting for contract revenues and contract costs, the contractor must ensure that it has adequate systems and processes in place to accumulate costs incurred and estimate costs of completion for each contract. This is necessary because costs are not always expensed at the time they are incurred and revenues are not usually recognized when billings occur. The nature or complexity of these systems and processes depends on many factors including:

• The number of open contracts the contractor has at any point in time (e.g., a larger number of open contracts may require computerized cost accumulation and estimation processes whereas a smaller number of open contracts may only require manual cost accumulation and estimation processes); and

• The nature of the contractor's operations (e.g., if the contractor constructs very large, high-tech, complex pieces of equipment, a more elaborate cost accumulation and estimation process may be necessary).

The basic objective is to have systems and processes that provide adequate and consistent cost accumulation and estimation. Adequacy is measured by whether the information produced allows the contractor to properly account for each contract.

EXAMPLE: CONTRACT REVENUE AND COST ESTIMATION

Foster-Wheeler Form 10-K—Fiscal Year Ended December 28, 2007

We have numerous contracts that are in various stages of completion. Such contracts require estimates to determine the extent of revenue and profit recognition. We rely extensively on estimates to forecast quantities of labor (man-hours), materials and equipment, the costs for those quantities (including exchange rates), and the schedule to execute the scope of work including allowances for weather, labor and civil unrest. Many of these estimates cannot be based on historical data as most contracts are unique, specifically designed facilities. In determining the revenues, we must estimate the percentage-of-completion, the likelihood that the client will pay for the work performed, and the cash to be received net of any taxes ultimately due or withheld in the country where the work is performed. Projects are reviewed on an individual basis and the estimates used are tailored to the specific circumstances. In establishing these estimates, we exercise significant judgment, and all possible risks cannot be specifically quantified.

The percentage-of-completion method requires that adjustments or re-evaluations to estimated project revenues and costs, including estimated claim recoveries, be recognized on a project-to-date cumulative basis, as changes to the estimates are identified. Revisions to project estimates are made as additional information becomes known, including information that becomes available subsequent to the date of the consolidated financial statements up through the date such consolidated financial statements are filed with the Securities and Exchange Commission. If the final estimated profit to complete a long-term contract indicates a loss, provision is made immediately for the total loss anticipated. Profits are accrued throughout the life of the project based on the percentage-of-completion. The project life cycle, including project-specific warranty commitments, can be up to six years in duration.

The actual project results can be significantly different from the estimated results. When adjustments are identified near or at the end of a project, the full impact of the change in estimate is recognized as a change in the profit on the contract in that period. This can result in a material impact on our results for a single reporting period. In accordance with the accounting and disclosure requirements of the American Institute of Certified Public Accountants Statement of Position, or SOP, 81-1, "Accounting for Performance of Construction-Type and Certain Production-Type Contracts" and SFAS-154, "Accounting Changes and Error Corrections—a replacement of APB Opinion No. 20 and FASB Statement No. 3 ," we review all of our material contracts monthly and revise our estimates as appropriate. These estimate revisions, which include both increases and decreases in estimated profit, result from events such as earning project incentive bonuses or the incurrence or forecasted incurrence of contractual liquidated damages for performance or schedule issues, executing services and purchasing third-party materials and equipment at costs differing from those previously estimated, and testing of completed facilities which, in turn, eliminates or confirms completion and warranty-related costs. Project incentives are recognized when it is probable they will be earned. Project incentives are frequently tied to cost, schedule and/or safety targets and, therefore, tend to be earned late in a project's life cycle. There were 38, 29, and 45 separate projects each had final estimated profit revisions exceeding $1,000 in fiscal years 2007, 2006 and 2005, respectively. These changes in final estimated profits resulted in a net increase/(decrease) to contract profits of approximately $35,100, $(5,700), and $99,600 in fiscal years 2007, 2006, and 2005, respectively.

LOSS ON CONTRACTS

Regardless of the method used to account for the contract, a loss should be recognized when the current estimate of total contract revenue is less than the current estimate of total contract costs. This determination should be based solely on that contract's revenues and costs after combining or segmenting contracts into appropriate units of accounting, as discussed earlier in this chapter. A loss on one contract (or, if applicable, one segment of a contract) cannot be deferred because the expected income from another contract (or contract segment) will absorb or "cover" that loss (SOP 81-1, par. 85) (ASC 605-35-25-45).

The loss on a contract should be treated as part of the contract cost, not as a reduction of contract revenues or non-operating expense. The amount of the loss does not need to be broken out separately on the income statement unless it is material, unusual, or infrequent in nature. To the extent the loss is separately presented on the income statement, it should be reflected as a component of gross profit (SOP 81-1, par. 88) (ASC 605-35-45-1).

When a contract loss is recorded, the credit reflected on the balance sheet should be an offset to costs accumulated, if any exist or as a current liability. The current liability should be shown as a separate line item on the balance sheet if the amount is significant (SOP 81-1, par. 89) (ASC 605-35-45-2).

CHANGES IN ESTIMATES

Estimation is an integral part of contract accounting, particularly when using the percentage-of-completion method. The percentage-of-completion method requires estimates of total contract revenues, total contract costs, and progress toward completion. Changes in estimates should be accounted for under FAS-154 (ASC 250, *Accounting Changes and Error Corrections*) using the cumulative catch-up method. The cumulative catch-up method effectively provides for a true-up to the new estimate in the current period by calculating revenues, costs, and gross profit as if the new estimate were used from day one of the contract (SOP 81-1, par. 83) (ASC 605 35-25-86).

ILLUSTRATION: CHANGES IN ESTIMATES

Facts: Contractor J enters into a contract with Customer V to construct an office building. Performance under the contract is expected to span three years. Assume for purposes of this example that the contract falls within the scope of SOP 81-1 and that Contractor J meets the conditions required to apply the percentage-of-completion method and has decided to use Alternative A to calculate earned revenues and costs of earned revenue. The total amount initially due from Customer V under the contract is $10 million. The initial estimate of costs to construct the office building is $9 million. During Year 2, a change order is approved that results in an additional $500,000 of revenue under the contract. In addition, the combination of increased costs related to the change order as well as decreased costs due to construction efficiencies results in a net increase of $200,000 in the estimate of costs to construct the building. Other information necessary to determine earned revenues and costs of earned revenues for Year 1 and Year 2 of the contract is provided below.

	Year 1	Year 2
Total Expected Revenues	$10,000,000	$10,500,000
Total Expected Costs of Revenues	9,000,000	9,200,000
Total Expected Gross Profit	1,000,000	1,300,000
Expected Gross Profit Percentage	10%	12%
Percent Complete (calculated using an efforts-based input measure)	25%	70%

Accounting: The amount of Current Period Revenues and Current Period Costs using Alternative A for Years 1 and 2 are shown below.

	Year 1	Year 2
Revenues:		
Total Expected Revenues	$10,000,000	$10,500,000
Percent Complete	25%	70%
Cumulative Revenues	2,500,000	7,350,000
Revenues Earned in Prior Periods	—	2,500,000
Current Period Revenues	2,500,000	4,850,000
Costs of Revenues:		
Total Expected Costs	9,000,000	9,200,000
Percent Complete	25%	70%
Cumulative Costs of Revenues	2,250,000	6,440,000
Costs Recognized in Prior Periods	—	2,250,000
Current Period Costs	2,250,000	4,190,000
Current Period Gross Profit	250,000	660,000
Current Period Gross Profit Percentage	10%	14%
Cumulative Gross Profit Percentage	10%	12%

At the end of Year 2 the Cumulative Gross Profit Percentage is equal to the Expected Gross Profit Percentage. This is due to the cumulative catch-up adjustment effectively booked in Year 2. This adjustment resulted in a higher Current Period Gross Profit Percentage than the Cumulative Gross Profit Percentage in Year 2. The catch-up adjustment that was booked in Year 2 resulted in an additional $125,000 of revenues ($10,500,000 × 25% − $2,500,000), $50,000 of costs of revenues ($9,200,000 × 25% − $2,250,000) and $75,000 of gross profit in Year 2.

BALANCE SHEET PRESENTATION

Unique balance sheet presentation issues arise when accounting for an arrangement under both the percentage-of-completion and completed-contract methods. This is because costs are not always expensed at the time they are incurred and revenues are not usually recognized on a basis that is consistent with when billings occur.

Percentage-of-Completion Method

Accounting for a contract using the percentage-of-completion method raises two unique balance sheet presentation issues. One issue relates to the classification of the difference between current period actual contract costs incurred and those recognized as costs of sales. This difference should generally be classified as inventory. The second issue relates to the classification of the amount by which billings exceed revenues recognized and costs incurred but not yet expensed. This excess should be classified as a liability.

Completed-Contract Method

Under the completed-contract method, costs are accumulated on the balance sheet until the contract is complete or substantially complete. Similarly, amounts billed to customers are also deferred until the contract is complete or substantially complete. To the extent that the amount of accumulated costs exceeds the amount of advance (or progress) payments received or billed by the contractor, the excess should be reflected on the balance sheet as a current asset, separate from inventory. To the extent that the amount of advance (or progress) payments received or billed by the contractor exceeds the amount of accumulated costs, the excess should be reflected as a liability on the balance sheet.

☛ **PRACTICE POINTER:** The contract accounting literature specifies that costs incurred but not yet expensed and revenues billed but not yet recognized should be offset against one another. This is generally inappropriate for other transactions. In those situations, inventory or deferred costs and deferred revenue must be reported separately in most revenue arrangements.

SEC REGISTRANT ALERT: For receivables due under long-term contracts, SEC registrants must state separately in the balance sheet, or disclose in the notes to the financial statements, the following (REG S-X, Rule 5-02) (ASC 210-10-S99):

1. Balances billed but not paid by customers under retainage provisions (i.e., retainage receivables);

2. Amounts representing the recognized sales value of performance and such amounts that have not been billed and were not billable to customers at the date of the balance sheet; and

3. Billed or unbilled amounts representing claims or other similar items subject to uncertainty concerning their determination or ultimate realization.

EXAMPLE: PERCENTAGE-OF-COMPLETION BALANCE SHEET ACCOUNTS

Meadow Valley Corporation Form 10-K—Fiscal Year Ended December 31, 2007

The asset "costs and estimated earnings in excess of billings on uncompleted contracts" represents revenue recognized in excess of amounts billed. The liability "billings in excess of costs and estimated earnings on uncompleted contracts" represents billings in excess of revenues recognized.

5. Accounts Receivable, net:

Accounts receivable, net consists of the following:

	December 31, 2007	December 31, 2006
Contracts in progress	$14,156,776	$11,781,074
Contracts in progress—retention	5,297,883	3,928,480
Completed contracts	–	9,481
Completed contracts—retention	888,649	964,255

Other trade receivables	8,593,891	9,468,930
Other receivables	223,506	233,786
	29,160,705	26,386,006
Less: Allowance for doubtful accounts	(594,722)	(395,243)
	$28,565,983	$25,990,763

6. Contracts in Progress:

Costs and estimated earnings in excess of billings and billings in excess of costs and estimated earnings on uncompleted contracts consist of the following:

	December 31, 2007	December 31, 2006
Costs incurred on uncompleted contracts	$182,467,584	$ 200,904,026
Estimated earnings (loss) to date	14,965,044	17,742,674
	197,432,628	218,646,700
Less: billings to date	(208,113,722)	(225,758,594)
	$(10,681,094)	(7,111,894)

Included in the accompanying consolidated balance sheets under the following captions:

	December 31, 2007	December 31, 2006
Costs and estimated earnings in excess of billings on uncompleted contracts	$ 567,013	$ 1,254,860
Billings in excess of costs and estimated earnings on uncompleted contracts	(11,248,107)	(8,366,754)
	$(10,681,094)	$(7,111,894)

CHAPTER 10
SOFTWARE—A COMPLETE MODEL

CONTENTS

SURVEY OF APPLICABLE LITERATURE

SOP 97-2 (ASC 985, *Software*; 985-605) comprehensively addresses revenue recognition for companies that sell, license, lease, or otherwise earn revenue from computer software. Because revenue accounting for software is so thoroughly covered, companies generally need not look to SAB Topic 13, *Revenue Recognition* (ASC 605-10-S99) for guidance, except on a limited number of issues. Several other revenue recognition issues that are relevant to software have been addressed by the EITF, most notably scoping issues, including EITF 00-3 and EITF 03-5 (ASC 985-605-15-3). Significant software revenue implementation guidance was also provided by a Task Force organized by the AICPA. All of this guidance is included in the FASB Accounting Standards Codification (ASC).

☛ **PRACTICE POINTER:** The guidance published by the AICPA Task Force was published in the form of Technical Practice Aids (TPAs). TPAs have been published by the AICPA for many years and were never considered to be authoritative GAAP. However, the staff of the SEC had indicated that public companies were expected to follow the guidance in the software TPAs. When putting together the Codification, the FASB decided to include the guidance originally published in the software TPAs, making such guidance authoritative for all entities. Nonpublic entities that had not followed the guidance in the software TPAs have been provided transition provisions upon publication of the Codification so that they may adopt the software TPA guidance prospectively. No other AICPA TPAs have been included in the Codification.

LISTING OF APPLICABLE LITERATURE

Publication	ASC	ASC Topic	Subject
SOP 97-2	985-605	Software	Software Revenue Recognition
ARB-45	605-35	Revenue Recognition	Long-Term Construction-Type Contracts
APB-29	845-10	Nonmonetary Transactions	Nonmonetary Transactions
FAS-5	450-20	Contingencies	Loss Contingencies
FAS-48	605-15-25	Revenue Recognition	Revenue Recognition When Right of Return Exists
FAS-86	985-330	Software	Costs of Computer Software to Be Sold, Leased, or Otherwise Marketed
FIN-45	460	Guarantees	Guarantees
FSP FIN 45-1	460-10-55-30 through 55-34	Guarantees	Accounting for Intellectual Property Infringement Indemnifications
SOP 81-1 (ASC)	605-35	Revenue Recognition	Construction-Type and Certain Production-Type Contracts
EITF 88-18	470-10-25	Debt	Sales of Future Revenues

EITF 00-3	985-605-15-3	Software	Arrangements That Include the Right to Use Software Stored on Another Entity's Hardware
EITF 00-21	605-25	Revenue Recognition	Revenue Arrangements with Multiple Deliverables
EITF 01-9	605-50	Revenue Recognition	Accounting for Consideration Given by a Vendor to a Customer (Including a Reseller of the Vendor's Products)
EITF 03-5	985-605-15-3	Software	Non-Software Deliverables in an Arrangement Containing More-Than-Incidental Software
SAB Topic 13	605-10-S99	Revenue Recognition	Revenue Recognition
TPA 5100.38	985-605-25-9 and 55-94	Software	Determination of Vendor-Specific Objective Evidence After the Balance Sheet Date
TPA 5100.39	985-605-55-4	Software	Indicators that Multiple Contracts Should be Viewed as Single Arrangements
TPA 5100.41	985-605-55-15	Software	Effect of Prepayments on Revenue Recognition
TPA 5100.43	985-605-55-77 and 55-78	Software	Promises to Correct Software Errors (Bug Fixes)
TPA 5100.45	985-605-55-99	Software	License Mix Arrangements
TPA 5100.46 & .47	985-845	Software	Nonmonetary Exchanges Involving Software
TPA 5100.49	985-605-55-74	Software	Post-Contract Customer Support When Contract Accounting Is Applied
TPA 5100.50	985-605-15-3	Software	Definition of More-Than-Insignificant Discount
TPA 5100.51	985-605-55-85	Software	Significant Incremental Discounts
TPA 5100.52	985-605-55-57	Software	Fair Value of PCS in a Perpetual License
TPA 5100.53	985-605-55-59	Software	Fair Value of PCS in a Short-Term Time-Based License

TPA 5100.54	985-605-55-62	Software	Fair Value of PCS in a Multi-Year Time-Based License
TPA 5100.55	985-605-55-68	Software	Fair Value of PCS with a Consistent Renewal Percentage (But Varying Renewal Dollar Amount)
TPA 5100.56	985-605-55-18	Software	Concessions
TPA 5100.57	985-605-55-22	Software	Overcoming Presumption of Concessions in Extended Payment Term Arrangements
TPA 5100.58	985-605-55-31	Software	Effect of Prepayments on Software Revenue Recognition—Transfer of Receivable Without Recourse
TPA 5100.59	985-605-55-26	Software	Subsequent Cash Receipt in an Extended Payment Term Arrangement
TPA 5100.60	985-605-55-34	Software	Customer Financing with No Software Vendor Participation
TPA 5100.61	985-605-55-36	Software	Effect of Prepayments on Software Revenue Recognition When Vendor Participates in Customer Financing
TPA 5100.62	985-605-55-40	Software	Indicators of Incremental Risk and Their Effect on the Evaluation of Whether a Fee Is Fixed or Determinable
TPA 5100.63	985-605-55-42	Software	Overcoming the Presumption that a Fee Is Not Fixed or Determinable When Vendor Participates in Customer Financing
TPA 5100.64	985-605-55-46	Software	Indicators of Vendor Participation in Customer Financing That May Not Result in Incremental Risk
TPA 5100.67	985-605-55-79	Software	Customer Acceptance
TPA 5100.68	985-605-55-64	Software	Fair Value of PCS in Perpetual and Multi-Year Time-Based Licenses
TPA 5100.69	985-605-55-97	Software	Delivery Terms

TPA 5100.70	985-605-55-101	Software	Effect of Commencement of an Initial License Term
TPA 5100.71	985-605-55-105	Software	Effect of Commencement of an Extension/Renewal License Term
TPA 5100.72	985-605-55-110	Software	Effect of Additional Product(s) in an Extension/Renewal of License Term
TPA 5100.73	985-605-55-115	Software	Arrangement Containing an Option to Extend a Time-Based License Indefinitely
TPA 5100.74	985-605-55-201	Software	Effect of Discounts on Future Products on the Residual Method
TPA 5100.75	985-605-55-70	Software	Fair Value of PCS Renewals Based on Users Deployed
TPA 5100.76	985-605-55-5	Software	Fair Value in Multiple-Element Arrangements that Include Contingent Usage-Based Fees

OVERVIEW

Transfers of rights to software are generally accomplished by licenses rather than by outright sales to provide additional legal protection to software vendors. Although software licenses may have terms similar to a lease, such as a limited term and periodic payments, the rights transferred under software licenses are substantially the same as those transferred in many product sales. Therefore, in many cases, delivery of a license to use software is evaluated under the Completed Performance model (see Chapter 3, "General Principles").

Software sales take many forms and vary in complexity. Certain software sales involve significant production, modification, or customization of software. These types of software sales should be accounted for under the long-term construction-type contract model (see "Contract Accounting for Software Arrangements" later in this chapter).

Revenue from each software or software-related element in an arrangement that does not involve significant production, modification, or customization of software should be recognized when the vendor has vendor-specific objective evidence (VSOE) of the fair value of all of the undelivered elements as well as all of the following criteria have been met for that element (see the "Multiple-Element Arrangements" section of this chapter for a discussion of when elements in a multiple-element arrangement involving software should be separated and if so, the allocation of revenue to each element in the arrangement):

1. Persuasive evidence of an arrangement exists.
2. The arrangement fee is fixed or determinable.
3. Delivery or performance has occurred.
4. Collectibility is reasonably assured.

These four criteria are the same criteria that must be met to recognize revenue in any transaction (see Chapter 3, "General Principles"). SOP 97-2 (ASC 985-605) provides a significant amount of guidance on how to apply the criteria in a software transaction.

SCOPE

SOP 97-2 (ASC 985-605), provides comprehensive guidance on software revenue recognition and was developed to address factors unique to the software industry. For example, one unusual factor of the software industry is that delivering additional units of the product (a piece of software) involves virtually no cost. As a result, some of the guidance in SOP 97-2 (ASC 985-605) is not consistent with that of other revenue recognition literature. Therefore, determining whether an arrangement is within the scope of SOP 97-2 (ASC 985-605) is extremely important.

SOP 97-2 (ASC 985-605) applies to revenue-producing activities that involve the licensing, sale, leasing, or other marketing of computer software (SOP 97-2, par. 2) (ASC 985-605-15-3). It focuses on the transaction rather than the type of company entering into it. Therefore, any company engaging in a software transaction should apply the guidance in this chapter. This includes companies that may not normally consider themselves software providers, such as companies that sell telecommunications or medical equipment that includes a significant software component.

> **SEC REGISTRANT ALERT:** The SEC staff has asked non-software companies, whose products include software that is more than incidental, to ensure that their revenue recognition practices are consistent with SOP 97-2 (ASC 985-605) *and* disclose that the company accounts for revenue under the provisions of SOP 97-2 (ASC 985-605).

Incidental Software

A product sale that includes only incidental software should not be accounted for as a sale of software. Indicators of whether software is incidental to a product as a whole include, but are not limited to (see SOP 97-2, fn. 2) (ASC 985-605-15-3 and 15-4):

1. *Whether the software is a significant focus of the marketing effort or is sold separately.* When a company makes software a significant focus of the marketing effort or sells such software separately, it indicates that the software has significant functionality and importance to the product as a whole. The evaluation of the significance of software in the marketing effort should consider representations made in product literature, websites, communications with the customer (including contract negotiations), and other advertising channels.

2. *Whether the vendor will provide software upgrades or telephone support to users relating to the operation of the software.* The obligation to provide these types of post-sale services may indicate that the software is more than incidental. The nature and relative significance of post-sale support services to the overall functionality of the product requires judgment and careful evaluation in making this determination. The distinction between warranties and post-sale support often is a critical component of this evaluation.

3. *Whether the vendor incurs significant costs that are within the scope of FAS-86 (ASC 985-330).* Logically, if the company incurs significant costs in developing the software portion of the product, software would be a significant component of the product or service. Another component of this evaluation is the cost of developing and providing post-sale support.

4. *Whether the software and/or post-sale support is sold separately or the customer acquires title to the software.* Such sales and the transfer of title would establish both separability and value to the customer independent of the functionality and features of the remainder of the product or service. The separate subsequent sale or renewal of post-sale support would be a very strong indicator of the significance of software.

ILLUSTRATION: INCIDENTAL SOFTWARE

EXAMPLE 1 (Adapted from SOP 97-2, Appendix A (ASC 985-605-55-126 through 55-129))

Facts: An automobile includes software that assists in the electronic fuel injection process and helps to run the electronic dashboard. This software is used solely in connection with operating the automobile and is not sold or marketed separately. Once installed, the software may or may not be updated for new versions (models) that the manufacturer subsequently develops. The automobile manufacturer's costs for the development and subsequent updates of the software are insignificant relative to the other development and production costs of the automobile.

Discussion: The sale of the car should not be accounted for in accordance with the literature on software revenue recognition because the software is incidental to the product as a whole. Although the software may be critical to the operation of the automobile, the software *enables* or assists in the operation rather than drives the automobile. The software itself is not the focus of the marketing effort, nor is it what the customer believes he or she is buying.

EXAMPLE 2

Facts: A company produces maps previously distributed in hard copy, but now puts the data on a CD along with software that allows the customer to generate customized maps of his or her route, including identification of key attractions, hotels, and the like along the route. These features are mentioned prominently in the promotional literature for the interactive atlas.

Discussion: The software revenue recognition literature is applicable because the software is not incidental to the product. Although some might argue that the product is maps, not software, the marketing of the product focuses on the interactive features made possible by the software. In this situation, the conclusion would not change, even if the software development costs were small and no post-sale upgrade or technical support were provided.

EXAMPLE 3

Facts: Company A manufactures a handheld personal organizer that includes a calendar, address book, calculator, and game modules. The personal organizer operates using a proprietary software operating system, for which upgrades are periodically made available on Company A's website. The operating system allows users to download other programs to the personal organizer to enhance its capabilities. The main points of differentiation between Company A's products and those of the competitors, aside from minor styling details, are the features and functionality of the operating system, including the number of additional programs that run on the system. Company A spends considerable time and effort in maintaining and upgrading its operating system so that it remains better than the competitors' systems.

Discussion: The software revenue recognition literature is applicable because the software is not incidental to the product. The operating system is a key point of differentiation between Company A's product and the competitors' products, and Company A spends time and effort to keep its product leading edge. In addition, upgrades are made available to users from time to time. All of this indicates that the software is more than incidental to the personal organizer.

OBSERVATION: Companies should periodically reevaluate the significance of embedded software to existing products. This is important because the evolution of additional features and functionality could make software that was once incidental significant to a product as a whole and thereby subject to the guidance in SOP 97-2 (ASC 985-605).

EXAMPLE: INCIDENTAL SOFTWARE

Pitney Bowes, Inc. Form 10-K—Fiscal Year Ended December 31, 2007

Embedded Software Sales

We sell equipment with embedded software to our customers. The embedded software is not sold separately, it is not a significant focus of the marketing effort and we do not provide post-contract customer support specific to the software or incur significant costs that are within the scope of SFAS 86. Additionally, the functionality that the software provides is marketed as part of the overall product. The software embedded in the equipment is incidental to the equipment as a whole such that SOP No. 97-2, Software Revenue Recognition, is not applicable. Sales of these products are recognized in accordance with either SEC Staff Accounting Bulletin (SAB) No. 104, Revenue Recognition, or SFAS No. 13, Accounting for Leases, for sales-type leases.

Software Used to Provide a Service

A company may provide a customer with services that require the use of software. As a result, it may be difficult to determine whether the transaction should be accounted for as the provision of a service, to which software revenue recognition guidance does not apply, or as the sale of software. The answer depends on whether the rights to use the software remain solely with the company or are transferred to the customer as part of the transaction. When these rights transfer to the customer, the transaction should be accounted for in accordance with SOP 97-2 (ASC 985-605).

ILLUSTRATION: DETERMINING WHETHER A TRANSACTION IS A SOFTWARE OR SERVICE TRANSACTION

Facts: Company I provides tax preparation services. Its services are based on a sophisticated software package that gathers and processes all of the necessary information to prepare a tax return. Customers may use Company I's software in two ways. A customer may purchase a copy of the software from

Company I, download the software onto their computer, input the necessary information, and generate their tax return. If the customer chooses this option, he or she obtains a copy of the software that remains on his or her computer.

Alternatively, a customer may log on to Company I's website and for a fee, set up a user account and input the necessary information in an online form. Through an automated process, that information is then input into a version of Company I's software running on Company I's system and a tax return is generated, which the customer may then download and file online. If the customer chooses this option, he or she does not obtain a copy of the software and is only entitled to use the online tax preparation service.

Discussion: The first type of transaction above represents the sale of software and should be accounted for under SOP 97-2 (ASC 985-605) because the customer obtains the right to use the software. However, in the second transaction, the customer does not obtain the right to use the software. Instead, the customer only has the right to obtain a service provided by Company I.

Hosted Software Arrangements

Some computer software providers offer arrangements whereby users do not take possession of the software. Rather, the software application resides on the vendor's or a third party's hardware and the customer accesses and uses the software on an as-needed basis. These arrangements, often called hosting or application service provider arrangements, may or may not include a license to the software and the customer may or may not have an option to take delivery of the software.

Because the customer in a hosted software arrangement does not install the software on its own computer system, it is not clear whether the customer has purchased software or merely the right to a service. The EITF concluded that a hosting arrangement is only considered a sale of software if all of the following are true (EITF 00-3, par. 5) (ASC 985-605-15-3):

1. The customer has the contractual right to take possession of the software at any time during the hosting period;

2. The customer will not incur a significant penalty (in terms of cost and value in use) if it exercises its right to take possession of the software; and

3. It is feasible for the customer to either run the software on its own hardware or contract with another party unrelated to the vendor to host the software.

An arrangement meeting the above criteria should be accounted for as a multiple-element arrangement (see "Multiple-Element Arrangements" later in this chapter), the two elements being the software product and the hosting service (EITF 00-3, par. 6) (ASC 985-605-55-124). The multiple-element arrangement guidance in SOP 97-2 should be applied to this type of arrangement, because the hosting services are considered software-related (see "Software-Related Elements" later in this chapter).

> **OBSERVATION:** Even in this situation, revenue should not be recognized upon delivery of the software unless VSOE exists for the hosting element (at inception, the undelivered element) in the arrangement. Unless the company sells hosting services separately, VSOE of fair value likely does not exist (see "Multiple-Element Arrangements" later in this chapter for further discussion).

A hosting arrangement that does not meet all three of the above criteria should be accounted for as a contract to provide a service, not as a sale of software (see Chapter 6, "Service Deliverables"). This makes it unlikely that any revenue will be recognized at the inception of the arrangement.

Pursuant to the Issue Consensus, even if the customer has the option to take delivery of the software, the seller must still account for the transaction as the provision of a service unless it is "feasible" for the customer to take delivery and thus end the hosting arrangement, without a "significant penalty." The EITF noted that a significant penalty exists if the customer does not have the ability to take delivery of the software without incurring significant cost or has that ability but would experience a significant diminution in utility or value of the software if the hosting arrangement were ended (EITF 00-3, par. 5) (ASC 985-605-55-122).

The following are some examples of situations in which it is either not feasible for the customer to take possession of the software or a "significant penalty" exists:

- The vendor's software runs only on specialized hardware and most individual customers need to use only a small portion of the hardware's capacity. In addition, no significant third parties provide hosting services using this specialized hardware. In this instance, it is not feasible for most customers to take delivery because it would not be economical for the customer to purchase the hardware.

- The hosting arrangement has a three-year term and may not be cancelled without payment of the remaining hosting fees. Assuming the fair value of the hosting is significant either on its own or in relation to the overall arrangement, the requirement to continue paying for hosting not being received would be a significant penalty.

- A customer is entitled to upgrades of the software if it pays to have the seller host the software and is not entitled to those upgrades (and cannot purchase them) if it ends the hosting arrangement. If upgrades are expected to be important to the customer, the fact that it can obtain them only if it pays for hosting constitutes a significant penalty for ending the hosting arrangement.

- To use a key function of the software, it is necessary that the user communicate with other users of the same software and that communication is facilitated through the hosted environment. Although the customer may have the right to take delivery of the software and cancel the hosting arrangement, it would lose access to the online community if it chooses to cancel the hosting.

EXAMPLE: HOSTING ARRANGEMENTS

Computer Programs and Systems, Inc. Form 10-K—Fiscal Year Ended December 31, 2007

The Company accounts for ASP contracts in accordance with the EITF 00-3, Application of AICPA Statement of Position 97-2 to Arrangements That Include the Right to Use Software Stored on Another Entity's Hardware. EITF 00-3 states that the software element of ASP services is covered by SOP 97-2 only "if the customer has the contractual right to take possession of the software at any time during the hosting period without significant penalty and it is feasible for the customer to either run the software on its own hardware or contract with another party related to the vendor to host the software." Each ASP contract includes a system purchase and buyout clause, and this clause specifies the total amount of the system buyout. In addition, a clause is included which states that should the system be bought out by the customer, the customer would be required to enter into a general support agreement (for post-contract support services) for the remainder of the original ASP term. Accordingly, the Company has concluded that ASP customers do not have the right to take possession of the system without significant penalty (i.e., the purchase price of the system), and thus ASP revenue of CPSI does not fall within the scope of SOP 97-2. In accordance with SAB No. 104, revenue is recognized when the services are performed.

Software-Related Elements

In Issue 03-5 (ASC 985-605-15-3), the EITF concluded that when an arrangement includes software that is more than incidental (see previous discussion), all software-related elements in the arrangement must also be accounted for under SOP 97-2

(ASC 985-605). Software-related elements include, but are not limited to, software-related products and services, such as upgrades/ enhancements and PCS (discussed later in this chapter), as well as any non-software deliverable(s) for which a software deliverable is essential to the non-software deliverable's functionality (for a discussion of "essential to the functionality," see "Multiple-Element Arrangements" later in this chapter). An example of a non-software deliverable where software is essential to that non-software deliverable's functionality is the hardware associated with the handheld personal organizer discussed in Example 3 in the "Incidental Software" Illustration, earlier in this chapter. As a result, both the software that runs the handheld personal organizer, as well as the hardware that encases that software, falls within the scope of SOP 97-2 (ASC 985-605). Alternatively, if a carrying case for the handheld personal organizer were also included in the arrangement, it would not be accounted for pursuant to SOP 97-2 (ASC 985-605) unless the handheld personal organizer was essential to the carrying case's functionality.

> **PRACTICE ALERT:** The effect of this guidance is that a significant number of arrangements that are primarily hardware in nature are nonetheless accounted for under the provisions of SOP 97-2 (ASC 985-605). Because the software revenue recognition guidance was written specifically with software in mind, applying it to hardware arrangements can be difficult and produce unexpected results. In large part because of these concerns, the EITF, in Issue 09-3, *Application of AICPA Statement of Position 97-2 to Certain Arrangements That Include Software Elements*, is rethinking this guidance. See Chapter 13, "Future Expectations and Projects," for further discussion.

EXAMPLE: SOFTWARE-RELATED ELEMENTS

Keynote Systems, Inc. Form 10-K—Fiscal Year Ended September 30, 2007

Ratable License Revenue: Ratable licenses revenue consists of sales of our mobile automated test equipment, maintenance, engineering and minor consulting services associated with Keynote SIGOS System Integrated Test Environment ("SITE"). We frequently enter into multiple element arrangements with mobile customers, for the sale of our automated test equipment, including both hardware and software licenses, consulting services to configure the hardware and software (implementation or integration services), post contract support (maintenance) services, training services and other minor consulting services. These multiple element arrangements are within the scope of SOP No. 97-2, and EITF 03-5. This determination is based on the hardware component of our multiple element arrangements being deemed to be a software related element. In addition, customers do not purchase the hardware without also purchasing the software, as well as the software and hardware being sold as a package, with payments due from the customer upon delivery of this hardware and software package.

PERSUASIVE EVIDENCE OF AN ARRANGEMENT

The evaluation of the persuasive evidence of an arrangement is the same in a software environment as in any other revenue transaction. Software companies, like non-software entities, should evaluate this criterion based on their standard business practices. If obtaining written contracts is the software vendor's customary business practice, the persuasive evidence of an arrangement criterion has been met only when both parties have signed and executed the written contract (SOP 97-2, par. 15) (ASC 985-605-25-16). Regardless of how an arrangement is documented, the documentation must be in place before any revenue can be recognized. For additional discussion, see Chapter 3, "General Principles."

Documentation of persuasive evidence can take on added significance for a software vendor, because a sale of software generally results in almost zero cost of sales. Therefore, any revenue recognized has nearly a 100% corresponding effect on margins and both operating and pre-tax income.

> ☛ **PRACTICE POINTER:**   Software companies that sell large software packages are likely to have a small number of individual transactions, each of which is significant to the company's revenue and net income. Because of the significant effect that a revenue transaction may have on net income, these vendors (and their salespeople) may feel pressured to close a transaction before the end of a fiscal quarter or fiscal year, especially if the company is publicly traded. Therefore, companies should have strong internal controls to ensure that appropriate documentation is received before the end of the period for all transactions from which revenue is recognized.

EXAMPLE: PERSUASIVE EVIDENCE OF AN ARRANGEMENT

Red Hat, Inc. Form 10-K—Fiscal Year Ended February 28, 2008

Revenue Recognition

The Company recognizes revenue in accordance with Statement of Position No. 97-2, Software Revenue Recognition ("SOP 97-2"), as amended by

Statement of Position No. 98-4, Deferral of the Effective Date of a Provision of SOP 97-2, and Statement of Position No. 98-9, Modification of SOP 97-2, and Staff Accounting Bulletin No. 101, as amended by Staff Accounting Bulletin No. 104. The Company establishes persuasive evidence of an arrangement for each type of revenue transaction based on either a signed contract with the end customer, a click-through contract on the Company's website whereby the customer agrees to the Company's standard subscription terms, signed or click-through distribution contracts with original equipment manufacturers ("OEMs") and other resellers, or, in the case of individual training seats, through receipt of payment which indicates acceptance of the Company's training agreement terms.

FIXED OR DETERMINABLE FEES AND COLLECTIBILITY

In most cases, the fixed or determinable fees and collectibility criteria are applied to software arrangements in the same manner they are applied to product or service transactions. Thus, if a portion of the fee is contingent upon future events, such as the software helping the customer achieve cost reductions, the contingent portion of the fee should not be recognized until the contingency is resolved.

Transaction-Based Pricing Arrangements

A simple example of a software arrangement with a contingent fee is one where some, or all, of the fee is based on the volume of transactions or amount of information processed. For example, a banking software package may be sold for a fixed fee of $1,000,000 plus an additional payment of one cent for every processed transaction. In this case, the $1,000,000 fixed fee may be recognized upon delivery (provided all other criteria have been met), but the additional one cent per transaction fee cannot be recognized until the transactions are actually processed. This is the case even if the vendor has no further obligations and can reasonably estimate the number of transactions that will be processed.

Extended Payment Terms

SOP 97-2 (ASC 985-605) specifically discusses the application of the fixed or determinable criterion to software arrangements with extended payment terms. Although such terms must be evaluated in any revenue transaction to determine whether they introduce a contingency or raise the risk of nonpayment, extended payment terms in a software environment raise the risk that a concession, such as an additional software product or user license, will be granted to ensure payment of the previously agreed-upon amount. This risk is especially high in the software industry because of rapid technological change and the fact that the cost of providing a concession may be insignificant. As a result, software sales that include extended payment terms must be critically evaluated to determine whether they meet the fixed or determinable criterion.

Because of the higher risk of concessions in software arrangements, SOP 97-2 (ASC 985-605) specifies that a presumption exists that the fee in a software transaction is not fixed or determinable if a significant portion of the payment is due beyond the earlier of the expiration of the license or one year following delivery (SOP 97-2, pars. 27–28) (ASC 985-605-25-33 and 25-34).

EXAMPLES: EXTENDED PAYMENT TERMS

Rightnow Technologies, Inc. Form 10-K—Fiscal Year Ended December 31, 2007

If an arrangement includes a right of acceptance or a right to cancel, revenue is recognized when acceptance is received or the right to cancel has expired. If the fee for the license has any payment term that is due in excess of the Company's normal payment terms (over 90 days), the fee is considered to not be fixed or determinable, and the amount of revenue recognized (a) for perpetual license arrangements is limited to the amount currently due from the customer, or (b) for term license or subscription arrangements is limited to the lesser of the amount currently due from the customer or a ratable portion of the total unallocated arrangement fee.

Oracle, Inc. Form 10-K—Fiscal Year Ended May 31, 2007

We assess whether fees are fixed or determinable at the time of sale and recognize revenue if all other revenue recognition requirements are met. Our standard payment terms are net 30; however, terms may vary based on the country in which the agreement is executed. Payments that are due within six months are generally deemed to be fixed or determinable based on our successful collection history on such arrangements, and thereby satisfy the required criteria for revenue recognition.

The presumption, however, may be overcome if persuasive evidence demonstrates that the vendor has a business practice of using extended payment terms and has been successful in collecting under the original terms, without providing any concessions. If the presumption cannot be overcome due to a lack of such evidence, revenue should be recognized as payments become due, assuming that all other revenue recognition criteria have been met (SOP 97-2, pars. 28–29) (ASC 985-605-25-34 and 25-35).

OBSERVATION: Because of the conclusion that payment terms exceeding one year create a presumption that the fee is not fixed or determinable, a company with no history of successfully collecting under such arrangements must recognize revenue as payments become due, even though delivery has occurred and the customer is creditworthy. In fact, strong creditworthiness does not help a company overcome this presumption because the concern is that a concession will be provided, not that the customer will become unable to pay.

☛ **PRACTICE POINTER:** These provisions are often misinterpreted to permit immediate recognition, upon delivery, of any payments due within one year, even if other payments extend beyond one year. The basis for conclusions that was published when SOP 97-2 (ASC 985-605) was issued, makes clear that recognition of *any* revenue is prohibited until payments become due unless the presumption discussed above is overcome.

ILLUSTRATION: ONE-YEAR PRESUMPTION

Facts: Vendor S sells a perpetual license to one of its software products for a fee of $10,000,000. Payment terms are $2,500,000 upon delivery and another $2,500,000 every six months thereafter. Thus, $2,500,000 of the fee (the final payment) is due more than one year after delivery. Vendor S does not have a history of using extended payment term arrangements, but the customer in this arrangement is very creditworthy and has used Vendor S's products for a long time without complaints. There are no return, acceptance, or other provisions in the arrangement that raise additional questions regarding the customer's obligation to pay the license fee.

Discussion: Because Vendor S has no history of using extended payment terms, the fact that a significant (25%) portion of the fee is due more than one year after delivery means that Vendor S may only recognize revenue as payments become due. Thus, Vendor S may only recognize $2,500,000 upon delivery, even though $7,500,000 is due within one year of delivery. The creditworthiness of the customer and Vendor S's strong relationship with the customer do not change this conclusion.

Overcoming the Presumption That the Fee in an Extended Payment Term Arrangement Is Not Fixed or Determinable

Concessions (TPA 5100.56) (ASC 985-605-55-18 through 55-21) To overcome this presumption, a company must have persuasive evidence, based on historical practice, of its ability to collect under the original terms of extended payment arrangements without granting concessions. Concessions by a software vendor may take many forms. Essentially, any change to an arrangement that reduces the total revenue to be recognized, extends the payment terms, increases the customer's rights, or increases the vendor's obligations constitutes a concession. For example, the following would all be considered concessions:

- Extending payment due dates in the arrangement;
- Decreasing total payments due under the arrangement;
- Paying financing fees on a customer's financing arrangement that were not contemplated in the original arrangement;
- Accepting returns beyond those provided for in the terms of the original arrangement;
- Providing discounted or free post-contract customer support that was not included in the original arrangement;
- Providing other discounted or free services, upgrades, or products that were not included in the original arrangement;
- Extending the timeframe for a reseller to sell the software or an end user to use the software; and
- Extending the geographic area in which a reseller is allowed to sell the software, or the number of locations in which an end user can use the software.

Relevant historical experience   (TPA 5100.57) (ASC 985-605-55-22 through 55-25) To have a history of successfully collecting under the original payment terms without making concessions, a vendor must have collected all payments as due under comparable arrangements without providing concessions. For example, a vendor that sells software with three-year payment terms, but has only been doing so for the past year, could not have sufficient history, even if it has yet to encounter any difficulties.

In order to determine whether the company's historical experience is based on sufficiently similar arrangements, the following factors should be considered:

- *Type or class of customer.*
- *Types of products.*
- *Stage of product life cycle*—The later in a product's life cycle that an arrangement is entered into, the higher the likelihood of the product becoming technologically obsolete during the payment period.
- *Elements included in the arrangement*—The inclusion of significant rights to services or discounts on future products in

some arrangements, but not others, could indicate that there is a significant difference between these arrangements. For example, an arrangement that does not include bundled post-contract customer support (PCS) and rights to additional software products would not be comparable to arrangements that included these rights.

- *Length of payment terms.*

- *Economics of license arrangement*—License arrangements that include significant discounts from list prices may not be comparable to those that do not.

Revenue Recognition When Payments Become Due

If, at the inception of an arrangement, a fee in a software arrangement with extended payment terms is not deemed fixed or determinable (e.g., if the presumption cannot be overcome), revenue must be recognized as payments become due. However, if the payment terms are changed, it may not be clear when revenue should be recognized.

If a customer makes payments early (e.g., to avoid financing costs), revenue should be recognized when the payments are received, because the fact that the customer has received payments indicates that the fee is now fixed or determinable (TPA 5100.41) (ASC 985-605-55-15).

However, the presumption that the licensing fee is not fixed or determinable is *not* overcome if the vendor receives cash from selling the receivable under the extended payment term arrangement to a third party, even if the sale is without recourse to the vendor. The difference between this situation and the one in the previous paragraph is that the transfer of the extended payment term arrangement does not change the nature or structure of the transaction between the vendor and customer. Therefore, the presumption that the fee is not fixed or determinable is not overcome by any transaction between the vendor and a third party. Instead, the sale of the right to receive payments from the customer should be accounted for under EITF 88-18 (ASC 470-10-25) (see Chapter 11, "Presentation") (TPA 5100.58) (ASC 985-605-55-31; 985-605-55-32).

Cash Received after Balance Sheet Date

The determination of whether the fee in an extended payment term arrangement is fixed or determinable must be made at the outset of the arrangement. Subsequent cash receipts do not change this conclusion. Thus, a payment (even a full payment) received after the end of a reporting period cannot be used to justify the recognition of revenue in that reporting period. Instead, a payment received after period end should be recognized in the next period (i.e., the period the payment was made) (TPA 5100.59) (ASC 985-605-55-26 through 55-30).[1]

Customer Financing with Software Vendor Participation

To receive payment on normal terms, a software vendor may help the customer obtain financing from a third party. If the vendor's participation results in incremental risk that a refund or concession will be provided to either the end-user or financing party, the financing arrangement should be evaluated to determine whether it creates extended payment terms. For example, if the financing arrangement between the company and the third-party lender extends for greater than one year after delivery, a presumption would exist that the fee is not fixed or determinable. If the software vendor cannot overcome this presumption, revenue should be recognized as payments become due and payable from the customer to the financing party, provided all other revenue recognition requirements have been met. Therefore, a payment received by the vendor at contract inception would be reported as deferred revenue until the customer's payments to the financing party become due.

Any one of the following conditions or actions results in incremental risk and a presumption that the fee is not fixed or determinable (TPAs 5100.61 and 5100.62) (ASC 985-605-55-38 through 55-41):

1. Provisions that require the software vendor to indemnify the financing party against claims (when such indemnifications are greater than similar indemnifications included in the company's standard arrangements with customers).

2. Provisions that require the software vendor to make representations to the financing party related to customer acceptance of the software that are above and beyond any written acceptance documentation that the software vendor has already received from the end user customer.

3. Provisions that obligate the software vendor to take actions against the customer on behalf of the financing party, or to refuse further business from the customer, in the event that the customer defaults under the financing arrangements, unless, as part of the original arrangement, the customer explicitly

---

[1] Collecting a payment after the end of the period is a "Nonrecognized Subsequent Event," as discussed in paragraph 10 of FAS-165, *Subsequent Events* (ASC 855). Nonrecognized subsequent events "provide evidence with respect to conditions that did *not* exist at the date of the balance sheet but arose after the balance sheet date."

authorizes the software vendor to take such actions without penalty.

4. Provisions that require the software vendor to guarantee, certify, or otherwise attest to the financing party that the customer meets the financing party's qualification criteria.

5. Provisions that require the software vendor to guarantee the customer's indebtedness to the financing party.

6. The software vendor has previously provided concessions to customers or financing parties to facilitate or induce payment.

When a software arrangement involves an indemnification or a guarantee as discussed in items 1 and 5 above, the provisions of FIN-45 (ASC 460) may apply. This depends on whether the existence of the indemnification or guarantee precludes revenue recognition. If the indemnification or guarantee leads to a conclusion that the fee is not fixed or determinable, the provisions of FIN-45 (ASC 460) do not apply. However, if the presumption can be overcome (i.e., the fee is fixed or determinable despite the existence of the indemnification or guarantee), the provisions of FIN-45 (ASC 460) should be considered.

When the presumption related to an indemnification can be overcome, FSP FIN 45-1 (ASC 460-10-55-30 through 55-34) indicates that a software licensing agreement that indemnifies the licensee against liability and damages (including legal defense costs) arising from any claims of patent, copyright, trademark or trade secret infringement by the software vendor's software falls within the scope of FIN-45 (ASC 460) from a disclosure perspective, but not from an initial recognition and measurement perspective. As a result, although the indemnification must be disclosed, its fair value should not be initially recognized nor should it be treated as a separate element in a multiple-element arrangement. See Chapter 12, "Disclosures."

In other situations in which the presumption is overcome, all of the provisions of FIN-45 (ASC 460) may apply. In this case, the arrangement may contain two elements: the software and the guarantee. Further analysis is required to determine whether the guarantee is a separable element. See Chapter 4, "Multiple-Element Arrangements," regarding the scope of FIN-45 (ASC 460) and the accounting for multiple-element arrangements where one of the elements is a guarantee. Also, see Chapter 12 for the disclosure requirements of FIN-45 (ASC 460).

U.S. generally accepted accounting principles (GAAP) also identifies several actions that the vendor may take that do not result in any incremental risk (TPA 5100.64) (ASC 985-605-55-46):

- The software vendor introduces the customer and financing party, facilitates their discussions, provides the financing party with information on behalf of the customer and assists the customer in filling out applications, as long as the vendor does not attest in any manner that the customer meets the financing party's qualification criteria.

- The software vendor makes representations to the financing party similar to representations included in the arrangement with the customer.

- The vendor takes actions that were explicitly authorized by the customer in the original arrangement to terminate the license agreement and/or any related services, or to not enter into another arrangement for the same or similar product.

- The vendor grants customary recourse provisions to its customer related to warranties for defective software.

Cancellation and Customer Acceptance Clauses

Cancellation clauses should be evaluated to determine their substance. For example, a cancellation clause that is short-term and subjective in nature should be evaluated as a right of return (see "Rights to Exchange or Return Software" later in this chapter). However, a clause that allows a customer to cancel the arrangement only if the software does not meet standard specifications should be evaluated as a warranty. The treatment of warranties in a software transaction is the same as it is in the sale of any other product (see Chapter 5, "Product Deliverables") (SOP 97-2, par. 31) (ASC 985-605-25-37).

Certain cancellation and customer acceptance clauses may raise uncertainty about whether the transaction is complete. After delivery, if uncertainty exists about customer acceptance of the software, license revenue should not be recognized until acceptance occurs. This will often be the case when a customer acceptance clause is based on customer or arrangement-specific criteria that cannot be evaluated until the software is installed and operating in the customer's environment (SOP 97-2, par. 20) (ASC 985-605-25-21). For further information on these and other customer acceptance clauses, see Chapter 5.

If a software sale is cancelable after delivery, the fixed or determinable condition is not met until the cancellation privileges lapse. If the cancellation privileges lapse ratably, then the fee becomes fixed or determinable ratably. For example, software sold on a three-year term license, with payments due at the beginning of each year, might have a cancellation provision that enables the customer to terminate its license after two years and avoid making the license fee payment for year 3. If this is the case, revenue related to year 3 cannot be recognized until the cancellation right lapses, even if the vendor has sufficient history to overcome the presumption that the fee is not fixed or determinable because of extended payment terms.

Price Protection

Price protection provides the buyer with a credit for any price decreases that occur during a specified period of time or until the buyer resells the products. In these situations, revenue should be recognized net of the estimated amount to be refunded under the price protection, assuming the refund amount can be reasonably and reliably estimated and that the other conditions for revenue recognition have been met. When there are significant uncertainties related to the seller's ability to maintain its prices, refunds may not be reasonably and reliably estimable. If refunds cannot be reliably estimated, revenue should not be recognized until reliable estimates can be made or the price protection lapses (SOP 97-2, par. 30) (ASC 985-605-25-36).

EXAMPLE: PRICE PROTECTION

Electronic Arts, Inc. Form 10-K—Fiscal Year Ended March 31, 2009

Product Revenue: Product revenue, including sales to resellers and distributors ("channel partners"), is recognized when the above criteria are met. We reduce product revenue for estimated future returns, price protection, and other offerings, which may occur with our customers and channel partners.

. . .

We estimate potential future product returns, price protection and stock-balancing programs related to product revenue. We analyze historical returns, current sell-through of distributor and retailer inventory of our products, current trends in retail and the video game segment, changes in customer demand and acceptance of our products and other related factors when evaluating the adequacy of our sales returns and price protection allowances. In addition, we monitor the volume of sales to our channel partners and their inventories as substantial overstocking in the distribution channel could result in high returns or higher price protection costs in subsequent periods.

DELIVERY

Products

The primary software product element is the license which is usually delivered on a disk, tape, or other storage media. Software elements may also be delivered electronically, via e-mail or the internet. Generally, the product element in a software arrangement is fairly easy to identify, and will be accounted for in the same manner as any non-software product (i.e., delivery of software generally occurs when the product is transferred to the customer). Exceptions to this fundamental principle are also the same as in other product transactions and include consignment shipments, bill and hold sales, and product financing arrangements. When software is to be delivered on a physical storage medium such as a disk, tape, or hard drive, the financial reporting provisions relating to title or delivery to an alternate site also apply. For information on all these topics, see Chapter 5, "Product Deliverables." Special considerations related to the delivery of software are discussed further below.

As discussed earlier in this chapter under "Software-Related Elements," if a non-software product (e.g., computer hardware) is included in an arrangement with a software product that is more than incidental and essential to the functionality of the non-software product, then the non-software product is considered software related. Software-related products should be evaluated using the same principles as the actual software.

Electronic Delivery

When software is delivered electronically, the delivery criterion is considered to have been met when the customer either downloads the software, or has been provided with access codes that permit the immediate possession of the software on the customer's hardware pursuant to an agreement or purchase order for the software (SOP 97-2, par. 18) (ASC 985-605-25-18).

Multiple Licenses of the Same Product

Some software arrangements involve multiple copies or licenses of the same software. These arrangements may specify the number of copies the customer may use, or allow the customer to use an unlimited number of copies (a site license). As long as the arrangement does not have a variable fee arrangement (i.e., one based on the number of copies ordered), delivery of all copies of a particular piece of software occurs when the first copy or product master is delivered to the customer. In these arrangements, duplication, even if it is to be performed by the vendor, is incidental to the arrangement, and the fee is payable even if no additional copies are requested. The estimated costs of duplication should be accrued at the time revenue is recognized if the vendor is responsible for duplication (SOP 97-2, par. 21) (ASC 985-605-25-23).

Multiple-copy software arrangements may also be structured so that, although the customer has the right to multiple (or perhaps unlimited) copies of the software, the fee varies based on the number of copies the customer deploys as an end-user, or sells to end-users as a reseller. As a result, delivery only occurs as the copies are made by the user or sold by the reseller. In this type of arrangement, the fee for the additional copies is not fixed or determinable until the copies are made or sold (SOP 97-2, par. 21) (ASC 985-605-25-24).

Authorization Codes or Keys

Some vendors use electronic "locks" to prevent unauthorized users from accessing the software. Thus, a user must not only have a copy of the software, but also have the correct authorization code, or "key," to use the software. Typically, software installed without a permanent key will work for a short period of time before it becomes locked. In software arrangements involving the use of keys, delivery of all keys is not necessarily required to satisfy the delivery condition. The software may be considered delivered as long as the customer has a version that is fully functional except for the permanent key or additional keys necessary for reproduction and the customer's payment obligation is not contingent in any way upon the delivery of additional keys. However, if a vendor only uses keys selectively, this may be evidence that collectibility is questionable or that the product has only been delivered for demonstration purposes (SOP 97-2, pars. 24–25) (ASC 985-605-25-27 through 25-29).

ILLUSTRATION: AUTHORIZATION CODES

EXAMPLE 1

Facts: A vendor includes 20 optional functions on a CD which contains its licensed software product. Keys control access to the optional functions and are provided if and when the customer orders and agrees to pay for these functions. The vendor estimates that the customer will purchase three optional functions.

Discussion: Revenue for each optional function should be recognized when evidence of an order exists and the key is delivered to the user. Although the user has received a fully functional version of the licensed software, the user has not agreed to license the additional functions. Therefore, no evidence of an arrangement exists, and revenue for the optional functions may not be recognized when the CD-ROM is delivered.

EXAMPLE 2

Facts: A software vendor's product requires an authorization code to work after being installed on a new computer. The code necessary to activate the software changes daily. The vendor enters into a license arrangement with a user and delivers a disk containing the product. The customer will handle installation of the product and is instructed to contact the vendor for the daily key on the day of installation. The customer is required to pay for the software 30 days after delivery, whether or not it has installed the software.

Discussion: The version of the software that has been delivered is fully functional except for the installation key, and the customer's payment obligation is not contingent upon either installation of the software or delivery of the key. Therefore, revenue may be recognized upon delivery of the software assuming all other revenue recognition conditions have been met.

Delivery before License Period Begins

If software is physically delivered and all other revenue recognition criteria are met, but the customer's license to use the software has not yet begun, revenue should not be recognized because the customer does not yet have the legal right to use the software. Effective delivery does not occur in these situations until the license term begins (TPA 5100.70; SAB Topic 13A3d) (ASC 985-605-55-101 through 55-104; 605-10-S99, A3d).

"Delivery" When License Period Is Extended

When a term license to a software product is extended, the vendor must determine whether the extension results in the provision of additional products and whether the extension occurs before the original term license lapses (TPAs 5100.70, 5100.71, and 5100.72) (ASC 985-605-55-105 through 55-114).

When an active term license is extended and no additional products will be provided, the vendor should recognize the fee when the extension is executed, even if that date is before the extension period begins.

When a term license has lapsed (i.e., it is inactive), any purported extension of that license should be treated as a new initial arrangement, not an extension of an existing arrangement. In these situations, the guidance in the section, "Delivery before License Period Begins," should be followed.

When an active term license is extended and an additional product will be provided, the extension fee should be allocated between the software product that was the subject of the original license (original product) and the software product added in the extension (new product) based on the guidance in the "Multiple-Element Arrangements" section of this chapter. The vendor should recognize the amount allocated to the original product when the extension arrangement is executed if all other revenue recognition criteria have been met. The vendor should recognize the amount allocated to the new product when all of the revenue recognition criteria have been met related to that new product.

> **OBSERVATION:** Arrangements may contain an option to extend a time-based license indefinitely for an additional fee. This fee is essentially the same as the additional fee related to an extension/renewal of a license. The right associated with each fee is the same—the right to continue to use the product

the customer already has access to as part of the original or base arrangement. Therefore, the additional fee related to the option should be accounted for the same way as a fee received in connection with the extension/renewal of a license. However, if exercise of the option requires another delivery of the software media (e.g., due to a self-destruct or similar mechanism in the original software media delivered), then delivery of the software media must occur before the revenue related to the extension/renewal can be recognized (TPA 5100.73) (ASC 985-605-55-115 through 55-118).

Delivery of a Beta Version or an Earlier Release

When the version of the software ordered by the customer is not immediately available because it is still in development or testing before commercial release, the vendor may deliver a beta (or test) version of the product, or an earlier release (e.g., version 5.5 instead of 6.0) so that the customer has a product to use until the ordered version becomes available.

Delivery of a beta version or earlier release does not constitute delivery of the product the customer ordered. As a result, the vendor may not recognize revenue because it has not substantially completed its obligations under the arrangement.

Upgrades

SOP 97-2 (ASC 985-605) defines an upgrade as: "An improvement to an existing product that is intended to extend the life or improve significantly the marketability of the original product through added functionality, enhanced performance, or both." Upgrades are often a key aspect of a software arrangement because software products are often upgraded over time (e.g., from version 1.0 to version 2.0). The accounting for upgrades depends upon whether the upgrade is specified or unspecified.

Specified upgrades are treated as separate elements of the arrangement (see guidance later in this chapter under "Multiple-Element Arrangements" for purposes of determining whether specified upgrades should be treated separately for accounting purposes). Delivery of specified upgrades can generally be determined in the same manner as delivery of products. Unspecified upgrades are discussed below under "Post-Contract Customer Support (PCS)."

Post-Contract Customer Support (PCS)

In contrast to specified upgrades, unspecified upgrades are treated as a component of post-contract customer support (PCS). PCS includes telephone support, correction of errors (bug fixing or debugging), and unspecified (when- and if-available) product upgrades and enhancements developed by the vendor during the period in which the PCS is provided. These services and upgrades are generally described in the PCS arrangement. Sometimes, a limited period of PCS is included with the purchase of a license to software. This initial period of PCS, even though it may be provided to all purchasers, is considered an element in a multiple-element arrangement (see guidance later in this chapter under "Multiple-Element Arrangements" for purposes of determining whether PCS should be treated separately for accounting purposes).

> **OBSERVATION:** Although an arrangement to provide unspecified upgrades and enhancements is accounted for as PCS, an arrangement that only requires the vendor to provide "bug fixes" that correct errors in the operation of the software should be accounted for as a warranty, pursuant to FAS-5 (TPA 5100.43) (ASC 985-605-55-77 and 55-78) (see Chapter 5, "Product Deliverables").

The portion of the fee allocated to PCS should be recognized as revenue ratably over the term of the PCS arrangement because there is generally no better estimate of the manner in which such services will be provided. However, revenue should be recognized in proportion to the expenses expected to be incurred for the PCS services if sufficient vendor-specific historical evidence exists demonstrating that costs to provide PCS are incurred on other than a straight-line basis (SOP 97-2, pars. 56–57) (ASC 985-605-25-67 and 25-68).

> **OBSERVATION:** Because predicting the costs to be incurred in developing unspecified upgrades is extremely difficult, PCS is almost always recognized on a straight-line basis over the PCS period.

In rare circumstances, PCS is considered insignificant to the arrangement and delivery is not required to recognize the revenue allocated to it. PCS revenue may be recognized at the same time as the portion of the fee allocated to the software product if *all* of the following conditions are met (SOP 97-2, par. 59) (ASC 985-605-25-71):

1. *The PCS fee is included with the initial licensing fee.* Arrangements where PCS fees are charged for an optional period do not qualify.

2. *The PCS included with the initial license is for one year or less.* This condition is met if the arrangement includes post-delivery telephone support for an unspecified period of time, but the vendor's history shows that substantially all of the support is provided within the first year after delivery.

3. *The estimated cost of providing PCS during the arrangement is insignificant.* Historical experience in providing PCS to similar customers on similar software products is necessary to reach this conclusion.

4. *If unspecified upgrades are included in the PCS arrangement, such upgrades historically have been and are expected to continue to be minimal and infrequent.* This determination should consider the content of the upgrades in addition to the number.

If PCS revenue is recognized upon the delivery of the software, the vendor must accrue all estimated costs of providing the PCS at the same time (SOP 97-2, par. 59) (ASC 985-605-25-72).

EXAMPLE: DESCRIPTION OF PCS

Oracle, Inc. Form 10-K—Fiscal Year Ended May 31, 2007

The vast majority of our software license arrangements include software license updates and product support, which are recognized ratably over the term of the arrangement, typically one year. Software license updates provide customers with rights to unspecified software product upgrades, maintenance releases and patches released during the term of the support period. Product support includes internet access to technical content, as well as internet and telephone access to technical support personnel located in our global support centers. Software license updates and product support are generally priced as a percentage of the net new software license fees. Substantially all of our customers purchase both software license updates and product support when they acquire new software licenses. In addition, substantially all of our customers renew their software license updates and product support contracts annually.

Subscriptions

A software vendor may agree to deliver one or more software products or licenses currently and unspecified additional software products in the future. For example, the vendor may agree to deliver all new products to be introduced over the next three years. Such arrangements are treated as subscriptions and are conceptually similar to a magazine or other subscription. A subscription is different from a PCS arrangement (that includes unspecified upgrades and enhancements) because the future deliverables include or are products with their own functionality, rather than upgrades to already existing products.

In a subscription, the customer is entitled to the delivery of products made available during some period of time. Delivery (use by the customer) occurs ratably throughout the period once the first product has been provided to the customer. As a result, no allocation of revenue should be made to any of the software products. Even if the vendor has no obligation to develop additional products and in fact does not intend to develop any products, delivery under a subscription still occurs and revenue is recognized ratably, beginning with the delivery of the first product (SOP 97-2, pars. 48–49) (ASC 985-605-25-58 and 25-59).

> **OBSERVATION:** Because a subscription typically involves rights to future software products that have not yet been developed, VSOE of fair value of these unspecified products would not exist at the outset of the arrangement. In the absence of these special provisions for subscriptions, no revenue would be recognized until the end of the subscription term.

Software-Related Services

Software-related services other than PCS may also exist in an arrangement and include training, installation, or consulting. Consulting services often involve implementation support, software design or development, and customization or modification of licensed software. When software-related services meet the criteria to be accounted for separately (see "Multiple-Element Arrangements" below), they are considered delivered as the services are performed. If no pattern of performance is discernable, software-related services are considered delivered ratably as they are provided.

> **OBSERVATION:** As discussed above, PCS may be considered incidental to the arrangement under limited circumstances, such that revenue allocated to it may be recognized when the software product is delivered. This exception does not apply to any other software-related services.

MULTIPLE-ELEMENT ARRANGEMENTS

Software transactions may involve more than one deliverable including different software products, upgrades, enhancements, or other software-related services, such as training, installation, consulting, and post-contract customer support. The deliverables may also include non-software related products and services. When the transaction involves multiple-elements, the fee from the arrangement must be allocated to the various deliverables, so that the proper amount can be allocated to each element and recognized as revenue as that element is delivered.

Determining the Model to Apply

As discussed in Chapter 4, "Multiple-Element Arrangements," EITF 00-21 (ASC 605-25) does not apply to arrangements that fall entirely within the scope of other literature. As a result, arrangements that fall within the scope of SOP 97-2 (ASC 985-605) are not subject to the requirements of EITF 00-21 (ASC 605-25) and the multiple-element arrangement guidance in SOP 97-2 (ASC 985-605) should be applied. However, when an arrangement has elements that fall within the scope of SOP 97-2 (ASC 985-605) as well as other elements, EITF 00-21 (ASC 605-25) should be applied to separate the SOP 97-2 (ASC 985-605) elements (hereafter referred to as "software elements" in this section) and the non-software elements. Further separation of the software elements is governed by the separation guidance in SOP 97-2 (ASC 985-605), which we will also refer to as the software multiple-element model.

Multiple-element software arrangements may include software that is (a) more than incidental but that does not involve significant production, modification, or customization and (b) software that is more than incidental and does involve significant production, modification, or customization. Revenue in an arrangement that includes only software elements should be recognized in accordance with the guidance in SOP 97-2 (ASC 985-605). Revenue in an arrangement with only software that requires significant production, modification, or customization services should be recognized using the contract accounting model provided in SOP 81-1 (ASC 605-35). Additional discussion related to these two classes of software is provided below, including the accounting implications of multiple-element arrangements with both classes of software. In addition, a detailed discussion regarding the application of contract accounting to software that requires significant production, modification, or customization is provided later in this chapter in the section titled "Contract Accounting for Software Arrangements."

To ensure that the proper multiple-element guidance is applied to an arrangement involving software and/or software-related elements, it is essential to understand whether the elements fall within the scope of SOP 97-2 (ASC 985-605) or other literature. The following discussion addresses the various types of software and software-related elements that may be included in a multiple-element arrangement and how to determine which guidance is applicable.

Incidental Software

Incidental software, as discussed earlier in this chapter, does not fall within the scope of SOP 97-2 (ASC 985-605) and should not be considered a separate element in the arrangement.

Software and Software-Related Elements

When sold on a standalone basis, software that is more than incidental and does not involve significant production, modification, or customization falls within the scope of SOP 97-2 (ASC 985-605). If a multiple-element arrangement includes two or more software elements, the software multiple-element model should be applied to determine whether these elements should be treated separately for accounting purposes.

When software is essential to the functionality of another element in the arrangement, the other element is considered software-related (EITF 03-05) (ASC 985-605-15-3). If a multiple-element arrangement consists only of software and software-related elements, the software multiple-element model should be applied to determine whether these elements should be treated separately for accounting purposes.

However, if a multiple-element arrangement consists of (a) a software element and/or a software-related element, and (b) one or more other element(s), then the multiple-element model in EITF 00-21 (ASC 605-25) should be applied to determine whether the software (and software-related) elements can be separated from the non-software (and non-software related) elements for accounting purposes.

Software and Software-Related Elements Requiring Significant Production, Modification, or Customization

When sold on a standalone basis, this class of software and the related production, modification, or customization services must be accounted for using the contract accounting methods prescribed under SOP 81-1 (ASC 605-35), percentage of completion or completed contract. This class of software and software-related elements includes (a) other elements in the arrangement that are essential to the functionality of the software requiring significant production, modification, or customization and (b) other elements in the arrangement to which that software is essential to their functionality, with the possible exception of PCS, as discussed below. If a multiple-element arrangement includes software and software-related elements requiring significant production, modification, or customization, the software multiple-element model should be applied to determine whether the elements should be treated separately for accounting purposes. The rationale here is that although SOP 97-2 (ASC 985-605) requires the use of contract accounting, the elements remain software elements.

However, if a multiple-element arrangement consists of (a) software and software-related element(s) that must be accounted for using contract accounting and (b) another element(s) that would not fall within the scope of SOP 97-2 (ASC 985-605) on a standalone basis, then EITF 00-21 (ASC 605-25) should be applied to determine whether these elements should be treated separately for accounting purposes (see Chapter 4, "Multiple-Element Arrangements").

> **SEC REGISTRANT ALERT:** In a December 2003 speech, an SEC staff member communicated that "the consensus reached by the EITF requires that the EITF 00-21 (ASC 605-25) criteria be applied in bundled arrangements involving significant customization of software to determine whether SOP 81-1 (ASC 605-35) deliverables should be separated from the [other] deliverables." This conclusion is different from the one in TPA 5100.49 (ASC 985-605-55-74; 985-605-55-75), which effectively indicates that the multiple-element model in SOP 97-2 (ASC 985-605) should be applied to separate PCS-related services from a multiple-element arrangement including software that involves significant production, modification, or customization and PCS. We believe that although software requiring significant production, modification, or customization must be accounted for under contract accounting, the software remains a SOP 97-2 (ASC 985-605) element. Therefore, the guidance in EITF 00-21 (ASC 605-25) would apply to multiple-element arrangements, including software (regardless of whether significant production, modification, or customization is needed) and one or more non-software elements.

PCS

Generally, PCS is not essential to the functionality of the software to which it relates (and the software generally has value to the customer on a standalone basis absent the PCS). Absent any general or specific return/refund rights that could affect the analysis, PCS should typically be treated as a separate element for accounting purposes provided appropriate fair value evidence exists to allocate arrangement consideration between the PCS and the other elements in the arrangement. If an arrangement includes software (including or limited to any software requiring significant production, modification, or customization) and PCS, the software multiple-element arrangement model should be used to separate the elements for accounting purposes.

A vendor may enter into an arrangement that includes software requiring significant production, modification, or customization and PCS and may conclude that those elements should not be separated for accounting purposes. In this case, using a Proportional Performance model to recognize revenue for the bundled set of elements would most likely be inappropriate because of the difficulties that arise in estimating costs associated with certain activities covered by PCS, such as telephone support and delivery of unspecified upgrades (i.e., "when-and-if-available" upgrades). Therefore, a Completed Performance model would likely be used to recognize revenue for the bundled set of elements.

ILLUSTRATION: DETERMINING THE APPROPRIATE
MULTIPLE-ELEMENT ARRANGEMENT GUIDANCE TO APPLY

EXAMPLE 1

Facts: A multiple-element arrangement includes off-the-shelf software (i.e., software that is more than incidental but does not require significant production, modification, or customization) and computer hardware. The off-the-shelf software is not essential to the functionality of the computer hardware.

Discussion: Since the software falls within the scope of SOP 97-2 (ASC 985-605) and the hardware does not, the multiple-element model in EITF 00-21 (ASC 605-25) should be applied to determine whether the two elements should be treated separately for revenue recognition purposes.

EXAMPLE 2

Facts: A multiple-element arrangement includes off-the-shelf software (i.e., software that is more than incidental but does not require significant production, modification, or customization) and computer hardware. The off-the-shelf software is essential to the functionality of the computer hardware.

Discussion: The computer hardware is a software-related element because the software is essential to its functionality. Since both elements therefore fall within the scope of SOP 97-2 (ASC 985-605), the multiple-element model in SOP 97-2 (ASC 985-605) should be applied to determine whether the two elements should be treated separately for revenue recognition purposes.

EXAMPLE 3

Facts: A multiple-element arrangement includes software that will be significantly modified and customized as part of the multiple-element arrangement and computer hardware. The significantly modified and customized software is not essential to the functionality of the computer hardware and the computer hardware is not essential to the functionality of the significantly modified and customized software.

Discussion: The arrangement effectively has three deliverables: (1) the software that will be significantly modified and customized, (2) the services that will be performed to significantly modify and customize the software, and (3) the computer hardware. The software and services to significantly modify and customize the software would be treated as a single element (that must be accounted for in accordance with SOP 81-1 (ASC 605-35)) if the software does not have standalone value to the customer without the modification and customization. However, because the software is not essential to the functionality of the computer hardware, the computer hardware is not a software-related element. As one element falls within the scope of SOP 97-2 (ASC 985-605) and one element does not, the multiple-element arrangement model in EITF 00-21 (ASC 605-25) should be applied to determine whether the software element and the computer hardware should be treated separately for revenue recognition purposes.

EXAMPLE 4

Facts: A multiple-element arrangement includes software that will be significantly modified and customized as part of the multiple-element arrangement and computer hardware. The significantly modified and customized software is essential to the functionality of the computer hardware.

Discussion: The arrangement effectively has three deliverables: (1) the software that will be significantly modified and customized, (2) the services that will be performed to significantly modify and customize the software, and (3) the computer hardware. The software and services to significantly modify and customize the software would be treated as a single software element if the software does not have standalone value to the customer without the modification and customization. In addition, the computer hardware is considered a software-related element since the software is essential to its functionality. Because both elements fall within the scope of SOP 97-2 (ASC 985-605), the software multiple-element arrangement model should be applied to determine whether the elements should be separated.

SUMMARY

Is the hardware software-related (i.e., is the software essential to the functionality of the hardware)?

		Yes	No
Is the vendor providing significant production, modification, or customization services in connection with the software sale?	Yes	Software Multiple-Element Model (Example 4)	EITF 00-21 (ASC 605-25) Multiple-Element Model (Example 3)
	No	Software Multiple-Element Model (Example 2)	EITF 00-21 (ASC 605-25) Multiple-Element Model (Example 1)

The remainder of this section discusses the software multiple-element model.

DISCLOSURE ALERT: See Chapter 12, "Disclosures," for information about required disclosures.

SEC REGISTRANT ALERT: In early 2003, the SEC staff issued a Report Pursuant to Section 704 of the Sarbanes-Oxley Act of 2002 (the Section 704 Report). In compiling the information in this Report, the SEC staff studied enforcement actions filed during the period July 31, 1997, through July 30, 2002. The greatest number of enforcement actions brought by the SEC related to improper revenue recognition. One of the common revenue recognition issues highlighted in the Section 704 Report related to improper recognition of revenue from multiple-element arrangements or bundled contracts. One of the two actions discussed in the Section 704 Report in this regard involved improper allocation of arrangement consideration and the other involved improper separation of interdependent elements. This finding is a strong indication that more attention should be given to accounting for multiple-element arrangements.

In addition, in early 2003, the SEC staff issued the Summary by the Division of Corporation Finance of Significant Issues Addressed in the Review of the Periodic Reports of the Fortune 500 Companies (the Fortune 500 Report). This report resulted from the SEC's Division of Corporation Finance's (Corp Fin) review of all annual reports filed by Fortune 500 companies. The report provides insight into areas commonly questioned by Corp Fin during its reviews of annual reports. One area specifically mentioned in the Fortune 500 Report relates to accounting for multiple-element arrangements. Corp Fin specifically indicated that companies in the computer software, computer services, and computer hardware industries could improve their disclosures by expanding the discussion related to multiple-element arrangements.

Defining the Arrangement When Multiple Contracts Exist

A number of requirements in software revenue recognition affect multiple-element arrangements, but not single-element arrangements. In addition, there are times when the inclusion or exclusion of an element within an arrangement can significantly affect the accounting for the other elements of the arrangement (e.g., one undelivered element for which vendor-specific objective evidence (see below) of fair value does not exist prohibits recognition of revenue upon delivery of, or completion of performance for, other elements). For these reasons, it is important to properly identify the "arrangement" (i.e., identify all the elements of deliverables) or properly identify the unit of accounting, which is the starting point for allocating revenue to individual elements.

SOP 97-2 (ASC 985-605) requires vendors to account for the substance or the economics of the agreement, rather than merely the contractual terms of the agreement. Even if different elements are documented in multiple contracts, a multiple-element arrangement that includes only software and/or software-related elements must be accounted for using the appropriate multiple-element provisions of SOP 97-2 (ASC 985-605). Therefore, contracts should be evaluated together when they are, in substance, part of one arrangement. Some indicators or factors that might indicate that multiple contracts are substantively part of the same arrangement include (TPA 5100.39 and FAS-133 Guide, Question K-1) (ASC 985-605-55-4):

- *Timing of execution of the contracts:*
  - The contracts or agreements are negotiated or executed within a short time frame of each other.
- *Substance and the composition of the contract:*
  - The contracts relate to the same elements or what is, in essence, the same project.
  - The different elements are closely interrelated or interdependent in terms of design, technology, or function.
  - One or more elements in one contract or agreement are essential to the functionality of an element in another contract.
- *Arrangement consideration and payment terms:*
  - The fee for one or more contracts or agreements is subject to refund or forfeiture or other concession if another contract is not completed satisfactorily.
  - Payment terms under one contract or agreement coincide with performance criteria of another contract or agreement.
- *Definition of contract and customer:*
  - The negotiations are conducted jointly with two or more parties (e.g., from different divisions of the same company) to do what, in essence, is a single project.

EXAMPLE: DEFINING THE ARRANGEMENT

Rightnow Technologies, Inc. Form 10-K—Fiscal Year Ended December 31, 2007

Separate contracts with the same customer that are entered into at or near the same time are generally presumed to have been negotiated together and are combined and accounted for as a single arrangement.

> **OBSERVATION:**   SOP 81-1 (ASC 605-35) also contains guidance to aid in the determination as to when two or more contracts should be segregated or combined. See Chapter 9, "Contract Accounting."

Allocating Revenue Among Elements

If vendor-specific objective evidence (VSOE) of fair value (as discussed below) exists for all elements, the arrangement consideration should be allocated to the individual elements based on their relative fair values. However, the full fair value of a specified upgrade right should be allocated to that right, regardless of any discount inherent in the total arrangement. The remainder of the arrangement consideration (total fee or arrangement consideration less the full fair value of the upgrade right) is allocated on the basis of the relative fair values (as supported by VSOE) of each of the individual elements. The discount is therefore allocated pro rata across each of the other elements (SOP 97-2, par. 11) (ASC 985-605-25-8). The discount is not allocated to the upgrade right.

If VSOE of fair value exists for all undelivered elements, but does not exist for one or more delivered elements, the arrangement consideration should be allocated to the various elements of the arrangement under the residual method. Under this method, the amount of arrangement consideration allocated to the delivered elements should be the total arrangement consideration less the aggregate fair values of the undelivered elements. Thus, any potential discount on the arrangement taken as a whole is allocated entirely to the delivered elements. This ensures that the amount of revenue recognized at any point in time is not overstated. If the sum of the fair values of the undelivered elements is greater than the total arrangement consideration, no revenue may be recognized, despite the fact that one or more elements have already been delivered (SOP 97-2, par. 12 (ASC 985-605-25-10 and 25-11).

> **OBSERVATION:**   The residual method works in only one direction. It works only when VSOE of fair value exists for all undelivered elements. If VSOE of fair value exists for delivered elements, but does not exist for one or more undelivered elements, the residual method cannot be used because it is not possible, in the absence of VSOE of fair value of the undelivered elements, to ensure that all of the potential discount in the arrangement is allocated to the delivered elements. See TPA 5100.74 (ASC 985-605-55-88 through 55-92).

Once the fee in an arrangement has been allocated among elements based on the appropriate method, the allocation should not be subsequently changed, even if the company changes its pricing (SOP 97-2, par. 10) (ASC 985-605-25-7).

If VSOE of fair value does not exist for one or more undelivered elements, no revenue from the arrangement may be recognized until either sufficient VSOE exists to allocate revenue based on one of the methods described above or the last element in the arrangement is delivered. Establishment of VSOE (e.g., by separately selling an element) after the end of an accounting period but before financial statements are prepared is not sufficient to permit revenue recognition during the accounting period in question (TPA 5100.38) (ASC 985-605-25-9 and ASC 985-605-55-94).[2]

> **OBSERVATION:** Some software arrangements are very complex and include a large number of elements. If VSOE of fair value of even one undelivered element does not exist, no revenue may be recognized until VSOE of fair value for that element does exist, or the element is delivered. Therefore, no matter how immaterial a particular undelivered element is to an entire arrangement, the lack of VSOE of fair value for it can delay revenue recognition.

> **SEC REGISTRANT ALERT:** In a December 2007 speech, the SEC Staff discussed revenue recognition for hardware deliverables in software arrangements. SEC Staff indicated that when the remaining undelivered elements are multiple units of the same hardware product for which no VSOE exists, it may be acceptable to recognize revenue from the entire arrangement on a proportionate basis, as the units of hardware are delivered. This recognition pattern is similar to that specified in SOP 97-2 (ASC 985-605) for situations where no VSOE exists for any deliverables and the only undelivered element is PCS. In such a situation, revenue from the entire arrangement would be recognized proportionately (ratably) over the period of PCS.

Multiple-Product and Multiple-Copy Fixed-Fee Arrangements

Some software arrangements provide customers with the right to reproduce or obtain copies, at specified prices per copy, of several software products for a fixed fee. In these arrangements, the fixed fee is payable regardless of the number of copies of the various products that are eventually used and payment is not tied to deployment or use of the copies. Although the price per copy is fixed at the inception of the arrangement, the arrangement fee cannot be

---

[2] Establishing VSOE after period-end is also a nonrecognized subsequent event, as discussed in footnote 1.

allocated to the individual products because the revenue allocable to each software product depends on the choices to be made by the customer in the future regarding how many of each product will be used (or resold, if the customer is a reseller). These arrangements may also include the rights to select copies of products that are not available at the inception of the arrangement.

Because the minimum fee is fixed in these arrangements and is not dependent upon duplication or the selection of the number of copies of each product to be used, all revenue should be recognized when the first or master copy of all products that are part of the arrangement has been delivered, provided all other revenue recognition criteria have been met. Until then, revenue should be recognized as copies of delivered products are made.

> **OBSERVATION:** In this case, the stated contract prices are used to recognize revenue, regardless of the fair value of each product and regardless of whether VSOE of fair value exists. This is a unique feature of the accounting for fixed minimum, multi-product, multi-copy arrangements in which the customer chooses how many copies of each product to use. This use of contractually stated amounts to recognize revenue may not be analogized to for other types of arrangements.

Certain arrangements may impose a maximum on the number of copies of a particular product that the customer may select. If all undelivered products in an arrangement are subject to such maximums, any revenue in excess of the specified prices per copy multiplied by the applicable maximums should be recognized as revenue provided all other revenue recognition criteria have been met (SOP 97-2, pars. 43–47) (ASC 985-605-25-52 through 25-57).

ILLUSTRATION: PER COPY PRICES IN A MULTIPLE-PRODUCT, MULTIPLE-COPY, FIXED-FEE ARRANGEMENT

(Adapted from SOP 97-2, Appendix A (ASC 985-605-55-134 through 55-144))

EXAMPLE 1

Facts: A vendor enters into an arrangement under which a customer has the right to make copies of Product A at $100 a copy, copies of Product B at $200 a copy, or copies of Product C at $50 a copy until such time as the customer has made copies aggregating $100,000 based on the per copy prices. The customer is obligated to pay the $100,000 immediately, without regard to when it makes copies of the three products. The first copy of Products A and B are delivered immediately, but Product C is not available yet.

No portion of the fee allocable to copies made of Products A and B is refundable if Product C is not delivered, nor is there any obligation to deliver Product C if copies of Products A and B aggregating $100,000 have been made. None of the products are essential to the functionality of any of the other products. The maximum number of copies of Product C that can be made is 500.

Discussion: Because the first copy of Product C has not yet been delivered, the maximum amount of the fee that may be used for Product C must be deferred. Thus, $25,000 (500 copies × $50 per copy) must be deferred. The remaining $75,000 of revenue should be recognized when the first copies of Products A and B are delivered to the customer. The $25,000 allocated to Product C would be recognized upon delivery of the first copy of that product. If the customer duplicates enough copies of Products A and B such that the revenue allocable to those products exceeds $75,000, the additional revenue should be recognized as the additional copies are made.

EXAMPLE 2

Facts: Assume the same facts as in the preceding example, except the arrangement does not state a maximum number of copies of Product C that can be made.

Discussion: Because no limit on the number of copies of Product C exists, the customer could, in theory, use the entire fixed fee to purchase copies of Product C. Therefore, revenue should only be recognized as copies of Products A ($100 of revenue per copy) and B ($200 of revenue per copy) are made, until the first copy of Product C is delivered, at which point, any remaining revenue should be recognized.

License Mix Arrangements

In some cases, a fixed fee, multi-product, multi-copy arrangement may allow a user to change or alternate its use of multiple products or licenses (license mix) even after the customer makes its initial choice.

Software sold under a license mix arrangement is considered delivered for accounting purposes once the first or master copy of each product is delivered. In addition, remixing is not considered an exchange or a return of software because the master or first copy of all products has been licensed and delivered and the customer has the right to use them. Nor is a remix right considered the right to obtain additional products or licenses, as long as the remix rights do not allow the customer to increase the aggregate value of the licenses it uses at a particular time. Therefore, as long as all other revenue recognition criteria are met, revenue from a remix arrangement may be recognized upon delivery of the first or master copy of each product (TPA 5100.45) (ASC 985-605-55-99 and 55-100).

However, if the remix provisions allow the customer to receive the rights to use products that do not exist at the initiation of the arrangement, the arrangement should be treated as a subscription (see "Subscriptions" earlier in this chapter).

ILLUSTRATION: REMIX RIGHTS

EXAMPLE 1

Facts: A vendor enters into an arrangement under which a customer has the right to make copies of Product A at $100 a copy, copies of Product B at $200 a copy, or copies of Product C at $50 a copy until such time as the customer has made copies aggregating $100,000 based on the per copy prices. The customer is obligated to pay the $100,000 immediately, without regard to when it makes copies of the three products. The customer initially selects 200 copies of Product B ($40,000), 250 copies of Product A ($25,000), and 700 copies of Product C ($35,000).

After the initial selection, the customer has the right, for three years, to change its use of Products A, B, and C by giving up licenses of one in exchange for licenses of another based on the ratio of the prices stated in the arrangement. For example, the customer can give up one copy of Product B in exchange for two copies of Product A or four copies of Product C.

Discussion: Once a copy of each of the products has been delivered, the remix rights do not affect the recognition of revenue under the contract since the remix rights do not extend to any additional products and the aggregate value of the software under the arrangement is limited to the $100,000 fee.

EXAMPLE 2

Facts: Same as Example 1, except that the customer may exchange each copy of Product B it initially chooses for five copies of Product C.

Discussion: In this case, the customer can obtain additional value based on exercising its remix rights. The 1,000 copies of Product C that could be obtained by giving up 200 copies of Product B have a value of $50,000, while the 200 copies of Product B that would be given up have a value of $40,000. Thus, the additional value that the customer can realize is $10,000. That amount should be deferred to account for these rights when revenue is recognized under the arrangement.

EXAMPLE 3

Facts: Same as Example 1, except that the remix rights will also pertain to any other products that the vendor develops during the remix period, based on the list prices of these products as compared to the contractual prices of Products A, B, and C.

Discussion: Because the remix rights apply to future products, the arrangement should be treated as a subscription, meaning that the $100,000 fee should be recognized ratably over three years.

Vendor-Specific Objective Evidence (VSOE) of Fair Value

General

SOP 97-2 (ASC 985-605) limits the information that a company may use to establish the fair value of a particular element. This information, which is called vendor-specific objective evidence (VSOE) of fair value, is limited to:

1. The price charged when the same element is sold separately.

2. For an element not yet being sold separately, the price established by management having the relevant authority; it must be probable that the price, once established, will not change before the separate introduction of the element into the marketplace.

Separate prices stated in an arrangement are not relevant in determining the fair value of the individual elements, because such prices, having been negotiated as part of the arrangement as a whole, do not necessarily represent bargained-for prices for each individual element. As such, they may not represent fair value (SOP 97-2, par. 10) (ASC 985-605-25-6).

The definition of VSOE also prohibits the use of surrogate prices, such as prices charged by a competitor for similar products or industry averages, to determine fair value. This is because software produced by different vendors, even if they are designed for the same purpose, invariably has inherent differences. Using competitor prices as evidence of fair value would essentially result in those differences being ignored. For that reason, the evidence must be vendor-specific (SOP 97-2, par. 100).

SOP 97-2 (ASC 985-605) also prohibits the use of methods such as "cost plus a normal profit margin" to support fair value. In part, this is because it is difficult to establish both "cost" and a "normal profit margin" in a software environment. The direct cost of software products is very low because almost all of the cost is incurred as the software is developed. Once the software has been developed, additional copies can be produced at almost no cost. Therefore, the notion of a "normal profit margin" is virtually nonexistent.

Allocating revenue to each element based on the combined profit margin in the arrangement is also unacceptable. This type of allocation would not result in the correct assignment of fair value to individual elements, because each element is normally expected to have a different profit margin. For example, software products have an almost nonexistent direct cost component, but services have a significant direct cost component.

Although many other methods for allocating the arrangement fee to the individual elements were suggested during the development of SOP 97-2 (ASC 985-605), none of them are currently allowed. Therefore, software vendors often conclude that insufficient evidence exists (i.e., there is no VSOE of fair value) to allocate the arrangement fee to the individual elements.

EXAMPLE: VSOE OF FAIR VALUE

BMC Software, Inc. Form 10-K—Fiscal Year Ended March 31, 2008

Revenue Recognition

Software license revenue is recognized when persuasive evidence of an arrangement exists, delivery of the product has occurred, the fee is fixed or determinable, collection is probable and vendor-specific objective evidence (VSOE) of the fair value of undelivered elements exists. As substantially all of the Company's software licenses are sold in multiple-element arrangements that include either maintenance or both maintenance and professional services, the Company uses the residual method to determine the amount of license revenue to be recognized. Under the residual method, consideration is allocated to undelivered elements based upon VSOE of the fair value of those elements, with the residual of the arrangement fee allocated to and recognized as license revenue. The Company has established VSOE of the fair value of maintenance through independent maintenance renewals, which demonstrate a consistent relationship of pricing maintenance as a percentage of the discounted or undiscounted license list price. VSOE of the fair value of professional services is established based on daily rates when sold on a stand-alone basis.

The Company is unable to establish VSOE of fair value for all undelivered elements in arrangements that include software products for which maintenance pricing is based on both discounted and undiscounted license list prices, certain arrangements that include unlimited licensing rights and certain arrangements that contain rights to future unspecified software products as part of the maintenance offering. If VSOE of fair value of one or more undelivered elements does not exist, license revenue is deferred and recognized upon delivery of those elements or when VSOE of fair value can be established, or if the deferral is due to the factors described above, license revenue is recognized ratably over the maintenance term in the arrangement.

In its time-based license agreements, the Company is unable to establish VSOE of fair value for undelivered maintenance elements because the contractual maintenance terms in these arrangements are the same duration as the license terms, and VSOE of fair value of maintenance cannot be established. Accordingly, license fees in time-based license arrangements are recognized ratably over the term of the arrangement.

Matrix Pricing

In some cases, pricing may be based on combinations of multiple factors. For example, certain arrangements are priced based on the type of customer or the number of users that will be granted access to the licensed products. In these arrangements, a software vendor may, as part of its standard pricing policy, offer a reduced per user price to companies purchasing a greater number of user licenses or a greater number of products. SOP 97-2 does allow these types of pricing policies to be taken into account when determining the fair value of an element in an arrangement (SOP 97-2, par. 10) (ASC 985-605-25-7).

ILLUSTRATION: VSOE OF FAIR VALUE BASED ON MULTIPLE FACTORS

Facts: A software vendor generally sells a single license to its product for $100. However, as part of its standard price list, not-for-profit entities receive a 10% discount on every license. In addition, any customer purchasing over 100 licenses at once receives a 10% discount off of the otherwise applicable price.

Discussion: Standard discounts imply that the vendor is selling to different classes of customers. Therefore, the vendor really has a matrix of VSOE of fair values for its product. Because the discounts are standard, they should be considered in assessing the VSOE of fair value. This vendor's VSOE of fair value is as follows:

	Not-for-Profits	Other Customers
Less than 100 licenses	$90 per license	$100 per license
100 licenses or more	$81 per license	$90 per license

Specified Upgrades

Specified upgrades are treated as separate elements in an arrangement. Therefore, VSOE of fair value for an undelivered specified upgrade must exist before any revenue may be recognized. VSOE of fair value for a specific upgrade is the fee charged to existing users of the software product who separately purchase the upgrade. However, if the software vendor provides the upgrade free of charge to all users of the product (e.g., by providing a free download on its Internet site) regardless of whether the users have a contractual right to the upgrade, VSOE is zero and revenue need not be deferred when rights to the upgrade are specifically included in an arrangement.

> ☛ **PRACTICE POINTER:** Many upgrades are neither sold separately nor provided free of charge to all users, regardless of the contractual arrangements. Instead, customers generally obtain such rights by purchasing post-contract customer support (see the next section for the accounting for such arrangements) or negotiating these rights in the original license arrangement. As a result, VSOE of fair value for a specified upgrade often does not exist. Many companies, as a matter of policy, do not include specific upgrade rights in their arrangements to sell software. However, each contract should be reviewed to determine whether specific upgrade rights are granted. It is also important to determine whether the vendor has a history of providing and charging for upgrades regardless of whether the upgrades are included in its arrangements.

SOP 97-2 (ASC 985-605) contains two special provisions on the allocation of the arrangement fee to a specified upgrade. First, no portion of any discount in a multiple-element arrangement should be allocated to a specified upgrade right. Therefore, if an arrangement includes a specified upgrade for which VSOE of fair value exists, the full fair value must be allocated to the upgrade. This is similar to the application of the residual method when VSOE of fair value does not exist for one or more delivered elements. Second, when sufficient vendor-specific experience exists to reasonably estimate breakage (the percentage of customers that are not expected to exercise the upgrade right), the fee allocated to the upgrade right should be reduced to reflect that estimated breakage (SOP 97-2, pars. 36–37) (ASC 985-605-25-45).

> **OBSERVATION:** The concept of reducing the amount allocated to an undelivered element to reflect expected breakage is an issue that arises frequently in multiple-element arrangements. Although there is some judgment that can be applied in non-software arrangements (see Chapter 3, "General Principles"), SOP 97-2 (ASC 985-605) only allows the application of breakage in the context of specified upgrades. Therefore, when an arrangement includes an additional product, rather than an upgrade, revenue must be allocated to the additional product as if all users will request it, even if the vendor reasonably believes that some will not (i.e., no breakage may be incorporated in the allocation of revenue).

PCS

A limited period of PCS is often included with a software license. As discussed earlier, if PCS is included in an arrangement with software, the software multiple-element arrangement model should be applied to determine whether the software and PCS should be treated separately for accounting purposes. PCS should be treated as a separate element for accounting purposes when VSOE of its fair value exists. Determining whether VSOE of fair value exists for PCS is discussed below. PCS should be analyzed in this manner even though it may be provided to all purchasers. In rare circumstances, however, PCS is considered insignificant to the arrangement and delivery is not required to recognize the revenue allocated to it (see additional discussion of this issue in the section above, "Post-Contract Customer Support (PCS)").

In general, an arrangement that includes software (including software that requires significant production, modification, or customization) and an initial PCS period will also stipulate that the customer may purchase additional periods of PCS, at a specified renewal rate, when the initial "free" period expires. The specified renewal rate provides VSOE of fair value of the PCS services, unless the renewal rate is not substantive (SOP 97-2, par. 57) (ASC 985-605-25-67).

> **OBSERVATION:** Vendors should note that documentation is generally required to demonstrate that substantially all customers generally renew at or close to the specified renewal rates.

ILLUSTRATION: ALLOCATION OF ARRANGEMENT FEE BETWEEN LICENSE AND PCS

For purposes of these examples, assume that the software does not involve significant production, modification, or customization.

EXAMPLE 1

Facts: A vendor licenses software to a user along with one year of PCS for $90,000. VSOE of fair value for the software is $85,000 and PCS is renewable on an annual basis for $15,000 per year.

Discussion: The PCS renewal rate is considered substantive and provides VSOE of fair value for the PCS. Therefore, there is sufficient VSOE to allocate the fee between the software and the PCS. The fair value of the two elements is $100,000, meaning there is a 10% discount in the arrangement. This discount should be allocated across the two elements as follows:

	License	PCS	Total
Fair Value	$85,000	$15,000	$100,000
Less: 10% Discount	−8,500	−1,500	−10,000
Revenue	$76,500	$13,500	$90,000

EXAMPLE 2

Facts: A vendor licenses software to a user along with one year of PCS for $90,000. PCS is renewable on an annual basis for $15,000 per year. The vendor does not have VSOE of fair value for the software because it is never sold separately (it is always sold with PCS).

Discussion: The PCS renewal rate is substantive and considered to be VSOE of fair value for the PCS. Therefore, there is sufficient VSOE to allocate the fee using the residual method. In this case, $15,000 of the arrangement fee is deferred, representing the full fair value of the undelivered element, PCS. The remaining $75,000 is allocated to the software element.

Note that there is no way to determine the size of the discount in this example.

EXAMPLE 3

Facts: A software vendor typically prices annual PCS at 13% of its standard perpetual license fee. The VSOE of fair value for the software is $100,000. The vendor enters into an arrangement that includes a perpetual license to its software and one year of PCS for $102,000. The stated renewal rate for PCS is $2,000.

Discussion: The $2,000 should not be considered to be VSOE of fair value for the PCS, as the renewal rate is not substantive. In this situation, the company should look to its standard renewal rates that are used in other arrangements to find VSOE of fair value. Therefore, the fair value of PCS is $13,000 per year. In allocating the license fee, the vendor would need to estimate how many years of discounted PCS the customer would be expected to buy. Typically, the estimate used would be the remaining product life of the software product. Thus, if the product has a five-year remaining life, revenue would be allocated as follows:

	Payments	Fair Value
Software	$102,000	$100,000
Expected Five Years of PCS	8,000	65,000
Total	$110,000	$165,000

This results in an implied discount in the arrangement of 33.33%. Therefore, when revenue is recognized on the sale of software, $66,667 should be recognized. The remainder of the upfront fee ($110,000 − $66,667 = $43,333 or $65,000 less a 33.33% discount) should be deferred and recognized over the anticipated five-year PCS period ($43,333/5, or $8,666.60 of PCS revenue will be recognized each year).

An arrangement may include two different pricing methodologies related to PCS renewals. For example, an arrangement may include (1) a perpetual software license with a three-year unlimited deployment period and (2) PCS where the renewal fee is fixed in the second and third year of the arrangement, but varies in the fourth year and thereafter, depending on the number of software copies deployed. In this situation, a vendor should consider whether there is any basis to determine which of the PCS renewal pricing methodologies represents VSOE of fair value. Much of the time, no basis upon which to make such a determination will exist. However, if sufficient objective evidence exists to support the assertion that the renewal rate in the fourth year and thereafter is more likely than not (i.e., a likelihood of greater than 50%) to approximate or be less than the amount charged in the second and third years, the PCS renewal rates for the second and third years would constitute VSOE of fair value of PCS (TPA 5100.75) (ASC 985-605-55-70 through 55-73).

Implied PCS arrangements When an arrangement does not explicitly include rights to PCS, but the vendor has a historical pattern of providing (or an intention to provide) the customer with support services and/or unspecified upgrades, an implied PCS arrangement exists and should be considered an element in the arrangement.

In other situations, the arrangement may include a period of PCS that begins some time after product delivery, presumably to coincide with the installation or deployment of the product by the customer. However, because such arrangements almost invariably entitle the customer to unspecified upgrades introduced during the intervening period and because other support is generally provided during this period as well, an arrangement with a delayed PCS commencement date should be considered to include PCS during the intervening period. For example, an arrangement that includes one year of PCS that begins three months after product delivery (with no charge for those three months) should be accounted for as an arrangement that includes 15 months of PCS. The arrangement fee should be allocated accordingly (SOP 97-2, par. 56) (ASC 985-605-55-70 through 71).

Renewal rates based on a percentage of license fee Some vendors have a practice of charging for PCS renewals at a rate calculated as a consistent percentage of the net license fee, which may vary from arrangement to arrangement. Thus, the PCS renewal rates, expressed in terms of actual dollars rather than percentages, will be different across arrangements. As long as each of the arrangements includes a renewal fee based on a consistent percentage of the license fee that is substantive, that renewal rate may be treated as VSOE of fair value for the arrangement (TPA 5100.55) (ASC 985-605-55-68 and 55-69).

VSOE of PCS for term licenses Although perpetual licenses are the more common type of software license arrangement, term licenses are also used. In a term license, the software product can only be used for a limited period of time. In order to continue using the product after the term expires, the customer must enter into a new license (or extend the old one). Many term licenses of software include PCS for the entire period. In these licenses, there is no renewal rate for PCS and VSOE of fair value for PCS does not exist. Although the company might look to its standard PCS renewal rate in perpetual licenses of the same product as evidence of fair value, the fair value for PCS in a term license is likely to be different because of the period during which any upgrades or technical advice will be useful to the customer. Therefore, PCS in a term license and PCS in a perpetual license of the same product are not considered the same element. As a result the separate sales price (renewal rate) of PCS in a perpetual license is not VSOE of fair value for PCS in a term license of the same product (TPA 5100.68) (ASC 985-605-55-64 through 55-67).

☛ **PRACTICE POINTER:** Several other TPAs address PCS issues in term licenses. These TPAs apply to limited circumstances and are not discussed here. However, the guidance has been incorporated into the ASC.

EXAMPLE: VSOE of PCS

Cognos, Inc. Form 10-K—Fiscal Year Ended February 27, 2007

As required by SOP 97-2, the Corporation establishes VSOE of fair value for each element of a contract with multiple elements (i.e., delivered and undelivered products, support obligations, education, consulting, and other services). The Corporation determines VSOE for service elements based on the normal pricing and discounting practices for those elements when they are sold separately. For PCS, VSOE of fair value is based on the PCS rates contractually agreed to with customers, if the rate is consistent with our customary pricing practices. Absent a stated PCS rate, a consistent rate which represents the price when PCS is sold separately based on PCS renewals is used.

We have historically used two forms of contract terms regarding PCS: contracts which include a stated PCS rate (either a stated renewal rate or a stated rate for the first year PCS bundled with the software license); and contracts which do not state a PCS rate. For contracts which include a stated renewal rate, we use the contractually stated renewal rate to allocate arrangement consideration to the undelivered PCS at the inception of the arrangement and recognize such consideration ratably over the PCS term provided that the stated rate is substantive and consistent with our customary pricing practices. Historically, there has been a high correlation between the amounts allocated to PCS in the initial software licensing arrangement for such arrangements and the amounts at which PCS is renewed.

For contracts that have a stated first year PCS rate, we use such stated prices to allocate arrangement consideration to the undelivered PCS at the inception of the arrangement and recognize such consideration ratably over the PCS term, provided that it is substantive and consistent with our customary pricing practices, as this is typically the rate at which PCS will be renewed. Historically, there has been a high correlation between the amounts allocated to PCS in the initial software licensing arrangement for such arrangements and the amounts at which PCS is renewed.

For contracts which do not state a PCS rate, we allocate a consistent percentage of the license fee to PCS in the first year of such arrangements based on a substantive rate at which our customer experience indicates customers will typically agree to renew PCS. Historically, there has been a high correlation between the mean of amounts allocated to PCS in the initial software licensing arrangement for such arrangements and the mean of amounts at which PCS is renewed.

We stratify our customers into three classes in determining VSOE of fair value for PCS. The classifications are based on the amount of software license business (i.e., software license revenues), life-to-date, that has previously been obtained from the respective customers. For each class of customer, a range of prices exists which represents VSOE of fair value for PCS for that class of customer.

When PCS in individual arrangements is stated below the lower limits of our acceptable ranges by customer class, we adjust the percentage allocated for support upwards to the low end of the applicable range by customer class. This adjustment allocates additional revenue from license revenue to deferred PCS revenue which is amortized over the life of the PCS contract, which is typically one year. If the stated PCS is above the reasonable range, no adjustment is made and the deferred PCS revenue is measured at the contracted percentage.

Services

VSOE of fair value for service elements is more easily determined because services can usually be purchased separately. For example, many software vendors offer training and consultation services on system integration that can be purchased for a specific amount after the software has been delivered or installed. Other services, such as software customization, however, may not have VSOE of fair value, because they are undertaken only as part of a comprehensive arrangement to design, develop, and deliver a customized software package. As discussed below, the existence of such services in an arrangement may require the use of contract accounting.

Elements Essential to the Functionality of One Another

In general, once revenue is allocated to each of the elements in an arrangement, revenue recognition for that element is evaluated without regard to the other elements. However, in determining whether an element in a multiple-element arrangement has been delivered, the delivery of an element is considered not to have occurred if there are undelivered elements that are essential to the functionality of the delivered element, because the customer would not have the full use of the delivered element (SOP 97-2, par. 13) (ASC 985-605-25-12). For example, no revenue should be recognized upon delivery of a software upgrade if the base package has not yet been delivered.

Service Elements Essential to the Functionality of Software

An important factor to consider in determining whether services are essential to the functionality of any other element is whether the software included in the arrangement is considered core or off-the-shelf software. Core software is software that a vendor uses in creating other software. It is not sold as is because customers cannot use it unless it is customized to meet system objectives or customer specifications. Design and customization services are almost always essential to the functionality of core software included in the same arrangement (SOP 97-2, pars. 68–69) (ASC 985-605-25-81 through 25-83).

In contrast, off-the-shelf software is software the customer can use with no significant changes in the underlying code. In some instances, an arrangement may include delivery of off-the-shelf software along with integration or other services that do not affect the operation of the off-the-shelf software. In these cases, the services may not be essential to the functionality of the software. However, if significant modifications or additions to software that is normally considered off-the-shelf software are necessary to meet the customer's purpose (e.g., changing or making additions to the software because it would not be usable in its off-the-shelf form in the customer's environment), the software should be considered core software for purposes of that arrangement. As such, the services included in the arrangement would be considered essential to the functionality of the software (SOP 97-2, pars. 68–69) (ASC 985-605-25-81 through 25-83).

A service element should only be separately accounted for if it is separately identified in the arrangement such that the arrangement fee would be expected to vary based on whether it was included (SOP 97-2, par. 65) (ASC 985-605-25-78). For example, assume that an arrangement calls for the delivery of a software package that interfaces with a certain report writer system and that the off-the-shelf version of the software does not interface with that report writer. Because the arrangement does not specifically identify the development of the interface as a separate implementation service, this service cannot be accounted for separately. Instead, the service and the product must be accounted for on a combined basis under contract accounting. However, if the arrangement had called for the delivery of the off-the-shelf product and implementation services to build the interface to the report writer, the product and service could possibly be accounted for separately.

Other factors should also be considered in evaluating whether a service element is essential to the functionality of the other elements of an arrangement. For example, the following factors are indicative of services that are essential to the functionality of other elements (SOP 97-2, par. 70) (ASC 985-605-25-84):

1. *Building complex interfaces is necessary for the vendor's software to be functional in the customer's environment.* If the software is not sold by third parties, there may be no party other than the vendor that can design and develop such complex interfaces.

2. *The timing of payments for the software is coincident with performance of the services.* This would seem to indicate that the customer does not have full use of the software until the services are complete. This factor only indicates that services are essential to the software's functionality if the dollar amount of payments, whose timing is tied to the services, is greater than the amount of revenue allocated to the services.

3. *Milestones or customer-specific acceptance criteria affect the realizability of the software-license fee.* If the customer has negotiated the right to reject the software if the services are not performed to its satisfaction, this would seem to indicate that the customer believes the services are essential to the functionality of the software.

Conversely, the following factors are indicative that the services are not essential to the functionality of the software (SOP 97-2, par. 71) (ASC 985-605-25-85):

1. *The services are available from other vendors.* If this is true, then the customer could have obtained any services necessary to use the software for its purposes without the involvement of the vendor.

2. *The services do not carry a significant degree of risk or unique acceptance criteria.* Services that are routine in nature are not likely to be essential to the software's functionality.

3. *The software vendor is an experienced provider of the services.* This indicates a low risk related to the provision of the services.

4. *The vendor is providing primarily implementation services that do not affect the operation of the software.* Services, such as loading of software, training of customer personnel, data conversion, report writing and the documentation of procedures, are not generally essential to operating the software.

5. *Customer personnel are dedicated to participate in the services being performed.* The dedication of customer personnel may indicate that services from the vendor are not absolutely necessary.

If a service element is determined to be essential to the functionality of the software in an arrangement, the software product and service elements should be accounted for on a combined basis, using contract accounting. The application of contract accounting to a software arrangement is discussed later in this chapter.

Nonservice Elements

Except for undelivered service elements, U.S. GAAP does not provide significant guidance on how to determine whether one element is essential to the functionality of another. However, many of the same concepts that are relevant in determining whether an undelivered service is essential to the functionality of a delivered element are also relevant when the undelivered element is a product. If an undelivered element other than a service is essential to the functionality of a delivered element, revenue from the delivered element should be deferred until the element essential to its functionality is also delivered.

EXAMPLES: SOFTWARE AND SERVICES

Oracle, Inc. Form 10-K—Fiscal Year Ended May 31, 2007

Many of our software arrangements include consulting implementation services sold separately under consulting engagement contracts. Consulting revenues from these arrangements are generally accounted for separately from new software license revenues because the arrangements qualify as service transactions as defined in SOP 97-2. The more significant factors considered in determining whether the revenue should be accounted for separately include the nature of services (i.e., consideration of whether the services are essential to the functionality of the licensed product), degree of risk, availability of services from other vendors, timing of payments and impact of milestones or acceptance criteria on the realizability of the software license fee. Revenues for consulting services are generally recognized as the services are performed. If there is a significant uncertainty about the project completion or receipt of payment for the consulting services, revenue is deferred until the uncertainty is sufficiently resolved. We estimate the proportional performance on contracts with fixed or "not to exceed" fees on a monthly basis utilizing hours incurred to date as a percentage of total estimated hours to complete the project. We recognize no more than 90% of the milestone or total contract amount until project acceptance is obtained. If we do not have a sufficient basis to measure progress towards completion, revenue is recognized when we receive final acceptance from the customer. When total cost estimates exceed revenues, we accrue for the estimated losses immediately using cost estimates that are based upon an average fully burdened daily rate applicable to the consulting organization delivering the services. The complexity of the estimation process and factors relating to the assumptions, risks and uncertainties inherent with the application of the proportional performance method of accounting affects the amounts of revenue and related expenses reported in our consolidated financial statements. A number of internal and external factors can affect our estimates, including labor rates, utilization and efficiency variances and specification and testing requirement changes.

If an arrangement does not qualify for separate accounting of the software license and consulting transactions, then new software license revenue is generally recognized together with the consulting services based on contract accounting using either the percentage-of-completion or completed-contract method. Contract accounting is applied to any arrangements: (1) that include milestones or customer specific acceptance criteria that may affect collection of the software license fees; (2) where services include significant modification or customization of the software; (3) where significant consulting services are provided for in the software license contract without additional charge or are substantially discounted; or (4) where the software license payment is tied to the performance of consulting services.

Refund Provisions Based on Undelivered Elements

Revenue allocated to a delivered element is not considered collectible to the extent that it is subject to forfeiture, refund, or other concession in the event of non-performance on other elements in the arrangement. These forfeiture provisions may or may not be explicitly documented in the arrangement. Nonetheless, revenue should be considered subject to forfeiture, refund, or other concession, unless management does not intend to accept returns or grant concessions under these circumstances. In addition, a review of all available evidence should persuasively support this position.

If the vendor has a historical pattern of making refunds or granting concessions on delivered elements not required under the original provisions of its arrangements, due to non-delivery of other elements, no other evidence is persuasive enough to reach a conclusion that revenue in current arrangements with similar elements is not subject to forfeiture. Therefore, no revenue should be recognized until all of the elements are delivered (SOP 97-2, par. 14) (ASC 985-605-25-13).

ILLUSTRATION: TIMING OF REVENUE RECOGNITION WHEN SPECIFIED DAMAGES ARE INCLUDED IN A MULTIPLE-ELEMENT ARRANGEMENT

Facts: Company X enters into a contract to deliver two off-the-shelf software elements, A and B, for $1,000,000. Company X appropriately allocates $600,000 of the fee to Element A and $400,000 to Element B based on VSOE of fair value. The agreement stipulates that Company X must pay a $550,000 penalty if it does not deliver Element B by a specified date. Element A has already been delivered, but Element B has not.

Accounting: The portion of the fee allocated to Element A that is subject to forfeiture if Element B is not delivered is not considered collectible until Element B is delivered. Therefore, Company X may only recognize revenue upon the delivery of Element A to the extent that revenue is not refundable. In this case, the penalty for failing to deliver Element B on a timely basis ($550,000) exceeds the portion of the fee allocated to Element B ($400,000) by $150,000. Therefore, only $450,000 of the $600,000 otherwise allocable to Element A may be recognized. If Company X receives payments of greater than $450,000 before Element B is delivered, the excess should be reflected as deferred revenue.

RECOGNITION WHEN ELEMENTS ARE ACCOUNTED FOR TOGETHER

There are several situations discussed above in which revenue from two separate deliverables cannot be separated for recognition purposes. The appropriate recognition pattern for such situations depends on the mix of elements in the multiple-element arrangement or portion of a multiple-element arrangement that cannot be further separated.

> **PRACTICE ALERT:** A unique cost deferral issue may arise in the application of specific refund right provisions under EITF 00-21 (ASC 605-25) (see Chapter 4, "Multiple-Element Arrangements"). When a specific refund right results in some

or all of the amount otherwise allocable to a delivered element not being allocated, should some portion or all of the delivered element's cost be deferred? This issue, however, occurs infrequently in software transactions, given the nature of software development costs. See Chapter 8, "Miscellaneous Issues" for additional discussion of this issue.

Multiple-Element Arrangement Includes Software Elements and Non-Software Elements

As discussed earlier in this chapter, separation of a multiple-element arrangement that includes software elements and non-software elements should be based on the guidance in EITF 00-21 (ASC 605-25). If the application of EITF 00-21 (ASC 605-25) results in a conclusion that the elements should not be separated, the general revenue recognition principles apply to the bundled arrangement. In other words, software accounting guidance should not be applied to determine when revenue should be recognized because the bundled group of elements falls outside the scope of SOP 97-2 (ASC 985-605). Additional recognition guidance for elements subject to EITF 00-21 (ASC 605-25) that should not be treated separately for accounting purposes is provided in Chapter 4, "Multiple-Element Arrangements."

Multiple-Element Arrangement Includes Software Elements Requiring Significant Production, Modification, or Customization and Non-Software Elements

The guidance in EITF 00-21 (ASC 605-25) applies to the separation of the deliverables in a multiple-element arrangement that includes software requiring significant production, modification, or customization, other software-related elements and non-software elements. If the application of EITF 00-21 (ASC 605-25) results in a conclusion that the elements should not be separated, it is usually appropriate to apply general revenue recognition principles to the bundled arrangement. It is generally inappropriate to apply contract accounting to the bundled group of elements for purposes of determining when revenue should be recognized because some the elements fall outside the scope of SOP 81-1 (ASC 605-35). Additional recognition guidance for elements subject to EITF 00-21 (ASC 605-25) that should not be treated separately for accounting purposes is provided in Chapter 4, "Multiple-Element Arrangements."

Multiple-Element Arrangement Includes Only Software Elements Requiring Significant Production, Modification, or Customization and Software-Related Elements

The software multiple-element model should be used to separate the deliverables in a multiple-element arrangement that includes only software requiring significant production, modification, or customization and software-related elements. If application of the guidance in SOP 97-2 (ASC 985-605) results in a conclusion that the elements should not be separated, the revenue recognition principles in SOP 81-1 (ASC 605-35) should be applied to the bundled group of elements. The general provisions of SOP 81-1 (ASC 605-35) are discussed in detail in Chapter 9, "Contract Accounting," and specific issues related to the application of these provisions to software arrangements are discussed in the following section entitled "Contract Accounting for Software Arrangements."

Multiple-Element Arrangement Includes Only Software and Software-Related Elements

The accounting for a multiple-element arrangement that includes only software and software-related elements should be based on the software multiple-element model. If application of this model results in a conclusion that the elements should not be separated, the revenue recognition principles in SOP 97-2 (ASC 985-605) should be applied to the bundled group of elements.

When the elements cannot be separated for accounting purposes, revenue recognition for the bundled group of deliverables must be based on the reason for inability to separate the elements. Some of these reasons and the effects they have on recognizing revenue are explained below.

Sufficient VSOE of Fair Value Does Not Exist

When sufficient VSOE of fair value does not exist to allocate revenue among software and software-related elements, revenue is generally recognized upon delivery of the final element for which VSOE of fair value does not exist, presuming that all other revenue recognition criteria have been met. Upon delivery of the final element, either the seller's performance under the arrangement will be complete or all of the remaining items will be those for which VSOE of fair value exists. This will allow the company to apply the residual method.

Thus, if an arrangement consists of only software and PCS and there is insufficient VSOE of fair value to allocate revenue among the elements, revenue from the entire arrangement must be recognized as the PCS is delivered—in most cases, ratably over the PCS period. Similarly, if the only undelivered element in an arrangement is a software-related service that is not essential to the functionality of the software, all revenue from the arrangement would be recognized as the service is performed, or, if no pattern of performance can be discerned, on a straight-line basis over the period during which the service is performed (SOP 97-2, par. 12) (ASC 985-605-25-10).

If the final element to be delivered is a software-related product or specified upgrade for which VSOE of fair value does not exist, all revenue from the arrangement must be deferred until this final product or upgrade is delivered, even if the vendor believes that the product's value is not material to the arrangement.

An Element Is Essential to the Functionality of Another Element

When an undelivered software or software-related element is essential to the functionality of a delivered element, revenue allocated to the delivered element may not be recognized. If the delivered element is a software product and the undelivered element essential to the product's functionality is a software-related service, contract accounting for the product and service must be used (SOP 97-2, par. 64) (ASC 985-605-25-77) (see "Contract Accounting for Software Arrangements" below). When an undelivered software or software-related product is essential to the functionality of a delivered software or software-related product, revenue allocated to both products should be recognized, assuming all other revenue recognition criteria have been met, when the second product is delivered.

CONTRACT ACCOUNTING FOR SOFTWARE ARRANGEMENTS

If an arrangement to deliver software, either alone or together with other software-related products or services, requires significant production, modification, or customization of software, the service element cannot be accounted for separately. In these cases, the arrangement should be accounted for using long-term contract accounting, in conformity with ARB-45 and the relevant guidance in SOP 81-1 (ASC 605-35). Contract accounting is discussed in detail in Chapter 9, "Contract Accounting." However, the application of contract accounting to software arrangements presents unique issues, which are discussed here.

> ☛ **PRACTICE POINTER:** Unlike the software revenue recognition guidance, the percentage-of-completion method of contract accounting permits revenue recognition before complete delivery occurs. Therefore, the use of contract accounting might be attractive to a company that enters into an arrangement to sell a software product that is not yet complete. However, transactions that normally are accounted for as product sales may not be accounted for under contract accounting to avoid the delivery requirements normally associated with product sales (SOP 97-2, par. 74) (ASC 985-605-25-88).

Measuring Progress under the Percentage-of-Completion Method

The diverse approaches used to measure progress toward completion under the percentage-of-completion method may be grouped into two broad categories: (1) input measures, which are measurements made in terms of efforts devoted to the contract, such as costs, labor hours or other inputs, and (2) output measures, which are indices of results achieved, such as units produced or contract milestones.

Output Measures

Output measures are not easily applied to software arrangements because it is difficult to establish relevant measures. However, if the transaction requires delivery of multiple modules, output may be measured based on delivery of individual modules. If reliable output measures cannot be established, input measures should be used (SOP 97-2, par. 85) (ASC 985-605-25-96).

Input Measures

Although costs incurred may be a good measure of progress on a software arrangement, labor hours often are the best measure of progress for projects involving labor-intensive software customization. When input measures based on costs incurred are used, the contract accounting guidance notes that only costs that relate to contract performance should be included in the measurement. For example, software customization projects begin with core software. As the software was not produced for the purpose of the particular contract, no value should be assigned to it in measuring progress-toward completion (SOP 97-2, pars. 81–84) (ASC 985-605-25-97 through 25-100).

RIGHTS TO EXCHANGE OR RETURN SOFTWARE

As part of an arrangement, a software vendor may provide the customer with a right to return or exchange software. The accounting for return rights in a software arrangement is generally similar to that used for return rights on any other product, and that accounting is addressed in FAS-48 (ASC 605-15-25). The accounting for exchange rights, however, depends on whether the right is limited to an exchange for a product of similar price, features, and functionality. An exchange right that meets these criteria does not receive accounting recognition because it is not considered substantive. However, any other exchange right should be accounted for as a return right.

Distinguishing Among Return, Exchange, and Additional Product Rights

In certain situations, a return or exchange right allows the customer to obtain a new software product and retain the right to use the original product. This is not an exchange or return right at all, but is instead a right to an additional software product. The additional product should be treated as an additional element of the arrangement (SOP 97-2, par. 50) (ASC 985-605-25-60).

When the customer is not contractually entitled to continue using the original software product, the right is either an exchange or a return right. Although it is sometimes difficult to determine which of the two it is, the following situations are clear:

1. If the customer with the return or exchange right is a reseller rather than an end-user, the right is accounted for as a right of return.

2. If the right allows an end-user to return the software and get anything in exchange other than another software product (e.g., services or PCS), the right is accounted for as a right of return.

Rights that allow an end-user to exchange the software for another software package are accounted for as exchange rights if the software the user is entitled to receive has similar price, functionality and features as the software the user will give up. Whether this is the case is a matter of judgment. However, if the product that is available to the user in the exchange has not yet been developed and the company expects to incur significant costs in development of that product, it should not be considered to have similar price, features, and functionality to the product delivered to the customer (SOP 97-2, par. 51) (ASC 985-605-25-61).

The most common situation that qualifies for accounting as an exchange is a platform-transfer right, which is the right to exchange a software product for a product marketed under the same name that operates on a different operating system or on different hardware, but otherwise has the same features and functionality (SOP 97-2, par. 52) (ASC 985-605-25-62; 985-605-25-63).

Accounting for Exchange Rights

The existence of a right that allows an end-user to exchange software for software of similar price, features and functionality does not affect the accounting for a software arrangement. As a result, revenue may be recognized when each of the revenue recognition criteria is met with respect to the original software product deliverable.

Accounting for Return Rights

Like return rights in non-software arrangements, a right to return software should be evaluated to determine its substance. If the return right is limited to situations where the software does not operate according to published specifications, it should be treated as a warranty. Warranties on software products are treated the same as warranties on any other products (see Chapter 5, "Product Deliverables").

A right to return software that does not meet customer- or arrangement-specific operating specifications should be treated as a customer acceptance clause. A return right that is of sufficient length to be something other than a period that allows the customer to determine whether software is functional for the customer's purpose should be treated as a cancellation clause (see "Fixed or Determinable Fees and Collectibility" in this chapter for discussion of the accounting for each of these clauses).

Other return rights on software should generally be accounted for in the same manner as similar rights in product arrangements. Information on how to account for these rights can be found in Chapter 5, "Product Deliverables." However, to recognize revenue when a right of return exists, the vendor must be able to reasonably estimate the amount of returns. Due to the rapid introduction and replacement of software products, historical experience may not be relevant in estimating returns on current sales. In this situation, it is unlikely that returns can be estimated and revenue could not be recognized upon delivery.

EXAMPLE: STOCK BALANCING RIGHTS

Citrix Systems, Inc. Form 10-K—Fiscal Year Ended December 31, 2007

In the normal course of business, the Company is not obligated to accept product returns from its distributors under any other conditions, unless the product item is defective in manufacture, but it does provide most of its distributors with stock balancing and price protection rights. Stock balancing rights permit distributors to return products to the Company up to the forty-fifth day of the fiscal quarter, subject to ordering an equal dollar amount of its other products prior to the last day of the same fiscal quarter. Price protection rights require that the Company grants retroactive price adjustments for inventories of its products held by distributors or resellers if it lowers its prices for such products. Product items returned to the Company under the stock balancing program must be in new, unused and unopened condition. The Company establishes provisions for estimated returns for stock balancing and price protection rights, as well as other sales allowances, concurrently with the recognition of revenue. The provisions are established based upon consideration of a variety of factors, including, among other things, recent and historical return rates for both, specific products and distributors, estimated distributor inventory levels by product, the impact of any new product releases and projected economic conditions. Actual product returns for stock balancing and price protection provisions incurred are, however, dependent upon future events, including the amount of stock balancing activity by distributors and the level of distributor inventories at the time of any price adjustments. The Company continually monitors the factors that influence the pricing of its products and distributor inventory levels and makes adjustments to these provisions when it believes actual returns and other allowances could differ from established reserves. The Company's ability to recognize revenue upon shipment to distributors is predicated on its ability to reliably estimate future stock balancing returns. If actual experience or changes in market condition impairs the Company's ability to estimate returns, it would be required to defer the recognition of revenue until the delivery of the product to the end-user. Allowances for estimated product returns amounted to approximately $1.7 million at both December 31, 2007 and December 31, 2006. The Company has not reduced and has no current plans to reduce its prices for inventory currently held by distributors. Accordingly, there were no reserves required for price protection at December 31, 2007 and 2006. The Company also records estimated reductions to revenue for customer programs and incentive offerings including volume-based incentives. If market conditions were to decline, the Company could take actions to increase its customer incentive offerings, which could result in an incremental reduction to revenue at the time the incentive is offered.

SALES INCENTIVES

General

Companies that sell packaged software to consumers, either directly or through retailers, often use sales incentives such as rebates. The accounting for such incentives has been addressed in EITF 01-9 (ASC 605-50). The EITF's conclusions in this area are discussed in detail in Chapters 8, "Miscellaneous Issues," and Chapter 11, "Presentation." The application of these conclusions to software arrangements does not pose any unique issues.

Discounts on Future Purchases

In connection with the licensing of an existing product, a vendor might offer a discount (coupon) on future purchases of additional licenses of the same product or on other products or services. If this discount is insignificant, it does not require accounting recognition. However, if the discount is more than insignificant, it creates a presumption that there is an additional element in the arrangement. The authoritative guidance exists on a number of issues regarding the accounting for discounts on future purchases.

Significant Incremental Discounts

A discount with respect to future purchases that is provided in a software arrangement indicates that another element is present in a software arrangement if the discount meets all of the following criteria (TPA 5100.50) (ASC 985-605-15-3; 985-605-55-87):

1. *It is incremental to the range of discounts reflected in the pricing of the other elements of the arrangement.* If the customer was able to negotiate a 30% discount on the price of the elements in the current arrangement, offering a 30% discount on additional elements does not appear to grant the customer anything that would not otherwise have been available.

2. *It is incremental to the range of discounts typically given in comparable transactions.* A discount that is not incremental to discounts typically given in comparable transactions (e.g., volume purchase discounts comparable to those generally provided in comparable transactions) does not confer any additional value to the customer other than what was already given.

3. *It is significant.* Judgment is required when assessing whether an incremental discount is significant.

4. *It is not limited to additional copies of products licensed by and delivered to the customer under the same arrangement.* As discussed above under "Delivery," additional copies of delivered software are not considered undelivered element. Rather, this situation should be accounted for as an arrangement in which the fee depends upon the number of copies ordered and duplicated. The amount of the fee contingent upon future duplication should not be recognized until the contingency is resolved. However, there need not be any deferral of the initial licensing fee to recognize the discount on the additional copies.

Accounting for Significant Incremental Discounts

The overriding concept in a software arrangement that includes the right to a significant incremental discount on a future purchase of products or services is that a proportionate amount of this discount should be applied to each element in the arrangement based on the relative fair value. Applying this guidance when all of the elements are known and have VSOE of fair value is relatively straightforward.

However, if either the future elements to which the discount applies are not specified in the arrangement (e.g., a customer is allowed a discount on any future purchases) or VSOE of fair value of the future elements does not exist, the concept in the preceding paragraph becomes difficult to apply. In these situations, if the maximum amount of the incremental discount on the future purchases is quantifiable, this amount should be allocated to the elements in the current arrangement and the future purchases, assuming that the customer will purchase the minimum amount necessary to utilize the maximum discount.

If the maximum amount of the significant incremental discount on future purchases is not quantifiable (e.g., the discount can be used on all purchases within a specified period of time and there is no limit on the amount of purchases), revenue allocated to each element in the arrangement should be reduced by the rate of the discount.

If the residual value method is used to allocate arrangement consideration in a multiple-element arrangement that includes a discount on future purchases, the discount offered in the initial arrangement should be computed by comparing the published list price of the delivered elements to the residual value attributable to these elements. If the discount on future purchases is significant and incremental to the discount computed for the initial arrangement, the software vendor should apply the significant and incremental discount on future purchases to the initial arrangement (TPA 5100.74) (ASC 985-605-55-88 through 55-91).

The portion of the fee that is deferred as a result of the significant incremental discount on future purchases should be recognized as revenue proportionately as the future purchases are delivered (assuming all other revenue recognition criteria are met) so that a consistent discount rate is applied to all purchases under the arrangement. If the future purchases are not limited by quantity of product(s) or service(s), the portion of the fee that is deferred as a result of the presence of a significant incremental discount should be recognized as revenue as a subscription (TPA 5100.51) (ASC 985-605-55-85).

ILLUSTRATION: SIGNIFICANT INCREMENTAL DISCOUNTS

(Adapted from TPAs 5100.51 and 5100.74) (ASC 985-605-55-185 through 55-203)

(For purposes of these examples, VSOE of fair value equals list price and all of the software products do not involve significant production, modification, or customization.)

EXAMPLE 1

Facts: A software vendor sells Product A for its list price of $40 along with a right to a discount of $30 on another of its software products, Product B, which has a list price of $60. The $30 discount on Product B is a significant incremental discount that would not normally be given in comparable transactions.

Accounting: The vendor should allocate the $30 discount across Product A and Product B. The overall discount is 30%, calculated as the ratio of the discount ($30) to the fair values of the products ($40 + $60 = $100). Therefore, upon the delivery of Product A, the vendor would recognize $28 (a 30% discount off of $40) of revenue and defer $12. If the customer uses the discount and purchases Product B, the vendor would recognize $42 in revenue upon delivery of Product B ($30 in cash received plus the $12 previously deferred). If the discount expires unused, the $12 in deferred revenue would be recognized at that time.

EXAMPLE 2

Facts: A software vendor sells Product A for its list price of $40 along with a right to a discount of $20 on any one of its other software products, Products B through Z. The list prices of Products B through Z range from $40 to $100. The $20 discount is a significant incremental discount that would not normally be given in comparable transactions.

Accounting: The vendor should allocate the $20 discount across Product A and the assumed purchase of whichever of Product B through Z has the lowest fair value ($40). The overall discount is 25% ($20/$80). Therefore, upon delivery of Product A, the vendor would recognize $30 in revenue, and defer $10. If the customer uses the discount and purchases the additional product with a fair value of $40, the vendor would recognize $30 in revenue upon its delivery (the $10 previously deferred and the additional cash license fee due of $20). If the discount expires unused, the $10 in deferred revenue would be recognized at that time.

EXAMPLE 3

Facts: A software vendor sells Product A for its list price of $40 along with a right to a discount of 50% off list price on any future purchases of its other software products, Products B through Z, with a maximum cumulative discount of $80. The 50% discount is a significant incremental discount that would not normally be given in comparable transactions.

Accounting: The vendor should assume that the customer will purchase additional products worth $160 in order to use the maximum $80 discount. Therefore, the vendor would allocate the $80 discount across Product A and the assumed additional products to be purchased. The overall discount is 40% ($80/$200). Therefore, upon the delivery of Product A, the vendor would recognize $24 of revenue and defer $16. If the customer uses the discount by purchasing additional products with fair values totaling $160, the vendor would recognize $96 in revenue upon delivery of those products ($80 in cash received plus the $16 previously deferred). If the discount expires unused, the $16 in deferred revenue would be recognized at that time.

EXAMPLE 4

Facts: A software vendor sells Product A for $60, which represents a 40% discount off its list price (VSOE) of $100. In the same transaction, it also provides the right to a discount of 50% off of the list price (VSOE) on any future purchases of units of Product B for the next six months with a maximum discount of $200. The discount of 50% on future purchases of units of Product B is a discount not normally given in comparable transactions.

Accounting: Because the discount offered on future purchases of Product B is not normally given in comparable transactions and is both significant and incremental in relation to the 40% discount, it must be accounted for as part of the original sale consistent with Example 3 above. The vendor should assume that the customer will make $400 in purchases of Product B in order to use the maximum discount of $200. Therefore, the vendor would allocate the $240 discount ($40 on Product A and $200 maximum on future purchases) across Product A and the assumed additional products to be purchased. The overall discount is 48% ($240/$500). Therefore, upon the delivery of Product A, the vendor would recognize $52 (a 48% discount off of Product A's fair value of $100) of revenue and defer $8. If the customer uses the discount by purchasing additional products with fair value totaling $400, the vendor would recognize $208 in revenue upon delivery of those products ($200 in cash received plus the $8 previously deferred). If the discount expires unused, the $8 in deferred revenue would be recognized at that time.

EXAMPLE 5

Facts: A software vendor sells Product A for its list price of $40 along with a right to a discount of 50% off list price on any future purchases of its other software products with no maximum cumulative discount. The 50% discount is a significant incremental discount that would not normally be given in comparable transactions.

Accounting: The vendor should apply the 50% discount to Product A and all future products purchased using the discount. Therefore, upon the delivery of Product A, the vendor would recognize $20 of revenue and defer $20. If the customer purchases additional products using the discount, the vendor would recognize revenue equal to the cash received upon the delivery of those products. The previously deferred $20 should be accounted for as a subscription and recognized pro rata over the discount period or, if no period is specified in the arrangement, over the estimated period during which additional purchases will be made.

EXAMPLE 6

Facts: A software vendor sells Product A, which has a list price of $100, for $30 along with the right to a discount of 70% off list price (VSOE) on any future purchases of its other software products for the next six months with no maximum cumulative discount.

Accounting: As the discount offered on future purchases over the next six months is equal to the discount offered on the current purchase (70%), there is no accounting necessary in the original sale for the discount offered on future purchases.

EXAMPLE 7

Facts: A software vendor sells Product A, which has a list price of $100, for $80. One year of PCS is included in the arrangement, and the customer may renew PCS following the initial year at a rate of $15. As part of the transaction, the customer receives the right to a 55% discount off of published list prices for the purchase of all new products released by the software vendor for two years, with no maximum cumulative discount. The software vendor does not have VSOE of fair value for Product A, as Product A is never sold separately.

Accounting: The residual value allocated to Product A is $65 ($80 arrangement fee less $15 PCS renewal rate). The discount on Product A is 35% ($35 discount on Product A ($100 list price less $65 allocated residual value) divided by $100 list price). The incremental discount offered on future purchases is 20% (55% discount on future purchases less 35% computed discount on Product A). If the software vendor concludes that this 20% incremental discount is significant, it will recognize revenue of $45 upon delivery of Product A, provided all other revenue recognition criteria have been met. The $45 ultimately allocated to Product A represents the $80 arrangement fee reduced by (a) $20 of additional discount (20% significant incremental discount off of $100 list price), and (b) $15 PCS renewal rate. The $20 additional discount is deferred and recognized pro rata over the two-year discount period. If the customer purchases additional products using the 55% discount, the software vendor should recognize revenue equal to the net fee attributable to those products when all of the revenue recognition criteria have been met.

NONMONETARY EXCHANGES INVOLVING SOFTWARE

Nonmonetary exchanges involving software are generally treated the same way as those involving other products or services. The guidance in APB-29 (ASC 845-10) is applied to determine whether the transaction should be recorded at historical cost or at fair value. If the transaction should be reported at fair value, then the software revenue recognition guidance is applied to determine whether the measured fair value can be recognized as revenue, or must be deferred until remaining obligations are completed (TPAs 5100.46 and 5100.47) (ASC 985-845).

> **OBSERVATION:** In an exchange in which either or both parties to the agreement do not plan to use or sell the products (or rights) they receive in the exchange, fair value is considered zero, because the transaction does not appear to have economic substance. Therefore, no revenue can ever be recognized in such a transaction.

Exchanging Software for Technology or Product to Be Sold

APB-29 (ASC 985-845-25-3) states that an exchange of inventory for inventory to be sold in the same line of business does not culminate an earnings process. Therefore, if a software vendor exchanges one or more software licenses (which are considered inventory for the purposes of applying this guidance) and receives in return the rights to technology or products that are to be sold, licensed, or leased in the same line of business as the software licenses delivered in the exchange, then the software vendor should record the exchange at historical cost, which is likely to be zero.

However, if the technology or products received by the software vendor in the exchange are to be sold, licensed, or leased in a different line of business from the software licenses delivered, the exchange should be recorded at fair value, as long as VSOE of fair value exists. If VSOE of fair value does not exist, the transaction should be recorded at historical cost, because APB-29 (ASC 985-845-25-5) indicates that historical cost must be used if fair value cannot be reasonably determined and SOP 97-2 (ASC 985-605) limits the determination of fair value of software to VSOE.

> **OBSERVATION:** APB-29 (ASC 845-10) requires that the fair value of a nonmonetary transaction be determinable within reasonable limits. VSOE of fair value is the only way to satisfy this requirement for software and software-related elements included in a nonmonetary transaction.

Exchanging Software for Technology to Be Used Internally

When a software vendor licenses its externally sold software to a customer in exchange for a license to the customer's technology, which the software vendor intends to utilize internally (i.e., the software received will not be sold but instead used in the vendor's operations), the transaction should be recorded at fair value (provided that VSOE exists) because the exchange is one of inventory for a long-term asset, which should not be accounted for at historical cost under APB-29 (ASC 985-845-25-7).

DEFERRED COSTS

Revenue from a software sale may have to be deferred for a number of reasons. In many instances, the issue of whether related direct costs should be deferred is unimportant, because these costs are minimal. However, in certain arrangements, especially those involving payment of sales commissions, the direct and incremental costs of a software sale are significant. Because the deferral of costs is not addressed in SOP 97-2 (ASC 985-605) or any other software-specific guidance, the literature that applies to non-software transactions on this issue should be consulted. See Chapter 8, "Miscellaneous Issues," for further information.

ADDED CONSIDERATIONS IN RESELLER TRANSACTIONS

Consignment Arrangements

When a software vendor has a relationship with a reseller, terms of the arrangement or the customary business practices between the parties may indicate that a contractual sale actually functions more like a consignment, from which revenue should not be recognized. The factors that might result in a software transaction with a reseller being treated as a consignment are similar to those discussed in the "Consignment Sales" section of Chapter 5, "Product Deliverables." In these cases, revenue would not be recognized until the reseller sells the product to an end-user. This is commonly referred to as recognizing revenue upon "sell-through."

EXAMPLE: SELL-THROUGH REVENUE

Isilon Systems, Inc. Form 10-K—Fiscal Year Ended December 31, 2008

On sales to channel partners, we evaluate whether fees are considered fixed or determinable by considering a number of factors, including our ability to estimate returns, the geography in which a sales transaction originates, payment terms, and our relationship and past history with the particular channel partner. If fees are not considered fixed or determinable at the time of sale to a channel partner, revenue recognition is deferred until there is persuasive evidence indicating product has sold through to an end-user. Persuasive evidence of sell-through may include reports from channel partners documenting sell-through activity, copies of end-user purchase orders, data indicating an order has shipped to an end-user, cash payments or letters of credit guaranteeing cash payments or other similar information.

PCS Granted by Resellers

Some transactions give the reseller a right to upgrades or enhancements introduced between the time the reseller arrangement is entered into and the time the reseller sub-licenses the product to end-users. This right is often included even when upgrades and technical support will not be provided to the end-user. Such an arrangement, in which the reseller has the right to provide unspecified upgrades to its customers, is an implied PCS arrangement between the vendor and the reseller. Therefore, the arrangement fee must be allocated, based on VSOE of fair value, between the software product and the implied PCS arrangement. If VSOE of fair value for PCS does not exist, the entire arrangement fee should be recognized over the expected PCS term, which would generally be the period over which the reseller has the right to sell licenses to its customers that include unspecified upgrades developed before the sublicense is entered into (SOP 97-2, par. 62) (ASC 985-605-25-75).

CHAPTER 11
PRESENTATION

CONTENTS

BACKGROUND

Accounting standard setters have provided little, if any, guidance on income statement and balance sheet classification. However, the increasing emphasis on more sophisticated financial analysis has made it important for financial statement preparers to correctly classify income and cost items within the income statement, even when this does not change the reported gross margin, operating income or net income. In addition, the "deferred revenue" caption on the balance sheet has also received more attention because it is a liability usually settled by performance rather than a transfer of cash, which results in an increase in equity rather than a decrease in assets.

SURVEY OF APPLICABLE LITERATURE

Conceptual guidance on income statement classification is provided in CON-6, which distinguishes between (1) revenue and gains, and (2) expenses and losses. In addition, the SEC has issued guidelines for various income statement captions, including revenues, in REG S-X, Rule 5-03 (ASC 225, *Income Statement*; 225-10-S99-2). However, until late 1999, this constituted the only guidance that addressed financial statement classification.

Since then, the EITF has addressed income statement classification in a number of consensuses that are broadly applicable to a wide range of revenue transactions and industries. These issues address questions such as: (1) classification of payments from a company to its customers, (2) classification of taxes collected from customers and remitted to government authorities, (3) whether a company should recognize revenue on a gross or net basis, and (4) whether coupons, rebates, and other discounts should be reported as expenses or as reductions of revenue.

LISTING OF APPLICABLE LITERATURE

Publication	ASC	ASC Topic	Subject
CON-5	N/A	N/A	Recognition and Measurement in Financial Statements of Business Enterprises
CON-6	N/A	N/A	Elements of Financial Statements
FAS-13	840	Leases	Accounting for Leases
FAS-45	952-605	Franchisors	Franchise Fees
REG S-X, Rule 5-03	225-10-S99-2	Income Statement	Financial Statement Requirements, Commercial and Industrial Companies, Income Statements
AAG-CAS	924-605-45	Entertainment— Casinos	Promotional Allowances
EITF 88-18	470-10-25	Debt	Sales of Future Revenues
EITF 99-19	605-45	Revenue Recognition	Reporting Revenue Gross as a Principal versus Net as an Agent
EITF 00-10	605-45	Revenue Recognition	Shipping and Handling Fees and Costs
EITF 01-9	605-50	Revenue Recognition	Consideration Given by a Vendor to a Customer (Including a Reseller of the Vendor's Products)
EITF 01-14	605-45	Revenue Recognition	Income Statement Characterization of Reimbursements Received for "Out-of-Pocket" Expenses Incurred

EITF 02-3	932-330-35	Extractive Activities—Oil and Gas	Accounting for Derivative Contracts Held for Trading Purposes
EITF 02-16	605-50	Revenue Recognition	Accounting by a Customer (Including a Reseller) for Certain Consideration Received from a Vendor
EITF 03-10	605-50	Revenue Recognition	Accounting by Resellers for Sales Incentives Offered to Consumers by Manufacturers
EITF 03-11	815-10-55-62	Derivatives and Hedging	Reporting Realized Gains and Losses on Derivative Instruments That Are Not "Held for Trading Purposes"
EITF 06-1	605-50	Revenue Recognition	Accounting for Consideration Given by a Service Provider to a Manufacturer or Reseller of Equipment Necessary for an End-Customer to Receive Service from the Service Provider
EITF 06-3	605-45	Revenue Recognition	How Taxes Collected from Customers and Remitted to Governmental Authorities Should Be Presented in the Income Statement (That Is, Gross versus Net Presentation)
SAB Topic 8A	605-15-S99-2	Revenue Recognition	Retail Companies—Sales of Leased or Licensed Departments
SAB Topic 13	605-10-S99	Revenue Recognition	Revenue Recognition
TPA 5100.58	985-605-55-32	Software	Effect of Prepayments on Software Revenue Recognition—Transfer of Receivable without Recourse

REVENUES VERSUS GAINS

One of the key issues in income statement classification is whether a transaction that contributes to income should be reported as revenue or as a gain. CON-6 addresses the difference between revenues and gains by noting that "Revenues . . . result from an entity's ongoing major or central operations and activities . . ." while "Gains . . . result from entities' peripheral or incidental transactions" (CON-6, par. 87). CON-5 depicts revenues as a result of an "earnings process" involving activities specifically targeted toward bringing in that revenue, while "Gains commonly result from transactions and other events that involve no 'earnings process,' and for recognizing gains, being earned is generally less significant than being realized or realizable" (CON-5, par. 83b).

The application of this guidance depends on the unique facts and circumstances of a company's operations. In practice, it is generally easy to identify an entity's "ongoing major or central operations and activities." These activities usually include a company's main productive efforts and most of its transactions with other companies. For example, a manufacturer hires employees, buys raw materials, rents or purchases land, buildings, and equipment, and sells its output to customers. Its manufacturing operations convert purchased materials using production processes and facilities into a product that is sold at a price higher than the combined cost of the inputs. Other companies incur expenses and generate revenues differently—for example, retailers and distributors buy, transport, market, and sell goods, insurers charge customers to assume risks, and banks pay interest to depositors to have funds available to provide loans that earn greater interest (CON-6, par. 88).

Some companies engage in many different ongoing major or central activities. Any activity that the company performs repeatedly, expects to continue performing, and on which it focuses its resources and efforts may be an ongoing major line of business and, hence, an activity that generates revenues and expenses, rather than gains and losses.

Transactions that are not part of a company's ongoing major or central operations typically involve activities that are ancillary, but are still necessary. For example, a company that owns its office building may rent excess space to another entity. This rental income should not be reported as revenue. Similarly, a manufacturing or service company will typically invest cash rather than have it sit idle. The interest income earned should not be reported as revenue, even if it was earned on funds obtained from customer prepayments. Other transactions that produce gains (or losses) can be identified because they result from events over which the company has little control, such as currency fluctuations, strikes, natural disasters and related insurance recoveries, as well as changes in the fair value of assets and liabilities.

OBSERVATION: Many companies enter into arrangements that can result in the receipt of payments even though nothing of value is ever provided to the customer. This occurs when a customer returns a product or cancels a service but is required to pay a termination fee. In these and similar situations, the payments should be reported as a gain, rather than as revenue, because no earnings process occurred.

SEC REGISTRANT ALERT: In a December 2002 speech, the SEC staff highlighted the fact that revenues exclude equity in net income of investees, net gains or losses on sales of fixed assets or investments, and "other income."

EXAMPLE: PRESENTATION OF REVENUES VERSUS GAINS

IBM Corporation, Inc. Form 10-K—Fiscal Year Ended December 31, 2007

OBSERVATION: IBM's Consolidated Statement of Earnings shows the following sources of revenues: Services, Sales, and Financing. The Company, however, reports intellectual property and custom development income (IP&CDI), as well as asset sales and other nonrecurring gains (components of Other (income) and expense) under the caption Expense and Other Income. These sources of income are not classified as revenues by IBM because they are not considered part of the "ongoing major or central operations or activities" of the Company.

CONSOLIDATED STATEMENT OF EARNINGS

($ in millions except per share amounts)

FOR THE YEAR ENDED DECEMBER 31:	2007	2006	2005
Revenue:			
Services	**$54,057**	$48,328	$47,509
Sales	**42,202**	40,716	41,218
Financing	**2,526**	2,379	2,407
Total Revenue	**98,786**	91,424	91,134
Cost:			
Services	**39,160**	35,065	35,151
Sales	**16,552**	16,882	18,360
Financing	**1,345**	1,182	1,091
Total Cost	**57,057**	53,129	54,602
Gross Profit	**41,729**	38,295	36,532

Expense and Other Income:

Selling, general and administrative	**22,060**	20,259	21,314
Research, development and engineering	**6,153**	6,107	5,842
Intellectual property and custom development income	**(958)**	(900)	(948)
Other (income) and expense	**(626)**	(766)	(2,122)
Interest expense	**611**	278	220
Total Expense and Other Income	**27,240**	24,978	24,306

IBM describes IP&CDI as follows:

Intellectual Property and Custom Development Income

As part of the company's business model and as a result of the company's ongoing investment in research and development, the company licenses and sells the rights to certain of its intellectual property (IP) including internally developed patents, trade secrets and technological know-how. Certain transfers of IP to third parties are licensing/royalty-based and other transfers are transaction-based sales and other transfers. Licensing/royalty-based fees involve transfers in which the company earns the income over time, or the amount of income is not fixed or determinable until the licensee sells future related products (i.e., variable royalty, based upon licensee's revenue). Sales and other transfers typically include transfers of IP whereby the company has fulfilled its obligations and the fee received is fixed or determinable at the transfer date. The company also enters into cross-licensing arrangements of patents, and income from these arrangements is recorded only to the extent cash is received. Furthermore, the company earns income from certain custom development projects for strategic technology partners and specific clients. The company records the income from these projects when the fee is realized or realizable and earned, is not refundable and is not dependent upon the success of the project.

Intellectual Property and Custom Development Income

($ in millions)

FOR THE YEAR ENDED DECEMBER 31:	2007	2006	Yr. to Yr. Change
Sales and other transfers of intellectual property	**$138**	$167	(17.7)%
Licensing/royalty-based fees	**368**	352	4.6
Custom development income	**452**	381	18.8
Total	**$958**	$900	6.4%

The timing and amount of Sales and other transfers of IP may vary significantly from period to period depending upon timing of divestitures, industry consolidation, economic conditions and the timing of new patents and know-how development. There were no significant IP transactions in 2007 and 2006.

Other (Income) and Expense

Other (income) and expense includes interest income (other than from Global Financing external business transactions), gains and losses on certain derivative instruments, gains and losses from securities and other investments, gains and losses from certain real estate transactions, foreign currency transaction gains and losses, gains and losses from the sale of businesses and amounts related to accretion of asset retirement obligations.

GROSS VERSUS NET PRESENTATION OF REVENUE

General

EITF 99-19 (ASC 605-45) addresses a question that frequently arises for product resellers—should the entire amount received from an end-user be recorded as revenue and the amount paid to the supplier as cost of sales or just the net amount as revenue? The correct response, from a financial reporting standpoint, depends on (1) which party in the transaction (i.e., supplier or company) holds all or substantially all of risks and benefits related to the product or service, and (2) an evaluation of the contractual arrangements. Gross reporting treats the transaction as if the company purchased a product or service (thereby acquiring all or substantially all of the related risks and benefits) from the supplier and then sold that product or service to the end-user. Under net reporting, the transaction is recorded as if the end-user made a purchase from the supplier, with the company acting as a sales agent.

This question is common for companies that sell goods or services over the internet. Many Internet resellers do not stock inventory and arrange for third-party suppliers to drop-ship merchandise on their behalf. These companies may also sell services that will be provided by a third party. The difficulty in making the determination of gross versus net reporting is that many companies do not assume (a) all the risks and rewards of ownership of the products they sell before entering into the sales transaction or (b) all of the responsibility to provide the services they sell. Through contracts or by operation of the business, some or all of these risks and responsibilities remain with the supplier of the goods or services.

EITF 99-19 (ASC 605-45) applies to all industries and transaction types unless guidance is specifically provided in other authoritative literature.[1] The EITF's consensus on this question does not draw bright lines or provide objective answers. Rather, the EITF identified a number of indicators that a company should evaluate to determine whether it has taken on enough risks to be considered the principal in the transaction.

> **PRACTICE ALERT:** The EITF has addressed two gross versus net issues involving derivative instruments. EITF 02-3 (ASC 932-330-35) addresses gains and losses (realized and unrealized) on derivative instruments "held for trading purposes." The consensus in EITF 02-3 (ASC 932-330-35) requires these gains and losses to be shown net in the income statement, regardless of whether the derivative instrument is physically settled. EITF 03-11 (ASC 815-10-55-62) addresses realized gains and losses on physically settled derivative contracts *not* "held for trading purposes." The determination of whether realized gains and losses on such instruments should be reported on a gross or net basis is a matter of judgment that depends on the relevant facts and circumstances. In analyzing these facts and circumstances, the guidance in EITF 99-19 (ASC 605-45) and APB-29 (ASC 845-10), should be considered. If these issues are applicable to an entity's financial reporting, the final Abstracts should be consulted for additional information.

Indicators of Gross Revenue Reporting

1. *The company is the primary obligor in the arrangement.* The primary obligor is the party responsible for delivering the product or providing service to the customer. In substance, the primary obligor is the party to whom the customer looks for fulfillment and to ensure satisfaction. If this party is the company and not the supplier, the company is at risk for the full amount of the contract, not just a commission. Representations made by a company during marketing and the terms of the sales contract generally will provide evidence as to whether the company or the supplier is the primary obligor (EITF 99-19, par. 7) (ASC 605-45-45-4).

---

[1] For example, SOP 81-1 (ASC 952-605), FAS-45 (ASC 952-605), EITF 02-3 (ASC 932-330-35) and 03-11 (ASC 815-10-55-62) and the AICPA Audit and Accounting Guides for Casinos (ASC 924-605-45), include guidance on presenting revenue on a gross versus a net basis.

2. *The company has general inventory risk.* This risk exists when a company buys inventory to resell for a profit. Front-end inventory risk exists if a reseller maintains inventory of a product after taking title and assuming all risks and rewards of ownership *before* the product is ordered by a customer. Back-end inventory risk exists if the customer has a right of return and the reseller will take title to and assume the risks and rewards of ownership if the product is returned. In a service transaction, a similar risk exists if the reseller commits to purchase the service from its supplier before it has found customers. General inventory risk not mitigated by terms of the arrangement between the reseller and supplier is a strong indicator that the reseller should record revenue on a gross basis. However, factors that mitigate general inventory risk must be considered as well. For example, a company's risk may be reduced significantly or essentially eliminated if it has the right to return unsold products or receives inventory price protection from the supplier. Similarly, back-end inventory risk is mitigated if the company has the right to return any products returned by the customer to the supplier (EITF 99-19, par. 8) (ASC 605-45-45-5; 605-45-7).

3. *The company has the ability to determine the price at which it sells the product or service.* When a company has reasonable latitude to establish prices for the products and services, it is an indication that the company is acting as a principal, rather than as another company's agent (EITF 99-19, par. 9) (ASC 605-45-45-8).

4. *The company changes the product or performs part of the service.* If a company physically changes the product (beyond its packaging) or performs part of the service ordered by a customer, the company does not appear to act solely as an agent. In addition, this fact may indicate that the company is partially or fully responsible for fulfillment, potentially making it the primary obligor in the arrangement (EITF 99-19, par. 10) (ASC 605-45-45-9).

> ☛ **PRACTICE POINTER:** Transporting or repackaging the goods or providing marketing services does not demonstrate that this indicator of gross reporting exists, even when these actions add value to the product or service.

5. *The company has discretion in supplier selection.* When a company has multiple suppliers for a product or service ordered by a customer and discretion to select the supplier that will provide the product or service ordered by a customer, it is an indication that the company is acting as a principal (EITF 99-19, par. 11) (ASC 605-45-45-10).

6. *The company is involved in the determination of product or service specifications.* If a company must determine the nature, type, characteristics, or specifications of the product or service ordered by the customer, that fact might indicate that the company is primarily responsible for fulfillment (EITF 99-19, par. 12) (ASC 605-45-45-11).

7. *The company has physical loss inventory risk (after customer order or during shipping).* Physical loss inventory risk exists if the reseller holds title to the product at some point between the time an order is placed and the product is delivered. Because the risk of physical loss during this period is low, it is a weak indicator of gross reporting (EITF 99-19, par. 13) (ASC 605-45-45-12).

8. *The company has credit risk.* If a company assumes credit risk for the amount billed to the customer, that fact may provide evidence that the company has risks and rewards as a principal in the transaction. Credit risk exists if a company is responsible for collecting the sales price from a customer but must pay the supplier regardless of whether the sales price is fully collected. A requirement that a company return or refund only the net amount it earned in the transaction, if the transaction is cancelled or reversed, is not evidence of credit risk for the gross transaction. In some cases, credit risk may be mitigated such that this indicator is virtually meaningless—for example, if a customer pays by credit card and a company obtains authorization for the charge in advance of product shipment or service performance, credit risk has been substantially mitigated (EITF 99-19, par. 14) (ASC 605-45-45-13; 605-45-45-14).

Indicators of Net Revenue Reporting

1. *The supplier is the primary obligor in the arrangement.* If the supplier is responsible for fulfillment and customer satisfaction, the company may not have risks and rewards as a principal in the transaction and should therefore recognize only its net fee as revenue. Representations made by a company during marketing and the terms of the sales contract will generally provide evidence as to a customer's understanding of whether the company or the supplier is responsible for fulfillment (EITF 99-19, par. 15) (ASC 605-45-45-16).

2. *The amount the company earns per transaction is fixed (in dollars or as a percentage of the arrangement fee).* When a company earns a fixed dollar amount per customer transaction or a stated percentage of

the amount billed to a customer, this may indicate that the company is acting as an agent of the supplier (EITF 99-19, par. 16) (ASC 605-45-45-17).

3. *The supplier has credit risk.* If credit risk exists (i.e., the sales price has not been fully collected prior to delivering the product or service) but the supplier assumes that risk, the company may be acting as an agent of the supplier (EITF 99-19, par. 17) (ASC 605-45-45-18).

Evaluating the Indicators

Strong and Weak Indicators

The identity of the primary obligor in the transaction and front-end general inventory risk are strong indicators of the nature of the transaction. They help identify the bearer of key risks, such as the risk of market price declines, customer satisfaction, obsolescence, and excess inventory.

By contrast, physical loss inventory risk and credit risk are considered weak indicators. Because they relate to lower risks that are easily mitigated through the use of insurance or well-designed business practices, these indicators are rarely useful.

The importance of certain indicators depends on the specific facts and circumstances in a transaction. For example, back-end general inventory risk may be important when products with high values have low turnover and are often returned or rejected. This risk, however, may be a less significant indicator for low value products with high turnover, because one product can be used to fill a subsequent order.

> ☞ **PRACTICE POINTER:** By providing indicators of gross versus net reporting, EITF 99-19 (ASC 605-45) attempts to answer two basic questions.
>
> First, who does the end-customer believe it is buying from? If the end-customer believes it is buying from the company, the company is most likely the primary obligor and should report revenue on a gross basis. If the end-customer believes it is buying from the supplier, it is likely that net reporting for the company is appropriate.
>
> Second, is the company's customer the end-customer or the supplier? If the company's contracts refer to it as an agent or to the product supplier as the customer, it is likely that reporting on a net basis is appropriate.
>
> Answering these questions, however, does not eliminate the requirement that a company review the indicators in EITF 99-19 (ASC 605-45).

Transaction-by-Transaction Analysis

A company may operate as a principal (gross reporting) in some transactions and as an agent (net reporting) in others. For example, an office products company may maintain inventories of products of which large quantities are sold, such as pens, paper, and printer cartridges, but have other products, such as furniture and computers, drop-shipped from the supplier. In this instance, general inventory risk may only exist for the high-volume products. This distinction could result in different conclusions as to how to report these transactions.

EXAMPLE: GROSS VERSUS NET CONCLUSION DIFFERS FOR DIFFERENT TRANSACTIONS

Express Scripts, Inc. Form 10-K—Fiscal Year Ended December 31, 2007

Revenues related to the sale of prescription drugs by retail pharmacies in our networks consist of the amount the client has contracted to pay us (which excludes the co-payment) for the dispensing of such drugs together with any associated administrative fees. These revenues are recognized when the claim is processed. When we independently have a contractual obligation to pay our network pharmacy providers for benefits provided to our clients' members, we act as a principal in the arrangement and we include the total payments we have contracted to receive from these clients as revenue, and payments we make to the network pharmacy providers as cost of revenue in compliance with Emerging Issues Task Force ("EITF") Issue No. 99-19, *Reporting Gross Revenue as a Principal vs. Net as an Agent.* When a prescription is presented by a member to a retail pharmacy within our network, we are solely responsible for confirming member eligibility, performing drug utilization review, reviewing for drug-to-drug interactions, performing clinical intervention, which may involve a call to the member's physician, communicating plan provisions to the pharmacy, directing payment to the pharmacy and billing the client for the amount they are contractually obligated to pay us for the prescription dispensed, as specified within our client contracts. We also provide benefit design and formulary consultation services to clients. We have separately negotiated contractual relationships with our clients and with network pharmacies, and under our contracts with pharmacies we assume the credit risk of our clients' ability to pay for drugs dispensed by these pharmacies to clients' members. Our clients are not obligated to pay the pharmacies as we are primarily obligated to pay retail pharmacies in our network the contractually agreed upon amount for the prescription dispensed, as specified within our provider contracts. In addition, under most of our client contracts, we realize a positive or negative margin represented by the difference between the negotiated ingredient costs we will receive from our clients and the separately negotiated ingredient costs we will pay to our network pharmacies. These factors indicate we are a principal as defined by EITF 99-19 and, as such, we record ingredient cost billed to clients in revenue and the corresponding ingredient cost paid to network pharmacies in cost of revenues.

If we merely administer a client's network pharmacy contracts to which we are not a party and under which we do not assume credit risk, we record only our administrative fees as revenue. For these clients, we earn an administrative fee for collecting payments from the client and remitting the corresponding amount to the pharmacies in the client's network. In these transactions we act as a conduit for the client. Because we are not the principal in these transactions, drug ingredient cost is not included in our revenues or in our cost of revenues.

Revenues from our SAAS segment also are derived from the distribution of pharmaceuticals requiring special handling or packaging where we have been selected by the pharmaceutical manufacturer as part of a limited distribution network, the distribution of pharmaceuticals through Patient Assistance Programs where we receive a fee from the pharmaceutical manufacturer for administrative and pharmacy services for the delivery of certain drugs free of charge to doctors for their low-income patients, sample fulfillment and sample accountability services. Revenues include administrative fees received from pharmaceutical manufacturers for dispensing or distributing consigned pharmaceuticals requiring special handling or packaging and administrative fees for verification of practitioner licensure and distribution of consigned drug samples to doctors based on orders received from pharmaceutical sales representatives. We also administer sample card programs for certain manufacturers and include the ingredient costs of those drug samples dispensed from retail pharmacies in SAAS revenues, and the associated costs for these sample card programs in cost of revenues. Because manufacturers are independently obligated to pay us and we have an independent contractual obligation to pay our network pharmacy providers for free samples dispensed to patients under sample card programs, we include the total payments from these manufacturers (including ingredient costs) as revenue, and payments to the network pharmacy provider as cost of revenue. These transactions require us to assume credit risk.

Brightpoint, Inc. Form 10-K—Fiscal Year Ended December 31, 2007

Revenue Recognition

The Company recognizes revenue in accordance with SEC Staff Accounting Bulletin (SAB) 104, *Revenue Recognition.* Revenue is recognized when the title and risk of loss have passed to the customer, there is persuasive evidence of an arrangement, delivery has occurred or services have been rendered, the sales price is fixed or determinable, and collectibility is reasonably assured. The amount of revenue is determined based on either the gross method or the net method. The amount under the gross method includes the value of the product sold while the amount under the net method does not include the value of the product sold.

For distribution revenue, which is recorded using the gross method, the criteria of SAB 104 are generally met upon shipment to customers, including title transfer; and therefore, revenue is recognized at the time of shipment. In some circumstances, the customer may take legal title and assume risk of loss upon delivery; and therefore, revenue is recognized on the delivery date. In certain countries, title is retained by the Company for collection purposes only, which does not impact the timing of revenue recognition in accordance with the provisions of SAB 104. Sales are recorded net of discounts, rebates, returns and allowances. The Company does not have any material post-shipment obligations (e.g. customer acceptance) or other arrangements. A portion of the Company's sales involves shipments of products directly from its suppliers to its customers. In such circumstances, the Company negotiates the price with the supplier and the customer, assumes responsibility for the delivery of the product and, at times, takes the ownership risk while the product is in transit, pays the supplier directly for the product shipped, establishes payment terms and bears credit risk of collecting payment from its customers. In addition, the Company bears responsibility for accepting returns of products from the customer in these arrangements. Under these arrangements, the Company serves as the principal with the customer, as defined by Emerging Issues Task Force (EITF) Issue No. 99-19, *Reporting Revenue Gross as a Principal versus Net as an Agent*, and therefore recognizes the sale and cost of sale of the product upon receiving notification from the supplier that the product has shipped or in cases of FOB destination, CIP destination, or similar terms, the Company recognizes the sales upon confirmation of delivery to the customer at the named destination.

For logistic services revenue, the criteria of SAB 104 are met when the Company's logistic services have been performed and, therefore, revenue is recognized at that time. In general, logistic services are fee-based services. The Company has certain arrangements for which it records receivables, inventory and payables based on the gross amount of the transactions; however, the Company records revenue for these logistic services at the amount of net margin because it is acting as an agent for mobile operators as defined by EITF 99-19. The Company also records revenue from the sale of prepaid airtime within logistic services. In certain circumstances, the Company recognizes revenue for the sales of prepaid airtime using the gross method (based on the full sales price of the airtime to its customers) because the Company has general inventory risk, latitude in setting price and other gross reporting indicators as defined by EITF 99-19. If all of the Company's prepaid airtime transactions that are currently recorded using the gross method were accounted for using the net method, logistic services revenue would have been lower by $90.2 million, $121.7 million and $136.7 million for 2007, 2006 and 2005.

In other logistic services arrangements, the Company receives activation commissions for acquiring subscribers on behalf of mobile operators through its independent dealer/agents. In the event activation occurs through an independent dealer/agent, a portion of the commission is passed on to the dealer/agent. These arrangements may contain provisions for additional residual commissions based on subscriber usage. These agreements may also provide for the reduction or elimination of activation commissions if subscribers deactivate service within stipulated periods. The Company recognizes revenue for activation commissions upon activation of the subscriber's service and residual commissions when earned. An allowance is established for estimated wireless service deactivations as a reduction of accounts receivable and revenues. In circumstances where the Company is acting as an agent for mobile operators as defined by EITF 99-19, the Company recognizes the revenue using the net method. Performance penalty clauses may be included in certain contracts whereby the Company provides logistic services. In general, these penalties are in the form of reduced per unit fees or a specific dollar amount. In the event the Company has incurred performance penalties, revenues are reduced accordingly within each calendar month.

Financial Statement Presentation

Companies with Both Gross and Net Transactions

When a company records some transactions in gross terms and others in net terms, it may be necessary to report revenue for each type of transaction separately and break out cost of sales in a similar fashion. This enables financial statement users to properly evaluate gross margins on the two types of transactions.

In addition, SEC registrants are also required to report revenue from the sale of products and from the provision of services separately (REG S-X, Rule 5-03(b)(1)) (ASC 225-10-S99-2). Because commissions and fees earned from activities reported net are service revenues, separate presentation of revenues from transactions reported gross (product revenues) and transactions reported net (service revenues) may be required.

EXAMPLE: DISCLOSURE OF REVENUE RECOGNIZED NET

Best Buy Co., Inc. Form 10-K—Fiscal Year Ended February 28, 2009

We sell service contracts such as for phone or television service, as well as extended warranties, that typically have terms that range from three months to four years. In jurisdictions where we are deemed to be the obligor on the contract, service revenue is recognized in revenue ratably over the term of the service contract. In jurisdictions where we sell service contracts or extended warranties on behalf of an unrelated third party, where we are not deemed to be the obligor on the contract, commissions are recognized in revenue at the time of sale. Commissions from the sale of extended warranties represented 2.0%, 2.1% and 2.2% of revenue in fiscal 2009, 2008 and 2007, respectively.

Disclosure of Gross Activity for Transactions Reported Net

The EITF noted that although disclosure of gross transaction volume for these revenues is not required by U.S. generally accepted accounting standards (GAAP), it may be useful to financial statement users. However, if the gross amounts are disclosed, they should not be characterized as revenues. In addition, the presentation should not result in the gross activity being presented in the income statement such that it begins a column that sums to net income or loss (EITF 99-19, par. 20) (ASC 605-45-50-1).

Leased Departments

Department stores and other retailers customarily lease portions of their store space to specialty retailers. For example, higher-end department stores often lease space to companies that specialize in displaying and selling cosmetics, or designing and selling wedding dresses. Smaller retailers may allow vending machines owned by another party to be placed in their stores. The store (lessor) typically receives a lease payment from the company leasing the space (lessee). Revenue from the leased part of the store goes to the lessee (which is also responsible for the costs of running its leased portion of the store).

Because the store/lessor has virtually no involvement in product purchasing, pricing, or sales, these types of arrangements generally require the lessee to record sales on a gross basis, with the store only recording its net lease receipts as revenue. Furthermore, these arrangements generally meet the definition of a lease and are therefore within the scope of FAS-13 (ASC 840). The department store or other retailer should include only the rental income, if the arrangement is a lease, or service revenue, if the arrangement is not a lease, as part of its revenues (SAB Topic 8A) (ASC 605-15-S99-2).

ILLUSTRATION: ASSESSMENT OF GROSS VERSUS NET REPORTING INDICATORS

EXAMPLE 1

Facts: Company A runs a catalog business that sells home products, such as rugs, sheets, and towels. Company A does not manufacture any of these products, but has instead compiled products from various manufacturers in its catalog. Each product in the catalog identifies the unique supplier, because the identity of the supplier is a factor that customers use to select products to order. Company A does not maintain inventories but does take title to the products ordered by customers at the point of shipment from suppliers. Title is passed to the customer upon delivery. The gross sales price is charged to the customer's credit card prior to shipment and Company A is the merchant of record. Company A must pay its suppliers even if the credit card amount cannot be collected. Suppliers determine product sales prices and Company A retains a fixed percentage of the sales price and remits the balance to the supplier. The catalog and sales contracts clearly indicate that Company A is not responsible for the quality or safety of the products and that the customer must contact the supplier directly regarding complaints, warranty issues, and returns.

Discussion: Although indicators of gross reporting exist for physical loss inventory risk (during shipping) and credit risk (for collecting amounts charged to credit cards), these indicators do not overcome the stronger indicators that revenues should be reported net. The critical indicators of net reporting are that the supplier, not the company, is the primary obligor and that the amount earned by the company is a fixed percentage of the sales price.

EXAMPLE 2

Facts: Same as in Example 1, except that (1) Company A sets product sales prices, and thereby earns a profit on any amounts in excess of its agreed-upon purchase price with the supplier, and (2) although Company A does not offer a warranty on the products it sells, it does provide a "Satisfaction Guaranteed or Your Money Back" right of return, even when it has no similar right of return with its suppliers.

Discussion: In addition to physical loss inventory risk (during shipping) and credit risk (for collecting amounts charged to credit cards) that exists in Example 1, other gross indicators include both back-end general inventory risk and the pricing latitude of Company A. In addition, the right of return provisions make less clear the identity of the primary obligor. Therefore, gross reporting is appropriate for Company A.

EXAMPLE 3

Facts: Company B is a travel consolidator that negotiates with major airlines to obtain access to airline tickets at reduced rates that are not available to travelers who buy tickets directly from the airlines. Company B determines the prices at which it will sell the airline tickets. The reduced rate paid to an airline by Company B for each ticket sale is negotiated and agreed to in advance and Company B commits to purchase a specific number of tickets for specific flights. Company B must pay for these tickets regardless of whether it is able to resell them. Customers pay for airline tickets using credit cards and Company B is the merchant of record. Although credit card charges are pre-authorized, there are occasional losses that result from disputed charges for which Company B bears the risk of loss. Company B utilizes electronic ticketing and, therefore, no risk of physical loss exists. Company B facilitates the resolution of customer complaints if the customer is dissatisfied with the airline, but Company B's responsibility ends at successfully booking the reservation. The airline is responsible for fulfilling all obligations associated with the ticket.

Discussion: Company B should use gross reporting because it has general inventory risk (a strong indicator of gross reporting) by committing to purchase tickets before it resells them. Company Bs latitude to set ticket prices, also suggests gross reporting because the amount it earns will vary. In addition, Company B has credit risk for collecting customer credit card charges, although this is a weak indicator of gross reporting. An indicator of net reporting also exists because the airlines provide the transportation and are the primary obligors. However, the gross reporting indicators in this case outweigh the fact that the supplier is the primary obligor.

EXAMPLE 4

Facts: Same as Example 3, except that Company B is only required to pay for tickets that it resells to customers.

Discussion: Company B should report revenues net. As in Example 3, the fact that the airline is the primary obligor is a strong indicator of net reporting. There are two indicators of gross reporting in this example—pricing latitude and credit risk. However, these indicators do not overcome the strong net indicator of the supplier being the primary obligor. The strong indicator of gross reporting—general inventory risk—present in Example 3 is not present here.

PAYMENTS FROM A VENDOR TO A CUSTOMER

In many instances, a vendor makes a payment to one of its customers because the vendor is purchasing a product or service from its customer (i.e., the two parties are customers of one another) or the payment is a sales incentive, the main purpose of which is to convince the customer to purchase (or continue purchasing) the vendor's products or services. Payments may include, for example, cash discounts, coupons, rebates, "free" products or services, or equity instruments. In some cases, a vendor will make payments to its customer's customer (an indirect customer of the vendor). For example, the manufacturer of a grocery product may issue coupons that are redeemed by a consumer, even though the manufacturer's customer is the grocery store.

Other common arrangements that involve payments from vendors to customers include:

- Cooperative advertising arrangements, in which a vendor agrees to make payments to its customer if the customer features the vendor's products in its advertising.

- Slotting fees, in which a vendor makes a payment to a retailer so that the retailer will stock the manufacturer's product in its stores, sometimes in a particular location.

- Buydowns, in which a vendor makes a payment to a retailer that makes some amount of purchases at agreed-upon prices.

- Rebates, in which a customer, usually an indirect customer, may send in a form to request a return of a portion of the purchase price of the product or service.

The vendor's (including service providers) and customer's accounting has been addressed in four separate EITF issues (ASC 605-50).

Vendor Classification

The vendor classification model must be applied to all payments made by a company to one of its customers (or an affiliate of that customer) regardless of whether the payments are contractually linked to the revenue. In addition, the guidance applies whether the consideration is given to direct or indirect customers of the vendor, and whether the consideration is in the form of cash, equity, or a product or service. Furthermore, it applies to payments made to customers who will alter the product before reselling it (e.g., a cooperative advertising payment from a computer chip manufacturer to one of its PC manufacturer customers).

> **OBSERVATION:** The model developed in EITF 01-9 (ASC 605-50) must be applied to payments made to both direct and indirect (i.e., further down the distribution chain) customers to prevent a vendor from changing the reporting of a sales incentive without changing its substance. For example, a vendor could achieve essentially the same result by (1) selling its product at a $1 discount to list price, (2) selling the product

at list price and providing a $1 rebate to its direct customer, or (3) selling the product at list price and providing a $1 rebate to a customer further down the distribution chain. An approach that requires revenue reduction in some, but not all, of these arrangements would result in different income statement characterization for sales incentives that are essentially the same.

SEC REGISTRANT ALERT: Round-trip transactions have received a significant amount of attention by the SEC staff and were an area of focus in the SEC staff's Report Pursuant to Section 704 of the Sarbanes-Oxley Act of 2002 (the Section 704 Report), issued in early 2003. In compiling the information in the Section 704 Report, the SEC staff studied enforcement actions filed during the period July 31, 1997, through July 30, 2002. In addition, round-trip transactions have also been a focus in recent SEC staff speeches. The Section 704 Report describes round-trip transactions as transactions that "involve simultaneous pre-arranged sales transactions often of the same product in order to create a false impression of business activity and revenue." A payment from a vendor to its customer should be analyzed carefully to ensure that the payment is not merely one leg in a round-trip transaction. See Chapter 8, "Miscellaneous Issues," for additional discussion regarding nonmonetary transactions.

Consideration in the Form of Cash or Equity

EITF 01-9 (ASC 605-50) begins with the presumption that a cash or equity payment by a vendor to a customer (as noted above, "customer" includes both direct and indirect customers) should be accounted for as a reduction in revenues. However, the presumption is overcome if both of the following are true (EITF 01-9, par. 9) (ASC 605-50-45-2):

1. The vendor receives, or will receive, an identifiable benefit (goods or services) in exchange for the consideration. To meet this condition, the identified benefit must be sufficiently separable from the customer's purchase of the vendor's products such that the vendor could have purchased the identified benefit from somebody other than one of its customers.

2. The vendor can reasonably estimate the fair value of the benefit identified under the first condition.

EXHIBIT 11-1
CHARACTERIZATION OF PAYMENTS FROM VENDOR TO
CUSTOMER

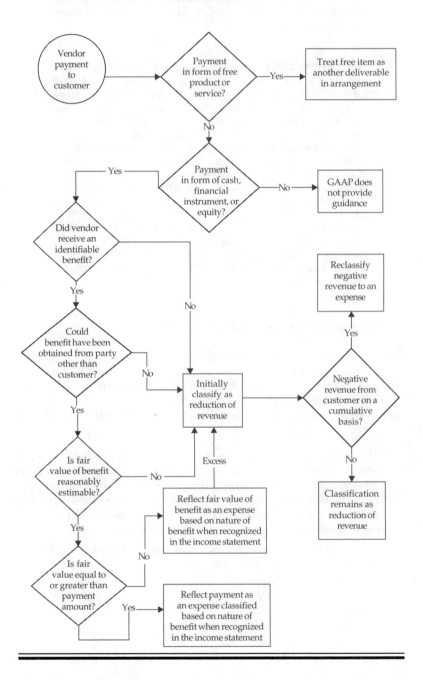

OBSERVATION: The first criterion is meant to ensure that the two transactions (the sale to the customer and the purchase from it) are separable. The second criterion ensures that the net fee can be appropriately allocated to the events, based on relative fair values. These two criteria are similar to the criteria necessary to separate deliverables in a multiple-element arrangement (see Chapter 4, "Multiple-Element Arrangements").

If both criteria are met, the lesser of the amount paid to the customer and the fair value of the benefit received may be classified as an expense when recognized in the income statement, while any amount paid in excess of the fair value of the benefit received must be characterized as a reduction of revenue (EITF 01-9, par. 9) (ASC 605-50-45-2). Any amount that can appropriately be characterized as an expense when recognized in the income statement should be included in an expense caption based on the nature of the identifiable benefit received. For example, if the identifiable benefit is advertising, the amount characterized as an expense should be included in a sales and marketing expense (or similar) caption.

If either of the two criteria is not met, the entire payment must be characterized as a reduction of revenue. Determining whether the criteria are met requires analysis of all available information.

☛ **PRACTICE POINTER:** When the payment from the vendor is in the form of equity instruments, a question arises about the date to use in valuing the instruments. Regardless of whether the cost of the instruments should be treated as an expense or a reduction of revenues, the value should be measured based on the guidance of EITF Issue 96-18, *Accounting for Equity Instruments That Are Issued to Other Than Employees for Acquiring, or in Conjunction with Selling, Goods or Services* (ASC 505, *Equity*; 505-50).

Consideration in the Form of "Free" Products or Services

If the sales incentive is a free product or service, the cost of the free product or service should be classified as an expense when recognized in the income statement. The "free" item is considered an additional deliverable in the exchange transaction and not a refund of any amount charged to the customer. Although the EITF did not reach a consensus on the income statement classification of the cost of the "free" products or services, in most cases, this expense should be classified as part of cost of sales (EITF 01-9, par. 10) (ASC 605-50-45-3).

SEC REGISTRANT ALERT: The SEC Observer indicated that the SEC staff believes that any expense associated with a "free" product or service delivered at the time of sale of another product or service should be classified as cost of sales.

EXAMPLE: VENDOR CLASSIFICATION OF PROMOTIONAL ALLOWANCES

Boston Beer Company, Inc. Form 10-K—Fiscal Year Ended December 29, 2007

The Company reimburses its wholesalers and retailers for promotional discounts, samples and certain advertising and marketing activities used in the promotion of the Company's products. The reimbursements for discounts to wholesalers are recorded as reductions to net revenue. The Company has sales incentive arrangements with its wholesalers based upon performance of certain marketing and advertising activities by the wholesalers. Depending on applicable state laws and regulations, these activities promoting the Company's products may include, but are not limited to, the following: point-of-sale merchandise placement, product displays and promotional programs at retail locations. The costs incurred for these sales incentive arrangements and advertising and promotional programs are included in advertising, promotional and selling expenses during the period in which they are incurred. Total advertising and sales promotional expenditures of $64.2 million, $58.5 million and $55.7 million were included in advertising, promotional and selling expenses in the accompanying consolidated statements of income for fiscal years 2007, 2006 and 2005, respectively. Of these amounts, $5.4 million, $5.6 million and $4.2 million related to sales incentives, samples and other promotional discounts and $29.5 million, $28.8 million and $26.3 million related to advertising costs for fiscal years 2007, 2006 and 2005, respectively.

The Company conducts certain advertising and promotional activities in its wholesalers' markets and the wholesalers make contributions to the Company for such efforts. Reimbursements from wholesalers for advertising and promotional activities are recorded as reductions to advertising, promotional and selling expenses.

Customer Classification

General Model

Cash or equity consideration received from a vendor is presumed to be a reduction of cost of sales when it is recognized in the income statement (prior to recognition in the income statement, the payment would be recognized as a reduction of inventory or prepayments for services). This presumption can only be overcome if the customer can demonstrate that the payment relates to either (1) assets or services provided by the customer to the vendor (in which case the payment is treated as revenue when recognized in the income statement) or (2) a reimbursement of costs incurred by the customer to sell the vendor's products (in which case the payment is treated as a reduction of the related cost when recognized in the income statement) (EITF 02-16, par. 4) (ASC 605-50-45-13).

To conclude that the payment relates to the sale of assets or services by the customer to the vendor, the vendor must receive an identifiable benefit (goods or services) in exchange for the consideration. To be considered an identifiable benefit, the customer should be able to: (1) illustrate that it would have entered into an exchange transaction with another (nonvendor) party to provide that benefit, and (2) determine the fair value of the benefit. If the amount of the payment from the vendor is greater than the fair value of the identifiable benefit provided to the vendor, the excess should be reflected as a reduction of cost of sales when recognized in the income statement (EITF 02-16, par. 5) (ASC 605-50-45-14).

To demonstrate that the payment relates to a reimbursement of costs incurred by the customer to sell the vendor's products or services, the customer must incur an incremental, identifiable cost. If the amount of the payment from the vendor is greater than the incremental, identifiable cost incurred by the customer, the excess should be reflected as a reduction of cost of sales when recognized in the income statement (EITF 02-16, par. 6) (ASC 605-50-45-15).

EXAMPLE: CUSTOMER CLASSIFICATIONS OF PROMOTIONAL ALLOWANCES

SUPERVALU, INC. Form 10-K—Fiscal Year Ended February 28, 2009

Vendor Funds

The Company receives funds from many of the vendors whose products the Company buys for resale in its stores. These vendor funds are provided to increase the sell-through of the related products. The Company receives vendor funds for a variety of merchandising activities: placement of the vendors' products in the Company's advertising; display of the vendors' products in prominent locations in the Company's stores; supporting the introduction of new products into the Company's retail stores and distribution system; exclusivity rights in certain categories; and to compensate for temporary price reductions offered to customers on products held for sale at retail stores. The Company also receives vendor funds for buying activities such as volume commitment rebates, credits for purchasing products in advance of their need and cash discounts for the early payment of merchandise purchases. The majority of the vendor fund contracts have terms of less than a year, with a small proportion of the contracts longer than one year.

The Company recognizes vendor funds for merchandising activities as a reduction of Cost of sales when the related products are sold in accordance with Emerging Issues Task Force ("EITF") Issue No. 02-16, *Accounting by a Customer (Including a Reseller) for Certain Consideration Received from a Vendor.*

Vendor funds that have been earned as a result of completing the required performance under the terms of the underlying agreements, but for which the product has not yet been sold, are recognized as reductions of inventory. The amount and timing of recognition of vendor funds as well as the amount of vendor funds remaining in ending inventory requires management judgment and estimates. Management determines these amounts based on estimates of current year purchase volume using forecast and historical data and review of average inventory turnover data. These judgments and estimates impact the Company's reported operating earnings and inventory amounts. The historical estimates of the Company have been reliable in the past, and the Company believes the methodology will continue to be reliable in the future. Based on previous experience, the Company does not expect there will be a significant change in the level of vendor support. However, if such a change were to occur, cost of sales and advertising expense could change, depending on the specific vendors involved. If vendor advertising allowances were substantially reduced or eliminated, the Company would consider changing the volume, type and frequency of the advertising, which could increase or decrease its advertising expense. Similarly, the Company is not able to assess the impact of vendor advertising allowances on creating additional revenues as such allowances do not directly generate revenue for the Company's stores. For fiscal 2009, a 100 basis point change in total vendor funds earned, including advertising allowances, with no offsetting changes to the base price on the products purchased, would impact gross profit by 10 basis points.

Vendor's Sales Incentives Offered Directly to Consumers

A vendor may issue sales incentives that a consumer will present to a reseller for redemption (e.g., manufacturer's coupons redeemed by retailers when presented by consumers). Resellers facilitate the redemption of these incentives by acting as middlemen or agents between the vendor and consumer. If these types of sales incentive arrangements possess the following characteristics, they are not treated as sales incentives by the reseller (EITF 03-10, pars. 5-6) (ASC 605-50-45-19):

- The incentive can be presented by a consumer to resellers that accept manufacturer's incentives as partial (or full) payment of the price charged by the reseller for the vendor's product.

- The incentive results in the reseller receiving a direct reimbursement from the vendor (or a clearinghouse authorized by the vendor) based on the face amount of the incentive.

- The incentive was not influenced by or negotiated in conjunction with any other incentive arrangements between the vendor and the reseller (i.e., the incentive is between the manufacturer and the consumer).

- The reseller is acting in the capacity of an agent for the vendor (either expressly or implied) in redeeming the incentive presented by the consumer.

These characteristics are intended to identify those sales incentives where a reseller receives a payment from the vendor solely to reimburse it for acting as the vendor's agent in redeeming a sales incentive that is between the vendor and consumer. Requiring a reseller to record this type of sales incentive as a reduction in cost of sales would not properly reflect the reseller's role in the transaction.

If a sales incentive possesses all of the above characteristics, the reseller should account for its involvement in the redemption on the balance sheet. The appropriate balance sheet treatment is to record a receivable, in the amount of the sales incentive (from the vendor at the time of the sale to the consumer), with the full sales price included as revenue. If a sales incentive does not possess all of these characteristics, the reseller should apply the model in EITF 02-16 (ASC 605-50-45-13). Application of this model to a manufacturer's coupon that lacks one or more of the characteristics discussed above would likely result in the recognition of the vendor's payment to the reseller as a reduction in cost of sales on the reseller's income statement. It is highly unlikely that such an incentive would meet the criteria to be treated as revenue or a selling cost reimbursement when recognized in the reseller's income statement.

EXAMPLES: VENDOR'S SALES INCENTIVES

BJ's Wholesale Club Form 10-K—Fiscal Year Ended February 2, 2008

Manufacturers' Incentives Tendered by Consumers

At the beginning of 2004, we adopted the provisions of EITF Issue No. 03-10, *Application of EITF Issue No. 02-16 by Resellers to Sales Incentives Offered to Consumers by Manufacturers* (EITF 03-10), which provides guidance for the reporting of vendor consideration received by a reseller as it relates to manufacturers' incentives (such as rebates or coupons) tendered by consumers. We include such vendor consideration in revenues only if all of the criteria defined in EITF 03-10 are met. Otherwise, such consideration is recorded as a decrease in cost of sales.

Application to Certain Common Arrangements

The guidance in EITF 01-9 and 02-16 (ASC 605-50) applies to any situation in which payments are made from a vendor to a customer. Application of these models to several common types of arrangements is discussed below.

Cooperative Advertising Arrangements

In a cooperative advertising arrangement, the vendor makes a payment to a customer for including the vendor's products in the customer's advertising.

Vendor classification Such arrangements may seem to meet the first criterion of the model in EITF 01-9 (ASC 605-50-45-2). Because the vendor can separately purchase advertising from, for example, a newspaper, magazine, or radio station, a cooperative advertising arrangement would appear to include an identifiable benefit that could have been obtained from a party other than the customer. However, the substance of some cooperative advertising arrangements makes it difficult to ascertain the identifiable benefit. For example, some arrangements do not specify the amount or type of advertising the customer must purchase to qualify for the cooperative payment. In other arrangements, the payment amount is determined by the total purchases made by the customer, which makes the arrangement appear similar to a volume discount or rebate. For a cooperative advertising arrangement to meet the second criterion of the model in EITF 01-9 (ASC 605-50-45-2)— reasonable estimate of fair value of the benefit received—it is generally necessary for the arrangement to specify the type and volume of advertising to be provided. Without this information, fair value cannot be determined. If both criteria are met, the vendor's payment should be reflected as a cost incurred, to the extent it does not exceed the estimated fair value of the advertising received. If the amount of the vendor's payment exceeds the estimated fair value of the advertising received, then (a) the estimated fair value of the advertising received should be reflected as a cost incurred and (b) the excess of the vendor's payment over the estimated fair value of the advertising received should be reflected as a reduction of revenue.

EXAMPLE: COOPERATIVE ADVERTISING AND BUYDOWN PROGRAMS

Helen of Troy Limited Form 10-K—Fiscal Year Ended February 29, 2008

We offer our customers certain incentives in the form of cooperative advertising arrangements, volume rebates, product markdown allowances, trade discounts, cash discounts and slotting fees. We account for these incentives in accordance with Emerging Issues Task Force Issue No. 01-9, *Accounting for Consideration Given by a Vendor to a Customer* (EITF 01-9). In instances where the customer is required to provide us with proof of performance, reductions in amounts received from customers as a result of cooperative advertising programs are included in our consolidated statements of income on the line entitled "Selling, general, and administrative expenses" ("SG&A").

Other reductions in amounts received from customers as a result of cooperative advertising programs are recorded as reductions of net sales. Markdown allowances, slotting fees, trade discounts, cash discounts and volume rebates are all recorded as reductions of net sales. Customer incentives included in SG&A were $12,161, $12,568 and $12,124 for the fiscal years 2008, 2007, and 2006, respectively.

Customer classification   In cooperative advertising arrangements, the customer may be able to demonstrate that the payment relates to the reimbursement of advertising costs if there is an incremental, identifiable cost related to selling the vendor's products or services. If the customer has documentation to support the incremental and identifiable nature of the cost, the vendor's payment should be reflected as a reduction in that cost. Any amount of the vendor's payment in excess of the reimbursed cost should be reflected as a reduction of cost of sales. The cost reimbursement reduction should be reflected in the sales and marketing expense (or similar) line item on the income statement. If the customer does not have documentation to support the incremental and identifiable nature of the cost, it must recognize the vendor's payment as a reduction of cost of sales.

ILLUSTRATION: COOPERATIVE ADVERTISING ARRANGEMENTS

EXAMPLE 1

Facts: Company D provides satellite television services. It sells the hardware (a satellite dish and receivers) necessary to receive its services through retailers that sell the hardware and arrange installation. The hardware is purchased from Company D and retailers receive an advertising allowance of $100 for each receiver sold and activated. This allowance is shown as a deduction on the related invoice. The retailers are expected to include Company D's products and service in local advertisements. However, retailers are not required and do not provide any documentation to Company D on how the advertising allowance was used.

Vendor Classification Discussion: The first condition of the EITF 01-9 model is not met. Company D cannot identify the benefit that has been received because retailers do not provide documentation of any advertising. Therefore, the allowances should be characterized as a reduction of revenue in Company D's income statement.

Customer Classification Discussion: The retailers do not have documentation to support the incremental, identifiable nature of the costs incurred to sell Company D's products and services required by the model in

EITF 02-16 (ASC 605-50-45-15). Therefore, the payments should be characterized as a reduction of cost of sales when recognized in the retailers' income statements.

EXAMPLE 2

Facts: Company E provides satellite television services. It sells the hardware (a satellite dish and receivers) necessary to receive its services through retailers that sell the hardware and arrange installation. The hardware is purchased from Company E and retailers receive an advertising allowance of $100 for each receiver sold and activated. This allowance is shown as a deduction on the related invoice. Retailers are required by their contract with Company E to use the advertising allowance to advertise Company E's products and services and to provide documentation of these expenditures to Company E.

Vendor Classification Discussion: Company E receives an identifiable benefit (advertising) from the retailers that is sufficiently separable from the retailers' purchases of Company E's products. Company E could have purchased advertising from another party that does not purchase Company E's satellite dishes and receivers. Therefore, the first condition in the EITF 01-9 (ASC 605-50-45-2) model is met. Because Company E receives documentation of the advertising expenditures, it can likely estimate the fair value of the benefit received based on the prices charged for similar advertising. Thus, the second condition can likely be met. As a result, the lesser of the fair value of the advertising and the amount of the allowance would be characterized as an expense. If the amount of the allowance exceeds the fair value of the benefit, this excess would be characterized as a reduction of revenue.

Customer Classification Discussion: The retailers have documentation to support the incremental, identifiable nature of the advertising costs incurred to sell Company E's products and services as required by the model in EITF 02-16 (ASC 605-50-45-15). As a result, the lesser of the amount of the payment or the amount of the related advertising costs is recognized as a reduction in advertising expense when recognized in the retailers' income statements. Any amount of the payment in excess of the related advertising costs is recognized as a reduction of cost of sales when recognized in the retailers' income statements.

Slotting Fees and Allowances

The terms "slotting allowances" and "slotting fees" describe a family of practices that involve payments by manufacturers and wholesalers to persuade downstream resellers to stock, display, and support particular products. They are most commonly used by grocery retailers who are asked to stock a new product or to devote a certain amount of shelf space to a product or family of products. Slotting fees are increasingly used for other retail products as well, such as computer software, compact discs, books, magazines, apparel, over-the-counter drugs, and tobacco products.

Vendor classification Because of the nature of slotting fees and allowances, it is almost impossible for the first criterion in EITF 01-9 (ASC 605-50-45-2) to be met. Although a vendor might argue that a slotting fee gives an identifiable advertising benefit due to greater awareness of the product, this benefit can only be obtained from the customer. In other cases, a slotting fee might provide the vendor with exclusivity in its product category in a particular store. Although exclusivity might be an identifiable benefit, it can only be obtained from the customer. As a result, the first criterion is not met. In addition, the second criterion would be difficult to meet, because of the extreme variation in slotting fee amounts, and the fact that such payments are never made to parties that are not also customers of the payer.

EXAMPLE: TRADE PROMOTION, SLOTTING FEES, AND COUPON PROGRAMS

Spectrum Brands Form 10-K—Fiscal Year Ended September 30, 2007

The Company also enters into various arrangements, primarily with retail customers, which require the Company to make upfront cash, or "slotting" payments, to secure the right to distribute through such customers. The Company capitalizes slotting payments, provided the payments are supported by a time or volume based arrangement with the retailer, and amortizes the associated payment over the appropriate time or volume based term of the arrangement. The amortization of slotting payments is treated as a reduction in Net sales and a corresponding asset is reported in Deferred charges and other in the accompanying Consolidated Balance Sheets.

Customer classification The nature of slotting fees and allowances makes it difficult for a customer to demonstrate that it is either providing an identifiable benefit to the vendor or incurring an incremental, identifiable cost related to selling the vendor's products or services. This is because the customer will most likely be unable to prove that it could enter into an exchange transaction with the same terms as a slotting fee arrangement with parties other than its vendors. Similarly, the cost of the space provided by the customer to the vendor in a slotting fee arrangement would not be considered an incremental, identifiable cost. As a result, slotting fees and allowances should almost always be treated as a reduction in cost of sales in the income statement.

Some argue that slotting fees should be accounted for as a cost incurred by a vendor to lease shelf space from a retailer. Although certain slotting fee arrangements are indeed written in the form of a lease, they generally do not provide the vendor/lessee with the right to access and use the shelves for a specified period of time. Instead, control of the shelf space continues to be retained by the retailer. In addition, a true lease would give the vendor/lessee ownership of the products on the shelf, because the vendor/lessee would control the space and the receipts from the sale of these products would belong to the vendor/lessee. However, in a slotting arrangement, proceeds from the sale of such products are recorded as the retailer's revenues. For these reasons, a slotting fee arrangement does not meet the accounting definition of a lease, even if its legal form appears to be one.

> **OBSERVATION:**   Certain retailers lease a portion of the store to a provider of products. However, in these situations, the retailer only receives lease revenue, not the revenue from the sale of products, and the lessee controls the products in the leased portion of the store (see "Leased Departments" earlier in this chapter).

Coupons and Rebates

Coupons and consumer rebates are the most widely used sales incentives. Some coupons and rebates are offered by a retailer directly to the consumer; others are given by product manufacturers to the end consumer, even though the consumer purchases the product through a retail reseller.

Vendor classification   Coupon or rebate offers are promotions instituted and managed by marketing departments and are considered a marketing expense. As a result, in the absence of any accounting guidance, many vendors reported the costs of these discounts as a marketing expense and recorded the normal selling price of the related products or services as revenue. However, based on the model in EITF 01-9 (ASC 605-50-45-2), coupons and rebates must be characterized as a reduction in revenue, because there is no separately identifiable benefit received by the vendor.

EXAMPLE: CLASSIFICATION OF COUPONS

Revlon Consumer Products Corporation Form 10-K—Fiscal Year Ended December 31, 2007

Net sales is comprised of gross revenues less expected returns, trade discounts and customer allowances, which include costs associated with off-invoice mark-downs and other price reductions, as well as trade promotions and coupons. These incentive costs are recognized at the later of the date on which the Company recognizes the related revenue or the date on which the Company offers the incentive.

Customer classification   The consumer should treat the cash payment received from the vendor or the redemption value provided by the reseller as a reduction of cost of sales based on the model in EITF 02-16 (ASC 605-50-45-13). This is because the consumer does not provide any products or services to the vendor in return for the payment and the payment does not relate to a reimbursement of any particular cost.

If a reseller is involved in redeeming the coupon, the reseller's treatment of the reimbursement from the vendor depends on whether the coupon or rebate possesses the characteristics discussed earlier under "Vendor's Sales Incentives Offered Directly to Consumers." If the coupon or rebate possesses these characteristics, the retailer would account for the coupon or rebate on its balance sheet rather than on its income statement. If the coupon or rebate does not possess these characteristics, the model in EITF 02-16 (ASC 605-50-45-13) would apply and payment from the vendor would be recorded as a reduction in cost of sales. In many cases, the retailer receives a "fee" for redeeming coupons. This fee should be analyzed to determine whether it should be recognized as revenue or as a reduction in cost of sales or another cost altogether. Generally, the analysis of this "fee" under EITF 02-16 (ASC 605-50-45-13) would not result in a reduction to cost of sales because (a) the related activity does not provide an identifiable benefit to the vendor and (b) the customer has not incurred an incremental, identifiable cost related to that activity.

Buydowns

Buydown programs generally involve a vendor agreeing to compensate a retailer for lower-than-expected per unit revenue from certain products during a specified time period. In return, the retailer agrees to run a promotion for the vendor's product involving a reduced selling price, rebate, or some other discount. In contrast to cooperative advertising, buydown programs generally do not require expenditures by the retailer for advertising or promotion. Buydowns are known by different names in various industries. For example, the "factory to dealer incentives" often mentioned in automobile advertisements are a form of buydown program.

Vendor classification   Much like a coupon or rebate, payments under a buydown program are always considered a reduction in revenue rather than an expense, because there is no separable identifiable benefit received from the customer as required by the model in EITF 01-9 (ASC 605-50-45-2).

Customer classification   Much like a coupon or rebate where only the vendor and consumer are involved, payments under a buydown program are always a cost of sales reduction under the model in EITF 02-16 (ASC 605-50-45-13) because no products or services are provided by the customer to the vendor and because the payment does not relate to reimbursement of any particular cost.

ILLUSTRATION: CLASSIFICATION OF PAYMENTS FROM VENDORS TO CUSTOMERS

EXAMPLE 1

Facts: Company Z markets and sells a popular brand of peanuts. One of Company Z's contracts makes it the exclusive peanut supplier for a major airline. Company Z sells its peanuts to the airline at discounted prices. In addition, Company Z agrees to purchase a minimum amount of airline tickets from the airline to be used for travel by Company Z's personnel. If Company Z does not purchase the minimum amount of travel by the end of any year of the contract, it must make an additional payment for the shortfall. The prices Company Z pays for plane tickets are comparable to those available to the general public.

Vendor Classification Discussion: With respect to the air travel, Company Z receives an identifiable benefit from the airline. This benefit is sufficiently separable from the airline's purchase of Company Z's peanuts because Company Z could have used any other airline for its corporate travel. Therefore, the first condition in EITF 01-9 (ASC 605-50-45-2) is met. The second condition is also met because the fair value of the plane tickets can be determined based on the prices paid by the general public for similar tickets. As Company Z pays these same amounts, as long as Company Z actually uses at least the minimum purchase requirement for corporate travel, all of the payments to the airline may be characterized as expenses. If Company Z is required to make a payment at year-end due to a shortfall in travel purchases, the amount of the shortfall would be characterized as a reduction in revenue, because it would represent a payment that is over and above the fair value of the benefit received.

Company Z may also believe it is obtaining other benefits from the airline, such as exclusivity and visibility to a captive audience, but these benefits are not separable from the sales arrangement, nor could their fair value be determined. As a result, no amount of the shortfall payment could be classified as an expense based on this rationale.

Customer Classification Discussion: With respect to the air travel, the airline is providing a service that it would offer to other, non-vendor customers. In addition, the airline is providing this service to Company Z at prices comparable to those available to the general public. As a result, if Company Z actually uses at least the minimum purchase requirement for corporate travel, all of the payments to the airline may be classified as revenue by the airline based on the model in EITF 02-16. (ASC 605-50-45-13) To the extent that Company Z is required to make a payment at year-end due to a shortfall in travel purchases, the amount of the shortfall payment would be characterized as a reduction in the cost of the peanuts.

EXAMPLE 2

Facts: Company Y makes frozen desserts and sells them through grocery and warehouse stores. As part of an arrangement to sell a large quantity of products to a large grocery store chain, Company Y agrees to reimburse the chain for special display freezers that will display Company Y's products. The freezers will include Company Y's logo on the outside and will have racking and other components specifically designed to highlight Company Y's products. The grocery chain will pay an independent third party to design and build the freezers. Company Y and the grocery store chain believe that the new display freezers will increase sales of Company Y products at the chain's stores. However, the grocery store chain has no obligation to continue purchasing Company Y's products.

Vendor Classification Discussion: The first condition in EITF 01-9 (ASC 605-50-45-2) is not met because Company Y does not receive an identifiable benefit that is sufficiently separable from the arrangement to sell products to the grocery store chain. Company Y could only enter into such an arrangement with a reseller of its products. The consideration therefore should be characterized as a reduction in revenue.

Customer Classification Discussion: If the chain has support for the amount it spends to purchase the freezers from the independent third party such that the cost is identifiable and incremental under the model in EITF 02-16 (ASC 605-50-45-15), it should recognize the payment from Company Y as a reduction in the cost of these freezers when recognized in the income statement.

EXAMPLE 3

Facts: Company Y makes frozen desserts and sells them through grocery and warehouse stores. As part of an arrangement to sell a large quantity of products to a grocery store chain, Company Y agrees to give special display freezers to the chain to display Company Y's products. The freezers include Company Y's logo on the outside and have racking and other components specifically designed to highlight Company Y's products. Company Y currently owns the freezers, as it purchased them from an independent third party and modified them as necessary to effectively display its products. Company Y and the grocery chain believe that the new display freezers will increase sales of Company Y's products at the chain's stores. However, the grocery store chain has no obligation to continue purchasing Company Y's products.

Vendor Classification Discussion: The consideration that Company Y gives to the chain consists of "free" products (the freezers). Consideration in the form of "free" products or services is treated as a deliverable in the arrangement under the model in EITF 01-9 (ASC 605-50-45-3), rather than as a refund of revenue. Therefore, Company Y should record the cost of the freezers as an expense when recognized in its income statement. In addition, a portion of the revenue from the arrangement should be allocated to the freezers.

Customer Classification Discussion: EITF 02-16 (ASC 605-50-15-2) does not address situations where consideration received by the customer is other than cash or equity. Therefore, the customer's accounting treatment of the "free" freezers should be based on all available facts and circumstances.

EXAMPLE 4

Facts: Company G is an auto manufacturer that sells its products to consumers through a network of dealers. Company G plans to run a nationwide promotion in which its dealers will stay open late for a two-week period and purchasers will receive factory rebates on vehicles purchased during the same two-week period. Company G agrees to reimburse its dealers for the extra payroll costs they will incur during the promotion for keeping the dealerships open longer.

Vendor Classification Discussion: The first condition in EITF 01-9 (ASC 605-50-45-2) is not met because Company G does not receive an identifiable benefit that is sufficiently separable from Company G's sale of automobiles to the dealer. The payroll reimbursements should therefore be characterized as a reduction in revenue on Company G's income statement.

Customer Classification Discussion: If the dealers can demonstrate that the additional payroll costs incurred are identifiable and incremental under the model in EITF 02-16 (ASC 605-50-45-15), the payment from Company G should be recognized as a reduction in payroll costs in the income statement. The dealers will need to consider the nature of their payroll costs when determining whether these costs are identifiable and incremental. Hourly wages would be considered incremental; salaries would not. In addition, most benefit-related payroll costs would most likely not be considered incremental. If the amount of the payment from Company G is greater than the amount of identifiable and incremental reimbursed costs, the excess should be reflected as a reduction in cost of sales.

NEGATIVE REVENUE

Because revenue only relates to amounts received from customers, negative revenue should generally not exist. However, negative revenue might exist for a reporting period or a particular transaction under several circumstances. For example, if a company underestimates the amount of returns it will receive on sales with return rights, it will eventually need to reverse some previously recognized revenue when the additional returns occur. Negative revenue can also exist because of payments made by a vendor to the customer that exceed the revenue from that customer but do not provide a separately identifiable benefit, as discussed above. For example, a company may agree to pay an upfront slotting allowance to have its products sold in a store for the first time. If the initial product order is less than the slotting fee, negative revenues would result.

As part of its deliberations on payments from vendors to customers, the EITF considered whether the existence of negative revenue for a reporting period, a transaction, or some other segment of a company's transactions should be recharacterized as an expense. The EITF concluded that negative revenue amounts may only be reclassified as an expense if, at a particular point in time, the company would have recognized negative revenue for a specific customer on a cumulative basis since it began selling to the customer (EITF 01-9, par. 17) (ASC 605-50-45-7). This is consistent with the model for classifying payments made to customers because it analyzes the vendor-customer relationship as a whole, rather than on a transaction-by-transaction or other basis.

Based on this conclusion, it is clear that a payment at the inception of a customer relationship, and before the customer makes any commitment to purchase products or services from the vendor could be recharacterized as an expense, even if there is no separately identifiable benefit. However, this recharacterization would not be appropriate to the extent that the customer contractually agrees to make future purchases from the vendor as part of the arrangement including the upfront payment, and it is probable that such purchases will be in amounts greater than the upfront payment (EITF 01-9, par. 18) (ASC 605-50-45-9). In this event, the payment to the customer would result in an asset, rather than an immediate expense. The asset would be amortized (as a reduction of revenue) as the customer makes the related purchases.

The evaluation of whether negative revenue results from cost recognition on a cumulative basis should be made whenever any cost must be recorded in the income statement. Thus, any additional revenues received from the customer at a later date would not result in a "re-reclassification" of the negative revenue that was previously reclassified as an expense.

ILLUSTRATION: NEGATIVE REVENUE

EXAMPLE 1

Facts: Company C provides computer technology support services to large corporations. Company C enters into an arrangement with Customer D to provide information technology troubleshooting and installation support. Company C will charge specified hourly rates for various services that Customer D may ask it to perform. Customer D agrees to publicize its relationship with Company C through the issuance of a press release, to inform all of its personnel of the arrangement with Company C, to allow Company C to meet with its employees to "pitch" its capabilities and to ensure that Company C's dedicated technology support phone number for Customer D is conspicuously placed throughout Customer D's facilities. In part to defray the costs Customer D will incur in these activities, Company C makes a $500,000 payment to Customer D at the inception of the arrangement. However, Customer D also uses other technology support companies and will continue to do so even after the relationship with Company C is put into place. As a result, Customer D does not guarantee any level of purchases from Company C.

Discussion: The $500,000 payment would normally be treated as a reduction of revenue, because Company C gets no separately identifiable benefit in exchange. However, because this payment is made before any revenue is received from Customer D, it results in negative revenue from Customer D on a cumulative basis. Because there is negative cumulative revenue and because Customer D has not contractually agreed to make future purchases from Company C, the entire $500,000 payment may be recharacterized as an expense. Even when revenue is received from Customer D in the future, the $500,000 payment may remain classified as an expense, as the negative revenue model cannot be applied retroactively.

EXAMPLE 2

Facts: Same as Example 1, except that Customer D had previously used Company C as a service provider and has purchased $800,000 in services from Company C over the past two years. The new arrangement raises Company C's profile significantly with Customer D. Company C believes that the additional publicity from Customer D will result in more business for Company C, rather than other technology support providers.

Discussion: As in Example 1, there is no separately identifiable benefit from the $500,000 payment, so it should be initially characterized as a reduction in revenue. In addition, even though Customer D makes no purchases at the time the new contract is signed, it has made $800,000 in purchases from Company C in the past. On a cumulative basis, Company C has positive revenue of $300,000 from Customer D. Therefore, the $500,000 payment should remain classified as a revenue reduction, even if it results in negative revenue for the reporting period.

EXAMPLE 3

Facts: Same as in Example 1, except that Customer D guarantees that it will purchase at least $800,000 in services from Company C over the next two years.

Discussion: There is no separately identifiable benefit from the $500,000 payment, so it should be initially characterized as a reduction in revenue. Because the contract includes a commitment to make purchases, Company C should consider these purchases in its determination of whether it is appropriate to recharacterize the payment as an expense. Because the committed purchases are greater than the upfront payment, the payment should not be recharacterized as an expense. In this case, Company C would likely conclude that the purchase commitment from Customer D represents an asset. The $500,000 would therefore be capitalized and amortized pro rata as a reduction in revenue over the $800,000 in purchases by Customer D.

PAYMENTS BY A SERVICE PROVIDER TO A MANUFACTURER OR A RESELLER

Certain services are provided through equipment that must be purchased by the end-customer. The equipment may be manufactured, distributed, and sold by third parties to end-users without the direct participation of the service providers. A service provider may offer incentives to manufacturers or resellers to reduce the cost of such equipment to the end-customer thereby increasing the demand for and sales of the service.

The financial reporting guidance of Issue 01-9 (ASC 605-50-45-2 and 45-3) must be used to determine whether the consideration given by the service provider to the manufacturer or reseller should be treated as "cash consideration" or "other than cash consideration" when that consideration can be linked contractually to the benefit received by the customer of the service provider (EITF 06-1, par. 4) (ASC 605-50-25-14).

The Task Force also decided that the characterization of the consideration (as "cash consideration" or "other than cash consideration") should be based on the form of the consideration directed by the service provider to be provided to the service provider's customer (EITF Issue 06-1, par. 4) (ASC 605-50-25-16).

EXAMPLE: INCENTIVE PAYMENTS BY A SERVICE PROVIDER

Sirius Satellite Radio, Inc. Form 10-K—Fiscal Year Ended December 31, 2007

Critical Accounting Policies and Estimates

Revenue Recognition

Revenue from subscribers consists of subscription fees; revenue derived from our agreement with Hertz; nonrefundable activation fees; and the effects of rebates.

We recognize subscription fees as our service is provided to a subscriber. We record deferred revenue for prepaid subscription fees and amortize these prepayments to revenue ratably over the term of the respective subscription plan.

At the time of sale, vehicle owners purchasing or leasing a vehicle with a subscription to our service typically receive between a six month and one year prepaid subscription. We receive payment from automakers for these subscriptions in advance of our service being activated. Such prepayments are recorded to deferred revenue and amortized ratably over the service period upon activation and sale to a customer. We also reimburse automakers for certain costs associated with the SIRIUS radio installed in the applicable vehicle at the time the vehicle is manufactured. The associated payments to the automakers are included in subscriber acquisition costs. Although we receive payments from the automakers, they do not resell our service; rather, automakers facilitate the sale of our service to our customers, acting similar to an agent. We believe this is the appropriate characterization of our relationship since we are responsible for providing service to our customers, including being obligated to the customer if there was interruption of service.

Equipment revenue from the direct sale of SIRIUS radios and accessories is recognized upon shipment, net of discounts and rebates. Shipping and handling costs billed to customers are recorded as revenue. Shipping and handling costs associated with shipping goods to customers are recorded to cost of equipment.

Summary of Significant Accounting Policies

Subscriber Acquisition Costs

Subscriber acquisition costs include hardware subsidies paid to radio manufacturers, distributors, and automakers, including subsidies paid to automakers that include a SIRIUS radio and a prepaid subscription to our service in the sale or lease price of a new vehicle; subsidies paid for chip sets and certain other components used in manufacturing radios; device royalties for certain SIRIUS radios; commissions paid to retailers and auto-makers as incentives to purchase, install, and activate SIRIUS radios; prod-uct warranty obligations; provisions for inventory allowance; and compensation costs associated with stock-based awards granted in connec-tion with certain distribution agreements. The majority of subscriber acquisi-tion costs are incurred in advance of acquiring a subscriber. Subscriber acquisition costs do not include advertising, loyalty payments to distributors and dealers of SIRIUS radios, and revenue share payments to automakers and retailers of SIRIUS radios.

Subsidies paid to radio manufacturers and automakers are expensed upon shipment or installation. Commissions paid to retailers and automakers are expensed either upon activation or sale of the SIRIUS radio. Chip sets that are shipped to radio manufacturers and held on consignment are recorded as inventory and expensed as subscriber acquisition costs when placed into production by radio manufacturers. Costs for chip sets not held on consignment are expensed as subscriber acquisition costs when the chip sets are shipped to radio manufacturers.

In September 2006, the FASB issued EITF No. 06-01, *Accounting for Con-sideration Given by a Service Provider to Manufacturers or Resellers of Equipment Necessary for an End-Customer to Receive Service from the Service Provider.* The EITF concluded that if consideration given by a service provider to a third-party manufacturer or a reseller that is not the service provider's customer can be linked contractually to the benefit received by the service provider's customer, a service provider should account for the consideration in accordance with EITF No. 01-09, *Accounting for Consider-ation Given by a Vendor to a Customer.* EITF No. 06-01 is effective for annual reporting periods beginning after June 15, 2007. We have adopted EITF No. 06-01 for the year ended December 31, 2007. The adoption of EITF No. 06-01 did not have a material impact on our consolidated results of operations or financial position.

PRESENTATION OF CERTAIN COSTS BILLED TO CUSTOMERS

Shipping and Handling

Many companies sell goods that are shipped directly to customers and charge a separately identified "shipping and handling" fee on the customer invoice. Other companies do not charge a separate fee and instead advertise "free" shipping. When a separate shipping and han-dling charge is included, the method of determining the amount of the charge varies. Some companies merely pass through third-party ship-ping charges, while others attempt to recover a portion of their inter-nal costs as well. Other companies charge shipping and handling fees on a basis that bears no relation to the costs incurred.

The EITF concluded that amounts billed to a customer for shipping and handling should be classified as revenue in the income statement. The conclusion is partially based on the fact that a company has the ability to alter its pricing between its product prices and its shipping and handling charge to achieve similar results (EITF 00-10, par. 5) (ASC 605-45-45-20).

The EITF also concluded that shipping and handling costs should be classified as an expense. Therefore, it is not appropriate to offset shipping and handling costs incurred and shipping and handling revenue received against one another in the income statement. Rather, the two must each be reported separately (EITF 00-10, par. 6) (ASC 605-50-45-21). This conclusion is consistent with the conclusions reached on reporting revenue gross versus net. The seller acts as a principal in purchasing the shipping from the postal service or private shipping company and in the transaction with the customer. Therefore, shipping and handling costs and revenues should not be reported on a net basis, even if the cost is merely "passed through" to the customer without any markup.

> **DISCLOSURE ALERT:** If shipping and handling costs are classified within cost of sales on the income statement, no separate disclosure of these costs is required. However, if shipping and handling costs are significant and are not classified within cost of sales, the amount must be disclosed and the line item in which they are included must be identified (ASC 605-45-50-2).

EXAMPLE: SHIPPING AND HANDLING COSTS

Colgate-Palmolive, Inc. Form 10-K—Fiscal Year Ended December 31, 2007

Shipping and handling costs may be reported as either a component of cost of sales or selling, general and administrative expenses. The Company reports such costs, primarily related to warehousing and outbound freight, in the Consolidated Statements of Income as a component of Selling, general and administrative expenses. Accordingly, the Company's gross profit margin is not comparable with the gross profit margin of those companies that include shipping and handling charges in cost of sales. If such costs had been included in cost of sales, gross profit margin as a percent of sales would have decreased by 790 bps from 56.2% to 48.3% in 2007 and decreased 770 bps and 750 bps in 2006 and 2005, respectively, with no impact on reported earnings.

Out-of-Pocket Expenses

Service providers often incur incidental expenses while performing work for their clients. These "out-of-pocket" expenses include travel costs (e.g., hotel charges, airline tickets, car rentals, meals) and costs of supplies, printing and copying. In many cases, the customer reimburses the service provider for these costs, in addition to the agreed-upon service fee. In other cases, the arrangement fee is stated as a single figure that includes both out-of-pocket costs and the service fee.

Prior to 2001, there was no specific accounting guidance on how to characterize out-of-pocket costs and the related reimbursements. Many companies that routinely billed such costs to their customers accounted for the reimbursements as an offset to the related expenses. This was viewed as appropriate because it resulted in gross margins that included the service fee and the related direct costs of providing the service, without a gross-up for out-of-pocket costs. When companies used this accounting policy, some disclosed the amount of out-of-pocket expenses that had been netted against reimbursements; others did not.

The EITF addressed the income statement classification of reimbursements for out-of-pocket expenses in EITF 01-14 (ASC 605-45-45-23) and concluded that these reimbursements should be characterized as revenue, rather than as an offset against the related expenses. This is consistent with the conclusion reached on how to account for shipping and handling costs and is based on the principles underlying gross versus net revenue reporting. The EITF concluded that with respect to the purchase of travel, supplies, and other out-of-pocket costs, the service provider acts as a principal, not as an agent. Furthermore, the EITF decided that the customer does not purchase the travel or supplies, but only the services offered by the service provider. As a result, out-of-pocket costs are like any other cost incurred in providing the service; the fact that the arrangement fee varies based on the amount of such costs should not cause the accounting to be any different.

EXAMPLE: OUT-OF-POCKET EXPENSES

GP Strategies Corporation Form 10-K—Fiscal Year Ended December 31, 2007

As part of the Company's on-going operations to provide services to its customers, incidental expenses, which are commonly referred to as "out-of-pocket" expenses, are billed to customers, either directly as a pass-through cost or indirectly as a cost estimated in proposing on fixed-price contracts. Out-of-pocket expenses include expenses such as airfare, mileage, hotel stays, out-of-town meals and telecommunication charges. The Company's policy provides for these expenses to be recorded as both revenue and direct cost of services in accordance with the provisions of EITF 01-14, *Income Statement Characterization of Reimbursements Received for "Out-of-Pocket" Expenses Incurred.*

Sales and Excise Taxes

Sales and excise taxes are taxes based on sales or purchase activity. Although various names are used, this discussion refers to sales taxes as a tax on the purchaser and excise taxes as a tax on the seller. In most jurisdictions, the selling party remits both sales and excise taxes to the government. For sales taxes, the seller acts as a collection agent when it charges the customer and remits this amount to the government.

Because sales taxes are imposed on the purchaser, the conceptually correct accounting would have the seller not record such amounts on the income statement at all. Any amounts collected would be recorded as a payable to the government that is settled upon payment.

Excise taxes, however, are imposed on the seller of goods or services and therefore could appropriately be classified as an expense in cost of sales. Alternatively, because these taxes are not discretionary and reduce the amount of revenue that is available to cover the company's expenses (unless they can be passed on to the end-customer), it has also been acceptable to report excise taxes as a reduction of revenue.

For companies that do business in a number of jurisdictions that have transaction-based taxes like sales and excise taxes, tracking whether the tax is legally imposed on the seller or the purchaser of the goods and services, in order to get the conceptually correct accounting in each jurisdiction, might be difficult. EITF 06-3 (ASC 605-45-15-2) concludes that, rather than determining how to record each tax in each jurisdiction, the income statement presentation of taxes is an accounting policy decision that should be disclosed as required by APB Opinion 22 (ASC 235, *Notes to Financial Statements*). The EITF also decided not to require companies to reevaluate existing accounting policies.

Disclosure of the amounts of taxes in interim and annual financial statements is required, if significant, for any of these taxes reported gross (ASC 605-45-50-4).

> **DISCLOSURE ALERT:**   SEC registrants must disclose the amount of excise taxes included in revenue if the amount exceeds 1% of sales. The classification of excise tax payments should also be disclosed (REG S-X, Rule 5-03) (ASC 225-10-S99-2).

EXAMPLES: SALES AND EXCISE TAXES

Murphy Oil Corporation Form 10-K—Fiscal Year Ended December 31, 2007

Excise taxes collected on sales of refined products and remitted to governmental agencies are not included in revenues or in costs and expenses.

Sunoco, Inc. Form 10-K—Fiscal Year Ended December 31, 2007

Consumer excise taxes on sales of refined products and merchandise are included in both revenues and costs and expenses, with no effect on net income.

Valero Energy Corporation Form 10-K—Fiscal Year Ended December 31, 2007

In June 2006, the FASB ratified its consensus on EITF Issue No. 06-3, *How Taxes Collected from Customers and Remitted to Governmental Authorities Should Be Presented in the Income Statement (That Is, Gross versus Net Presentation)* (EITF No. 06-3). The scope of EITF No. 06-3 includes any tax assessed by a governmental authority that is imposed concurrent with or subsequent to a revenue-producing transaction between a seller and a customer. For taxes within the scope of this issue that are significant in amount, the consensus requires the following disclosures: (i) the accounting policy elected for these taxes and (ii) the amount of the taxes reflected gross in the income statement on an interim and annual basis for all periods presented. The disclosure of those taxes can be provided on an aggregate basis. We adopted the consensus effective January 1, 2007. We present excise taxes on sales by our U.S. retail system on a gross basis with supplemental information regarding the amount of such taxes included in revenues provided in a footnote on the face of the income statement. All other excise taxes are presented on a net basis in the income statement.

Consolidated statements of Income

(Millions of Dollars)	2007	2006	2005
Operating revenues (2)	$95,327	$87,640	$80,616
Supplemental information:			
(2) Includes excise taxes on sales by our U.S. retail system	$0.8	$0.8	$0.8

UNCOLLECTIBLE AMOUNTS AND BAD DEBTS

As noted throughout this product, one of the criteria for revenue recognition is that collectibility must be reasonably assured. When collectibility is in doubt, it is not acceptable for a company to recognize revenue along with a bad debt expense. Although presenting both amounts would result in a correct calculation of operating income, it would inappropriately overstate revenue by including revenue that has not met the collectibility criterion.

Even when revenue is considered collectible and can be recognized when the other criteria have been met, circumstances may subsequently arise that make payment unlikely. When this occurs, a company may need to recognize bad debt expense. Bad debts can be distinguished from sales that do not meet the collectibility criterion because bad debts result from sales that were considered collectible at the time of delivery but became uncollectible sometime thereafter. The classification of bad debt expenses is not specified in U.S. GAAP, although the SEC requires them to be presented as expenses (generally selling or marketing expenses) rather than as a reduction of revenue (REG S-X, Rule 5-03(b)(5)) (ASC 225-10-S99-2).

Readers also should refer to Chapter 3, "General Principles," and the Covad Communications Form 10-K—Fiscal Year Ended December 31, 2007 example on revenue recognition when collectibility is not reasonably assured.

BALANCE SHEET PRESENTATION

Accounting guidance on the classification of cash received in advance of revenue recognition (deferred revenue) is still somewhat scarce. Although the deferred revenue liability caption is acknowledged in several FASB and EITF pronouncements, no literature actually describes what liabilities qualify as "deferred revenue."

Cash Received Before Revenue Recognition (Deferred Revenue)

Many reasons have been provided throughout this product to explain why, under certain circumstances, revenue recognition should be prohibited even after cash is received. When this occurs, a liability must be recorded for the cash received in excess of whatever revenue can be recognized. For example, when a right of return exists, no revenue is recognized if returns cannot be reliably estimated. As a result, any amounts received must be recognized as a liability. When returns can be estimated, revenue can only be recognized up to the extent of expected returns. Therefore, if full payment is made, a portion will still need to be reflected as a liability.

When these deferred liabilities are recognized, a question arises as to how they should be characterized. Possible characterizations include deferred revenue, a deposit liability, debt, or a contra-receivable account.

In general, amounts classified as deferred revenue should be ultimately expected to result in revenue recognition. Thus, advance payments that are received before services are performed are usually classified as deferred revenue because these amounts will be recognized as revenue upon performance of the service. Similarly, payments received upon delivery of a product, where revenue recognition is prohibited due to a customer acceptance clause, may be characterized as deferred revenue in the balance sheet.

Any amounts that are expected to be refunded to a customer may not be included in deferred revenue. For example, revenue that is not recognized based on expected returns should be classified in a separate monetary liability account, labeled with a caption such as "customer deposits" (SAB Topic 13A4a, ques. 1) (ASC 605-10-S99, A4a, ques. 1). It is also not acceptable to reflect a product return liability as an offset to accounts receivable. This is because the reserve for product returns is an estimate of cash that will be returned to customers—it is not a valuation account related to the accounts receivable balance.

The following chart lists some of the common reasons for revenue to be deferred once cash has been received and identifies whether it is generally appropriate to record the related liability as deferred revenue. When the reason for the deferral is that the revenue has not yet been earned, the liability may be reflected as deferred revenue. However, if the reason for the deferral is related to a concern about whether the fee is fixed or determinable or whether a true sale has occurred, the liability should not be characterized as deferred revenue.

Reason for Deferral	Deferred revenue?
Estimated returns or price protection when estimates can be made	N
Right of return or price protection exists and no estimate can be made	N
Estimated refunds under sales incentives	N
Product not yet delivered	Y
Service not yet performed	Y
Standard warranty when estimate of costs cannot be made	Y

Reason for Deferral	Deferred revenue?
Extended warranty	Y
Product financing arrangement	N
No persuasive evidence of an arrangement	N
Refundable deposit against variable fee	N
Product delivered—awaiting acceptance	Y
Delivered element in a multiple-element arrangement does not have value to the customer on a standalone basis	Y
Insufficient evidence of fair value to allocate revenue in a multiple-element arrangement	N
No revenue is allocated to the delivered element in a multiple-element arrangement that meets the criteria to be accounted for separately, or only a portion of the revenue that would otherwise have been allocated to the delivered element is ultimately allocated to the delivered element, due to all or a portion of the payment for that delivered element being contingent upon delivery of an as-yet-undelivered element	Note 1

Note 1: Generally, the liability in this situation should be characterized as deferred revenue. However, classification of the liability may be affected by the approach taken to account for the totality of the arrangement (i.e., it may be affected by the approach taken to account for both the revenue and cost elements of the arrangement). For a discussion of the revenue accounting in this situation, see Chapter 4, "Multiple-Element Arrangements." For a discussion of how costs associated with the delivered element are treated in this situation, see Chapter 8, "Miscellaneous Issues."

Accounts Receivable and Deferred Revenue

There are situations when it is unclear whether deferred revenue, or another liability, should be recognized. For example, consider a transaction in which delivery has occurred, there is a right of return, returns cannot be estimated and payment, although due under normal terms, has not yet been received. Because returns cannot be estimated, no revenue may be recognized (see Chapter 5, "Product Deliverables") and the inventory shipped should remain on the seller's books. However, a final sales agreement does exist and, except for the right of return, the fee is fixed or determinable. Therefore, it may not be clear whether a receivable should be recorded, with an offsetting entry to either deferred revenue or another liability account.

The SEC staff believes that it is generally not appropriate to record a receivable in this case. Because the conditions for revenue recognition have not yet been met and payment not made, neither party has fulfilled its obligations under the contract. As a result, SEC registrants should treat the contract as an executory contract under which neither party has performed. This treatment results in neither a receivable nor a liability in the financial statements. This position is consistent with TPA 5100.58 (ASC 985-605-55-32) where the AICPA Task Force on software revenue recognition issues effectively concluded that a receivable does not exist (and therefore cannot be considered transferred for accounting purposes) when revenue cannot be recognized due to extended payment terms.

The SEC staff's position is generally preferable for private companies. However, private companies may recognize these receivables if they meet the definition of an asset in CON-6, which requires the customer to be unconditionally obligated to pay the receivable balance.

> ☛ **PRACTICE POINTER:** Although the receivable and related deferred revenue may not be reflected in the financial statements, a company may wish to record these entries in its internal records to ensure that receivables are properly tracked and that obligations related to potential returns are considered. When the receivable and deferred revenue are not reflected in the financial statements, a company using this procedure should ensure that these assets and liabilities are eliminated.
>
> This is particularly important because financial statement users generally assume that amounts shown as deferred revenue have already been paid. As a result, recording deferred revenue when payment has not yet been received may cause a user to misunderstand the company's cash flow position.

Sales of Future Revenue

In certain situations, a company may receive payment from a third party and agree to pay the third party for a defined period a specified percentage or amount of the revenue, or of a measure of income, of a particular product line, business segment, trademark, patent, or contractual right. For example, a sale of future revenue occurs when a company sells its rights to receive payments from a customer to a third party before the revenue related to these payments has been recognized.

EITF 88-18 (ASC 470-10-25) addresses the classification of the amounts received by the company in these situations. The nature of the payment generally precludes immediate recognition in income due to the payments owed to the third-party investor. In most cases, these payments cannot be classified as deferred revenue, but should instead be reflected as debt. Any of the following factors creates a presumption that classification as debt is required (EITF 88-18) (ASC 470-10-25-2):

1. The transaction does not purport to be a sale (that is, the form of the transaction is debt).

2. The enterprise has significant continuing involvement in the generation of the cash flows due the investor (for example, active involvement in the generation of the operating revenues of a product line, subsidiary, or business segment).

3. The transaction is cancelable by either the enterprise or the investor through payment of a lump sum or other transfer of assets by the enterprise.

4. The investor's rate of return is implicitly or explicitly limited by the terms of the transaction.

5. Variations in the enterprise's revenue or income underlying the transaction have only a trifling impact on the investor's rate of return.

6. The investor has any recourse to the enterprise relating to the payments due the investor.

CLASSES OF REVENUE

When a company gets its revenue from different product or service categories, separate presentation of revenue from each category may be appropriate. This is especially true if the various categories of sales transactions are expected to have different gross margins or other economic characteristics. In SEC filings, separate presentation of revenues and related cost of sales is required for each of the following categories of transactions:

1. Tangible product sales;

2. Public utility operations;

3. Rentals;

4. Service transactions; and

5. All other sources (REG S-X, Rule 5-03(b)(1)) (ASC 225-10-S99-2).

> **DISCLOSURE ALERT:** See Chapter 12, "Disclosures," for information about required disclosures.

> **SEC REGISTRANT ALERT:** In a December 2007 speech, the SEC Staff discussed whether revenue from product and service deliverables can be displayed separately on the income statement when a vendor is unable to separate a multiple element arrangement. SEC Staff indicated that separate display of

product and service revenue may be appropriate when the vendor has a reasonable basis for developing a separation methodology and it can be consistently applied, clearly disclosed and not misleading. However, a systematic allocation with no basis other than consistency or based on contractually stated amounts would likely be insufficient.

EXAMPLE: PRESENTATION OF MULTIPLE CLASSES OF REVENUE

IBM Corporation, Inc. Form 10-K—Fiscal Year Ended December 31, 2007

($ in millions except per share amounts)

FOR THE YEAR ENDED DECEMBER 31:	2007	2006	2005
Revenue:			
Services	**$54,057**	$48,328	$47,509
Sales	**42,202**	40,716	41,218
Financing	**2,526**	2,379	2,407
Total Revenue	**98,786**	91,424	91,134
Cost:			
Services	**39,160**	35,065	35,151
Sales	**16,552**	16,882	18,360
Financing	**1,345**	1,182	1,091
Total Cost	**57,057**	53,129	54,602
Gross Profit	**41,729**	38,295	36,532

CHAPTER 12
DISCLOSURES

CONTENTS

BACKGROUND

Disclosures related to sales transactions and revenue recognition policies continue to receive tremendous scrutiny from regulators and users of financial statements. The frequency, number, and critical nature of highly publicized restatements in recent years related to revenue recognition is a primary reason for this high level of scrutiny. This chapter provides a detailed discussion of revenue-related disclosure requirements. No single accounting standard provides comprehensive guidance and, as a result, disclosure requirements are scattered across the authoritative literature. Consequently, some requirements are very general (i.e., they apply to all types of sales transactions), whereas others are very specific (i.e., they apply to only certain types of sales transactions). In addition to the disclosure requirements in the authoritative literature, which are applicable to all companies, the SEC requires additional disclosures from publicly traded companies.

> **OBSERVATION:** Revenue-related disclosures provide the user of the financial statements with critical information related to the types and terms of the sales transactions entered into by the company. The preparer should, therefore, consider the user's perspective when evaluating the need for and content of these disclosures.

GENERAL DISCLOSURE REQUIREMENTS

LISTING OF APPLICABLE LITERATURE

Publication	ASC	ASC Topic	Subject
APB-22	235-10	Notes to Financial Statements	Disclosure of Accounting Policies
APB-28	270-10-50	Interim Reporting	Interim Financial Reporting
FAS-57	850-10	Related Party Disclosures	Related Party Disclosures
FAS-131	280-10	Segment Reporting	Segments Reporting
FAS-144	205-20-50	Presentation of Financial Statements	Discontinued Operations
FAS-154	205-10	Presentation of Financial Statements	Accounting Changes and Error Corrections
SOP 94-6	275-10	Risks and Uncertainties	Disclosure of Certain Significant Risks and Uncertainties
EITF 99-19	605-45-50	Revenue Recognition	Reporting Revenue Gross as a Principal versus Net As an Agent
EITF 00-10	605-45-50	Revenue Recognition	Shipping and Handling Fees and Costs
REG S-X, Rule 4-08	235-10-S99	Notes to Financial Statements	Financial Statement Requirements, Rules of General Application, General Notes to Financial Statements
REG S-X, Rule 5-03	225-10-S99-2	Income Statement	Financial Statement Requirements, Commercial and Industrial Companies, Income Statements
SAB Topic 13	605-10-S99	Revenue Recognition	Revenue Recognition

Accounting Policies

General

Companies are required to disclose the significant accounting policies used in the preparation of their financial statements (APB-22, par. 12) (ASC 235-10). Preparers must consider the following issues to determine whether a revenue recognition accounting policy should be disclosed:

- Is all or some portion of the revenue recognition accounting policy based on a selection from acceptable alternatives?
- Is all or some portion of the revenue recognition accounting policy industry-specific?
- Is all or some portion of the revenue recognition accounting policy an unusual or innovative application of generally accepted accounting principles?

If the answer to any of these questions is "yes," the revenue recognition accounting policy must be disclosed. Based on these parameters, it would be an extremely rare situation where revenue recognition is not a required component of a company's accounting policies footnote. One such situation would be a development stage company that has not yet started generating revenue. However, even a development stage company should discuss the accounting policy it expects to follow once it commences its revenue-generating activities.

> **SEC REGISTRANT ALERT:** The SEC staff has communicated its observations and requirements related to revenue recognition accounting policy disclosures in a variety of ways—SAB Topic 13, *Revenue Recognition* (ASC 605-10-S99), the Summary by the Division of Corporation Finance of Significant Issues Addressed in the Review of the Periodic Reports of the Fortune 500 Companies (the Fortune 500 Report), SEC staff speeches, a "Cautionary Advice," and a Proposed Rule.
>
> In SAB Topic 13 (ASC 605-10-S99), the SEC staff states that it would always expect a registrant to disclose its revenue recognition accounting policies given the judgment ordinarily exercised in accounting for sales transactions (SAB Topic 13B, ques. 1) (ASC 605-10-S99, B, ques. 1).
>
> In early 2003 the SEC staff issued the Fortune 500 Report. This report resulted from the SEC's Division of Corporation Finance's (Corp Fin) review of all annual reports filed by Fortune 500 companies. The Fortune 500 Report provides insight into areas commonly questioned by Corp Fin during its reviews of annual reports. One area specifically mentioned in the Fortune 500 Report relates to revenue recognition accounting policy disclosures. A common request from Corp

Fin was for companies to expand or clarify their revenue recognition accounting policy disclosures. Corp Fin highlighted certain industries in the Fortune 500 Report as those that require specific improvements in their revenue recognition accounting policy disclosures:

- *Computer software, computer services, computer hardware, and communications equipment*—Expanded disclosure for software and multiple-element arrangements.

- *Capital goods, semiconductors, and electronic instruments and controls*—Improved disclosures for deferred revenue, revenue recognition for products with return or price protection features, requirements for installation of equipment, and other customer acceptance provisions.

- *Energy*—Improved disclosures of the material terms of energy contracts.

- *Pharmaceutical and retail*—Improved disclosures related to accounting for product returns, discounts and rebates, and co-op advertising arrangements with retail companies.

The SEC staff, in speeches given in December 2002, observed that revenue recognition accounting policy disclosures should be more complete and precise. Specifically, the SEC staff suggested that revenue recognition accounting policy disclosures:

- Address all material revenue streams;

- Consider whether the sources of revenue described in the notes parallel those discussed in the business section;

- Discuss explicit or implicit acceptance conditions, contingencies, or other circumstances that could affect the timing and amount of revenue recognized;

- Address multiple-element arrangements; and

- Describe the basis for gross or net presentation.

Additional disclosures regarding revenue recognition may be required in the MD&A as a component of the disclosure of critical accounting policies. Pursuant to the December 2001 "Cautionary Advice" release, companies were requested to discuss their critical accounting policies beginning with December 31, 2001, 10-K filings. A Proposed Rule was issued in April 2002 that would formally require this discussion in future filings.

The SEC guidance describes critical accounting policies as policies that are both:

... important to the portrayal of the company's financial condition and results, and they require management's most difficult, subjective or complex judgments, often as a result of the need to make estimates about the effect of matters that are inherently uncertain.

Given this description, revenue recognition would qualify as a critical accounting policy for many public companies.

In December 2003, the SEC issued Release No. 33-8350, *Interpretation—Commission Guidance Regarding Management's Discussion and Analysis of Financial Condition and Results of Operations*, which incorporated components of the Proposed Rule. Most of the guidance in the Proposed Rule has not yet been finalized by the SEC, however, and it is not clear whether—and, if so, when—the SEC will finalize the remaining guidance in the Proposed Rule. In the meantime, SEC registrants still should ensure that they take into consideration the guidance in the SEC's Cautionary Advice when preparing their annual reports and should follow the progress of the critical accounting policies Rule Proposal. Information regarding both the Cautionary Advice and the Proposed Rule is available on the SEC's web site at http://www.sec.gov.

Multiple Revenue Streams

Companies engaging in multiple types of sales transactions should disclose the accounting policies related to each significant type of sales transaction (SAB Topic 13B, ques. 1) (ASC 605-10-S99, B, ques. 1). For example, if a company has one product-selling division and one service-selling division, and each division accounts for a significant percentage of total sales, the company should disclose the revenue recognition accounting policies for both the product-related and service-related revenue streams.

EXAMPLE: MULTIPLE REVENUE STREAMS

Eastman Kodak Company Form 10-K—Fiscal Year Ended December 31, 2007

The Company's revenue transactions include sales of the following: products; equipment; software; services; equipment bundled with products and/or services and/or software; integrated solutions; and intellectual property licensing. The Company recognizes revenue when realized or realizable and earned, which is when the following criteria are met: persuasive evidence of an arrangement exists; delivery has occurred; the sales price is fixed or determinable; and collectibility is reasonably assured. At the time revenue is recognized, the Company provides for the estimated costs of customer incentive programs, warranties and estimated returns and reduces revenue accordingly.

For product sales, the recognition criteria are generally met when title and risk of loss have transferred from the Company to the buyer, which may be upon shipment or upon delivery to the customer site, based on contract terms or legal requirements in certain jurisdictions. Service revenues are recognized as such services are rendered.

For equipment sales, the recognition criteria are generally met when the equipment is delivered and installed at the customer site. Revenue is recognized for equipment upon delivery as opposed to upon installation when there is objective and reliable evidence of fair value for the installation, and the amount of revenue allocable to the equipment is not legally contingent upon the completion of the installation. In instances in which the agreement with the Customer contains a customer acceptance clause, revenue is deferred until customer acceptance is obtained, provided the customer acceptance clause is considered to be substantive. For certain agreements, the Company does not consider these customer acceptance clauses to be substantive because the Company can and does replicate the customer acceptance test environment and performs the agreed upon product testing prior to shipment. In these instances, revenue is recognized upon installation of the equipment.

Revenue for the sale of software licenses is recognized when: (1) the Company enters into a legally binding arrangement with a customer for the license of software; (2) the Company delivers the software; (3) customer payment is deemed fixed or determinable and free of contingencies or significant uncertainties; and (4) collection from the customer is reasonably assured. If the Company determines that collection of a fee is not reasonably assured, the fee is deferred and revenue is recognized at the time collection becomes reasonably assured, which is generally upon receipt of payment. Software maintenance and support revenue is recognized ratably over the term of the related maintenance period.

The Company's transactions may involve the sale of equipment, software, and related services under multiple element arrangements. The Company allocates revenue to the various elements based on their fair value. Revenue allocated to an individual element is recognized when all other revenue recognition criteria are met for that element.

The timing and the amount of revenue recognized from the licensing of intellectual property depend upon a variety of factors, including the specific terms of each agreement and the nature of the deliverables and obligations. When the Company has continuing obligations related to a licensing arrangement, revenue related to the ongoing arrangement is recognized over the period of the obligation. Revenue is only recognized after all of the following criteria are met: (1) the Company enters into a legally binding arrangement with a licensee of Kodak's intellectual property, (2) the Company delivers the technology or intellectual property rights, (3) licensee payment is deemed fixed or determinable and free of contingencies or significant uncertainties, and (4) collection from the licensee is reasonably assured.

Changes in Estimates

Revenue recognition and reporting require various estimates. Examples include estimates of (1) returns for product sales, (2) revenues, costs to complete, and percentage-of-completion for construction contracts, (3) price protection liabilities for product or service sales, and (4) settlements under cost reimbursement arrangements. Estimates, by their very nature, are subject to change. Disclosure regarding a change in estimate generally is not required for routine estimates. However, to the extent a change in a routine estimate is material, disclosure is required. Disclosure also is required if the change in estimate affects several future periods. These disclosures should consist of the effect on income from continuing operations, net income (or, when appropriate, changes in the applicable net assets or performance indicator), and any related per share amounts of the current period.

Certain changes may not have a material effect in the period of change but are reasonably certain to have a material effect in later periods. These changes in estimate must be described in disclosures whenever the financial statements of the period of the change are presented. (FAS 154, par. 22) (ASC 250, *Accounting Changes and Error Corrections*; 250-10-50-1).

> **SEC REGISTRANT ALERT:** SEC registrants must disclose material changes in estimated product returns (SAB Topic 13B, ques. 1) (ASC 605-10-S99, B, ques. 1).

EXAMPLES: CHANGE IN ESTIMATE

Trimeris, Inc. Form 10-K—Fiscal Year Ended December 31, 2007

The Research Agreement

Research, or the process of identifying clinical candidates, is generally distinct from the advanced testing of these compounds, a process referred to herein as development (see discussion above "Development Expenses"). In the Company's collaboration with Roche, the identification of compounds that may become clinical candidates had been governed by a separate research agreement and the work by the parties was performed according to an agreed upon research plan. In 2001, the Company entered into a research agreement (the "Research Agreement") with Roche to discover, develop and commercialize novel generations of HIV fusion inhibitor peptides. In September 2006, we announced that our Research Agreement with Roche to co-develop a novel next generation fusion inhibitor ("NGFI") was extended through December 31, 2008. The development work covered under the Research Agreement had focused on two distinct peptide classes, exemplified by TRI-999 and TRI-1144, as NGFI candidates. Based on the results of certain preclinical studies, TRI-1144 met the criteria established by Trimeris and Roche for further development and was being advanced as the lead preclinical NGFI candidate. TRI-999 did not satisfy these criteria and will not be further developed. In addition, the Company has the option to participate in the co-development and commercialization of certain Roche-developed fusion inhibitor peptides. In order to exercise its option, the Company must pay Roche a one-time, lump sum payment of $4.5 million, per candidate.

On March 13, 2007, the Company entered into an agreement with Roche that amended the terms of the Research Agreement whereby all rights, joint patents and other intellectual property rights to the NGFI peptides falling under the Research Agreement, which includes the lead drug candidate, TRI-1144, reverted to Trimeris. As a result of this agreement, the Company accelerated revenue, into the first quarter of 2007, for those milestone payments being amortized over the length of the research and development period of the NGFI peptides because our period of joint development ended.

In 2006, we recognized approximately $1.7 million more in milestone revenue when compared to 2005. In January 2006, Roche agreed to pay the Company $2.5 million for the results of research that was performed outside the research plan during 2005. This payment did not become due until January 2006 upon the next generation peptides passing Roche's internal review and is distinct from the milestone payments that were made under the Development and License Agreement. In February 2006, Trimeris received this payment and initially recognized it as a component of revenue over the term of the annual 2006 research plan. During the third quarter of 2006, we extended our Research Agreement with Roche from January 1, 2007 to December 31, 2008. In March 2007, the Research Agreement was amended and as a result the Company accelerated revenue, into the first quarter of 2007, for those milestone payments being amortized over the length of the research and development period of the NGFI peptides because our period of joint development had ended.

Risks and Uncertainties

The two primary types of revenue-related risks and uncertainties that must be disclosed relate to the uncertainties inherent in making estimates and the risks inherent in the concentration of business activities.

Estimates

As discussed earlier in this chapter, accounting for sales transactions often requires the use of estimates. For example, when products are sold with return rights, the company must be able to make reasonable and reliable estimates of expected returns prior to recognizing any revenue. A company must disclose any significant estimates involved in accounting for revenues, including the nature of the related uncertainty and an indication that it is at least reasonably possible that a change in those estimates will occur in the near term (SOP 94-6, pars. 12–14) (ASC 275-10-50-6 through 50-15). In the case of significant estimates of product returns, a company should disclose the existence and nature of the return right, and the fact that it is at least reasonably possible that a change in product return estimates will occur in the near term. In addition, a company is encouraged, but not required, to disclose (a) the factors that cause its estimates to be sensitive to change and (b) the risk-reduction techniques it uses to mitigate losses or the uncertainties that may result from future events (SOP 94-6, pars. 14–15) (ASC 275-10-50-10 and 50-11)

EXAMPLES: USE OF SIGNIFICANT ESTIMATES

EMCOR Group, Inc. Form 10-K—Fiscal Year Ended December 31, 2007

Revenue Recognition

Revenues from long-term construction contracts are recognized on the percentage-of-completion method. Percentage-of-completion is measured principally by the percentage of costs incurred to date for each contract to the estimated total costs for such contract at completion. Certain of our electrical contracting business units measure percentage-of-completion by the percentage of labor costs incurred to date for each contract to the estimated total labor costs for such contract. Revenues from services contracts are recognized as services are provided. There are two basic types of services contracts: (a) fixed-price facilities services contracts which are signed in advance for maintenance, repair and retrofit work over periods typically ranging from one to three years (pursuant to which our employees may be at a customer's site full time) and (b) services contracts which may or may not be signed in advance for similar maintenance, repair and retrofit work on an as needed basis (frequently referred to as time and material work). Fixed price facilities services contracts are generally performed over the contract period, and, accordingly, revenue is recognized on a pro-rata basis over the life of the contract. Revenues derived from other services contracts are recognized when the services are performed in accordance with Staff Accounting Bulletin No. 104, "Revenue Recognition, revised and updated." Expenses related to all services contracts are recognized as incurred. Provisions for estimated losses on uncompleted long-term contracts are made in the period in which such losses are determined. In the case of customer change orders for uncompleted long-term construction contracts, estimated recoveries are included for work performed in forecasting ultimate profitability on certain contracts. Due to uncertainties inherent in the estimation process, it is reasonably possible that completion costs, including those arising from contract penalty provisions and final contract settlements, will be revised in the near-term. Such revisions to costs and income are recognized in the period in which the revisions are determined.

Qwest Communications International, Inc. Form 10-K—Fiscal Year Ended December 31, 2007

Customer arrangements that include both equipment and services are evaluated to determine whether the elements are separable based on objective evidence. If the elements are deemed separable and separate earnings processes exist, total consideration is allocated to each element based on the relative fair values of the separate elements and the revenue associated with each element is recognized as earned. If separate earnings processes do not exist, total consideration is deferred and recognized ratably over the longer of the contractual period or the expected customer relationship period. We believe that the accounting estimates related to estimated lives and to the assessment of whether bundled elements are separable are "critical accounting estimates" because: (i) they require management to make assumptions about how long we will retain customers; (ii) the assessment of whether bundled elements are separable is subjective; (iii) the impact of changes in actual retention periods versus these estimates on the revenue amounts reported in our consolidated statements of operations could be material; and (iv) the assessment of whether bundled elements are separable may result in revenue being reported in different periods than significant portions of the related Costs.

As the telecommunications market experiences greater competition and customers shift from traditional land based telecommunications services to wireless and Internet-based services, our estimated customer relationship period could decrease and we will accelerate the recognition of deferred revenue and related costs over a shorter estimated customer relationship period.

Concentrations

A company may concentrate its revenue-related business activities by (1) selling only to a particular customer or a small group of customers, (2) selling only a limited number of products or services, or (3) limiting the market or geographic area in which it operates (SOP 94-6, par. 22) (ASC 275-10-50-18 through 50-22). While these types of concentrations may represent prudent business decisions, they ultimately carry with them the acceptance of concentration risk. A company that bears concentration risks may be required to disclose those risks if (1) the concentrations make the company vulnerable to the risk of a near-term severe financial statement impact, and (2) it is at least reasonably possible that the events that could cause the severe impact will occur in the near term (SOP 94-6, par. 21) (ASC 275-10-50-16).

EXAMPLES: CUSTOMER CONCENTRATION RISK

Mattel, Inc. Form 10-K—Fiscal Year Ended December 31, 2007

A small number of customers account for a large share of Mattel's net sales and accounts receivable. For 2007, Mattel's three largest customers, Wal-Mart, Toys "R" Us and Target, in the aggregate, accounted for approximately 41% of net sales, and its ten largest customers, in the aggregate, accounted for approximately 50% of net sales. As of December 31, 2007, Mattel's three largest customers accounted for approximately 34% of net accounts receivable, and its ten largest customers accounted for approximately 45% of net accounts receivable. The concentration of Mattel's business with a relatively small number of customers may expose Mattel to a material adverse effect if one or more of Mattel's large customers were to experience financial difficulty.

Arris Group, Inc. Form 10-K—Fiscal Year Ended December 31, 2007

Our two largest customers (including their affiliates, as applicable) are Comcast and Time Warner Cable. From time-to-time, the affiliates included in our revenues from these customers have changed as a result of mergers and acquisitions. Therefore the revenue for our customers for prior periods has been adjusted to include, on a comparable basis for all periods presented, the affiliates currently understood to be under common control. Our sales to these customers for the last three years were:

	Years Ended December 31,		
	2007	2006	2005
	(in millions)		
Comcast	$ 395.2	$ 345.8	$ 163.3
% of sales	39.8%	38.8%	24.0%
Time Warner Cable	$ 106.4	$ 82.8	$ 72.3
% of sales	10.7%	9.3%	10.6%

Note: The Company operates in three distinct segments: Broadband Communications Systems (BCS), Access, Transport and Supplies (ATS) and Media & Communication Systems (MCS).

	Net Sales For the Year Ended December 31,			Increase (Decrease) Between Periods 2007 vs. 2006		2006 vs. 2005	
	2007	2006	2005	$	%	$	%
Segment:							
BCS	$859.2	$766.5	$561.0	$ 92.7	12.1%	$205.5	36.6%
ATS	130.6	123.6	118.1	7.0	5.7%	5.5	4.7%
MCS	2.4	1.5	1.3	0.9	60.0%	0.2	15.4%
Total	$992.2	$891.6	$680.4	$100.6	11.3%	$211.2	31.0%

The table below sets forth our domestic and international sales for the three years ended December 31, 2007, 2006, and 2005 (in millions, except percentages):

	Net Sales For the Year Ended December 31,			Increase (Decrease) Between Periods 2007 vs. 2006		2006 vs. 2005	
	2007	2006	2005	$	%	$	%
Domestic International:	$724.1	$668.1	$495.8	$ 56.0	8.4%	$172.3	34.8%
Asia Pacific	42.0	52.9	51.1	(10.9)	(20.6)	1.8	3.5
Europe	98.6	75.0	67.4	23.6	31.5	7.6	11.3
Latin America	71.5	41.7	25.0	29.8	71.5	16.7	66.8
Canada	56.0	53.9	41.1	2.1	3.9	12.8	31.1
Total international	268.1	223.5	184.6	44.6	20.0%	38.9	21.1%
Total	$999.2	$891.6	$680.4	$100.6	11.3%	$211.2	31.0%

Related Party Transactions

The existence of related party transactions raises many questions. What is the nature of the transactions? How significant are the transactions to the company's business? Do the transactions occur on an arm's-length basis? To help address these and other questions, a company is required to disclose certain information regarding revenue-generating transactions with related parties. This information includes (1) the nature of the company's relationship with the related party, (2) the nature of the sales transaction itself, (3) any other information necessary to gain an understanding of the effects the transaction has on the financial statements, (4) the dollar amount of sales transactions to related parties for each of the income statements presented, and (5) period-over-period changes in sales terms with the related parties. These disclosure requirements do not apply to sales transactions that occur in the ordinary course of business or those that are eliminated in consolidation (FAS-57, par. 2) (ASC 850-10-50-1).

When making related party disclosures, a company should take care not to inappropriately represent that transactions with related parties occurred on an arm's-length basis. Such a representation should only be made if it can be substantiated (FAS-57, par. 3) (ASC 850-10-50-5).

> **SEC REGISTRANT ALERT:** In SEC filings, the amount of related party sales should be disclosed on the face of the income statement and statement of cash flows, and the amount of related party accounts receivable should be disclosed on the face of the balance sheet (REG S-X, Rule 4-08(k)) (ASC 235-10-S99). This disclosure is required even if the sales were in the ordinary course of business.
>
> In addition, in early 2003, the SEC staff issued the Report Pursuant to Section 704 of the Sarbanes-Oxley Act of 2002 (the Section 704 Report). In compiling the information in the Section 704 Report, the SEC staff studied enforcement actions filed during the period July 31, 1997, through July 30, 2002. One of the areas of improper accounting where a significant number of enforcement actions were brought by the SEC related to disclosure of related party transactions. The SEC staff noted in the Section 704 Report that "Failure to disclose related party transactions hides material information from shareholders and may be an indicator of weaknesses in internal control and corporate governance procedures." This finding is a strong indication that more attention should be given to identifying and disclosing related party transactions.

EXAMPLE: RELATED PARTY SALES

Acxiom Corporation Form 10-K—Fiscal Year Ended March 31, 2009

The Company leased an aircraft from a business owned by a former officer and director. Rent expense under this lease was approximately $0.9 million for the years ended March 31, 2008 and 2007. The lease has been terminated.

The Company paid $0.6 million in fiscal 2007 in NASCAR sponsorship fees to a company which was partially owned by the son of a former officer of the Company until January 2004. Since January 2004, neither the former officer nor his son has an ownership interest in the sponsored company. However, the sponsored company has other ongoing business relationships with both the officer and his son. In return for the sponsorship, the Company received publicity for the Acxiom brand and hospitality facilities for customers at race events.

The Company has an agreement to sell Acxiom products and services to a company whose majority shareholder is a family member of a former officer and director of the Company. Under the agreement, the Company received revenues of approximately $2.6 million in fiscal 2008 and $2.2 million in fiscal 2007. The accounts receivable balance was approximately $0.9 million at March 31, 2008.

Seasonal Revenue

Certain companies experience seasonality in their revenue streams. For example, if a company sells natural gas to residential customers in Illinois where the climate requires significant usage in winter but not summer (because electricity is primarily used to cool homes), the company would expect to sell significantly higher volumes of natural gas in the winter months. If this fact is not explained in the company's interim results, financial statement users may not gain insight into what annual revenues will look like. Therefore, companies that experience seasonality in their revenue streams must disclose the seasonal nature of their activities and consider providing supplemental information in their interim reports consisting of revenues for the 12-month period ended at the interim date for the current and prior years (APB-28, par. 18) (ASC 270-10-45-11).

EXAMPLE: SEASONAL REVENUE

Reddy Ice Holdings, Inc. Form 10-K—Fiscal Year Ended December 31, 2007

The packaged ice business is highly seasonal, characterized by peak demand during the warmer months of May through September, with an extended peak selling season in the southern United States. Approximately 68%, 70%, 70% and 69% of our annual revenues occurred during the second and third calendar quarters in each of 2007, 2006, 2005 and 2004. For information on our revenues per quarter for each of 2007, 2006 and 2005, see Note 15 to our audited financial statements included under Item 8. As a result of seasonal revenue declines and a less than proportional decline in expenses during the first and fourth quarters, we typically experience lower margins resulting in losses during these periods. In addition, because our operating results depend significantly on sales during our peak season, our quarterly and annual results of operations may fluctuate significantly as a result of adverse weather during this peak selling period if the weather is unusually cool or rainy on a national or regional basis.

Presentation-Related Disclosures

Gross versus Net

As discussed in Chapter 11, "Presentation," a company may be required to report revenues on a net basis. For example, a travel agent that bears minimal or no risks related to the airline tickets it sells, must report as revenue only the commission it receives for selling the airline ticket, not the price of the airline ticket itself. In this and other situations where companies are required to report revenues on a net basis, the company is permitted, but not required, to disclose the gross transaction volume related to these net revenues. If gross amounts are disclosed, care should be taken such that these amounts would not be construed as either revenues or part of the total net income or loss (EITF 99-19) (ASC 605-45-50-1).

EXAMPLE: GROSS VS. NET

Priceline.com, Inc. Form 10-K—Fiscal Year Ended December 31, 2007

Merchant Revenues and Cost of Merchant Revenues

Name Your Own Price Services: Merchant revenues and related cost of revenues are derived from transactions where priceline.com is the merchant of record and, among other things, selects suppliers and determines the price it will accept from the customer. The Company recognizes such revenues and costs if and when it fulfills the customer's nonrefundable offer. Merchant revenues and cost of merchant revenues include the selling price and cost, respectively, of the travel services and are reported on a gross basis. In very limited circumstances, priceline.com makes certain customer accommodations to satisfy disputes and complaints. The Company accrues for such estimated losses and classifies the resulting expense as adjustments to merchant revenue and cost of merchant revenues. Pursuant to the terms of the Company's hotel service, its hotel suppliers are permitted to bill the Company for the underlying cost of the service during a specified period of time. In the event that the Company is not billed by its hotel supplier within the specified time period, the Company reduces its cost of revenues by the unbilled amounts.

Merchant Price-Disclosed Hotel Service: Merchant revenues for the Company's merchant price-disclosed hotel service are derived from transactions where its customers purchase hotel rooms from hotel suppliers at disclosed rates which are subject to contractual arrangements. Charges are billed to customers at the time of booking and are included in Deferred Merchant Bookings until the customer completes his or her stay. Such amounts are generally refundable upon cancellation prior to stay, subject to cancellation penalties in certain cases. Merchant revenues and accounts payable to the hotel supplier are recognized at the conclusion of the customer's stay at the hotel. The Company records the difference between the selling price and the cost of the hotel room as merchant revenue.

Agency Revenues and Cost of Agency Revenues

Agency revenues are derived from travel related transactions where the Company is not the merchant of record and where the prices of the services sold are determined by third parties. Agency revenues include travel commissions, customer processing fees and global distribution system ("GDS") reservation booking fees and are reported at the net amounts received, without any associated cost of revenue. Such revenues are recognized by the Company when the customer completes their travel.

Shipping and Handling Costs

As discussed in Chapter 11, "Presentation," a company is required to present shipping and handling fees charged to customers as revenue and the related shipping and handling costs it incurs as expense. If the shipping and handling costs are classified within cost of sales on the income statement, no disclosure of such costs is required. If such costs are significant and are not classified within cost of sales, then the amount of shipping and handling costs must be disclosed and the line item in which they are included must be identified (EITF 00-10) (ASC 605-45-50-2).

EXAMPLES: SHIPPING AND HANDLING COSTS

Helen of Troy Limited Form 10-K—Fiscal Year Ended February 29, 2008

Shipping and handling expenses are included in our consolidated statements of income on the "Selling, general, and administrative" expenses line. These expenses include distribution center costs, third party logistics costs and outbound transportation costs. Our expenses for shipping and handling totaled $51,944, $58,863, and $51,017 during fiscal years 2008, 2007 and 2006, respectively. We bill our customers for charges for shipping and handling on certain sales made directly to consumers and retail customers ordering relatively small dollar amounts of product. Such charges are recorded as a reduction of our shipping and handling expense and are not material in the aggregate.

Amazon.com, Inc. Form 10-K—Fiscal Year Ended December 31, 2007

Shipping Activities

Outbound shipping charges to customers are included in "Net sales" and were $740 million, $567 million and $511 million for 2007, 2006 and 2005. Outbound shipping-related costs are included in "Cost of sales" and totaled $1.2 billion, $884 million and $750 million for 2007, 2006 and 2005. The net cost to us of shipping activities was $434 million, $317 million and $239 million for 2007, 2006 and 2005.

Excise Taxes

As discussed in Chapter 11, sales or excise taxes that relate directly to sales may be presented as reductions of revenue instead of as an expense. The classification of payments received for such taxes should be disclosed. If significant, the amount included in revenue on a gross basis must be disclosed (ASC 605-45-50-4). SEC registrants must disclose the amount of excise taxes included in revenue if that amount exceeds 1% of sales (REG S-X, Rule 5-03) (ASC 225-10-S99-2).

EXAMPLE: EXCISE TAXES

Murphy Oil Corporation Form 10-K—Fiscal Year Ended December 31, 2007

Revenue Recognition

Excise taxes collected on sales of refined products and remitted to governmental agencies are not included in revenues or in costs and expenses.

Business Segments

Excise taxes on petroleum products of $2,070,077,000, $1,741,707,000 and $1,459,713,000 for the years 2007, 2006 and 2005, respectively, that were collected by the Company and remitted to various government entities were excluded from revenues and costs and expenses.

Other

FAS-131 (ASC 280) requires SEC registrants to disclose certain information by segment. Certain revenue-related information is required as part of those disclosures (ASC 280-10-50-21, 22; 280-10-50-30, 32; 280-10-50-40 through 50-42).

FAS-144 (ASC 205-20) requires the disclosure of certain information related to discontinued operations. Certain revenue-related information is required as part of those disclosures (ASC 205-20-50-6).

SPECIFIC DISCLOSURE REQUIREMENTS

The authoritative literature requires other disclosures that are intended to provide users of financial statements with incremental information about specific sales transactions and the related revenue accounting issues. Many of these disclosure requirements have been promulgated by SEC staff through SAB Topic 13 (ASC 605-10-S99), announcements at EITF meetings, and in documents published by the SEC's Division of Corporation Finance. Although these disclosure requirements are not mandatory for private companies, private entities should strongly consider applying them for the benefit of financial statement users.

LISTING OF APPLICABLE LITERATURE

Publication	ASC	ASC Topic	Subject
APB-29	845-10-50	Nonmonetary transactions	Accounting for Nonmonetary Transactions
FAS-68	730-20-50	Research and Development	Research and Development Arrangements
FIN-45	460-10	Guarantees	Guarantees
EITF 99-17	605-20-50	Revenue Recognition	Accounting for Advertising Barter Transactions
EITF 00-8	505-50-50	Equity	Accounting for an Equity Instrument to Be Received in Conjunction with Providing Goods or Services
EITF 00-21	605-25-50	Revenue Recognition	Revenue Arrangements with Multiple Deliverables
ITC	N/A	N/A	FASB Invitation to Comment: Accounting for Certain Service Transactions
SAB Topic 13	605-10-S99	Revenue Recognition	Revenue Recognition
CIRP-8/01	N/A	N/A	SEC Division of Corporation Finance—Current Issues and Rulemaking Projects (August 2001)
EITF D-96	605-20-S99	Revenue Recognition	Accounting for Management Fees Based on a Formula

Multiple-Element Revenue Arrangements

Many sales transactions involve more than one element or deliverable. For example, a company may sell equipment and services to install the equipment. The revenue recognition policy, and the timing of revenue recognition, for each of those elements may be different, such that the allocation of revenue between or among elements would have a major effect on the amount of revenue that should be recognized in an accounting period. This requires consideration of how to separate the elements and allocate the amount of consideration to each element. As it relates to multiple-element arrangements, a vendor should disclose the following (EITF 00-21, par. 18) (ASC 605-25-50):

- The accounting policy for recognition of revenue from multiple-element arrangements (e.g., whether deliverables are separable into units of accounting); and

- The description and nature of such arrangements, including performance-, cancellation-, termination-, or refund-type provisions.

The SEC has also commented on required disclosures in multiple-element arrangements and noted that the following should be included:

- The nature of a company's contractual arrangements that result in the performance of multiple revenue-generating activities, including the type of products and services to be delivered,

- Whether the arrangements requiring multiple deliverables consist of more than one unit of accounting and the basis for this conclusion,

- How revenues are allocated between separate units of accounting when there is more than a single unit, and

- The impact on the timing of revenue recognition of applying EITF 00-21 (ASC 605-25).

In addition, the accounting policy followed for each unit-of-accounting should be described in the vendor's accounting policy disclosures discussed earlier in this chapter. For example, if a multiple-element arrangement involves the sale and installation of equipment and the multiple-element arrangement is separated for accounting purposes, the accounting policy disclosures should cover the individual accounting policies for each separate element.

SEC REGISTRANT ALERT: SEC registrants must disclose how multiple-element arrangements are determined and valued (SAB Topic 13B, ques. 1) (ASC 605-10-S99, B, ques. 1).

In addition, in early 2003 the SEC staff issued the Summary by the Division of Corporation Finance of Significant Issues Addressed in the Review of the Periodic Reports of the Fortune 500 Companies (the Fortune 500 Report). This report resulted from the SEC's Division of Corporation Finance's (Corp Fin) review of all annual reports filed by Fortune 500 companies. The report provides insight into areas commonly questioned by Corp Fin during its reviews of annual reports. One area specifically mentioned in the Fortune 500 Report relates to accounting for multiple-element arrangements. Corp Fin specifically indicated that companies in the computer software, computer services, computer hardware, and communications equipment industries could improve their disclosures by expanding the discussion related to multiple-element arrangements.

EXAMPLE: SEPARATION OF ELEMENTS

Salesforce.com, Inc. Form 10-K—Fiscal Year Ended January 31, 2008

Revenue Recognition: We recognize revenue in accordance with the provisions of SAB 104 and EITF 00-21.

Consulting services and training revenues are accounted for separately from subscription and support revenues when these services have value to the customer on a standalone basis and there is objective and reliable evidence of fair value of each deliverable. When accounted for separately, revenues are recognized as the services are rendered for time and material contracts, and when the milestones are achieved and accepted by the customer for fixed price contracts. The majority of our consulting service contracts are on a time and material basis. Training revenues are recognized after the services are performed. For revenue arrangements with multiple deliverables, such as an arrangement that includes subscription, premium support, consulting or training services, we allocate the total amount the customer will pay to the separate units of accounting based on their relative fair values, as determined by the price of the undelivered items when sold separately.

In determining whether the consulting services can be accounted for separately from subscription and support revenues, we consider the following factors for each consulting agreement: availability of the consulting services from other vendors, whether objective and reliable evidence for fair value exists for the undelivered elements, the nature of the consulting services, the timing of when the consulting contract was signed in comparison to the subscription service start date, and the contractual dependence of the subscription service on the customer's satisfaction with the consulting work. If a consulting arrangement does not qualify for separate accounting, we recognize the consulting revenue ratably over the remaining term of the subscription contract. Additionally, in these situations we defer the direct costs of the consulting arrangement and amortize those costs over the same time period as the consulting revenue is recognized. The deferred cost on our consolidated balance sheet totaled $13,922,000 at January 31, 2008 and $5,232,000 at January 31, 2007.

Nonmonetary Revenue Transactions

In general, a company should disclose both the nature of these transactions and the basis for recognizing revenues (APB-29, par. 28) (ASC 845-10-50). The EITF has addressed the accounting for two specific types of nonmonetary revenue transactions—those where equity instruments are received and barter transactions involving advertising.

> **PRACTICE ALERT:** Round-trip transactions receive a significant amount of attention by the SEC staff and were an area of focus in the SEC staff's 2003 Report Pursuant to Section 704 of the Sarbanes-Oxley Act of 2002 (the Section 704 Report). In compiling the information in the Section 704 Report, the SEC staff studied enforcement actions filed during the period July 31, 1997, through July 30, 2002. In addition, round-trip transactions have also been a focus in SEC staff speeches. The SEC staff characterizes round-trip transactions in the Section 704 Report as transactions that "involve simultaneous pre-arranged sales transactions often of the same product in order to create a false impression of business activity and revenue." The SEC staff cited a number of enforcement actions in the Section 704 Report where registrants inappropriately used round-trip transactions to boost revenue. Essentially, the types of round-trip transactions identified by the SEC staff in the Section 704 Report should be treated as nonmonetary transactions (see Chapter 8, "Miscellaneous Issues," regarding accounting for nonmonetary transactions). To the extent a registrant enters into round-trip transactions, appropriate disclosure is required.

Equity Instruments Received in Conjunction with Providing Goods or Services

When a company receives equity instruments in exchange for providing goods or services, it should disclose the amount of gross operating revenue recognized as a result of such transactions (EITF 00-8) (ASC 505-50-50).

EXAMPLE: EQUITY INSTRUMENTS IN EXCHANGE FOR SERVICES

Radio One, Inc. Form 10-K—Fiscal Year Ended December 31, 2007

In January 2004, together with an affiliate of Comcast Corporation and other investors, the Company launched TV One, an entity formed to operate a cable television network featuring lifestyle, entertainment and news-related programming targeted primarily towards African-American viewers.

The Company also entered into separate network services and advertising services agreements with TV One in 2003. Under the network services agreement, which expires in January 2009, the Company is providing TV One with administrative and operational support services. Under the advertising services agreement, the Company is providing a specified amount of advertising to TV One over a term of five years ending in January 2009. In consideration for providing these services, the Company has received equity in TV One and receives an annual fee of $500,000 in cash for providing services under the network services agreement.

The Company is accounting for the services provided to TV One under the advertising and network services agreements in accordance with EITF Issue No. 00-8, *Accounting by a Grantee for an Equity Instrument to Be Received in Conjunction with Providing Goods or Services.* As services are provided to TV One, the Company is recording revenue based on the fair value of the most reliable unit of measurement in these transactions. For the advertising services agreement, the most reliable unit of measurement has been determined to be the value of underlying advertising time that is being provided to TV One. For the network services agreement, the most reliable unit of measurement has been determined to be the value of the equity received in TV One. As a result, the Company is re-measuring the fair value of the equity received in consideration of its obligations under the network services agreement in each subsequent reporting period as the services are provided. The Company recognized approximately $4.3 million, $2.9 million and $2.7 million of revenue relating to these two agreements for the years ended December 31, 2007, 2006 and 2005, respectively.

Advertising Barter Transactions

A company that enters into advertising barter transactions should disclose the amount of revenue and expense recognized from these arrangements. If the facts and circumstances did not permit the company to record revenue or expense for some or all of these transactions (e.g., fair values were not determinable in accordance with the literature), the company should disclose information such as the volume and type of advertising surrendered and received (EITF 99-17) (ASC 605-20-50).

EXAMPLE: ADVERTISING BARTER TRANSACTIONS

Time Warner Inc. Form 10-K—Fiscal Year Ended December 31, 2007

Barter Transactions

Time Warner enters into transactions that either exchange advertising for advertising ("Advertising Barter") or advertising for other products and services ("Non-advertising Barter"). Advertising Barter transactions are recorded at the estimated fair value of the advertising given in accordance with the provisions of EITF Issue No. 99-17, *Accounting for Advertising Barter Transactions*. Revenues for Advertising Barter transactions are recognized when advertising is provided, and services received are charged to expense when used. Non-advertising Barter transactions are recognized by the programming licensee (e.g., a television network) as programming inventory and deferred advertising revenue at the estimated fair value when the product is available for telecast. Barter programming inventory is amortized in the same manner as the non-barter component of the licensed programming, and advertising revenue is recognized when delivered. From the perspective of the programming licensor (e.g., a film studio), incremental licensing revenue is recognized when the barter advertising spots received are either used or sold to third parties. Revenue from barter transactions is not material to the Company's consolidated statement of operations for any of the periods presented herein.

Guarantees and Indemnifications

Scope

As discussed in Chapter 4, "Multiple-Element Arrangements," revenue arrangements may include guarantees or indemnifications from one party to the other. Extensive disclosures are required for guarantees and indemnifications that fall within the scope of FIN-45 (ASC 460). Guarantees and indemnifications that possess any of the following characteristics fall within the scope of FIN-45 (ASC 460) for disclosure purposes, except as described further below (FIN-45, par. 3) (ASC 460-10-15-4):

- Contracts that contingently require the guarantor to make payments (either in cash, financial instruments, other assets, shares of its stock, or provision of services) to the guaranteed party based on changes in an underlying that is related to an asset, liability, or equity security of the guaranteed party.

- Contracts that contingently require the guarantor to make payments (either in cash, financial instruments, other assets, shares of its stock, or provision of services) to the guaranteed party based on another entity's failure to perform under an obligating agreement (performance guarantees).

- Indemnification agreements (contracts) that contingently require the indemnifying party (the guarantor) to make payments to the indemnified party (guaranteed party) based on changes in an underlying that is related to an asset, liability, or equity security of the indemnified party.

- Indirect guarantees of the indebtedness of others even though the payment to the guaranteed party may not be based on changes in an underlying that is related to an asset, liability, or equity security of the guaranteed party.

FIN-45 (ASC 460) does not apply to certain types of guarantees or indemnifications that have one of the above characteristics, in many cases because the accounting and disclosure for the excluded items is covered in other literature. The guarantees and indemnifications that possess one of the above characteristics that are sometimes included in revenue arrangements and are excluded include (FIN-45, par. 6) (ASC 460-10-15-7):

- Guarantees of the residual value of leased property at the end of a lease term by the lessee if the lessee accounts for the lease as a capital lease.

- Guarantees involved in leases that are accounted for as contingent rent.

- Guarantees (or indemnifications) that are issued by either an insurance company or a reinsurance company and accounted for under the related industry-specific authoritative literature, including guarantees embedded in either insurance contracts or investment contracts.

- Vendor rebates where the contract contingently requires the vendor to make payments to the customer based on the customer's sales revenues, number of units sold, or similar events.

- Guarantees (or indemnifications) whose existence prevents the guarantor from being able to either account for a transaction as the sale of an asset or recognize the profit from that sale transaction. An example of this situation is a software arrangement where the software vendor participates in the customer's financing through either (a) indemnifying the financing party against claims beyond the software vendor's standard indemnifications or (b) guaranteeing the customer's loan with the financing party. In these situations, a presumption exists that the fee in the arrangement is not fixed or determinable. If the presumption cannot be overcome, revenue is not recognized until the fee can be deemed fixed or determinable (see Chapter 10, "Software—A Complete Model"). In this situation, it is the guarantee or indemnification that prohibits the recognition of revenue. As a result, the guarantee or indemnification does not fall within the scope of FIN-45 (ASC 460).

Despite these exclusions, many guarantees and indemnifications included in sales arrangements are subject to FIN-45 (ASC 460). Examples include product warranties; a manufacturer's guarantee of a loan from a third-party lender to its customer to buy the manufacturer's product; and an indemnification in a software licensing agreement that indemnifies the licensee against liability and damages arising from any claims of patent, copyright, trademark, or trade secret infringement by the software vendor's software. Other guarantees and indemnifications included in sales arrangements are discussed in Chapter 4, "Multiple-Element Arrangements."

Disclosures

When a guarantee or indemnification is subject to FIN-45 (ASC 460), the guarantor is required to disclose the following information about each guarantee, or each group of similar guarantees, even if the likelihood of the guarantor having to make any payments under the guarantee is remote (FIN-45, par. 13) (ASC 460-10-50-4):

- The nature of the guarantee, including the approximate term of the guarantee, how the guarantee arose, and the events or circumstances that would require the guarantor to perform under the guarantee.

- Except for product warranties and similar guarantees (which are discussed below), the maximum potential amount of future payments (undiscounted) the guarantor could be required to make under the guarantee. That maximum potential future payment should not be reduced by the effect of any amounts recoverable under recourse or collateralization provisions in the guarantee (the disclosure of which is addressed below in the fourth bullet point). When the terms of the guarantee provide for no limitation to the maximum potential future payments under the guarantee, that fact must be disclosed. When the guarantor is unable to develop an estimate of the maximum potential amount of future payments under its guarantee, the guarantor must disclose the reasons why it cannot estimate this amount.

- The nature of (1) any recourse provisions that would enable the guarantor to recover from third parties any amount paid under the guarantee and (2) any assets held either as collateral or by third parties that, upon the occurrence of any triggering event or condition under the guarantee, the guarantor can obtain and liquidate to recover all or a portion of the amounts paid under the guarantee. The guarantor must indicate, if estimable, the approximate extent to which the proceeds from liquidation of those assets would be expected to cover the maximum potential amount of future payments under the guarantee.

EXAMPLE: INDEMNIFICATIONS

TiVo Inc. Form 10-K—Fiscal Year Ended January 31, 2008

The Company undertakes indemnification obligations in its ordinary course of business. For instance, the Company has undertaken to indemnify its underwriters and certain investors in connection with the issuance and sale of its securities. The Company has also undertaken to indemnify certain customers and business partners, for among other things, the licensing of its products, the sale of its DVRs, and the provision of engineering and consulting services. Pursuant to these agreements, the Company may indemnify the other party for certain losses suffered or incurred by the indemnified party in connection with various types of claims, which may include, without limitation, intellectual property infringement, advertising and consumer disclosure laws, certain tax liabilities, negligence and intentional acts in the performance of services and violations of laws, including certain violations of securities laws with respect to underwriters and investors. The term of these indemnification obligations is generally perpetual. The Company's obligation to provide indemnification would arise in the event that a third party filed a claim against one of the parties that was covered by the Company's indemnification obligation. As an example, if a third party sued a customer for intellectual property infringement and the Company agreed to indemnify that customer against such claims, its obligation would be triggered.

The Company is unable to estimate with any reasonable accuracy the liability that may be incurred pursuant to its indemnification obligations. A few of the variables affecting any such assessment include but are not limited to: the nature of the claim asserted, the relative merits of the claim, the financial ability of the party suing the indemnified party to engage in protracted litigation, the number of parties seeking indemnification, the nature and amount of damages claimed by the party suing the indemnified party and the willingness of such party to engage in settlement negotiations. During the period of calendar year 2002 through 2006, the Company incurred legal fees in the amount of $6.1 million in connection with the indemnification and defense of a claim against one of its manufacturers of which approximately $50,000 was related to fiscal year 2007. In the quarter ended April 30, 2007 we incurred

$1.5 million in expenses in connection with one of our customer's settlement of a legal dispute. However, these indemnification obligations were not typical of the Company's indemnity liability and do not necessarily provide a reasonable measure of liability that may be expected to be incurred pursuant to its indemnification obligations. Due to the nature of the Company's potential indemnity liability, its indemnification obligations could range from immaterial to having a material adverse impact on its financial position and its ability to continue operation in the ordinary course of business.

Under certain circumstances, the Company may have recourse through its insurance policies that would enable it to recover from its insurance company some or all amounts paid pursuant to its indemnification obligations. The Company does not have any assets held either as collateral or by third parties that, upon the occurrence of an event requiring it to indemnify a customer, the Company could obtain and liquidate to recover all or a portion of the amounts paid pursuant to its indemnification obligations.

The disclosure of the maximum potential amount of future payments is not required for product warranties and similar guarantees related to the performance of nonfinancial assets owned by the guaranteed party. Instead, the guarantor is required to disclose the following information (FIN-45, par. 14) (ASC 460-10-50-8):

- The guarantor's accounting policy and methodology used in determining its liability for product warranties (including any liability, for example, deferred revenue, associated with extended warranties), and

- A rollforward of the changes in the aggregate product warranty liability for the reporting period. That rollforward should present the beginning balance of the liability, the reductions in that liability for payments made (in cash or in kind) under the warranty, the changes in the liability for accruals related to product warranties issued during the reporting period, the changes in the liability for accruals related to pre-existing warranties (including adjustments related to changes in estimates), and the ending balance of the liability.

EXAMPLE: PRODUCT WARRANTIES

A.T. Cross Company, Form 10-K—Fiscal Year Ended December 29, 2007

Warranty Costs

Cross branded writing instruments are sold with a full warranty of unlimited duration against mechanical failure, accessories are sold with a one-year warranty against mechanical failure and defects in workmanship and timepieces are warranted to the original owner to be free from defects in material and workmanship for a period of ten years. Costa Del Mar sunglasses are sold with a lifetime warranty against defects in materials or workmanship. Estimated warranty costs are accrued at the time of sale. The most significant factors in the estimation of warranty cost liabilities include the operating efficiency and related cost of the service department, unit sales and the number of units that are eventually returned for warranty repair. The current portions of accrued warranty costs were $4 million at December 29, 2007 and December 30, 2006, respectively, and were recorded in accrued expenses and other liabilities. The following chart reflects the activity in aggregate accrued warranty costs:

| | Years Ended | | |
	December 29, 2007	December 30, 2006	December 31, 2005
(Thousands of Dollars)			
Accrued Warranty Costs—Beginning of Year	$1,736	$1,919	$2,138
Warranty costs paid	(534)	(673)	(459)
Warranty costs accrued	413	406	454
Impact of changes in estimates and assumptions	115	84	(214)
Accrued Warranty Costs— End of Year	$1,730	$1,736	$1,919

Contingencies Related to Revenue Recognition

Any number of contingencies may be present in a revenue transaction—for example, rights of return or refund, customer acceptance conditions, warranties, and price protection. The resolution of these contingencies may have a material effect on the financial statements of future periods. Companies should strongly consider whether the potential effects of these contingencies are significant enough to warrant disclosure.

> **SEC REGISTRANT ALERT:** When such contingencies exist, SEC registrants are required to disclose the following information: (1) the accounting treatment afforded the contingency, (2) significant assumptions used in accounting for the contingency, (3) material changes in the contingency, and (4) reasonably likely uncertainties that may affect the contingency (CIRP-8/01).

In addition, in early 2003 the SEC staff issued the Summary by the Division of Corporation Finance of Significant Issues Addressed in the Review of the Periodic Reports of the Fortune 500 Companies (the Fortune 500 Report). This report resulted from the SEC's Division of Corporation Finance's (Corp Fin) review of all annual reports filed by Fortune 500 companies. The report provides insight into areas commonly questioned by Corp Fin during its reviews of annual reports. One area specifically mentioned in the Fortune 500 Report relates to accounting for certain contingencies. Corp Fin specifically indicated that companies in certain industries could improve their disclosures related to contingencies such as price protection and product returns. Specifically:

- Companies in the capital goods, semiconductor, and electronic instruments and controls industries could improve their disclosures related to revenue recognition for products with return or price protection features and customer acceptance provisions.

- Companies in the pharmaceutical and retail industries could improve their disclosures related to product returns, discounts, rebates, and co-operative advertising arrangements.

EXAMPLE: PRODUCT RETURN AND CONTRACTUAL ALLOWANCE CONTINGENCIES

Intersil Corporation Form 10-K—Fiscal Year Ended December 28, 2007

The Company's sales to international distributors are made under agreements which permit limited stock return privileges and pricing credits. Revenue on these sales is recognized upon shipment, at which time title passes. The Company estimates international distributor returns and pricing credits based on historical data and current business expectations and provides an allowance based on these estimated returns. The international distributor allowances are made up of two components that are reasonably estimable:

International price protection allowance—protects the distributors' gross margins in the event of falling prices. This allowance is based on the relationship of historical credits issued to distributors in relation to historical inventory levels and price paid by the distributor as applied to current inventory levels.

International stock rotation allowance—protects distributors for certain unsold inventories of our products which they hold. This allowance is based on the percentage of sales made to certain international distributors.

Fees for Services

In general, a service provider should disclose information concerning unearned service revenues and deferred costs of services, including an indication of the periods in which the related services will be performed (ITC, par. 26). Depending on the nature of the service provided and the terms of the arrangement, additional disclosures may also be required. These situations are discussed below.

> **SEC REGISTRANT ALERT:** If an SEC registrant recognizes revenues from service fees over the service period based on progress towards completion or based on separate contract elements or milestones, the registrant must disclose how revenues from service fees are measured. This should include, but may not be limited to, the following:
>
> 1. How progress is measured (cost-to-cost, time-and-materials, units-of-delivery, units-of-work-performed);
>
> 2. Types of contract payment milestones and how they relate to substantive performance and revenue recognition events;
>
> 3. Whether contracts with a single counterparty are combined or bifurcated;
>
> 4. Contract elements permitting separate revenue recognition and how they are distinguished;
>
> 5. Whether the relative fair value or residual method is used to allocate contract revenue among elements; and
>
> 6. Whether fair value is determined based on vendor-specific evidence or by other means (CIRP-8/01).

Contingent Fees—Management Fees Based on a Formula

Given that acceptable alternatives may exist to account for management fees based on a formula, a company must disclose the accounting policy it elects to account for such fees.

> **SEC REGISTRANT ALERT:** SEC registrants are also required to disclose whether they have recorded any revenue at risk due to future performance contingencies, the nature of the contracts giving rise to the contingencies, and, if material, the amount of any such revenue recorded (EITF D-96) (ASC 605-20-S99).

EXAMPLE: MANAGEMENT FEES BASED ON A FORMULA

Marriott International, Inc. Form 10-K—Fiscal Year Ended December 28, 2007

Management fees comprise a base fee, which is a percentage of the revenues of hotels, and an incentive fee, which is generally based on hotel profitability.

Base Management and Incentive Management Fees: We recognize base management fees as revenue when earned in accordance with the contract. In interim periods and at yearend, we recognize incentive management fees that would be due as if the contract were to terminate at that date, exclusive of any termination fees payable or receivable by us.

Refundable Service Fees

The accounting for refundable service fees is not discussed in the accounting literature. Therefore, whatever policy is applied to these transactions is a choice among available alternatives. Companies with a significant amount of refundable service transactions should therefore disclose the policy used to account for them, in accordance with APB-22 (ASC 235-10).

> **SEC REGISTRANT ALERT:** To the extent an SEC registrant provides services where the fees are refundable, it must disclose the accounting policy followed to account for those refundable fees. The registrant must also provide a rollforward of the unearned revenue and refund obligations liabilities. Such rollforwards should consist of the balance at the beginning of the period, the amount of cash received from customers, the amount of revenue recognized in earnings, the amount of refunds paid, other adjustments (explained), and the balance at the end of the period (SAB Topic 13A4a, ques. 1) (ASC 605-10-S99, A4a, ques. 1).

EXAMPLE: REFUNDABLE FEES

BlackRock, Inc., Form 10-K—Fiscal Year Ended December 31, 2007

Revenue Recognition

Investment advisory and administration fees are recognized as the services are performed. Such fees are primarily based on pre-determined percentages of the market value of the assets under management ("AUM") or, in the case of certain real estate clients, net operating income generated by the underlying properties. Investment advisory and administration fees are affected by changes in AUM, including market appreciation or depreciation and net subscriptions or redemptions. Investment advisory and administration fees for mutual funds are shown net of fees waived pursuant to expense limitations or for other reasons. Certain real estate fees are earned upon the acquisition or disposition of properties in accordance with applicable investment management agreements and are generally recognized at the closing of the respective real estate transactions.

The Company contracts with third parties and related parties for various mutual fund administration and shareholder servicing to be performed on behalf of certain funds managed by the Company. Such arrangements generally are priced as a portion of the Company's management fee paid by the fund. In certain cases, the fund takes on the primary responsibility for payment for services such that BlackRock bears no credit risk to the third party. The Company accounts for such retrocession arrangements in accordance with EITF No. 99-19, *Reporting Revenue Gross as a Principal versus Net as an Agent*, and has recorded its management fees net of retrocessions. Retrocessions for the years ended December 31, 2007 and 2006 were $780,416 and $156,014, respectively, and were reflected net in investment advisory and administration fees on the consolidated statements of income. The Company did not enter into any retrocession arrangements prior to 2006. The Company also receives performance fees or an incentive allocation from alternative investment products and certain separate accounts. These performance fees generally are earned upon exceeding specified investment return thresholds. Such fees are recorded upon completion of the measurement period.

The Company receives carried interest from certain alternative investments upon exceeding performance thresholds. BlackRock may be required to return all, or part, of such carried interest depending upon future performance of these investments. BlackRock records carried interest subject to such claw-back provisions as revenue on its consolidated statements of income upon the earlier of the termination of the alternative investment fund or when the likelihood of claw-back is mathematically improbable. The Company records a deferred carried interest liability to the extent it receives cash or capital allocations prior to meeting the revenue recognition criteria. At December 31, 2007 and 2006, the Company had $28,567 and $0, respectively of deferred carried interest recorded in other liabilities on the consolidated statements of financial condition.

Research and Development Activities

When a company is engaged in performing research and development activities for others, it should disclose the significant terms of these arrangements (including royalty agreements, purchase provisions, license agreements, and commitments to provide additional funding or services). It should also disclose the amount of revenue earned and costs incurred under such contracts. If a company has entered into more than one such arrangement, it may exercise judgment in aggregating the arrangements for disclosure purposes (FAS-68, par. 14) (ASC 730-20-50).

> **SEC REGISTRANT ALERT:** SEC registrants must also disclose how they apply their revenue recognition policies for each major revenue stream (e.g., research and development services, license agreements, product sales, consulting) and payment form (e.g., upfront fees, milestone fees, royalty payments) in their research and development arrangements. If different revenue recognition policies are followed for a particular major revenue stream or payment form due to varying facts and circumstances, or contractual terms, each policy should be separately described. In many cases, especially for recognition of milestone payments, it will be necessary to discuss the facts and circumstances resulting in the culmination of the earnings process (CIRP-8/01).

EXAMPLE: COLLABORATION AND LICENSE AGREEMENT

Trimeris, Inc. Form 10-K—Fiscal Year Ended December 31, 2007

Through December 31, 2007 the Company has received a $10.0 million license fee, research milestone payments of $15 million and $3.3 million in manufacturing milestones related to Roche achieving certain production levels. The license fee and research milestones were recorded as deferred revenue and were being recognized ratably over the research and development period. The manufacturing milestones were also recorded as deferred revenue and are being recognized ratably over the patent term associated with these milestones, or November 2014.

At the time of the license fee payment, Roche was granted a warrant to purchase Trimeris stock. The fair value of the warrant, $5.4 million, was credited to additional paid-in capital in 1999, and as a reduction of the $10 million license fee payment.

Bill and Hold Sales Transactions

When revenue is recognized before delivery in a product sale, a company is exposed to greater risks than in a transaction where revenue is only recognized after delivery. Therefore, a company that recognizes revenue before delivery in bill and hold transactions should disclose this policy if the amount of revenue recognized in bill and hold transactions is material.

SEC REGISTRANT ALERT: When revenue is recognized on bill and hold sales, registrants should disclose the risks and uncertainties surrounding warehousing arrangements with distributors and their potential effect on the financial statements. This disclosure might include the registrant's relationship with distributors, that fixed commitments to purchase goods are obtained prior to revenue recognition, whether the registrant has modified its normal billing and credit terms, or that the distributor carries the risk of decline in the market value of bill and hold inventory.

INDUSTRY-SPECIFIC DISCLOSURE REQUIREMENTS

All companies, regardless of industry affiliation, are subject to the general and specific disclosure requirements discussed in the previous sections of this chapter. In addition to these requirements, the authoritative literature mandates incremental disclosures for certain industries. The industry-specific disclosure requirements for construction contractors and franchisors are discussed below. In addition, a list of authoritative literature with other industry-specific disclosure requirements is also provided.

LISTING OF APPLICABLE LITERATURE

Publication	ASC	ASC Topic	Subject
ARB-43	912	Contractors— Federal Government	Government Contractors
ARB-45	605-35-50	Revenue Recognition	Long-Term Construction-Type Contracts
FAS-45	952-605-50	Franchisors	Franchise Fee Revenue
FAS-69	932	Extractive Activities—Oil and Gas	Disclosures about Oil and Gas Producing Activities, an amendment of FASB Statements 19, 25, 33, and 39
FAS-71	980	Regulated Operations	The Effects of Certain Types of Regulation
SOP 81-1	605-35-50	Revenue Recognition	Construction-Type and Certain Production-Type Contracts

SOP 01-6	942	Financial Services— Depository and Lending	Accounting by Certain Entities (Including Entities with Trade Receivables) That Lend to or Finance the Activities of Others
AAG-BRD	940	Financial Services—Brokers and Dealers	Brokers and Dealers in Securities
AAG-CON	910	Contractors— Construction	Construction Contractors
AAG-FGC	912	Contractors— Federal Government	Federal Government Contractors
AAG-HCO	954	Health Care Entities	Health Care Organizations
ARA-1991	N/A	N/A	Frequent Flyer Programs
REG S-X, Rule 5-02	210-10-S99	Balance Sheet	Financial Statement Requirements, Commercial and Industrial Companies, Balance Sheets
SAB Topic 8B	605-15-S99-3	Revenue Recognition	Retail Companies Finance Charges

Construction Contractors

In general, a construction contractor should disclose the basic accounting policy it has adopted to account for revenues from construction contracts. This disclosure should include a discussion of the method used to (1) account for construction-related revenues and costs (e.g., percentage-of-completion, completed contract) and (2) segment or combine construction contracts for accounting purposes (ARB-45, par. 15; SOP 81-1, par. 21) (ASC 605-35-50-1). To the extent the contractor deviates from its basic accounting policy (because the facts and circumstances and relevant accounting literature support such a deviation), that deviation should be disclosed (SOP 81-1, pars. 25 and 31) (ASC 605-35-50-3; 605-35-50-5).

Percentage-of-Completion

Contractors must disclose the method(s) used to measure progress toward completion (e.g., effort expended, units produced) (SOP 81-1, par. 45) (ASC 605-35-50-2).

Completed Contract

The contractor must disclose the criteria used to determine when a contract is "complete" (SOP 81-1, par. 52) (ASC 605-35-50-4).

Claims

To the extent a contractor recognizes revenue related to a claim, the amounts recorded should be disclosed (SOP 81-1, par. 65) (ASC 605-35-50-6). To the extent a contractor does not meet the requirements to record the claim or the amount of the claim exceeds the recorded contract costs, the contractor should consider whether disclosure of the related contingent asset is required (SOP 81-1, par. 67) (ASC 605-35-50-8). If a contractor adopts a policy of not recognizing revenue related to a claim until the amounts have been received or awarded, that policy should be disclosed (SOP 81-1, par. 66) (ASC 605-35-50-7). See the Jacobs Engineering disclosure of claims in Chapter 9, "Contract Accounting."

Subsequent Events

Events occurring after the date of the financial statements that are outside the normal exposure and risk aspects of the contract should be disclosed as subsequent events (SOP 81-1, par. 82) (ASC 6050-35-50-10).

Costs

Given the uniqueness of accounting for construction contract costs, there are incremental disclosure requirements related to these costs. These requirements include disclosing total contract costs related to unapproved change orders, claims or other items subject to similar uncertainties surrounding their determination or realizability. In addition to the aggregate amount, the contractor should also disclose (1) the nature and status of the significant items included in the total and (2) the basis on which these amounts are recorded (e.g., cost or realizable value). To the extent progress payments have been netted against contract costs at the balance sheet date, the contractor should disclose those netted amounts as well (AAG-CON, chap. 6, par. 21) (ASC 910-20-50).

For precontract costs (as defined in SOP 81-1) or other costs deferred as a result of an unapproved change order, the contractor should disclose its deferral policy and the related amounts (AAG-CON, chap. 6, par. 21) (ASC 910-20-50).

> **SEC REGISTRANT ALERT:** Registrants are also required to make the following disclosures related to contract costs: (1) when program accounting is applied, the assumptions used, including total units estimated to be sold under the program, units delivered, and units on order, (2) amounts of manufacturing and other costs incurred on long-term contracts carried forward under the "learning curve" concept put forth in SOP 81-1 and the portion of those costs that would not be absorbed in cost of sales on existing firm orders, (3) amounts that are not expected to be recorded under contract, and (4) the elements of deferred costs (REG S-X, Rule 5-02.6) (ASC 210-10-S99).

Receivables

The unique nature of accounting for construction contracts also results in receivable balances with attributes that may not necessarily be found in receivables related to normal product or service sales. This gives rise to incremental disclosure requirements related to construction contract receivables. These requirements include disclosing the following receivable balances as of the balance sheet date (AAG-CON, chap. 6, pars. 24–28) (ASC 910-310-50-1 through 50-3):

1. For billed or unbilled amounts subject to uncertainty regarding their determination or realizability (e.g., unapproved change orders, claims) the contractor must disclose, either on the face of the balance sheet or in a note thereto, (a) the amount, (b) a description of the nature and status of the significant items included in the amount, and (c) the portion, if any, expected to be collected after one year.

2. For other unbilled amounts, the contractor must disclose (a) the amounts, (b) a general description of the prerequisites for billing, and (c) the portion, if any, expected to be collected after one year.

3. For retainages billed but not collected, a contractor must disclose, either on the face of the balance sheet or in a note thereto, (a) the amounts included, (b) the portion (if any) expected to be collected after one year, and, (c) if practicable, the years in which the amounts are expected to be collected.

In addition, to the extent receivables include amounts with maturities beyond one year, the following should be disclosed: (a) the amount that matures after one year, (b) if practicable, the amounts maturing in each year, and (c) either (i) the related interest rates, (ii) an indication of the average interest rate on all receivables, or (iii) the range of rates on all receivables (AAG-CON, chap. 6, par. 27) (ASC 910-310-50-4).

SEC REGISTRANT ALERT: The SEC staff requires all registrants (i.e., all commercial and industrial companies, not just those considered long-term contractors) that enter into long-term contracts to make the same disclosures required of a construction contractor. For purposes of this view the SEC staff defines long-term contracts as (1) all contracts accounted for under the percentage-of-completion method and (2) any contracts or programs accounted for on the completed contract basis that involve material amounts of inventories or unbilled receivables and that will be performed over a period in excess of 12 months (REG S-X, Rules 5-02.3 and 5-02.6) (ASC 210-10-S99).

Franchisors

Franchise agreements capture the significant commitments and obligations of the franchisor. The nature of these commitments and obligations, whether or not they have been provided, should be disclosed by the franchisor (FAS-45, par. 20) (ASC 952-440-50).

Franchise Fees

As it relates specifically to franchise fees, the franchisor must disclose the following:

1. Information about any franchise fee revenue being recognized on the cost recovery or installment basis due to collectibility concerns (FAS-45, par. 21) (ASC 952-605-50-1); and

2. The portion of franchise fees represented by initial rather than continuing franchise fees (FAS-45, par. 22) (ASC 952-605-50-2).

Regarding initial franchise fees, the following disclosures should also be made, if significant:

1. Relative contribution of initial franchise fees to net income; and

2. Likelihood that initial franchise fees will decline in the future due to sales predictably reaching a saturation point (FAS-45, par. 22) (ASC 952-605-50-2).

Franchisor-Owned versus Franchised Outlets

Franchisors must present specific information for both franchisor-owned outlets and franchised outlets. This information includes revenue- and cost-related information for each outlet group. In addition, to the extent there are significant changes in the number of franchisor-owned or franchised outlets during the period, the number of franchises sold and purchased must be disclosed along with the number of franchisor-owned and franchised outlets in operation (FAS-45, par. 23) (ASC 952-605-50-3).

EXAMPLE: FRANCHISE FEES

McDonald's Corporation Form 10-K—Fiscal Year Ended December 31, 2007

Revenue Recognition

The Company's revenues consist of sales by Company-operated restaurants and fees from restaurants operated by franchisees/licensees and affiliates. Sales by Company-operated restaurants are recognized on a cash basis. Revenues from franchised and affiliated restaurants include continuing rent and royalties and initial fees. Foreign affiliates and developmental licensees pay a royalty to the Company based upon a percent of sales, as well as initial fees. Continuing rent and royalties are recognized in the period earned. Initial fees are recognized upon opening of a restaurant, which is when the Company has performed substantially all initial services required by the franchise arrangement.

Franchise Arrangements

Individual franchise arrangements generally include a lease and a license and provide for payment of initial fees, as well as continuing rent and royalties to the Company based upon a percent of sales with minimum rent payments that parallel the Company's underlying leases and escalations (on properties that are leased). McDonald's franchisees are granted the right to operate a restaurant using the McDonald's System and, in most cases, the use of a restaurant facility, generally for a period of 20 years. Franchisees pay related occupancy costs including property taxes, insurance and maintenance. In addition, in certain markets outside the U.S., franchisees pay a refundable, noninterest-bearing security deposit. Foreign affiliates and developmental licensees pay a royalty to the Company based upon a percent of sales, as well as initial fees.

The results of operations of restaurant businesses purchased and sold in transactions with franchisees, affiliates and others were not material to the consolidated financial statements for periods prior to purchase and sale.

Revenues from franchised and affiliated restaurants consisted of:

In millions	2007	2006	2005
Rents and royalties	$6,118.3	$5,441.3	$5,061.4
Initial fees	57.3	51.5	38.0
Revenues from franchised and affiliated restaurants	$6,175.6	$5,492.8	$5,099.4

Future minimum rent payments due to the Company under existing franchise arrangements are:

In millions	Owned sites	Leased sites	Total
2008	$ 1,120.1	$ 933.4	$ 2,053.5
2009	1,084.3	905.8	1,990.1
2010	1,045.2	874.5	1,919.7
2011	995.6	838.2	1,833.8
2012	959.3	$809.0	$ 1,768.3
Thereafter	7,117.7	5,414.8	12,532.5
Total minimum payments	$12,322.2	$9,775.7	$22,097.9

At December 31, 2007, net property and equipment under franchise arrangements totaled $10.9 billion (including land of $3.3 billion) after deducting accumulated depreciation and amortization of $5.8 billion.

CHAPTER 13
FUTURE EXPECTATIONS AND PROJECTS

CONTENTS

BACKGROUND

Financial reporting issues in revenue recognition have increasingly occupied standard-setters in recent years. As a result, standard-setters around the world have undertaken a wide range of revenue-related projects. Some of the projects are designed to interpret existing standards, while others are designed to develop new reporting frameworks. Several projects with broad applicability are currently under way and will likely occupy standard-setters for many years.

In addition to improving financial reporting, one of the objectives of the current projects is international convergence. In 2002, the FASB and the IASB agreed that a principal goal of each organization was international convergence. The two boards have pooled their resources and efforts on several significant projects, including the major revenue recognition project discussed in this chapter.

This chapter provides an overview of current revenue recognition standard-setting activities. However, readers should regularly review FASB Action Alerts, IASB Insights, IFRIC Updates, and the minutes of FASB, IASB, EITF, and IFRIC meetings to follow the progress of and actively participate in these activities on a real-time basis.

PROJECTS WITH BROAD APPLICABILITY

Revenue Recognition Project

In early 2002, the FASB issued a prospectus regarding adding a project to its agenda dealing with liability and revenue recognition. The FASB received over 30 response letters to this prospectus. Given this response, the continued public scrutiny of revenue recognition accounting policies, and the lack of an overall revenue recognition framework, the FASB decided in May 2002 to add a revenue recognition project to its agenda.

Goals of the Project

The primary goal of this project is to develop a comprehensive revenue recognition framework that provides broadly applicable guidance on the subject of revenue recognition. Four goals of this project that are complementary to the primary goal are to:

1. Converge U.S. and international standards;
2. Eliminate inconsistencies in the existing conceptual guidance and standard-level authoritative literature as well as in practice;
3. Develop a single comprehensive model; and
4. Develop conceptual guidance that will provide an overall framework to address future issues.

Convergence   The FASB and the IASB have agreed to reduce or eliminate differences across the standards they issue and those in use today.

Eliminate inconsistencies   As discussed throughout this product, existing revenue recognition guidance generally focuses on specific transactions or issues. Although the guidance is reasonable for the given circumstances, it is not consistent across the board. For example, the accounting treatments for standard and separately priced extended warranties (see Chapter 5, "Product Deliverables," and Chapter 6, "Service Deliverables") are inconsistent, as standard warranties are never treated separately for accounting purposes from the related product or service, while extended warranties always are. Another example is the estimation of the effects of future events. SOP 81-1 (ASC 605-35) (see Chapter 9, "Contract Accounting"), generally encourages the estimation of revenue on contracts for which the ultimate amount of revenue may vary, while SOP 97-2, (ASC 985, *Software*; 985-605) (see Chapter 10, "Software—A Complete Model"), and SAB Topic 13, (ASC 605-10-S99) generally discourage or prohibit such estimation. The FASB hopes to identify, reconcile, and eliminate these and other inconsistencies in the existing literature that addresses revenue recognition.

Develop a comprehensive model   Because so much of the existing revenue recognition literature addresses only narrow issues or specific transactions, there are many transactions for which no authoritative literature exists. Although existing literature can often be applied by analogy, it is often not clear whether the analogy is appropriate, or, in cases where two or more potential analogies exist, which analogy is best. In addition, as discussed further below, the FASB's conceptual framework provides inconsistent guidance on the definition of revenues and how those revenues should be recognized. By creating a comprehensive model, the FASB hopes to provide the framework and the guidance to allow questions to be answered in all transactions under the same principles, rather than the haphazard approach that exists today.

Provide a framework to address future issues   One of the reasons the current literature on revenue recognition is not consistent from pronouncement to pronouncement is that the framework in the concept statements is not robust enough to ensure that the accounting standard-setters use the same underlying analysis to answer questions. This became apparent in the EITF's deliberations on certain revenue-related issues. The EITF is, in general, not supposed to address issues for which a framework does not exist in the authoritative literature. It has, arguably, ventured beyond its normal scope to provide needed guidance on sales incentives (EITF Issue No. 01-9) (ASC 605-50) and multiple-element arrangements (EITF Issue No. 00-21) (ASC 605-25). However, the lack of a framework in which to operate has resulted in the EITF's deliberations on these issues taking far longer than the deliberations on most EITF issues. The FASB hopes to provide a robust framework that will allow transaction or issue-specific questions to be answered in an effective and efficient manner in the future.

Project History

Initially, the FASB simultaneously addressed revenue recognition using both top-down and bottom-up approaches. The top-down approach addressed broad conceptual issues related to recognition and measurement of revenue. The bottom-up approach focuses first on existing authoritative literature for specific transactions and then on nonauthoritative practices that are regarded as accepted practices. The FASB Staff has developed a comprehensive inventory of the guidance and related practice. That work was completed in August 2003 and has enabled the identification of accounting models and classes of transactions that are expected to inform the development of a comprehensive revenue recognition standard.

Conceptual Framework

The FASB has concluded that inconsistencies in its conceptual framework have contributed to the difficulties involved in revenue recognition accounting. These inconsistencies relate to the discussion of revenue in CON-5 and CON-6. CON-6 defines revenues in terms of changes in assets and liabilities, that is, revenues are generated when assets increase or liabilities decrease (the "Asset/Liability Approach"). CON-5, however, defines revenues in terms of the earnings process (the "Earnings Approach"). The Earnings Approach is the approach used in all of the current literature addressing or dealing with different aspects of revenue recognition (see Chapter 3, "General Principles"). This explains why the focus in the current literature is so often on defining the earnings process and determining when it has been completed.

In October 2004, the FASB and the IASB began work on a joint project to develop an improved and common conceptual framework. The project considers certain recognition and measurement issues that previously had been included in the revenue recognition project.

The Fair Value and Customer Consideration Models

Until May 2005, the FASB and the IASB ("the Boards") pursued a revenue recognition model that measured assets and liabilities at fair value (the FV model) for the following reasons: (a) applying the CON-5 Earnings Approach to revenue recognition conflicts with the definitions of assets and liabilities in CON-6 (e.g., CON-5 may result in deferral of revenue, however, "deferred revenue" may not be a liability as defined in CON-6); (b) it is difficult, if not impossible, to define and apply consistently the concepts of "earning" and "realization"; and (c) application of the Earnings Approach takes on added complexities when multiple-element arrangements are involved. The Boards had agreed that the FV of performance obligations should be measured as the amount the reporting entity would have to pay an unrelated entity to assume legal responsibility for the performance of its remaining obligations. However, substantive concerns were voiced regarding practical problems in the development of reasonable estimates of FV and resulting patterns of revenue recognition.

Those concerns resulted in the formulation of a variant of the fair value model, called the customer consideration model, wherein performance obligations would be measured using an allocation of the customer consideration amount rather than an estimated fair value. In October 2006, the Boards decided on a comprehensive development of both models rather than treating the customer consideration model as a compromise approach. The work on these two models was completed in July 2007, and the Boards discussed the two models from October 2007 to May 2008.

These discussions produced a single contract-based revenue recognition principle. The Boards considered the two measurement approaches, customer consideration, and fair value, within the contract-based revenue recognition principle. The Boards subsequently decided to develop the initial due process document focusing on the customer consideration model, as that model is likely to be easier to apply and is more consistent with current revenue recognition practices. The Boards issued a discussion paper on this in December 2008.

The contract-based revenue recognition model is based on the rights of the customer and the performance obligations of the vendor in a contract. A contract may, therefore, be an asset or a liability of an entity as a result of the remaining rights and performance obligations in a contract. At the inception of a contract, the customer consideration measurement approach measures the rights in terms of the consideration paid or promised by the customer.

The consideration is allocated (at the inception of the contract) to the individual performance obligations pro rata on the basis of the entity's observed or estimated selling prices of the goods or services underlying the performance obligations. Goods or services are treated as separate performance obligations only if they must be transferred to the customer at different times. Performance obligations are initially measured at inception. The Boards continue to debate remeasurement criteria and timing.

In the contract-based revenue recognition model using a customer consideration measurement approach:

- Revenue is recognized only when a performance obligation is satisfied,

- In general, revenue is not recognized when a contract is obtained. However, recognition may occur close to contract inception so long as a performance obligation is satisfied;

- Unless the performance obligations are considered onerous at contract inception, no asset or liability would be recognized at contract inception. Only payment or performance gives rise to a contract asset or liability; and

- The customer consideration measures the total revenue recognized over the life of the contract.

Timing

While the Boards' official project plans call for issuance of a converged revenue recognition standard in 2011, it seems increasingly unlikely that this will be achieved, given the amount of work that still needs to be done, including the analysis of comments on the discussion paper, continued deliberations, the issuance of an exposure draft, and consideration of comments on that document, redeliberations, and the issuance of a final standard. Thus, the timing of any final standards is uncertain.

> **OBSERVATION:** The discussion paper issued by the Boards explains and illustrates the contract-based revenue recognition model using the customer consideration approach. Interested constituents should follow the activities related to this project very closely and provide feedback to the FASB. The Boards' websites (http://www.fasb.org and http://www.iasb.org) should be consulted for updates on decisions reached and current and future discussion topics.

Financial Statement Presentation

The FASB added a project dealing with financial performance reporting to its agenda in 2001, and the IASB joined the project in 2004. The Boards also formed an international joint advisory group to analyze issues on reporting financial performance and comprehensive income. This group will advise the Boards as they discuss and decide upon the agreed-upon issues in this project.

The objective of this project relates to presenting higher quality and more meaningful and useful information in financial statements that would augment the ability of users of financial statements to better understand (1) an entity's past and current financial position, and (2) changes in the entity's financial position due to past operating, financing, and other activities. The project is intended to allow users to improve their assessment of the amount, timing, and uncertainty of an entity's future cash flows.

Current Direction and International Convergence

The Boards issued a discussion paper on this project in October 2008 that addresses:

- The composition of a complete set of financial statements.
- The requirements for the presentation of comparative financial information.

- The principles that should be used for aggregating and disaggregating information on the financial statements. This issue may affect revenue line items that should be included in the financial statements (e.g., product-related revenues vs. service-related revenues).

- The totals and subtotals (e.g., categories such as business and financing) that should be reported on the financial statements. This issue will likely determine the categories, totals, and subtotals in which the different elements of revenue should be included.

- Presentation of a direct-method statement of cash flows.

Timing

The Boards' current project plans call for completion of this project in 2011.

INDUSTRY-SPECIFIC PROJECTS

As discussed above, the FASB's approach to issuing standards in its revenue recognition project will first involve working through general revenue recognition principles and concepts that will be broadly applicable to all (or virtually all) revenue transactions. This work is expected to result ultimately in an amendment to CON-5 and the issuance of a general principles standard. The FASB will also need to decide whether the existing industry-specific revenue recognition standards should also be revised or superseded.

As illustrated throughout this book, there are a significant number of original pronouncements dealing with revenue recognition on an industry-specific basis.

OTHER PROJECTS

The following revenue-related EITF issues were discussed recently by the EITF and will likely lead to new revenue recognition guidance in the near future:

- EITF Issue No. 08-1, *Revenue Recognition Arrangements with Multiple Deliverables;*

- EITF Issue No. 08-9, *Milestone Method of Revenue Recognition;* and

- EITF Issue No. 09-3, *Application of AICPA Statement of Position 97-2 to Certain Arrangements That Include Software Elements*.

EITF Issue No. 08-1

Revenue arrangements may involve multiple payment streams for a single unit of accounting or a single deliverable. For example, a vendor may provide payroll tax services for an upfront payment plus monthly fees based on the number of transactions processed. Other revenue arrangements may include two or more deliverables (performance obligations or units of accounting) but the vendor may be unable to separate the deliverables and must account for the arrangement as a single unit of accounting because one or more delivered items do not have standalone value and/or the vendor does not have sufficient fair value evidence for one or more of the undelivered elements.

During the March 2008 EITF meeting the Task Force discussed two issues:

> Issue 1—Whether, under certain facts and circumstances, it may be acceptable to use a multiple attribution model to account for a single unit of accounting consisting of a single deliverable

> Issue 2—Whether, under certain facts and circumstances, it may be acceptable to use a multiple attribution model to account for a single unit of accounting consisting of multiple deliverables.

After additional work by the EITF and a Working Group formed to consider this issue, EITF 08-1 has become a project that entirely reconsiders EITF 00-21 (ASC 605-25) (see Chapter 4, "Multiple Element Arrangements"). Eventually, the EITF decided to amend the guidance in Issue 00-21 (ASC 605-25) and remove the requirement for objective and verifiable evidence of fair value for the undelivered elements of the arrangement as a condition of recognizing revenue on delivered items. In addition, the EITF decided that the current fair value terminology in Issue 00-21 (ASC 605-25) is no longer appropriate because EITF 00-21 (ASC 605-25) does not use the term "fair value" consistent with its definition in FAS-157 (ASC 820, *Fair Value Measurements and Disclosures*). Instead, references to "fair value" will be replaced with "selling price" to avoid confusion.

The new guidance is likely to require that deliverables be separated into multiple units of accounting as long as the delivered items have stand-alone value to the customer and the consideration that would be allocated to those deliverables is not contingent upon delivery of other items in the future. Allocation of revenue to the various deliverables would be based on estimated selling prices of the individual deliverables. Companies would be directed to use their best estimates of estimated selling prices, incorporating whatever information is available. Existing examples in Issue 00-21 (ASC 605-25) will be updated and additional examples illustrating how an entity might develop the estimated selling price for the undelivered unit of accounting will be added. With this new guidance, there would never be a situation in which revenue could not be recognized on delivered units of accounting because of a lack of sufficient evidence of the value of the undelivered items.

This represents a very significant change to U.S. GAAP. If the EITF finalizes the issue consistent with its tentative conclusions, the new guidance would be effective for fiscal years beginning on or after June 15, 2010, with earlier application permitted.

EITF Issue No. 08-9

EITF Issue No. 08-9, *Milestone Method of Revenue Recognition*, addresses issues that often arise in research and development arrangements, such as those discussed in the "Research and Development Arrangements" section of Chapter 6, "Service Deliverables." Specifically, EITF 08-9 considers whether the "milestone-based method" discussed in that section is acceptable and, if so, how it should be applied.

In the application of the proportional performance method of revenue recognition, the fixed or determinable fees associated with an arrangement generally do not include consideration tied to the future achievement of milestones. However, once achieved, the additional consideration becomes fixed or determinable and is then recognizable. Under the milestone method, the additional consideration earned from achievement of the milestone is viewed as being indicative of the value provided to the customer by completion of that milestone, rather than an additional amount of revenue applied to all of the services under the contract.

The EITF has tentatively agreed that the application of the milestone-based method is acceptable when the milestones are substantive. Substantive milestones, consistent with the discussion in Chapter 6, are those:

1. For which there is substantial uncertainty at the date the arrangement is entered into that the event will be achieved;

2. That can only be achieved based in whole or in part on the vendor's performance; and

3. That would result in additional payments to the vendor if achieved.

The EITF continues to discuss this issue and will likely finalize it sometime in 2009.

EITF Issue No. 09-3

This issue considers whether to change SOP 97-2 (ASC 985-605) to remove from its scope products that include both software and hardware. As discussed in Chapter 10, "Software—A Complete Model," SOP 97-2 (ASC 985-605) severely limits the information that can be considered sufficient evidence of fair value of undelivered software elements. Other parts of the software revenue recognition guidance are also quite restrictive. These restrictions produce results that some believe are not consistent with the economics of the underlying contracts, and the distortion can be much greater when there is hardware with significant incremental costs involved in the transaction.

The EITF is currently considering whether and how to remove from the scope of the software revenue recognition guidance those arrangements that largely are made up of hardware, but also include software, such as smart phones and other software-enabled devices. This could significantly change the accounting for these arrangements. The EITF will likely reach a conclusion on whether SOP 97-2 (ASC 985-605) should be modified sometime in 2009.

Cross-Reference

ORIGINAL PRONOUNCEMENTS TO
2010 *REVENUE RECOGNITION GUIDE*

This locator provides instant cross-references between an original pronouncement and the chapter(s) in this publication in which the pronouncement is covered. Original pronouncements are listed chronologically on the left and the chapter(s) in which they appear in the 2010 *Revenue Recognition Guide* on the right. To find where in the 2010 *Revenue Recognition Guide* a topic from the FASB Accounting Standards Codification is discussed, please use the topical index that follows this cross-reference index.

ACCOUNTING RESEARCH BULLETINS (ARBs)

(Accounting Research Bulletins 1–42 were revised, restated, or withdrawn at the time ARB No. 43 was issued.)

ORIGINAL PRONOUNCEMENT	2010 *REVENUE RECOGNITION GUIDE* REFERENCE
ARB-43, Ch. 4 Restatement and Revision of Accounting Research Bulletins, Chapter 4, Inventory Pricing	Miscellaneous Issues, ch. **8**
ARB-43, Ch. 11 Restatement and Revision of Accounting Research Bulletins, Chapter 11, Government Contracts	Contract Accounting, ch. **9**
ARB-45 Long-Term Construction-Type Contracts	General Principles, ch. **3** Contract Accounting, ch. **9** Software—A Complete Model, ch. **10** Disclosures, ch. **12**

ACCOUNTING PRINCIPLES BOARD OPINIONS (APBs)

ORIGINAL PRONOUNCEMENT	2010 *REVENUE RECOGNITION GUIDE* REFERENCE
APB-10 Omnibus Opinion—1966, Installment Method of Accounting	General Principles, ch. **3**

APB-21
Interest on Receivables and Payables

Product Deliverables, ch. **5**
Service Deliverables, ch. **6**
Intellectual Property Deliverables, ch. **7**

APB-22
Disclosure of Accounting Policies

Disclosures, ch. **12**

APB-28
Interim Financial Reporting

Disclosures, ch. **12**

APB-29
Accounting for Nonmonetary
Transactions

Miscellaneous Issues, ch. **8**
Software—A Complete Model, ch. **10**
Disclosures, ch. **12**

FINANCIAL ACCOUNTING STANDARDS BOARD
STATEMENTS (FASs)

ORIGINAL PRONOUNCEMENT	2010 *REVENUE RECOGNITION GUIDE* REFERENCE

FAS-5
Accounting for Contingencies

General Principles, ch. **3**
Multiple-Element Arrangements, ch. **4**
Product Deliverables, ch. **5**
Service Deliverables, ch. **6**
Contract Accounting, ch. **9**
Software—A Complete Model, ch. **10**

FAS-13
Accounting for Leases

General Principles, ch. **3**
Multiple-Element Arrangements, ch. **4**
Intellectual Property Deliverables, ch. **7**
Presentation, ch. **11**

FAS-45
Accounting for Franchise Fee Revenue

Multiple-Element Arrangements, ch. **4**
Intellectual Property Deliverables, ch. **7**
Presentation, ch. **11**
Disclosures, ch. **12**

FAS-48
Revenue Recognition When Right of
Return Exists

General Principles, ch. **3**
Multiple-Element Arrangements, ch. **4**
Product Deliverables, ch. **5**
Service Deliverables, ch. **6**
Intellectual Property Deliverables, ch. **7**
Software—A Complete Model, ch. **10**

FAS-49
Accounting for Product Financing
Arrangements

General Principles, ch. **3**
Product Deliverables, ch. **5**

FAS-57
Related Party Disclosures

Disclosures, ch. **12**

FAS-60
Accounting and Reporting by Insurance
Enterprises

Miscellaneous Issues, ch. **8**

FAS-66
Accounting for Sales of Real Estate

General Principles, ch. **3**
Multiple-Element Arrangements, ch. **4**

FAS-68
Research and Development Arrangements

Service Deliverables, ch. **6**
Disclosures, ch. **12**
Future Expectations and Projects, ch. **13**

FAS-71
Accounting for the Effects of Certain
Types of Regulation

General Principles, ch. **3**

FAS-86
Accounting for the Costs of Computer
Software to Be Sold, Leased, or Otherwise
Marketed

Software—A Complete Model, ch. **10**

FAS-91
Accounting for Nonrefundable Fees and
Costs Associated with Originating or
Acquiring Loans and Initial Direct Costs
of Leases, an amendment of FASB State-
ments No. 13, 60 and 65 and a rescission of
FASB Statement No. 17

Miscellaneous Issues, ch. **8**

FAS-98
Accounting for Leases, an amendment of
FASB Statements No. 13, 66, and 91 and a
rescission of FASB Statement No. 26 and
Technical Bulletin No. 79-11

Intellectual Property Deliverables, ch. **7**

FAS-131
Disclosure about Segments of an Enterprise and Related Information

Disclosures, ch. **12**

FAS-133
Accounting for Derivative Instruments
and Hedging Activities

General Principles, ch. **3**
Multiple-Element Arrangements, ch. **4**
Presentation, ch. **11**

FAS-140
Accounting for Transfers and Servicing of
Financial Assets and Extinguishments of
Liabilities, a replacement of FASB
Statement No. 125

General Principles, ch. **3**
Service Deliverables, ch. **6**
Miscellaneous Issues, ch. **8**
Future Expectations and Projects, ch. **13**

FAS-144
Accounting for the Impairment or
Disposal of Long-Lived Assets

Disclosures, ch. **12**

FAS-153
Exchanges of Nonmonetary Assets, an
amendment of APB Opinion No. 29   Miscellaneous Issues, ch. **8**

FAS-154
Accounting Changes and Error Correc-
tions, a replacement of APB Opinion
No. 20 and FASB Statement No. 3   Disclosures, ch. **12**

FASB INTERPRETATIONS (FINs)

ORIGINAL PRONOUNCEMENT

2010 *REVENUE RECOGNITION GUIDE* REFERENCE

FIN-45
Guarantor's Accounting and Disclosure
Requirements for Guarantees, Including
Indirect Guarantees of Indebtedness of
Others, an interpretation of FASB State-
ments No. 5, 57, and 107 and rescission of
FASB Interpretation No. 34

Multiple-Element Arrangements, ch. **4**
Product Deliverables, ch. **5**
Service Deliverables, ch. **6**
Intellectual Property Deliverables, ch. **7**
Software—A Complete Model, ch. **10**
Disclosures, ch. **12**

FASB TECHNICAL BULLETINS (FTBs)

ORIGINAL PRONOUNCEMENT

2010 *REVENUE RECOGNITION GUIDE* REFERENCE

FTB 90-1
Accounting for Separately Priced
Extended Warranty and Product
Maintenance Contracts

Product Deliverables, ch. **5**
Service Deliverables, ch. **6**
Miscellaneous Issues, ch. **8**

FASB STAFF POSITIONS (FSPs)

ORIGINAL PRONOUNCEMENT

2010 *REVENUE RECOGNITION GUIDE* REFERENCE

FSP FIN 45-1
Accounting for Intellectual Property In-
fringement Indemnifications under FASB
Interpretation No. 45, *Guarantor's Ac-
counting and Disclosure Requirements for
Guarantees, Including Indirect Guarantees of
Indebtedness of Others*

Multiple-Element Arrangements, ch. **4**
Intellectual Property Deliverables, ch. **7**
Software—A Complete Model, ch. **10**

FSP FIN 45-2
Whether FASB Interpretation No. 45,
Guarantor's Accounting and Disclosure
Requirements for Guarantees, Including Indir-
ect Guarantees of Indebtedness of Others,
Provides Support for Subsequently
Accounting for a Guarantor's Liability at
Fair Value   Multiple-Element Arrangements, ch. **4**

FASB STAFF IMPLEMENTATION GUIDES

| | 2010 *REVENUE RECOGNITION* |
| ORIGINAL PRONOUNCEMENT | *GUIDE* REFERENCE |

FAS-133 Guide
Guide to Implementation of Statement 133
on Accounting for Derivative Instruments
and Hedging Activities   Multiple-Element Arrangements, ch. **4**

FASB CONCEPTS STATEMENTS (CONs)

| | 2010 *REVENUE RECOGNITION* |
| ORIGINAL PRONOUNCEMENT | *GUIDE* REFERENCE |

CON-5
Recognition and Measurement in Finan-
cial Statements of Business Enterprises   A Brief Survey of Revenue-Related Literature,
                                              ch. 2
                                              General Principles, ch. 3
                                              Multiple-Element Arrangements, ch. 4
                                              Product Deliverables, ch. 5
                                              Service Deliverables, ch. 6
                                              Miscellaneous Issues, ch. 8
                                              Presentation, ch. 11
                                              Future Expectations and Projects, ch. 13

CON-6
Elements of Financial Statements   A Brief Survey of Revenue-Related Literature,
                                              ch. 2
                                              Multiple-Element Arrangements, ch. 4
                                              Miscellaneous Issues, ch. 8
                                              Presentation, ch. 11
                                              Future Expectations and Projects, ch. 13

FASB INVITATION TO COMMENT (ITC)

| | 2010 *REVENUE RECOGNITION* |
| ORIGINAL PRONOUNCEMENT | *GUIDE* REFERENCE |

ITC
FASB Invitation to Comment: Accounting
for Certain Service Transactions   Service Deliverables, ch. **6**
                                              Disclosures, ch. **12**

AICPA STATEMENTS OF POSITION (SOPs)

ORIGINAL PRONOUNCEMENT	2010 *REVENUE RECOGNITION GUIDE* REFERENCE
SOP 81-1 Accounting for Performance of Construction-Type and Certain Production-Type Contracts	General Principles, ch. **3** Multiple-Element Arrangements, ch. **4** Service Deliverables, ch. **6** Contract Accounting, ch. **9** Software—A Complete Model, ch. **10** Disclosures, ch. **12** Future Expectations and Projects, ch. **13**
SOP 94-6 Disclosure of Certain Significant Risks and Uncertainties	Disclosures, ch. **12**
SOP 97-2 Software Revenue Recognition	General Principles, ch. **3** Multiple-Element Arrangements, ch. **4** Intellectual Property Deliverables, ch. **7** Contract Accounting, ch. **9** Software—A Complete Model, ch. **10** Future Expectations and Projects, ch. **13**
SOP 00-2 Accounting by Producers or Distributors of Films	General Principles, ch. **3** Multiple-Element Arrangements, ch. **4** Intellectual Property Deliverables, ch. **7**
SOP 04-2 Accounting for Real Estate Time-Sharing Transactions	Future Expectations and Projects, ch. **13**

AICPA AUDIT AND ACCOUNTING GUIDES (AAGs)

ORIGINAL PRONOUNCEMENT	2010 *REVENUE RECOGNITION GUIDE* REFERENCE
AAG-CAS Audits of Casinos	Presentation, ch. 11
AAG-CON Audit and Accounting Guide for Construction Contractors	Contract Accounting, ch. **9** Disclosures, ch. **12**
AAG-FGC Audit and Accounting Guide for Audits of Federal Government Contractors	Contract Accounting, ch. **9**

AICPA TECHNICAL PRACTICE AIDS (TPAs)

ORIGINAL PRONOUNCEMENT	2010 *REVENUE RECOGNITION GUIDE* REFERENCE
TPA 5100.38 Determination of Vendor-Specific Objective Evidence After the Balance Sheet Date	Software—A Complete Model, ch. **10**
TPA 5100.39 Indicators that Multiple Contracts Should be Viewed as Single Arrangements	Multiple-Element Arrangements, ch. **4** Software—A Complete Model, ch. **10**
TPA 5100.41 Effect of Prepayments on Revenue Recognition	Software—A Complete Model, ch. **10**
TPA 5100.43 Promises to Correct Software Errors (Bug Fixes)	Software—A Complete Model, ch. **10**
TPA 5100.45 License Mix Arrangements	Software—A Complete Model, ch. **10**
TPA 5100.46 &.47 Nonmonetary Exchanges Involving Software	Software—A Complete Model, ch. **10**
TPA 5100.49 Accounting for Post-Contract Customer Support When Contract Accounting Is Applied	Software—A Complete Model, ch. **10**
TPA 5100.50 Definition of More-Than-Insignificant Discount	Miscellaneous Issues, ch. **8** Software—A Complete Model, ch. **10**
TPA 5100.51 Accounting for Significant Incremental Discounts	Miscellaneous Issues, ch. **8** Software—A Complete Model, ch. **10**
TPA 5100.55 Fair Value of PCS with a Consistent Renewal Percentage (But Varying Renewal Dollar Amount)	Software—A Complete Model, ch. **10**
TPA 5100.56 Concessions	Software—A Complete Model, ch. **10**
TPA 5100.57 Overcoming Presumption of Concessions in Extended Payment Term Arrangements	Software—A Complete Model, ch. **10**
TPA 5100.58 Effect of Prepayments on Software Revenue Recognition—Transfer of Receivable Without Recourse	Software—A Complete Model, ch. **10** Presentation, ch. **11**

TPA 5100.59
Subsequent Cash Receipt in an Extended
Payment Term Arrangement   Software—A Complete Model, ch. **10**

TPA 5100.61
Effect of Prepayments on Software
Revenue Recognition When Vendor
Participates in Customer Financing   Software—A Complete Model, ch. **10**

TPA 5100.62
Indicators of Incremental Risk and Their
Effect on the Evaluation of Whether a Fee
Is Fixed or Determinable   Software—A Complete Model, ch. **10**

TPA 5100.64
Indicators of Vendor Participation in
Customer Financing That Do Not Result
in Incremental Risk   Software—A Complete Model, ch. **10**

TPA 5100.68
Fair Value of PCS in Perpetual and
Multi-Year Time-Based Licenses   Software—A Complete Model, ch. **10**

TPA 5100.70
Effect of Commencement of an Initial
License Term   Software—A Complete Model, ch. **10**

TPA 5100.71
Effect of Commencement of an Extension/
Renewal License Term   Software—A Complete Model, ch. **10**

TPA 5100.72
Effect of Additional Product(s) in an
Extension/Renewal of License Term   Software—A Complete Model, ch. **10**

TPA 5100.73
Arrangement Containing an Option to
Extend a Time-Based License Indefinitely   Software—A Complete Model, ch. **10**

TPA 5100.74
Effect of Discounts on Future Products on
the Residual Method   Software—A Complete Model, ch. **10**

TPA 5100.75
Fair Value of PCS Renewals Based on
Users Deployed   Software—A Complete Model, ch. **10**

CONSENSUS POSITIONS OF THE EMERGING
ISSUES TASK FORCE (EITFs)

ORIGINAL PRONOUNCEMENT	2010 *REVENUE RECOGNITION GUIDE* REFERENCE

EITF 85-20
Recognition of Fees for Guaranteeing a
Loan   Multiple-Element Arrangements, ch. **4**

EITF 88-18
Sales of Future Revenues

Service Deliverables, ch. **6**
Software—A Complete Model, ch. **10**
Presentation, ch. **11**

EITF 91-6
Revenue Recognition of Long-Term Power
Sales Contracts

Service Deliverables, ch. **6**

EITF 91-9
Revenue and Expense Recognition for
Freight Services in Process

Service Deliverables, ch. **6**

EITF 93-11
Accounting for Barter Transactions
Involving Barter Credits

Miscellaneous Issues, ch. **8**

EITF 95-1
Revenue Recognition on Sales with a
Guaranteed Minimum Resale Value

Product Deliverables, ch. **5**

EITF 95-4
Revenue Recognition on Equipment Sold
and Subsequently Repurchased Subject to
an Operating Lease

Product Deliverables, ch. **5**

EITF 99-5
Accounting for Pre-Production Costs
Related to Long-Term Supply
Arrangements

Miscellaneous Issues, ch. **8**

EITF 99-17
Accounting for Advertising Barter
Transactions

Miscellaneous Issues, ch. **8**
Disclosures, ch. **12**

EITF 99-19
Reporting Revenue Gross as a Principal
versus Net as an Agent

Presentation, ch. **11**
Disclosures, ch. **12**

EITF 00-3
Application of AICPA Statement of
Position 97–2 to Arrangements That
Include the Right to Use Software Stored
on Another Entity's Hardware

Intellectual Property Deliverables, ch. **7**
Software—A Complete Model, ch. **10**

EITF 00-8
Accounting by a Grantee for an Equity
Instrument to Be Received in Conjunction
with Providing Goods or Services

Miscellaneous Issues, ch. **8**
Disclosures, ch. **12**

EITF 00-10
Accounting for Shipping and Handling
Fees and Costs

Presentation, ch. **11**
Disclosures, ch. **12**

EITF 00-21
Revenue Arrangements with Multiple
Deliverables

Multiple-Element Arrangements, ch. **4**
Service Deliverables, ch. **6**

EITF 03-12
Impact of FASB Interpretation No. 45 on
Issue No. 95–1   Product Deliverables, ch. **5**

EITF 04-13
Accounting for Purchases and Sales of
Inventory with the Same Counterparty   Miscellaneous Issues, ch. **8**

EITF 06-01
Accounting for Consideration Given
by a Service Provider to Manufacturers   General Principles, ch. **3**
or Resellers of Equipment Necessary   Presentation, ch. **11**
for an End-Customer to Receive
Service from the Service
Provider

EITF 06-03
How Taxes Collected from
Customers and Remitted to
Governmental Authorities Should
Be Presented in the Income Statement
(That Is, Gross versus Net   Presentation, ch. **11**
Presentation)

EITF 07-1
Accounting for Collaborative Arrange-
ments Related to the Development and
Commercialization of Intellectual
Property   Intellectual Property Deliverables, ch. **7**

EITF 08-1
Revenue Arrangements with Multiple
Deliverables   Future Expectations, ch. **13**

EITF 08-9
Milestone Method of Revenue Recognition   Future Expectations, ch. **13**

EITF 09-3
Applicability of SOP 97-2 to Certain
Arrangements That Include Software
Elements   Future Expectations, ch. **13**

SEC RULES AND REGULATIONS (REGs)

ORIGINAL PRONOUNCEMENT   2010 *REVENUE RECOGNITION*
                                                 GUIDE REFERENCE

REG S-X, Rule 4-08
Financial Statement Requirements, Rules
of General Application, General Notes to
Financial Statements   Disclosures, ch. **12**

REG S-X, Rule 5-02
Financial Statement Requirements,
Commercial and Industrial Companies,
Balance Sheets   Contract Accounting, ch. **9**
                                                 Disclosures, ch. **12**

CR.12 *Cross-Reference*

REG S-X, Rule 5-03
Financial Statement Requirements,
Commercial and Industrial Companies,
Income Statements   Presentation, ch. 11
                                         Disclosures, ch. 12

FRR 23
The Significance of Oral Guarantees to the
Financial Reporting Process   General Principles, ch. 3

SEC STAFF ACCOUNTING BULLETINS (SABs)

ORIGINAL PRONOUNCEMENT	2010 *REVENUE RECOGNITION GUIDE* REFERENCE

SAB Topic 13
Revenue Recognition   Introduction, Ch. 1
                                         A Brief Survey of Revenue-Related
                                         Literature, ch. 2
                                         General Principles, ch. 3
                                         Multiple-Element Arrangements, ch. 4
                                         Product Deliverables, ch. 5
                                         Service Deliverables, ch. 6
                                         Intellectual Property Deliverables, ch. 7
                                         Miscellaneous Issues, ch. 8
                                         Software—A Complete Model, ch. 10
                                         Presentation, ch. 11
                                         Disclosures, ch. 12
                                         Future Expectations and Projects, ch. 13

SAB Topic 8A
Retail Companies—Sales of Leased or
Licensed Departments
                                         A Brief Survey of Revenue-Related
                                         Literature, ch. 2
                                         Presentation, ch. 11

SEC STAFF POSITIONS

ORIGINAL PRONOUNCEMENT	2010 *REVENUE RECOGNITION GUIDE* REFERENCE

EITF D-96
Accounting for Management Fees Based
on a Formula   General Principles, ch. 3
                                         Disclosures, ch. 12

SEC CURRENT ISSUES AND RULEMAKING PROJECTS (CIRPs)

ORIGINAL PRONOUNCEMENT	2009 *REVENUE RECOGNITION GUIDE* REFERENCE
CIRP 8/01 SEC Division of Corporation Finance— Current Issues and Rulemaking Projects (August 2001)	Disclosures, ch. **12**

SEC STAFF REPORTS

ORIGINAL PRONOUNCEMENT	2010 *REVENUE RECOGNITION GUIDE* REFERENCE
Fortune 500 Report Summary by the Division of Corporation Finance of Significant Issues Addressed in the Review of the Periodic Reports of the Fortune 500 Companies	Introduction, ch. **1** Multiple-Element Arrangements, ch. **4** Product Deliverables, ch. **5** Service Deliverables, ch. **6** Software—A Complete Model, ch. **10** Disclosures, ch. **12**
Section 704 Report Report Pursuant to Section 704 of the Sarbanes-Oxley Act of 2002	Introduction, ch. **1** General Principles, ch. **3** Multiple-Element Arrangements, ch. **4** Product Deliverables, ch. **5** Miscellaneous Issues, ch. **8** Software—A Complete Model, ch. **10** Presentation, ch. **11** Disclosures, ch. **12**
Section 108(d) Study Study Pursuant to Section 108(d) of the Sarbanes-Oxley Act of 2002 on the Adoption by the United States Financial Reporting System of a Principles-Based Accounting System	A Brief Survey of Revenue-Related Literature, ch. **2**

INDEX